Psychological Approaches to Pain Management

PSYCHOLOGICAL APPROACHES TO PAIN MANAGEMENT

A Practitioner's Handbook

Edited by
ROBERT J. GATCHEL
DENNIS C. TURK

THE GUILFORD PRESS
New York   London

©1996 The Guilford Press
A Division of Guilford Publications, Inc.
72 Spring Street, New York, NY 10012

Printed in the United States of America

This book is printed on acid-free paper.

Last digit is print number: 9 8 7 6 5 4 3 2

Library of Congress Cataloging-in-Publication Data

Psychological approaches to pain management : a practitioner's
    handbook / edited by Robert J. Gatchel and Dennis C. Turk.
        p.   cm.
    Includes bibliographical references and index.
    ISBN 0-89862-292-1
    1. Pain–Treatment–Handbooks, manuals, etc. 2. Pain–
Psychological aspects–Handbooks, manuals, etc.
3. Psychotherapy–Handbooks, manuals, etc. I. Gatchel,
Robert J., 1947- . II. Turk, Dennis C.
    [DNLM: 1. Pain–psychology–handbooks. 2. Pain–therapy–
handbooks. 3. Chronic Disease–psychology–handbooks.
4. Chronic Disease–therapy–handbooks. 5. Psychotherapy–
handbooks.   WL 39 p974 1996]
RB127.P82   1996
616'.0472–dc20
DNLM/DLC
for Library of Congress   95-26230
                                                          CIP

Contributors

Janet R. Abrams, PsyD, Fred Hutchinson Cancer Research Center and Department of Psychiatry and Behavioral Sciences, University of Washington School of Medicine, Seattle, Washington

John G. Arena, PhD, Pain Evaluation and Intervention Program, Department of Veterans Affairs Medical Center and Medical College of Georgia, Augusta, Georgia

Pat M. Beaupré, PhD, Department of Psychiatry and Behavioral Sciences and Pain Management Program, Duke University Medical Center, Durham, North Carolina

Edward G. Blanchard, PhD, Center for Stress and Anxiety Disorders, State University of New York at Albany Medical College, Albany, New York

Laurence A. Bradley, PhD, Division of Clinical Immunology and Rheumatology, University of Alabama at Birmingham, Birmingham, Alabama

Joseph R. Dane, PhD, Departments of Anesthesiology and Psychiatric Medicine, Cancer Center, University of Virginia Medical Center, Charlottesville, Virginia

Douglas E. DeGood, PhD, Departments of Anesthesiology and Psychiatric Medicine, Pain Management Center, University of Virginia Medical Center, Charlottesville, Virginia

Robert H. Dworkin, PhD, Departments of Anesthesiology and Psychiatry, College of Physicians and Surgeons, Columbia University, New York, New York

Michael Feuerstein, PhD, Center for Occupational Rehabilitation, University of Rochester Medical Center, Rochester, New York; Departments of Medical and Clinical Psychology and Preventive Medicine and Biometrics, Uniformed Services University of the Health Sciences

Robert J. Gatchel, PhD, Departments of Psychiatry and Rehabilitation Science, University of Texas Southwestern Medical Center at Dallas, Dallas, Texas

Karen M. Gil, PhD, Department of Psychology, University of North Carolina at Chapel Hill, Chapel Hill, North Carolina

Roy C. Grzesiak, PhD, Department of Psychiatry, New Jersey Medical School, and Center for TMJ and Orofacial Pain Management, New Jersey Dental School, University of Medicine and Dentistry of New Jersey, Newark, New Jersey; Department of Psychiatry and Behavioral Health, Overlook Hospital, Summit, New Jersey; Pain Management Center, The Rehabilitation Institute at Morristown Memorial Hospital, Morristown, New Jersey

Loretta M. Hillier, MA, Paediatric Pain Program, Child Health Research Institute, and Department of Paediatrics, University of Western Ontario, London, Ontario, Canada

Mark P. Jensen, PhD, Department of Rehabilitation Medicine, University of Washington, Seattle, Washington

William J. Kee, PhD, Department of Physical Medicine and Rehabilitation, Medical University of South Carolina, Charleston, South Carolina

Francis J. Keefe, PhD, Department of Psychiatry and Behavioral Sciences and Pain Management Program, Duke University Medical Center, Durham, North Carolina

Robert D. Kerns, PhD, Psychology Service, Department of Veterans Affairs Medical Center, West Haven, Connecticut; Departments of Psychiatry, Neurology, and Psychology, Yale University, New Haven, Connecticut

John A. Kubinski, PhD, Department of Anesthesiology/Critical Care Medicine and Pain Evaluation and Treatment Institute, University of Pittsburgh School of Medicine, Pittsburgh, Pennsylvania

Steven J. Linton, PhD, Department of Occupational and Environmental Medicine, Örebo Medical Center, Örebo, Sweden

Patricia A. McGrath, PhD, Paediatric Pain Program, Child Health Research Institute, and Department of Paediatrics, Univerisity of Western Ontario, London, Ontario, Canada

Susan J. Middaugh, PhD, Department of Physical Medicine and Rehabilitation, Medical University of South Carolina, Charleston, South Carolina

Kim L. Pawlick, PhD, Department of Anesthesiology, Medical University of South Carolina, Charleston, South Carolina

Annette Payne, PhD, Psychology Service, Department of Veteran Affairs Medical Center, West Haven, Connecticut; Department of Psychiatry, Yale University, New Haven, Connecticut

Peter B. Polatin, MD, Department of Psychiatry, University of Texas Southwestern Medical Center at Dallas, Dallas, Texas

Thomas E. Rudy, PhD, Departments of Anesthesiology/Critical Care Medicine and Psychiatry and Pain Evaluation and Treatment Institute, University of Pittsburgh School of Medicine, Pittsburgh, Pennsylvania

Steven H. Sanders, PhD, Pain and Health Management, Duluth, Georgia; Department of Rehabilitation Medicine, Emory University School of Medicine, Atlanta, Georgia

Karen L. Syrjala, PhD, Fred Hutchinson Cancer Research Center and Department of Psychiatry and Behavioral Sciences, University of Washington School of Medicine, Seattle, Washington

Dennis C. Turk, PhD, Departments of Psychiatry and Anesthesiology and Pain Evaluation and Treatment Institute, University of Pittsburgh School of Medicine, Pittsburgh, Pennsylvania

Gregg M. Ury, PsyD, Department of Psychiatry, College of Physicians and Surgeons, Columbia University, New York, New York

David A. Williams, PhD, Division of Behavioral Medicine, Georgetown University Medical Center, Washington, DC

Thomas R. Zastowny, PhD, Center for Occupational Rehabilitation and Department of Psychiatry, University of Rochester Medical Center, Rochester, New York

Preface

Perhaps the most universal form of stress encountered is pain. No other physical symptom is more pervasive: Pain accounts for over 80% of all physician visits, affects over 50 million Americans, and costs over $70 billion annually in health care costs and lost productivity. With such astronomical figures, it is all too easy to lose sight of the incalculable human suffering of the patient and his or her family.

The quest to control pain has been a major human pursuit since earliest recorded history. Mention of pain treatment has been found in Egyptian papyri dating back to 4000 B.C. Yet, despite this lengthy history; advances in our knowledge of sensory physiology, anatomy, and biochemistry; and the development of potent analgesic medications and other innovative medical and surgical interventions, pain relief remains elusive for many patients. Indeed, pain management continues to be an extremely challenging problem for the sufferer, his or her family members, health care providers, and society in general.

Systematic attempts to treat pain have been closely aligned with how pain is conceptualized and evaluated. Traditionally, the focus in medicine has been on the cause of the pain reported, with the assumption that there is a physical basis for the pain and that once this is identified, the source can be either eliminated or blocked by medical or surgical intervention. Consequently, assessment was focused on identifying the physical basis for the pain. In the absence of a physical basis, it was often the case that psychological causation was invoked; hence the term "psychogenic pain." Thus, the traditional view of persistent pain complaints was characterized by a simple dichotomy: The pain reported had either a physical basis or a psychological one.

More recently, these dichotomous views of pain have been shown to be incomplete and inadequate. There is no question that physical factors contribute to pain symptoms; nor is there any argument that psychological factors, including secondary gain, may play a part in the symptom reporting of some patients. However, it has become equally evident that numerous psychosocial factors frequently occur secondary to a trauma or disease. These psychosocial factors must be evaluated and treated in conjunction with the physical and predispositional psychological ones in order to ensure therapeutic success. Moreover, research has suggested that the social and familial context in which pain persists also plays a central role in the maintenance of disability.

These observations underscore the important role of mental health specialists in the assessment and treatment of patients with pain. Indeed, the role of mental health specialists has been noted in U.S. government publications such as the Social Security Administration's *Report of the Commission on the Evaluation of Pain* and the Institute of

Medicine's *Report on Pain and Disability*; it has also been noted by a private medical certifying agency, the Commission for the Accreditation of Rehabilitation Facilities. Moreover, the acknowledgment of the importance of psychological factors in pain has resulted in a large number of mental health specialists' evaluating and treating pain patients in specialized pain clinics, in a variety of medical settings, and in private practices. Recently, the American Psychological Association designated psychological treatment of chronic pain patients as one of the 25 areas for which there was empirical validation for psychological intervention. The demand for specialized services by mental health specialists has outpaced the availability of such mental health specialists with appropriate training and experience.

Although many published volumes have appeared on the topic of pain, most of these include only token chapters examining psychological issues. Only a few have focused exclusively on practical aspects of psychological pain management, and many of these were published over a decade ago. In recent years, there has been an explosion of research on psychological factors in pain, along with a large number of publications describing the efficacy of a range of psychologically based interventions. With the growth of such a research base, greater attention is now being given to a prescriptive approach whereby psychologically supported treatments are "tailored" to patients with identified characteristics.

What has been missing from the literature is a text that provides coverage of the range of relevant treatment-oriented topics, presented in sufficient depth and detail to provide practical information regarding psychological approaches to the management of patients suffering from diverse pain syndromes. In response to this need, the present handbook was designed to provide the most current material on many different types of treatment strategies. The emphasis in many chapters is on chronic pain, but acute pain, pain associated with cancer, and pain specifically connected with work-related injuries are considered as well. In addition, attention is given to the developmental issues associated with treatment of children and the elderly; a focus on families is also included. Finally, the increasingly important roles of the mental health specialist in pain consulting, prevention, and outcome evaluation are addressed.

It is our intention that this volume will bridge the gap between laboratory research and direct application to the clinical environment. The contributors, who are seasoned clinicians as well as known and respected scholars in the field, were carefully selected. They were given the task of writing chapters for practitioners who desire information about the most effective, empirically documented methods of pain management that can be applied in the clinical arena. We requested that each contributor provide brief scholarly overviews of the most recent developments in the area, followed by their comprehensive, expert recommendations and specific clinical details of how to manage pain most effectively. That is, we asked them to describe the nuts and bolts of treatment in depth. They all did outstanding jobs in fulfilling this task. This handbook will therefore be of particular relevance and interest to clinicians, whether they see only a small number of pain patients or whether the majority of their practice is devoted to this population. It provides practical clinical information and guidelines, which can help the practitioner understand the most heuristic ways of managing pain and interfacing with the medical environment. Moreover, the details presented should inform clinical investigators about a number of areas in which clinical insights have revealed important issues in need of empirical testing and support. In the current health care environment, outcome research will be essential to support the role of psychological factors in pain and to demonstrate the efficacy and cost-effectiveness of treatments that integrate psychological with physical modalities.

A comprehensive handbook of this type is not possible without help from many gifted individuals. All of the contributors were very diligent in providing outstanding "state-of-the-art" chapters in a timely manner. We would also like to thank and acknowledge the help and support we received from the staff of Guilford Publications, particularly from Jodi Creditor and Seymour Weingarten. Finally, preparation of this text and the timeliness in bringing it to fruition were greatly aided by the efforts of Carol Gentry.

—ROBERT J. GATCHEL
DENNIS C. TURK

Contents

Part III
SPECIAL POPULATIONS AND TOPICS

Psychological Approaches to Pain Management

PART I

CONCEPTUAL
AND PSYCHOLOGICAL
DIAGNOSTIC ISSUES

CHAPTER 1

Biopsychosocial Perspective on Chronic Pain

Dennis C. Turk

Chronic pain is a demoralizing situation that confronts the individual sufferer not only with the stress created by pain, but with many other continuing stressors that compromise all aspects of his or her life. Living with chronic pain requires considerable emotional resilience and tends to deplete the individual's emotional reserve. There is a continuing quest for relief that often remains elusive; this can lead to feelings of demoralization, helplessness, hopelessness, and outright depression. Moreover, chronic pain taxes not only the individual, but the capacity of significant others who provide support. Health care providers share patients' and families' feelings of frustration as the patients' reports of pain continue, despite the providers' best efforts and at times in the absence of any pathology that is sufficient to account for the pain reported.

On a societal level, pain creates a burden in lost productivity, tax revenue, health care expenses, and disability benefits. Third-party payers are confronted with escalating medical costs, disability payments, and frustration when patients remain disabled despite extensive treatment and rehabilitation efforts. Thus, pain is a major health problem in society that affects millions of people and costs billions of dollars, in addition to the incalculable human suffering.

Although pain has existed since time immemorial, the prevalence of pain, advances in knowledge of the physical mechanisms, development of sophisticated laboratory diagnostic procedures, and development of innovative medical and surgical treatments; there is currently no treatment available that consistently and permanently alleviates pain for all patients. The intention of this chapter is to examine how psychological and social factors can be integrated with physical factors within a biopsychosocial framework that can serve as a way to understand chronic pain and disability. Research focusing specifically on psychological and social factors is reviewed, and the implications of these factors for treatment and rehabilitation are described. The factors discussed here underlie the treatment approaches described in other chapters contained in this volume.

THE NEED FOR AN ALTERNATIVE TO THE DISEASE MODEL

The biomedical model of pain—which dates back to the ancient Greeks and was codified by Descartes in the 17th century—assumes that an individual's complaints should result from a specific disease state represented by disordered biology, the diagnosis of which is confirmed by data from objective tests of physical damage and impairment. More specifically, positive tests should confirm a diseased organ or organ system that cannot perform the biological functions necessary to maintain health. Subsequent medical interventions are specifically directed toward correcting the organic dysfunction or pathology. Despite advances in understanding of anatomy, biochemistry, and neurophysiology, there is general agreement that physical factors cannot completely account for reported physical symptoms. Highly diverse responses to objectively the same physical perturbations and identical treatments have been noted clinically and have been documented in many empirical investigations.

In the case of chronic pain, the failure of purely physiological explanations for symptoms has been widely reported. Although they are related, the associations between physical impairments on the one hand and pain report and disability on the other have been shown to be modest at best (Magora & Schwartz, 1980; Waddell & Main, 1984). Identified physical pathology does not predict severity of pain or level of disability; moreover, pain severity is not adequate to explain psychological distress or the extent of disability observed.

The question that remains to be answered is this: What factors can account for the highly varied individual expression of subjective experience and behavioral responses? From the perspective of the disease model, accompanying features of chronic conditions, such as sleep disturbance, depression, psychosocial disability, and pain, are not viewed as pathognomonic of a particular disease. Rather, they are viewed as reactions to the disease and are thus considered of secondary importance. It is assumed that once the disease is "cured," these secondary reactions will disappear. If they do not, then speculations are raised as to psychological causation. Thus, traditional medicine has adopted a dichotomous view in which symptoms are either somatogenic *or* psychogenic. Although evidence to support this dichotomy is lacking, the view remains pervasive.

The recognition that substantial numbers of people suffer from persistent pain that is refractory to available medical and surgical treatments, and the fact that functional disability often appears to be in excess of what might be expected on the basis of physical pathology alone, have led to the realization that others factors must contribute to pain experience and response. The biomedical model has been criticized because of its failure to account for psychological and psychosocial variables in health and disease, or for the dynamic interaction of these variables with pathophysiological factors (Engel, 1977). Specifically, problems arise when patients' complaints and ailments are not commensurate with the degree of observable pathology. In this circumstance, which is common in such chronic pain conditions as back pain, headache, fibromyalgia, and temporomandibular disorders (TMDs), the patient's presentation does not yield clues that are clearly related to the biomedical model.

Chronic pain is more than a physical symptom. Its continuous presence creates widespread manifestations of suffering, including demoralization and affective disturbance; preoccupation with pain; limitation of personal, social, and work activities; increased use of medications and of health care services; and a generalized adoption of the sick role (Parsons, 1958). Although the importance of such factors has been acknowledged for some time, only within the last three decades have systematic attempts been made to incorporate these factors within comprehensive models of pain (see Turk, in press, for a review). The dissatisfaction with the conventional model of pain led in the 1960s to a seminal event: the formulation of the gate control theory of pain by Melzack and his colleagues (Melzack & Casey, 1968; Melzack & Wall, 1965).

THE GATE CONTROL THEORY OF PAIN

The first attempt to develop an integrative model designed to address the problems created by unidimensional models and to integrate physiological and psychological factors was the gate control theory proposed by Melzack and his colleagues (Melzack & Casey, 1968; Melzack & Wall, 1965). Perhaps the most important contribution of this theory has been the way it has changed thinking about pain perception. Melzack and Casey (1968) have differentiated three systems related to the processing of nociceptive stimulation—sensory-discriminative, motivational-affective, and cognitive-evaluative—all of which are thought to contribute to the subjective experience of pain. Thus, the gate control theory specifically includes psychological factors as an integral aspect of the pain experience. It also emphasizes central nervous system (CNS) mechanisms and provides a physiological basis for the role of psychological factors in chronic pain.

The gate control model describes the integration of peripheral stimuli with cortical variables, such as mood and anxiety, in the perception of pain. This model contradicts the notion that pain is either somatic or psychogenic, and instead postulates that both factors have either potentiating or moderating effects on pain perception. From the gate control perspective, the experience of pain is an ongoing sequence of activities—largely reflexive in nature at the outset, but modifiable even in the earliest stages by a variety of excitatory and inhibitory influences, as well as the integration of ascending and descending CNS activity. The process results in overt expressions communicating pain and strategies by the individual to terminate the pain. In addition, considerable potential for shaping of the pain experience is implied, because the gate control theory invokes the continuous interaction of multiple systems (sensory-physiological, affect, cognition, and ultimately behavior).

Melzack and colleagues' (Melzack & Casey, 1968; Melzack & Wall, 1965) emphasis on the modulation of inputs in the dorsal horn of the spinal cord and the dynamic role of the brain in pain processes and perception has resulted in the integration of psychological variables (e.g., past experience, attention, and other cognitive activities) into current research and therapy on pain. Prior to this formulation, psychological processes were largely dismissed as reactions to pain. This new model was the first to suggest that cutting or blocking neurological pathways is inadequate, because numerous other factors modulate the input. Perhaps the major contribution of the gate control theory has been its highlighting of the CNS as an essential component in nociceptive processing and perception.

The physiological details of the gate control model have been challenged, and it has been suggested that the model is incomplete (Nathan, 1976; Price, 1987; R. F. Schmidt, 1972). As additional knowledge has been gathered since the original formulation in 1965, specific points of posited mechanisms have been disputed and have required revision and reformulation (Nathan, 1976; Wall, 1989). Overall, however, the gate control theory has proved remarkably resilient and flexible in the face of accumulating scientific data and challenges to it; it still provides a "powerful summary of the phenomena observed in the spinal cord and brain, and has the capacity to explain many of the most mysterious and puzzling problems encountered in the clinic" (Melzack & Wall, 1982, p. 261). This theory has had enormous heuristic value in stimulating further research in the basic science of pain mechanisms. It has also given rise to new clinical treatments, including neurophysiologically based procedures (e.g., neural stimulation techniques, from peripheral nerves and collateral processes in the dorsal column of the spinal cord; North, 1989), pharmacological advances (Abram, 1993), behavioral treatments (Fordyce, Roberts, & Sternbach,

1985), and interventions targeting modification of attentional and perceptual processes involved in the pain experience (Turk, Meichenbaum, & Genest, 1983). After the gate control theory was proposed, no one could continue trying to explain pain exclusively in terms of peripheral factors.

THE BIOPSYCHOSOCIAL PERSPECTIVE: A BASIC DESCRIPTION

People differ markedly in how frequently they complain about physical symptoms, in their propensity to visit physicians when experiencing identical symptoms, and in their response to the same treatments (Desroaches, Kamen, & Ballard, 1967; Zborowski, 1969). Often the nature of patients' responses has little to do with their objective physical condition (Mechanic, 1962). For example, White, Williams, and Greenberg (1961) noted that fewer than one-third of individuals with clinically significant symptoms consult a physician. Conversely, from 30% to 50% of patients who seek treatment in primary care do not have specific diagnosable disorders (Dworkin & Massoth, 1994), and for up to 80% of people complaining of back pain, no physical basis for the pain can be identified (Deyo, 1986).

The distinction between "disease" and "illness" is crucial to understanding chronic pain. Disease is generally defined as an "objective biological event" that involves disruption of specific body structures or organ systems caused by pathological, anatomical, or physiological changes (Mechanic, 1986). In contrast to this customary view of physical disease, illness is defined as a "subjective experience or self-attribution" that a disease is present; it yields physical discomfort, emotional distress, behavioral limitations, and psychosocial disruption. In other words, illness refers to how the sick person and members of his or her family and wider social network receive, live with, and respond to symptoms and disability. It has been commonly observed clinically and in empirical studies that for many chronic conditions, the expressions of symptoms, related psychological distress, and extent of disability are only loosely related to observable pathophysiology (Magora & Schwartz, 1980; Waddell & Main, 1984).

In contrast to the biomedical model's emphasis on disease, the biopsychosocial model focuses on illness—the result of a complex interaction of biological, psychological, and social variables. From this perspective, the diversity in illness expression (which includes its severity, duration, and consequences for the individual) is accounted for by the interrelationships among biological changes, psychological status, and the social and cultural contexts that shape the patient's perception and response to illness.

The biopsychosocial way of thinking about the differing responses of patients to symptoms and the presence of chronic conditions is based on an understanding of the dynamic nature of these conditions. That is, by definition, chronic syndromes extend over time. Therefore, these conditions need to be viewed longitudinally as ongoing, multifactorial processes in which there is a dynamic and reciprocal interplay among biological, psychological, and social factors that shapes the experience and responses of patients (Dworkin, Von Korff, & LeResche, 1992). Biological factors may initiate, maintain, and modulate physical perturbations; psychological factors influence the appraisal and perception of internal physiological signs; and social factors shape the behavioral responses of patients to the perceptions of their physical perturbations.

Conversely, psychological factors may affect biology by affecting hormone production (e.g., Bandura, O'Leary, Taylor, Gauthier, & Gossard, 1987) and the autonomic nervous system (e.g., Flor, Turk, & Birbaumer, 1985). Behavioral responses may also affect biological factors, as when an individual decides not to engage in certain activities to reduce the symptoms. That is, avoidance of noxious symptoms is a powerful motivator. Failure to engage in physical activities, as in the case of a person with back pain, will result in physical deconditioning that may exacerbate nociceptive stimulation.

The picture is not complete unless we consider the direct effects of disease factors and treatment upon cognitive and behavioral factors. Biological factors and medications (e.g., steroids, opioids) may affect the ability to concentrate, cause fatigue, and influence individuals' interpretation of their state as well as of their ability to engage in certain activities.

At different points during the evolution of a disease or impairment, the weighting of these physical, psychological, and social factors may change. For example, during the acute phase of a syndrome biological factors may predominate, but over time psychological and social factors may assume a disproportionate role in accounting for symptoms and disability. Moreover, there is considerable heterogeneity in behavioral and psychological manifestations of dysfunction, both across persons with comparable symptoms and within the same individual overtime (Crook, Weir, & Tunks, 1989). Thus, there is not only variability in responses between people with the same diagnosis, but variability in the same individual throughout the course of a disease.

To understand the variable responses of patients to chronic conditions, it is essential that biological, psychological, and social factors all be considered. Moreover, a longitudinal perspective is essential: A cross-sectional approach will only permit consideration of these factors at a specific point in time, and chronic conditions are not stable but continue to evolve over time. What is observed at any one point in time is the adaptation of the individual to interacting biological, personal, and environmental factors. Thus, the hallmarks of the biopsychosocial perspective are (1) integrated action, (2) reciprocal determinism, and (3) evolution. No single factor in isolation—pathophysiological, psychological, or social—will adequately explain chronic pain status. This can be contrasted with the traditional biomedical model, whose emphasis on the somatogenic–psychogenic dichotomy is too narrow in scope to accommodate the complexity of chronic pain.

The biopsychosocial model suggests that elements of symptom reporting and disability are common to all clinically important pain conditions. Moreover, the model suggests that common elements shared by diverse pain conditions should be more evident at behavioral and psychosocial levels. For example, the emergence of maladaptive chronic pain behaviors implies a spread of effect beyond the biological level, such that, whatever their pathophysiological status, individuals with chronic pain may share behavioral, psychological, and social characteristics. Simultaneously, the biopsychosocial model allows pain conditions to retain unique pathobiological characteristics (e.g., musculoskeletal or neurological components) that are specific to a given disease or anatomical site.

Research supporting the role of a common set of psychological and social factors across diagnoses has been reported by several investigators. For example, a colleague and I (Turk & Rudy, 1988) used cluster analyses of patients' responses to the West Haven–Yale Multidimensional Pain Inventory (WHYMPI; Kerns, Turk, & Rudy, 1985) to discover empirically three subgroups of a heterogeneous sample of chronic pain patients, based on psychosocial and behavioral factors. In a subsequent study, we (Turk & Rudy, 1990) showed that covariance structures of WHYMPI scores were similar for back pain, headache, and TMD pain patients, resulting in similar profiles regardless of the anatomical site of pain. The percentages of patients with the different diagnoses varied; however, regardless of physical diagnosis, significant numbers of patients were classified within one of these three subgroups. These results have been replicated in several additional studies using very different pain samples (Jamison, Rudy, Penzien, & Mosely, 1994; Talo, 1992; Walter & Brannon, 1991).

Consistent with our results, Von Korff, Dworkin, and LeResche (1990) demonstrated that different measures of pain experience (e.g., intensity, interference, duration, persistence) showed similar intercorrelations across back pain, headache, abdominal pain, chest pain, and TMD pain; they also found that it was useful to employ consistent criteria for classification of chronic pain patients, regardless of the anatomical site of pain. These results suggest that a standard set of criteria for grading chronic pain and dysfunction can be applied to primary care back pain, headache, and TMD pain patients, and that such a classification yields groups that are similar in terms of unemployment rates, depression, use of opioids, and use of pain-related health care (Von Korff, Ormel, Keefe, & Dworkin, 1992).

As noted earlier, psychological factors and social factors have been viewed as reactions to disease and trauma in the traditional disease model, and thus have been considered of secondary importance. However, a voluminous literature has been generated since the 1960s supporting the significant role of psychological and social factors in the severity, maintenance, and exacerbation of pain. Despite the proliferation of research, these factors often are not incorporated within the treatment of chronic pain patients. In the remainder of this chapter, some of the social and psychological factors whose roles have been implicated in pain and disability are discussed, and their implications for treatment are described.

SUPPORT FOR THE IMPORTANCE
OF NONPHYSIOLOGICAL FACTORS

The history of medicine is replete with descriptions of diverse treatment modalities believed to be appropriate for treating pain, many of which are now known to have little therapeutic merit, and some of which may actually have been harmful to patients (Turk et al., 1983). In fact, Chapin (1915) suggested that, in many instances, not complying with physicians' therapeutic recommendations might be the best thing for patients to do!

Prior to the second half of the 19th century and the advent of research on sensory physiology, much of the pain treatment arsenal was composed of treatment modalities that had no direct mode of action upon organic mechanisms associated with the source of the pain. Yet, despite the absence of an adequate physiological basis, these treatments proved to have some therapeutic merit, at least for some patients. The effects were despairingly referred to as "placebo effects" or "psychological cures," with the implicit message being that the symptoms alleviated by such measures must be psychological (i.e., imaginary).

The same labels and the same message have been applied to some more modern treatment modalities. Although some of these sophisticated treatment regimens are based on specific knowledge of physiology, the mode of action may be unrelated to modification of physiological processes. For example, in a study of headache patients treated with pharmacological preparations, Fitzpatrick, Hopkins, and Harvard-Watts (1983) concluded that although a large number of patients benefited from the drug treatment, most of the improvement appeared to be unrelated to the pharmacological action per se. Similarly, biofeedback has been reported to be of potential benefit for a wide range of disorders, from headaches to TMDs to back pain; the actual effect of biofeedback, however, may be unrelated to modification of physiological activity (Blanchard, 1987; Burdette & Gale, 1988; Holroyd et al., 1984).

Deyo, Walsh, and Martin (1990) studied a group of patients with intractable low back pain, whose mean duration of symptoms was over 4 years. Given the long duration of symptoms, few improvements would be expected in the absence of an efficacious treatment. Following treatment with transcutaneous electrical nerve stimulation (TENS), patients experienced statistically significant and substantial improvements in overall functioning, physical functioning, and pain severity. However, the same results were produced with *sham* TENS. No statistically significant differences were obtained between the groups that received the true and sham TENS.

The importance of nonspecific (psychological) effects has been demonstrated in other areas of medicine, where there are objective signs of specific conditions (Coronary Drug Project Research Group, 1980). For example, in a large-scale trial of drug treatment for coronary artery disease, one group of subjects received placebo therapy. The placebo patients were divided into two subgroups: those who were compliant with the placebo treatment (taking more than 80% of the pills) and those who were noncompliant (taking less than 80% of the medication). After the investigators adjusted for a large number of cardiovascular risk factors, including previous myocardial infarction, congestive heart failure, hypertension, and diabetes, they found an enormous difference in mortality between the compliant and noncompliant subgroups: The compliant group's mortality rate at 5 years was less than half that of the noncompliant group. Here the outcome was not something as subjective as pain, but death! One explanation for these results is that people who are compliant are different from those who are noncompliant—different in health attitudes and behaviors (psychological and social factors). (For reviews of other medical and surgical studies reporting similar results, see Epstein & Cluss, 1982, and Roberts, Kewman, Mercier, & Hovell, 1993.)

Some pain syndromes seem responsive to almost any treatment. For example, Greene and Laskin (1974) followed 100 patients with TMDs from 6 months to 8 years following a diverse set of treatments, including analgesic medication, minor tranquilizers, physical exercises, intraoral appliances, injections into muscles and nerves, physical therapy modalities, and psychological counseling, along with various "placebo" treatments (inert drugs, nonoccluding bite plates, mock equilibration of the bite, and nonfunctional biofeedback). These investigators reported that 92% of the patients had no or only minor recurrences of symptoms. These treatments were all given in combination with reassurances, explanation for self-management, and a "general attitude of sympathetic understanding" (Greene & Laskin, 1974, p. 1367). Thus the common factors for the diverse set of successful treatments were nonspecific features. Should this be taken as an indication that TMDs are psychological and have no physical basis? Absolutely not; rather, they point up the important role of nonphysiological factors in the maintenance of these symptoms and responses to treatment.

SOCIOCULTURAL AND LEARNING FACTORS

Common-sense beliefs about illness and physicians are based both on prior experience and on social and cultural transmission of beliefs and expectancies. Ethnic group membership influences how one perceives, labels, responds to, and communicates various symptoms, as well as from whom one elects to obtain care when it is sought, and the types of treatments received (Mechanic, 1978). Several authors have specifically noted the importance of sociocultural factors in beliefs about and responses to pain (e.g., Lipton & Marbach, 1984; Wolff & Langley, 1968; Zborowski, 1969). Social factors influence how families and local groups respond to and interaction with patients (see discussion of operant conditioning below). Furthermore, ethnic expectations and sex and age stereotypes may influence the practitioner–patient relationship (Harkins, 1988; Melding, 1991; Turk, Okifuji, & Scharff, 1994, 1995).

Social Learning Mechanisms

The role of social learning has received some attention in the development and maintenance of chronic pain states. From this perspective, pain behaviors may be acquired through observational learning and modeling processes. That is, individuals can learn responses that were not previously in their behavioral repertoire by observing others who respond in these ways. Bandura (1969) has described and documented the important role of observational learning in many areas of human functioning.

Children acquire attitudes about health and health care, the perception and interpretation of symptoms and physiological processes, and appropriate responses to injury and disease from their parents and social environment; thus, they may be more or less likely to ignore or overrespond to symptoms they experience (Pennebaker, 1982). Culturally acquired perception and interpretation of symptoms determine how people deal with illness (Nerenz & Leventhal, 1983). The observation of others in pain is an event that captivates attention. This attention may have survival value: It may help children to avoid experiencing more pain and help them to learn what to do about acute pain.

There is ample experimental evidence of the role of social learning from controlled pain studies in the laboratory (Craig, 1986, 1988); there is also some evidence based on observations of patients' behaviors in naturalistic and clinical settings (Christensen & Mortensen, 1975; Fagerhaugh, 1975). For example, Vaughan and Lanzetta (1980, 1981) demonstrated that physiological responses to pain stimuli may be vicariously conditioned during observation of others in pain. Richard (1988) found that children of chronic pain patients chose more pain-related responses to scenarios presented to them and were more external in their health locus of control than were children with healthy or diabetic parents. Moreover, teachers rated the pain patients' children as displaying more illness behaviors (e.g., complaining, whining, days absent, visits to school nurse) than children of healthy controls.

Thus, expectancies and actual behavioral responses to nociceptive stimulation are based at least partially on prior learning history. This may contribute to the marked variability in response to objectively similar degrees of physical pathology noted by health care providers.

Operant Learning Mechanisms

Long ago, Collie (1913) discussed the effects of environmental factors in shaping the experience of people suffering with pain. However, a new era in thinking about pain began with Fordyce's (1976) description of the role of operant factors in chronic pain. The operant approach stands in marked contrast to the disease model of pain described earlier.

In the operant formulation, behavioral manifestations of pain rather than pain per se are central. It is suggested that when an individual is exposed to a stimulus that causes tissue damage, the immediate response is withdrawal or an attempt to escape from the noxious sensations. This may be accomplished through avoiding activity believed to cause or exacerbate pain, seeking help to reduce symptoms, and so forth. These behaviors are observable, and consequently are subject to the principles of learning.

The operant view proposes that acute "pain behaviors," such as limping to protect a wounded limb from producing additional nociceptive input, may come under the control of external contingencies of reinforcement and thus develop into chronic pain problems. Pain behaviors (e.g., complaining, inactivity) may be positively reinforced directly, for example, by attention from a spouse or health care providers. Pain behaviors may also be maintained by the escape from noxious stimulation through the use of drugs or rest, or the avoidance of undesirable activities such as work.

In addition, "well behaviors" (e.g., activity, working) may not be sufficiently reinforcing, and the more rewarding pain behaviors may therefore be maintained. The pain behaviors originally elicited by organic factors may thus come to occur totally or in part in response to reinforcing environmental events. Because of the consequences of specific behavioral responses, it is proposed that pain behaviors may persist long after the initial cause of the pain is resolved or greatly reduced.

The operant conditioning model does not concern itself with the initial cause of pain. Rather, it considers pain an internal subjective experience that may be maintained even after an initial physical basis for it is resolved. Again, this model focuses on overt manifestations of pain and suffering expressed as pain behaviors, such as limping, moaning, and avoiding activity. Emphasis is placed on the communicative function of these behaviors. Thus, in one sense, the operant conditioning model can be viewed as analogous to the psychogenic model described earlier. That is, psychological factors are treated as secondary reactions to sensory stimulation, rather than as factors directly involved in the perception of pain per se.

Several studies have provided evidence that supports the underlying assumptions of the operant conditioning model. For example, Cairns and Pasino (1977) and Doleys, Crocker, and Patton (1982) showed that pain behaviors (specifically, inactivity) could be decreased and well behaviors (specifically, activity) could be increased by verbal reinforcement with or without feedback and by the setting of exercise quotas. Block, Kremer, and Gaylor (1980) demonstrated that pain patients reported differential levels of pain in an experimental situation, depending upon whether they knew they were being observed by their spouses or by ward clerks. Pain patients with nonsolicitous spouses reported more pain when neutral observers were present than when the spouses were present. When solicitous spouses were present, pain patients reported more pain than in the neutral-observer condition.

Romano et al. (1992) videotaped patients and their spouses engaged in a series of cooperative household activities, and recorded patients' pain behaviors and spouses' responses. Sequential analyses showed that spouses' solicitous behaviors were more likely to precede and follow pain behaviors in pain patients than in healthy controls. Two additional studies (Flor, Kerns, & Turk, 1987; Turk, Kerns, & Rosenberg, 1992) found that chronic pain patients reported more intense pain and less activity when they indicated that their spouses were solicitous. These three studies suggest that spouses can serve as discriminative stimuli for the display of pain behaviors by chronic pain patients, including their reports of pain severity.

The operant view has also generated what has proven to be an effective treatment for select samples of chronic pain patients (Keefe, Dunsmore, & Bennett, 1992; Keefe & Williams, 1989; see Sanders, Chapter 5, this volume). Treatment focuses on extinction of pain behaviors and positive reinforcement of well behaviors.

Although operant factors undoubtedly play a role in the maintenance of disability, the operant conditioning model to explain the experience of pain has been criticized for its exclusive focus on motor pain behaviors, failure to consider the emotional and cognitive aspects of pain (A. J. M. Schmidt, 1985a, 1985b; A. J. M. Schmidt, Gierlings, & Peters, 1989; Turk & Flor, 1987), and failure to treat the subjective experience of pain (Kotarba, 1983).

Respondent Learning Mechanisms

Factors contributing to chronicity that have previously been conceptualized in terms of operant learning may also be initiated and maintained by respondent conditioning (Gentry & Bernal, 1977). Fordyce, Shelton, and Dundore (1982) have hypothesized that intermittent sensory stimulation from the site of bodily damage, environmental reinforcement, or successful avoidance of aversive social activity is not necessarily required to account for the maintenance of avoidance behavior or protective movements. Avoidance of activities has been shown to be related more to anxiety about pain than to actual reinforcement (Linton, 1985).

Lenthem, Slade, Troup, and Bentley (1983) and Linton, Melin, and Götestam (1984) have suggested that once an acute pain problem exists, fear of motor activities that the patient *expects* to result in pain may develop and motivate avoidance of activity. Nonoccurrence of pain is a powerful reinforcer for reduction of activity. Thus, the original respondent conditioning may be followed by an operant learning process whereby the nociceptive stimuli and the associated responses need no longer be present for the avoidance behavior to occur. In acute pain states it may be useful to reduce movement, and consequently to avoid pain, in order to accelerate the healing process. Over time, however, anticipatory anxiety related to activity may develop and act as a conditioned stimulus for sympathetic activation (the conditioned response), which may be maintained after the original unconditioned stimulus (injury) and unconditioned response (pain and sympathetic activation) have subsided (Lenthem et al., 1983; Linton et al., 1984; Philips, 1987a).

Pain related to sustained muscle contractions may, however, also be conceptualized as an unconditioned stimulus in the case where no acute injury is present; sympathetic activation and tension increases may be viewed as unconditioned responses that may elicit more pain, and conditioning may proceed in the same fashion as outlined above. Thus, although the original association between pain and pain-related stimuli results in anxiety regarding these stimuli, with time the expectation of pain related to activity may lead to avoidance of adaptive behaviors even if the nociceptive stimuli and the related sympathetic activation are no longer present.

In acute pain, many activities that are otherwise neutral or pleasurable may elicit or exacerbate pain, and are thus experienced as aversive and avoided. Over time, more and more activities may be seen as eliciting or exacerbating pain and will be avoided (stimulus generalization). Fear of pain may become conditioned to an expanding number of situations. Avoided activities may involve simple motor behaviors, but also work, leisure, and sexual activity (Philips, 1987a). In addition to the avoidance learning, pain may be exacerbated and maintained in these encounters with potentially pain-increasing situations because of the anxiety-related sympathetic activation and muscle tension increases that may occur in anticipation of pain and also as a consequence of pain (Flor, Birbaumer, & Turk, 1990). Thus, psychological factors may directly affect nociceptive stimulation and need not be viewed as only reactions to pain. I return to this point later in the chapter.

The persistence of avoidance of specific activities will reduce disconfirmations that are followed by corrected predictions (Rachman & Arntz, 1991). The prediction of pain promotes pain avoidance behavior, and overpredictions of pain promote excessive avoidance behavior, as demonstrated in studies by A. J. M. Schmidt (1985a, 1985b). Insofar as pain avoidance succeeds in preserving the overpredictions from repeated disconfirmation, they will continue unchanged (Rachman & Lopatka, 1988). By contrast, repeatedly engaging in behavior that produces significantly less pain than was predicted will be followed by adjustments in subsequent predictions, which also become more accurate. These increasingly accurate predictions will be followed by increasingly appropriate avoidance behavior—even by elimination of all avoidance if that is appropriate. These observations add support to the importance of physical therapy, with patients progressively increasing their activity levels despite their fears of injury and discomfort associated with renewed use of deconditioned muscles.

Thus, from a respondent conditioning perspective, the patient may have learned to associate increases in pain with all kinds of stimuli that were originally associated with nociceptive stimulation (stimulus generalization). Sitting, walking, cognitively demanding work or social interaction, sexual activity, or even thoughts about these activities may increase anticipatory anxiety and concomitant physiological and biochemical changes (Philips, 1987a). Subsequently, patients may display maladaptive responses to many stimuli and reduce the frequency of their performance of many activities other than those that initially induced pain. The physical abnormalities often observed in chronic pain patients (e.g., distorted gait, decreased range of motion, muscular fatigue) may thus actually be secondary to changes initiated in behavior through learning. As the pain symptoms persist, more and more situations may elicit anxiety and anticipatory pain and depression, because of the low rate of reinforcement obtained when behavior is greatly reduced (cf. Lethem et al., 1983). With chronic pain, the anticipation of suffering or prevention of suffering may be sufficient for the long-term maintenance of avoidance behaviors.

PSYCHOLOGICAL FACTORS

Cognitive Factors

As noted earlier, individuals are not passive responders to physical sensation; rather, they actively seek to make sense of their experience. They appraise their conditions and decide by matching sensations to some pre-existing implicit model whether a particular sensation is a symptom of a particular physical disorder that requires attention. Thus, to some extent, each individual functions with a uniquely constructed reality. When information is ambiguous, he or she relies on general attitudes and beliefs based on prior learning history. These beliefs determine the meaning and significance of the problems, as well as the perceptions of appropriate treatment. If we accept the premise that pain is a complex, subjective phenomenon that is uniquely experienced by each individual, then knowledge about idiosyncratic beliefs, appraisals, and coping repertoires becomes critical for optimal treatment planning and for accurately evaluating treatment outcome (Reesor & Craig, 1988).

A great deal of research has been directed toward identifying cognitive factors that contribute to pain and disability (e.g., Jensen, Turner, Romano, & Karoly, 1991; Turk & Rudy, 1986, 1992). These studies have consistently demonstrated that patients' attitudes, beliefs, and expectancies about their plight, themselves, their coping resources, and the health care system affect their reports of pain, activity, disability, and response to treatment (Flor & Turk, 1988; Jensen, Turner, & Romano, 1994a; Tota-Faucette, Gil, Williams, & Goli, 1993).

Beliefs about Pain

Clinicians working with chronic pain patients are aware that patients having similar pain histories and reports of pain may differ greatly in their beliefs about their pain. Certain beliefs may lead to maladaptive coping, exacerbation of pain, increased suffering, and greater disability.

Pain is likely to produce considerably more suffering and behavioral dysfunction if it is interpreted as signifying ongoing tissue damage than if it is viewed as being the result of a stable problem that may improve, although the amount of nociceptive input in the two cases may be equivalent (Spiegel & Bloom, 1983). Patients who believe that their pain is likely to persist may be quite passive in their coping efforts and fail to make use of cognitive or behavioral strategies to cope with pain. Patients who consider their pain to be an unexplainable mystery may negatively evaluate their own abilities to control or decrease pain, and may be less likely to rate their coping strategies as effective in controlling and decreasing pain (Williams & Keefe, 1991; Williams & Thorn, 1989).

Moreover, patients' beliefs about the implications of a disease can affect their perception of symptoms. For example, only rarely is pain the primary symptom that brings cancer patients to seek medical attention; however, the frequency of pain complaints appears to increase significantly following the diagnosis of cancer (Woodforde & Fielding, 1979). Spiegel and Bloom (1983) reported that the pain severity ratings of cancer patients could be predicted by the use of analgesics and by the patients' affective state, but also by their interpretations of pain. Patients who attributed their pain to a worsening of their underlying disease experienced more pain than did patients with more benign interpretations, despite the same level of disease progression. Cassell (1982) cited an example of a patient whose pain could easily be controlled with codeine when he attributed it to sciatica, but required significantly greater amounts of opioids to achieve the same degree of relief when he attributed it to metastatic cancer.

A person's cognitions (beliefs, appraisals, expectancies) regarding the consequences of an event and his or her ability to deal with it are hypothesized to affect functioning in two ways: They may have a direct influence on mood and an indirect one through their impact on coping efforts.

The presence of pain may change the way individuals process pain-related and other information. For example, the presence of chronic pain may focus attention on all types of bodily signals. Arntz and Schmidt (1989) have suggested that the processing of internal information may become disturbed in chronic pain patients. It is possible that pain patients become preoccupied with and overemphasize physical symptoms and interpret them as painful stimulation, although they may be less able then healthy controls to differentiate threshold levels. Studies of patients with diverse conditions (e.g., irritable bowel syndrome, Whitehead, 1980; fibromyalgia, Tunks, Crook, Norman, & Kalasher, 1988; angina pectoris, Droste & Roskamm, 1983; headaches, Borgeat, Hade, Elie, & Larouche, 1984) have supported the presence of what appears to be a hypersensitivity characterized by a lowered threshold for labeling stimuli as noxious. Patients may interpret pain symptoms as indicative of an underlying disease, and they may do everything to avoid pain exacerbation, most often by resorting to inactivity. For example, in acute pain states, bed rest is often prescribed to relieve pressure on the spine. Patients may begin to ascribe to a belief that any movement of the back may worsen their condition, and they may still maintain this belief in the chronic state, when inaction is not only unnecessary but harmful.

In a set of studies, A. J. M. Schmidt (1985a, 1985b) found that patients with low back pain demonstrated poor behavioral persistence in various exercise tasks, and that their performance on these tasks was independent of physical exertion or actual self-reports of pain, but rather was related to *previous* pain reports. These patients appeared to have a negative view of their abilities and expected increased pain if they performed physical exercises. In another study, Council, Ahern, Follick, and Cline (1988) found that 83% of patients with low back pain reported that they were unable to complete a movement sequence including leg lifts and lateral bends because of *anticipated* pain; only 5% were unable to perform the activities because of actual lack of ability. Thus, the rationale for their avoidance of exercise was not the presence of pain, but their *learned expectation* of heightened pain and accompanying physical arousal, which might further exacerbate pain and reinforce the patients' beliefs regarding the pervasiveness of their disability. These results are consistent with the respondent learning factors described above. A. J. M. Schmidt has postulated that patients' negative perceptions of their capabilities for physical performance form a vicious circle, with the failure to perform activities reinforcing the perception of helplessness and incapacity.

Jensen, Turner, Romano, and Lawler (1994b) demonstrated that patients' beliefs that emotions affected their pain, that others should be solicitous when they experienced pain, and that they were disabled by pain were positively associated with psychosocial dysfunction. Patients who believed that they were disabled by pain and that they should avoid activity because pain signified damage were more likely to reveal physical disability than were patients who did not hold these beliefs. Similarly, Slater, Hall, Atkinson, and Garfin (1991) reported that patients' beliefs about their pain and disability were significantly related to actual measures of disability, but not to physicians' ratings of disease severity.

As Pennebaker, Gonder-Frederick, Cox, and Hoover (1985) showed, once cognitive structures (based on memories and meaning) about a disease are formed, they become stable and are very difficult to modify. Patients tend to avoid experiences that could invalidate their beliefs, and they guide their behavior in accordance with these beliefs even in situation where the beliefs are no longer valid. Consequently, as noted above in regard to the role of respondent conditioning, they do not receive corrective feedback.

In addition to beliefs about the ability to function despite pain, beliefs about pain per se appear to be of importance in understanding patients' response to treatment, compliance with treatment, and disability. For example, Schwartz, DeGood, and Shutty (1985) presented patients with information about the role of cognitive, affective, and behavioral factors and their own role in the rehabilitation process. They found that patients who rated the information as applicable to their pain condition had much better treatment outcomes. Those who disagreed with the concepts presented were found at follow-up to have higher levels of pain, lower levels of activity, and a high degree of dissatisfaction.

The results of several studies suggest that when successful rehabilitation occurs, there appears to be an important cognitive shift—a shift from beliefs about helplessness and passivity to resourcefulness and ability to function regardless of pain. Consistent with the central role of a cognitive shift in rehabilitation, Herman and Baptiste (1981) noted that successes and failures in their treatment program could be distinguished most prominently on the basis of changed versus unchanged thought patterns relative to the prospect of living useful lives despite pain. Williams and Thorn (1989) found that chronic pain patients who believed that their pain was an "unexplained mystery" reported high levels of psychological distress and pain, and also showed poorer treatment compliance, than patients who believed that they understood their pain.

In an innovative process study designed to evaluate the direct association between patients' beliefs and pain symptoms, Newton and Barbaree (1987) used a modified thought-sampling procedure to evaluate the nature of patients' cognitions during and immediately following headache, both prior to and following treatment. Results indicated significant changes in certain aspects of headache-related thinking in the treated groups compared to the control group. Reduction in negative appraisal ("It's getting worse," "There is nothing I can do") and increase in positive appraisal of treated subjects, indicated that these subjects were evaluating headaches in a more positive fashion. Newton and Barbaree (1987) noted that patients who reported the largest positive shift in appraisal also reported the greatest reduction in headache intensity. Treated patients also reported experiencing significantly fewer headache days per week and lower intensity of pain than untreated controls. Correlational analyses suggested that complaints of more intense pain were associated with more negative appraisals of headache episodes. Similar results were reported in a study (Flor & Turk, 1988) in which the negative thoughts of patients with back pain and rheumatoid arthritis (RA) predicted pain, disability, and physician visits.

The results of the Newton and Barbaree (1987) study support the argument that changes in cognitive reactions to headache may underlie headache improvement (see also Blanchard, 1987; Holroyd & Andrasik, 1982). There appears to be strong evidence pointing toward a reduction in negative appraisal as representing the potential change mechanism in many outcome studies of pain treatment. In considering the efficacy of biofeedback for back pain patients, Nouwen and Solinger (1979) concluded that "simultaneous accomplishment of muscle tension reduction and lowering reported pain convinced patients that muscle tension, and subsequently pain, could be controlled. ... As self-control could not be demonstrated in most patients, it seems plausible that the feeling of self-control, rather than actual control of physiological functions or events is crucial for further reductions" (p. 110). In other words, it appears that the extent to which voluntary control over muscles has been achieved dictates the outcome, which is not, however, necessarily accompanied by lasting reductions in muscular reactivity.

Similar to Nouwen and Solinger's (1979) interpretation, Blanchard (1987) speculated that for headache patients the maintenance of treatment effects endures in spite of almost universal cessation of regular home practice of biofeedback, because the self-perpetuating cycle of chronic headache has been broken. The experience of headache serves as a stressor, which in part causes a future headache. It may also serve to maintain improper consumption of analgesic medication, the cessation of which can lead to "rebound headache." By the end of biofeedback treatment, when the patient has experienced noticeable headache relief, it is as if the patient has redefined himself or herself as someone able to cope with headaches. As a consequence, one source of stress is removed, and the patient copes with recurrences more adaptively.

Clearly, it appears essential for patients with chronic pain to develop adaptive beliefs about the relation among impairment, pain, suffering, and disability, and to de-emphasize the role of experienced pain in their regulation of functioning. In fact, results from numerous treatment outcome studies have shown that changes in pain level do not parallel changes in other variables of interest, including activity level, medication use, return to work, rated ability to cope with pain, and pursuit of further treatment (see the recent meta-analysis reported by Flor, Fydrich, & Turk, 1992).

Beliefs about Controllability

There is evidence that the explicit expectation of uncontrollable pain stimulation may cause the following nociceptive input to be perceived as more intense (Leventhal & Everhart, 1979). Thus, patients who have associated activity with pain may expect heightened levels of pain when they attempt to get involved in activity, and then may actually perceive higher levels of pain or avoid activity altogether. There are many laboratory studies demonstrating that controllability of aversive stimulation reduces its impact (e.g., Flor & Turk, 1988; Jensen & Karoly, 1991; Main & Waddell, 1991; Wells, 1994).

Chronic pain patients typically perceive a lack of personal control, which probably relates to their ongoing but unsuccessful efforts to control their pain. A large proportion of chronic pain patients tend to believe that they have limited ability to exert control over their pain (Turk & Rudy, 1988). Such negative, maladaptive appraisals about their situation and their personal efficacy may reinforce the experience of demoralization, inactivity, and overreaction to nociceptive stimulation commonly observed in chronic pain patients (Biedermann, McGhie, Monga, & Shanks, 1987).

The relationship between perceived controllability and pain has been demonstrated in a variety of chronic pain syndromes. Mizener, Thomas, and Billings (1988) demonstrated that successfully treated migraine headache patients reported correlations between reduction in headache activity and increases in perceived control over physiological activity and their health in general. We (Flor & Turk, 1988) examined the relationship among general and situation-specific pain-related thoughts, conceptions of personal control, pain severity, and disability levels in patients with chronic low back pain and RA. The general and situation-specific convictions of uncontrollability and helplessness were more highly related to pain and disability than were disease-related variables for both samples. The combination of both situation-specific and general cognitive variables explained 32% and 60% of the variance in pain and disability, respectively. The addition of disease-related variables improved the predictions only marginally. Jensen and Karoly (1991) have shown that patients' beliefs about the extent to which they can control their pain are associated with such outcome variables as medication use, activity levels, and psychological functioning.

Self-Efficacy

Closely related to the sense of control over aversive stimulation is the concept of "self-efficacy." A self-efficacy expectation is defined as a personal conviction that one can successfully execute a course of action (i.e., perform required behaviors) to produce a desired outcome in a given situation. This construct has been demonstrated as a major mediator of therapeutic change.

Bandura (1977) has suggested that if an individual has sufficient motivation to engage in a behavior, the individual's self-efficacy beliefs are what determine his or her choice of activities to initiate, the amount of effort he or she will expend, and how long he or she will persist in the face of obstacles and aversive experiences. Efficacy judgments are based on the following four sources of information regarding one's capabilities, in descending order of impact: (1) one's own past performance at the task or similar tasks; (2) the performance accomplishments of others who are perceived to be similar to oneself; (3) verbal persuasion by others that one is capable; and (4) perception of one's own state of physiological arousal, which is in turn partly determined by prior efficacy estimation. Performance mastery experience can be created by encouraging patients to undertake subtasks that are increasingly difficult or close to the desired behavioral repertoire. From this perspective, the occurrence of coping behaviors is conceptualized as being mediated by the individual's beliefs that situational demands do not exceed his or her coping resources.

Dolce, Crocker, Moletteire, and Doleys (1986b) and Litt (1988) reported that low self-efficacy ratings regarding pain control are related to low pain tolerance, and that they are better predictors of tolerance than are objective levels of noxious stimuli. Several studies have also obtained self-efficacy ratings from pain patients and related them to patients' ability to control pain. For example, Manning and Wright (1983) obtained self-efficacy ratings from women expecting their first child concerning their ability to have a medication-free childbirth. These ratings were good predictors of medication use and time in labor without medication. Similarly, Council et al. (1988) had patients rate their self-efficacy as well as expectancy of pain related to the performance of movement tasks. Patients' performance levels were highly related to patients' self-efficacy expectations, which in turn appeared to be determined by patients' expectancy of pain levels.

Converging lines of evidence from investigations of both laboratory and clinical pain indicate that perceived self-efficacy operates as an important cognitive factor in pain control (e.g., Bandura et al., 1987; Lorig, Chastain, Ung, Shoor, & Holman, 1989), adaptive psychological functioning (e.g., Lorig et al., 1989; Rosensteil & Keefe, 1983; Spinhoven, Ter Kuile, Linssen, & Gazendam, 1989), disability (e.g., Dolce, Crocker, & Doleys, 1986a; Lorig et al., 1989), impairment (e.g., Lorig et al., 1989), and treatment outcome (e.g., O'Leary, Shoor, Lorig, & Holman, 1988; Philips, 1987b). What are the mechanisms that account for the observed association between self-efficacy and behavioral outcome? Cioffi (1991) has suggested that at least four psychological processes may be responsible: (1) As perceived self-efficacy decreases anxiety and its concomitant physiological arousal, the person may approach the task with less potentially distressing physical information to begin with; (2) the efficacious person is able to willfully distract attention from potentially threatening physiological sensations; (3) the efficacious person perceives and is distressed by physical sensations, but simply persists in the face of them (stoicism); and (4) physical sensations are neither ignored nor necessarily distressing, but rather are relatively free to take on a broad distributions of meanings (change interpretations).

Bandura (1977) has suggested that those techniques that most enhance mastery experiences will be the most powerful tools for bringing about behavior change. He has proposed that cognitive variables are the primary determinants of behavior, but that these variables are most affected by performance accomplishments. The studies on headache, back pain, and RA cited above appear to support Bandura's supposition.

Cognitive Errors

In addition to specific self-efficacy beliefs, a number of investigators have suggested that a common set of "cognitive errors" will affect perceptions of pain, affective distress, and disability (Lefebvre, 1981, Smith, Aberger, Follick, & Ahern, 1986a; Smith, Follick, Ahern, & Adams, 1986b; Smith, Peck, Milano, & Ward, 1990). A cognitive error may be defined as a negatively distorted belief about oneself or one's situation.

Lefebvre (1981) developed a Cognitive Errors Questionnaire to assess cognitive distortions in back pain patients. He found that patients with chronic low back pain were particularly prone to such cognitive errors as "catastrophizing" (self-statements, thoughts, and images anticipating negative outcomes or aversive aspects of an experience, or misinterpreting the outcome of an event as extremely negative); "overgeneralization" (assuming that the outcome of one event necessarily applies to the outcome of future or similar events); "personalization" (interpreting negative events as reflecting personal meaning or responsibility); and "selective abstraction" (selectively attending to negative aspects of experience). Dufton (1989) reported that persons experiencing chronic pain had a tendency to make cognitive errors related to the emotional difficulties associated with living with pain, rather than to the pain intensity alone; moreover, those who made such errors were more depressed.

As is the case with self-efficacy, specific cognitive errors and distortions have been linked consistently to depression (e.g., Gil, Williams, Keefe, & Beckham, 1990; Lefebvre, 1981; Slater et al., 1991), self-reported pain severity (e.g., Gil et al., 1990; Keefe & Williams, 1989), and disability (e.g., Flor & Turk, 1988; Smith et al., 1986b) in chronic pain patients. Such negative thoughts (1) predict long-term adjustment to chronic pain; (2) may mediate a portion of the relationship between disease severity and adjustment; and (3) make a unique contribution (over and above other cognitive factors) to the prediction of adjustment (Smith et al., 1990).

Catastrophizing appears to be a particularly potent cognitive error that greatly influences pain and disability (Keefe et al., 1990a, 1990b). Several lines of research, including experimental laboratory studies of acute pain with normal volunteers and field studies with patients suffering clinical pain, have indicated that catastrophizing and adaptive coping strategies (see below) are important in determining the reaction to pain.

Two findings from laboratory studies are particularly important. Individuals who spontaneously utilized fewer catastrophizing self-statements and/or more adaptive coping strategies rated experimentally induced pain as lower and tolerated painful stimuli longer than did those who indicated they engaged in more catastrophizing thoughts (Heyneman, Fremouw, Gano, Kirkland, & Heiden, 1990; Spanos, Horton, & Chaves, 1975). Individuals who spontaneously utilized more catastrophizing self-statements reported more pain in several acute and chronic pain studies, as well as more distress and disability (Butler, Damarin, Beaulieu, Schwebel, & Thorn, 1989; Flor & Turk, 1988; Main & Waddell, 1991; Martin, Nathan, Milech, & Van Keppel, 1989; Turner & Clancy, 1986; Wells, 1994).

Butler et al. (1989) demonstrated that in the case of postsurgical pain, cognitive coping strategies and catastrophizing thoughts correlated significantly with medication, pain reports, and nurses' judgments of patients' pain tolerance. Turner and Clancy (1986) showed that during cognitive-behavioral treatment, reductions in catastrophizing were significantly related to increases in pain tolerance and reductions in physical and psychosocial impairment. They also showed that following cognitive-behavioral treatment, reductions in catastrophizing were related to reductions in pain intensity and physical impairment. As noted earlier, we (Flor & Turk, 1988) found that in low back pain sufferers and RA patients, significant percentages of the variance in pain and disability were accounted for by cognitive factors that we labeled catastrophizing, helplessness, adaptive coping, and resourcefulness. In both the low back pain and the RA groups, the cognitive variables of catastrophizing and adaptive coping had substantially more explanatory power than did disease-related variables or impairment. Finally, Keefe, Brown, Wallston, and Caldwell (1989) found that RA patients who reported high levels of pain, physical disability, and depression indicated excessive catastrophizing ideation on questionnaires administered 6 months earlier.

Coping

Self-regulation of pain and its impact depend upon individuals' specific ways of dealing with pain, adjusting to pain, and reducing or minimizing the pain and distress caused by pain—in other words, their coping strategies. Coping is assumed to be manifested by spontaneously employed purposeful and intentional acts, and it can be assessed in terms of overt and covert behaviors. Overt behavioral coping strategies include rest, medication, and use of relaxation. Covert coping strategies include various means of distracting oneself from pain, reassuring oneself that the pain will diminish, seeking information, and problem solving. Particular strategies need not always be adaptive or maladaptive. Coping strategies are thought to act to alter both the perception of pain intensity and the ability to manage or tolerate pain and to continue everyday activities (Turk et al., 1983).

Studies have found active coping strategies (efforts to function in spite of pain or to distract oneself from pain, such as engaging in activity or ignoring pain) to be associated with adaptive functioning, and passive coping strategies (such as depending on others for help in pain control and restricting one's activities) to be related to greater pain and depression (Brown & Nicassio, 1987; Brown, Nicassio, & Wallston, 1989; Lawson, Reesor, Keefe, & Turner, 1990; Tota-Faucette et al., 1993). However, beyond this, there is no evidence supporting the greater effectiveness of any one active coping strategy compared to any other (Fernandez & Turk, 1989). It seems more likely that different strategies will be more effective than others for some individuals at some times, but not necessarily for all individuals all of the time.

A number of studies have demonstrated that if individuals are instructed in the use of adaptive coping strategies, the rating of intensity of pain decreases and tolerance of pain increases (for a review, see Fernandez & Turk, 1989). The most important factor in poor coping appears to be the presence of catastrophizing, rather than differences in the nature of specific adaptive coping strategies (e.g., Heyneman et al., 1990; Martin et al., 1989). Turk et al. (1983) concluded that "what appears to distinguish low from high pain tolerant individuals is their cognitive processing, catastrophizing thoughts and feelings that precede, accompany, and follow aversive stimulation" (p. 197).

Affective Factors

Pain is ultimately a subjective, private experience, but it is invariably described in terms of sensory and affective properties. As defined by the International Association for the Study of Pain, "[Pain] is unquestionably a sensation in a part or parts of the body but it is also always unpleasant and therefore also an emotional experience " (Merskey, 1986, p. S217). The central and interactive roles of sensory information and affective state are supported by an overwhelming amount of evidence (Fernandez & Turk, 1992).

The affective components of pain include many different emotions, but they are primarily negative in quality. Anxiety and depression have received the greatest amount of attention in chronic pain patients. The importance of anxiety in the maintenance of chronic pain has been described above. Research suggests that from 40% to 50% of chronic pain patients suffer from depression. In the majority of cases, depression appears to be patients' reaction to their plight. Some have suggested that chronic pain is a form of masked depression; although this may be true in a small number of cases, the research on this topic does not suggest that depression precedes the development of chronic pain (Turk & Salovey, 1984).

Given what has been discussed above, it is not surprising that a large number of chronic pain patients are depressed. It is interesting to ponder the other side of the coin: Given the nature of the symptom and the problems created by chronic pain, how is it that all such patients are *not* depressed? My colleagues and I (Rudy, Kerns, & Turk, 1988; Turk et al., 1994, 1995) examined this question and determined that patients' appraisals of the impact of the pain on their lives and of their ability to exert any control over the pain and their lives mediated the pain–depression relationship. That is, those patients who felt that they could continue to function despite their pain, and that they could maintain some control despite their pain, did not become depressed.

Anger has been widely observed in individuals with chronic pain (e.g., Kinder & Curtiss, 1988; Schwartz, Slater, Birchler, & Atkinson, 1991). Summers, Rapoff, Varghese, Porter, and Palmer (1992) examined patients with spinal cord injuries and found that anger and hostility explained 33% of the variance in pain severity. Pilowsky and Spence (1975) found an incidence of "bottled-up anger" in 53% of chronic pain patients. Kerns, Rosenberg, and Jacob (1994) found that the internalization of angry feelings accounted for a significant proportion of variances in measures of pain intensity, perceived inter-ference, and reported frequency of pain behaviors. Corbishley, Hendrickson, and Beutler (1990) reported that even though chronic pain patients in psychotherapy might present an image of themselves as even-tempered, 88% of the patients treated acknowledged their feelings of anger when these were explicitly sought.

Frustrations related to persistence of symptoms, limited information on etiology, and repeated treatment failures, along with anger toward employers, the insurance provider, the health care system, family members, and themselves, all contribute to the general dysphoric mood of these patients. The impact of anger and frustration on exacerbation of pain and treatment acceptance has not received much attention, but it would not be unreasonable to expect that the presence of anger may serve as a complicating factor—increasing autonomic arousal and blocking motivation and acceptance of treatments oriented toward rehabilitation and disability management rather than cure, which are often the only treatments available for chronic pain (Fernandez & Turk, 1995).

Personality Factors

The search for specific personality factors that may predispose individuals to develop chronic pain problems has been a major emphasis of psychosomatic medicine. Studies have attempted to identify a specific "migraine personality," an "RA personality," and a more general "pain-prone personality" (Blumer & Heilbronn, 1982). By and large, these efforts have received little support and have been challenged (Turk & Salovey, 1984). However, on the basis of their prior experiences, people develop idiosyncratic ways of interpreting information and coping with stress. There is no question that these unique patterns will have an effect on their perceptions of and responses to the presence of pain.

Many studies have attempted to use different measures of psychopathology to pre-dict pain patients' responses to conservative and surgical interventions, but discussion of this topic is beyond the scope of this chapter. Several papers have reviewed this extensive literature (e.g., Bradley, Haile, & Jaworski, 1992; Love & Peck, 1987; McCreary, 1993; see also Gatchel, Chapter 2, this volume).

THE EFFECT OF PSYCHOLOGICAL AND SOCIAL FACTORS ON PAIN

Psychological and social factors may act indirectly on pain and disability by reducing physical activity, and consequently reducing muscle flexibility, muscle tone, strength, and physical endurance. Fear of reinjury, fear of loss of disability compensation, and job dis-satisfaction can also influence the return to work. Several studies have suggested that psychological factors, particularly cognitive factors, may also have a direct effect on physiological parameters associated more directly with the production or exacerbation of nociception. Cognitive interpretations and affective arousal may directly affect physiology by increasing sympathetic nervous system arousal (Bandura, Taylor, Williams, Mefford, & Barchas, 1985), production of endogenous opioids (endorphins) (Bandura et al., 1987), and elevated levels of muscle tension (Flor et al., 1985, Flor, Birbaumer, Schugens, & Lutzenberger, 1992).

Effect of Thoughts on Sympathetic Arousal and Muscle Tension

Circumstances that are appraised as potentially threatening to safety or comfort are likely to generate strong physiological reactions. For example, Rimm and Litvak (1969) demonstrated that subjects exhibited physiological arousal when they only thought about or imagined a painful stimulus. Barber and Hahn (1962) showed that subjects' self-reported discomfort and physiological responses (frontalis electromyographic [EMG] activity, heart rate, skin conductance) were similar when they imagined taking part in a cold-pressor test and when they actually participated in it. In patients suffering from recurrent migraine headaches, Jamner and Tursky (1987) observed increases in skin conductance related to the processing of words describing migraine headaches.

Chronic increases in sympathetic nervous system activation, known to increase skeletal muscle tone, may set the stage for hyperactive muscle contraction and possibly for the persistence of a contraction following conscious muscle activation. Excessive sympathetic arousal and maladaptive behaviors are viewed as the immediate precursors of muscle hypertonicity, hyperactivity, and persistence. These in turn may be the proximate causes of chronic muscle spasm and pain. It is not unusual for persons in pain to exaggerate or amplify the significance of their problem and needlessly "turn on" their sympathetic nervous systems (Ciccone & Grzesiak, 1984). In this way, cognitive processes may influence sympathetic arousal and thereby predispose individuals to further injury or otherwise complicate the process of recovery.

Several studies support the direct effect of cognitive factors on muscle tension. For example, we (Flor et al., 1985) demonstrated that discussing stressful events and pain produced elevated levels of EMG activity localized to the site of back pain patients' pain. The extent of abnormal muscular reactivity was better predicted by depression and cognitive coping style than by pain demographic variables (e.g., number of surgeries or duration of pain). Flor et al. (1992) replicated these results and extended them to patients with TMDs. For this group, imagery reconstruction of episodes and pain produced elevated tension in the facial muscles.

Although "causal" pain eliciting psychophysiological mechanisms (e.g., elevated EMG) may exist, only one longitudinal study has been directly reported that directly tested the causal relationship. This study found no consistent muscle hyperactivity during headache attacks compared to pain-free baseline; it found no differences in EMG activity between tension-type headache patients and controls; and EMG did not covary with stress, negative affect, or pain (Hatch et al., 1991). Moreover, the natural evolution and course of many chronic pain syndromes are unknown. At the present time, it is probably more appropriate to refer to abnormal psychophysiological patterns as antecedents of chronic pain states or to view them as consequences of chronic pain that subsequently maintain or exacerbate the symptoms, rather than to assign them any direct etiological significance.

Effects of Thoughts on Biochemistry

Bandura et al. (1987) directly examined the role of central opioid activity in cognitive control of pain. They provided subjects with instructions and practice in using different coping strategies for alleviating pain, including diversion of attention from pain sensations to other matters, vivification of engrossing imagery, dissociation of the limb in pain from the rest of the body, transformation of pain sensations into nonpain sensations, and self-encouragement of coping efforts. They demonstrated that (1) self-efficacy increased with cognitive training, (2) self-efficacy predicted pain tolerance, and (3) naloxone (an opioid antagonist) blocked the effects of cognitive control. The third result specifically implicates the direct effects of thoughts on the endogenous opioids. Bandura et al. (1987) concluded that the physical mechanism by which self-efficacy influences pain perception may be at least partially mediated by the endogenous opioid system. This conclusion fits well with the data of Maier, Dugan, Grau, and Hyson (1984), who showed that uncontrollability of a stressor elicited opioid-mediated hypoalgesia. Opioid release was closely related to psychological factors, specifically subjects' sense of control.

O'Leary et al. (1988) provided cognitive-behavioral stress management treatment to RA patients. RA is an autoimmune disease that may result from impaired functioning of the suppressor T-cell system. Enhancement of self-efficacy (expectations about the ability to control pain and disability) was correlated with treatment effectiveness: Those with higher self-efficacy and greater self-efficacy enhancement displayed greater numbers of suppressor T-cells (a direct effect of self-efficacy on physiology). Increased self-efficacy for functioning was also significantly associated with decreased disability and joint impairment.

Much more research is required before confidence can be placed in the direct effects of thoughts on physical mechanisms, inducing nociception. However, the large body of research in psychoneuroimmunology attests to the direct role of psychological factors in the body's immune system. The results of the handful of studies available would seem to indicate that further research examining the direct effects of thoughts on the physiology known to be associated with pain—namely, sympathetic nervous system activity and the endorphins—would be a fruitful endeavor.

IMPLICATIONS FOR TREATMENT

Pain is a subjective perceptual event that is not solely dependent on the extent of tissue damage or organic dysfunction. The intensity of pain reported and the responses to the perception of pain are influenced by a wide range of factors, such as meaning of the situation, attentional focus, mood, prior learning history, cultural background, environmental contingencies, social supports, and financial resources, among others. These factors were viewed until fairly recently as reactions to pain and thus as of secondary importance. The research reviewed in this chapter, however, demonstrates that these factors can play a role in the etiology, severity, exacerbation, and maintenance of pain, suffering, and disability.

Treatment based on the biopsychosocial perspective must not only address the biological basis of symptoms; it must incorporate the full range of social and psychological factors that have been shown to affect pain, distress, and disability. Therefore, treatment should be designed not only to alter physical contributors but also to change the patient's behaviors, regardless of the patient's specific pathophysiology and without necessarily controlling pain per se (Fordyce, 1976; Turk et al., 1983).

Treatment from the biopsychosocial perspective focuses on providing the patient with techniques to gain a sense of control over the effects of pain on his or her life, as well as on actually modifying the affective, behavioral, cognitive, and sensory facets of the experience. Behavioral experiences help to show patients that they are capable of more than they assumed they were, thus increasing their sense of personal competence. Cognitive techniques help to place affective, behavioral, cognitive, and sensory responses under a patient's control. The assumption is that long-term maintenance of behavioral changes will occur only if the patient has learned to attribute success to his or her own efforts. There are suggestions that these treatments can result in changes in beliefs about pain, coping style, and reported pain severity, as well as in direct behavior changes (Dolce et al., 1986b; Turner & Clancy, 1986, 1988). Treatment that results in increases in perceived control over pain and decreases in catastrophizing has also been associated with decreases in pain severity ratings and functional disability (Jensen et al., 1991; Turner, 1991).

An important implication of the biopsychosocial perspective is the need first to identify the relevant physical, psychological, and social characteristics of patients, and then to develop treatments matched to patients' characteristics and to evaluate their efficacy. The ultimate aim is the prescription of treatment components that have been shown to maximize outcome for different subsets of patients (Turk, 1990).

SUMMARY AND CONCLUSIONS

The biomedical factors that may have initiated a patient's original report of pain play less and less of a role in disability over time, although secondary problems associated with deconditioning may exacerbate and serve to maintain the problem. Inactivity leads to increased focus on and preoccupation with the body and pain, and these cognitive/attentional changes increase the likelihood of misinterpreting symptoms, the overemphasis on symptoms, and the patient's self-perception as disabled. Reduction of activity, anger, fear of reinjury, pain, loss of compensation, and an environment that perhaps unwittingly supports the "pain patient role" can impede alleviation of pain, successful rehabilitation, reduction of disability, and improvement in adjustment.

The variability of patients' responses to nociceptive stimuli and treatment is somewhat more understandable when we consider that pain is a personal experience influenced by attention, meaning of the situation, and prior learning history, as well as physical pathology. In the majority of cases, biomedical factors appear to instigate the initial report of pain; over time, however, psychosocial and behavioral factors may serve to maintain or exacerbate levels of pain and to influence adjustment and disability, as noted above. Pain that persists over time should not be viewed as either solely physical or solely psychological. Rather, the experience of pain is a complex amalgam maintained by an interdependent set of biomedical, psychosocial, and behavioral factors, whose relationships are not static but evolve and change over time. The various interacting factors that affect an individual with chronic pain suggest that the phenomenon is quite complex and requires a biopsychosocial perspective.

From the biopsychosocial perspective, each of these factors contributes to the experience of pain and the response to treatment. Pain is neither solely somatically based nor solely psychologically based; the interaction among the various factors is what produces the subjective experience of pain. There is a synergistic relationship whereby psychological and socioenvironmental factors can modulate nociceptive stimulation and the response to treatment. In turn, nociceptive stimulation can influence patients' appraisals of their situation and the treatment, their mood states, and the ways they interact with significant others, including medical practitioners. An integrative, biopsychosocial model of chronic pain needs to incorporate the mutual interrelationships among physical, psychological, and social factors and the changes that occur among these relationships over time (Flor et al., 1990; Turk & Rudy, 1991). A model that focuses on only one of these three core sets of factors will inevitably be incomplete.

REFERENCES

Abram, S. E. (1993). Advances in chronic pain management since gate control. *Regional Anesthesia, 18*, 66–81.

Arntz, A., & Schmidt, A.J.M. (1989). Perceived control and the experience of pain. In A. Steptoe & A. Appels (Eds.), *Stress, personal control and health* (pp. 131–162). Chichester, England: Wiley.

Bandura, A. (1969). *Principles of behavior modification.* New York: Holt, Rinehart & Winston.

Bandura, A. (1977). Self-efficacy: Toward a unifying theory of behavior change. *Psychological Review, 84*, 191–215.

Bandura, A., O'Leary, A., Taylor, C. B., Gauthier, J., & Gossard, D. (1987). Perceived self-efficacy and pain control: Opioid and nonopioid mechanisms. *Journal of Personality and Social Psychology, 53*, 563–571.

Bandura, A., Taylor, C. B., Williams, S. L., Mefford, I. N., & Barchas, J. D. (1985). Catecholamine secretion as a function of perceived coping self-efficacy. *Journal of Consulting and Clinical Psychology, 53*, 406–414.

Barber, T., & Hahn, K. W. (1962). Physiological and subjective responses to pain producing stimulation under hypnotically-suggested and waking-imagined "analgesia." *Journal of Abnormal and Social Psychology, 65*, 411–418.

Biedermann, H. J., McGhie, A., Monga, T. N., & Shanks, G. L. (1987). Perceived and actual control in EMG treatment of back pain. *Behaviour Research and Therapy, 25*, 137–147.

Blanchard, E. B. (1987). Long-term effects of behavioral treatment of chronic headache. *Behavior Therapy, 18*, 375–385.

Block, A. R., Kremer, E. F., & Gaylor, M. (1980). Behavioral treatment of chronic pain: Variables affecting treatment efficacy. *Pain, 8*, 367–375.

Blumer, D., & Heilbronn, M. (1982). Chronic pain as a variant of depressive disease: The pain-prone disorder. *Journal of Nervous and Mental Disease, 170*, 381–406.

Borgeat, F., Hade, B., Elie, R., & Larouche, L. M. (1984). Effects of voluntary muscle tension increases in tension headache. *Headache, 24*, 199–202.

Bradley, L. A., Haile, J. M., & Jaworski, T. M. (1992). Assessment of psychological status using interviews and self-report instruments. In D.C. Turk & R. Melzack (Eds.), *Handbook of pain assessment* (pp. 193–213). New York: Guilford Press.

Brown, G. K., & Nicassio, P. M. (1987). Development of a questionnaire for the assessment of active and passive coping strategies in chronic pain patients. *Pain, 31*, 53–62.

Brown, G. K., Nicassio, P. M., & Wallston, K. A. (1989). Pain coping strategies and depression in rheumatoid arthritis. *Journal of Consulting and Clinical Psychology, 57*, 652–657.

Burdette, B. H., & Gale, E. N. (1988). The effects of treatment on masticatory muscle activity and manbidular posture in myofascial pain-dysfunction patients. *Journal of Dental Research, 67*, 1126–1130.

Butler, R., Damarin, F., Beaulieu, C., Schwebel, A., & Thorn, B. E. (1989). Assessing cognitive coping strategies for acute post-surgical pain. *Psychological Assessment: A Journal of Consulting and Clinical Psychology, 1*, 41–45.

Cairns, D., & Pasino, J. (1977). Comparison of verbal reinforcement and feedback in the operant treatment of disability of chronic low back pain. *Behavior Therapy, 8*, 621–630.

Cassell, E. J. (1982). The nature of suffering and the goals of medicine. *New England Journal of Medicine, 396*, 639–645.

Chapin, C. V. (1915). Truth in publicity. *American Journal of Public Health, 5*, 453–502.

Christensen, M. F., & Mortensen, O. (1975). Long-term prognosis in children with recurrent abdominal pain. *Archives of Disease in Childhood, 51*, 110–114.

Cioffi, D. (1991). Beyond attentional strategies: A cognitive-perceptual model of somatic interpretation. *Psychological Bulletin, 109*, 25–41.

Ciccone, D. S., & Grzesiak, R. C. (1984). Cognitive dimensions of chronic pain. *Social Science and Medicine, 19*, 1339–1345.

Collie, J. (1913). *Malingering and feigned sickness.* London: Edward Arnold.

Corbishley, M., Hendrickson, R., & Beutler, L. (1990). Behavior, affect, and cognition among psychogenic pain patients in group expressive psychotherapy. *Journal of Pain and Symptom Management, 5*, 241–248.

Coronary Drug Project Research Group. (1980). Influence of adherence to treatment and response of cholesterol on mortality in the Coronary Drug Project. *New England Journal of Medicine, 303*, 1038–1043.

Council, J. R., Ahern, D. K., Follick, M. J., & Kline, C. L. (1988). Expectancies and functional impairment in chronic low back pain. *Pain, 33*, 323–331.

Craig, K. D. (1986). Social modeling influences: Pain in context. In R. A. Sternbach (Ed.), *The psychology of pain* (2nd ed., pp. 67–95). New York: Raven Press.

Craig, K. D. (1988). Consequences of caring: Pain in human context. *Canadian Psychologist, 28*, 311–321.

Crook, J., Weir, R., & Tunks, E. (1989). An epidemiologic follow-up survey of persistent pain sufferers in a group family practice and specialty pain clinic. *Pain, 36*, 49–61.

Desroaches, H. F., Kaiman, B. D., & Ballard, H. T. (1967). Factors influencing reporting of physical symptoms by aged patients. *Geriatrics, 22*, 169–175.

Deyo, R. A. (1986). The early diagnostic evaluation of patients with low back pain. *Journal of General Internal Medicine, 1*, 328–338.

Deyo, R. A., Walsh, N. E., Martin, D. (1990). A controlled trial of transcutaneous electrical nerve stimulation (TENS) and exercise for chronic low back pain. *New England Journal of Medicine, 322*, 1627–1634.

Dolce, J. J., Crocker, M. F., & Doleys, D. M. (1986a). Prediction of outcome among chronic pain patients. *Behaviour Research and Therapy, 24*, 313–319.

Dolce, J. J., Crocker, M. F., Moletteire, C., & Doleys, D. M. (1986b). Exercise quotas, anticipatory concern and self-efficacy expectancies in chronic pain: A preliminary report. *Pain, 24*, 365–375.

Doleys, D. M., Crocker, M., & Patton, D. (1982). Response of patients with chronic pain to exercise quotas. *Physical Therapy, 62*, 1112–1115.

Droste, C., & Roskamm, H. (1983). Experimental pain measurement inpatients with asymptomatic myocardial ischemia. *Journal of the American College of Cardiology, 1*, 940–945.

Dufton, B. D. (1989). Cognitive failure and chronic pain. *International Journal of Psychiatry in Medicine, 19*, 291–297.

Dworkin, S. F., & Massoth, D. L. (1994). Temporomandibular disorders and chronic pain: Disease or illness? *Journal of Prosthetic Dentistry, 7*, 29–38.

Dworkin, S. F., Von Korff, M., & LeResche, L. (1992). Epidemiologic studies of chronic pain: A dynamic-ecologic perspective. *Annals of Behavioral Medicine, 14*, 3–11.

Engel, G. L. (1977). The need for a new medical model: A challenge for biomedical science. *Science, 196*, 129–136.

Epstein, L. H., & Cluss, P. A. (1982). A behavioral medicine perspective on adherence to long-term medical regimens. *Journal of Consulting and Clinical Psychology, 50*, 950–971.

Fagerhaugh, S. (1975). Pain expression and control on a burn care unit. *Nursing Outlook, 22*, 645–650.

Fernandez, E., & Turk, D. C. (1989). The utility of cognitive coping strategies for altering perception of pain: A meta-analysis. *Pain, 38*, 123–135.

Fernandez, E., & Turk, D. C. (1992). Sensory and affective components of pain: Separation and synthesis. *Psychological Bulletin, 112*, 205–217.

Fernandez, E., & Turk, D. C. (1995). The scope and significance of anger in the experience of chronic pain. *Pain, 61,* 165–175.

Fitzpatrick, R. M., Hopkins, A. P., & Harvard-Watts, O. (1983). Social dimensions of healting: A longitudinal study of outcomes of medical management of headaches. *Social Science and Medicine, 17,* 501–510.

Flor, H., Birbaumer, N., Schugens, M. M., & Lutzenberger, W. (1992). Symptom-specific psychophysiological responses in chronic pain patients. *Psychophysiology, 29,* 452–460.

Flor, H., Birbaumer, N., & Turk, D. C. (1990). The psychobiology of chronic pain. *Advances in Behaviour Research and Therapy, 12,* 47–84.

Flor, H., Fydrich, T., & Turk, D. C. (1992). Efficacy of multidisciplinary pain treatment centers: A meta-analytic review. *Pain, 49,* 221–230.

Flor, H., Kerns, R. D., & Turk, D. C. (1987). The role of spouse reinforcement, perceived pain, and activity levels of chronic pain patients. *Journal of Psychosomatic Research, 31,* 251–259.

Flor, H., & Turk, D. C. (1988). Chronic back pain and rheumatoid arthritis: Predicting pain and disability from cognitive variables. *Journal of Behavioral Medicine, 11,* 251–265.

Flor, H., Turk, D. C., & Birbaumer, N. (1985). Assessment of stress-related psychophysiological responses in chronic pain patients. *Journal of Consulting and Clinical Psychology, 35,* 354–364.

Fordyce, W. E. (1976). *Behavioral methods for chronic pain and illness.* St. Louis, MO: C.V. Mosby.

Fordyce, W. E., Roberts, A. H., & Sternbach, R. A. (1985). The behavioral management of chronic pain: A response to critics. *Pain, 22,* 113–125.

Fordyce, W. E., Shelton, J., & Dundore, D. (1982). The modification of avoidance learning pain behaviors. *Journal of Behavioral Medicine, 4,* 405–414.

Gentry, W. D., & Bernal, G. A. A. (1977). Chronic pain. In R. Williams & W. D. Gentry (Eds.), *Behavioral approaches to medical treatment* (pp. 171–182). Cambridge, MA: Ballinger.

Gil, K. M., Williams, D. A., Keefe, F. J., & Beckham, J. C. (1990). The relationship of negative thoughts to pain and psychological distress. *Behavior Therapy, 21,* 349–352.

Greene, C. S., & Laskin, D. M. (1974). Long-term evaluation of conservative treatments for myofascial pain dysfunction syndrome. *Journal of the American Dental Association, 89,* 1365–1368.

Harkins, S. W. (1988). Pain in the elderly. In R. Dubner, G. F. Gebhart, & M. R. Bond (Eds.), *Proceedings of the Vth World Congress on Pain* (pp. 355–367). Amsterdam: Elsevier.

Hatch, J. P., Prihoda, T. J., Moore, P. J., Cyr-Provost, M., Borcherding, S., Boutros, N. N., & Seleshi, E. (1991). A naturalistic study of the relationship among electromyographic activity, psychological stress, and pain in ambulatory tension-type headache patients and headache-free controls. *Psychosomatic Medicine, 53,* 576–584.

Herman, E., & Baptiste, S. (1981). Pain control: Mastery through group experience. *Pain, 10,* 79–86.

Heyneman, N. E., Fremouw, W. J., Gano, D., Kirkland, F., & Heiden, L. (1990). Individual differences in the effectiveness of different coping strategies. *Cognitive Therapy and Research, 14,* 63–77.

Holroyd, K. A., & Andrasik, F. (1982). Do the effects of cognitive therapy endure? A two-year follow-up of tension headache sufferers treated with cognitive therapy or biofeedback. *Cognitive Therapy and Research, 6,* 325–333.

Holroyd, K. A., Penzien, D. B., Hursey, K. G., Tobin, D. L., Rogers, L., & Holm, J. E. (1984). Change mechanisms in EMG biofeedback training: Cognitive changes underlying improvements in tension headache. *Journal of Consulting and Clinical Psychology, 52,* 1039–1053.

Jamison, R. N., Rudy, T. E., Penzien, D. B., & Mosely, T. H. (1994). Cognitive-behavioral classification of chronic pain: Replication and extension of empirically-derived patient profiles. *Pain, 57,* 233–239.

Jamner, L. D., & Tursky, B. (1987). Syndrome-specific descriptor profiling: A psychophysiological and psychophysical approach. *Health Psychology, 6,* 417–430.

Jensen, M. P., & Karoly, P. (1991). Control beliefs, coping effort, and adjustment to chronic pain. *Journal of Consulting and Clinical Psychology, 59,* 431–438.

Jensen, M. P., Turner, J. A., & Romano, J. M. (1994a). Correlates of improvement in multidisciplinary treatment of chronic pain. *Journal of Consulting and Clinical Psychology, 62,* 172–179.

Jensen, M. P., Turner, J. A., Romano, J. M., & Karoly, P. (1991). Coping with chronic pain: A critical review of the literature. *Pain, 47,* 249–283.

Jensen, M. P., Turner, J. A., Romano, J. M., & Lawler, B. K. (1994b). Relationship of pain-specific beliefs to chronic pain adjustment. *Pain, 57,* 301–309.

Keefe, F. J., Brown, G. K., Wallston, K. S., & Caldwell, D. S. (1989). Coping with rheumatoid arthritis pain: Catastrophizing as a maladaptive strategy. *Pain, 37,* 51–56.

Keefe, F. J., Caldwell, D. S., Williams, D. A., Gil, K. M., Mitchell, D., Robertson, C., Martinez, S., Nunley, J., Beckham, J. C., Crisson, J. E., & Helms, M. (1990a). Pain coping skills training in the management of osteoarthritis knee pain: A comparative approach. *Behavior Therapy, 21,* 49–62.

Keefe, R. J., Caldwell, D. S., Williams, D. A., Gil, K. M., Mitchell, D., Robertson, C., Martinez, S., Nunley, J., Beckham, J. C., Crisson, J. E., & Helms, M. (1990b). Pain coping skills training in the management of osteoarthritis knee pain: II. Follow-up results. *Behavior Therapy, 21,* 435–447.

Keefe, F. J., Dunsmore, J., & Burnett, R. (1992). Behavioral and cognitive-behavioral approaches to chronic pain: Recent advances and future directions. *Journal of Consulting and Clinical Psychology, 60,* 528–536.

Keefe, F. J., & Williams, D. A. (1989). New directions in pain assessment and treatment. *Clinical Psychology Review, 9,* 549–568.

Kerns, R. D., Rosenberg, R., & Jacob, M. C. (1994). Anger expression and chronic pain. *Journal of Behavioral Medicine, 17,* 57–68.

Kerns, R. D., Turk, D. C., & Rudy, T. E. (1985). West Haven–Yale Multidimensional Pain Inventory (WHYMPI). *Pain, 23,* 345–356.

Kinder, B. N., & Curtiss, G. (1988). Assessment of anxiety, depression, and anger in chronic pain patients: Conceptual and methodological issues. In C. D. Spielberger & J. N. Butcher (Eds.), *Advances in personality assessment* (pp. 651–661). Hillsdale, NJ: Erlbaum.

Kotarba, J. A. (1983). *Chronic pain: Its social dimensions.* Beverly Hills, CA: Sage.

Lawson, K., Reesor, K. A., Keefe, F. J., & Turner, J. A. (1990). Dimensions of pain-related cognitive coping: Cross validation of the factor structure of the Coping Strategies Questionnaire. *Pain, 43,* 195–204.

Lefebvre, M. F. (1981). Cognitive distortion and cognitive errors in depressed psychiatric low back pain patients. *Journal of Consulting and Clinical Psychology, 49,* 517–525.

Lenthem, J., Slade, P. O., Troup, J. P. G., & Bentley, G. (1983). Outline of a fear-avoidance model of exaggerated pain perception. *Behaviour Research and Therapy, 21,* 401–408.

Leventhal, H., & Everhart, D. (1979). Emotion, pain and physical illness. In C. E. Izard (Ed.), *Emotion and psychopathology* (pp. 263–299). New York: Plenum Press.

Linton, S. J. (1985). The relationship between activity and chronic back pain. *Pain, 21,* 289–294.

Linton, S. J., Melin, L., & Götestam, K. G. (1984). Behavioral analysis of chronic pain and its management. In M. Hersen, R. Eisler, & P. Miller (Eds.), *Progress in behavior modification* (Vol. 18, pp. 1–42). New York: Academic Press.

Lipton, J. A., & Marbach, J. J. (1984). Ethnicity and the pain experience. *Social Science and Medicine, 19,* 1279–1298.

Litt, M. D. (1988). Self-efficacy and perceived control: Cognitive mediators of pain tolerance. *Journal of Personality and Social Psychology, 54,* 149–160.

Lorig, K., Chastain, R. L., Ung, E., Shoor, S., & Holman, H. R. (1989). Development and evaluation of a scale to measure perceived self-efficacy in people with arthritis. *Arthritis and Rheumatism, 32,* 37–44.

Love, A. W., & Peck, C. L. (1987). The MMPI and psychological factors in chronic low back pain: A review. *Pain, 28,* 1–12.

Magora, A., & Schwartz, A. (1980). Relation between the low back pain syndrome and X-ray findings. *Scandinavian Journal of Rehabilitation Medicine, 12,* 9–15.

Maier, S. F., Dugan, J. W., Grau, R., & Hyson, A. S. (1984). Learned helplessness, pain inhibition and the endogenous opioids. In M. Zeiler & P. Harzem (Eds.), *Advances in the analysis of behavior* (Vol. 7, pp. 102–114). New York: Wiley.

Main, C. J., & Waddell, G. (1991). A comparison of cognitive measures in low back pain: Statistical structure and clinical validity of initial assessment. *Pain, 46*, 287–298.

Manning, M. M., & Wright, T. L. (1983). Self-efficacy expectancies, outcome expectancies, and the persistence of pain control in childbirth. *Journal of Personality and Social Psychology, 45*, 421–431.

Martin, P. R., Nathan, P., Milech, D., & Van Keppel, M. (1989). Cognitive therapy vs. self-management training in the treatment of chronic headaches. *British Journal of Clinical Psychology, 28*, 347–361.

McCreary, C. P. (1993). Psychological evaluation of chronic pain with the MMPI. *Pain Digest, 3*, 246–251.

Mechanic, D. (1962). The concept of illness behavior. *Journal of Chronic Disease, 15*, 189–194.

Mechanic, D. (1978). Effects of psychological distress on perceptions of physical health and use of medical and psychiatric facilities. *Journal of Human Stress, 4*, 26–32.

Mechanic, D. (1986). Illness behavior: An overview. In S. McHugh & T. M. Vallis (Eds.), *Illness behavior: A multidisciplinary model* (pp. 101–110). New York: Plenum Press.

Melding, P. S. (1991). Is there such a thing as geriatric pain? *Pain, 46*, 119–121.

Melzack, R., & Casey, K. L. (1968). Sensory, motivational and central control determinants of pain: A new conceptual model. In D. Kenshalo (Ed.), *The skin senses* (pp. 423–443). Springfield, IL: Charles C Thomas.

Melzack, R., & Wall, P. D. (1965). Pain mechanisms: A new theory. *Science, 50*, 971–979.

Melzack, R., & Wall, P. D. (1982). *The challenge of pain.* New York: Basic Books.

Merskey, H. (1986). Classification of chronic pain: Description of chronic pain syndromes and definitions of pain terms. *Pain*, Suppl. 3, S1–S225.

Mizener, D., Thomas, M., & Billings, R. (1988). Cognitive changes of migraineurs receiving biofeedback training. *Headache, 28*, 339–343.

Nathan, P. W. (1976). The gate control theory of pain: A critical review. *Brain, 99*, 123–158.

Newton, C. R., & Barbaree, H. E. (1987). Cognitive changes accompanying headache treatment: The use of a thought-sampling procedure. *Cognitive Therapy and Research, 11*, 635–652.

Nerenz, D. R., & Leventhal H. (1983). Self-regulation theory in chronic illness. In T. Burish & L.A. Bradley (Eds.), *Coping with chronic illness* (pp. 13–37). Orlando, FL: Academic Press.

North, R. B. (1989). Neural stimulation techniques. In C.D. Tollison (Ed.), *Handbook of chronic pain management* (pp. 136–146). Baltimore: Williams & Wilkins.

Nouwen, A., & Solinger, J. W. (1979). The effectiveness of EMG biofeedback training in low back pain. *Biofeedback and Self-Regulation, 4*, 103–111.

O'Leary, A., Shoor, S., Lorig, K., & Holman, H. R. (1988). A cognitive-behavioral treatment for rheumatoid arthritis. *Health Psychology, 7*, 527–544.

Parsons, T. (1958). Definitions of health and illness in the light of American values and social structure. In E. G. Jaco (Ed.), *Patients, physicians, and illness* (pp. 3–29). New York: Free Press.

Pennebaker, J. W. (1982). *The psychology of physical symptoms.* New York: Springer-Verlag.

Pennebaker, J. W., Gonder-Frederick, L., Cox, D. J., & Hoover, C. W. (1985). The perception of general versus specific visceral activity and the regulation of health-related behavior. *Advances in Behavioral Medicine, 1*, 165–198.

Philips, H. C. (1987a). Avoidance behaviour and its role in sustaining chronic pain. *Behaviour Research and Therapy, 25*, 273–279.

Philips, H. C. (1987b). The effects of behavioural treatment on chronic pain. *Behaviour Research and Therapy, 25*, 365–377.

Pilowsky, I., & Spence, N. D. (1975). Patterns of illness behaviour in patients with intractable pain. *Journal of Psychosomatic Research, 19*, 279–287.

Price, D. D. (1987). *Psychological and neural mechanisms of pain.* New York: Raven Press.

Rachman, S., & Arntz, A. (1991). The overprediction and underprediction of pain. *Clinical Psychology Review, 11*, 339–356.

Rachman, S., & Lopatka, C. (1988). Accurate and inaccurate predictions of pain. *Behaviour Research and Therapy, 26*, 291–296.

Reesor, K. A., & Craig, K. (1988). Medically incongruent chronic pain: Physical limitations, suffering and ineffective coping. *Pain, 32*, 35–45.

Richard, K. (1988). The occurrence of maladaptive health-related behaviors and teacher-related conduct problems in children of chronic low back pain patients. *Journal of Behavioral Medicine, 11*, 107–116.

Rimm, D. C., & Litvak, S. B. (1969). Self-verbalizations and emotional arousal. *Journal of Abnormal Psychology, 74*, 181–187.

Roberts, A. H., Kewman, D. G., Mercier, L., & Hovell, M. (1993). The power of nonspecific effects in healing: Implications for psychological and biological treatments. *Clinical Psychology Review, 13*, 375–392.

Romano, J. M., Turner, J. A., Friedman, L. S., Bulcroft, R. A., Jensen, M. P., Hops, H., & Wright, S. F. (1992). Sequential analysis of chronic pain behaviors and spouse responses. *Journal of Consulting and Clinical Psychology, 60*, 777–782.

Rosensteil, A. K., & Keefe, F. J. (1983). The use of coping strategies in chronic low back pain patients: Relationship to patient characteristics and current adjustment. *Pain, 17*, 33–44.

Rudy, T. E., Kerns, R. J., & Turk, D. C. (1988). Chronic pain and depression: Toward a cognitive-behavioral mediation model. *Pain, 35*, 179–183.

Schmidt, A. J. M. (1985a). Cognitive factors in the performance of chronic low back pain patients. *Journal of Psychosomatic Research, 29*, 183–189.

Schmidt, A. J. M. (1985b). Performance level of chronic low back pain patients in different treadmill test conditions. *Journal of Psychosomatic Research, 29*, 639–646.

Schmidt, A. J. M., Gierlings, R. E. H., & Peters, M. L. (1989). Environment and interoceptive influences on chronic low back pain behavior. *Pain, 38*, 137–143.

Schmidt, R. F. (1972). The gate control theory of pain: An unlikely hypothesis. In R. Jansen, W. D. Keidel, A. Herz, C. Streichele, J. P. Payne, & R. A. P. Burt (Eds.), *Pain: Basic principles, pharmacology, therapy* (pp. 57–71). Stuttgart, Germany: Thieme.

Schwartz, D. P., DeGood, D. E., & Shutty, M. S. (1985). Direct assessment of beliefs and attitudes of chronic pain patients. *Archives of Physical Medicine and Rehabilitation, 66*, 806–809.

Schwartz, L., Slater, M. A., Birchler, G., & Atkinson, J. H. (1991). Depression in spouses of chronic pain patients: The role of pain and anger, and marital satisfaction. *Pain, 44*, 61–67.

Slater, M. A., Hall, H. F., Atkinson, J. H., & Garfin, S. R. (1991). Pain and impairment beliefs in chronic low back pain: Validation of the Pain and Impairment Relationship Scale (PAIRS). *Pain, 44*, 51–56.

Smith, T. W., Aberger, E. W., Follick, M. J., & Ahern, D. L. (1986a). Cognitive distortion and psychological distress in chronic low back pain. *Journal of Consulting and Clinical Psychology, 54*, 573–575.

Smith, T. W., Follick, M. J., Ahern, D. L., & Adams, A. (1986b). Cognitive distortion and disability in chronic low back pain. *Cognitive Therapy and Research, 10*, 201–210.

Smith, T. W., Peck, J. R., Milano, R. A., & Ward, J. R. (1990). Helplessness and depression in rheumatoid arthritis. *Health Psychology, 9*, 377–389.

Spanos, N. P., Horton, C., & Chaves, J. F. (1975). The effects of two cognitive strategies on pain threshold. *Journal of Abnormal Psychology, 84*, 677–681.

Spiegel, D., & Bloom, J. R. (1983). Pain in metastatic breast cancer. *Cancer, 52*, 341–345.

Spinhoven, P., Ter Kuile, M. M., Linssen, A. C. G., & Gazendam, B. (1989). Pain coping strategies in a Dutch population of chronic low back pain patients. *Pain, 37*, 77–83.

Summers, J. D., Rapoff, M. A., Varghese, G., Porter, K., & Palmer, K. (1992). Psychological factors in chronic spinal cord injury pain. *Pain, 47*, 183–189.

Talo, S. (1992). *Psychological assessment of functioning in chronic low back pain patients.* Turku, Finland: Social Insurance Institute.

Tota-Faucette, M. E., Gil, K. M., Williams, F. J., & Goli, V. (1993). Predictors of response to pain management treatment: The role of family environment and changes in cognitive processes. *Clinical Journal of Pain, 9*, 115–123.

Tunks, E., Crook, J., Norman, G., & Kalasher, S. (1988). Tender-points in fibromyalgia. *Pain, 34,* 11–19.

Turk, D. C. (1990). Customizing treatment for chronic pain patients: Who, what and why. *Clinical Journal of Pain, 6,* 255–270.

Turk, D. C. (in press). Physiological and psychological bases of pain. In A. Baum, T. Revenson, & J. Singer (Eds.), *Handbook of health psychology.* Hillsdale, NJ: Erlbaum.

Turk, D. C., & Flor, H. (1987). Pain > pain behaviors: The utility and limitations of the pain behavior construct. *Pain, 31,* 277–295.

Turk, D. C., Kerns, R. D., & Rosenberg, R. (1992). Effects of marital interaction on chronic pain and disability: Examining the down-side of social support. *Rehabilitation Psychology, 37,* 259–274.

Turk, D. C., Meichenbaum, D., & Genest, M. (1983). *Pain and behavioral medicine: A cognitive-behavioral perspective.* New York: Guilford Press.

Turk, D. C., Okifuji, A., & Scharf, L. (1994). Assessment of older women with chronic pain. *Journal of Women and Aging, 6,* 25–42.

Turk, D. C., Okifuji, A., & Scharff, L. (1995). Chronic pain and depression: Role of perceived impact and perceived control in different age cohorts. *Pain, 61,* 93–102.

Turk, D. C., & Rudy, T. E. (1986). Assessment of cognitive factors in chronic pain: A worthwhile enterprise? *Journal of Consulting and Clinical Psychology, 54,* 760–768.

Turk, D. C., & Rudy, T. E. (1988). Toward an empirically derived taxonomy of chronic pain patients: Integration of psychological assessment data. *Journal of Consulting and Clinical Psychology, 56,* 233–238.

Turk, D. C., & Rudy, T. E. (1990). Robustness of an empirically derived taxonomy of chronic pain patients. *Pain, 43,* 27–36.

Turk, D. C., & Rudy, T. E. (1991). Persistent pain and the injured worker: Integrating biomedical, psychosocial, and behavioral factors. *Journal of Occupational Rehabilitation, 1,* 159–179.

Turk, D. C., & Rudy, T. E. (1992). Cognitive factors and persistent pain: A glimpse into Pandora's box. *Cognitive Therapy and Research, 16,* 99–112.

Turk, D. C., & Salovey, P. (1984). "Chronic pain as a variant of depressive disease": A critical reappraisal. *Journal of Nervous and Mental Disease, 172,* 398–404.

Turner, J. A. (1991). Coping and chronic pain. In M. R. Bond, J. E. Charlton, & C. J. Woolf (Eds.), *Proceedings of the VIth World Congress on Pain* (pp. 219–227). Amsterdam: Elsevier.

Turner, J. A., & Clancy, S. (1986). Strategies for coping with chronic low back pain: Relationship to pain and disability. *Pain, 24,* 355–363.

Turner, J. A., & Clancy, S. (1988). Comparison of operant behavioral and cognitive-behavioral group treatment for chronic low back pain. *Journal of Consulting and Clinical Psychology, 56,* 261–266.

Vaughan, K. B., & Lanzetta, J. T. (1980). Vicarious instigation and conditioning of facial expressive and autonomic responses to a model's expressive display of pain. *Journal of Personality and Social Psychology, 38,* 909–923.

Vaughan, K. B., & Lanzetta, J. T. (1981). The effect of modification of expressive displays on vicarious emotional arousal. *Journal of Experimental Social Psychology, 17,* 16–30.

Von Korff, M., Dworkin, S., & LeResche, L. (1990). Graded chronic pain status: An epidemiologic evaluation. *Pain, 40,* 279–291.

Von Korff, M., Ormel, J., Keefe, F. J., & Dorkin, S. F. (1992). Grading severity of chronic pain: Concepts, use, and validity. *Pain, 50,* 133–149.

Waddell, G., & Main, C. J. (1984). Assessment of severity in low back disorders. *Spine, 9,* 204–208.

Wall, P. D. (1989). The dorsal horn. In P. D. Wall & R. Melzack (Eds.), *Textbook of pain* (2nd ed., pp. 102–111). New York: Churchill Livingstone.

Walter, L., & Brannon, L. A. (1991). A cluster analysis of the Multidimensional Pain Inventory. *Headache, 31,* 476–479.

Wells, N. (1994). Perceived control over pain: Relation to distress and disability. *Research in Nursing and Health, 17,* 295–302.

White, K. L., Williams, F., & Greenberg, B. G. (1961). The ecology of medical care. *New England Journal of Medicine, 265*, 885–886.

Whitehead, W. E. (1980). Interoception. In R. Holzl & W. E. Whitehead (Eds.), *Psychophysiology of the gastrointestinal tract* (pp. 145–161). New York: Plenum Press.

Williams, D. A., & Keefe, F. J. (1991). Pain beliefs and the use of cognitive-behavioral coping strategies. *Pain, 46*, 185–190.

Williams, D. A., & Thorn, B. E. (1989). An empirical assessment of pain beliefs. *Pain, 36*, 251–258.

Wolff, B. B., & Langley, S. (1968). Cultural factors and the response to pain: A review. *American Anthropologist, 70*, 494–501.

Woodeforde, J. M., & Fielding, J. R. (1970). Pain and cancer. *Journal of Psychosomatic Research, 14*, 365–370.

Zborowski, M. (1969). *People in pain*. San Francisco: Jossey-Bass.

CHAPTER 2

Psychological Disorders and Chronic Pain

Cause-and-Effect Relationships

Robert J. Gatchel

With the introduction of the gate control theory of pain by Melzack and Wall (1965), the scientific community came to accept the central importance of psychological factors in the pain perception process. As a result, there has been a great deal of research attempting to isolate the psychological characteristics associated with chronic pain patients. For example, the Minnesota Multiphasic Personality Inventory (MMPI) has been widely used to delineate these psychological characteristics. This early work attempted to differentiate "functional" pain from "organic" pain. However, Sternbach (1974) challenged the utility and validity of attempting to make a functional–organic dichotomy when dealing with chronic pain. Chronic pain is a complex psychophysiological behavior pattern that cannot be broken down into distinct psychological and physical components. As discussed in Chapter 1 by Turk, the biopsychosocial conceptual model of pain includes physical, psychological, and social elements; thus, it replaces the overly simplistic physical disease model of pain with an alternative multidimensional model. In the biopsychosocial model, psychological and social factors are viewed as intricately related to the pain perception process. As pain becomes more chronic, these factors play an increasingly dominant role in the maintenance of pain behavior and suffering. In this chapter, I discuss the issue of one of the important concomitants that clinicians must be prepared to deal with when treating chronic pain patients—psychopathology. In connection with this, the complex "chicken-or-egg" question of what occurs first—the chronic pain or psychopathology—is addressed.

PSYCHOLOGICAL CONCOMITANTS OF PAIN

There is evidence to suggest that because of the failure of attempts to alleviate their pain, chronic pain patients develop specific psychological problems that distinguish them from acute pain patients. For example, Sternbach, Wolf, Murphy, and Akeson (1973) compared the MMPI profiles of a group of patients with acute low back pain (pain present for less than 6 months) to those of a group of patients with chronic low back pain (pain present for more than 6 months). Results indicated significant differences between the two groups on the first three clinical scales (Scale 1, Hypochondriasis; Scale 2, Depression; and Scale

3, Hysteria). The combined elevation of these three scales is often referred to as the "neurotic triad," since it is commonly found in neurotic individuals who are experiencing a great deal of anxiety. (Another typical pattern is the "conversion V," in which Scales 1 and 3 are more elevated than Scale 2.) These results indicate that during the early stages of pain, major psychological problems are not produced by it. However, as the pain becomes chronic in nature, psychological changes begin to occur. These changes are probably attributable to the constant discomfort, despair, and preoccupation with the pain that come to dominate the lives of these patients. This may produce a "layer" of behavioral/psychological problems over the original nociception or pain experience itself. As Sternbach (1974) noted in his description of chronic pain sufferers:

> Pain patients frequently say that they could stand their pain much better if they could only get a good night's sleep. They feel as though their resistance is weakened by their lack of sleep. They never feel rested. They feel worn down, worn out, exhausted. They find themselves getting more and more irritable with their families, they have fewer and fewer friends, and fewer and fewer interests. Gradually as time goes on, the boundaries of their world seem to shrink. They become more and more preoccupied with the pain, less and less interested in the world around them. The world begins to center around home, doctor's office, and pharmacy. (p. 7)

My colleagues and I obtained a similar pattern of results from patients with chronic low back pain participating in an intensive 3-week rehabilitation program (Barnes, Gatchel, Mayer, & Barnett, 1990). In this study, patients were administered the MMPI before the start of the program. Results clearly showed that the first three clinical scales were significantly elevated in these chronic patients before the start of the treatment program, as would be expected on the basis of past clinical research (such as that reported by Sternbach et al., 1973). However, at a 6–month follow-up after successful completion of this program (which produced successful rehabilitation and return to work in the great majority of these patients), scores on the three scales were significantly decreased to normal levels. Thus, these results again suggest that elevations of scores are most likely caused by the trauma and stress associated with the chronic pain condition, and not by stable psychological traits. When patients are successfully treated, these clinically significant elevations disappear.

These findings indicate that one of the consequences of dealing with chronic pain is the development of emotional reactions such as anxiety and dysphoria, produced by the long-term "wearing down" effects and drain of psychological resources. Again, the data suggest that this may produce a layer of behavioral and psychological problems over the original nociception or pain experience itself. Indeed, it is generally accepted that chronic pain is a complex behavior that does not merely result from some specific structural cause. When the chronic pain is effectively treated, many of the problematic psychosocial symptoms tend also to be alleviated.

A CONCEPTUAL MODEL OF THE TRANSITION FROM ACUTE TO CHRONIC PAIN

Elsewhere, I have presented a broad conceptual model of three stages that may be involved in the transition of acute low back pain into chronic low back pain disability and accompanying psychosocial distress (Gatchel, 1991). To summarize, and as presented in

Figure 2.1, it is proposed that Stage 1 is associated with emotional reactions such as fear, anxiety, and worry as a consequence of the perception of pain during the acute phase. Pain or hurt is usually associated with harm, and so there is a natural emotional reaction to the potential for physical harm. If the pain persists past a reasonable acute period of time (2 to 4 months), this leads to the progression into Stage 2. This stage is associated with a wider array of behavioral and psychological reactions and problems, such as learned helplessness/depression, distress/anger, and somatization, that are the result of suffering with the now more chronic nature of the pain. It is hypothesized that the form these problems take depends primarily upon the premorbid or pre-existing personality/psychological characteristics of the individual, as well as current socioeconomic and other environmental conditions. Thus, in an individual with premorbid depression who is seriously affected economically by losing a job because of the pain and disability, the depressive symptomatology will be greatly exacerbated during this stage. Similarly, an individual with premorbid hypochondriacal characteristics who receives a large amount of secondary gain for remaining disabled will probably display a great deal of somatization and symptom magnification.

This model does *not* propose that there is one primary pre-existing "pain personality." It is assumed that there is a general nonspecificity in terms of the relationship between personality/psychological problems and pain. This is in keeping with a great deal of research, which has not found any such consistent personality syndrome (Mayer & Gatchel, 1988). Moreover, even though a relationship is usually found between pain and certain psychological problems such as depression (Romano & Turner, 1985), the nature of the relationship between the two variables remains inconclusive. Some, but not all, patients develop depression secondary to chronic pain. Others show depression as

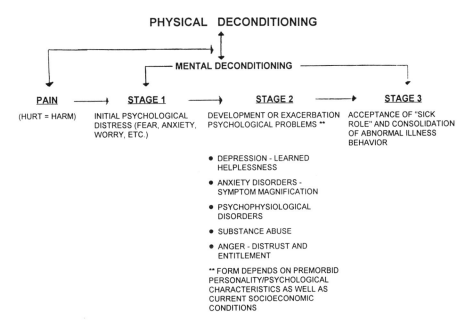

FIGURE 2.1. A conceptual model of the transition from acute to chronic pain. From Gatchel (1991). Copyright 1991 by Lea & Febiger. Adapted by permission.

the primary syndrome, of which pain is a symptom. Moreover, factors that mediate the relationship between depression and pain remain largely unknown (Turk & Rudy, 1988).

In a study initially evaluating one aspect of this "chicken-or-egg" question, we (Polatin, Kinney, Gatchel, Lillo, & Mayer, 1993) assessed 200 patients with chronic low back pain (pain disability present for an average of well over 1 year) for current and lifetime psychiatric syndromes, using a structured psychiatric interview to make *Diagnostic and Statistical Manual of Mental Disorders*, third edition, revised (DSM-III-R) Axis I and Axis II diagnoses. Results revealed that even when the somewhat controversial category of somatoform pain disorder was excluded, 77% of patients met lifetime diagnostic criteria and 59% demonstrated current symptoms for at least one psychiatric diagnosis. The most common of these were major depressive disorder, substance abuse, and anxiety disorders. In addition, 51% met criteria for at least one personality disorder. All of these prevalence rates were significantly greater than the base rate for the general population. These are strikingly high rates of psychopathology in this chronic pain population (an issue to which I return later in this chapter). More important, however, was the finding that of those patients with a positive lifetime history for psychiatric syndromes, 54% of those with major depression, 94% of those with substance abuse, and 95% of those with anxiety disorders had experienced these syndromes *before* the onset of their back pain. These are the first results to suggest that certain psychiatric syndromes appear to precede chronic low back pain (substance abuse and anxiety disorders), whereas others (specifically, major depression) develop either before or after the onset of low back pain. The interesting aspect of these findings was that major depression was demonstrably high in chronic low back pain patients, and patients appeared to be divided almost equally between those who had depression before the onset of low back pain and those in whom depression developed after the onset of low back pain. Obviously, a prospective study is needed to substantiate these retrospective-recall results more clearly, since the findings cannot definitively answer the question of whether psychopathological disorders in chronic pain patients are consequences of experiencing the chronic pain or whether pre-existing disorders act as "predispositions" for pain to become chronic.

To return to the proposed conceptual model, it is assumed that patients "bring with them" certain predisposing personality/psychological characteristics that differ from one patient to the next, and that may be exacerbated by the stress of attempting to cope with the chronic pain. Indeed, the relationship between stress and exacerbation of mental health problems has been documented in the scientific literature (e.g., Barrett, Rose, & Klerman, 1979).

This conceptual model proposes that as the "layer" of behavioral/psychological problems persists, it leads to the progression into Stage 3, which can be viewed as the acceptance or adoption of a "sick role" during which patients are excused from their normal responsibilities and social obligations. This may become a potent reinforcer for not becoming "healthy." The medical and psychological "disabilities" or "abnormal illness behaviors" (Pilowsky, 1978) are consolidated during this phase. Moreover, if compensation issues are present they can also serve as disincentives for becoming well again, because compensation is a critical factor in the persistence of disabilities (Beals, 1984). Research has consistently demonstrated the important psychological changes that occur as a pain patient progresses from the acute to more chronic phases, such as the MMPI changes documented by Hendler (1982).

This conceptual model also proposes that superimposed on these three stages is what is known as the "physical deconditioning syndrome" (Mayer & Gatchel, 1988). This refers to a significant decrease in physical capacity (strength, flexibility, and endurance) resulting from disuse and resultant atrophy of the injured area. There is usually a two-way pathway between the physical deconditioning and the stages described above. For example, research has clearly demonstrated that physical deconditioning can "feed back" and negatively affect the emotional well-being and self-esteem of individuals (Gatchel, Baum, & Krantz, 1989). This can lead to further psychological sequelae. Conversely, negative emotional reactions such as depression can significantly "feed back" to physical functioning—for example, by decreasing the motivation to get involved in work or recreational activities, and thereby contributing further to physical deconditioning.

BASE RATES OF PSYCHOPATHOLOGY

When one views results from the National Institute of Mental Health (NIMH) epidemiological study on 1-month prevalence of various mental disorders in the general population (Regier et al., 1988), it is not surprising that chronic pain patients are often found to have psychiatric problems, since the base rates for such problems in the general population are quite high. For example, these statistics indicate that the prevalence rates for anxiety disorders and mood disorders are 7.3% and 5.1% of the population, respectively. The rate for symptoms of schizophrenia is 0.7%, and that for abuse of alcohol and drugs is about 3.8%. Overall, 15.4% of the noninstitutionalized population has some significant mental health disorder. In an earlier study of *lifetime* prevalences of these disorders assessed across three sites, there were even higher rates (Robins et al., 1984). One can easily argue that these disorders will become greatly exacerbated under the stress of chronic pain disability.

The NIMH prevalence statistics do not take into account the probably equally prevalent personality disorders, such as antisocial, borderline, and paranoid personalities. There are also data to suggest that patients with codiagnoses on Axis I and Axis II (DSM-III-R) have a poor prognosis and higher relapse rate than comparable patients without an Axis II diagnosis (e.g., Joffe & Regan, 1988; Fyer, Frances, Sullivan, Hurt, & Clarkin, 1988). Thus, a personality disorder together with a major psychiatric illness may be an especially poor prognostic sign, and perhaps an index of greater vulnerability to major stressors such as chronic pain and disability.

DATA SUPPORTING THE CONCEPTUAL MODEL

Although there has been little research directly addressing the model reviewed above, an investigation by Blanchard, Kirsch, Applebaum, and Jaccard (1989) provided some indirect support with one type of chronic pain—chronic headache. These authors appropriately noted that a direct answer to the question of whether psychological disturbances often seen in chronic headache are the consequences of years of living with the chronic pain, or are predisposing factors in the initial development of the pain, awaits a prospective longitudinal study. However, they took an initial step in attempting to answer this question indirectly, through a series of statistical analyses of cross-sectional data on a large number of headache patients of various ages and at different points in their lifetime course of headaches. Although these investigators point out that such analyses must be viewed as quite tentative, some modest support was found for the hypothesis that pre-existing psychopathology may be a significant factor in "causing" chronic headache. Such results are quite intriguing and are partly in keeping with the present conceptual model.

The Polatin et al. (1993) study, reviewed earlier, also provides some additional support for this model. In a more recent study, we (Gatchel, Polatin, & Kinney, 1995) attempted to determine whether a comprehensive evaluation of psychosocial and personality characteristics is useful in characterizing those patients with acute low back pain who subsequently develop chronic pain disability problems (as measured by work status at 6 months after evaluation). In this study, an initial sample of 324 patients was evaluated, with all patients being administered a standard battery of psychological assessment tests (the Structured Clinical Interview for DSM-III-R [SCID], the MMPI, and the Million Visual Pain Analogue Scale) within 6 weeks of acute back pain onset. All patients were symptomatic with lumbar pain syndrome for no more than 6 weeks. A structured telephone interview was conducted 6 months after the psychological assessment in order to evaluate return-to-work status, as well as any recurrence of back pain or a new back injury. Logistic regression analyses, conducted to differentiate between those patients who were back at work at 6 months versus those who were not because of the original back injury, revealed the importance of three psychosocial measures: level of self-reported pain and disability, the presence of a DSM-III-R Axis II personality disorder, and scores on Scale 3 (Hysteria) of the MMPI. The model that was generated classified 88% of the cases correctly.

The self-report pain and disability analogue score was found to be an extremely robust risk variable in this study. In other studies, too, subjectively reported high severity of pain and disability has been well recognized as a potentially important secondary predictor variable (i.e., predicting those with an acute episode who subsequently develop chronic problems), as well as a tertiary predictor variable (i.e., predicting those with chronic problems who do not respond to treatment) (e.g., Biering-Sorensen, 1983; Mooney, Cairns, & Robertsen, 1975; Lancourt & Kettelhut, 1992).

In terms of the other psychosocial variables found to be important, Scale 3 of the MMPI has also been reported to be a primary predictor variable for the development of low back pain in uninjured workers in a large-scale study of Boeing employees (Bigos et al., 1991). For Axis II personality disorders, it was interesting that no *specific* type of personality disorder was found to predict chronicity, but rather any personality disorder in general. This suggests that an Axis II diagnosis may reflect a general deficit in coping skills that is linked to chronic disability. Indeed, Millon (1981) notes that a major characteristic of individuals with personality disorders is an inadequate coping style. Moreover, the DSM-III-IV (American Psychiatric Association, 1994) explicitly defines a personality disorder in terms of traits or styles that "are inflexible and maladaptive and cause significant functional impairment or subjective distress" (p. 630). As such, one would expect independent evaluation of coping styles to further document these skills deficits in individuals with personality disorders.

In fact, there has been a growing literature demonstrating a relationship between ineffective pain coping strategies and chronic pain (e.g., Turk & Rudy, 1986; Kleinke, 1994). Much of the research has been correlational in nature, although there is evidence to suggest that patients who are taught effective pain coping strategies can deal more effectively with their pain (e.g., Keefe et al., 1990). It therefore appears to be quite important to measure both personality disorders and coping skills. Surprisingly, to date there has been an almost total lack of research directly evaluating the relationship between the two. Future research will need to remedy this void. A review of coping measures that can be used in such pain-related research, as well as in clinical practice, has been provided by DeGood and Shutty (1992).

THE "PSYCHOSOCIAL DISABILITY FACTOR"

The results of the Gatchel et al. (1995) study clearly demonstrate the presence of a robust "psychosocial disability factor" among injured workers who are likely to develop chronic low back pain disability problems. Such results again highlight the fact that chronic pain disability reflects more than just the presence of some physical symptomatology or a single psychosocial characteristic; it is a complex psychosocioeconomic phenomenon. In fact, some investigators have argued that only about one-half of the total disability phenomenon in someone complaining of chronic back pain can be attributed to physical impairment (e.g., Waddell, Main, Morris, DiPaola, & Gray, 1984). Indeed, physical findings, such as radiographic results, have not been found to be reliable indices of low back pain (Mayer & Gatchel, 1988). Most cases of low back pain are ill defined and physically unverifiable, and are often classified as "soft-tissue injuries" that cannot be visualized or verified on physical examination. Even the correlation between radiographically documented disc space narrowing and disc rupture level in proven disc herniation is less than 50% (Pope, Frymoyer, & Andersson, 1984). Moreover, in a recent magnetic resonance imaging study by Jensen et al. (1994), significant spinal abnormalities were found in patients who were *not* experiencing back pain. A similar dissociation between self-reports of pain and actual physical abnormalities has been found in other chronic pain conditions, such as temporomandibular disorders (Moss & Garrett, 1984).

Emotional or psychological characteristics make a significant contribution in characterizing which injured workers will develop chronic low back pain disability. This is *not* to suggest that these patients are "malingerers." Psychosocial factors can interact with physical symptoms to contribute to disability. Such psychosocial factors will need to receive additional careful attention in the primary care setting. Medical evaluation will need be required to take into account more than pure biomechanical factors in assessing low back pain. Indeed, today it is generally accepted that the phenomenon of pain is much more than a purely physical process.

In passing, it should be noted that no specific Axis I disorders were found to be predictive of failure to return to work in the Gatchel et al. (1995) study, as one might expect on the basis of the conceptual model I have presented of the transition from acute to chronic pain. However, it must be kept in mind that this model does not propose that psychopathology *causes* chronic pain. Rather, if psychopathology is present in a chronic pain patient, then the form displayed depends upon the premorbid characteristics of the particular patient. During the evaluation of the early acute stage, many Axis I symptoms may still be relatively "dormant" and may not express themselves until the stress of more chronic experiences with pain and disability begin to dominate the lives of such patients. Moreover, in this study, the 6-month follow-up period used may still have been in the subacute phase of disability, and more chronic disability effects and their psychopathology correlates may not be fully evident at the 6-month mark. Indeed, in a recent classification model of low back pain disability development proposed by Krause and Ragland (1994), chronic disability effects appear to begin between 6 and 18 months after initial injury. If one were to evaluate patients at 18 months, when they are well into the chronic phase, one would expect clear evidence of Axis I psychopathology. My colleagues and I are currently planning such an evaluation, which should provide a stronger test of the relationship between psychopathology and truly chronic pain disability. We are also conducting a similar investigation of another disabling pain syndrome—temporomandibular disorders.

Finally, we have begun to analyze data from a large cohort of over 400 patients, who were available for a structured interview at 1 year after their initial injury, in order to assess return-to-work status as well as any recurrence of back pain or a new back injury (Gatchel, Polatin, & Mayer, in press). In addition, complete information about the status of workers' compensation or personal injury insurance claims was also collected at this point in time (such data were not available during the 6-month evaluation). Preliminary analysis has revealed the continued importance of self-reported pain and disability analogue scores and of Scale 3 of the MMPI. Moreover, workers' compensation/personal injury insurance status appears to be another powerful predictor variable. This is not surprising, since, as noted earlier, it has been shown that compensation cases (if present) can serve as powerful disincentives or barriers to recovery that maintain disability (e.g., Beals, 1984).

TREATMENT IMPLICATIONS: ACUTE STAGE

What implications do these results have for the treatment of pain? There can be little doubt that such psychosocial variables are important not only in pain perception, but also in the subsequent development of pain-related disability. As in other areas of the growing field of health psychology and behavioral medicine, medical personnel will need to be concerned with the psychological characteristics of their patients in order to prevent costly effects (both economic and human productivity losses) of prolonged bouts of pain disability. Many patients whose pain later becomes chronic may "bring with them" certain premorbid or predisposing psychological/personality characteristics or disorders (a diathesis) that are exacerbated by the stress of attempting to cope with pain. Thus, early intervention may be important for more effective management of these patients. Within this diathesis–stress model, though, there are also other factors that can lead to chronicity; a number of important socioeconomic and environmental variables can significantly contribute to it (e.g., secondary gain, such as workers' compensation). These predisposed patients, however, are the ones who have the greater likelihood of subsequently becoming the difficult-to-treat chronic patients. Finally, this is not to say that these predisposing factors make chronic pain cases "functional" disorders or that chronic pain is "all in the patient's head." The chronic problem represents a complex interaction between physical and psychosocioeconomic variables.

At this point it is useful to differentiate among "primary," "secondary," and "tertiary" care, because the type of psychological treatment required for each form of care is substantially different. As reviewed by Mayer et al. (1995) in discussing spine rehabilitation, *primary* care is applied usually to acute cases of pain of limited severity. Basic symptom control methods are used in relieving pain during the normal early healing period. Often, some psychological reassurance that the acute pain episode is temporary and will soon be resolved is effective. *Secondary* care represents "reactivation" treatment administered to those patients who do not improve simply through the normal healing process. It is administered during the transition from acute (primary) care to the return to work. Such rehabilitation is designed to promote return to productivity before advanced deconditioning and significant psychosocial barriers to work return occur. At this phase, more active psychological intervention may need to be applied to those individuals who do not appear to be progressing. Finally, *tertiary* care is an interdisciplinary and intensive treatment requiring medical direction. It is intended for those patients suffering the effects of deconditioning and chronic disability. In general, it differs from secondary treatment in regard to the intensity of rehabilitation services required, including psychological and disability management.

In terms of primary and secondary care, the clinician must be aware of many psychological factors that can contribute to an acute pain episode's becoming subacute and then chronic. A patient may progress through a number of stages (reviewed previously) as his or her pain and disability becomes more chronic. These may create formidable barriers to recovery if they are not effectively dealt with. These barriers to recovery include the psychosocial variables discussed earlier, as well as functional, legal, social, and work-related issues that can significantly interfere with the patient's return to full functioning and a productive lifestyle. Treatment personnel must also be alert to potential secondary gains of continued disability, whether these are legal, financial, job-related, or familial. It is important that members of the treatment team be knowledgeable about all psychosocial issues while the patient is in rehabilitation. This knowledge allows staff members not only to understand and serve the patient better, but also to be more effective in problem solving if the patient's physical progress is slow or nonexistent. At other times, real interfering circumstances may be used as "smoke screens" or excuses for suboptimal performance and failure to adhere to the treatment regimen. Indeed, failure to make physical progress generally indicates psychosocial barriers to recovery. These barriers to recovery issues must be effectively assessed and brought to the attention of the entire treatment team. Steps can then be taken to understand their origins and avoid their interference with treatment goals.

In a recent review of epidemiological studies, Sanders (1995) has begun to delineate a number of risk factors or barriers to recovery that have been found to be associated with an increased likelihood of an acute low back pain episode's developing into chronic disability (Table 2.1). Sanders argues that a risk factor model similar to a cardiovascular disease risk factor model should be employed in the area of pain, for more effective early detection, prevention, and intervention. As can be seen, a number of risk factors or barriers have been consistently found across a number of epidemiological studies to be important. These may provide important "flags" for clinicians to be aware of, in order to anticipate important barriers to recovery in the treatment setting.

The transition from the acute to the more subacute stage at about 3 months is a point at which psychopathology may begin to emerge as a potentially significant barrier to recovery. Of course, explaining to the patient that psychological and emotional factors

TABLE 2.1. Risk Factors for Low Back Pain and Chronic Disability

Risk factor	Occurrence of	
	Low back pain	Chronic disability (failure to return to work)
Back pain history	Yes	?
Job dissatisfaction	Yes	?
Smoking	Yes	?
Blue-collar work	Yes	?
MMPI Scale 3 elevation	Yes	Yes
Depression	?	Yes
Low activity–high pain behavior	?	Yes
Negative beliefs for pain and activity	?	Yes

Note. From Sanders (1995). Copyright 1995 by the American Pain Society. Adapted by permission.

are invariably involved in the pain syndrome must be done in such a manner as not to alienate the patient into assuming, "The clinician thinks the pain is all in my head." Figure 2.2 presents a diagram that can be shown to patients to explain this relationship. Physical changes attributable to injury and their aftereffects (e.g., disruption in activities of daily living such as work and play) can lead to emotional changes. Such emotional changes, which result from the forced decrease in everyday activities, can produce significant emotional distress such as increased anxiety, depression, and anger. This emotional distress in turn can lead to increased psychophysiological tension and stress. Such stress and tension can substantially affect pain threshold and exacerbation, ultimately feeding back and affecting physical functioning and changes. The cycle can also work in the opposite direction, with physical changes affecting pain threshold and exacerbation, leading to increased psychophysiological stress and tension, producing additional emotional distress and changes, which can in turn produce disruptions in activities of daily living (e.g., depression may decrease interest in getting involved in work or social activities). Once the cycle is completed, it can begin at any new point in the interrelated process and start the whole vicious cycle over again. If this process is explained in an appropriate and clinically sensitive manner, the patient will become more receptive to the role that psychosocial stress factors can play in contributing to (*not* causing) the pain and disability process. Patients can also be shown a diagram depicting the many factors that can affect the stress/tension–pain cycle (see Figure 2.3).

TREATMENT IMPLICATIONS: CHRONIC STAGE

In Table 2.1, Sanders also highlights those risk factors (based upon a summary of epidemiological studies) that appear to be important for treatment outcome with chronic back pain patients. Psychopathology is included in the list. Indeed, as we have seen, when patients reach the more chronic stages of pain, there is usually some significant psychopathology that needs to be dealt with and that may impede the rehabilitation process. A

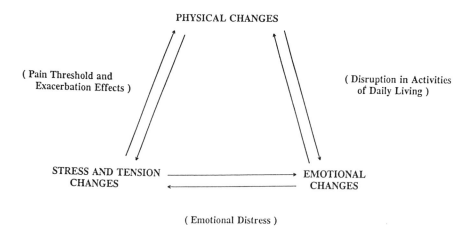

FIGURE 2.2. The cycle of physical changes, emotional changes, and psychophysiological stress and tension changes in the chronic pain process. From Mayer and Gatchel (1988). Copyright 1988 by Lea & Febiger. Adapted by permission.

FIGURE 2.3. Factors magnifying the stress–pain cycle. From Mayer and Gatchel (1988). Copyright 1988 by Lea & Febiger. Adapted by permission.

recent study (Gatchel, Polatin, Mayer, & Garcy, 1994), however, indicates that these high rates of psychopathology alone in pain patients do not have to interfere significantly with their effective rehabilitation. Although this study was not a randomized treatment evaluation study, it did evaluate a total of 152 patients with chronic low back pain for psychopathology, upon the patients' entering an intensive 3-week functional restoration treatment program developed by Mayer and Gatchel (1988). All patients were assessed for the presence of Axis I and Axis II disorders with the SCID at the start of the treatment program. They were subsequently tracked for 1 year after program completion, with treatment outcome being defined as return to work at this 1-year time period. Results demonstrated that although over 90% of patients obtained at least one Axis I diagnosis, and over 50% obtained at least one Axis II diagnosis, neither type nor degree of psychopathology was significantly predictive of a patient's capacity to return successfully to work.

These results again indicate that one of the important reasons why the treatment of chronic pain patients has traditionally been so challenging is the high prevalence of emotional distress and psychopathology commonly found in these patients. This comorbidity clearly highlights the fact that members of the pain treatment staff must be sensitive to high rates of psychopathology, and must be prepared to utilize mental health professionals to assist them in stabilizing these patients. One of the major factors that makes a functional restoration program or other tertiary multidisciplinary programs so time-intensive and professional-staff-intensive is the need to address such psychopathology carefully in order to manage these patients effectively during the program. Programs that do not have an adequate mental health component may well be doomed to failure in the treatment of chronic pain patients. This is not to say that such rehabilitation programs should be developed to try to "cure" such psychopathology. Rather, the philosophy of a tertiary treatment program such as a functional restoration program is that many of these patients were likely to have been functioning adequately before the onset of their pain disabilities, in spite of any psychopathology. The aim of the program is to provide a multidisciplinary disability management approach to use in a spirit of crisis intervention, in order to *manage* these patients better. Indeed, there has been an increase in the development of effective brief or short-term therapeutic approaches to replace the traditional long-term therapies that have been used in the past (e.g., Dattilio & Freeman, 1994; Strupp & Binder, 1984; Budman & Gurman, 1988; Puryear, 1988). Moreover, the recent development of brief cognitive-behavioral techniques for pain management (see Bradley, Chapter 6, this volume) also fits this philosophy well. Many of these chronic patients may still have some signs of psychopathology after finishing the program (as they may also have had before their injury or pain episode), but they no longer have the chronic pain disability that has seriously interfered with their working lives.

THE DSM-IV MULTIAXIAL CLASSIFICATION SYSTEM OF PSYCHOPATHOLOGY

Since psychopathology is so often associated with chronic pain, an important question clinicians must face is this: Should psychopathology be routinely assessed in chronic pain patients, and, if so, what is the best method of assessing it? Unfortunately, the answer to this question is often based on financial considerations, and not purely on what is best for the patient and for the most effective rehabilitation planning. Many third-party payers are reluctant to approve various psychological services because of their outdated "functional" view of pain, as well as their concerted attempts to curb costs. In such cases, it is up to the ingenuity and clinical skill of therapists to screen patients as effectively as possible in the limited time allowable. There are many brief psychological screening tests, such as the Symptom Checklist 90—Revised (SCL-90-R) and the short version of the MMPI, that can help flag some potentially significant psychological disturbance. The reader is referred to an edited text by Turk and Melzack (1992), which reviews the wide array of assessment methods that can be used with pain patients.

If there are no restrictions on psychological evaluation, it may be advantageous to use standardized nomenclature to assess for the presence of psychopathology. Indeed, Reich, Rosenblatt, and Tupin (1983) originally argued that a uniform diagnostic nomenclature needs to be utilized in order to develop a more accurate means for classifying patients with chronic pain. They suggested that the DSM-III (now the DSM-IV; American Psychiatric Association, 1994) is an extremely useful way to categorize chronic pain patients. They have pointed out that the DSM multiaxial classification criteria allow clinicians and researchers to consider both physiological and psychological components of chronic pain in a systematized manner. This can be done with a greater degree of replication than any currently available descriptive method permits. The DSM-IV sorts the physical, psychological, and historical components of the problem behavior into five categories or axes. The first axis (Axis I) is used to designate major clinical disorders such as schizophrenia, mood disorders, and substance-related disorders, as well as other conditions that may be the focus of clinical attention (such as academic or occupational problems). Axis II designates personality disorders (e.g., obsessive-compulsive personality disorder, antisocial personality disorder) and mental retardation. Axis III denotes the patient's general medical condition. The DSM-IV considers knowledge of the general physical health of the person as a major part of the total diagnostic picture and as potentially relevant for better understanding or managing the individual's mental disorder. A patient with an intracapsular derangement, for example, would have that diagnosis listed under Axis III. *International Classification of Diseases*, 9th Revision, Clinical Modification (ICD-9-CM) codes are used. Axis IV enables the clinician to rate specific psychosocial or environmental events that are judged to be significant contributors to the diagnosis, treatment, or prognosis of the present disorder. For example, death of a spouse, financial loss, or job termination may have etiological significance and therefore may be considered a psychosocial stressor. Finally, Axis V (Global Assessment of Functioning, or GAF) allows the clinician to rate his or her overall judgment of a patient's psychological, social, and occupational functioning on a scale (the GAF Scale) that assesses mental health–illness. Ratings on this scale are made for the current period (at the time of the evaluation).

Thus, a primary strength of the DSM-IV is that it allows multiaxial diagnoses. By ensuring that a diagnosis is based on all five axes, the DSM-IV reduces the probability that a single diagnostic category will be used to represent a unique individual. The fact that patients with a similar psychiatric diagnosis differ markedly on a host of dimensions was often lost in traditional diagnostic systems. However, unlike prior systems, the DSM-IV has a better-delineated internal structure, with individual diagnoses defined in a relatively precise manner. It also, for the first time, provides a method by which to integrate concurrent psychiatric and physiological diagnoses. As Reich et al. (1983) have noted, this more precise classification of psychological and medical diagnoses of patients with chronic pain syndromes will aid significantly in expanding our knowledge of these syndromes, as well as increasing our therapeutic skills in treating them.

However, despite the suggestion by Reich et al. (1983) on the potential usefulness of the DSM nomenclature for classifying chronic pain patients, only a few studies have utilized it (e.g., Fishbain, Goldberg, Meagher, Steele, & Rosomoff, 1986; Katon, Egan, & Miller, 1985; Large, 1986). These studies clearly indicate that chronic pain patients are likely to meet DSM criteria for specific psychiatric diagnoses, with estimates of Axis I diagnoses in chronic pain patients ranging from 86.5% (Katon et al., 1985) to 90% (Large, 1986). In addition, it has been found that 60% (Fishbain et al., 1986) to 69% (Reich et al., 1983) of all chronic pain patients meet criteria for more than one Axis I disorder. Finally, it has been shown that from 40% (Large, 1986) to 59% (Fishbain et al., 1986) of these patients have an Axis II disorder. Thus, these results are in keeping with the recognition that chronic pain patients often suffer from a variety of psychiatric and personality disorders, although the exact nature of the associations is currently not known.

One major problem in the studies reviewed above, though, has been the use of loosely semistructured psychiatric interviews in determining the DSM diagnoses. These studies used clinical interviews based on DSM flowsheets to arrive at the diagnoses. However, since the manner in which such clinical interviews are conducted can vary greatly from clinician to clinician, it is difficult to make comparisons of the reliability and validity of the diagnoses across these studies. As a means of overcoming this major problem, the use of *structured* clinical interviews has been advocated. One such interview is the SCID (Spitzer, Williams, Gibbon, & First, 1988). In my colleagues' and my studies reviewed in this chapter, the SCID was used.

The SCID was developed to be used by clinically trained mental health professionals who have experience doing unstructured diagnostic interviews and a basic knowledge of psychopathology in the DSM, and was designed to help such clinicians make a rapid and valid assessment of DSM diagnoses on Axes I and II. This is accomplished by the use of screening questions and skip-out instructions, so that an interviewer does not spend time asking about symptoms that are not diagnostically relevant. However, when a screening question is endorsed, patients are asked the same set of questions in order to rule a particular DSM diagnosis either in or out.

There are three standard versions of the instrument available for diagnosing the major Axis I and Axis II disorders. The SCID-P (Patient version) was designed for use with psychiatric inpatients; it may also be used in other situations in which there is often a need for a differential diagnosis of a psychotic disorder. The SCID-OP (Outpatient version) was designed for use with psychiatric outpatients in settings in which psychotic disorders can be expected to be rare and a detailed assessment of psychotic symptoms is not necessary. Finally, the SCID-NP (Nonpatient version) was developed for use in studies in which the subjects are not identified as psychiatric patients (e.g., community surveys, research in primary care settings, etc.).

In clinical studies, the SCID has the advantage over semistructured interviews of ensuring that patients are asked the same questions for a particular diagnosis. Moreover, the SCID I (for Axis I diagnoses) has a further advantage in that research has shown it to have good reliability (Williams et al., 1992) and promising validity (Skodol, Rosnick, Kellman, Oldham, & Hyler, 1988). Although research on the SCID II (for Axis II diagnoses) suggests that it may not be equally sensitive for discriminating among different types of personality disorders (Skodol et al., 1988), it again has major advantages over semistructured procedures. In future studies, if investigators use the same diagnostic interview, it will be much easier to compare results across different clinical settings and populations. Indeed, this was a major intent of the developers of the SCID.

Another important advantage of the SCID is that it allows a determination of current and lifetime diagnoses. It also makes it possible to establish whether the current pain episode was present before or after the occurrence of the psychopathology. This may be important information in helping to determine the degree of treatment support that may be needed to manage the psychopathology while the pain problem is being treated (this is further discussed later in the chapter).

It should be noted that the SCID is not the only structured interview technique for making DSM diagnoses. For example, the Diagnostic Interview Schedule (DIS) has also been widely used (e.g., Robins, Helzer, Croughan, & Ratcliff, 1981). The DIS is likewise a highly structured interview that requires specialized training to administer. There is also a computerized version of it (C-DIS). The reliability and validity of the DIS have been shown to be quite acceptable in a number of studies (e.g., Helzer, Spitznagel, & McEvoy, 1987; Robins et al., 1981). The one disadvantage of the DIS when compared to the SCID is the lack of supplementary source material that one has available when making SCID diagnoses (e.g., additional questions to clarify differential diagnoses; challenges to inconsistencies in self-reports). To date, there have been no studies directly comparing the SCID and the DIS in terms of relative degree of reliability and validity.

OTHER TREATMENT ISSUES

Finally, besides the important issue of considering the role that psychopathology plays in chronic pain, clinicians need to be aware of a number of other psychosocial treatment issues pertaining to chronic pain patients. One such issue is that of discordance among medical/administrative diagnostic concepts. In an earlier report noting the problem of discordance in evaluation of chronic low back pain, Waddell (1987) indicated that although correlations are found among impairment, pain, and disability, there is not perfect overlap among these categories. Figure 2.4 is a depiction of his characterization of their relationship. As can be seen, although they are all logically and clinically related to one another, there is usually not a 1:1:1 relation among them. The wide individual differences in this discordance from one patient to the next make this imperfect correlation even more complex. Therefore, treatment personnel need to be aware of the varying relationships among these concepts. Attempts to develop an algorithm or model to help guide and predict the therapeutic process on the basis of measurement of these various components have not been successful (Gatchel, 1991). Another important issue that needs to

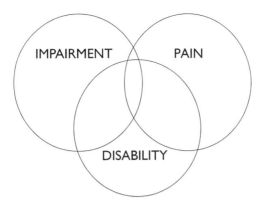

FIGURE 2.4. Waddell's conceptualization of the overlap among impairment, pain, and disability. From Gatchel (1994). Copyright 1994 by the American Pain Society. Adapted by permission.

be addressed is what role psychopathology plays in affecting the degree of discordance displayed.

The reader should also be aware of the definitions of the three categories or concepts mentioned above, since they are fundamentally different. "Impairment" is a medical term used to refer to an alteration of the patient's usual health status (i.e., some anatomical or pathological abnormality) that is evaluated by medical means. The evaluation of impairment is solely a medical responsibility in which there is an attempt to evaluate structural limitations objectively. Unfortunately, though, no technology currently exists that would allow impairment evaluation to be totally accurate or objective; at present, such evaluation relies upon methods that are not highly reliable and are often subject to examiner bias. "Disability" is an administrative term that refers to the diminished capacity or inability to perform certain activities of everyday living. Disability evaluations, too, are not totally reliable and are subject to various examiner and patient response biases. The assessment of disability is usually based upon subjective report measures. Finally, "pain" is a psychophysiological concept based primarily upon experiential or subjective evaluation. It is likewise often difficult to quantify in an objective or reliable manner.

As I have noted elsewhere (Gatchel, 1994), a fundamental problem associated with using these three concepts is that of measurement. Rather than being actual entities or "things" that can be tied to one specific, "touchable" property (such as size or weight), these three categories or concepts should be viewed as hypothesized constructs that are inferred on the basis of relationships among objects or events, and that appear to account for some important form of behavior or outcome. Just as "intelligence," "stress," and "essential hypertension" are constructs used to account for some observed behavior or medical phenomenon, so too are "impairment," "disability," and "pain" also constructs. The construct of impairment, for example, is used to account for some inferred pathological or anatomical dysfunction assumed to have a negative effect on current health status or behavior. The construct of disability, in turn, is often used to infer whether an individual can perform activities required for gainful employment. The construct of pain is many times used to infer the presence of some psychophysiological mechanism that leads to a patient's complaints and inhibition of behavior. Of course, if one uses a construct to explain some form of behavior, it is essential to develop a precise operational definition of it and to employ objective and quantifiable behavioral referents as measures of that construct. Unfortunately, however, this remains a major problem in the field. To date, numerous operational definitions have been proposed for these three constructs, and the measurements developed for their evaluation have not always been shown to be reliable or valid.

As noted earlier, another factor that makes the study and measurement of these constructs so difficult is that one cannot always assume that these three broad constructs will be highly correlated with one another. One patient may verbally report a significant amount of pain, but yet may show very little impairment that can be objectively evaluated, with disability perhaps lying somewhere in between the two in terms of severity. Another patient may report little pain, but may display great disability and some impairment. Needless to say, it is important to assess all three constructs in specific situations whenever possible, with the expectation that there may be complex interactions among them that may differ from one patient to the next, as well as from one time to the next. Moreover, an issue that has not received much empirical attention to date is the role that psychopathology plays in this relationship process.

WHAT COMPONENT OR CONSTRUCT
IS THE MOST HEURISTIC TO USE
IN "DRIVING" THE TREATMENT PROCESS?

There has traditionally been a great deal of debate as to what component of behavior or construct one should focus on in order to maximize treatment effectiveness. Fordyce (see Fordyce, Roberts, & Sternbach, 1985) has been a pioneer in the field involving the behavioral assessment and treatment of chronic pain. His approach was based upon the operant conditioning model of behavior advocated by psychologists such as B. F. Skinner (1974). Sanders comprehensively reviews the rudiments of this orientation in Chapter 5 of this volume. Fordyce has emphasized that it is not enough simply to evaluate and attempt to modify an individual's subjective experience of pain. One must comprehensively evaluate pain *behavior* or behavioral functioning, because such behavior can be more objectively and reliably evaluated. This approach can be viewed as focusing primarily on observable and objectively evaluated function (Mayer & Gatchel, 1988). Relying upon simple subjective self-report of pain or disability, or issues of psychopathology, and allowing these to "drive" the treatment process has not been proven to be effective. This is not to say that the other components, such as self-reports of pain and disability, are not important; however, they are made subordinate to the construct of function. Concentrating on overt behavior or function shows more promise because of the ability to quantify it objectively and reliably. Indeed, in the Gatchel et al. (1994) study reviewed earlier, functional restoration was found to be effective regardless of the degree of patient psychopathology, because function "drove" the rehabilitation process. Psychopathology needs to be effectively managed during rehabilitation, but it should not "drive" the rehabilitation process. The clinician also does not ignore signs of psychopathology. The treatment team must be prepared to manage such signs effectively as the patient progresses through the rehabilitation process.

As Hazard (1994) has noted, it is extremely important to develop a successful therapeutic alliance between the chronic pain patient and the practitioner. According to Hazard, this can be accomplished by setting mutually acceptable tripartite goals of pain relief, improved functional capacity, and socioeconomic recovery. Indeed, a positive therapeutic alliance has been demonstrated to be important in the treatment of most medical conditions (Gatchel et al., 1989). However, for the most systematic application of a treatment method, the focus on the best available objective measure available—function—is most likely to lead to positive results. Whenever in doubt, the clinician should use the most objective measure available. A distinct advantage of this is that it keeps both the therapist and patient consistent in their focus on a behavior or function that can be reliably measured and "fed back" to both. Again, this is not to say that the therapist ignores self-reports of pain and disability. Indeed, it is difficult to dissuade chronic pain patients from their goal of pain relief. However, it is made subordinate to the construct of function in the therapist's overall treatment strategy. Of course, this may not successfully "capture" all patients. For a certain percentage of patients, there may be significant barriers to recovery, such as secondary gain issues that cannot be overcome even after careful negotiation of goals. In such cases, the specific biases of the rehabilitation specialist will then determine what goal or category will be used to document failure. Such "losses" are inevitable in an environment in which significant psychosocioeconomic issues often overshadow the medical vagaries of a case.

The functional restoration treatment program mentioned earlier, which has been demonstrated to be a highly efficacious rehabilitation approach with chronic low back pain disability, and which has been replicated across different clinical sites and countries, is based on the premise that objectively evaluated functional behavior should be the focus of rehabilitation (Bendix & Bendix, 1994; Hazard et al., 1989; Mayer et al., 1985, 1987). Across these studies, 1-year return-to-work rates average 80–85% for the once recalcitrant, chronic, mostly workers' compensation samples of blue-collar workers treated in these program studies. This form of rehabilitation is effective because function "drives" the treatment process. The subjective components of pain and disability are then seen to change concurrently when functioning is positively altered. However, we have found that there will usually be no major change in the subjective expression of pain and disability without an improvement in functional level. Focusing on function allows the entire treatment and patient team to "stay on track" and avoid issues that may disrupt the therapeutic milieu and the requisite clear-cut boundaries of a successful rehabilitation approach. Thus, the three goals of treatment delineated by Hazard (1994) always need to be considered. However, the clear focus on the most objectively quantified and meaningful behavior will increase the probability of rehabilitation success with the greatest proportion of patients. Moreover, with appropriate treatment personnel, psychopathology need not impede the rehabilitation process, as was demonstrated in the Gatchel et al. (1994) study.

SUMMARY AND CONCLUSIONS

As pain becomes more chronic, psychosocial variables play an increasingly dominant role in the maintenance of pain behavior and suffering. I have presented a conceptual model of the transition from acute to chronic pain, in which it is assumed that the type of psychological distress displayed by patients whose pain becomes subacute or chronic depends upon the premorbid or pre-existing personality/psychological characteristics of each individual. One of the major psychosocial concomitants or sources of distress clinicians must be prepared to deal with when treating chronic pain patients is psychopathology. Preliminary research addressing the complex "chicken-or-egg" question of what occurs first—the chronic pain or psychopathology—suggests that either may occur first, depending upon the form of psychopathology. Regardless of the direction of this relationship, however, clinicians need to evaluate the presence of psychopathology (a structured method for DSM diagnosis, the SCID, has been reviewed), and be prepared to manage it effectively during the course of rehabilitation. The increase in recent years in the development of effective brief or short-term therapeutic approaches coincides nicely with the philosophy of effective management of psychopathology while rehabilitation of the chronic pain disability occurs. In terms of rehabilitation, I have argued that function should "drive" the treatment process, rather than self-report of pain or disability. When such is the case (as exemplified by a functional restoration treatment approach), the probability of rehabilitation success is greatly increased, regardless of the presence of psychopathology.

ACKNOWLEDGMENT

Much of my research reported in this chapter was supported by grants from the National Institutes of Health (Nos. MH46452, MH01107, and DE10713).

REFERENCES

American Psychiatric Association. (1994). *Diagnostic and statistical manual of mental disorders* (4th ed.). Washington, DC: Author.

Barnes, D., Gatchel, R. J., Mayer, T. G., & Barnett, J. (1990). Changes in MMPI profiles of chronic low back pain patients following successful treatment. *Journal of Spinal Disorders, 3*, 353–355.

Barrett, J. F., Rose, R. M., & Klerman, G. L. (Eds.). (1979). *Stress and mental disorder.* New York: Raven Press.

Beals, R. K. (1984). Compensation and recovery from injury. *Western Journal of Medicine, 40*, 276–283.

Bendix, T., & Bendix, A. (1994, June). *Different training programs for chronic low back pain: A randomized, blinded one-year follow-up study.* Paper presented at the annual meeting of International Society for the Study of the Lumbar Spine, Seattle, WA.

Biering-Sorensen, F. (1983). A prospective study of LBP in a general population: II. Location, character, aggravating and relieving factors. *Scandinavian Journal of Rehabilitation Medicine,* 15–81.

Bigos, S. J., Battie, M. C., Spengler, D. M., Fisher, L. D., Fordyce, W. E., Hansson, T. H., Nachemson, A. L., & Wortley, M. D. (1991). A prospective study of work perceptions and psychosocial factors affecting the report of back injury. *Spine, 16*, 1–6.

Budman, S. H., & Gurman, A. S. (1988). *Theory and practice of brief therapy.* New York: Guilford Press.

Blanchard, E. B., Kirsch, C. A., Applebaum, K. A., & Jaccard, J. (1989). Role of psychopathology in chronic headache: Cause or effect? *Headache, 29*, 295–301.

Dattilio, F. M., & Freeman, A. (Eds.). (1994). *Cognitive-behavioral strategies in crisis intervention.* New York: Guilford Press.

DeGood, D. E., & Shutty, M. S. (1992). Assessment of pain beliefs, coping, and self-efficacy. In D. C. Turk & R. Melzack (Eds.), *Handbook of pain assessment.* New York: Guilford Press.

Fishbain, D. A., Goldberg, M., Meagher, B. R., Steele, R., & Rosomoff, H. (1986). Male and female chronic pain patients categorized by DSM-III psychiatric diagnostic criteria. *Pain, 26*, 181–197.

Fordyce, W. E., Roberts, A., & Sternbach, R. (1985). The behavioral management of chronic pain: A response to critics. *Pain, 22*, 112–125.

Fyer, M. R., Frances, A. J., Sullivan, T., Hurt, S. W., & Clarkin, J. (1988). Comorbidity of borderline personality disorder. *Archives of General Psychiatry, 45*, 348–352.

Gatchel, R. J. (1991). Early development of physical and mental deconditioning in painful spinal disorders. In T. G. Mayer, V. Mooney, & R. J. Gatchel (Eds.), *Contemporary conservative care for painful spinal disorders.* Philadelphia: Lea & Febiger.

Gatchel, R. J. (1994). Occupational low back pain disability: Why function needs to "drive" the rehabilitation process. *American Pain Society Journal, 3*, 107–110.

Gatchel, R. J., Baum, A., & Krantz, D. (1989). *An introduction to health psychology* (2nd ed.). New York: McGraw-Hill.

Gatchel, R. J., Polatin, P. B., & Kinney, R. K. (1995). Predicting outcome of chronic back pain using clinical predictors of psychopathology: A prospective analysis. *Health Psychology, 14*, 415–420

Gatchel, R. J., Polatin, P. B., & Mayer, T. G. (in press). The dominant role of psychosocial risk factors in the development of chronic low back pain disability. *Spine.*

Gatchel, R. J., Polatin, P. B., Mayer, T. G., & Garcy, P. D. (1994). Psychopathology and the rehabilitation of patients with low back pain disability. *Archives of Physical Medicine and Rehabilitation, 75*, 666–670.

Hazard, R. G. (1994). Occupational low back pain: The critical role of functional goal setting. *American Pain Society Journal, 3*, 102–107.

Hazard, R. G., Fenwick, J. W., Kalisch, S. M. (1989). Functional restoration with behavioral support: A one-year prospective study of patients with chronic low-back pain. *Spine, 14*, 157–161.

Helzer, J. E., Spitznagel, E. L., & McEvoy, L. (1987). The predictive validity of lay Diagnostic Interview Schedule diagnoses in the general population: A comparison with physician examiners. *Archives of General Psychiatry, 44*, 1069–1077.

Hendler, N. H. (1982). The four stages of pain. In N. H. Hendler, D. M. Long, & T. N. Wise (Eds.), *Diagnosis and treatment of chronic pain.* Littleton, MA: PSG.

Jensen, M. C., Brant-Zawadzki, M. N., Obuchowski, N., Modic, M. T., Malkasian, D., & Ross, J. S. (1994). Magnetic resonance imaging of the lumbar spine in people without back pain. *New England Journal of Medicine. 331*, 69–73.

Joffe, R. T., & Regan, J. J. (1988). Personality and depression. *Journal of Psychiatric Research, 22*, 279–286.

Katon, W., Egan, K., & Miller, D. (1985). Chronic pain: Lifetime psychiatric diagnoses and family history. *American Journal of Psychiatry, 142*, 1156–1160.

Keefe, F. J., Caldwell, D. S., Williams, D. A., Gil, K. M., Mitchell, D., Robertson, C., Martinez, S., Nunley, J., Beckham, J. C., Crisson, J. E., & Helms, M. (1990). Pain coping skills training in the management of osteoarthritic knee pain: A comparative study. *Behavior Therapy, 21*, 49–62.

Kleinke, C. L. (1994). MMPI scales as predictors of pain-coping strategies preferred by patients with chronic pain. *Rehabilitation Psychology, 39*, 123–128.

Krause, N., & Ragland, D. R. (1994). Occupational disability due to low back pain: A new interdisciplinary classification used in a phase model of disability. *Spine, 19*, 1011–1020.

Lancourt, J., & Kettelhut, M. (1992). Predicting return to work for lower back pain patients receiving worker's compensation. *Spine, 17*(6), 629–640.

Large, R. G. (1986). DSM-III diagnosis in chronic pain: Confusion or clarity? *Journal of Nervous and Mental Disease, 174*, 295–303.

Mayer, T. G., & Gatchel, R. J. (1988). *Functional restoration for spinal disorders: The sports medicine approach.* Philadelphia: Lea & Febiger.

Mayer, T. G., Gatchel, R. J., Kishino, N. D., Keeley, J., Capra, P., Mayer, H., Barnett, J., & Mooney, V. (1985). Objective assessment of spine function following industrial injury: A prospective study with comparison group and one-year follow-up. *Spine, 10*, 482–492.

Mayer, T. G., Gatchel, R. J., Mayer, H., Kishino, N. D., Keeley, J., & Mooney, V. (1987). A prospective two year study of functional restoration in industrial low back injury. *Journal of the American Medical Association, 258*, 1763–1767.

Mayer, T. G., Polatin, P., Smith, B., Smith, C., Gatchel, R., Herring, S., Hall, H., Donaldson, R., Dickey, J., & English, W. (1995). Spine rehabilitation: Secondary and tertiary nonoperative care. *Spine, 20*, 2060–2066.

Melzack, R., & Wall, P. (1965). Pain mechanisms: A new theory. *Science, 50*, 971–979.

Millon, T. (1981). *Disorders of personality: DSM-III, Axis II.* New York: Wiley.

Mooney, V., Cairns, D., & Robertson, J. (1975). The psychological evaluation and treatment of the chronic low back pain patient: A new approach (Part II). *Orthopedic Nurses Association Journal, 2,* 187–189.

Moss, R. A., & Garrett, J. C. (1984). Temporomandibular joint dysfunction syndrome and myofascial pain dysfunction syndrome: A critical review. *Journal of Oral Rehabilitation, 11,* 3–28.

Pilowsky, I. (1978). A general classification of abnormal illness behavior. *British Journal of Medical Psychiatry, 51,* 131–137.

Polatin, P. B., Kinney, R. K., Gatchel, R. J., Lillo, E., & Mayer, T. G. (1993). Psychiatric illness and chronic low back pain. *Spine, 18,* 66–71.

Pope, M., Frymoyer, J. W., & Andersson, G. (1984). *Occupational low back pain.* New York: Praeger.

Puryear, D. A. (1988). *Helping people in crisis.* San Francisco: Jossey-Bass.

Regier, D. A., Boyd, J. H., Burke, J. D., Rae, D. S., Myers, J. K., Kramer, M., Robins, L. N., George, L. K., Karno, M., & Locke, B. Z. (1988). One-month prevalence of mental disorders in the United States. *Archives of General Psychiatry, 45,* 977–986.

Reich, J., Rosenblatt, R. M., & Tupin, J. (1983). DSM-III: A new nomenclature for classifying patients with chronic pain. *Pain, 16,* 201–206.

Robins, L. N., Helzer, J. E., Weissman, M. M., Orvaschel, D. A., Gruenberg, E., Burke, J. D., & Regier, D. A. (1984). Lifetime prevalence of specific psychiatric disorders in three sites. *Archives of General Psychiatry, 41,* 949–958.

Robins, L. N., Helzer, J. E., Croughan, J., & Ratcliff, K. S. (1981). National Institute of Mental Health Diagnostic Interview Schedule. *Archives of General Psychiatry, 38,* 381–389.

Romano, J. M., & Turner, J. A. (1985). Chronic pain and depression: Does the evidence support a relationship? *Psychological Bulletin, 97,* 18–34.

Sanders, S. H. (1995). Risk factors for the occurrence of low back pain and chronic disability. *American Pain Society Bulletin, 5,* 1–5.

Skinner, B. F. (1974). *About behaviorism.* New York: Knopf.

Skodol, A. E., Rosnick, L., Kellman, D., Oldham, J. M., & Hyler, S. E. (1988). Validating structured DSM-III-R personality assessments using longitudinal data. *American Journal of Psychiatry, 145,* 1297–1299.

Spitzer, R. L., Williams, J. B. W., Gibbon, M., & First, M. (1988). *Structured Clinical Interview for DSM-III-R.* New York: New York State Psychiatric Institute.

Sternbach, R. A. (1974). *Pain patients: Traits and treatments.* New York: Academic Press.

Sternbach, R. A., Wolf, S. R., Murphy, R. W., & Akeson, W. H. (1973). Traits of pain patients: The low-back "loser." *Psychosomatics, 14,* 226–229.

Strupp, H. H., & Binder, J. L. (1984). *Psychotherapy in a new key: A guide to time-limited dynamic psychotherapy.* New York: Basic Books.

Turk, D. C., & Melzack, R. (Eds.). (1992). *Handbook of pain assessment.* New York: Guilford Press.

Turk, D. C., & Rudy, T. E. (1986) Assessment of cognitive factors in chronic pain: A worthwhile enterprise? *Journal of Consulting and Clinical Psychology, 54,* 760–768.

Turk, D. C., & Rudy, T. E. (1988). Toward an empirically derived taxonomy of chronic pain patients: Integration of psychological assessment data. *Journal of Consulting and Clinical Psychology, 56,* 233–238.

Waddell, G. (1987). Clinical assessment of lumbar impairment. *Clinical Orthopedic Related Research, 221,* 110–120.

Waddell, G., Main, C. J., Morris, E. W., DiPaola, M., & Gray, I. C. (1984). Chronic low back pain, psychologic distress, and illness behavior. *Spine, 9,* 209–213.

Williams, J. B. W., Gibbon, M., First, M. B., Spitzer, R. L., Davies, M., Borus, J., Howes, M. J., Kane, J., Pope, H. G., Rounsaville, B., & Wittchen, H. U. (1992). The Structured Clinical Interview for DSM-III-R (SCID): II: Multisite test–retest reliability. *Archives of General Psychiatry, 49,* 630–636.

PART II

TREATMENT APPROACHES

CHAPTER 3

Acute Pain Management

David A. Williams

The role of the health psychologist is less central in the management of acute pain than it is in the management of chronic or persistent pain. This is true in part because of the wealth of pharmacological agents capable of bringing about rapid relief from pain for many acute pain conditions. By definition, acute pain is brief, and therefore front-line assessment and treatment with pharmacological agents are typically carried out by nursing staff and attending physicians.

This is not to say that the health psychologist plays no role in the management of acute pain. On the contrary, research contributions from health psychology have identified better methods of pain assessment, highlighted the role of behavioral and emotional modulation of acute pain, explored the role of the family in assisting children undergoing painful medical procedures, and further defined the role of beliefs in the perception of pain. Health psychologists have also been helpful in developing and supporting public policy regarding improved and timely delivery of acute pain management technology for pain sufferers. Clinically, health psychologists play a valued role as consultants to private practitioners or to more structured acute pain services. Some medical procedures cannot offer the amount of pain relief desired by a patient, and some patients are excessively anxious, intolerant of medications, or philosophically opposed to standard medical procedures. These and other special situations complicate the usually effective technology of acute pain control. In such cases, the perspective and skill of the doctoral-level health psychologist is greatly needed and complements routine pharmacological approaches.

This chapter provides a brief overview of acute pain from both a philosophical and a pathophysiological perspective. Following the overview, current clinical issues relevant to the management of acute pain are explored, and examples of treatment options are provided. A case example is given for each clinical issue. The chapter concludes with practical recommendations for integrating the skills of the health psychologist into settings where acute pain is treated.

ACUTE PAIN FROM PHILOSOPHICAL AND PATHOPHYSIOLOGICAL PERSPECTIVES

A Philosophical Perspective

Pain as a Complementary Life Force

Historical accounts from as early as 5 B.C. indicate that acute pain was considered a natural part of everyday life. During the Middle Ages, Christian societies gave pain religious value as a sign of future reward in heaven. During the Renaissance and Classical periods, pain was viewed as a means of compelling the senses to obey reason, promoting moral and spiritual growth, and paying penance for one's sins. During the 18th, 19th, and early 20th centuries, pain was viewed as a means of stirring weak or dormant vital forces in the body and was considered necessary for the promotion of healing. (For a more detailed discussion of views of pain throughout history, see Rey, 1993.)

Pain as a Destructive Life Force

Modern Western society has adopted a very different view of acute pain. Today there is a strong sentiment that pain is rarely beneficial to the sufferer, and health care professionals are encouraged to offer the greatest degree of pain relief that can be provided safely. This view of acute pain is best articulated in a U.S. Department of Health and Human Services publication, *Acute Pain Management: Operative or Medical Procedures and Trauma* (Agency for Health Care Policy and Research [AHCPR], 1992). The American Pain Society, a multidisciplinary professional society for pain specialists, has similarly published guidelines for acute pain management and for cancer pain (American Pain Society, 1992).

The strong movement for better pain management stems in part from an acknowledgment within the medical community that far too many individuals are being undertreated for their pain. In 1989 there were 23.3 million surgical operations in the United States. It is estimated that at least half of these procedures were accompanied by higher-than-necessary acute pain because of inadequate pain management (Peebles & Schneiderman, 1991). Undermedication stems in part from an underreporting of pain by pain patients. Some patients resist asking for narcotic medications because they fear addiction or believe that they should be able to tolerate pain on their own. Many physicians also fear the addictive potential of narcotic analgesics and do very little to dispel the myth of widespread addiction. Although some patients, particularly those who have a history of addiction problems, will go on to develop an addiction to opiates, the number of patients who actually develop opiate addictions is quite low (e.g., 19 out of 22,000) (Porter & Jick, 1980; S. Perry & Heidrich, 1982; Taub, 1982; Krames, 1993). To help address the issue of undermedicating acute pain, multiple health care disciplines and agencies have taken steps to educate their members and patients regarding this issue (e.g., surgery and anesthesia, Royal College of Surgeons, 1990; urology, Portnoy, 1990; G. D. Phillips & Cousins, 1986; nursing, American Nurses Association, 1991; the U.S. Department of Health and Human Services, AHCPR, 1992; and professionl pain societies, American Pain Society, 1992; International Association for the Study of Pain, Ready & Edwards, 1992). Another reason acute pain is undermanaged is the underreferral of pain cases to those clinicians most capable of addressing pain (i.e., pain specialists). It is estimated that clinical pain specialists are consulted in only 4–7% of pain cases (H. Taylor, 1985).

A Pathophysiological Perspective

Prevalence

The first U.S. national survey on the prevalence of pain was conducted in 1985 by Lou Harris and Associates and was sponsored by the Bristol–Myers Company. The results were reported in a book titled *The Nuprin Pain Report* (H. Taylor, 1985). To summarize some of the findings from this survey, most respondents reported experiencing different types of pain each year, with a modal duration of 1–5 days. Pain resulted in a loss of over 650 million workdays in 1985, and the cost to the public was $65 billion in lost work productivity.

The Stages of Acute Pain

Wall (1979; see also Bonica, 1990) proposed that following an acute injury, there are three stages of response: immediate, secondary, and tertiary. Immediately after injury, the individual may report the absence of pain. The absence of pain may represent an adaptive biological function that permits the individual to fight, escape, or seek help, and thus ultimately promotes survival after injury. The secondary phase is marked by tissue damage, pain, and anxiety. It is during this phase that the individual can mentally process the events leading up to the injury and recruit coping responses to get recovery under way. The tertiary stage is marked by limited activity, excessive sleep, poor appetite, and diminished attention span. These aspects of the tertiary stage of acute pain are similar to the neurovegetative signs of depression. If they are time-limited, the aspects of the tertiary stage can serve the protective functions of limiting mobility and preparing the body for recovery.

Psychophysiological and Psychological Responses to Acute Pain

As noted in Wall's (1979) theory, the human response to acute pain is both physiological and psychological. Acute pain is associated with increased sympathetic tone, including vasoconstriction of the skin, the splanchnic region, and nonpriority organs. It is also associated with increased cardiac output, increased blood pressure and viscosity, increased metabolic rate and oxygen consumption, decreased gastric tone and emptying, and decreased urinary tract tone and evacuation. Endocrine and metabolic responses to acute pain include increases in catabolic substances such as adrenocorticotropic hormone, cortisol, antidiuretic hormone, growth hormone, catecholamines, cyclic adenosine monophosphate, renin, angiotensin II, glucagon, aldosterone, and IL-1 (Interleukin-1) and decreases in immunological competence and anabolic substances such as insulin and testosterone (Bonica, 1990; Carron, 1989; Dionne, 1992).

Acute pain is also associated with emotional arousal. Anxiety, depression, anger, and fear are perhaps the four most prominent emotions that affect acute pain. Of these emotions, anxiety is the best studied for acute pain (Chapman & Turner, 1990; Gil, 1992). Anxiety is associated both with increased pain perception and with complicating factors that increase the risk to physical health and prolongation of the pain experience. Bonica (1990) cites several examples of how anxiety associated with acute pain can further complicate a clinical picture: (1) Anxiety causes cortically mediated increases in blood viscosity and clotting time, fibrinolysis, and platelet aggregation, leading to increased risk of thromboembolism; (2) anxiety can cause a 50–200% increase in the neuroendocrine secretion of catecholamines and cortisol, resulting in significant increases in cardiac output, abnormally high sympathetic tone, shock, excessive vasoconstriction, intestinal ischemia, and hypoxic tissue damage; and (3) anxiety can cause 5- to 20-fold increases in ventilation, with the potential of respiratory alkalosis. Moreover, anxiety can lower the pain threshold, causing the patient to interpret any sensation as pain—a problem that can limit a physician's ability to complete an invasive procedure (Dworkin, 1967). As several dentists have reported, "No technique, no device, no magic solution will anesthetize patients who are so distraught and upset that they interpret any stimulus as pain" (Walton & Torabinejad, 1992, p. 97).

ASSESSMENT AND TREATMENT ISSUES RELEVANT TO THE HEALTH PSYCHOLOGIST

In the bulk of this chapter, I explore several prominent clinical issues that are at the forefront of psychological research in the area of acute pain management. Following a brief discussion of each clinical issue, a case example helps to define the various challenges facing the clinician, and treatment options are presented for addressing each issue. This chapter is written under the assumption that the reader is familiar with chronic pain management techniques and therefore seeks to augment that knowledge with nuances relevant to the management of acute pain.

The Underreporting of Acute Pain

The pain of surgery produces autonomic, psychological, immunological, and behavioral responses that can delay or inhibit normal healing. Fortunately, many techniques are available that can suppress pain such as scheduled intravenous analgesics, patient-controlled analgesia (PCA), stimulation therapy, nerve blocks, epidural narcotics, and interpleural analgesia (Carron, 1989). Although the technology behind these methods is good, clinicians are reliant upon subjective reports of pain from their patients in order to use this technology effectively. For the health psychologist familiar with chronic pain patients, the problem of underreported pain may seem ironic. In fact, however, the underreporting of acute pain is what can lead to needless pain escalation and physical complications.

Case Example

> Mary, aged 47, was a socially and philosophically conservative individual who tried hard to please the people around her. Despite her outward desire to please others, she did hold strong opinions about the way others acted. For example, she had little tolerance for the woman in her neighborhood who monopolized conversations with discussions of her physical ailments. Similarly, she was offended by the lifestyle of a 26-year-old neighbor suspected of alcohol use, recreational drug use, and liberal philosophical leanings. When Mary visited her doctor, she tried to be a good patient by making as few demands on him as possible. Thus, when her doctor suggested that she receive a hysterectomy, she asked very few questions about the surgery; instead, she followed the adage of "Doctor knows best." With satisfactory but minimal discussion, therefore, Mary agreed to surgery. The surgery went well, and Mary's doctor asked her afterward, "How is your pain?" Fearing the lifestyle of narcotic addicts and wanting to appear cooperative for her doctor, she replied "OK." Shortly thereafter, a nurse asked her to rate her pain on a 0- to 10-point scale. To this request, she replied, "5." Following discharge, a third party queried Mary about her pain relief following surgery. To this she replied, "The pain was horrible, but I'm fine now. I'm just glad it's over."

Mary's case was fraught with problems that plague acute pain assessment: (1) poor choice of pain assessment instruments, (2) inconsistent methods of assessing pain over time, and (3) failure to teach the patient prior to surgery how to report pain.

Poor Choice of Assessment Instruments

The single best measure of pain and suffering is still the patient's self-report (AHCPR, 1992). How physicians obtain that self-report, however, varies widely in practice. Price, Bush, Long, and Harkins (1994) sampled 218 physicians and found that in practice 56% preferred numerical rating scales (NRSs), 19.5% preferred verbal rating scales (VRSs), and only 7% preferred visual analogue scales (VASs).

An NRS asks patients to rate the intensity of their pain in terms of a numerical value (e.g., 0–10). The endpoints typically have verbal descriptors such as "no pain" and "worst pain" (see Figure 3.1). NRSs have demonstrated good validity as measures of pain intensity, having strong correlations with other intensity measures (e.g., Jensen, Karoly, & Braver, 1986). Their advantages include ease of administration and ease of scoring. An NRS can be completed in under 10 seconds and can be given repeatedly over time. Scoring is simple, since the circled response represents the pain intensity. NRSs exist with all possible distributions of numbers; the most common are 0–10 and 0–100 scales. The 0–100 scale is recommended, since this scale more closely approximates a continuous distribution and provides more response categories (Karoly & Jensen, 1987). Disadvantages of NRSs stem mainly from the inability of some patients (e.g., older adults and members of some cultural groups) to conceptualize pain, a bodily sensation, as a number.

A VRS asks patients to use one word from a list of adjectives to rate their pain intensity. Each adjective has associated with it an intensity score. When the patient chooses an adjective, the clinician must then transform the adjective into a standardized quantita-

The 0–10 Numeric Rating Scale (NRS):

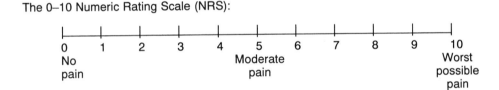

```
|—|—|—|—|—|—|—|—|—|—|
0   1   2   3   4   5   6   7   8   9   10
No              Moderate            Worst
pain              pain              possible
                                     pain
```

12-point Verbal Rating Scale (VRS)
(from Tursky, Jamner, & Friedman, 1982)
  Not noticeable
  Just noticeable
  Very weak
  Weak
  Mild
  Moderate
  Strong
  Intense
  Very strong
  Severe
  Very intense
  Excruciating

Visual Analogue Scale (VAS):

                                                  Worst
No ———————————————————————— possible
pain   pain

FIGURE 3.1. Acute pain measurement tools.

tive pain intensity score. Like NRSs, VRSs have been developed with varying numbers of adjectives. Figure 3.1 displays a 12-point VRS developed by Tursky, Jamner, and Friedman (1982). This method of pain assessment has demonstrated high correlations with the more time-consuming and empirically rigorous cross-modality-matching method of pain assessment. VRSs have advantages similar to those of NRSs: They demonstrate good convergent and discriminant validity with other pain measures, and show sensitivity to treatment effects (Karoly & Jensen, 1987). A VRS is a bit more difficult to administer, in that it should be administered in written rather than oral form. Committing a 12-adjective VRS to memory is difficult for both the patient and clinician. The VRS also has the added step for the clinician of transforming the chosen adjective into a number. Compared to the many NRS versions, a VRS has a limited range of possible responses (e.g., 12 adjectives vs. 100 numbers on an NRS). It has been noted that patients tend to use the middle adjectives more frequently than the endpoints; this further limits the available range of responses. A final disadvantage of this approach is relevant to the health psychologist researcher: The VRS produces categorical data, thus limiting analyses to nonparametric options.

A VAS is a straight line, usually 10 cm in length, with verbal descriptors much like those of an NRS at the endpoints (see Figure 3.1). The patient is asked simply to place a mark on the line that indicates the intensity of pain. Despite the simplicity of the VASs, they are used less frequently by clinicians, in part because scoring a VAS requires an extra step that the other measures do not include. Specifically, the clinician must use a ruler to measure the distance of the mark on the line in order to quantify the pain intensity; this step takes some time and introduces the possibility of the clinician's making a measurement error into the accuracy of the pain assessment. Price et al. (1994) suggested a solution to this drawback—a mechanical VAS. A mechanical VAS is a standard VAS with a ruler encased in a sleeve, making pain measurement quick and accurate for the clinician. A mechanical VAS has the added psychometric advantage of possessing good ratio scale properties. A VAS is also a useful pain assessment method in work with children, who may not be able to conceptualize pain as a number or be able to make the fine verbal discrimination of pain intensity required by a VRS (Varni, Jay, Masek, & Thompson, 1986). Despite its potential advantages with children, a VAS still tends to be difficult for some older patients to understand.

Inconsistent Methods of Assessing Pain over Time

In Mary's case, the doctor did not use any empirically studied method of pain assessment. His use of a simple verbal response to identify her level of pain could not be quantified and invited miscommunication. The nurse in this example used an NRS. The use of two different pain assessment methods made it difficult to assess the progression of the patient's pain over time. Inconsistent intervals for assessing pain also provide opportunities for pain to escalate out of control, particularly in patients who act stoically and wait for someone to ask before they report their pain. It is recommended that pain be assessed by one of the quantifiable methods described above at the following points: (1) preoperatively; (2) at regular intervals postoperatively (e.g., every 2 hours while the patient is awake during the first 24 hours); (3) with each new report of pain; and (4) shortly after the administration of an analgesic, to determine its effect on the pain (AHCPR, 1992). It should be noted that reliance on persons other than the patient for pain report is discouraged. For example, in a sample of 119 nurse observers and 119 abdominal surgical patients, nurses tended to underestimate severe pain and overestimate mild pain (Zalon, 1993).

Failure to Teach Patients How to Report Pain Prior to Surgery

The accuracy of self-reported pain can improve if patients are educated in how to report pain and encouraged to report pain when it exists. In a national survey of 1,006 adults conducted by the Opinion Research Corporation, 65% of the respondents reported that they avoided talking about pain because they did not want to be seen as complainers (see Brody, 1994). The AHCPR (1992) guidelines for acute pain management recommend gathering a detailed pain history prior to surgery, under the assumption that much of acute pain control takes place prior to the surgery. Our program at Georgetown University Medical Center uses the following brief outline as a guide for gathering such information before surgery.

1. How does the patient typically express pain? Examples:
   Screaming, talking.
   Holding painful area.
   Exaggerated movements.
   Crying, grimacing.
2. How does the patient cope with pain? Examples:
   Behavioral: Increased activity, self-talk, self-isolation, seeking out others.
   Cognitive: Ignoring the pain, distraction, rationalization/control.
   Affective: Anxiety, fear, worry, calm, humor.
3. How has pain affected the patient in the past? Examples:
   Behavioral: Decreased activity, sleep disruption, job problems.
   Cognitive: Decreased concentration, decreased motivation.
   Affective: Anxiety, fear, worry, irritability, depression.
4. What are the patient's attitudes toward pain and pain control? Examples:
   "Pain is needed for healing."
   "Pain should be suffered quietly."
   "Narcotics will cause addiction."
   "I'll be out of control if I'm placed on narcotics."
   "Only wimps use pain medication."
   "I want all the drugs the doctor can muster."
5. What are the patient's family's attitudes toward pain and pain control? Examples:
   The patient may want good pain relief, but the family may be opposed to narcotic analgesics.
   The patient may want to use only hypnosis for pain control, but the family may discredit hypnosis as ineffective.

Each of the issues listed above can inhibit accurate reporting of pain, and thus can limit the ability of the hospital staff to manage pain effectively. In Mary's case, prior knowledge of her disdain for individuals who complained of pain could have alerted the hospital staff that she was likely to underreport her pain. Her opposition to psychotropic substances and association of psychotropic substances with her 26-year-old neighbor could have also alerted the hospital staff that she might harbor fears about narcotic use that could lead to her avoidance of asking for relief by underreporting pain.

During the preoperative period, patients can be allowed to choose which type of pain measurement tool they wish to use. It is a good idea to train each patient in the use of the chosen tool prior to surgery. This avoids confusion and miscommunication following surgery, when accurate pain assessment is essential for proper pain control. A VAS in particular may require some additional training, especially for older patients prior to surgery.

In some cases, patients flatly refuse to use available analgesics. Such patients may fear addiction, fear that the doctor will overmedicate them so that they won't be any trouble, fear side effects such as nausea or dysphoria, or simply want to tough it out. In these cases, a brief presurgical education session can help to alter attitudes and beliefs that may be obstructing the patients' willingness to receive the safest possible relief from pain. In a study of 166 surgical patients, 24% of the patients were undermedicated by the patients' choice. Reasons for refusing medication included fear of toxicity, fear of addiction, not wanting to disturb the nurse, and the belief that pain is normal and healthy. Following a brief educational intervention, 75% of those refusing medication were then willing to experience better management of their pain (Wilder-Smith & Schuler, 1992).

The health psychologist may be consulted in the development of a presurgical educational course for patients. The following topics and facts should be addressed in such a course.

1. *The fear of addiction.* Patients should be told that addiction to narcotics is most likely to occur in individuals with a history of addictive problems (e.g., alcohol, recreational drugs, etc.). Furthermore, opiate addiction has a very low prevalence, as pointed out earlier in this chapter.

2. *The fear of toxicity.* Patients need to know that scheduled administration of analgesics (e.g., through PCA) allows for lower doses to be used. Moreover, there are benefits in reporting even slight pain to the hospital staff. Early pain reporting allows lower doses of analgesics to be used; waiting until pain is severe means that higher doses will be needed.

3. *The fear of being a bother to the staff.* Patients need to be told that the staff genuinely wants to know about their pain. This can be presented in the context of the patients' being collaborators in helping the pain service do its job properly. In fact, not informing the pain service staff about pain actually *causes* problems, rather than relieving any burden on the staff. To circumvent the issue of bothering the staff, the educational session is a good time to ask patients which form of pain assessment is preferred, train them in the use of the assessment tool they choose, familiarize them with the pain assessment schedule, and let them know of their responsibility to indicate changes in pain between scheduled assessment periods.

4. *The desire to be stoic.* Some patients assume that pain is normal and therefore can't hurt them in the long run. However, as indicated in the discussion of pathophysiology earlier in this chapter, many natural but unhealthy responses occur in a body experiencing acute pain. The fact that pain is natural doesn't make it desirable, and now empirical research backs up what common sense suggests: Pain is a good thing to avoid if at all possible.

The Need for Brief Coping Skills

Many medical and dental procedures involve some element of pain. Currently, pharmacological agents are the treatments of choice for assisting most patients through procedures that involve moderate to severe pain. When pain is expected to be mild, some patients prefer to play an active role in their own pain management by using nonpharmacological self-management techniques. However, other patients prefer to deal with any level of pain by avoiding the necessary medical or dental attention altogether. The health psychologist can be a valuable consultant to medical and dental personnel when they are dealing with the latter two types of patients. The psychologist can train the more active patients in pain self-management techniques, and can also help the avoidant patients to deal with the fear and anxiety associated with seeking the procedures they need. In many complicated clinical situations, the health psychologist uses therapy skills to decrease pain through anxiety reduction, rather than direct modification of the pathophysiology (Gatchel, 1992).

Case Example

> Roger hadn't been to his dentist for 3 years. One day he noticed a slight pain in one of his molars when he chewed. Roger disliked the pain in his mouth, but had a greater dislike of the pain that could accompany a visit to the dentist. Roger therefore avoided going to the dentist, even though he realized that something was wrong with his tooth. Roger's strategy worked as long as the pain remained mild; after 6 months the pain become intense, however, and he was forced to visit his dentist. Unfortunately, his delay had turned a simple dental problem into a major one, and now he had to experience considerably more pain than he would have if he had visited the dentist sooner.

Roger's plight illustrates two problems that can be addressed by the health psychologist working from the perspective of preventive health care: (1) avoidance of both preventive and curative care, because of fear of the acute pain accompanying diagnostic or treatment procedures; and (2) the need for brief nonpharmacological methods of pain control that a patient can use in order to get through medical and dental procedures.

Avoidance of Preventive and Treatment Procedures

Roger is not alone in his avoidance of his dentist. In fact, it has been estimated that 12–15% of the U.S. population never goes to a dentist (Sokol, Sokol, & Sokol, 1985). A primary reason for the avoidance is fear. Gatchel and others (1983) determined that in a random sample, 11.7% of the responders had high dental fear and an additional 17.5% had moderate dental fear. Moreover, 50% of the responders in these two groups had not been to the dentist in over 1 year and could be classified as dental avoiders.

It is well recognized that anxiety reduces the pain threshold; however, the anticipation of pain is not the only source of anxiety that can act to increase pain perception. There are many sources of fear in a dentist's office, including the sounds and sights of the dental tools and the sight of the dentist himself or herself. A relatively new source of fear is the required use of personal protective equipment (PPE) as a precaution against HIV infection. Dentists now wear gloves, mask, and protective eyewear when working. For some patients, these new devices appear threatening, add an interpersonal barrier between the dentist and patient, and raise fears of AIDS. In studies with both adults and children, PPE has been identified as another source of anxiety that can affect treatment and potentially pain perception in the dentist's office (Glaros & Gadbury-Amyot, 1993; Siegel, Smith, Cantu, & Posnick, 1992).

Avoidance of necessary procedures because of the fear of pain is not limited to the dental clinic. In an era when more data are available than ever before about the importance of early detection of breast cancer, some women are avoiding diagnostic mammography because of the pain the procedure causes. A review of the literature found that pain was reported by 1–62% of patients undergoing this procedure (Keefe, Hauck, Egert, Rimer, & Kornguth, 1994). Although the pain of a diagnostic procedure may not seem remotely comparable to the pain and suffering associated with cancer, 77% of women indicating that they would not undergo a future mammogram also rated their mammogram discomfort as "very uncomfortable" or "intolerable" (Jackson, Lex, & Smith, 1988).

The health psychologist can play two important roles in situations such as these. By reducing anxiety that may be contributing to health care avoidance, the psychologist plays a preventive role: Fearful patients are helped to obtain treatment before more serious and painful pathology develops. Also by reducing anxiety, the health psychologist helps to reduce the psychophysiological arousal that is associated with decreased pain thresholds and tolerances. Gatchel (1980) described the use of systematic desensitization to reduce dental anxiety in a group of dental avoiders. Eighty-eight percent of the group of dental avoiders benefited from this psychological intervention. More recently, attempts have been made to put fear reduction strategies on videotape for patients to view either prior to or during dental procedures. Videotaped relaxation techniques were found to benefit patients who were mildly to moderately avoidant of dental procedures, but did not benefit severely avoidant patients (Gatchel, 1986). Severely avoidant patients are likely to require more intensive contact with the health psychologist for therapeutic strategies more specific to the treatment of anxiety disorders.

The Need for Brief Nonpharmacological Methods of Managing Acute Pain

Roger might be surprised to find that dentists are using more than needles and Novocain for pain relief these days. Many dentists are utilizing brief hypnotic procedures, distraction techniques such as providing patients with small headphones playing music or soothing sounds, or using humor to distract their patients from pain. Here, I describe several nonpharmacological methods of pain management that can be used to assist patients through painful medical and dental procedures. The strategies (though in part overlapping) are grouped into the following categories: information-based strategies, relaxation and distraction strategies, and more intensive therapeutic techniques.

Information-Based Strategies. Sometimes simply educating patients about the sights and sounds they are going to experience helps to relieve the anxiety associated with a particular procedure and helps to decrease reported pain. An example of this comes from a sample of adult dental patients who were given a running commentary of the procedures they were undergoing, as well as descriptions of the sensations they were likely to experience. Compared to control subjects who were not given any commentary or description of sensations, the informed patients reported significantly decreased anxiety and pain levels associated with their dental procedures (Wardle, 1983).

Childbirth is another acutely painful experience in which the dissemination of preparatory information can help to reduce pain. Empirical studies have found that women in early labor experience less pain when maintaining a vertical rather than a horizontal position, as long as such a position does not compromise a mother or child in any way (Melzack, 1993). Early labor constitutes a considerable portion of the entire labor experience, and therefore this simple bit of information can help to reduce the overall pain experienced during the early stages of a potentially lengthy ordeal.

Information-based strategies may be limited in their incremental utility as pain reducers, though they are easy to teach and decidedly useful as adjuncts to pharmacological methods of acute pain management. Prepared childbirth training is a common, time-intensive, nonpharmacological information-based strategy that, when critically evaluated, was shown to result in a significant but minimal 10% reduction in sensory and affective pain scores (Melzack, Taenzer, Feldman, & Kinch, 1981).

Relaxation and Distraction Strategies. The following are three brief relaxation/distraction strategies that can be used to assist patients undergoing acutely painful medical and dental procedures. The first of these is a technique developed by McCaffery and Beebe (1989); it relies upon jaw relaxation, deep breathing, and clearing of the mind. The patient is asked to do the following:

> "Let your lower jaw drop slightly, as though you were starting a small yawn." Keep your tongue quiet and resting on the bottom of your mouth. Breathe slowly, evenly, and rhythmically: Inhale, exhale, and rest. Now allow yourself to stop forming words with your lips and stop thinking in words."

This technique is easy for the hospital staff to teach, and patients can readily understand the instructions. The technique is very brief and can be applied in almost any clinic where acute pain is associated with medical procedures.

The second technique to be discussed here is a brief relaxation strategy developed and used in the Behavioral Medicine Pain Program at Georgetown University Medical Center. It is called the "mini-TRIP" (TRIP stands for "tension-reducing imagery practice"; it incorporates deep breathing, jaw and body relaxation, and brief imagery. "Trip" is an appropriate label for this technique, since many patients describe feeling as if they took a brief vacation from their pain while using this technique. The instructions given to patients are as follows.

> "The mini-TRIP is a brief self-management strategy for pain control. You should practice this technique 5–10 times before your planned medical [dental] procedure.
>   The mini-TRIP consists of seven steps:
>
>   1. Decide to take a mini-TRIP by stopping all other activities and thoughts. Decide where your trip will take you (e.g., the beach, the mountains, your backyard, an abstract location or experience).
>   2. Take a deep breath.
>   3. Purse your lips and slowly exhale your first deep breath through the small opening created by your lips. As you slowly exhale, say the word "Relax" to yourself.
>   4. After this first deep breath, let your jaw relax and go slack. Future deep breaths will be taken normally.
>   5. Relax your jaw and then allow the feeling of relaxation to travel downward from your jaw to the rest of your body. Allow the feeling of relaxation to wash like a wave over your entire body. As the wave travels down your body, make each breath you take a deep one. [Steps 1–5 can be accomplished in the first 15 seconds of the mini-TRIP.]
>   6. Begin your imagery. Make the image as rich as possible by using all of your senses. For example, if you are imagining a beach, allow yourself to *see* the clouds, the water, the sand, and the sky. *Hear* the waves, the sea gulls, and the wind. *Feel* the sand on your feet, the sea breeze on your face, and the waves wetting your ankles. *Smell* the ocean mist and the sweet coconut smell of suntan oil, and *taste* the salt on

your lips. Bring this image into your mind quickly and intensely, so that your mind is highly distracted for a brief period of time.

7. Time to come home. After about 30–60 seconds, return your attention to your surroundings. Try to maintain the relaxed feelings you achieved on the trip, now that you are conscious of your previous surroundings. Even though this moment's trip is over, you are never far away from your next one."

The mini-TRIP can be a helpful nonpharmacological adjunct for getting patients through venipunctures, dental procedures, injections, and spinal taps, among other procedures. The imagery portion of the mini-TRIP can be extended for use with longer medical procedures, such as burn debridement and brief surgeries.

A third brief intervention for acute pain is known as "positive emotion induction" (PEI; Bruehl, Carlson, & McCubbin, 1993). Unlike the two techniques just presented, this technique does not use deep breathing or body relaxation. It is similar to the mini-TRIP in that it uses multiple senses to distract the mind; however, it emphasizes emotional induction based on memories rather than fantasy.

The patient is told that feelings of discomfort are influenced by the thoughts and emotions experienced during the painful event. Catastrophic thoughts such as "I can't stand this" should be avoided, as these thoughts may increase discomfort. Focusing the mind on pleasant ideas should help reduce discomfort. Prior to a painful procedure, the patient can be asked to practice PEI by thinking of a pleasant memory of an event in the patient's own life. The psychologist should help the patient to recall the memory as vividly as possible by incorporating all five senses into the memory. For example, the patient can reconstruct a memory of eating a good meal. Once the patient is comfortable with the memory, the patient should recall it just prior to the start of the painful procedure. The patient can be encouraged to increase his or her focus on the memory throughout the duration of the brief painful procedure.

The pain-reducing effects of PEI have been compared to those of simple deep breathing strategies. Bruehl et al. (1993) found that subjects randomly assigned to PEI or deep breathing reported lower pain ratings, fear, and anxiety with PEI. The deep breathing group demonstrated greater blood pressure recovery following the painful event, but did not report decreased pain ratings.

The clinician will want to evaluate the merits of each of these three relaxation/distraction strategies. The jaw relaxation technique is by far the quickest and easiest to teach; its focus is on deep breathing and body relaxation. Given the findings of Bruehl et al. (1993), this technique would be expected to reduce the psychophysiological response to pain, but may not alter overall perception of pain. This conclusion is supported by another study with cardiac surgery patients, who demonstrated reductions in psychophysiological responding with the use of deep breathing relaxation techniques, but reported no decrease in pain sensation (Miller & Perry, 1990). Conversely, PEI, with its focus on emotions and distraction, was associated with reduced pain report but did not alter psychophysiological arousal. The inability of this technique to reduce psychophysiological arousal can probably be attributed to the absence of deep breathing and relaxation components. The mini-TRIP combines the deep breathing, bodily relaxation, imagery, and distraction components of the other two strategies, in an attempt to reduce both the psychophysiological arousal and the pain, fear, and anxiety associated with acute pain. The disadvantages of the mini-TRIP are that it is a bit more complicated to teach and has a few more instructions for the patient to follow than the other two methods.

More Intensive Therapeutic Techniques. Some pain conditions, procedures, and/or patients will require more extensive training in relaxation or anxiety reduction strategies prior to undergoing a painful medical procedure. This training can be costly and therefore is typically not used for routine medical procedures. When the management of a nonroutine case presents itself, or a patient specifically requests a nonpharmacological pain management strategy, these more extensive training sessions tend to pay off. As discussed more fully in Chapters 8 and 9 of this book, EMG-assisted relaxation (biofeedback) and hypnotherapy-assisted relaxation and imagery can prepare the exceptional acute pain patient more fully than the brief strategies just discussed.

One procedure for which more intensive therapeutic techniques are appropriate is the removal of dead or damaged tissue from severe burns (debridement). Removing the tissue is an acutely painful procedure that can last up to several hours each day. The procedure involves immersing the burned body area (in cases of extensive burns, most of the body) in a tank of water. The immersion itself can be painful, since new skin growth may be hyperesthesic to tactile stimulation. The burn victim then soaks for a time, allowing the skin to become moist and loose. The patient is then removed from the water, and a nurse specialist peels off the dead and damaged tissue and other foreign material. The peeling of the tissue is the part of debridement that is especially painful for most patients. Given the length of the debridement procedure, brief relaxation techniques are not likely to be sufficient. A health psychologist can assist a burn patient during this procedure by teaching the patient hypnotic strategies to enhance distraction and relaxation. Unlike a patient facing an elective medical procedure, who can learn pain control techniques prior to the medical procedure, the burn victim will need to learn the relaxation techniques as treatment progresses. For this reason, there is a clear need for the health psychologist to be an active member of the acute pain service and participate as a team member on the inpatient burn unit.

Tips for using hypnosis during burn debridement include the following:

1. The therapist should use the hypnotic induction technique with which he or she is most comfortable. It should be kept in mind, however, that the subject will be either sitting in a tub of water, or lying on a table while a nurse specialist weilds a knife under bright lights. The patient should generally close his or her eyes, and the therapist speaking in a readily audible voice helps initiate the procedure in this less-than-ideal setting for relaxation. It should be noted that eye-rolling techniques may not be possible for some patients with facial burns, and active Ericksonian techniques may not work as well in this environment filled with distractions. The therapist should allow his or her voice to serve as a focus for the patient, to help initiate reductions in psychophysiological arousal, anxiety, and fear as the debridement procedure begins.

2. Following a deepening strategy, the therapist can take the patient on a 20-minute progressive muscle relaxation exercise, beginning with the feet and working up to the head. However, the patient's preference for this strategy should always be determined. Some patients find this very relaxing, but others find the body focus to be pain-enhancing, and therefore it should be avoided with them.

3. Most patients will tolerate and enjoy a lengthy guided imagery experience. Focusing on the therapist's voice helps to keep them distracted and calm during the ongoing procedure. Some special considerations will need to be taken into account for burn victims. One of the most common images nonburn patients use for relaxation is the warm, sunny beach. Many burn patients dislike this image, as imagery involving heating or chilling is not relaxing to them. Instead, images that involve neutral temperatures; soothing, silky textures; and pleasant memories, tastes, and smells can be emphasized. The thera-

pist will probably need to have many different images in mind, since the ability of a burn patient to focus on any one image for a prolonged period of time may be limited. Some patients like to hear the same sequence of images each day, so that they can learn to anticipate the conclusion of that day's debridement when they hear the "final" image.

4. With chronic pain conditions, there is an emphasis on teaching patients self-management skills so that they can soon become their own therapists. With severe burns, however, patients may need the added distraction of the therapist to focus their thoughts adequately for the duration of the debridement procedure. Self-hypnosis and self-management may take longer to work effectively when painful procedures are both daily and lengthy.

General Comments. There is general agreement that preparing a patient with coping skills such as brief relaxation, distraction, and imagery; information; and/or more extensive hypnotic and anxiety-reducing skills (e.g., systematic desensitization) helps to reduce the discomfort of painful medical and dental procedures. In comparison to patients receiving routine medical management, patients who are psychologically prepared have been found to have less anxiety, report lower pain, require less opioid medication and sedatives, experience fewer complications, and have shorter recovery periods (Gil, 1984; Schultheis, Peterson, & Selby, 1987; Suls & Wan, 1989). These nonpharmacological strategies facilitate acute pain management and should be standard components of comprehensive pain treatment. The health psychologist plays an invaluable role by providing direct services or by serving as a consultant who can coordinate training and integration of these services for the medical community.

Cognitive Factors That Can Impede Adequate Pain Control

It has long been appreciated that beliefs can augment or degrade health and the healing process (D. P. Phillips, Ruth, & Wagner, 1993; S. E. Taylor, 1989; Lipowski, 1970; Mechanic, 1977; Anderson, 1993; Felten, 1993; Ornish, 1993). D. P. Phillips et al. (1993) compared the death rates of 28,169 adult Chinese-Americans with 412,632 matched white controls. The more strongly individuals were attached to Chinese beliefs about death, the more years of life were lost. Commenting on this report, a reviewer stated, "The belief systems people hold and the manner in which individuals interpret the world and their place in it can have profound consequences for their health" (O'Boyle, 1993, p. 1127). Beliefs about pain similarly appear to be associated with increases in pain intensity and functioning. In a sample of 49 patients hospitalized for acute burn injuries, patients' beliefs that they were to blame for the injuries were found to be significantly associated with increased pain behavior, poorer adherence to treatment essential for healing, and greater depression (Kiecolt-Glaser & Williams, 1987). These analyses were controlled for both the severity of the burns and the time since admission. This study supports the need to address not only the emotional factors affecting pain, but also beliefs and other cognitive factors that appear to influence pain and suffering.

Case Example

Sheryl was a 30-year-old female who experienced tension headaches once or twice per month. Each headache tended to last 3–4 hours and to remit with the use of over-the-counter medication. Sheryl reported excruciating pain, as well as intense emotional suffering, while the headaches were present. Despite her knowledge that her previous headaches had been caused by tension, she interpreted each new head-ache as proof that she had a life-threatening brain tumor. With each new headache, she feared that this time the headache would never go away.

Patients may develop numerous pain-specific beliefs. Just a few of many possible examples are these: "My pain will be with me for the rest of my life," "My pain will be enduring but intermittent in nature," and "I am responsible for the pain I'm experiencing." Recent explorations into the impact of pain-specific beliefs have found that beliefs can mediate pain perception, use of coping strategies, and adjustment to life events associated with pain and discomfort (Williams & Thorn, 1989; Williams & Keefe, 1991; Jensen, Turner, Romano, & Lawler, 1994; Williams, Robinson, & Geisser, 1994).

Beliefs about the Duration of Pain

One specific belief that might have increased Sheryl's pain and discomfort was the belief that her pain would be enduring for the rest of her life. Beliefs about the duration of pain have been found to be associated with pain reports even when the actual pain stimulus and duration of pain have been held constant. In a normal, healthy sample exposed to experimental cold-pressor pain, the belief in greater pain duration was associated with increased reported pain intensity. In this study, the pain stimulus and the actual duration of pain were identical for all subjects at the point of comparison (i.e., 2 minutes), but the subjects believing that the pain trial would last a fixed 3 minutes reported significantly lower pain ratings than the subjects believing that the pain trial was open-ended (Williams & Thorn, 1986). Similar results were obtained in a replication of this pain study, using an ischemic pain stimulus (Thorn & Williams, 1989).

These findings highlight the potential importance of viewing pain as a fixed-duration rather than an open-ended experience. This finding is particularly helpful in assisting patients through painful medical and dental procedures where they can be told the likely duration of the pain ahead of time. The belief that pain will be of a finite duration helps patients to develop concrete goals for coping with the pain. Patients believing the pain to be open-ended may be expected to have more difficulty using goal-directed coping strategies, since the time frame for the pain is ambiguous. Being able to cope with pain in a time-limited fashion versus an open-ended fashion was found to significantly improve the use of pain coping skills, reduce headache activity, and decrease medication use in a randomly assigned sample of headache sufferers (James, Thorn, & Williams, 1993). Thus, if patients can be helped to view pain (even continuous pain) in terms of discrete time durations, coping may be more effective and pain reduction more likely. The following, derived from the James et al. (1993) study, is an example of how patients can be trained to use cognitive coping for acute pain in a discrete, time-limited fashion.

Setting Time Goals for Coping Strategies

Prior to a painful procedure, the health psychologist may want to assess the repertoire of skills for coping with acute pain that a given patient brings to the medical setting. A coping assessment tool developed and designed for use with acute pain populations is the Cognitive Coping Strategies Inventory (CCSI; Butler, Damarin, Beaulieu, Schwebel, & Thorn, 1989). This assessment tool has clinically validated scales corresponding to the categories of coping strategies described by Turk, Meichenbaum, and Genest (1983).

Feedback from the CCSI can be shared with the patient in a presurgical training session. The focus of this discussion should be on identifying favored coping strategies for the patient and assessing how each strategy works for the patient. For a patient who lacks coping strategies, time can be taken to expose the patient to several potential strategies, such as distraction, the mini-TRIP, or PEI.

The patient should then be given time-limited goals for practicing the coping strategies. For example, the patient may be told to practice relaxation strategies twice a day for 10 minutes each. This is an improvement over instructing the patient to practice for as long as possible or giving no instructions for the duration of practice at all. The health psychologist may want to tailor the time goal for coping strategy use around the duration of the upcoming painful procedure. The goal for using the coping strategy should be slightly longer than the anticipated duration of the procedure. If the procedure is lengthy, several strategies should be taught, each with its own time goal for being practiced and used.

Who Controls Acute Pain?

"To control" means "to regulate, influence, or direct." In the past, medical professionals assumed control over patients' pain. Today, however, with hospital stays becoming shorter, the patient and the patient's family are being asked to play an emerging role in acute pain management. It is reassuring that at a time when cost containment is forcing more responsibility onto the patient, there is theoretical support for such practice. For example, numerous studies have documented that possessing an internal locus of control over health events is associated with decreased pain, less distress, and better use of coping strategies in chronic pain populations (see Jensen, Turner, Romano, & Karoly, 1991, for a review). On the surface, the concept of giving control to the patient sounds good and makes for good marketing of self-control technology. Policy, however, should be driven by empirical support, and currently the clinical data are equivocal (see below). It appears that simply giving control to the patient is not enough to ensure good pain management. Clearly, more empirical research is needed in this area of acute pain management.

Case Example

Bob underwent surgery and was given a PCA pump to manage his pain. PCA is best used with cognitively intact patients who can administer their own analgesics via a button on the PCA pump. PCA provides patients with control over their medication, and supposedly relieves the anxiety of having to wait for a nurse to administer intramuscular analgesics. Through frequent self-administration of small amounts of analgesics, patients theoretically avoid the need for less frequent but much larger doses of narcotics, thus reducing the overall need for narcotics (Carron, 1989). Prior to surgery, Bob was cognitively intact and enjoyed learning how to use the PCA device. He also scored a perfect 100% on the brief PCA exam the nurse gave him following her instructions. Thus, one would assume that Bob, trained and armed with his PCA button, was technologically and intellectually poised for good pain management following his surgery. However, despite his initial enthusiasm for controlling his own pain and despite his knowledge of PCA operation, Bob undermedicated himself and experienced inadequate postsurgical pain control. Upon questioning, it was learned that Bob felt abandoned by the nursing staff once he demonstrated competence with his PCA device. The added responsibility of controlling his own pain at a time when he was weak, afraid, and vulnerable acted to increase his anxiety and pain perception rather than to decrease it.

Two questions emerge from the case of Bob. First, if patients are adequately trained on PCA, why do some patients still undermedicate themselves? Second, what role does social support play in anxiety reduction and acute pain management?

Patient Undermedication on PCA

Does giving control to the patient really reduce anxiety, thereby reducing pain and the need for narcotic analgesics? Common sense and theory suggest that it should; however, empirical studies suggest that the relationship among control, anxiety, pain, and narcotic use is more complex than originally suspected. One fascinating finding is that despite patients' having more control with PCA, they frequently fail to titrate their analgesia to adequate blood concentrations, resulting in pain relief that is inadequate and not significantly different from the relief provided by intramuscular injections (Welchew, 1983). Thus, simply giving patients control over their analgesics does not ensure adequate pain relief. In fact, up to a fourfold variation in analgesic requirements has been observed in postoperative patients using PCA (Tamsen, Hartvig, Fagerlund, & Dalstrom, 1982). This finding suggests that the control offered by PCA may not adequately neutralize the effect of anxiety on pain and analgesic usage. Indeed, in a study of 99 females undergoing hysterectomy, patients' need for control was positively associated with increased pain ratings, morphine use, and PCA demands (F. Perry, Parker, White, & Clifford, 1994).

In a sample of 80 adult patients using PCA after orthopedic surgery, anxiety was still found to be a primary predictor of postoperative pain level (Gil, Ginsberg, Muir, Sykes, & Williams, 1990). The anxious patients in this study also tended to make more PCA demands. Since this study was associational, it is difficult to determine whether patients with greater pain made more demands and were more anxious or whether being more anxious lead to greater PCA demands and greater pain. Either way, however, the control associated with the PCA did not seem to influence the association between anxiety and pain. Similar findings were obtained in a postsurgical adolescent population (Gil, Ginsberg, Muir, Sullivan, & Williams, 1992).

In Bob's case, something other than his need for control was blocking his motivation to utilize the technology available to him for adequate pain control. For the sake of comparison, Bob might be likened to the laboratory animal that has learned to perform a task and has operational equipment, but still emits no response. How do we explain this state of affairs? Thorndike (discussed in Bolles, 1975) introduced the law of "readiness," which suggests that simply having circumstances that are satisfactory for a response is insufficient unless the subject is ready to emit the response. For example, an animal may know how to eat and food may be present, but no eating response will occur until the animal is hungry. It is quite possible that for some postsurgical patients, the desire for personal control over pain is not present following surgery. The postsurgical state of weakness and vulnerability produces dependency and a need for nurturance in some patients, rather than self-sufficiency. Thus, these patients are not in a state of "readiness" to take control for their own pain management. Being forced to take control at a time when they desire the support of others may introduce more anxiety and pain, rather than providing relief.

For Bob, taking personal control over pain and receiving desired attention from the nursing staff seemed incompatible. It is important, however, that in actual practice these two pain management issues work in tandem to reduce patient anxiety and pain. The efficiency and freedom PCA offers clinicians should not be used to reduce staff or reassign personnel. When it comes to anxiety reduction, it is doubtful that a computer chip and a hand-held button will ever adequately substitute for the calming rapport of a well-trained nursing staff. As described earlier, the use of scheduled nurse visits to monitor postsurgical pain, as well as general conversation during those visits, can assist in anxiety reduction via human contact for the patient.

Social Support: The Emerging Role of the Family in Acute Pain

Not too many years ago, an individual undergoing surgery would be in the hospital for several days or weeks. This protracted stay in the hospital allowed the patient to recover under observation, to undergo psychological adjustment to the trauma just experienced by the body, and to reunite with family members and friends who could come and show support during the recovery and healing process. Today, hospital stays are briefer than ever before. Same-day surgical units are common in hospitals, and patients do most of their recovery at home, unattended by professionals. If patients undergoing procedures are sent home with training in self-management techniques, they may be able to reduce their anxiety and pain further through the social support offered by family members. This prospect, of course, depends upon the pre-existing relationships in the family. In a study with postsurgical adolescents, the patients who reported having good, supportive family relationships reported lower procedural pain (Gil et al., 1992).

Postsurgical care is a new responsibility for many family members. Often little direction is given to a family caregiver, and concerns abound in the minds of both the patient and the caregiver as to what needs to be done and how pain should be managed. Gedaly-Duff and Ziebarth (1994) identified several concerns of mothers who were placed in the role of caring for their children soon after surgery for removal of adenoids and tonsils. Prior to surgery, mothers tended to underestimate the amount of pain their children would experience. This initial underestimation later resulted in the mothers' assuming that their children were exaggerating pain when they rated it at higher levels. Mothers also tended to fear drug addiction in their children and would purposely fail to administer analgesics at recommended dosages and frequencies. Instead, they would tend to stretch the time interval between dosages or switch to non-narcotic medications until the children's verbal or behavioral pain cues increased. Requests by the children for the narcotic analgesic were interpreted as addiction rather than as inadequate dosing on the part of the parents. This trial-and-error approach to pain management is another example of needless pain that could have been avoided if the mothers' anxiety and concerns had been appropriately addressed.

In a fascinating and methodologically sophisticated study, the impact of children's social environment on pain was analyzed during painful medical procedures (Blount et al., 1989). In this study, audiotapes were made of the verbal interactions of hospital staff members, and parents, with children undergoing bone marrow aspirations and lumbar punctures. The patterns of adult–child verbal interaction revealed that adult reassurances, apologies to the child for the pain, and giving control over the pain to the child typically preceded greater distress. Improved pain coping was typically preceded by adult commands to utilize prepared coping strategies, by non-procedure-related talk, and by humor directed to the child.

Studies like the one by Blount et al. challenge traditional views that presuppose the giving of control and stating of reassurances to be helpful in pain and anxiety reduction. The health psychologist may play an active role not only in teaching coping strategies to children, but also in educating parents about the types of verbal support that can be most helpful to children during painful procedures.

Clinical Summary of the Issues

There is an emerging understanding that simple education is important but not sufficient in order to ensure that acute pain technology is properly used. Anxiety and fear in both the patients and caregivers must be addressed in order for the technology to be used properly. The health psychologist plays an invaluable role both in developing anxiety reduction techniques and in delivering these services to patients with pain and to the caregivers who must help manage the patient. Frequently the fears associated with pain and narcotic use will not respond to a simple, rational explanation of the facts. Rather, a clinician trained in addressing the multidimensional aspects of pain (i.e., sensory, affective, cognitive, social, and behavioral; Melzack & Katz, 1994) must address these issues with the patient and patient's family.

THE HEALTH PSYCHOLOGIST AS A MEMBER OF AN ACUTE PAIN SERVICE

The concept of the acute pain service has evolved through a recognition that the skills of pain control practiced by anesthesiologists in the operating room could benefit patients with acute pain outside of surgery (White, 1989). The typical acute pain service is composed of anesthesiologists and nurses who are specially trained in the techniques of pharmacological remediation of acute pain (Ready, 1989; Petrakis, 1989). Recently, health psychologists have begun to be employed by these services, usually on a consultative basis. As this chapter has outlined, pain control is a two-way street, with the acute pain service and technology on one side and the patient on the other. The patient brings into the pain clinic not only a pain complaint, but also the possibility of misinformation, anxiety, and beliefs that can render the service's pain control technology useless. The health psychologist acts as a bridge between these two parties when a patient-based factor interferes or threatens to interfere with adequate pain management.

Although the role of the health psychologist is well recognized in chronic pain management (e.g., Fields, 1991), it is less well recognized in acute pain problems. Because acute pain management is more procedure-based than chronic pain management, there are some barriers for psychologists to overcome if they want to play a more prominent role. These barriers consist largely of concerns that the involvement of psychologists will slow down patient flow and add cost to the procedures, making acute pain services less attractive to third parties interested in cost reduction. For this reason, psychologists are now typically employed as consultants and utilized only for the truly exceptional cases. This is unfortunate, since less exceptional cases can also benefit from the care and skills of the health psychologist. The burden is once again on psychologists to demonstrate the value of their services. Psychologists must continue to demonstrate large-scale empirical support for both the effectiveness of their work and the benefits of including their services in a patient's overall medical care.

REFERENCES

Agency for Health Care Policy and Research (AHCPR). (1992). *Acute pain management: Operative or medical procedures and trauma* (Clinical Practice Guideline No. 1, AHCPR Publication No. 92-0032). Rockville, MD: U.S. Department of Health and Human Services.

American Nurses Association. (1991). *Position statement on the registered nurse's (RN) role in the management of patients receiving I.V. conscious sedation for short-term therapeutic, diagnostic, or surgical procedures*. Kansas City, MO: Author.

American Pain Society. (1992). *Principles of analgesic use in the treatment of acute pain and chronic cancer pain: A concise guide to medical practice* (3rd ed.). Skokie, IL: Author.

Anderson, R. (1993). The healing environment. In B. Moyers (Ed.), *Healing and the mind* (pp. 25–45). New York: Basic Books.

Blount, R. L., Corbin, S. M., Sturges, J. W., Wolfe, V. V., Prater, J. M., & James, L. D. (1989). The relationship between adults' behavior and child coping and distress during BMA/LP procedures: A sequential analysis. *Behavior Therapy, 20*, 585–601.

Bolles, R. C. (1975). *Learning theory*. New York: Holt, Rinehart & Winston.

Bonica, J. J. (1990). General considerations of acute pain. In J. J. Bonica (Ed.), *The management of pain* (2nd ed., pp. 159–179). Philadelphia: Lea & Febiger.

Brody, J. (1994, July 13). A new type of over-the-counter pain reliever. *The New York Times*, p. C12.

Bruehl, S., Carlson, C. R., & McCubbin, J. A. (1993). Two brief interventions for acute pain. *Pain, 54*, 29–36.

Butler, R. W., Damarin, C. B., Beaulieu, C. L., Schwebel, A. I., & Thorn, B. E. (1989). Assessing cognitive coping strategies for acute post-surgical pain. *Psychological Assessment: A Journal of Consulting and Clinical Psychology, 1*, 41–45.

Carron, H. (1989). Extension of pain relief beyond the operating room. *Clinical Journal of Pain, 5*, S1–S4).

Chapman, C. R., & Turner, J. A. (1990). Psychologic and psychosocial aspects of acute pain. In J. J. Bonica (Ed.), *The management of pain* (2nd ed., pp. 122–132). Philadelphia: Lea & Febiger.

Dionne, R. A. (1992). New approaches to preventing and treating postoperative pain. *Journal of the American Dental Association, 123*(6), 27–34.

Dworkin, S. F. (1967). Anxiety and performance in the dental environment: An experimental investigation. *Journal of the American Society of Psychosomatic Dentistry and Medicine, 14*, 88–102.

Felten, D. (1993). The brain and the immune system. In B. Moyers (Ed.), *Healing and the mind* (pp. 213–237). New York: Basic Books.

Fields, H. L. (1991). *Core curriculum for professional education in pain*. Seattle, WA: International Association for the Study of Pain Publications.

Gatchel, R. J. (1980). Effectiveness of procedures for reducing dental fear: Group-adminstered desensitization and group education and discussion. *Journal of the American Dental Association, 101*, 634–637.

Gatchel, R. J. (1986). Impact of a video taped fear reduction program on people who avoid dental treatment. *Journal of the American Dental Association, 112*, 218–221.

Gatchel, R. J. (1992). Managing anxiety and pain during dental treatment. *Journal of the American Dental Association, 123*, 37–41.

Gatchel, R. J., & Others. (1983). The prevalence of dental fear and avoidance: A recent survey study. *Journal of the American Dental Association, 107*, 609–610.

Gedaly-Duff, V., & Ziebarth, D. (1994). Mothers' management of adenoid–tonsillectomy pain in 4- to 8-year-olds: A preliminary study. *Pain, 57*, 293–299.

Gil, K. M. (1984). Coping with invasive medical procedures: A descriptive model. *Clinical Psychology Review, 4*, 339–362.

Gil, K. M. (1992). Psychological aspects of acute pain. In R. S. Sinatra, A. H. Hord, B. Ginsberg, & L. M. Preble (Eds.), *Acute pain: Mechanisms and management*. St. Louis, MO: Mosby–Year Book.

Gil, K. M., Ginsberg, B., Muir, M., Sullivan, F., & Williams, D. A. (1992). Patient controlled analgesia: The relationship of psychological factors to pain and analgesic use in adolescents with postoperative pain. *Clinical Journal of Pain, 8,* 215–221.

Gil, K. M., Ginsberg, B., Muir, M., Sykes, D., & Williams, D. A. (1990). Patient controlled analgesia in postoperative pain: The relation of psychological factors to pain and narcotic use. *Clinical Journal of Pain, 6,* 137–142.

Glaros, A. G., & Gadbury-Amyot, C. C. (1993). How personal protective equipment affects perceptions of dentists. *Journal of the American Dental Association, 124,* 82–88.

Jackson, V. P., Lex, A. M., & Smith, D. J. (1988). Patient discomfort during screen-film mammography. *Radiology, 168,* 421–423.

James, L. D., Thorn, B. E., & Williams, D. A. (1993). Goal specification in cognitive-behavioral therapy for chronic headache pain. *Behavior Therapy, 24,* 305–320.

Jensen, M. P., Karoly, P., & Braver, S. (1986). The measurement of clinical pain intensity: A comparison of six methods. *Pain, 27,* 117–126.

Jensen, M. P., Turner, J. A., Romano, J. M., & Karoly, P. (1991). Coping with chronic pain: A critical review of the literature. *Pain, 47,* 249–283.

Jensen, M. P., Turner, J. A., Romano, J. M., & Lawler, B. K. (1994). Relationship of pain-specific beliefs to chronic pain adjustment. *Pain, 57,* 301–309.

Karoly, P., & Jensen, M. P. (1987). *Multimethod assessment of chronic pain*. Elmsford, NY: Pergamon Press.

Keefe, F. J., Hauck, E. R., Egert, J., Rimer, B., & Kornguth, P. (1994). Mammography pain and discomfort: A cognitive-behavioral perspective. *Pain, 56,* 247–260.

Kiecolt-Glaser, J., & Williams, D. A. (1987). *Self-blame, compliance, and distress among burn patients. Journal of Personality and Social Psychology, 53,* 187–193.

Krames, E. (1993, Spring). Implantable pain management: An overview. *Lifeline* (The Newsletter of the National Chronic Pain Outreach Association, Inc.).

Lipowski, Z. J. (1970). Physical illness, the individual and the coping process. *Psychiatry and Medicine, 1,* 91–102.

McCaffery, M., & Beebe, A. (1989). *Pain: Clinical manual for nursing practice*. St. Louis, MO: C.V. Mosby.

Mechanic, D. (1977). Illness behavior, social adaptation, and the management of illness. *Journal of Nervous and Mental Disease, 165*(2), 79–87.

Melzack, R. (1993). Labour pain as a model of acute pain. *Pain, 53,* 117–120.

Melzack, R., & Katz, J. (1994). Pain measurement in persons in pain. In P. Wall & R. Melzack (Eds.), *Textbook of pain* (3rd ed., pp. 337–351). Edinburgh: Churchill Livingstone.

Melzack, R., Taenzer, P., Feldman, P., & Kinch, R. A. (1981). Labour is still painful after prepared childbirth training. *Canadian Medical Association Journal, 125,* 357–363.

Miller, K. M., & Perry, P. A. (1990). Relaxation technique and postoperative pain in patients undergoing cardiac surgery. *Heart and Lung, 19,* 136–146.

O'Boyle, C. A. (1993). Diseases with passion. *Lancet, 342,* 1126–1127.

Ornish, D. (1993). Changing life habits. In B. Moyers (Ed.), *Healing and the mind* (pp. 87–113). New York: Doubleday.

Peebles, R. J., & Schneiderman, D. S. (1991). *Socio-economic factbook for surgery, 1991–92*. Chicago: American College of Surgeons.

Petrakis, J. K. (1989). Acute pain services in a community hospital. *Clinical Journal of Pain, 5,* S34–S41.

Perry, F., Parker, R. K., White, P. F., & Clifford, A. (1994). Role of psychological factors in postoperative pain control and recovery with patient-controlled analgesia. *Clinical Journal of Pain, 10,* 57–63.

Perry, S., & Heidrich, G. (1982). Management of pain during debridement: A survey of U.S. burn units. *Pain, 13,* 267–280.

Phillips, D. P., Ruth, T. E., & Wagner, L. M. (1993). Psychology and survival. *Lancet, 342*, 1142–1143.

Phillips, G. D., & Cousins, M. J. (1986). Practical decision making. In J. M. Cousins & G. D. Phillips (Eds.), *Acute pain management* (pp. 275–290). New York: Churchill Livingstone.

Porter, J., & Jick, H. (1980). Addiction rare in patients treated with narcotics. *New England Journal of Medicine, 302*, 123.

Portnoy, R. K. (1990). Chronic opioid therapy in non-malignant pain. *Journal of Pain Symptom Management, 5*, S46–S62.

Price, D. D., Bush, F. M., Long, S., & Harkins, S. W. (1994). A comparision of pain measurement characteristics of mechanical visual analogue and simple numerical rating scales. *Pain, 56*, 217–226.

Ready, L. B. (1989). Acute pain services: An academic asset. *Clinical Journal of Pain, 5*, S28–S33.

Ready, L. B., & Edwards, W. T. (1992). *Management of acute pain: A practical guide*. Seattle, WA: International Association for the Study of Pain Press.

Rey, R. (1993). *History of pain*. Paris: Editions La Decouverte.

Royal College of Surgeons of England, the College of Anesthetists. (1990). *Report of the Working Party on Pain after Surgery*. London: Royal College of Surgeons.

Schultheis, K., Peterson, L., & Selby, V. (1987). Preparation for stressful medical procedures and person × treatment interactions. *Clinical Psychology Review, 7*, 329–352.

Siegel, L .J., Smith, K. E., Cantu, G. E., & Posnick, W. R. (1992). The effects of using infection-control barrier techniques on young children's behavior during dental treatment. *Journal of Dentistry for Children, 59*, 17–22.

Sokol, D., Sokol, J., & Sokol, C. (1985). A review of nonintrusive therapies used to deal with anxiety and pain in the dental office. *Journal of the American Dental Association, 110*, 217–222.

Suls, J., & Wan, C. K. (1989). Effects of sensory and procedural information on coping with stressful medical procedures and pain: A meta-analysis. *Journal of Consulting and Clinical Psychology, 57*, 372–379.

Tamsen, A., Hartvig, P., Fagerlund, C., & Dahlstrom, B. (1982). Patient controlled analgesic therapy: Part II. Individual analgesic demand and analgesic plasma concentrations of pethidine in postoperative pain. *Clinical Pharmacokinetics, 7*, 164–175.

Taub, A. (1982). Opioid analgesics in the treatment of chronic intractable pain of non-neoplastic origin. In L. M. Kitihata & D. Collins (Eds.), *Narcotic analgesics in anesthesiology* (pp. 199–208). Baltimore: Williams & Wilkins.

Taylor, H. (1985). *The Nuprin pain report*. New York: Louis Harris & Associates.

Taylor, S. E. (1989). *Positive illusions: Creative self-deception and the healthy mind*. New York: Basic Books.

Thorn, B. E., & Williams, G. A. (1989). Goal specification alters perceived pain intensity and tolerance latency. *Cognitive Therapy and Research, 13*, 171–183.

Turk, D. C., Meichenbaum, D., & Genest, M. (1983). *Pain and behavioral medicine: A cognitive-behavioral perspective*. New York: Guilford Press.

Tursky, B., Jamner, L. D., & Friedman, R. (1982). The pain perception profile: A psychophysical approach to the assessment of pain report. *Behavior Therapy, 13*, 376–394.

Varni, J. W., Jay, S. M., Masek, B. J., & Thompson, K. L. (1986). Cognitive-behavioral assessment and management of pediatric pain. In A. D. Holzman & D. C. Turk (Eds.), *Pain management: A handbook of psychological treatment approaches* (pp. 168–192). Elmsford, NY: Pergamon Press.

Wall, P. D. (1979). On the relation of injury to pain: The John J. Bonica Lecture. *Pain, 6*, 253–264.

Walton, R. E., & Torabinejad, M. (1992, May). Managing local anesthesia problems in the endodonic patient. *Journal of the American Dental Association, 123*, 97–102.

Wardle, J. (1983). Psychological management of anxiety and pain during dental treatment. *Journal of Psychosomatic Research, 27*, 399–402.

Welchew, E. A. (1983). On-demand analgesia: A double blind comparison of on-demand intravenous fentanyl with regular intramuscular morphine. *Anaesthesia, 38*, 19–25.

White, P. F. (1989). Current and future trends in acute pain management. *Clinical Journal of Pain, 5*, S51–S58.

Wilder-Smith, C. H., & Schuler, L. (1992). Postoperative analgesia: Pain by choice? The influence of patient attitudes and patient education. *Pain, 50,* 257–262.

Williams, D. A., & Keefe, F. J. (1991). Pain beliefs and the use of cognitive-behavioral coping strategies. *Pain, 46,* 185–190.

Williams, D. A., Robinson, M. E., & Geisser, M. E. (1994). Pain beliefs: Assessment and utility. *Pain, 59,* 71–78.

Williams, D. A., & Thorn, B. E. (1986). Can research methodology affect treatment outcome? A comparison of two cold pressor test paradigms. *Cognitive Therapy and Research, 10,* 539–546.

Williams, D. A., & Thorn, B. E. (1989). An empirical assessment of pain beliefs. *Pain, 36,* 351–358.

Zalon, M. L. (1993). Nurses' assessment of postoperative patients' pain. *Pain, 54,* 329–334.

CHAPTER 4

Enhancing Motivation to Change in Pain Treatment

Mark P. Jensen

Pain clinicians and researchers have many reasons to be proud. They have eased the pain and suffering of countless individuals through the development, refinement, and provision of a great variety of pain treatments. Most of these treatments, such as biofeedback, relaxation training, coping skills training, and multidisciplinary treatment, have all been shown to be effective in controlled studies (e.g., Flor, Haag, & Turk, 1986; Härkäpää, Mellin, Järvikoski, & Hurri, 1990; Keefe et al., 1990; Mellin, Härkäpää, Hurri, & Järvikoski, 1990; Philips, 1988; Sargent, Solbach, Coyne, Spohn, & Segerson, 1986). That is, *on average*, individuals who received these treatments have done significantly better than those who did not receive treatment.

Unfortunately, despite the growing research base that supports the effectiveness of current pain treatments on average, there remain many individuals who do not improve or who relapse (Turk, 1990; Turk & Rudy, 1991). There are numerous possible explanations for treatment failure, including the likelihood that some treatments are effective only for subgroups of pain sufferers (Turk, 1990). Another possible explanation concerns *motivation* for treatment (Karoly, 1980). To the extent that an intervention requires a patient to be an active participant, treatment should be effective only for those individuals who demonstrate a willingness (motivation) to participate. If this is true, then assessing and enhancing client motivation prior to treatment should help to reduce treatment failure.

On the assumption that client motivation is an important component of behavior change, William Miller and his colleagues (Miller, 1983a, 1983b; Miller & Rollnick, 1991; Miller, Zweben, DiClemente, & Rychtarik, 1992) have been developing an approach to clinician–client interactions that focuses on enhancing clients' motivation to change. This approach, called "motivational enhancement therapy" (MET) was initially developed to help problem drinkers cut down on or abstain from drinking alcohol (Bien, Miller, & Boroughs, 1993; Brown & Miller, 1993; Miller, 1983a; Miller & Baca, 1983; Miller, Benefield, & Tongigan, 1993; Miller, Sovereign, & Krege, 1988). Recently, however, MET has also been used to help individuals change a number of other problem behaviors (e.g., heroin dependency, HIV risk behaviors, child sexual abuse; see Miller & Rollnick, 1991).

The purpose of this chapter is to introduce pain clinicians to the principles and strategies of MET, and to explore how this approach may be used to facilitate changes in health behaviors thought to influence the long-term adaptation to pain conditions. Because MET focuses on client motivation, it may be used in a variety of settings and in conjunction with a variety of interventions. For the purposes of this chapter, *motivation* refers to "the probability that a person will enter into, continue, and adhere to a specific change strategy" (Miller & Rollnick, 1991, p. 19). Motivation is demonstrated by what a client *does*, not by what he or she *says*.

MET assumes that for the most part, people know how to engage in adaptive behaviors. Concerning adaptive responses to pain, for example, nearly everyone with a pain problem knows how to exercise (e.g., walk), to relax, or to "say no" to suggestions that they take pain-contingent medications. A lack of skill or knowledge, then, may not explain people's choice to display maladaptive responses to pain. Some of these individuals may lack motivation to engage in adaptive coping strategies. MET strategies, as applied to chronic pain problems, are designed primarily to address this motivational problem. In MET, the role of the clinician/therapist is to provide an environment that will lead to a greater probability that the client will respond in an adaptive way—that is, an environment that increases motivation.

My primary hope is that this chapter will interest pain clinicians in incorporating MET strategies into their practice, so as to increase the chances that their clients will follow through with recommendations for those changes deemed necessary for treatment success. In the long run, I hope that the ideas expressed here will encourage more systematic empirical investigations into the application of these strategies with chronic pain patients. The chapter begins with an outline of the stages-of-change model and a review of the assumptions upon which MET is based. The remainder (and bulk) of the chapter presents the principles and therapeutic strategies of MET. Throughout, the discussion focuses on how these strategies can be applied to the treatment of pain problems.

STAGES OF CHANGE

MET is based on the assumption that people vary in the degree to which they are ready to engage in new adaptive behaviors. This assumption has been supported in the research of DiClemente and Prochaska (1982), who have identified specific stages through which people move as they change from maladaptive to adaptive behaviors (graphically presented in Figure 4.1). According to this model, each stage poses different challenges for the

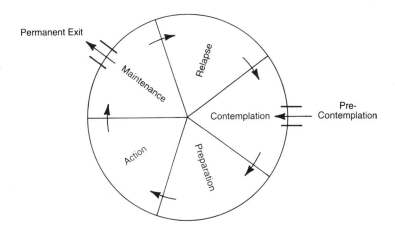

FIGURE 4.1. Prochaska and DiClemente's stage model of the process of change. Adapted from Miller and Rollnick (1991). Copyright 1991 by The Guilford Press. Adapted by permission.

individual, which need to be addressed before that person can move on to the next stage (Prochaska, DiClemente, & Norcross, 1992a). People who are not considering any changes in their behavior are in the *precontemplation* stage. Such individuals do not perceive a need for change. Precontemplators will show active resistance to change when and if they feel coerced into changing some behavior that other people, not they themselves, view as a problem. Although precontemplators may feel miserable, this is very different than serious contemplation of specific behavioral changes that may be necessary in order to feel better. *Contemplation* is a stage in which a person sees the need to change and is seriously considering making some change in the near future, but has yet to commit to that change. Contemplators are in a state of weighing the pros and cons of changing their behavior. *Preparation* (also known as the *decision-making* or *determination* stage) involves both an intention to make changes and initial behavioral steps in the direction of change. The fourth stage, *action*, is evidenced by concrete activities (modification of one's own behavior or environment) that will lead to the desired change. Individuals in the fifth stage, called *maintenance*, are making active efforts to sustain the changes made in the action stage. Those unable to sustain the changes they have made are said to be in the stage of *relapse*. From there, they may re-enter the change cycle at any point (e.g., give up and become precontemplators or start right back in again at the action stage).

Some important characteristics of the stages-of-change model influence how a clinician might think about and intervene with individuals engaging in problem behaviors. First, the model predicts who is most likely to benefit from interventions that require a patient or client to take action. People in different change stages should evidence different treatment success rates, with those in the action stage more likely to benefit than those in the precontemplation stage. Treatment outcome research supports this prediction for both smoking cessation (Ockene, Ockene, & Kristellar, 1988; Prochaska & DiClemente, 1992) and weight control (Prochaska, Norcross, Fowler, Follick, & Abrams, 1992b). The implication of this finding is that the same treatment should *not* be automatically provided to everyone who is engaging in a problem behavior. Rather, treatment should be tailored to each client's readiness stage. Those in the preparation or action stage should be provided with specific advice, recommendations, and encouragement on how to make behavior changes. However, those in the precontemplation or contemplation stage should first be provided with therapeutic responses that will facilitate their moving into the preparation and action stages. When they reach the later stages, they should then be provided with an intervention designed to teach or encourage adaptive pain management. In fact, once they are ready to take action, some clients may not need any other treatment; they may be able to follow through with recommendations for adaptive pain management on their own. In support of this idea, and on the basis of research with smokers, Prochaska et al. (1992a) note that merely helping clients move from one change stage to the next *doubles* their chances of taking action to quit smoking within the next 6 months. The specific clinician tasks associated with each change stage, according to MET procedures (Miller & Rollnick, 1991), are listed in Table 4.1.

Another important implication of the stages-of-change model is its recognition that relapse is a part of the change process. For example, in their initial research, Prochaska and DiClemente (1982) found that smokers tended to move through the various stages from three to seven times (on average, four) before finally quitting smoking for good (see also Schachter, 1982). For many clients, relapse can be predicted, prepared for, and (perhaps most importantly) learned from, so that relapse is less likely to occur next time.

TABLE 4.1. Stages of Change and Therapist Tasks

Client's stage	Clinician's motivational tasks
Precontemplation	Raise doubt—increase the client's perception of the risks and problems associated with the current behavior.
Contemplation	Tip the balance—evoke reasons to change, risks of not changing; strengthen the client's self-efficacy for change of current behavior.
Preparation	Help the client to determine the best course of action to take in seeking change.
Action	Help the client to take steps toward change.
Maintenance	Review progress. Renew motivation and commitment as needed.
Relapse	Help the client review the processes of contemplation, determination, and action, without becoming stuck or demoralized because of relapse.

Note. Adapted from Miller and Rollnick (1991). Copyright 1991 by The Guilford Press. Adapted by permission.

BASIC ASSUMPTIONS OF MOTIVATIONAL ENHANCEMENT THERAPY

The MET clinician has a single major purpose: to provide clients with a response, appropriate to the clients' stage of readiness to change, that will facilitate movement through the stages toward maintenance of some adaptive behavior. This requires an ongoing assessment of each client's readiness to change, as well as flexible and timely application of therapeutic strategies chosen specifically for that client to enhance movement through the change cycle. However, MET has some assumptions that should be explicitly acknowledged. First the clinician assumes that the behavior change being encouraged is actually beneficial for the client. There is little controversy regarding the need to change most of the problem behaviors to which MET approaches have already been applied (e.g., smoking, problem drinking, heroin abuse, HIV risk behaviors). However, there remains some controversy concerning the relative adaptiveness or maladaptiveness of specific behaviors related to pain problems. For example, although opioid medication use is strongly discouraged in some treatment programs (Loeser, Seres, & Newman, 1990), some clinicians believe that there is a place for opioid medications for some individuals suffering from chronic nonmalignant pain (France, Urban, & Keefe, 1984; Schofferman, 1993). Even exercise, which may be considered an essential component of multidisciplinary pain treatment (Loeser et al., 1990), has not necessarily been shown to be important to short-term treatment effectiveness (Jensen, Turner, & Romano, 1994). There is a strong need in the pain treatment literature for well-designed research that will identify which client behaviors are most adaptive and most maladaptive for which individuals suffering from pain problems. This research may then be used as a guide for clinicians who are in a position to encourage or discourage specific responses to pain. In the meantime, we clinicians must base our beliefs about which client behaviors are most adaptive on clinical experience and our theoretical model of pain.

In the absence of clear empirical guidelines concerning which pain-related behaviors to encourage or discourage in the individuals we serve, perhaps the role of the clinician should be to help motivate the client to try *something different* from what he or she is currently doing or has tried in the past, and then to monitor the effects of this change on the functioning of this particular client. The clinician may thus assist the client to determine which behaviors seem to be most adaptive for him or her. In fact, given the fact that it is unlikely that specific coping responses are necessarily adaptive or maladaptive for all individuals at all times, such an individualized empirical approach may be useful even after more knowledge is obtained concerning the relative adaptiveness of specific pain responses on average. In any case, the clinician is in a position to provide specific treatments, and in order to ensure that the client gives the intervention an adequate trial, MET strategies may be used to prepare the client for and maximize adherence to a particular treatment regimen.

Although an assumption of MET is that clinician behavior plays a key role in the development and maintenance of client motivation, the approach paradoxically argues that the ultimate responsibility for change lies within the client. In short, the clinician's task is to enhance motivation; the client's task is to take action. MET clinicians actively avoid doing anything "for" clients or overtly and strongly advocating for any one particular action. Interestingly, it appears that placing more responsibility on the client for action actually increases rather than decreases the probability of behavior change (Miller et al., 1993).

As indicated above, another assumption of MET is that clinician behavior has a very strong influence on client behavior. Clinicians can therefore either help or hinder clients in making adaptive decisions. In fact, the whole rationale of MET procedures depends on the fact that clinician behavior has a significant impact on client motivation. Each MET strategy has been selected or developed because it has been demonstrated to influence the probability of client behavior change.

The remainder of this chapter presents the five basic principles of MET, the three phases of MET treatment, and the clinical strategies associated with each treatment phase. Throughout, specific examples illustrate how the approach may be applied in the treatment of individuals who experience pain. In the examples that follow, the "adaptive" pain responses to which the MET strategies are applied include exercise, relaxation, and avoidance of pain-contingent rest and medication use. However, it is important to acknowledge that these responses may not be adaptive for all individuals at all times. In order to provide examples of the MET approach, it has been necessary to select *some* behaviors to encourage and discourage. However, MET principles and strategies may be applied to *any* behavior.

FIVE PRINCIPLES OF MOTIVATIONAL ENHANCEMENT THERAPY

Miller and Rollnick (1991) list five principles or tasks that guide the MET clinician in all of his or her interactions with clients. The MET clinician should (1) express empathy, (2) develop discrepancy, (3) avoid argumentation, (4) roll with resistance, and (5) support self-efficacy.

Expressing Empathy

Accurate empathy has been described in detail by Carl Rogers and his students (see Gordon, 1970; Ivey, 1980; Rogers, 1957, 1959). It involves efforts to communicate respect for the client, and includes active support for the client's right to self-determination and direction. Skillful reflective listening that helps to clarify and amplify the client's own experiences and values is one of the most effective ways to provide an atmosphere of respect. In addition, empathic listening ensures that the clinician is aware of the client's thoughts, wishes, and concerns.

The important attitude underlying accurate empathy is acceptance without judgment, criticism, or blame. Such acceptance is not the same thing as agreement. It reflects a desire to understand the client's perspective, and a willingness to reflect that understanding back to the client. Interestingly, as Miller and Rollnick (1991) point out, this approach seems to have a paradoxical effect of freeing people to change, whereas a more judgmental approach, by forcing resistance, can actually inhibit change. If people feel understood and accepted for whatever position they take, they can spend more time considering what they want to do and less time defending what they are currently doing.

Developing Discrepancy

The second principle of MET is to develop discrepancy between the client's current behavior and important goals in the client's life. *How* the clinician helps the client develop this discrepancy is crucial. So-called "confrontational" approaches are to be avoided, since they often result in defensive client responses. Rather, the MET clinician encourages the client to talk about the problem, listens specifically for discrepancies between client goals and client problem behaviors (e.g., "I want to be able to work" and "I am not working because of my pain problem"), reflects back discrepancies that are verbalized, and encourages the client to elaborate these discrepancies. In this process, the client becomes increasingly aware of how his or her current behavior conflicts with important personal goals. Such a client should be more likely to consider changing behavior. Discrepancies are enhanced not by lecturing the client about the negative effects of his or her behaviors, but through careful questioning and listening that enables the client to discover and elaborate on the discrepancies for himself or herself.

Of course, many individuals with chronic pain already perceive a discrepancy between their current situation and their goals. Often such discrepancies are what motivated them to seek help in the first place. The clinician's task is to *increase* these discrepancies as a means of encouraging motivation to change. Also, individuals suffering from chronic pain may not see a connection between maladaptive strategies they themselves are using to manage the pain problem and disruption in their goals. They may attribute all or most of the disruption in their lives to pain, and therefore express a primary goal of pain relief. The goal of the MET clinician, in the context of pain treatment, is to help such a client increase his or her understanding of the impact of the client's own (problem) behaviors on pain and functioning, so that the client begins to express reasons for changing these behaviors. The skilled MET clinician works to alter client discrepancies in subtle ways, outlined below, without making the client feeling pressured or coerced. When this is done well, it is the client and not the clinician who expresses the reasons for and intention to change. The clinician's role is to help the client move through this process.

Avoiding Argumentation

The MET clinician avoids argumentation at all costs—especially that which might involve the clinician's arguing *for* a specific behavior change, resulting in the client's arguing *against* an adaptive behavior change. Argumentation often gives the client the opportunity to list reasons to avoid change, and may thus inhibit rather than promote change. MET assumes that client resistance is strongly influenced by clinician behavior. For example, resistance is likely when a clinician tries to pressure a client to make some change before that client feels ready to change. If a clinician finds that the client begins to argue against adaptive behavior change, that is a signal for the clinician to switch strategies.

Rolling with Resistance

Related to the principle of avoiding argumentation is the fourth MET principle: rolling with resistance. The MET clinician avoids argumentation by switching strategies. But what should the clinician switch strategies to? There are several responses to client resistance other than direct disagreement or arguing. These are described in more detail below, but they generally involve reframing or restating the client's comment(s) in such a way as to demonstrate the clinician's understanding of the client's ambivalence about change. Sometimes, when the clinician reflects back the client's resistant statement, the client may actually respond by taking on the other side of the argument that he or she just started and come up with arguments *for* behavior change.

Supporting Self-Efficacy

The fifth principle important to MET is self-efficacy. *Self-efficacy* may be defined as the belief in one's ability to perform a specific behavior (Bandura, 1977); it includes beliefs in one's capabilities and optimism about being successful in behavior change efforts. All efforts to express empathy, develop discrepancy, avoid argumentation, and roll with resistance may prove ineffective if the client does not believe he or she is capable of making the needed changes. Thus, an important aspect of MET is to make statements and ask questions that promote the client's hope that change is possible.

SPECIFIC MOTIVATIONAL STRATEGIES

The five principles of MET, outlined above, may be seen as the overriding tasks or goals of the MET clinician. The chapter now proceeds with a review of specific intervention strategies that are consistent with these principles. What makes these strategies "motivational" is that they have empirical support for influencing client behavior change. Miller and his colleagues have divided the process of MET into three phases, which generally reflect the progression of change stages from precontemplation through action and maintenance (Miller et al., 1992). The specific MET intervention strategies are organized under these treatment phases. Phase 1 strategies generally are best used with precontemplators and contemplators, and are designed to encourage clients to consider change. Phase 2 strategies may be used with contemplators who appear almost ready to make a commitment for change, and are designed to "tip the balance" from ambivalence about change to preparation. Phase 3 strategies are used in follow-up sessions, after the client has made a commitment to change and has had an opportunity to take action on that commitment.

Phase 1: Strategies That Enhance Motivation for Behavior Change

Miller et al. (1992) describe eight specific therapeutic strategies that encourage motivation to change. These strategies can be used with clients in the precontemplative stage, but are especially helpful for contemplators to move them toward preparation and action. In Phase 1 of MET, the clinician (1) elicits self-motivational statements, (2) listens with empathy, (3) questions, (4) presents personal feedback, (5) affirms the client, (6) handles resistance, (7) reframes, and (8) summarizes. Each of these strategies is described below and is illustrated by examples involving encouragement of adaptive pain coping.

Eliciting Self-Motivational Statements

Perhaps the skill that distinguishes the MET therapist most clearly from other clinicians is the extent to which he or she asks questions and listens to the client in such a way as to elicit self-motivational statements. *Self-motivational statements* may be defined simply as arguments for behavior change (e.g., "It's time I did something about this," "OK, I'm ready to try something new," "I can't go on like this any more").

A number of psychological theories provide a strong rationale for the importance of clients', not clinicians', arguing for change. For example, cognitive dissonance theory (Festinger, 1957) asserts that when people are enticed to make public statements that differ from their previous statements, their beliefs and values shift in the direction of the new statements. Similarly, self-perception theory (Bem, 1967) argues that people learn about themselves through their actions; people know what they believe by what they hear themselves say and see themselves do. The bottom line is that people seem to be more convinced by their own arguments and assertions than by those of other people, however "expert" those other people might be.

For the purposes of building client motivation to alter pain-related behaviors, then, the clinician's task is to elicit from the client statements that support the following:

1. The client's recognition of the full nature and extent of the problem.
2. The client's concern about how he or she is currently managing the problem.
3. The client's intention of changing in the direction of adaptive pain management.
4. The client's optimism that change is possible.

From the MET perspective, every time a client expresses such motivational statements, he or she is more likely to try a new approach. Such statements are characteristic of preparation and action.

There are two ways to begin to elicit such statements (Miller & Rollnick, 1991). First, the clinician can simply ask for self-motivational statements from the client. For example, a clinician might ask, "Tell me, what is it that you would like to change about what you are doing now to manage your pain problem?" A second strategy is to ask the client to express the positive aspects of some maladaptive behavior before asking about the costs of that behavior. Most of us engage in maladaptive behaviors for specific reasons. If nothing else, behaviors such as smoking, eating a high-calorie meal, and inactivity can feel good, or at least reduce the chances of feeling bad (in the short run). Asking clients to discuss their reasons for maladaptive behaviors, prior to discussing the costs, indicates an acceptance of the ambivalence that most contemplators feel about such behaviors. Moreover, if the major arguments for a maladaptive behavior are reviewed now, the client will probably not feel the need to bring up these arguments later; it frees him or her to discuss the "down side" at length. Either direct questioning or discussion of the pros and cons of a maladaptive behavior can then be followed up with further questions or empathic listening (described below), in order to encourage the client to elaborate on the motivational statements that emerge. Some specific questions that may elicit self-motivational statements among individuals with pain problems are presented in Table 4.2. Examples of possible dialogues between a clinician and a client [with comments in square brackets] in which these questions are used to elicit motivational self-statements follow.

Problem Recognition. The clinician can ask questions to determine whether the problem, as identified by the client, is getting worse over time rather than better. Frequently, clients report that their pain problem is getting worse, and this information can be used to begin to build a case for making some changes in how the problem is being addressed.

CLINICIAN: During the past several months, do you see your pain problem getting worse, getting better, or staying the same?

CLIENT: Oh, things are much worse.

CLINICIAN: What exactly—

CLIENT: Well, the pain has been getting worse and worse, and I am getting at the end of my rope. I just can't seem to handle it any more.

CLINICIAN: So the pain is getting worse? How much worse?

CLIENT: Well, not a lot, but my bad days seem to be happening a lot more often.

CLINICIAN: What is a bad day like for you? [Note: The clinician is seeking elaboration on exactly what is worse from the perspective of the client. Later, the clinician ought to try and find out what being "at the end of my rope" means for the client. This should help to clarify the client's emotional state, build rapport (because the clinician is clearly showing interest in what the client is experiencing), and help to place in the foreground a possible emotional cost of not changing.]

TABLE 4.2. Examples of Questions That May Evoke Self-Motivational Statements in Individuals with Pain Problems

1. *Problem recognition*
   Have things gotten better or worse in the past 6 months? [Follow up with questions about current coping strategies].
   What are you now doing to cope with or manage your pain problem? Is this working?
   What do you miss most about your life before the pain problem?
2. *Concern*
   What concerns you the most about your pain problem?
   What scares you about what might happen if you don't try a new approach to this problem?
3. *Intention to change*
   The fact that you are here suggests to me that you are interested in seeing things change. How would you like your life to be different?
   If you received treatment here, how would you know whether treatment was successful? What would be different in your life?
   Of the things that you have control over, what would you like to see change the most?
4. *Optimism*
   Have you tried _____ in the past? What was easy and what was difficult about this?
   What area of your life has not yet been touched by the pain problem?
   What evidence do you have in your life that you could succeed here?
   What will make [decreasing your medication use, engaging in an exercise program, etc.] easier for you?
   What aspect of your life do you feel the most control over?
   What things in your life have you absolutely refused to let the pain control?

Note. Adapted from Miller and Rollnick (1991). Copyright 1991 by The Guilford Press. Adapted by permisison.

Nearly every client uses *some* strategies to manage pain; some of these may be adaptive and some may be maladaptive. The clinician can use responses to questions about coping to reflect and emphasize (1) the usefulness of adaptive strategies, and (2) problems with and concerns about maladaptive ones. By asking about both the benefits and costs, the clinician can get a more balanced picture of the client's beliefs.

CLINICIAN: What do you do now to cope with or manage your pain problem?

CLIENT: Nothing seems to help. [Sometimes clients have a difficult time identifying what they do to try to cope with pain; some prodding may be needed to obtain a response.]

CLINICIAN: I noticed on your diaries that you take an opioid medication every day. Is this for pain?

CLIENT: Well, it sometimes takes the edge off the pain, but it doesn't seem to do anything else.

CLINICIAN: So the opioid helps a little, but it has not taken your pain away. [The clinician hears an ambivalent feeling and reflects this to emphasize ambivalence about opioid medication use.]

CLIENT: Yes, and I've had to take more and more to have any effect.

CLINICIAN: That must be very frustrating, to have the drug lose its effectiveness. [The clinician reflects a possible negative emotion and consequence associated with the use of opioid medication.] Are there any other problems with this medication? [The clinician asks the client to come up with additional problems.]

CLIENT: Well, my doctor keeps telling me she does not want to prescribe it, and my husband does not like me using drugs. Sometimes I take many more than I am supposed to, just to try and get some relief. [The client is cooperating nicely by providing a high number of motivational statements, each of which, as they are emphasized and elaborated, should lead him or her closer to making a decision to try something new.]

CLINICIAN: So let me see if I understand you correctly. On one hand, the opioid medication sometimes, but not always, takes the edge off your pain. On the other hand, it does not always work; it has not cured the pain problem; your physician is not comfortable prescribing this medication; your husband does not like you taking it; and you sometimes take more than you are supposed to. Which of these concerns you the most? [The clinician gives the client the opportunity to hear the client's own arguments against using the opioid medication again, and seeks information about which problems are of most concern to the client.]

CLIENT: I'm scared that the only thing that has helped will stop working altogether.

CLINICIAN: So the main problem with the medication you're taking is that it is not working as well as before; you're afraid that it might stop working eventually. Do I have this right?

CLIENT: Yes, but it is the only thing that helps even a little bit. [Despite the many problems with opioids, at this time in the interview the client is not yet ready to consider giving them up.]

CLINICIAN: Is there anything else about these medications that concerns you?

CLIENT: Not really. I just wish I could find something that would work.

CLINICIAN: What else have you tried?

Concern. Presumably, the client is concerned about the problem; otherwise, he or she would not be seeking assistance. Discussing how the client's life is different, and especially how it is worse, since the pain problem began can be one way to focus on reasons the client has for managing the pain better.

CLINICIAN: What concerns you most about your pain problem?

CLIENT: It's taken over my life. My pain has stopped me from playing with my kids, and I'm no longer working.

CLINICIAN: Which of these has been harder on you? [In order to help the client develop discrepancies, the clinician should always try to be aware of which problems are of primary concern to the client. These may or may not be the problems that the clinician may deem important.]

CLIENT: I really miss playing with my kids. I can't pick them up or run with them—it's like they don't have a mother any more. I'd give anything to be able to hold Alice on my lap again.

CLINICIAN: You really want to be a good parent. [The clinician reflects a potentially deeply held value to better understand what is important to the client, as well as to enhance the client's awareness of this value. Later, the client may identify maladaptive responses to pain (using excessive opioid or sedative medications, becoming increasingly inactive) that are inconsistent with this value.]

Chances are that if a client does nothing to change how he or she is managing the problem, or continues to seek invasive medical procedures that have not been recommended or have already been tried without success, the client will continue to have difficulties managing the pain problem. It is not usually difficult for clients to reach this conclusion, but some direct questions can help emphasize this fact.

CLINICIAN: What scares you about what might happen if you don't try a new approach to this problem?

CLIENT: I suppose things will continue to get worse.

CLINICIAN: In what ways? [The clinician asks the client to elaborate on the self-motivational statement indicating concern about inaction.]

Intention to Change. Asking clients to envision a life in which they are managing the pain problem better can help to begin to establish treatment goals that have meaning to the clients, and can also help to shift the clients in the direction of working toward those goals. Several simple questions may be used to elicit such statements, and the clinician can ask for elaboration or use reflective listening to obtain more detailed information.

CLINICIAN: The fact that you are here suggests to me that you are interested in seeing things change. How would you like your life to be different?

CLIENT: I would like to be pain-free. [The client begins by setting an unlikely goal, and also a goal that may be incompatible with an active lifestyle.]

CLINICIAN: I can certainly understand wanting to be free of pain. How would your life be different if your pain were to go away? [Rather than pointing out that total pain relief is unlikely—a point better made by the client than by the clinician—the clinician gives an empathetic response that shows an understanding of the client's stated wish, while still trying to elicit what a "better life" might look like.]

Optimism. It is not uncommon for individuals with pain problems to have tried adaptive strategies at some time previously, and to have had at least some success with these strategies. For example, some individuals naturally use distraction, and report that they feel better when they are actively engaged in an interesting task. Others report that they experience less pain when they are calm or relaxed. Still others may have tried and experienced an increase in confidence and strength as a result of exercise. Information concerning these past successes is important, and their empathic reflection can help to build optimism for success in the future.

CLINICIAN: I'm interested in hearing about your experience with exercise. Have you tried an exercise program since the onset of the pain problem? If you have, what was easy and what was difficult about this? [As is frequently the case, the clinician is interested in hearing "both sides of the story" about efforts to manage the problem in the past.]

CLIENT: Right after the surgery, my doctor wanted me to walk every day. I was able to do it at first—for about 3 months. But then I fell and had to stay in bed for several weeks. After that, I couldn't walk without a lot of pain.

CLINICIAN: So you were able to maintain a walking program for 3 months [The clinician reflects past success]. During this time, did your tolerance for walking change? [The clinician wants to know about the client's perceptions of the effects of the walking program. The clinician may reflect and/or ask for elaboration on perceived benefits and improvements. A lack of perceived benefit may be responded to with an affirmation (see below) that the client's ability to maintain the exercise program, despite immediate benefits, suggests a lot of determination.]

Given the potential importance that perceptions of control may have on the well-being of people with pain problems (Andrasik & Holroyd, 1980; Jensen et al., 1994; Affleck, Tennen, Pfeiffer, & Fifield, 1987; Crisson & Keefe, 1988, Lorig, Chastain, Ung, Shoor, & Holman, 1989), as well as the established connection between self-efficacy beliefs and adaptive pain-related behaviors (Jensen, Turner, & Romano, 1991; Dolce, Crocker, & Doleys, 1986; Council, Ahern, Follick, & Kline, 1988), clients are likely to benefit from increases in self-efficacy and perceived control over pain. Discussions that focus on those times when, or those activities in which, when self-control and self-efficacy were maximized should help to enhance clients' self-efficacy.

CLINICIAN: Sometimes people feel like their activities are controlled by their pain; at other times they feel like they are controlling what they do, despite the pain. What areas of your life have not yet been touched by the pain problem? That is, what things have stayed the same?

CLIENT: Well, I haven't been able to work because of pain, but I still insist on doing a lot of yardwork. I can't let my husband do *all* the work.

CLINICIAN: I'd like to hear more about how you've managed to do the yardwork despite pain. [And then after discussion of the yardwork, eliciting and praising the client's efforts to maintain some degree of functioning, the clinician can seek to identify other times when the client is able to function despite pain. This should remind the client of her abilities and resources for pain management.] Are there other areas of your life that you feel you've managed to keep on top of, despite the pain problem?

Some clients may feel that they are almost completely controlled by their pain problems, and it may therefore be difficult to elicit self-motivational statements that indicate self-efficacy. Nevertheless, it is true that clients, at least at some level, make choices about control. Emphasizing and reflecting statements that show an understanding of this type of control should also enhance self-efficacy.

CLINICIAN: Sometimes people feel like their activities are controlled by their pain; at other times they feel like they are controlling what they do, despite the pain. What areas of your life have not yet been touched by the pain problem? In other words, what things have stayed the same?

CLIENT: Nothing is the same. My pain controls everything I do.

CLINICIAN: Have you ever just decided to go ahead and do something despite the pain?

CLIENT: Oh yeah, I used to try and get my work done no matter what. Then the pain would get me, and I've had to learn to tone down my activities quite a bit.

CLINICIAN: So in the past, when you've tried to control over your activities, you've experienced increases in pain. At this point, if I am hearing you right, you maintain a low profile as one way to manage pain. [The clinician reflects the client's current pattern of decreased activity because of pain. However, by framing this as something the client does "at this point," the clinician hints at the possibility that the client may choose another way to handle activities in the future.]

In summary, the goal of the questions listed in Table 4.2 and discussed above is to elicit statements indicating problem recognition, concern about how things are going, intention to change, and optimism that change is possible. The clinician does not need to ask each and every question listed in Table 4.2, nor should he or she limit questions to those presented in Table 4.2. Rather, the clinician should seek to ask questions and listen carefully to the client's responses, so as to get to the most important reasons for change *from the perspective of the client*. This should result in the client's feeling more listened to and understood. Moreover, to the extent that a high number of self-motivational statements are elicited and resistance is minimized (Miller et al., 1993), then the client should be more motivated to try something new.

Listening with Empathy

According to MET principles, empathic listening, as originally described by Carl Rogers (Rogers, 1957, 1959), provides a therapeutic environment that is extremely important if not essential for helping individuals take on difficult behavior changes (Miller & Rollnick, 1991; Miller et al., 1992). This therapeutic strategy involves listening carefully to the client, and then reflecting accurately what the client has said. Empathic listening also acts to minimize client resistance. It is more difficult for clients to argue with someone who is seeking to understand them than with someone who is challenging them. Furthermore, and consistent with the MET goal of encouraging clients to convince themselves to engage in adaptive behaviors, reflective listening keeps clients talking and therefore helps the clinician avoid lecturing.

Given the high volume of both verbal and nonverbal communication that can occur with every client phrase, the clinician cannot hope to accurately reflect *everything* a client says. Through careful selection of what to reflect back to the client, reflective listening also may be used to emphasize and reinforce self-motivational statements. The example below illustrates how a clinician might use reflective listening to help a client clarify the costs of maladaptive pacing (periods of high activity followed by increases in pain followed by periods of inactivity).

CLINICIAN: Do you ever find that on some days when you are feeling better, you try and get a lot of things done that you have been unable to do, only to find you pay for this later by an increase in pain?

CLIENT: *(Nods vigorously and smiles.)*

CLINICIAN: I seem to have touched a chord. Tell me about that.

CLIENT: Sometimes I just get sick of not being able to do the dishes, so I will do them anyway. Then I feel excruciating pain for the next few days and I can't get anything done.

CLINICIAN: So other people have to do more.

CLIENT: Yes, until I can't stand it again; then I try to get as much done as I can before the pain stops me. Then I feel so much pain that I have to stop for a while.

CLINICIAN: I'm curious about how that feels for you.

CLIENT: I'm sick of it! I can't do the laundry without my pain killing me. I've completely given up working on my car.

CLINICIAN: There is a lot you would like to be able to do.

CLIENT: I would love to be able to just hold my children again. And I really miss . . .

The clinician in this example is seeking to discover what is important to the client that the pain problem interferes with. The fact that the client misses certain activities will become important information to summarize back to the client as he or she begins to consider trying alternative, adaptive coping strategies. Because it is more client-directed than direct questioning, empathic listening tends to elicit information that may be more relevant to the client's own perceived needs and desires. Empathic listening also tends to elicit emotionally richer information than does direct questioning. Such information is important for identifying the client's core values and primary interests. Given that empathic listening involves acceptance and a desire to clarify what the client is really saying, skillful empathic listening has the additional advantage of facilitating rapport. For these reasons, a substantial amount of the MET clinician's time is spent listening with empathy.

Questioning

There are at least two situations that call for direct questioning. First, direct questions can be used to elicit initial client responses, which can then be responded to with empathic listening. Many of the interactions presented above begin with such questions. A second way to use direct questioning is to ask a series of planned questions (an interview protocol) as a means of efficiently obtaining a great deal of specific information in a short period of time. In this case, the clinician needs to be aware that the client has less control over the interaction, so the information obtained may not seem as relevant to the client concerning his or her pain problem. Therefore, a long series of direct questions without empathic listening may result in increasing client resistance and should be avoided during most interactions. If the clinician chooses to ask a number of such questions in a series, he or she should watch carefully for signs of resistance, and interject empathic listening to minimize any resistance as the session progresses.

"What Seems to Increase Your Pain?" Given the likelihood that clients find pain punishing, knowledge concerning activities that are associated with increased pain gives the clinician knowledge about activities that are perhaps being consistently punished. A client's report indicating that specific activities are decreasing over time provides further evidence that these activities are being punished, perhaps by the increase in pain associated with them. Often these activities include standing, bending, and lifting. It is unfortunate when such behaviors are punished in the short run by increases in pain experience, because they are often beneficial in moderate amounts for the client in the long run. A challenge for the clinician is therefore to help the client develop rewards for these activities, as well as methods for short-circuiting the punishing qualities of pain experience that may accompany them. Rewards may include affirmations from a spouse and self-affirmations for engaging in the activity despite pain. Coping self-statements may decrease the punishing qualities of pain by reframing the pain experience (e.g., "Pain means that the activity is challenging the muscles that need to be challenged; it is a *good* pain," "Despite the pain, I am increasing my tolerance for standing; this will make it easier for me to return to work").

"What Decreases Your Pain?" It is possible that activities associated with decreased pain are negatively reinforced by this pain decrease. Such activities may include medication use, asking for and receiving a massage, and rest. If these activities are increasing over time, then this could be construed as further evidence that something, perhaps a decrease in pain, is reinforcing the behavior. To the extent that such activities are maladaptive in the long run, then the challenge for the client and clinician is to develop motivation for stopping or decreasing these activities, despite the presence of the reinforcement. This may include contingency management, the use of appropriate coping self-statements, and/or changes in beliefs about the meaning of the pain relief associated with these activities.

"What Is the Effect of Deep Relaxation on Your Pain Experience?" Clients who report a decrease in pain experience with relaxation may be in a better position to seriously consider relaxation training than individuals who report no change in pain experience with relaxation. To the extent that relaxation training may be a treatment option, knowledge concerning the client's experience and beliefs about relaxation is important.

"How Has the Pain Problem Affected Your Spouse?" MET assumes that clinician behavior influences client motivation to engage in new, adaptive pain management strategies. Consistent with the MET approach, and with current conceptions of chronic pain that focus on the importance of environmental influences on adaptation (Fordyce, 1976; Romano et al., 1992), information concerning the responses of other people to the person in pain is important in developing a viable treatment plan. For example, what, if anything, would a spouse gain or lose as the client begins to feel better? What could the client gain or lose from his or her spouse as the client starts to feel better?

"What Do You Think Is Causing Your Pain?" Clients often have strong beliefs about what is wrong with their bodies that is causing the pain (e.g., "a pinched nerve," "a bulging disk," "nerve damage"). These beliefs may or may not be consistent with what they have been told by physicians. Concerns and fears about the meaning of pain, unless understood and dealt with, can interfere with progress. This is especially important if progress is initially associated with greater pain, as is often the case with reactivation programs. The answers to questions concerning a client's beliefs about the cause of pain provide important clues to the frequency and amount of reassurance the client may need as treatment progresses. Simply asking "What do you think is causing your pain?" is the most direct way to elicit this information. However, in cases where there has been difficulty building rapport, asking this question has resulted in the answer, "I have no idea; I'm no doctor!" If it is suspected that rapport is not yet strong, the question can be broken in two: "What have you been told about the cause of your pain problem?" and "What do you think about this? Does any of it make sense to you?"

Direct questioning, especially if it can be done with sensitivity and willingness to hear the client's full response, is an important aspect of assessing motivation to change. Questions can be used to obtain information that can later be summarized, so as to encourage clients to get closer to the point of considering approaching their problem in a new way.

Presenting Personal Feedback

An additional Phase 1 strategy is that of providing feedback concerning the effects of the problem behavior on the client's life. When MET is used with problem drinking, for example, clients are given feedback (based on a pretreatment assessment) of their level of drinking relative to same-gender peers, level of intoxication, risk factors for problem drinking, negative consequences of drinking, blood test results, and neuropsychological test results (Miller et al., 1992). Feedback information concerning the effects of maladaptive pain responses would obviously differ from this. However, the primary goal of such feedback is the same: to bring into better focus discrepancies between what the client is doing now to manage the problem, and his or her personal goals and core values.

For the purposes of adaptive pain management, feedback given to clients may include (but is not necessarily limited to) the following:

> Level of physical functioning relative to same-age, same-gender, and same-level-of-pain-report peers (according to a standardized measure of physical functioning such as the Sickness Impact Profile; Bergner, Bobbitt, Carter, & Gilson, 1981).
> Level of psychological functioning relative to peers (according to a measure such as the Center for Epidemiologic Studies Depression Scale; Radloff, 1977).
> Use of opioid medications as a risk factor for increased pain over time.
> Use of sedative medications as a risk factor for decreased cognitive functioning.
> Presence of sleep disturbance (including sleep onset insomnia, early morning awakening, and nocturnal awakenings).
> Impact of pain problem on social role functioning, including family and work responsibilities.

Of course, in order for the clinician to provide feedback, information concerning each of the components of the feedback needs to be obtained prior to the feedback session. Much of this information may be obtained by administering standardized tests (e.g., the Sickness Impact Profile and the Center for Epidemiologic Studies Depression Scale, among many others) or specific items on questionnaires. Other information may be obtained in a prior interview. The key is to consolidate this information and then to present it in such a way as to encourage the client's motivation to change in the direction of more effective pain management, as well as to build hope that such efforts will be beneficial.

Once the feedback information to be provided has been consolidated, the clinician is ready to present this to the client. The most important, and most challenging, aspect of this portion of the session is the *way* feedback is presented. Each important piece of information (whether it is provided orally only, or on a sheet of information that summarizes the feedback) is reviewed with the client. Clients are given time to ask questions about and respond to the information provided. The clinician's task is to adapt the timing of feedback to fit each client's ability to process the information. Self-motivational statements that clients make during the feedback session should be accurately reflected as they occur. In addition, as the data are discussed, questions may be asked to elicit such motivational statements (e.g., "What do you think of this? Does it make sense to you?"). Client responses that reflect resistance to the information may be responded to with reflection or reframing (see below). Here are some examples of feedback that is likely to support greater client motivation to change:

CLINICIAN: (*Presenting feedback*) First, my reading of your medical record indicates that your physicians see you as medically stable. That is, although you continue to experience significant pain, they have not yet found a specific disease process that is causing the pain or that will seriously harm you, over and above the effect of pain on your life. They have no surgeries to offer that they feel will relieve your pain, and in fact they think that any surgery may make your problem worse. Also, there do not seem to be any additional medical tests that they are considering at this time. People have a lot of different responses to this type of information, from relief that they do not have some deteriorating disease to frustration that they do not have a specific diagnosis. What is your response to it? Does it make sense to you?

CLIENT: I'd rather have a diagnosis, but if my doctors don't know, they don't know. I know that something is wrong. [This response suggests something in between the belief in the traditional biomedical approach to pain (if it hurts, there must be a physical cause that can be found and fixed) and acceptance that the problem may not have a single specific diagnosis.]

CLINICIAN: Given all this, what are your thoughts and feelings about a new approach? I mean an approach where you stop looking to doctors for a diagnosis and for some treatment that will cure pain, and begin to think about ways to manage the pain so you can get on with your life—like working to be the parent you'd like to be? [Here the clinician presents the option of pain management, and raises one of the client's core values that emerged in earlier discussions.]

CLINICIAN: (*Presenting feedback*) From what you have said to me and your responses to the Sickness Impact Profile, it appears that your pain has had a profound impact on your life. Your percentile score of 75% indicates that you are more disabled than 75 out of 100 of the people we see here who have the same level of pain intensity.

CLIENT: I am more disabled than other people with the same pain level?

CLINICIAN: Yes. Does it make sense to you that different people can be affected differently by the same amount of pain? [The clinician here suggests the possibility that people can vary in their adaptation to pain, implicitly indicating that the client may be able to function better even with the same amount of pain. As always, making this suggestion and then asking the client whether the idea makes sense to him or her should make the idea easier to accept than lecturing would.]

CLIENT: I guess some people can handle pain more than others. I have a real hard time with pain. [The client seems to be heading in a direction of pain tolerance as a trait rather than a learned skill—an idea inconsistent with his or her learning how to tolerate pain well.]

CLINICIAN: I'm curious: In yourself, do you find that there are days when you seem to be better able to manage the pain? [This question is designed to encourage the client to consider the possibility that pain tolerance may not be consistent from day to day, and therefore may be changeable through purposeful efforts.]

A defensive response to feedback that the client is having a difficult time managing the pain's impact on his or her life, relative to other individuals reporting the same pain level, should be met with reflection rather than argumentation. Perhaps such a client needs additional reassurance that the clinician understands how difficult the pain problem is for the client:

CLIENT: I think I am doing as good as I can.

CLINICIAN: I actually think you've done very well, considering how difficult pain can be to deal with. You've kept up on a lot of yardwork, and you've made a lot of effort to continue to be as good a parent as you can for your children.

Some clients may also have a difficult time understanding the percentile concept, or the associated idea that individuals who report the same pain level can evidence substantially different responses to pain. However, attempts to lecture the client concerning this concept may backfire. Even if the client eventually gets the concept, the lecturing clinician runs the risk of alienating the client (Client: "My clinician talks down to me"). A response more consistent with the MET approach would be to reflect the client's concern, and to plan to discuss the possibility of differential adaptation to pain problems at a later time.

CLIENT: Anyone with as much pain as I have would have their life affected!

CLINICIAN: I have to agree with you. Pain problems have a big impact on people, and I think you are working hard to manage this as best you can right now.

Affirming the Client

The MET clinician seeks to affirm the client at every opportunity. Affirmations, in the form of direct compliments and praise, are thought to provide a more positive environment for change by increasing rapport, enhancing client self-esteem, encouraging client responsibility, and reinforcing client self-motivational statements (Miller et al., 1992). Affirming statements may be contrasted with reflective statements: The former are sincere expressions of the *clinician's* positive responses to the client, whereas the latter consist of efforts to reflect the *client's* concerns. Some examples of affirmations follow.

"You've been working very hard to maintain your activity despite the pain. I really respect that."

"You've been able to understand some difficult concepts—pain is a very complex thing."

"I'm impressed with the resourcefulness you've shown in coming up with some pain management strategies that work for you."

"You seem to have really thought hard today about the things you can do to make your life better."

Handling Resistance

Most psychological models of pain, or any model that includes recognition of a psychological component in pain problems, place important emphasis on what the client does and how the client thinks about the pain problem (e.g., Turk, Meichenbaum, & Genest, 1983). Therefore, for a large number of individuals seeking help, something about what they are doing or thinking about the pain problem may be contributing to their difficulties. However, there are probably legitimate reasons (at least in the clients' minds) for using maladaptive coping strategies or thinking maladaptive thoughts concerning the pain. One of these reasons may be simply lack of information or lack of skills. If this were the whole story, however, simple education programs or skill training should be enough to assist all individuals with pain problems. Other reasons for maladaptive responding exist, and one of these is clients' "resistance" to trying new, adaptive approaches.

Miller et al. (1992) define resistance as a set of specific client behaviors, such as interrupting, arguing, sidetracking, or defensive responding, that appear to be associated with poor treatment outcome. MET emphasizes the role of the clinician in affecting these resistant behaviors. In fact, resistant behavior is thought of more as a clinician problem than as a client problem. There is evidence to support this. For example, Miller et al. (1993) randomly assigned problem drinkers to a confrontational/directive or a motivational/reflective treatment condition. They found that the clients in the confrontational/directive condition displayed significantly more resistant responses than did those in the motivational/reflective condition. Moreover, resistant behaviors were subsequently associated with poor treatment outcome in the predicted direction. These findings should not surprise contemporary psychologists, who understand the profound impact that environment can have on human behavior. What can be difficult for many clinicians to comprehend is that clients may be resistant not because they do not "want to change," but because of the way clinicians are interacting with them to induce change.

A key MET concept in managing clients' resistant behaviors is to monitor interactions for such behaviors, and then to *change strategies* when such behaviors emerge. Clinician responses that tend to evoke resistance, and that therefore should be avoided, include arguing, criticizing, "warning" a client of negative consequences, active persuasion, analyzing or questioning possible reasons for resistance, confronting, or using sarcasm (Miller & Jackson, 1995; Miller et al., 1992). Any persuasion to be done is best done by the client, not the clinician.

Four strategies for dealing with resistance are simple reflection, double-sided reflection, shifting focus, and rolling with resistance (Miller & Rollnick, 1991).

CLIENT: I never exercised before I had a pain problem. I don't see how I can do it now!

CLINICIAN: Before you had a pain problem, you did not see any reason to exercise. Now, with the pain, it seems like a real challenge to you. [By reflecting the client's concerns, the clinician avoids telling the client "You can do it" and thereby avoids a series of "Yes, but" responses, in which the client systematically lists all his or her reasons for being unable to exercise. Acknowledging the perceived difficulty of exercising regularly can serve at least two purposes. First, it reflects what the client is saying, and so has the positive effects of accurate empathy. In addition, by reframing exercise as a "challenge" instead of the implied impossibility, the clinician may increase hope that such behavior is possible, and also help set up the client for affirmation later ("You have successfully overcome this challenge").]

CLIENT: If I exercise, it will just make my pain problem worse. That has always happened before.

CLINICIAN: Maybe it seems crazy to you that I think exercise might be worth another try, given some of the problems you've had with exercise in the past. [Although appropriate (i.e., gradually increasing and quota-based) reactivation is central to many chronic pain treatment programs, many clients express significant worry and concern about exercise. These concerns are realistic, given their previous attempts to exercise. Reflection allows such a client to hear that the clinician understands and acknowledges this concern.]

CLIENT: It is hard for me to imagine going without my pain medications.

CLINICIAN: You are worried about being able to manage your pain without medications, yet you also seem to be considering it. What are your worries, and also why are you even considering this at this time? [That the client states a difficulty thinking about going without medications suggests at least some effort to consider being medication-free. A double-sided reflection usually incorporates both sides of an argument. Double-sided reflective statements have at least two beneficial effects. First, they acknowledge that nearly any behavior change has both benefits and costs; to the extent that the client may have previously been unwilling to consider behavior change, a balanced view represents movement in an adaptive direction. Second, encouraging the client to consider both sides often elicits self-motivational statements, which can later be reflected back to the client.]

CLIENT: No matter what you say, as long as I have pain, I will never, ever give up my pain medications.

CLINICIAN: It seems to me that it is hard for you to imagine life without pain medications. A lot of people feel like this at first. But now is *not* the time to make any final decisions about how you want to handle this problem for the rest of your life. Today, let's just review what you are now doing to manage your pain. I hope that by doing this, I can begin to understand, from your perspective, which of these seem to be working. As we progress, I hope to learn if there are any coping strategies you are not currently using that you would be interested in learning more about. [It is important to avoid arguing strongly for a particular coping strategy. In order to avoid this, the clinician may choose to shift focus completely away from the issue when a client expresses strong resistant statements, and to focus instead on an issue that is more likely to result in self-motivational statements.]

CLIENT: No matter what you say, as long as I have pain, I will never, ever give up my pain medications.

CLINICIAN: You may be right. After we are through, you may decide to continue to seek prescriptions for pain medications. That choice will be yours to make. [A second way to manage confrontational statements is simply to acknowledge the possibility of their truth. By not arguing in response, a clinician avoids pushing a client into expressing all the reasons for not changing. However, even when rolling with the resistance (essentially, agreeing with some component of what the client is saying), the clinician has an opportunity to emphasize client choice, as well as the *possibility* that the client may chose to engage in the adaptive behavior sometime in the future.]

Reframing

Reframing involves providing the client with feedback that (1) puts the client's maladaptive behavior in a generally positive light, and (2) still allows for the possibility of behavior change. The rationale behind reframing is that if the client does not have to defend his or her current pattern of responses, then he or she will have more energy for changing those responses.

CLIENT: No matter what you say, as long as I have pain, I will never, ever give up my pain medication.

CLINICIAN: You sound to me like a person who can really commit yourself to an action, once you decide that it is good for you.

Summarizing

Toward the end of every session, it is important to set aside a time to summarize the basic content of the session for the client. A summary serves the primary purpose of allowing clients to hear their own self-motivational statements one more time. Miller et al. (1992) point out that elements of resistant statements should also be included, so that a client perceives that all of his or her statements have been heard. Nevertheless, it is important to emphasize, as much as possible, the self-motivational statements that were elicited during the session.

CLINICIAN: I'd like to try and summarize all of the points I've heard you make today. Please let me know if I have missed anything important. You told me that things have been getting worse, especially over the past few months, and you are now getting to the end of your rope. The pain has interfered with your being able to do a lot of household chores; being able to lift, hold, and play with your children; and being able to work. You especially miss being able to hold your children. You told me that it interferes with all recreational activities. You spend much more time sitting and lying down. This high degree of deactivation was confirmed by the test scores, which indicated that 75% of pain patients with pain as intense as yours are less disabled than you are. The pain has also had a big impact on your mood, and I told you that this was very common.

You cope with your pain problem primarily through rest and by using pain-contingent opioid medications. Although it is hard for you to think of changing these coping strategies, they do not seem to be fixing the problem. If anything, it has been getting worse over the past several months, and you anticipate that if you don't do anything to change the problem, it will continue to get worse. You've heard me tell you that our treatment program involves a structured reactivation program and gradual elimination of the opioid medications. Although this seemed to worry you when I first talked about it, you seemed to understand how people who go through this program are able to tolerate a lot more activity. Given that what you are currently doing does not seem to be working that well, you see yourself as possibly benefiting from a new approach. Is this a pretty good summary? Did I miss anything?

Summary of Phase 1 Strategies

The eight Phase 1 strategies are eliciting self-motivational statements, listening with empathy, asking open-ended questions, presenting personal feedback, affirming the client, handling resistance, reframing, and summarizing. These strategies are used by the MET clinician in the first session to enhance the client's motivation to change—that is, to increase the probability that the client will engage in an adaptive behavior change in the future. Because the clinician alternately leads and follows the client in this process, the pace that the client takes in moving toward the preparation and action stages is determined in large part by the client. Rapid progression (e.g., within minutes), as indicated by a lack of resistant statements and frequent self-motivational statements, suggests that the client may be ready to prepare to take action; in this case, the clinician should rapidly shift to Phase 2 strategies. Slower progress suggests that the client is still in the contemplation stage, and indicates that more time may be needed for Phase 1 intervention. Very slow progress (e.g., a dearth of self-motivational statements) suggests precontemplation, again indicating the need for additional Phase 1 strategies.

Because the client's responses to Phase 1 strategies provide information about readiness to change, these strategies are an excellent way to assess the client's stage of change. In this way, MET can be considered both an assessment *and* an intervention approach. As the client progresses through contemplation and begins to move to preparation, the clinician should switch strategies from those that enhance motivation (Phase 1) to those that strengthen a commitment to change (Phase 2).

Phase 2: Strategies That Strengthen Commitment for Behavior Change

The timing of the switch from Phase 1 to Phase 2 strategies is important. If the clinician switches strategies too early, while the client is still in the precontemplation stage, then the client will evidence resistance, and progression to the preparation and action stages will be hindered. On the other hand, if the client is already in the preparation stage, Phase 1 strategies that encourage contemplation may backfire by annoying the client. Consider, for example, a smoker who has decided that he or she must quit smoking, and who visits a health care provider in search of assistance. If the health care provider spends much of the time available for the visit reviewing with the client all the reasons for quitting smoking (focusing on reasons important to the health care provider and not necessarily to the smoker), time is wasted that might have been used for reviewing strategies and developing a plan for quitting. On the other hand, consider a precontemplative smoker who visits a health care provider for a diagnosis and possible treatment of an ear infection. If the clinician attempts to assist the client in developing a plan for quitting smoking, the client is likely to evidence significant resistance ("I came here for an antibiotic, not a lecture!"). Fitting the motivational strategy to the client, according to the stage of change the client is in, is essential to effective MET.

Once the clinician has determined that the time is right to use Phase 2 strategies, then he or she should (1) help the client to develop a plan for change, (2) communicate free choice, (3) discuss the consequences of changing versus not changing, (4) provide information and advice as requested, (5) roll with resistance, (6) complete a change plan worksheet, (7) recapitulate, and (8) ask for a commitment. Each of these strategies, as they may be used with an individual who experiences pain and who is considering making some life change(s) to become better able to manage the pain, is discussed below.

Developing a Plan for Change

A primary goal of Phase 2 strategies is the development of a behavior change plan to which the client can commit himself or herself. This discussion may begin with the client's asking about ideas for change (e.g., "So what exercises should I do, exactly?"). It can also be effective for the clinician to raise the issue of plan development. Clinician-initiated discussions usually begin with some questions, such as the ones that follow:

> "Given all of the things we've been talking about, what do you see as your options for making your life better? What do you think will work for you?"
> "At this point, what is your plan for managing this pain problem?"
> "What are you now thinking about exercise [your medication use, the possibility that relaxation will be helpful, etc.]?"
> "At this point, what is your thinking about how to turn all this around?"

The difference between these questions and Phase 1 questions should be obvious. Instead of eliciting self-motivational statements (Phase 1 strategy), the clinician is attempting to elicit specific ideas for behavior change. There is a shift from *why* the client should consider change to *how* the client will make changes. At this point, the clinician may consider offering direct suggestions. However, when advising a client, it is best to (1) ask permission first, (2) couch advice in terms of freedom of choice, and (3) offer several ideas from which the client can choose. The clinician should avoid attempts to convince the client of the relative effectiveness of one approach over another. The clinician's primary role is to facilitate the client in developing a plan that the client can become committed to trying.

Communicating Free Choice

In order to maximize self-motivation, and to facilitate the attribution of control to the client, the clinician should provide frequent reminders of the client's free choice in all aspects of his or her change plan. This can be difficult when working with clients in the context of quota-based (i.e., non-pain-contingent) as opposed to pain-contingent reactivation programs. In quota-based reactivation programs, clients are asked to exercise to a specific and gradually increasing level (e.g., "10 minutes of aerobics" or "12 partial sit-ups") every day, no matter how good or bad they feel (Fordyce, 1976). A not uncommon complaint about such a program from clients is "I can't believe you are making me do 10 minutes of aerobics, even though my pain is excruciating!" The implication of such a comment is that the responsibility for treatment (and therefore improvement) rests with the clinicians who make decisions about the quota levels. In such an instance, it is important to remind the client gently that he or she has a choice to engage in the quota-based exercise approach. A response that communicates this idea follows.

CLINICIAN: You are free to do whatever you think is best for you. Clearly, what you do will have consequences. I'm wondering whether you are still interested in trying the quota-based approach. What are your thoughts about the long-term consequences of sticking to the plan versus trying something different at this point? [A complaint about feeling controlled is an opportunity for the clinician to remind the client gently that how the client responds to his or her pain is up to him or her. In this example, concerns about the quota-based program may be used as an opportunity to review the concept of pain's being in control of the client's life (i.e., pain-contingent activity level) versus the client's being in charge (i.e., non-pain-contingent or goal-contingent activity). Again, it is important to avoid lecturing the client, and allow him or her to come up with the pros and cons of continuing with the treatment plan or not. Such discussions also allow for a review of the consequences of behavior change versus no behavior change—another Phase 2 strategy (discussed below).]

Reviewing Consequences of Change versus No Change

Another effective way to strengthen commitment to change (or commitment to continue with a change program that has begun but perhaps has hit a snag) is to review with the client the consequences of making the change versus not making the change. Most likely, the client will realize that not making any changes means life as before. Such a life is unsatisfactory for many of the clients clinicians see.

One way to do this is to ask the client to review both the pros and cons of changing. It is more likely than not that much information about this will have already been reviewed during Phase 1, when the negative impact of the pain problem was reviewed in detail with the client. Clients may choose to list in two columns on a piece of paper the benefits and costs (or pros and cons) of different options. Such lists—as long as the contents are generated by clients and not "fed" to them by clinicians, and as long as the benefits of behavior change outweigh the costs—should help strengthen clients' motivation to change or maintain a behavior change plan.

Providing Information and Advice

As clients with pain problems reach the preparation stage, or attempt to manage difficulties with a change plan that is in progress, they may ask for specific information and advice concerning how to proceed. Examples of informational questions asked by clients are as follows:

"What is the success rate of your program?"
"Will I be pain-free after completing your program?"
"Will I have to continue to exercise after I am done with your program?"

Questions asking for advice may include the following:

"What do you think I should do?"
"I'm worse now than before I started. What should I do now?"

One way to respond is to provide information based on personal experience or research, and then ask a follow-up question concerning what the client wishes to do. Whenever possible, the clinician should offer a number of possible suggestions (a "menu") from which the client can choose. This helps emphasize that it is the client's responsibility to decide.

CLINICIAN: I have seen people make different decisions; some have chosen to continue with their plan of increasing activity, while others have chosen to quit at this point and try something different. For the most part, in my experience, those people who have done the best in the long run have been those who have kept at their plan. But I also think that every person is different, and that you need to decide what will be best for you. After all, you're the one who will have to live with the consequences. For some people, staying with a pain management plan has been the biggest challenge of their lives, and they feel very proud that they are able to stick with it. In my experience, people who went back to their former ways of coping have not done very well. I suppose you could give up now, give up for a short while and try again later, keep trying for a short while and see how it goes, or make a commitment to keep trying for as long as it takes. Ultimately, it has to be your choice. What do you think the consequences of these choices are, and how does that fit with your long-term goals of returning to work and being a better parent?

If the client continues to ask for advice, it is fine to provide this. Some resistance on the clinician's part to giving advice may help to ensure that the client is interested in hearing what is being suggested, and not seeking to hear information that he or she can argue with. Examples of preliminary resistant responses are:

CLINICIAN: I want you to understand that I support your right to decide for yourself what to do, and I'm a little worried that you might feel some pressure to follow any advice that I give. I would only want to make specific suggestions if I can also communicate that I believe you should do what *you* think is best for you. Only you can decide how best to handle your life.

CLINICIAN: I can tell you what I think might be best in your situation, based on my experience with people like you. However, I also believe that each person is different and that what is best for one person may not necessarily be best for another. That is why any decision about what you will do has to be up to you. I am here to support you in the development of a plan that *you* support and are interested in trying.

If the client expresses the desire to know what the clinician thinks may be best for him or her, especially after the clinician communicates some resistance to providing advice, then short and clear advice statements are best. Here are some examples:

"I think you should maintain a regular exercise program."
"I think you should stop using opioid medications."
"I think you should practice relaxation strategies 30 minutes a day for 3 months, and then decide whether to continue."
"I think you should reward yourself for exercising by spending some time—say 30 minutes—doing something just for you, such as reading a novel or sitting in a warm bath."

In general, it is always a good idea to follow up any information and advice with questions that gauge the client's response. Such questions help to emphasize that it is the client's responsibility to make a final decision as to what he or she is going to do next:

"Does this make sense to you?"
"Do you have any questions about what I said?"
"Does what I said fit with your own experience?"

Rolling with Resistance

It is as important to roll with resistance during Phase 2 as it is in Phase 1. Some ambivalence about change, despite the client's statements indicating determination to try change, can be expected at every stage. Of course, a high level of resistance may indicate movement away from preparation and back into contemplation. In any case, resistant statements should still be responded to with reflection and reframing. At any stage, direct confrontation or challenging statements from the clinician should be avoided, because of the resistant responses such communications elicit in clients.

Using a Change Plan Worksheet

Throughout Phase 2 (which may last only one session), the clinician may choose to keep notes of the information provided by the client during this phase on a change plan worksheet (see Figure 4.2). This sheet can provide a structure for organizing the most important aspects of the clients goals and reasons for making changes. The six issues addressed on the worksheet are presented in Figure 4.2 and discussed below.

"The Changes I Want to Make Are . . ." Clear goals are important to effective behavior change plans. The goals should be ones identified by the client as important. However, among individuals suffering from chronic, nonmalignant pain, it is wise to avoid listing "decreased pain" as a primary goal for several reasons. Although many clients identify this as a primary goal at the beginning of treatment, few adaptive behaviors that are in the client's control have been shown to have a profound influence on pain intensity in the short run. Moreover, two responses to pain that are thought to be maladaptive (pain-contingent use of opioid medications and pain-contingent rest) often have the short-term effect of decreasing pain experience. Thus, a primary goal of "decreased pain," placed in a prominent position on the change plan worksheet, may actually work *against* long-term positive adaptation. Clients who insist on keeping pain reduction on the worksheet (some may, and it is important to respect their ultimate choice) may be willing to consider "minimization of pain in the long run" as one of several goals. To the extent that the client can identify goals over which he or she has some direct control, there are more chances for success.

"The Most Important Reasons Why I Want to Make These Changes Are . . ." Here is where the clinician can list the client's review of the pros and cons of behavior change versus no behavior change. The clinician should be sure to emphasize those reasons for behavior change that the client deems most important, especially those that are related to the client's core values.

"The Steps I Plan to Take in Changing Are . . ." Under this heading, the clinician should list the ideas the client has stated for making specific changes. Ideas initiated by the clinician may be included if the client has endorsed these as his or her own. The more specific these plans can be, the more helpful this section of the worksheet will be to the client.

"The Ways Other People Can Help Me Are . . ." Pain clinicians have long recognized the importance of other people's responses to the client in influencing client functioning (Flor, Kerns, & Turk, 1987; Flor, Turk, & Rudy, 1989; Fordyce, 1976; Romano et al., 1992). Discussing with the client, and with someone close to the client (e.g., a spouse) if

CHANGE PLAN WORKSHEET

The changes I want to make are:

The most important reasons why I want to make these changes are:

The steps I plan to take in changing are:

The ways other people can help me are:
    Person   Possible ways to help

I will know that my plan is working if:

Some things that could interfere with my plan are:

_____
                                    Your Signature

FIGURE 4.2. Change plan worksheet. Adapted from Miller, Zweben, DiClemente, and Rychtarik (1992).

such a person is available, specific steps that the other person can take to assist the client in making adaptive changes should increase the chances that such changes will actually occur.

"I Will Know That My Plan Is Working If . . ." Because making adaptive changes to pain problems can be challenging, it is important to identify signposts that indicate the client is going in the right direction. Such signposts can act as potential reinforcers for the efforts made, even if the final goal has not yet been reached. Some goals—for example, reactivation—tend to result in *increased* pain and discomfort before the client feels stronger. To the extent that this increase can be predicted, and even identified as a sign of progress (i.e., "Increased pain means that the muscles that need to be stronger are being challenged"), then clients may be reassured rather than frightened. Specific signs of progress ("Able to lift a bag of groceries," "Able to drive for 15 minutes") toward the final goal ("Able to go grocery shopping by myself") should also be included here.

"Some Things That Could Interfere with My Plan Are . . ." To the extent that clients can identify specific problems they may encounter, and come up with plans for addressing these problems, then specific hurdles may be avoided altogether or at least more easily dealt with.

Recapitulating

The recapitulating strategy for Phase 2 provides benefits similar to those of the summarizing strategy for Phase 1. Clients get to hear once again their reasons for making change and their plan for change. The change plan worksheet, used by the clinician to keep track of the issues raised by the client during Phase 2, may be used as a guide. An example of a recapitulation follows.

CLINICIAN: I think now is a good time to review what I have heard you say so far. First, it is clear that the pain problem has had a profound impact on your life, especially your ability to parent as you would like to; you've said several times that you miss being able to hold your children. You also miss being able to do more yardwork and to work outside the home. You seem to think at this point that your low level of physical fitness is contributing to the problem, and that things have not improved with using rest and opioid medications to manage this. If anything, in fact, things are getting worse.

You've mentioned three things that you want to change. First, you would like to be able to lift and carry your children. Second, you want to be able to "do your share" around the house. For you, this means being able do the household chores that were your responsibility prior to the pain problem. Finally, you said you want to get to the point where you can tolerate a full day of work.

You've discussed several ways to reach these goals. One is to continue as you have been, and just wait for the problem to "get better" on its own. You do not think this is a good option, based on your experience of not getting better. You have decided that a structured exercise program is more likely to make you stronger. One way to do this is to visit a physical therapist who specializes in working with individuals who have pain problems, and to do the majority of work on your own and at home. This appeals to you because of your independent nature. However, you are also worried about the increase in pain that might accompany such a program, and so you are also thinking about a more closely supervised program.

You've decided to begin by trying the home program and seeing how far you can get. If this is effective for reaching your goals, you would plan to continue this. If you run into problems, then you have decided to come see us again at the pain center, and discuss the possibility of a more closely supervised program. In any case, you plan to come back here in 4 weeks to discuss the progress you have made, and whether the home program is working for you. You've also mentioned some things that your spouse can do to help you. These include avoiding talking with you about how bad you feel, and to avoid recommending that you "take it easy" if he thinks you are hurting. You have also asked for occasional praise from your spouse for the exercising you plan to do. You understand that you will probably experience more pain as you get started, and that this is a sign that the muscles that need to be challenged are responding to the exercise program. Have I covered everything that is important? What have I missed?

Changes offered by the client concerning recapitulation should be incorporated into the change plan worksheet. The client should get a copy of the worksheet, and one should be included in his or her record.

Asking for a Commitment

The final strategy to employ with clients in Phase 2 is to ask them to commit themselves to the plan they have outlined. Miller at al. (1992) list several issues that may be worth exploring when obtaining a commitment. First, it is important to clarify what exactly a client intends to do. This is a good time to review the change plan worksheet, beginning with the responses to the "The steps I plan to take in changing are . . ." stem. Are the steps, as listed, actually what the client intends to do? The other components of the change plan worksheet should also be reviewed at this time, including perceptions of the benefits of change and the costs of inaction, and concerns about what might interfere with making the change and how to deal with these obstacles. Following this review, the clinician should simply ask the client for a commitment to follow through with his or her plan: "Are you ready to commit yourself to doing this?" If so, then the clinincian can ask the client to sign the change plan worksheet, give the client a copy, and retain a copy for the client's records.

If the client does not feel ready to commit to a plan of action at this time, then the clinician should ask the client what he or she would like to do now. Any pressure to "go ahead and try" some aspects of the plan (from the clinician) should be avoided. The client may wish to think about the plan until the next visit or session. No client should feel pushed into making a decision to change before he or she feels ready to do so, as this is likely to result in more rather than less resistance to change in the long run.

Summary of Phase 2 Strategies

Phase 2 strategies should be used with clients who are in the preparation or action stages. The primary purposes of Phase 2 strategies are to develop a behavior change plan and obtain a commitment to this plan. The strategies themselves are as follows: helping the client to develop a plan, communicating free choice, discussing the consequences of changing versus not changing, providing information and advice as requested, rolling with resistance, completing a change plan worksheet, recapitulating, and asking for a commitment. At the end of Phase 2, the client should have a plan to make one or more specific behavior changes, and should have expressed commitment to follow through on the plan. The next phase, Phase 3, involves following up with the client on his or her efforts.

Phase 3: Follow-Through Strategies

On the premise that the most difficult obstacle to making adaptive behavior changes is lack of motivation to change, and not a lack of information or skills, Phases 1 and 2 of MET strategies may be considered the most difficult and challenging for the clinician. Once motivation to change has been developed (Phase 1), and this motivation has been shaped into a clear plan of action and commitment to change (Phase 2), adaptive changes should occur. Phase 3, follow-up and follow-through, consists of only three basic strategies: reviewing progress, renewing motivation (if needed), and renewing commitment (if needed).

Reviewing Progress

The first thing to do in a follow-up session is to review the changes that have occurred, if any, since the last session. The clinician should review the specific commitment and plans made at the last session, and explore the progress that has been made toward the plan. Any and all approximations of progress should be praised and reinforced as much as possible. Although the occasional client appears annoyed with praise (making it necessary for the clinician to provide alternative creative reinforcers), most people appreciate acknowledgment of and praise for their efforts. It is appropriate to express such praise in as dramatic a way and for as long as the client and session will permit.

Renewing Motivation

An assessment of motivation to change may include a review of the behavioral indicants of motivation (as reflected in what the client has done since the last session), as well as the client's responses to questions concerning reasons for making or maintaining changes. Any indications of a decrease in motivation to change can be met with Phase 1 strategies to renew motivation, if needed.

Renewing Commitment

Finally, Phase 2 strategies may be used to refine the change plan worksheet (if needed) and obtain a commitment to follow through on the new plan.

WHAT IF MOTIVATIONAL ENHANCEMENT THERAPY DOES NOT WORK?

What should the clinician do if all efforts to increase a client's motivation to change and to solidify that motivation into a specific commitment fail? All clinicians have worked with clients in the precontemplative stage who continue to employ maladaptive coping strategies for pain management *and* appear to refuse to consider that what they are doing to manage the problem has a negative impact on their functioning. Such clients may not be interested in the MET approach, and become so annoyed with the MET strategies and questions that they refuse to make or keep appointments. Although ambivalence to change exists in all clients, some may simply not have the patience to work with a clinician to develop motivation and commitment to try a new approach. With such clients, I still seek to plant a seed of adaptive responding, even if only during a single interaction.

CLINICIAN: In the little time we have had to get to know each other, I hope you understand that I respect your right to make all decisions about how you will handle this problem. I hear you saying that you are convinced that another surgery has the best chances of making you feel better, and surgery is not something that we offer. If at some time in the future you become interested in considering other approaches to managing the pain, I want you to know that we are here to help you do that.

GENERAL SUMMARY AND CONCLUSIONS

The purpose of this chapter has been to introduce pain clinicians to the philosophy and strategies of MET. Although MET was initially developed to assist problem drinkers, this approach has been adapted to the treatment of other health-related problem behaviors (Miller & Rollnick, 1991). The MET approach appears to translate well to the treatment of pain problems, given the multiple motivational challenges that individuals who experience pain face in trying to develop and maintain adaptive responses to their problems. I have proposed that motivational problems may explain the lack of effectiveness of pain treatment programs for some individuals. Motivational problems may also explain relapse among some of the individuals for whom pain treatment was initially effective. For these individuals, the use of MET strategies may enhance the effectiveness of treatment among some, and perhaps prevent relapse among others.

Moreover, the MET approach is consistent with current multidisciplinary pain treatment practice (Loeser et al., 1990). Multidisciplinary treatment emphasizes the encouragement of pain coping responses over which the individual has control, such as exercise, appropriate pacing of activities, non-pain-contingent activity, and avoidance of responses that are outside of the direct control of the individual (e.g., pain-contingent opioid or sedative/hypnotic medication use, invasive procedures, and multiple medical tests). Successful outcome, and maintenance of gains once the person completes multidisciplinary treatment, thus depend on what the individual does or does not do.

MET, by emphasizing empathic listening, frequent client affirmations, gentle persuasion, and avoidance of argument, significantly reduces client resistance to clinician–client interactions. Clients whom others might have described as "bitter, angry, resentful, and resistant" are much easier to deal with when MET strategies are used. As a clinician working in this field, I have found that efforts to incorporate MET strategies into my interactions with clients have made my job much more pleasant; I do not have to fight with my clients any more.

It is possible that making the clinician's job more pleasant is the only impact that the use of MET strategies will have. However, I believe that this approach holds significant promise for increasing treatment effectiveness and clients' satisfaction with treatment, as well as for decreasing relapse. Models of empirical tests of MET strategies, comparing them to more traditional approaches, already exist in the literature (see Miller et al., 1993). Moreover, at least one research group has begun to explore the utility of the stages-of-change model with chronic pain patients (Snow et al., 1993). Pain clinicians and researchers have a long tradition of applying useful models and treatment strategies to ease the suffering of their clients. Perhaps MET will become one of these.

ACKNOWLEDGMENT

I am grateful to William R. Miller, Joan M. Romano, and Dawn Ehde for their extremely helpful comments on an earlier draft of this chapter.

REFERENCES

Affleck, G., Tennen, H., Pfeiffer, C., & Fifield, J. (1987). Appraisals of control and predictability in adapting to a chronic disease. *Journal of Personality and Social Psychology, 53*, 273–279.

Andrasik, F., & Holroyd, K. A. (1980). A test of specific and nonspecific effects in the biofeedback treatment of tension headache. *Journal of Consulting and Clinical Psychology, 48*, 575–586.

Bandura, A. (1977). Self-efficacy: Toward a unifying theory of behavioral change. *Psychological Review, 84*, 191–215.

Bem, D. J. (1967). Self-perception: An alternative interpretation of cognitive dissonance phenomena. *Psychological Review, 74*, 183–200.

Bergner, M., Bobbitt, R. A., Carter, W. B., & Gilson, B. S. (1981). The Sickness Impact Profile: Development and final revision of a health status measure. *Medical Care, 19*, 787–805.

Bien, T. H., Miller, W. R., & Boroughs, J. M. (1993). Motivational interviewing with alcohol outpatients. *Behavioural and Cognitive Psychotherapy, 21*, 347–350.

Brown, J. M., & Miller, W. R. (1993). Impact of motivational interviewing on participation and outcome in residential alcoholism treatment. *Psychology of Addictive Behaviors, 7*, 211–218.

Council, J. R., Ahern, D. K., Follick, M. J., & Kline, C. L. (1988). Expectancies and functional impairment in chronic low back pain. *Pain, 33*, 323–331.

Crisson, J. E., & Keefe, F. J. (1988). The relationship of locus of control to pain coping strategies and psychological distress in chronic pain patients. *Pain, 35*, 147–154.

DiClemente, C. C., & Prochaska, J. O. (1982). Self-change and therapy change of smoking behavior: A comparison of processes of change in cessation and maintenance. *Addictive Behaviors, 7*, 133–144.

Dolce, J. J., Crocker, M. F., & Doleys, D. M. (1986). Prediction of outcome among chronic pain patients. *Behaviour Research and Therapy, 24*, 313–319.

Festinger, L. (1957). *A theory of cognitive dissonance.* Stanford, CA: Stanford University Press.

Flor, H., Haag, G., & Turk, D. C. (1986). Long-term efficacy of EMG biofeedback for chronic rheumatic back pain. *Pain, 27*, 195–202.

Flor, H., Kerns, R. D., & Turk, D. C. (1987). The role of spouse reinforcement, perceived pain, and activity levels of chronic pain patients. *Journal of Psychosomatic Research, 31*, 251–259.

Flor, H., Turk, D. C., & Rudy, T. E. (1989). Relationship of pain impact and significant other reinforcement of pain behaviors: The mediating role of gender, marital status, and marital satisfaction. *Pain, 38*, 45–50.

Fordyce, W. E. (1976). *Behavioral methods for chronic pain and illness.* St. Louis, MO: C.V. Mosby.

France, R. D., Urban, B. J., & Keefe, F. J. (1984). Long-term use of narcotic analgesics in chronic pain. *Social Science in Medicine, 19*, 1379–1382.

Gordon, T. (1970). *Parent effectiveness training.* New York: Wyden.

Härkäpää, K., Mellin, G., Järvikoski, A., & Hurri, H. (1990). A controlled study on the outcome of inpatient and outpatient treatment of low back pain: Part III. Long term follow-up of pain, disability, and compliance. *Scandinavian Journal of Rehabilitation Medicine, 22*, 181–188.

Ivey, A. (1980). *Counseling and psychotherapy: Skills, theories and practice.* Englewood Cliffs, NJ: Prentice-Hall.

Jensen, M. P., Turner, J. A., & Romano, J. M. (1991). Self-efficacy and outcome expectancies: Relationship to chronic pain coping strategies and adjustment. *Pain, 44*, 263–269.

Jensen, M. P., Turner, J. A., & Romano, J. M. (1994). Correlates of improvement in multidisciplinary treatment of chronic pain. *Journal of Consulting and Clinical Psychology, 62*, 172–179.

Karoly, P. (1980). Person variables in therapeutic change and development. In P. Karoly & J. J. Steffen (Eds.), *Improving the long-term effects of psychotherapy* (pp. 195–261). New York: Gardner Press.

Keefe, F. J., Caldwell, D. S., Williams, D. A., Gil, K. M., Mitchell, D., Robertson, C., Martinez, S., Nunley, J., Beckman, J. C., Crisson, J. E., & Helms, M. (1990). Pain coping skills training in the management of osteoarthritis knee pain: A comparative study. *Behavior Therapy, 21,* 49–62.

Loeser, J. D., Seres, J. I., & Newman, R. I., Jr. (1990). Interdisciplinary, multimodal management of chronic pain. In J. J. Bonica, C. R. Chapman, W. E. Fordyce, & J. D. Loeser (Eds.), *The management of pain in clinical practice* (2nd ed., pp. 2107–2120). Philadelphia: Lea & Febiger.

Lorig, K., Chastain, R. L., Ung, E., Shoor, S., & Holman, H. R. (1989). Development and evaluation of a scale to measure perceived self-efficacy in people with arthritis. *Arthritis and Rheumatism, 32,* 37–44.

Mellin, G., Härkäpää, K., Hurri, H., & Järvikoski, A. (1990). A controlled study on the outcome of inpatient and outpatient treatment of low back pain: Part IV. Long term effects on physical measurements. *Scandinavian Journal of Rehabilitation Medicine, 22,* 189–194.

Miller, W. R. (1983a). Motivational interviewing with problem drinkers. *Behavioural Psychotherapy, 11,* 147–172.

Miller, W. R. (1983b). Motivation for treatment: A review with special emphasis on alcoholism. *Psychological Bulletin, 98,* 84–107.

Miller, W. R., & Baca, L. M. (1983). Two-year follow-up of bibliotherapy and therapist-directed controlled drinking training for problem drinkers. *Behavior Therapy, 14,* 441–448.

Miller, W. R., Benefield, R. G., & Tongigan, J. S. (1993). Enhancing motivation for change in problem drinking: A controlled comparison of two therapist styles. *Journal of Consulting and Clinical Psychology, 61,* 455–461.

Miller, W. R., & Jackson, K. A. (1995). *Practical psychology for pastors: Toward more effective counseling.* Englewood Cliffs, NJ: Prentice-Hall.

Miller, W. R., & Rollnick, S. (1991). *Motivational interviewing: Preparing people to change addictive behavior.* New York: Guilford Press.

Miller, W. R., Sovereign, R. G., & Krege, B. (1988). Motivational interviewing with problem drinkers: II. The drinker's check-up as a preventive intervention. *Behavioural Psychotherapy, 16,* 251–268.

Miller, W. R., Zweben, A., DiClemente, C. C., & Rychtarik, R. G. (1992). *Motivational enhancement therapy manual: A clinical research guide for therapists treating individuals with alcohol abuse and dependence* (DHHS Publication No. ADM 92–1894). Washington, DC: U.S. Government Printing Office.

Ockene, J., Ockene, I., & Kristeller, J. (1988). *The coronary artery smoking intervention study.* Worcester, MA: National Heart–Lung–Blood Institute.

Philips, H. C. (1988). Changing chronic pain experience. *Pain, 32,* 165–172.

Prochaska, J. O., & DiClemente, C. C. (1982). Transtheoretical therapy: Toward a more integrative model of change. *Psychotherapy: Theory, Research and Practice, 19,* 276–288.

Prochaska, J. O., & DiClemente, C. C. (1992). Stages of change in the modification of problem behaviors. In M. Hersen, R. N. Eisler, & P. M. Miller (Eds.), *Progress in behavior modification* (pp. 184–214). Sycamore, IL: Sycamore Press.

Prochaska, J. O., DiClemente, C. C., & Norcross, J. C. (1992a). In search of how people change: Applications to addictive behaviors. *American Psychologist, 47,* 1102–1114.

Prochaska, J. O., Norcross, J. C., Fowler, J. L., Follick, M. J., & Abrams, D. B. (1992b). Attendance and outcome in a work-site weight control program: Processes and stages of change as process and predictor variables. *Addictive Behaviors, 17,* 35–45.

Radloff, L. (1977). The CES-D scale: A self-report depression scale for research in the general population. *Applied Psychological Measurement, 1,* 385–401.

Rogers, C. R. (1957). The necessary and sufficient conditions for therapeutic personality change: *Journal of Consulting Psychology, 21,* 95–103.

Rogers, C. R. (1959). A theory of therapy, personality and interpersonal relationships as developed in the client-centered framework. In S. Koch (Ed.), *Psychology: The study of a science. Vol. 3. Formulations of the person and the social context* (pp. 184–256). New York: McGraw-Hill

Romano, J. M., Turner, J. A., Friedman, L. S., Bulcroft, R. A., Jensen, M. P., Hops, H., & Wright, S. F. (1992). Sequential analysis of chronic pain behaviors and spouse responses. *Journal of Consulting and Clinical Psychology, 60,* 777–782.

Sargent, J., Solbach, P., Coyne, L., Spohn, H., & Segerson, J. (1986). Results of a controlled, experimental, outcome study of nondrug treatments for the control of migraine headaches. *Journal of Behavioral Medicine, 9,* 291–323.

Schachter, S. (1982). Recidivism and self-cure of smoking and obesity. *American Psychologist, 37,* 436–444.

Schofferman, J. (1993). Long-term use of opioid analgesics for the treatment of chronic pain of nonmalignant origin. *Journal of Pain and Symptom Management, 8,* 279–288.

Snow, M. G., Kerns, R. D., Rosenberg, R., Jarvis, J. A., McCourt, M. S., & Prochaska, J. O. (1993). *Stages of change for chronic pain patients: Development of a questionnaire to assess readiness to change.* Poster presented at the 14th annual scientific sessions of the Society of Behavioral Medicine.

Turk, D. C. (1990) Customizing treatment for chronic pain patient: Who, what, and why. *Clinical Journal of Pain, 6,* 255–270.

Turk, D. C., Meichenbaum, D., & Genest, M. (1983). *Pain and behavioral medicine: A cognitive-behavioral perspective.* New York: Guilford Press.

Turk, D. C., & Rudy, T. E. (1991). Neglected topics in the treatment of chronic pain patients: Relapse, noncompliance, and adherence enhancement. *Pain, 44,* 5–28.

CHAPTER 5

Operant Conditioning with Chronic Pain

Back to Basics

Steven H. Sanders

Operant conditioning is an empirically based behavioral model of learning, which has evolved over the last 70 years into a major component of contemporary experimental *and* clinical psychology (see Lattal, 1992). Vast numbers of research and clinical articles regarding the basic principles and usage of operant conditioning have been written (for reviews, see Iverson, 1994; Goldfried & Davison, 1994; Lattal, 1992; Skinner, 1953, 1989). As any first-year psychology student is aware, the operant conditioning model is a basic type of learning paradigm for all forms of voluntary animal and human responses, as well as more automatic or generalized emotional responses (e.g., crying, withdrawal, facial grimacing, and fight-or-flight responses). Specifically, the theory of operant conditioning asserts that all overt behavioral responses are significantly influenced by their consequences and the surrounding context in which they are emitted.

In the late 1960s and through the mid-1970s, Fordyce and his colleagues (Fordyce, 1973, 1976; Fordyce, Fowler, & DeLateur, 1968) extended the tenets of operant conditioning to chronic pain. This extension was truly a revolutionary expansion and step forward in our understanding and treatment of patients suffering from chronic pain disorders. It ushered in an explosion of research and clinical application, which clearly established that operant conditioning concepts and procedures could be used with chronic pain patients to produce significant improvement (see Fordyce, 1988; Fordyce, Roberts, & Sternbach, 1985; Keefe, 1994; Keefe, Dunsmore, & Burnett, 1992; Linton, 1986; Linton, Melin, & Götestam, 1984; Sanders, 1979, 1985, 1989).

Given this impressive longitudinal evolution in the application of operant conditioning to chronic pain and the empirical demonstration of its value (with data continuing to accumulate; see Flor, Turk, & Rudy, 1989; Romano et al., 1992), the present chapter provides a review of this application. The chapter is not a comprehensive review of the scientific literature; rather, it describes the application of empirically based operant conditioning methods to chronic pain patients as this is currently being done in interdisciplinary clinical programs. Likewise, although the chapter focuses on the operant conditioning model of learning, this model should not be viewed and/or applied in isolation when one is trying to conceptualize or treat chronic pain patients. As noted some years ago (Sanders, 1985) and further delineated by contemporary learning theorists (see Staats, 1990, 1991), the learning/conditioning effects on patients with clinical pain are multileveled and interactional. They involve operant, respondent (Grant, 1964; Pavlov, 1927), and observational (Bandura, 1969, 1986) learning effects from antecedent and consequent stimulus conditions, often occurring in a social context. Take the following example:

> Consider the child who is taken to the doctor for an injection. It will be quite appropriate to conceptualize the injection, and simultaneous tissue damage and irritation as an unconditioned stimulus, subsequent crying by the child as a generalized reflex response and the hypodermic needle as a previously neutral stimulus. Thus, we have all the basic ingredients for a Pavlovian-B conditioning paradigm. It would not be long before the child engages in the crying behavior on seeing the now conditioned hypodermic needle stimulus. Likewise, let us assume that the crying behavior results in termination or delay of the injection. We now have all the elements for the acquisition of a conditioned escape response. Furthermore, let us assume that on the initial visit the child observes another child of the same age and sex crying prior to the injection which leads to a delay in the injection and social attention. This gives us the necessary elements for an observational learning paradigm. (Sanders, 1985, p. 60)

This example highlights the rather fluid and mixed learning effects across various conditioning models, including operant conditioning. Thus, all of the information offered on operant conditioning in this chapter needs to be viewed in light of its obvious interplay and combined effects with respondent and observational learning/conditioning models. (See Sanders, 1985, for more on this contemporary mixed/interactional learning model and chronic pain states.)

FUNDAMENTALS

Pain Behaviors

Overt "pain behaviors" and more adaptive overt "well behaviors" exhibited by chronic pain patients have been the focus of most research and clinical practice. Although there is ongoing controversy about the adequacy of concentrating just on overt behaviors (Craig, 1992; Keefe & Dunsmore, 1992a, 1992b; Merskey, 1992; Turk & Matyas, 1992), there is a general consensus that these behaviors are an important part of the clinical presentation.

From a practical standpoint, the most common and clinically relevant overt pain behaviors can be categorized as follows: (1) verbal pain responses, such as expressions of hurting, moaning, sighing, and expressions of pain through subjective intensity ratings; (2) nonverbal motor pain behaviors, such as limping, using a cane or brace, grimacing, and rubbing; (3) general activity level, sitting, and lying down; and (4) consumption of medications to control pain. The common defining quality of all pain behaviors is that they are "capable of being produced by relevant tissue damage or irritation" (Sanders, 1979, p. 252). The categories of overt pain behaviors just summarized are often exhibited by patients experiencing acute and chronic pain. Although they are certainly not exhaustive, they represent the most common behaviors observed. So-called "well behaviors" are typically just the opposite or reverse of the pain responses; they include such things as statements of reduced pain level, increase in general activity level, and increases in functional behaviors.

Although overt pain behaviors are the most obvious and clinically accessible, they are not the only responses occurring in someone experiencing clinical pain. Neurophysiological and cognitive/subjective responses are also present (Sanders, 1985, 1989). However, despite these other, more internal responses, the overt expressions of pain through behavior constitute the most salient and clinically relevant aspect of a patient's presentation. Without such overt expression, it would be extremely difficult to be aware of, much less to try and treat, clinical pain. Indeed, it might be argued that without overt pain behaviors there is no clinical pain. Although this is a rather extreme statement and does ignore the more internal responses seen with tissue damage and irritation, it does underscore the importance of overt pain behaviors in the constellation of clinical pain responses.

Reinforcement

The most fundamental paradigm within the operant conditioning model is that of "reinforcement" (for in-depth discussions, see Goldfried & Davison, 1994; Fordyce, 1976; Reynolds, 1968; Sanders, 1985, 1989; Skinner, 1953). Specifically, the reinforcement paradigm involves contingently following an overt behavior with the application or removal of something (consequence), which results in the maintenance and/or increase in the occurrence of the behavior. The *application* of something as a consequence is referred to as a "positive reinforcement paradigm," with the consequence typically being something the individual enjoys or derives pleasure from. The *removal* of something as a consequence is called a "negative reinforcement paradigm" and usually involves removal of an unpleasant experience or aversive situation. The negative reinforcement paradigm is also known as "escape/avoidance conditioning" (Grant, 1964; Sidman, 1962). Overt behavior in this paradigm occurs to permit the individual to escape or avoid the unpleasant experience. Escape/avoidance behavior is extremely resistant to change and typically requires some direct intervention.

The negative reinforcement paradigm is important in the development and maintenance of overt pain behaviors. For example, take the patient who has low back pain as the result of a lumbar disc herniation with radicular symptoms in the lower extremities. This patient has tried to ambulate independently and fallen down. We can assume that falling down and the ensuing increase in pain are rather unpleasant experiences. It is not uncommon for such a patient, particularly if falling down occurs more than once, to begin using a cane to help in ambulation. If the falling down with increase in pain is thus diminished and/or removed by using the cane (overt pain behavior), then it is quite likely that use of the cane will persist, because it is being negatively reinforced by supposedly reducing the occurrence of an unpleasant event. Likewise, this escape/avoidance behavior may well persist long past the actual need for the cane, because the patient has learned that such an overt pain behavior is "necessary" to avoid further falls and potential injury. As long as the patient continues to perceive that use of the cane prevents further falling, this behavior will persist indefinitely. Changing this overt pain behavior under this set of circumstances requires the specific application of operant conditioning techniques (Fordyce, Shelton, & Dundore, 1982).

This same overt pain behavior of using a cane may simultaneously be under the influence of a positive reinforcement paradigm. Let us assume that when the patient uses the cane, this results in the occurrence of increased social attention and in offers to assist from those around him or her. The patient may perceive these as positive social events (consequences), and they may be strong or potent enough to maintain and/or increase the patient's cane usage. The basic point here is that both reinforcement paradigms, as well as other learning principles to be discussed subsequently, can and often do operate simultaneously to influence overt pain behaviors.

Punishment

"Punishment" is a conditioning paradigm whereby an overt behavior is contingently followed by an aversive/unpleasant experience (consequence). Typically, if the aversive/unpleasant experience or consequence is strong enough and applied consistently, the overt behavior that precedes it will be reduced in frequency and/or will cease altogether under certain conditions. The difference between an unpleasant or aversive experience in this conditioning paradigm and one in the negative reinforcement paradigm is that the aversive experience is *applied* following the overt behavior with punishment. As with reinforcers, there are a host of possible punishments for a given person; however, the most common ones include social ridicule, interpersonal discord, stress, loss of social attention or recognition, loss of material possessions or resources, and the experience of pain (nociception) itself. One of the most frequently used types of punishments in changing overt behavior is the removal of enjoyable/pleasurable events contingent upon emission of a specific overt behavior.

The punishment paradigm can often be seen in operation with pain patients regarding the general reduction in overt well behaviors (e.g., walking and working). At the acute phase of an injury involving tissue damage and irritation, such behaviors as walking and working may result in a marked increase in nociception (punishment). Thus, these behaviors may be reduced and/or may cease completely.

Extinction

The systematic removal of the contingent relationship between an overt behavior and its positive or negative consequences is called "extinction." This paradigm typically results in a change in the overt behavior. If contingent positive or negative reinforcers are removed, the overt behavior usually shows a reduction. On the other hand, if contingent punishment is removed, the overt behavior may show an increase. As already implied, the major exception to this extinction effect is seen with learned escape/avoidance behavior. Even when the contingent relationship between the overt behavior and its consequence is removed, escape/avoidance behavior tends to persist indefinitely.

From the earlier example of using a cane to ambulate, it is fairly easy to see why escape/avoidance behavior is so resistant to an extinction effect. If the overt pain behavior enables the patient to successfully escape and then to avoid a particular negative consequence, the patient never "learns" that the aversive or negative consequence may not actually occur upon failing to engage in the avoidant overt pain behavior. Once true avoidance behavior has been conditioned, the actual presence of an unpleasant experience or aversive consequence is no longer needed. To change such behavior, it is often necessary to prevent or limit the avoidant response, so that the individual can learn that this does not result in the occurrence of the aversive/negative consequence (Sidman, 1962).

Discriminative Stimulus Control

There are abundant data showing that overt behaviors are influenced not only by their consequences, but also by the context or environmental surroundings in which they occur. Specifically, as Skinner (1953) and countless others have demonstrated, various stimuli in one's environment can acquire discriminative or cue-like properties. Given repeated pairings with a target behavior and a contingent consequence, these stimuli come to alert or signal the individual that emission of a given overt behavior is likely to result in a certain consequence. The influence these discriminative stimuli have on overt behavior can be quite strong; many behaviors are directed by these cues that signal the presence of various consequences for certain overt behavior.

For example, let's go back to the patient with low back pain patient who uses a cane to walk. It would not be surprising to find that this patient engages in this behavior of cane usage when out of the home or visiting the doctor's office, but does not do so (or does so less often) when in his or her home. In other words, being in or out of the home is a discriminative stimulus condition for use of the cane when walking. Likewise, take the patient who is using pain medication. This overt behavior may be under rather strong discriminative stimulus control regarding the time of day. That is, the use of pain medications may be much more likely at certain times of day (discriminative stimuli) than at others. In addition, it is not unusual to observe that various other overt pain behaviors show significant changes in rate, depending upon the presence of certain important individuals or the topic of discussion (Bayer, Baer, & Early, 1991; Block, Kremer, & Gaylor, 1980; Romano et al., 1992; Schwartz, Slater, & Birchler, 1994; White & Sanders, 1986).

Conditions for Effective Usage

For operant conditioning methods to be effective, certain "conditions" are typically needed. It is important to identify specific overt behaviors and effective positive or negative consequences for these behaviors. Likewise, these consequences need to be applied consistently and contingently upon the occurrence of the targeted overt behaviors. It is also advisable to administer consequences as soon as possible after a given overt behavior occurs. Although immediate application is preferable, it is not critical, as long as the patient is aware that administration of the consequence is contingent upon emission of the target overt behavior.

The application of shaping to the occurrence of or change in a given overt behavior is also quite important. "Shaping" refers to systematically reinforcing successive approximations of a given overt behavior until the complete response is seen (Reynolds, 1968). An example of shaping with a pain patient is gradually reinforcing more and more distance walked without the aid of a cane until the patient reaches the desired distance. If the patient is not reinforced until this upper-level distance is reached, it is very likely that he or she will never achieve it. This idea of rewarding parts or approximations of the desired behavior is a very important and often overlooked condition for effective usage of the operant model.

Operant methods should also be combined with other learning-based and behavioral techniques for maximum effectiveness. This is clearly the case in the treatment of chronic pain patients, where operant techniques are routinely combined with such behavioral procedures as relaxation training and modeling.

Functional Behavioral Analysis

A basic process of operant conditioning is the systematic analysis of overt behaviors and their controlling antecedent (discriminative) and consequent (reinforcing or punishing) stimulus conditions. Specifically, this involves identifying relevant overt target behaviors or the lack or absence thereof, discriminative stimuli, and consequent reinforcers or punishments that can be applied to influence the occurrence of the target behaviors. This information is commonly obtained through direct observation of the patient, behavioral assessment questionnaires, and/or self-monitoring by the patient. A thorough review of behavioral assessment methods and detailed functional behavioral analysis techniques is beyond the scope of this chapter. The reader is referred to a number of excellent references for a better understanding and review of such techniques and approaches in general, and as they might be applied to chronic pain patients in particular (Fordyce, 1976; Goldfried & Davison, 1994; Karoly, 1985; Keefe, 1994; Keefe & Williams, 1992; Lake, 1981; Linton et al., 1984; Sanders, 1979, 1985;).

Table 5.1 summarizes common overt pain behaviors seen with chronic pain patients, as well as various antecedent and consequent stimulus conditions that have often been found to influence and/or maintain these behaviors. Obviously, the table does not contain an exhaustive set of stimuli and behaviors; however, it is representative. Although the behaviors and stimuli outlined in the table are typical, they should not be assumed to exist in all patients. It is always advisable to determine their presence or absence on an individual basis, as well as to identify any other relevant and clinically important stimuli or behaviors.

APPLICATION OF OPERANT CONDITIONING TO CHRONIC PAIN PATIENTS

Why?

The question of why to use operant conditioning techniques with chronic pain patients, or the related question of why to focus on overt behaviors when dealing with a supposedly internal, subjective experience such as clinical pain, needs further discussion. Other than the obvious answer that operant conditioning methods have been clearly demonstrated to produce significant improvement (Fordyce, 1976; Geiger, Todd, Clarke, Miller, & Kori, 1992; Linton, 1986; Sanders, 1983a), recent studies underscore some other, more broad-based reasons for the use of operant conditioning with overt pain behaviors.

Studies have shown that although chronic pain patients who exhibit high rates of overt pain behaviors can benefit from interdisciplinary pain rehabilitation, less improvement is noted (Connally & Sanders, 1991). Also, unless pain behaviors are reduced, they constitute a risk factor for failure to return to work following a low back injury (Sanders, 1995). Operant conditioning is usually needed to accomplish a reduction in pain behav-

TABLE 5.1 Common Overt Pain Behaviors and Controlling Stimuli with Chronic Pain Patients

Antededent (discriminative) stimuli	Overt pain behaviors	Consequent (reinforcing) stimuli
Tissue damage, nociception	Moaning, sighing	Reduce/avoid: stressors,
Worksite	Pain complaints, crying	nociception, drug withdrawal,
Bed, stairs	Using cane/brace	anxiety/fear, more injury
Employer, spouse	Limping, guarding	Increase: social attention,
Doctor, lawyer	Rubbing, grimacing	economic gain
Car	Lying down, sitting	
Time of day	Taking medications	
Sexual arousal		
Movement		

iors. Likewise, studies have found that there is a poor relationship between overt activity level and subjective pain intensity in patients with chronic low back pain (Linton, 1985). Thus, those clinical interventions that focus on merely reducing subjective pain intensity and nociception do little to ensure a reciprocal increase in general activity level and other well behaviors. In addition, research has demonstrated significant differences in overt behavior and function among low back pain patients with similar physical findings from different countries and cultures (Sanders et al., 1992). This suggests rather potent and important sociocultural/environmental factors at work in need of better identification and possible control.

These data highlight the need for specific intervention with overt pain behaviors and the importance of such intervention in maximizing recovery, as well as the real possibility that major social and environmental factors influence overt pain behavior within and between cultures. Thus, operant conditioning principles have a fundamental place and role in the understanding and treatment of chronic pain patients.

When, Where, and How?

When

Operant conditioning is best applied when the following conditions have been satisfied: (1) Overt pain behaviors are present; (2) salient positive and negative reinforcers and/or punishments can be identified; (3) there is sufficient environmental control that antecedent and consequent stimulus conditions can be contingently applied; (4) the patient is not experiencing any major non-drug-related cognitive/learning impairment; and (5) the patient is willing to participate actively.

Table 5.2 outlines those basic conditions suggesting that an overt pain behavior is at least partially influenced by operant conditioning (Fordyce, 1976; Linton et al., 1984; Sanders, 1985, 1989). For a clinician to draw the conclusion that operant conditioning effects are significant, at least three of the basic indications outlined in Table 5.2 should be present. If all six are present, there is a very high probability that operant conditioning has influenced and is influencing overt pain behavior. Even if the basic indications are not present or not that obvious for a given patient, operant conditioning may still be quite appropriate in efforts to increase more adaptive well behaviors, such as walking without a cane, exercising, smiling/laughing, and working. Likewise, and as noted in Table 4.1, the presence of basic indicators in Table 5.2 does not exclude the real possibility that a patient may also be experiencing nociception from ongoing pathophysiology. However, even if nociception is present, operant conditioning techniques can be applied to change overt pain and well behaviors.

TABLE 5.2. Basic Indications for Operant Conditioning Effects in Chronic Pain Patients

1. Overt pain behavior is chronic (3 months or longer).
2. Overt pain behavior occurs as a function of the environment, time of day, or person(s) present (e.g., in the clinic, at night, with spouse present).
3. Overt pain behavior is acknowledged by others (family, friends, etc.).
4. Overt pain behavior is sometimes followed by positive or negative reinforcers.
5. Overt pain behavior is in excess of known physical findings.
6. Patient exhibits significant concern about increased pain with increased physical activity or return to work.

As a general rule, operant conditioning methods are relevant and useful with *most* chronic pain patients (with or without nociception), either to reduce one or more overt pain behaviors or to facilitate increases in those more adaptive well behaviors that will improve a patient's overall physical and emotional condition. Obviously, there are exceptions to this point. For example, in patients suffering from a terminal disease process such as cancer or AIDS, chronic pain may be part of the symptom complex during the final stages. However, even in these terminal situations, operant conditioning methods can be successfully applied at the earlier stages of the disease.

Where

Traditionally, much operant conditioning took place within a controlled, inpatient environment. Determining whether there is adequate environmental and stimulus control present for operant conditioning principles to be contingently applied can be difficult at times. For those patients showing poor cooperation and/or the presence of very potent controlling conditions in the natural environment, an inpatient setting can be the most effective venue. However, it is becoming increasingly clear that operant conditioning can be successfully applied on an outpatient basis with the cooperation of the patient and family. A thorough functional behavioral analysis will typically provide an answer to this question. (The case example provided later in this chapter illustrates this process.)

Thus, there are no hard and fast rules regarding the settings where operant conditioning techniques can be effectively applied. This is even true for the overt pain behavior of medication usage. Although those patients presenting with excessive pain medication (opioid) usage and physiological dependency are often treated within an inpatient setting, more and more of these patients are being successfully treated as outpatients. (Again, the subsequent case example illustrates this.) With the introduction of more stringent monitoring laws regarding administration of opioids in many states, it has become somewhat easier for treating physicians to maintain control over medication application on an outpatient basis. Thus, even reduction in pain medication usage in a physiologically dependent patient can be quite feasible in an outpatient setting, provided that frequent monitoring and contact take place. For those patients also showing excessive use of other medications such as sedative/hypnotics or alcohol, which are more readily available, initial inpatient application of operant methods to reduce this behavior and detoxify the patients is often required. In practice, however, inpatient intervention to apply operant conditioning techniques to pain and well behaviors (including medication consumption) in most well-organized interdisciplinary rehabilitation programs currently accounts for a very small percentage of patients seen.

How

Table 5.3 summarizes basic recommendations for applying operant conditioning to chronic pain patients as discussed in the existing literature and currently practiced (Fordyce, 1976; Keefe, 1994; Roberts, 1986; Sanders, 1989).

As the table notes, the first step in assessing a patient for treatment with operant conditioning is a functional behavioral analysis. This should be accompanied by identification of the extent of the patient's pathophysiology, which can be quite important in setting realistic upper limits for overall physical function. It is typically a good idea to have patients monitor their own behavior, at least for time standing and walking ("up-

TABLE 5.3. Summary of Recommendations for Applying Operant Conditioning to Chronic Pain Patients

Assessment

1. Perform a functional behavioral analysis on patient to identify relevant overt pain and well behaviors, controlling antecedent and consequent stimuli, and level of patient and family cooperation.
2. Identify the extent of physical pathology present, and incorporate it in setting realistic goals for behavioral change.
3. Continue to monitor amount of behavioral change during treatment, to allow meaningful decisions about effects.

Treatment

1. Use extinction to reduce overt pain behaviors (with response prevention if these are escape/avoidance behaviors), plus positive and negative reinforcement to increase well behaviors.
2. For reducing medication-taking behavior, use time-contingent delivery while reducing the amount of medication per dose or day.
3. For increasing general activity level, uptime, and physical exercise, use initial baseline levels and gradually increase these at preset amounts (determined with patient cooperation), with abundant reinforcement.
4. Use the concept of shaping or gradual change for well behaviors whenever possible.
5. Once behavioral increases are occurring consistently, slowly reduce the application of positive and/or negative reinforcement to a less frequent, varying schedule of about 50% occurrence for a given behavior.
6. Apply operant methods to *each* relevant overt pain and well behavior across as many different environmental conditions and people as posible, to maximize generalization and discriminative stimulus efforts.
7. Eliminate or reduce as many external controlling stimulus conditions maintaining overt pain behaviors outside the treatment environment as possible.
8. Enlist the cooperation of the patient and family whenever possible to directly apply operant conditioning methods to change behavior.
9. Give operant methods time to work, *and* be sure to follow patients for at least 3 to 6 months after active treatment to facilitate maintenance of change.
10. Use operant conditioning methods in concert with other behavioral/psychological and physical/medical treatments (e.g., relaxation, physical therapy, antidepressant and anti-inflammatory medications, and conservative medical procedures such as trigger point injections) within an interdisciplinary treatment approach.

time"), exercise repetitions and walking time and/or duration, use of medications, and subjective pain intensity levels. There are a number of well-seasoned, clinically tested self-monitoring formats available (see Fordyce, 1976; Keefe, 1994; Keefe et al., 1992; Karoly, 1985). For the most part, these involve having the patient keep some kind of diary of these various responses on an hourly to daily basis. Behaviors can be counted over time to compute rates; pain medication usage is usually monitored by type and amount of medication consumed over time, and subjective pain intensity levels are generally assessed via rating or visual analogue scales (Price, Bush, Long, & Hawkins, 1994; Steedman et al., 1992).

It is also advisable to have some more direct observation of relevant pain and well behaviors. Although there are several sophisticated and highly structured observational and/or automated recording systems (Craig, 1992; Keefe, Crisson, & Trainor, 1987; Sanders, 1980, 1983b) these are not typically used that often in clinical practice because of their complexity and/or cost. Thus, most direct behavioral observational systems employ a rather straightforward checklist filled out at various times by members of the clinical staff and/or the patient's family. Several independent observational rating scales to consider include the University of Alabama at Birmingham Pain Behavior Scale (Richards, Nepomuceno, Riles, & Suer, 1982) or the Pain Behavior Checklist (Turk, Wack, & Kerns, 1985). Whenever possible, direct observational methods should be administered at least at the beginning, middle, and end of active treatment.

Table 5.3's recommendations for treatment with operant conditioning should be considered generic and applicable across various types of chronic painful conditions. The first recommendation includes the use of response prevention with those overt pain behaviors that are escape/avoidance behaviors. Specifically, to continue with the example of the patient who uses a cane to ambulate, this may require asking the patient to walk short distances without the cane. In other words, the use of the cane behavior is prevented in a controlled fashion to allow the patient to experience and learn that walking without a cane is possible—and, more importantly, that using the cane is not a necessary behavior to prevent or escape increased pain and/or falling down.

In regard to Recommendation 2 for treatment, clinical observations and research have demonstrated that taking pain medications is also typically an escape/avoidance response. To change it, a form of response prevention (time-contingent application of medications) is often needed to eliminate the contingency between taking the medication and escape/avoidance of nociception and/or physical withdrawal symptoms (Bertzen & Götestam, 1987; White & Sanders, 1985). Although it is certainly possible for some patients to reduce their medication usage without changing administration to a time-contingent schedule, such a schedule is advisable most of the time.

Decades of basic and clinical research on the application of reinforcement schedules have consistently demonstrated that intermittent schedules of reinforcement produce stronger and longer-lasting behavioral patterns. Thus, as Recommendation 5 indicates, it is advisable not to reinforce desirable well behaviors continuously after they have been established. In addition, an intermittent schedule of reward is also much more consistent with natural environmental circumstances, where a behavior is rarely reinforced each time it occurs.

Recommendation 7 in Table 5.3 highlights the importance of trying to change those naturally occurring contingencies that may be maintaining certain pain behaviors and inhibiting well responses. These include such things as economic reinforcers, social attention and reinforcement at home, and/or escape/avoidance of work responsibilities and issues. This often requires involving family members, employers, coworkers, and the patient's attorney if there is one. Although it is not always possible to involve all these various individuals directly, the clinician should do so whenever it is feasible.

Recommendation 8 underscores the need to evaluate and enlist the cooperation of the patient. Contemporary operant conditioning theory clearly recognizes the possibility for self-application of techniques (Sanders, 1989). Thus, the idea of patients' reinforcing themselves for engaging in more appropriate behavior is certainly not only feasible but desirable. Such approaches are usually more appropriate toward the middle to end of initial intervention and during follow-up, when the patient is less likely to be in an environment rich with ongoing reinforcers.

The final recommendation in Table 5.3 again emphasizes the need for operant conditioning to be applied in the context of an interdisciplinary rehabilitation approach (Polatin, Chapter 12, this volume; Sanders & Brena, 1990). Without such an interface as a means of offering patients more traditional medical and physical interventions and instruction, operant conditioning methods in and of themselves are very difficult to apply across the spectrum of chronic pain patients.

CASE EXAMPLE

This section describes a patient treated in an interdisciplinary pain rehabilitation program, in which operant conditioning and other behavioral/psychological techniques and methods (e.g., relaxation training, bibliotherapy, modeling, stress management training) are concurrently applied. The intent of the example is not merely to demonstrate the efficacy of operant conditioning methods, but rather to show how such methods can be effectively used within an interdisciplinary treatment protocol.

Identification and Chief Complaint

The patient was a 46-year-old married black male with a high school education, presenting with a 1-year history of low back pain radiating into both lower extremities. He had sustained two separate lifting–twisting injuries to the low back over a 6-month interval on his job as a foreman in a textile plant. His back pain was described as a bilateral aching, grabbing sensation in the lumbar region, with some secondary shooting pains and residual dysesthesia in the lower extremities. He rated his pain at a 90% intensity level on a 0- to 100-point visual analogue scale, and indicated that the pain seemed to increase as his day progressed. A recent medical diagnostic workup (including magnetic resonance imaging and evaluation by a physician specializing in pain medicine) revealed a bulging disc at lumbar vertebrae 4–5 without herniation, multiple myofascial trigger points in the lumbar region, and some secondary sensory loss in the lower extremities consistent with episodic nerve fiber irritation at lumbar vertebrae 4–5. No significant muscle weakness was noted in the lower extremities, nor were there any other major neurological findings. Aside from his complaints of back pain, the patient was in good health. At the time of his referral, he was not working and on workers' compensation. He was thinking of applying for Social Security disability benefits as well.

Functional Behavioral Analysis

The patient's overt pain behaviors were significant and included marked gait distortions, use of a cane, guarding, grimacing, constant verbal complaints of pain, complaints of inability to function at home and work, ongoing expressions of fears that increased activity would injure him and/or significantly increase pain, requests for and consumption of pain medications at an increasing rate, and prolonged lying down and sitting at home. (Note: The overt pain behaviors and controlling stimuli were identified through an interview with the patient, observation of the patient during the initial evaluation process and physical exam, and an interview with the patient's wife.) The total time spent standing and walking ("uptime"), as recorded by the patient and corroborated by his wife, equaled less than 2 hours per day.

The patient's overt pain behaviors were consistently influenced by the following antecedent stimuli: movement (standing and walking behavior), presence of the patient's wife, being in the home environment, presence of a health care professional, riding in a car, any discussion of return to work or increase in activity, and presumably secondary nociception from myofascial dysfunction and mild nerve root irritation in the lumbar region. Controlling consequent stimuli included reduction and avoidance of the following: nociception, fear and anxiety concerning increased pain and additional injury, possible side effects from drug withdrawal, and physical demands and stress reported in his current work. Consequent stimuli also included an increase in social attention (the patient's wife attended to most of his needs and provided episodic low back massage) and sustained economic gains (the patient was continuing to receive 60% of his original salary and benefits, which were the only source of income for the family).

The patient was asked to begin daily monitoring of his uptime, general activity level, subjective pain intensity, and medication intake on an hourly basis throughout his participation in the pain rehabilitation program. He and his wife both expressed interest in making an effort to change his current behavioral pattern toward improved functioning and ability to manage his pain effectively with less medication. In addition, contact with the patient's employers revealed that they were willing to work with the patient on making the necessary job modifications to enable him to resume full-time work.

It is apparent that this patient was exhibiting all six of the basic indications for operant conditioning effects listed in Table 5.2. Moreover, additional psychological behavioral data gathered during the initial evaluation revealed that this patient was exhibiting very poor understanding regarding the nature and extent of his pathophysiology. He was also experiencing some depressive symptoms, including increasing feelings of sadness and indecision, poor appetite, and disturbed sleep. Although the symptoms had not yet reached a level warranting a diagnosis of major depression, this was certainly a distinct possibility as time progressed if the patient was left untreated.

Operant Conditioning Treatment

Given the initial willingness of the patient and his wife to work toward change, treatment was initiated on an outpatient basis for 3 days a week (6 to 8 hours per day). The patient participated for 15 treatment days over 6 weeks. His wife was also seen on a weekly basis; she received information regarding appropriate responses to the patient's overt pain behaviors, as well as social reinforcement support to maintain her behavioral changes.

All of the patient's pain behaviors were put on extinction regarding any social reinforcement in the treatment center or at home. Specifically, staff members and the patient's wife were instructed to observe various pain behaviors but not to offer any assistance or social attention upon their occurrence. In contrast, overt well behaviors (i.e., walking without a cane, general activity and uptime, verbal expressions of feeling better or doing better, increase in exercise tolerance, overall reductions in the quantity of pain medications consumed, and any verbal expressions of interest in returning to work) were consistently followed by social attention and praise. To ensure adequate reduction in pain medication usage, the patient was shifted to time-contingent delivery, with gradual reduction in daily amounts over the course of the 6-week period (see Hare & Lipman, 1990, for details on medication reduction protocols).

Passive physical therapy interventions (massage, ultrasound, heat/ice, etc.) and medical procedures (trigger point injections) were first determined to be clinically appropriate for the patient, and were then initially administered on a noncontingent basis to establish their effects. If the patient obtained some temporary reduction in subjective pain intensity, they were repeated on a limited basis, contingent upon the patient's consistently participating in an active physical therapy exercise program that would lead to an increase in exercise tolerance, general activity level, and uptime. It might appear at first that such a contingent application of these physical treatment modalities would constitute unethical withholding of care. However, the research literature indicates that just the opposite is true. Although these treatments can have some temporary pain-relieving effects, there is no empirical support for their long-term benefit with chronic pain patients when they are used in isolation. In contrast, there are data supporting the use of these methods in combination with active rehabilitation emphasizing increased physical functioning (Sanders & Brena, 1993). Thus, applying passive physical therapy or trigger point injections in isolation or not contingent upon a patient's active participation in a rehabilitation program leading to increased physical function would actually be inconsistent with the available scientific literature.

The escape/avoidance pain behaviors of walking with a cane and verbal expressions of fear regarding increased pain and injury with increased activity and/or return to work required additional interventions. The patient was started on a very low-level walking program (in concert with other physical therapy interventions—see below), in which he would walk on an indoor track measuring one-eighth of a mile for a preset number of three laps. This was based upon the patient's initial baseline data regarding his walking tolerance. Every other lap, the patient was to ambulate without the cane. Given his initial baseline data, this equaled half a lap before tolerance was noted. The amount of ambulation without the cane was set so as not to exceed this baseline tolerance and to allow the patient to succeed comfortably. Each lap completed was followed by encouragement and social praise from the staff; completion of half a lap without the use of the cane was immediately followed by additional praise and 2 minutes of rest. With completion of three laps, the patient was given additional praise and a 10-minute massage with ultrasound. If the patient complained of wanting to stop or of not being able to complete his walking with or without his cane, this was acknowledged in a neutral fashion, and he was instructed to continue walking to the preset criteria. In addition to the walking program, the patient engaged in other strength- and flexibility-building exercises at a preset level; reinforced gradual increase (shaping) of this behavior was employed.

All staff members and the wife consistently applied social reinforcers/praise any time they saw the patient walking without the cane, in as many environments as possible. Likewise, within discussion groups the patient's increase in well behaviors was acknowledged and praised. The patient was also started on a gradually increasing activity assignment schedule for standing and walking and for general activity outside the home. He was given assignments such as making one trip to the grocery store for at least 1 hour twice a week and not using the cane for ambulation while in the store. Successful completion of this behavior was followed by praise from his wife and the health care professionals, and by application of an enjoyable activity or event from a list that the patient had constructed himself. These activities included such things as having a favorite meal, watching a certain enjoyable TV program, listening to music, and having his wife administer a massage.

Furthermore, the patient was exposed to ambulating without a cane up and down stairs, riding and then driving in an automobile, and engaging in task-specific work behaviors simulated within the treatment center. Each of these behaviors was started at a very low level within the patient's capability, and was reinforced with praise, rest, and physical treatment contingent upon completion; again, a shaping concept was employed. Throughout this, overt pain behaviors were acknowledged in a neutral fashion but did not receive any consistent/contingent reinforcement. During the course of treatment, the patient was also instructed to visit his worksite with his wife, and to spend at least an hour interacting with coworkers without the use of a cane if possible. The wife, along with the patient, was instructed to provide information to the coworkers and employers regarding the nature and extent of his progress. With the patient's permission, this information was also communicated by the pain rehabilitation center staff to his employers prior to the patient's first visit. Information regarding possible job options and return to work was communicated by the patient and reinforced by the employers. Some of the specific actions required to engage in a modification of the patient's original job were incorporated into the patient's physical activity at the center and systematically reinforced. Approximately midway through the patient's course of treatment, reinforcers were reduced slowly so that the patient was not receiving these with each occurrence of a more appropriate well behavior. By the end of initial treatment, the level of reinforcement was gradually reduced to 50% of the original level.

Other Behavioral/Psychological and Physical/Medical Treatment

Concurrently with operant conditioning, the patient also participated in ongoing educational and supportive groups focused on providing basic information about the nature and extent of his injury and probable recovery, as well as social support and modeling effects from other patients. He received training in relaxation methods as well (see Arena & Blanchard, Chapter 8, this volume). Instruction in physical exercises that could significantly increase his overall muscle function and stamina was provided. Likewise, he participated in water exercises to enhance his ability to move without increased pain and to further reduce his concerns and fears about general activity. The patient was also started on nonsteroidal anti-inflammatory medication and antidepressant medication. As already noted, he received limited passive physical therapy modalities and a series of five sets of trigger point injections, contingent upon his active participation in physical rehabilitation leading to a gradual increase in overall activity. Possible vocational options were identified and outlined, involving both his existing work and other work skills. As noted earlier, the emphasis was on returning the patient to some kind of modified job within his current work environment.

Outcome and Follow-Up

At the conclusion of initial treatment, the patient was exhibiting significant improvement in his overall function and stamina: an average daily uptime equaling 5 hours; total elimination of his cane-walking behavior; a 50% increase in overall muscle strength and stamina, as measured by exercise level; reduction in pain medication usage to one 5-mg Lortab tablet twice a week; consistent demonstration of job-specific activity completion in the center for at least 2 consecutive treatment days; a 25% reduction in his subjective pain intensity rating; and improvement in overall mood. He was discharged on a home program of exercise, walking, anti-inflammatory and antidepressant medications, and resumption of modified work duties for an initial trial of 4 weeks. He was followed up every 2 weeks during the initial 6 weeks after completion of treatment to review his status, continue to reinforce change, and make any revisions in daily routine necessary. The patient's wife was seen on a monthly basis during this time to continue providing reinforcement and instruction regarding her efforts.

The patient was able to resume modified work successfully during the initial 4-week trial, and he continued in this capacity at six months after initial treatment. His medication usage remained stable, including continued use of Lortab during the first 4 weeks of follow-up, and only intermittent use thereafter (approximately one tablet twice a month during the first 6 months). Pain behaviors remained low, with continued maintenance of appropriate well behaviors.

At a 1-year follow-up, the patient had maintained his behavioral changes; however, he was not working because his plant had closed. His workers' compensation case had been settled prior to this, and he was actively engaged in trying to find other work. No signs of significant mood disturbance were found, with the exception of an understandable increase in distress about finding another job. The patient was encouraged to continue his successful maintenance of appropriate well behaviors, and was able to secure another job within his physical capabilities within 3 months. His antidepressant medication was discontinued slowly over the next 3 months, with the patient being seen at 3-month intervals during his second year of follow-up. He did experience episodic increases in his overall pain during this time; with some residual support and maintenance of his home exercise and activity program, he was able to reduce his pain effectively and maintain functional behavior. The total cost for this interdisciplinary pain rehabilitation, including follow-up, was $7,500 (in 1992 dollars).

Comments

The case just presented is not ideal; it illustrates that interdisciplinary pain rehabilitation (with or without operant conditioning) does not ensure that a patient will live "happily ever after." Rather, such intervention with operant conditioning as a basic component tends to increase the patient's ability to engage in those behaviors necessary to manage pain and function more effectively, in spite of the presence of residual chronic nociception. To a large extent, what is done is to help the patient change his or her environment and behavior sufficiently to sustain more adaptive responses (both physical and emotional) and to manage a chronic condition successfully.

Likewise, it is important to remember that the clinical application of operant conditioning does not necessarily require a research-grade demonstration of cause and effect between behaviors and controlling stimuli. If a contingent relationship can be identified and the conditions noted in Table 4.2 are met, it can be assumed that there is at least a potential cause-and-effect relationship. The actual research literature has clearly demonstrated these effects already; there is no need in clinical practice to repeat this. There is a need, however, to monitor each patient's responses. If no change results from the application of operant conditioning in concert with other interventions, then the treatment plan must be revised and reassessed. Operant conditioning with or without other interventions is not a cure-all, and should not be blindly applied and continued if changes in specific behaviors are not forthcoming within a reasonable amount of time. Sound clinical judgment, in keeping with the available data base, must always be applied.

CONCLUSIONS

From the present chapter, it should be clear that operant conditioning methods have become a fundamental part of successful pain rehabilitation for chronic pain patients. This is particularly true in regard to increasing patients' physical functioning (Fordyce, 1988; Keefe, 1994; Sanders, 1989). Given this, health care professionals who work with chronic pain patients are strongly urged to incorporate the basic operant conditioning methods outlined in this chapter into their treatment protocols.

A case can be made for a dominant focus on reduction in nociception and subjective pain intensity as a primary goal of pain rehabilitation. However, in today's health care market, such a primary goal is simply inadequate. Given the amount of money being spent on health care, virtually all of the major consumer groups (employers, insurance carriers, and state and federal government, as well as patients) are defining improvement in physical functioning and reduction in health care usage as major treatment outcome goals. Operant conditioning methods are fundamental to achieving these goals. Thus, although operant conditioning may seem less exciting than other psychological interventions (such as rational–emotive therapy, hypnosis, or biofeedback), it is a critical part of today's effective pain rehabilitation. The reader is strongly urged not to forget the basics of operant conditioning as empirically demonstrated in regard to chronic pain since the late 1960s.

It is also important that clinical psychologists not become complacent in their use of operant conditioning with chronic pain patients. There is a need for continuing research and continuing delineation of limits. It is possible to apply these techniques with chronic pain patients on an outpatient basis. However, as has already been shown on a limited basis (Cott, Anchel, Goldberg, Fabich, & Parkinson, 1990; Gauthier, Cote, & French, 1994; Nash & Holroyd, 1992), it may also be quite possible to extend operant conditioning and other behavioral strategies into the natural home environments of patients. Likewise, the more broad-based sociocultural/environmental factors (e.g., political and economic policies, medical community practices, cultural and religious practices, etc.) that influence overt pain and well behaviors need a great deal more research attention (Sanders et al., 1992). Indeed, in cases where these sociocultural/environmental factors and contingencies are extremely powerful, the application of operant conditioning and other behavioral techniques to chronic pain may have few if any prolonged effects.

Thus, the use of operant conditioning techniques with chronic pain patients is far from simple, either in concept or in practice. With proper attention and research, however, the future should be rich in opportunities to further understand this basic learning model and extend it into the natural environment, as well as to employ it at the cultural and societal levels. Such expanded application has the real potential to decrease the occurrence of debilitating pain behaviors and to increase well behaviors for millions of chronic pain patients in the United States and throughout the world.

REFERENCES

Bandura, A. (1969). *Principles of behavior modification*. New York: Holt, Rinehart & Wilson.

Bandura, A. (1986). *Social foundations of thought in action: A social cognitive theory*. Englewood Cliffs, NJ: Prentice-Hall.

Bayer, T. L., Baer, P. E., & Early, C. (1991). Situational and psychophysiological factors in psychologically induced pain. *Pain, 44*, 45–50.

Bertzen, D., & Götestam, K. G. (1987). Effects of on-demand or fixed-interval schedules in the treatment of chronic pain with analgesic compounds: An experimental comparison. *Journal Of Consulting and Clinical Psychology, 55*, 213–218.

Block, A. R., Kremer, E. F., & Gaylor, M. (1980). Behavioral treatment of chronic pain: The spouse as a discriminative cue for pain behavior. *Pain, 9*, 243–252.

Connally, G. H., & Sanders, S. H. (1991). Predicting low back pain patients' response to lumbar sympathetic nerve blocks and interdisciplinary pain rehabilitation: The role of pretreatment overt pain behavior and cognitive coping strategies. *Pain, 44*, 139–146.

Cott, R., Anchel, H., Goldberg, W. M., Fabich, M., & Parkinson, W. (1990). Non-institutional treatment of chronic pain by home management: An outcome study with comparison group. *Pain, 40*, 183–194.

Craig, K. D. (1992). Facial expression of pain: Better than a thousand words? *American Pain Society Journal, 1*, 153–162.

Flor, H., Turk, D. C., & Rudy, T. E. (1989). Relationship of pain impact and significant other reinforcement of pain behaviors: Mediating role of gender, marital status, and marital satisfaction. *Pain, 38*, 45–50.

Fordyce, W. E. (1973). An operant conditioning method for managing chronic pain. *Postgraduate Medicine, 53*, 123–138.

Fordyce, W. E. (1976). *Behavioral methods for chronic pain and illness.* St. Louis, MO: C. V. Mosby.

Fordyce, W. E. (1988). Pain and suffering: A reappraisal. *American Psychologist, 43*, 276–283.

Fordyce, W. E., Fowler, R., & DeLateur, B. (1968). An application of behavior modification technique to a problem of chronic pain. *Behaviour Research and Therapy, 6*, 105–107.

Fordyce, W. E., Roberts, A. H., & Sternbach, R. A. (1985). The behavioral management of chronic pain: Response to critics. *Pain, 22*, 113–125.

Fordyce, W. E., Shelton, J. L., & Dundore, D. E. (1982). The modification of avoidance learning pain behaviors. *Journal of Behavioral Medicine, 5*, 405–414.

Gauthier, J., Cote, G., & French, D. (1994). The role of home practice in the thermal biofeedback treatment of migraine headache. *Journal of Consulting and Clinical Psychology, 62*, 180–184.

Geiger, G., Todd, D. D., Clarke, H. B., Miller, R. P., & Kori, S. H. (1992). The effects of feedback and contingent reinforcement on the exercise behavior of chronic pain patients. *Pain, 49*, 179–185.

Goldfried, M. R., & Davison, G. C. (1994). *Clinical behavior therapy.* New York: Wiley.

Grant, D. A. (1964). Classical and operant conditioning. In A. W. Melton (Ed.), *Categories of human learning* (pp. 1–31). New York: Academic Press.

Hare, B. D., & Lipman, A. G. (1990). Uses and misuses of medication in the management of chronic, non-cancer pain. In B. D. Hare & P. G. Fine (Eds.), *Problems in anesthesia: Chronic pain* (pp. 577–594). Philadelphia: Lippincott.

Iverson, G. L. (1994). Will the real behaviorism please stand up? *The Behavior Therapist, 17*, 191–194.

Karoly, P. (1985). The assessment of pain: Concepts and procedures. In P. Karoly (Ed.), *Measurement strategies in health psychology* (pp. 461–516). New York: Wiley.

Keefe, F. J. (1994). Behavior therapy. In P. D. Wall & R. Melzack (Eds.), *Textbook of pain* (3rd ed., pp. 392–406). Edinburgh: Churchill Livingstone.

Keefe, F. J., Crisson, J. E., & Trainor, M. (1987). Observational methods for assessing pain: A practical guide. In J. A. Blumenthal & D. C. McKee (Eds.), *Applications in behavioral medicine and health psychology* (pp. 67–94). Sarasota, FL: Professional Resource Exchange.

Keefe, F. J., & Dunsmore, J. (1992a). Pain behavior: Concepts and controversies. *American Pain Society Journal, 1*, 92–100.

Keefe, F. J., & Dunsmore, J. (1992b). The multifaceted nature of pain behavior. *American Pain Society Journal, 1*, 112–114.

Keefe, F. J., Dunsmore, J., & Burnette, R. (1992). Behavioral and cognitive-behavioral approaches to chronic pain: Recent advances and future directions. *Journal of Consulting and Clinical Psychology, 60*, 528–536.

Keefe, F. J., & Williams, D. A. (1992). Assessment of pain behaviors. In D. C. Turk & R. Melzack (Eds.), *Handbook of pain assessment* (pp. 275–284). New York: Guilford Press.

Lake, A. E. (1981). Behavioral assessment considerations in the management of headache. *Headache, 21*, 170–178.

Lattal, K. A. (Ed.). (1992). Reflections on B. F. Skinner and psychology [Special issue]. *American Psychologist, 47*, 1269–1533.

Linton, S. J. (1985). The relationship between activity and chronic back pain. *Pain, 21*, 289–294.

Linton, S. J. (1986). Behavioral remediation of chronic pain: A status report. *Pain, 24*, 125–141.

Linton, S. J., Melin, L., & Götestam, K. G. (1984). Behavioral analysis of chronic pain and its management. In M. Hersen, R. M. Eisler, & P. M. Miller (Eds.), *Progress in behavior modification* (Vol. 18, pp. 1–42). New York: Academic Press.

Merskey, H. (1992). Limitations on pain behavior. *American Pain Society Journal, 1*, 101–104.

Nash, J. M., & Holroyd, K. A. (1992). Home-based behavioral treatment for recurrent headache: A cost-effective alternative? *American Pain Society Bulletin, 2*, 1–6.

Pavlov, I. P. (1927). *Conditioned reflexes.* London: Oxford University Press.

Price, D. D., Bush, F. M., Long, S., & Hawkins, S. W. (1994). A comparison of pain measurement characteristics of mechanical visual analog and simple numerical rating scales. *Pain, 56,* 217–226.

Reynolds, G. S. (1968). *A primer of operant conditioning.* Glenview, IL: Scott, Foresman.

Richards, J. S., Nepomuceno, C., Riles, M., & Suer, Z. (1982). Assessing pain behavior: The UAB Pain Behavior Scale. *Pain, 14,* 193–198.

Roberts, A. H. (1986). The operant approach to the management of pain and excess disability. In A. D. Holzman & D. C. Turk (Eds.), *Pain management: The handbook of psychological treatment approaches* (pp. 10–30). Elmsford, NY: Pergamon Press.

Romano, J. M., Turner, J. A., Friedman, L. S., Bulcroft, R. A., Jensen, M. P., Hops, H., & Wright, S. F. (1992). Sequential analysis of chronic pain behaviors and spouse responses. *Journal of Consulting and Clinical Psychology, 60,* 777–782.

Sanders, S. H. (1979). Behavioral assessment and treatment of clinical pain: Appraisal and current status. In M. Hersen, R. Eisler, & P. Miller (Eds.), *Progress in behavior modification* (Vol. 8, pp. 249–291). New York: Academic Press.

Sanders, S. H. (1980). Toward a practical instrument system for the automatic measurement of "up-time" in chronic pain patients. *Pain, 9,* 103–109.

Sanders, S. H. (1983a). Component analysis of a behavioral treatment program for chronic low back pain. *Behavior Therapy, 14,* 697–705.

Sanders, S. H. (1983b). Automated versus self monitoring of "up-time" in chronic low back pain patients: A comparative study. *Pain, 15,* 399–405.

Sanders, S. H. (1985). The role of learning in chronic pain states. In S. F. Brena & S. Chapman (Eds.), *Clinics in anesthesiology: Pain control* (pp. 57–73). Philadelphia: W. B. Saunders.

Sanders, S. H. (1989). Contingency management and the reduction of overt pain behavior. In D. Tollison (Ed.), *Handbook of chronic pain management* (pp. 210–221). Baltimore: Williams & Wilkins.

Sanders, S. H. (1995). Risk factors for the occurrence of low back pain and chronic disability. *American Pain Society Bulletin, 5,* 1–60.

Sanders, S. H., & Brena, S. F. (1990). Organization and operation of a comprehensive pain management center. In B. Hare & P. Fine (Eds.), *Problems in anesthesia: Chronic pain* (pp. 657–677). Philadelphia: Lippincott.

Sanders, S. H., & Brena, S. F. (1993). Empirically derived chronic pain patient subgroups: The utility of multidimensional clustering to identify differential treatment effects. *Pain, 54,* 51–56.

Sanders, S. H., Brena, S. F., Spier, C. J., Beltrutti, O., McConnell, H., & Quintero, O. (1992). Chronic low back pain patients around the world: Cross-cultural similarities and differences. *Clinical Journal of Pain, 8,* 317–323.

Schwartz, L., Slater, M. A., & Birchler, G. R. (1994). Interpersonal stress and pain behaviors in patients with chronic pain. *Journal of Consulting and Clinical Psychology, 62,* 861–864.

Sidman, M. (1962). Operant techniques. In A. J. Bachrach (Ed.), *Experimental foundations of clinical psychology* (pp. 170–210). New York: Basic Books.

Skinner, B. F. (1953). *Science and human behavior.* New York: MacMillen.

Skinner, B. F. (1989). *Recent issues in the analysis of behavior.* Columbus, OH: Charles E. Merrill.

Staats, A. W. (1990). Paradigmatic behavior therapy: A unified framework for theory, research, and practice. In G. H. Eifert & I. M. Evans (Eds.), *Unifying behavior therapy: Contributions of paradigmatic behaviorism* (pp. 14–54). New York: Springer.

Staats, A. W. (1991). Unified positivism and unification psychology: Fad or new field? *American Psychologist, 46,* 899–912.

Steedman, S. M., Middaugh, S. J., Kee, W. G., Carson, D. S., Harden, R. N., & Miller, M. C. (1992). Chronic pain medications: Equivalence levels and method of quantifying usage. *Clinical Journal of Pain, 8,* 204–214.

Turk, D. C., & Matyas, T. A. (1992). Pain related behaviors: Communication of pain. *American Pain Society Journal, 1,* 109–111.

Turk, D. C., Wack, J. T., & Kerns, R. D. (1985). An empirical examination of the "pain behavior" construct. *Journal of Behavioral Medicine, 8,* 119–130.

White, B., & Sanders, S.H. (1985). Differential effects on pain and mood in chronic pain patients with time- versus pain-contingent medication delivery. *Behavior Therapy, 16,* 28–38.

White, B., & Sanders, S. H. (1986). The influence on patient's pain intensity ratings of antecedent reinforcement of pain talk or well talk. *Journal of Behavior Therapy and Experimental Psychiatry, 17,* 155–159.

Cognitive-Behavioral Therapy for Chronic Pain

Laurence A. Bradley

"Cognitive-behavioral therapy" (CBT) for chronic pain is a term that covers a wide variety of interventions provided in diverse clinical environments. However, all CBT interventions share a set of theoretical assumptions regarding interactions among environmental events, cognitions, and behaviors that determine patients' subjective pain perceptions and their overt displays of pain. This chapter reviews these assumptions and describes the treatment components that are common to all CBT interventions. The chapter then examines the efficacy of these interventions and the important issue of treatment gain maintenance. Although CBT interventions have been used to treat patients with a wide variety of chronic pain syndromes, this chapter places particular emphasis on the use of these interventions for patients with rheumatological or gastroenterological illnesses. The chapter concludes with suggestions for helping patients maintain their improvements after treatment is completed.

FOUNDATIONS OF COGNITIVE-BEHAVIORAL THERAPY FOR CHRONIC PAIN

Background

Cognitive-behavioral therapy for chronic pain evolved from the development of CBT for behavioral and psychiatric disorders in the early 1970s (Holzman, Turk, & Kerns, 1986). All of the CBT approaches to these disorders and to chronic pain encompass the fundamental tenets of operant theory. That is, they acknowledge that changes in behavioral response rates are influenced by the presentation and withdrawal of positive reinforcement, as well as by the initiation or avoidance of negative reinforcement (Thorndike, 1913; Turk & Rudy, 1989). In addition, the CBT approaches posit that treatment outcomes may be improved and better maintained over time if attention is also devoted to cognitive and affective factors that influence behavior. This assumption is quite compatible with Melzack and Wall's (1965) gate control theory, which suggests that the perception of pain is the product of a complex interaction of afferent nociceptive stimuli and such modulating factors as efferent stimuli, environmental events, emotional reactions, and cognitions.

Primary Assumptions

There are five primary assumptions that underlie all CBT interventions (Turk & Rudy, 1989); Table 6.1 summarizes these. The first assumption is that individuals actively process information regarding internal stimuli and environmental events. That is, they appraise the meanings of events, using their learning histories as well as general information-processing strategies, and develop expectations concerning consequences that are likely to follow potential responses to the events. Thus, individuals' behaviors are influenced both by their expectations and by their perceptions of the consequences of their behaviors. For example, a woman's decision to seek health care for a painful disorder such as gastroesophageal reflux (i.e., heartburn) will be influenced by her learning history and expectations regarding (1) the severity and consequences of the chest pain symptoms; (2) the potential aversiveness of diagnostic procedures such as endoscopy; (3) the effectiveness of acid-suppressive medications that may be obtained over the counter versus treatments that must be prescribed or performed by physicians; and (4) the behavior of her physician. Moreover, once this woman chooses to care for herself or seek medical care, her decision to maintain or alter her health care behavior will be influenced by her perceptions of the consequences that follow this behavior.

The second assumption of CBT is that cognitions interact with emotional and physiological reactions as well as with behavior. Thus, individuals' thoughts may alter behavior by their influence on both emotional and physiological responses. These thoughts may also be influenced by emotional, physiological, and behavioral events. To extend the example given above, the subjective intensity of the woman's reflux symptoms may be amplified by high levels of anxiety and beliefs regarding the extent to which the symptoms represent a threat to her well-being (Bradley et al., 1993). This interaction, in turn, will influence her decision to seek medical care. If this woman obtains effective medical treatment for reflux and is reassured that the associated esophageal tissue damage will not progress further, her concerns regarding the threat posed by reflux symptoms will probably be minimal.

The third assumption is that there are reciprocal interactions between an individual's behavior and environmental responses. Thus, behavior may be influenced by the environment and may also shape environmental events. For example, the highly anxious woman

---

TABLE 6.1. Primary Assumptions of CBT

---

1. Individuals actively process information regarding internal stimuli and environmental events. Thus, their behaviors are influenced by their expectations and by their perceptions of the consequences of their behaviors.

2. Individuals' thoughts may alter behavior by their influence on emotional and physiological responses. These thoughts may also be influenced by emotional, physiological, and behavioral responses.

3. Individuals' behaviors may be influenced by the environment and may also shape environmental events.

4. Treatment interventions must address the emotional, cognitive, and behavioral dimensions of individuals' problems if they are to be effective.

5. Individuals must become active participants in treatment if they are to learn adaptive methods of responding to their problems.

Note. From Turk and Rudy (1989). Copyright 1989 by Williams & Wilkins, Inc. Adapted by permission.

with reflux symptoms may frequently seek treatment for these symptoms during stressful periods, despite the fact that the symptoms are not associated with objective evidence of esophageal acid exposure as measured by 24–hour pH monitoring (Bradley et al., 1993). This behavior may cause her physician to react quite negatively to her health concerns over time, because the physician may come to believe that she is a "somatizer" or prone to over-utilize the health care system. As treatment visits evoke increasingly skeptical or unproductive responses from her physician, the woman is likely to seek treatment from other health care providers or to reduce her usage of the medical system for reflux symptoms.

The fourth assumption of CBT is that effective treatment interventions must address the cognitive, emotional, and behavioral dimensions of the presenting problem. To illustrate this assumption, it is helpful to return once again to the example of the woman with symptoms of gastroesophageal reflux, high levels of anxiety, and normal levels of esophageal acid exposure. Persons with these characteristics are often identified as suffering from "functional heartburn." If this woman with functional heartburn seeks CBT, the therapist must attend to her beliefs about the meaning of the reflux symptoms, to her anxiety and other emotional responses, and to her usual behavioral strategies for reducing the symptoms. Thus, effective treatment should include education regarding the low threat to health associated with functional heartburn, as well as the association between this disorder and anxiety. In addition, effort should be devoted to reinforcing the woman's adaptive coping strategies and teaching her anxiety management skills (e.g., relaxation), which have been shown to reduce symptoms of heartburn and emotional distress (McDonald-Haile, Bradley, Bailey, Schan, & Richter, 1994). Particular emphasis should be placed on helping the woman substitute the use of relaxation and other positive coping strategies for frequent visits to health care providers.

The fifth and final assumption of CBT is that it is necessary to help individuals become active participants in learning adaptive methods of responding to their problems. Thus, it is essential to help the woman with functional heartburn to adopt the belief that she can work actively with her therapist to learn to monitor the internal or external events that are associated with pain episodes, and to prevent or reduce painful symptoms by employing relaxation and other coping skills.

The example reviewed above illustrates how the primary assumptions of CBT may be operationalized in understanding and treating the relatively circumscribed problems of gastroesophageal reflux and functional heartburn. These disorders are usually not accompanied by high levels of morbidity or functional disability. In contrast, therapists who treat patients with more complex pain syndromes, such as rheumatoid arthritis (RA), face the difficult problem of operationalizing the primary assumptions of CBT to alter the symptoms and maladaptive behaviors that are often associated with multiple physiological and psychosocial problems. The following discussion reviews the essential components of CBT interventions for chronic pain. These components are discussed in the context of a treatment protocol for patients with RA.

THE COGNITIVE-BEHAVIORAL APPROACH
TO THE TREATMENT OF CHRONIC PAIN

Goals and Objectives

Chronic pain syndromes, including those produced by chronic diseases such as RA, pose substantial difficulties both for patients and for their health care providers. The patients' difficulties may be attributed in part to the uncertainties associated with chronic pain and illness (Bradley & Kay, 1985). That is, patients usually cannot identify with certainty the causes, natural histories, or probable outcomes of their pain syndromes. As a result, such patients often exhibit high levels of psychological distress and functional disability, as well as maladaptive cognitions and behavioral strategies for coping with their pain. These patients are frequently demoralized and are reluctant to collaborate actively with health care providers, whom they may perceive as ineffective or uncaring (Turk & Rudy, 1989). In addition, the problems experienced by the patients tend to be exacerbated by negative changes in patients' relationships with family members, employers, and friends (Anderson, Bradley, Young, McDaniel, & Wise, 1985).

Physicians, psychologists, and other health care providers often do not know how to respond effectively to patients with chronic pain. The patients' demoralization and reluctance to collaborate are especially troublesome to traditional medical care providers, who expect their patients to cooperate with them and adhere to their therapeutic recommendations (Burish & Bradley, 1983). However, the CBT approach to chronic pain is based on the assumption that patients will enter treatment with the belief that many of their problems are unmanageable. The goals of CBT, then, are first to help patients develop the expectation that they can learn to manage their problems effectively, and then to provide them with the skills to respond effectively both to their current problems and to new difficulties that will arise after treatment termination. Four objectives must be met in order to accomplish the goals of CBT (Holzman et al., 1986):

1. Help patients alter their beliefs that their problems are unmanageable; that is, help them to become resourceful problem solvers, instead of remaining individuals with little hope of coping effectively with their pain, emotional distress, and other psychosocial difficulties.
2. Help patients learn to monitor their thoughts, emotions, and behaviors to identify relationships among these factors and environmental events, pain, emotional distress, and psychosocial difficulties.
3. Help patients learn to perform behaviors at appropriate times to cope effectively with pain, emotional distress, and psychosocial difficulties.
4. Help patients develop and maintain increasingly effective and adaptive ways of thinking, feeling, and responding, which can be used to cope with problems that may be experienced after treatment termination.

Numerous CBT interventions have been developed for a variety of chronic pain problems, such as low back pain (Linton, Bradley, Jensen, Spangfort, & Sundell, 1989), fibromyalgia (Nielson, Walker, & McCain, 1992), osteoarthritis (Keefe et al., 1990a, 1990b), and RA (Parker et al., 1988). Although these interventions differ on various dimensions, they share four essential components. Below, I describe these components and illustrate their operationalization in a CBT protocol developed for patients with RA (Bradley et al., 1987). It should be noted that the pain and psychosocial difficulties associated with RA represent an ideal model for discussing the CBT approach to chronic pain. That is, RA is a chronic illness characterized by an unknown etiology, an unpredictable course, and no known cure (Anderson et al., 1985). Patients with RA experience joint inflammation, pain, and functional disability that may vary greatly in severity over short time periods. Moreover, these patients are characterized by relatively shortened lifespans, particularly if they experience high levels of functional disability (Pincus & Callahan, 1992). Consequently, patients with RA often show high levels of psychological distress and perceive that they do not have adequate control of their symptoms and other problems related to their illness (Bradley, 1993).

Treatment Components

The four essential components of all CBT interventions are (1) education, (2) skills acquisition, (3) cognitive and behavioral rehearsal, and (4) generalization and maintenance. Table 6.2 outlines a 15-week CBT intervention that my colleagues and I have designed to reduce pain and psychological distress among patients with RA (Bradley et al., 1987). The table identifies the four components, as well as the aspects of treatment associated with each component. It should be noted that this CBT intervention requires spouses or significant others to meet in a series of ten 90-minute small-group sessions with the patients and the therapist. Spouse participation is not common to all CBT interventions; however, it has been shown that the participation of spouses tends to enhance treatment outcomes among patients with RA (Radojevic, Nicassio, & Weisman, 1992; see also Kerns & Payne, Chapter 11, this volume).

Education

The primary purposes of the educational component are to present a credible rationale for the CBT intervention, to elicit the active collaboration of patients and spouses with the therapist, and to help patients and spouses begin to alter negative perceptions regarding their abilities to manage the pain and psychosocial consequences of RA. It is especially important during the educational component to encourage the patients and spouses to adopt the belief that they can learn the skills necessary to cope better with the patients' pain and other illness-related problems. Therefore, we devote the first week's treatment session to a discussion of the medical and psychosocial consequences that are often associated with RA. Medical consequences include joint inflammation, pain, stiffness, fatigue, and destruction of bone and cartilage. These consequences may vary greatly in intensity over short and unpredictable time periods. In addition, rheumatoid nodules may develop on the skin surface, and some patients develop ocular problems such as keratoconjunctivitis, as well as pulmonary disease or pericarditis. With regard to psychosocial consequences, patients with RA frequently experience depression, anxiety, difficulty in performing activities of daily living, and negative beliefs about their abilities to manage the medical and psychosocial consequences of the disease.

Throughout this discussion, we attempt to conceptualize these consequences according to the fundamental assumptions of CBT described earlier. For example, we ask patients to describe their perceptions of the degree to which they can manage their pain and emotional reactions to RA. By fostering discussions among the patients and their spouses, we attempt to help them recognize that the unpredictable variations in joint inflammation and pain have a negative effect on their psychological status, as well as on their perceived abilities to control their symptoms and to function effectively. These negative consequences, in turn, may influence their health status. For example, reductions in perceived control following a series of flares in pain and inflammation may lead patients to fail to adhere to their prescribed medication or exercise regimens, and thus may further exacerbate disease activity. We then describe the major components of the CBT intervention to the patients and spouses, and explain how the components of the intervention are designed to help them maintain better control of their pain and psychological reactions.

One important component of the intervention is relaxation training. We explain that nearly all persons can learn to induce a relaxed state by using the techniques that we have available. Furthermore, we explain that we ultimately wish to teach the patients and spouses to use "short cuts" such as deep breathing and mental imagery, so that they may quickly

TABLE 6.2. A CBT Intervention for Patients with RA

Education

Week 1. Education and rationale
   A. Discuss the medical and psychosocial consequences of RA, according to the primary assumptions of CBT.
   B. Provide a credible rationale for use of the CBT intervention for pain and psychological distress.
Week 2. Discussion of patients' and spouses' behaviors
   A. Develop consensus that patients may learn to control their pain better and that spouses may learn to respond appropriately to patients' displays of high and low pain levels.
   B. Review the components of the CBT intervention and discuss how this intervention may help patients and spouses achieve their pain control goals.

Skills acquisition; cognitive and behavioral rehearsal

Week 3 First thermal biofeedback training session
   A. Identify target joint or muscle, and provide visual and auditory feedback regarding increases in skin surface temperature at the target.
   B. Give instruction in use of home thermal biofeedback unit and in daily practice of temperature control skills.
Week 4. First relaxation training session
   A. Provide progressive muscle relaxation training in group session.
   B. Give instruction in deep breathing and relaxation imagery.
   C. Provide relaxation audiocassettes, portable audiocassette recorders, and instructions for home practice of relaxation by patients and spouses.
Week 5. Second thermal biofeedback training session
   A. Continue practice of skin surface temperature control skills in the clinic and home environments.
Week 6. Second relaxation training session
   A. Patients and spouses provide progress reports on successes and difficulties in using relaxation, imagery, and biofeedback skills.
   B. Group members provide reinforcements for success and assist one another in solving problems related to usage of their skills.
   C. Instruction in relaxation and deep breathing, as well as relaxation and pain relief imagery.
   D. Assist patients and spouses in identifying arthritis-related problems, behavioral goals and strategies, and rewards for patients' use of their strategies.
Week 7. Third thermal biofeedback training session
   A. Continue practice of skin surface temperature control skills in the clinic and home environments.
   B. Decrease visual and auditory feedback in the clinic environment.
Week 8. Relaxation and behavioral goal setting
   A. Patients and spouses provide progress reports on successes and difficulties in using relaxation, imagery, biofeedback, and behavioral goal-setting skills.
   B. Instruct patients to place relaxation cues in their home and work environments.
   C. Assist patients and spouses in modifying behavioral goals and strategies, as well as rewards for patients' use of their strategies.
Week 9. Fourth thermal biofeedback training session
   A. Continue practice of skin surface temperature control skills in the clinic and home environments.
   B. Decrease visual and auditory feedback in the clinic environment.
Week 10. Relaxation and behavioral goal setting
   A. Patients and spouses provide progress reports on successes and difficulties in using relaxation, imagery, biofeedback, and behavioral goal-setting skills.

(continued)

Skills acquisition; cognitive and behavioral rehearsal (*continued*)

B. Assist patients and spouses in modifying behavioral goals and strategies, as well as rewards for patients' use of their strategies.
C. Instruct patients and spouses to identify additional arthritis-related problems, behavioral goals and strategies, and rewards for patients' use of their strategies.

Week 11. Relaxation and behavioral goal setting
A. Patients and spouses provide progress reports on successes and difficulties in using relaxation, imagery, biofeedback, and behavioral goal-setting skills.
B. Assist patients and spouses in modifying behavioral goals and strategies, as well as rewards for patients' use of their strategies.

Week 12. Relaxation and behavioral goal setting
A. Patients and spouses provide progress reports on successes and difficulties in using relaxation, imagery, biofeedback, and behavioral goal-setting skills.
B. Assist patients and spouses in modifying behavioral goals and strategies, as well as rewards for patients' use of their strategies.
C. Instruct patients and spouses to identify additional arthritis-related problems, behavioral goals and strategies, and rewards for patients' use of their strategies.
D. Instruct patients to remove relaxation cues from their home and work environments.

Week 13. Fifth thermal biofeedback training session
A. Continue practice of skin surface temperature control skills in the clinic and home environments.
B. Eliminate visual and auditory feedback in the clinic environment.

Generalization and maintenance

Week 14. Progress reports and planning for treatment termination
A. Patients and spouses provide progress reports on successes and difficulties in using relaxation, imagery, biofeedback, and behavioral goal-setting skills.
B. Assist patients and spouses in modifying behavioral goals and strategies, as well as rewards for patients' use of their strategies.
C. Ask patients and spouses to identify arthritis-related problems they expect to encounter after treatment is completed, and to describe behavioral goals and strategies as well as rewards that may help them cope with these problems.

Week 15. Progress reports and planning for treatment termination
A. Patients and spouses provide progress reports on successes and failures in using relaxation, imagery, biofeedback, and behavioral goal-setting skills.
B. Assist patients and spouses in modifying behavioral goals and strategies, as well as rewards for patients' use of their strategies.
C. Ask patients and spouses to identify arthritis-related problems they expect to encounter after treatment is completed, and to describe behavioral goals and strategies as well as rewards that may help them cope with these problems.
D. Make plans to telephone each patient once a month during the next 6 months to provide assistance in maintaining relaxation, imagery, biofeedback, and behavioral goal-setting skills.

induce a relaxed state in their home or work environments during periods of high stress or pain levels. This will allow them in many circumstances to reduce their stress and pain and thus cope in an adaptive manner with these unpleasant states.

Finally, in order to assess the patients' beliefs regarding the potential effectiveness of the CBT intervention, we ask them at the end of the first session to respond to three questions on a 1–7 rating scale:

1. How confident are you that this treatment will successfully help you cope more effectively with your RA?

2. How successful do you feel this treatment will be in decreasing the extent to which RA interferes with your work/social life?
3. How confident would you be in recommending this treatment to a friend who suffers with RA?

For each question, a 1 is the least positive response, a 4 is moderately positive, and a 7 is the most positive response. In our initial study of the efficacy of our CBT intervention (Bradley et al., 1987), our patients produced mean ($\pm SD$) responses to these questions of $5.82 \pm 1.2, 5.23 \pm 1.2$, and 6.29 ± 0.8, respectively. We felt confident, therefore, that these patients completed the first education session with very positive expectations that the CBT intervention would help them learn improved coping skills.

We devote the beginning of the second week's treatment session to a brief review of the issues noted above. We especially encourage the patients and spouses to ask questions that have occurred to them in discussing the previous week's session in their homes. This allows us to correct any misperceptions about RA or the CBT intervention that may have developed, and to engage the participants further in the treatment. We then lead an intensive discussion of the spouses' reactions to the patients' behavioral displays of pain. The first purpose of this discussion is to elicit the active participation of the spouses in the CBT intervention, since many spouses tend to believe that they play a minor role in the medical treatment of the patients' conditions. Moreover, we use this discussion to begin a process of reconceptualization about the role of spouse–patient interactions in the patients' pain experiences.

To begin the discussion, we ask the spouses to identify behaviors indicating that the patients are experiencing pain. These behaviors are recorded on a large chalkboard. We then ask them to identify their responses to the patients' pain behaviors; these responses are also recorded on the chalkboard. Next, we ask the spouses to identify the behaviors indicating that the patients are experiencing relatively low levels of pain, as well as their responses to these behaviors. Again, the behaviors and responses identified by the spouses are recorded on the chalkboard. Invariably, the spouses report 20 to 30 patient pain behaviors and 10 to 15 responses to these behaviors. However, they usually can identify only 5 to 10 behaviors denoting low pain levels and 3 to 5 responses to these behaviors. Indeed, the spouses often state that they are reluctant to respond positively to the expression of low pain levels, because they are afraid that encouragement of pleasurable activities (e.g., sexual relations) may evoke a pain flare. We then discuss with the participants the implications of the fact that the spouses' repertoires of behavioral responses to patients' pain behaviors are much larger and more varied than their repertoires of responses to relatively healthy behavior. This helps both the patients and spouses to understand that they are involved in a constant series of interactions involving beliefs, expectations, emotional reactions, and behaviors, which help determine the patients' pain experiences and both the patients' and spouses' responses to pain.

The results of this discussion allow us to lead the participants to agree that the major treatment goals should be to help patients learn to control their pain better, and to help both the patients and spouses learn methods that they can use together to cope better with pain and the other medical and psychosocial problems associated with RA. We also convey to the participants that achieving these goals will help them to live more fulfilling and active lives within the limitations imposed by the disease. We conclude the session by reviewing how the components of the CBT intervention can help the patients and spouses achieve their goals.

Skills Acquisition; Cognitive and Behavioral Rehearsal

The purpose of the skills acquisition component is to help patients and spouses engage actively in the process of learning new behaviors and cognitions that will help them better manage pain and other RA-related problems. This learning process cannot succeed if the preceding education component is ineffective or if the therapist cannot motivate patients and spouses to become active collaborators in treatment. Success is also is predicated upon the skill with which the therapist implements the cognitive and behavioral rehearsal component. The purpose of this component is to help patients and spouses practice and consolidate new pain management behaviors and cognitions, and to apply these effectively in their home and work environments.

Table 6.2 shows that these two intervention components are implemented in group and individual sessions conducted from the 3rd through the 13th weeks' sessions. With regard to the skills acquisition component, we first devote attention to helping patients learn self-regulation techniques that may enable them to reduce their pain. We feel it is quite important early in treatment to allow the patients to experience enhanced control over physiological and cognitive activity related to pain. That is, most patients enter treatment with the belief (formed by their learning histories) that they and their physicians cannot exert adequate control over the pain produced by RA. Thus, we feel that if the patients experience some increased control over their pain perceptions or physiological functions associated with pain during the earliest phase of treatment, their beliefs regarding their inability to manage their problems will be challenged. Thus, the patients will be more likely to adopt the belief that active participation in treatment will be beneficial to them.

Given this rationale, we dedicate the 3rd and 4th weeks' treatment sessions to training in thermal biofeedback and progressive muscle relaxation (see Arena & Blanchard, Chapter 8, this volume). During the third week, patients meet individually with one of the treatment team members for the first of five thermal biofeedback training sessions. We choose to provide biofeedback training because of the evidence that effective skin temperature control at affected joints reliably reduces pain among patients with RA (Achterberg, McGraw, & Lawlis, 1981). Each patient begins the first biofeedback session by identifying a joint or muscle for which he or she wishes to develop improved pain control. The patient then engages in a 60-minute training protocol in which he or she receives auditory and visual feedback regarding increases in skin surface temperature at the target joint or muscle. We implement cognitive and behavioral rehearsal of the biofeedback instruction in two ways. First, at the end of the initial training session, the patient learns to operate a small battery-powered biofeedback unit for home practice that provides visual feedback concerning changes in skin surface temperature. We instruct the patient to practice with the home biofeedback unit at least once each day. In addition, all patients engage in additional individualized thermal biofeedback training in 60-minute sessions at the 5th, 7th, 9th, and 13th weeks. During the course of these sessions we gradually decrease the frequency of feedback, to help patients learn to control skin temperature in the absence of visual or auditory cues outside of the laboratory.

We conduct the initial relaxation training session at the 4th week in a group meeting with patients and spouses. Both patients and spouses perform a modified version of Jacobson's (1938) progressive muscle relaxation protocol. It should be noted that nearly all patients with RA will experience increased pain if they attempt to tense and relax some muscle groups. Therefore, we instruct the participants that if they experience increased pain while tensing a muscle, they should immediately relax that muscle and not attempt to tense it again during future exercises. With this precautionary procedure, we find that almost all of our patients can achieve a relatively relaxed state, even if they cannot exert control over all muscles. Once a state of relaxation has been achieved, all participants engage in the first of several cognitive and behavioral rehearsal exercises based on a procedure described by Linton (1982). That is, we instruct the patients and spouses to breathe deeply and vividly imagine a scene from their life histories that they associate with deep relaxation or feelings of serenity (cf. Syrjala & Abrams, Chapter 9, this volume). We also ask them to focus their attention on the experience of enhanced relaxation when they imagine their respective scenes. This instruction assists the participants in diverting their attention from pain or other unpleasant feelings or thoughts, and reaffirms that they are very capable of controlling internal events. At the end of the session, we give the patients an audiocassette of the relaxation and deep breathing instruction, and ask them to practice their newly learned relaxation and imagery skills at least twice each day. We loan portable audiocassette players to patients who do not own home audio equipment. Finally, we instruct the spouses to practice relaxation at home with the patients. Our rationale is that spouses who experience the benefits of relaxation will tend to encourage the patients to participate actively in treatment and to adhere to home practice of biofeedback, relaxation, and future CBT assignments.

At the 6th week, patients and spouses participate in a second group relaxation training session. We first ask the patients to provide progress reports on the successes and difficulties they have encountered in practicing their relaxation, imagery, and biofeedback skills. We focus particular attention on their thoughts and feelings during these successes and failures. We also ask the patients to describe any environmental events that may have interacted with their thoughts, feelings, and behaviors. Moreover, we encourage the patients and spouses to provide verbal reinforcement to each other and to the other group members for their successes, as well as to suggest strategies that may help the group members resolve their practice difficulties. This allows us to engage in extensive cognitive restructuring with the patients. That is, we elicit patients' adaptive and maladaptive thoughts and feelings associated with their pain experiences, in order to reinforce their adaptive "internal dialogues" and alter their maladaptive dialogues.

For example, one patient reported that her grandchildren frequently interrupted her while she practiced relaxation in the living room of her home. The patient would feel obligated at these times to attend to her grandchildren, since she believed that their welfare took precedence over her pain and her need to practice relaxation. However, the patient also felt angry with her spouse for not assisting with the grandchildren, as she highly valued her treatment and relaxation periods. Nevertheless, the patient doubted whether she could master the relaxation training skills offered to her in treatment, because she could not conceive of a strategy for responding both to her grandchildren's needs and to her own. This situation was resolved with the help of another group member. In accord with this member's suggestion, the patient's spouse agreed to take charge of the grandchildren for two 1-hour periods each day, while the patient practiced relaxation and imagery in the bedroom with a portable audiocassette player loaned by the treatment team. Therefore, the patient was able to accomplish both her child care and home practice tasks, as well as to defuse her anger at her spouse. She also learned that it was appropriate and effective to elicit help from her spouse in order to respond adaptively to the demands of her grandchildren and those of the treatment team.

After the patients give their progress reports, we lead the group members through the relaxation protocol and ask them to use their imagery and deep breathing to enhance their perceptions of relaxation. We also ask them to develop and use another image drawn from their life histories—this time, an image involving warmth and relief from arthritis pain. For example, many patients develop images of lying in the sand at the seashore during the summer. We instruct the patients to focus on their images of warmth and pain relief as they perform relaxation and deep breathing during the group session and their home practices.

We continue to provide patients and spouses with cognitive and behavioral rehearsal instructions for relaxation throughout the remaining group sessions. In accord with Linton's (1982) procedure, we begin the 8th, 10th, 11th, and 12th weeks' sessions with progress reports similar to that initiated at the 6th week's group meeting. Again, participants provide one another with verbal reinforcements for their successes, and develop strategies for solving problems associated with the practice of biofeedback and relaxation. They also continue to discuss the interactions among their thoughts, feelings, and environmental events that occur during these success and failure experiences. In addition, we suggest at the 8th week that patients place cues, such as Post-It Notes, at various sites in their home and work environments. We instruct the patients that, whenever they see a cue, they are to scan their bodies for areas of muscle tension. If patients find one or more tension areas, they are to breathe deeply and use their imagery for 1–2 minutes in order to relax. The purpose of this procedure is to help patients learn to evoke feelings of relaxation quickly in multiple situations outside the treatment setting that are associated with increases in pain or muscle tension. The patients report their successes and difficulties in performing these procedures as well as the interactions among thoughts, feelings, and environmental events, at the 10th and 12th weeks' group meetings. At the end of the 12th week's session, we instruct the patients to continue the tension monitoring and breathing/imagery procedures in their home and work environments without the use of cues.

In addition to the biofeedback and relaxation training procedures described above, we devote part of the 6th week's session to teaching behavioral goal-setting skills to the patients and spouses. We have adapted an approach originally described by Turk, Meichenbaum, and Genest (1983), in which each patient and spouse agree to work together to help the patient cope better with a specific arthritis-related problem. Once the agreement is reached, we instruct the patient and spouse to formulate the problem in terms of observable behaviors. For example, nearly all participants agree that fatigue is an important problem affecting the patients and their relationships with their family members or friends. The participants identify many behavioral manifestations of fatigue; however, the most common behaviors involve bed rest and withdrawal from family activities.

After the problem behaviors are identified, we instruct the patients and spouses to agree upon a goal that the patients can attain during the week that may help them reduce the frequencies of these behaviors. We also ask them to agree upon a series of strategies the patients can use to achieve their goals, as well as upon rewards that can be provided to patients for using each strategy. These goals, strategies, and rewards are recorded in a written contract between each patient and spouse. For example, patients and spouses who report fatigue as a problem frequently identify spending more time together in leisure activities as a behavioral goal. Therefore, they usually develop written daily time schedules for patients' activity and rest periods, in an attempt to reduce patients' fatigue behaviors and create more opportunities for shared leisure activities. The rewards for following these time schedules often include verbal self-reinforcement, as well as allowing the patients to choose the leisure activities they desire.

Several features of the behavioral goal-setting procedure should be noted. First, it is a highly individualized procedure in which participants are encouraged to identify coping problems and behavioral goals that are relevant to them, regardless of whether or not they are frequently identified by other patients or spouses. Second, the procedure allows the therapist to engage in extensive cognitive restructuring with the patients and spouses. As the participants discuss the coping problems, the therapist may probe for the interactions among thoughts, feelings, and environmental events that influence these problems. These interactions may also affect the participants' abilities to identify appropriate goals or strategies for achieving these goals. The therapist must reinforce the participants for continuing to engage in adaptive thoughts and feelings, and must also help them to identify and practice internal dialogues to replace those that appear to be associated with increases in pain or other problems. The third important feature is that group participants observe each patient–spouse couple engage in this behavioral goal-setting and cognitive restructuring process during the treatment session. We encourage the couples to assist one another when they encounter difficulties. This allows each group member to learn goal-setting skills by observing others' behaviors, and to avoid the negative cognition that he or she alone is experiencing difficultly in setting and achieving goals.

At the conclusion of the meeting, we instruct the participants to engage in their behavioral strategies during the subsequent 2 weeks. We emphasize that patients should attempt to avoid negative thoughts and feelings about themselves when they have difficulty in achieving their goals. We also point out that all patients will experience some problems in performing the desired behaviors. At these times, the patients should attempt to replace negative thoughts with this cognition: "I can think of another behavior that I can perform to receive my reward and achieve my goal."

At the 8th week's group meeting, we ask the patients and spouses to discuss the successes and difficulties they have encountered in performing their behavioral goal-setting skills. We encourage them to modify their goals, behavioral strategies, and rewards with our help and with assistance from the other group members. At the conclusion of the meeting, we remind the patients to avoid negative cognitions and feelings as they attempt to implement their behavioral strategies during the next 2 weeks.

We repeat this procedure at the 10th, 11th, and 12th weeks' group meetings. Indeed, one of the advantages of performing CBT in groups is that most participants quickly learn to engage in cognitive restructuring with one another. The participants experience a great deal of satisfaction when they successfully help other group members to devise and perform an effective behavioral strategy, alter a negative interaction with a spouse, or replace a negative internal dialogue with more adaptive thoughts and feelings. For example, one of our most successful patients was a woman aged 26 who had suffered from RA since early childhood and who had experienced a large number of destructive changes in her joints. Despite her considerable pain, her physical disabilities, and the negative effects of RA on her future prospects for a career and marriage, this individual maintained remarkably positive thoughts and feelings about herself and was able to overcome substantial difficulties in achieving her behavioral goals. Thus, she served as a constant reminder to the other group participants that they also could attain the skills needed to cope effectively with their problems. Moreover, the group members greatly admired this young woman and enthusiastically attempted to adopt her suggestions for altering their internal dialogues, goals, behavioral strategies, and reward systems.

At the 10th and 12th weeks' meetings, we require the patients and spouses to identify new arthritis-related problems and to develop and implement appropriate goals, behavioral strategies, and rewards for coping with these problems. Thus, the patients are actively rehearsing strategies for three personal goals and assisting one another with a variety of goals and behavioral strategies as they enter the final phase of the CBT intervention.

Generalization and Maintenance

The purpose of the generalization and maintenance component is to help patients retain their learned skills and avoid increases in pain following treatment. Therefore, at the 14th and 15th weeks' group meetings, we ask the patients and spouses to discuss their beliefs and feelings regarding new problems they may encounter after the termination of the CBT intervention. These problems are often associated with possible increases in disease activity or disability with advancing age. Therefore, we ask them to describe possible goals, behavioral strategies, and rewards for coping with their anticipated problems. We also frequently encourage them to use their newly learned skills to cope with problems unrelated to RA that they may confront in the future. Finally, we make plans to telephone each patient once a month for the next 6 months, to provide them with assistance in maintaining their relaxation, imagery, biofeedback, and behavioral goal-setting skills.

There are three goals associated with the generalization and maintenance phase. First, it allows the patients and spouses to anticipate and plan for future events concerning their pain. This is critical, given that RA is a progressive, systemic illness that may vary greatly over time and rarely remits spontaneously. Second, it allows the therapist to provide patients with the realistic expectation that setbacks may occur, given that not all future negative events can be anticipated. We remind the patients that these setbacks should not be regarded as evidence of failure; instead, they should be viewed as cues to use their coping skills more effectively or to develop new goals, behavioral strategies, and reward systems with their spouses. Finally, we feel it is important during this phase to provide patients with some tangible evidence of the progress they have made during treatment. This encourages the patients to maintain the belief that their personal efforts have contributed to their improvements and that they are capable of responding effectively to future changes in their pain or psychosocial problems (Holzman et al., 1986). We provide this evidence by making pretreatment and posttreatment video recordings of patients as they engage in a 10-minute standardized sequence of walking, standing, reclining, and sitting behaviors (Bradley et al., 1987). At the end of treatment, we show each patient his or her personal video recordings and point out to them changes in the frequencies of specific pain behaviors (e.g., guarded movement) that have been identified and recorded by trained observers. Nearly all patients show less frequent or less dramatic pain behaviors from pretreatment to posttreatment, and they are delighted to observe marked changes in their behavior of which they were previously unaware.

THE EFFICACY OF COGNITIVE-BEHAVIORAL THERAPY FOR CHRONIC PAIN

My colleagues and I compared the efficacy of the CBT intervention described above to the effects produced by a 15-week group social support protocol for patients and their spouses, and to the effects of standard medical treatment (Bradley et al., 1987, 1988). We found that the CBT intervention, relative to the other treatment conditions, produced significant reductions in pain behavior and disease activity (i.e., number of painful joints) at posttreatment. The CBT intervention also produced a significant reduction in pain intensity ratings at posttreatment, relative to social support. Nevertheless, a 1-year follow-up assessment revealed that only the reduction in pain intensity ratings was maintained following the termination of treatment.

Several other investigators have reported that CBT interventions produce reductions in pain and disease activity among patients with RA (Applebaum, Blanchard, Hickling, & Alfonso, 1988; O'Leary, Shoor, Lorig, & Holman, 1988; Parker et al., 1988; Radojevic et al., 1992). All of these investigations have also shown that the effects of CBT tend to diminish over time. Parker et al. (1988), however, have demonstrated that patients who continue to practice their newly learned relaxation skills and coping strategies after treatment maintain their reductions in pain intensity at a 1-year follow-up.

In contrast to the findings noted above, Lorig, Mazonson, and Holman (1993) have found that their Arthritis Self-Management Program, based on the principles of CBT, produced significant reductions in pain ratings and arthritis-related physician visits among patients with RA and osteoarthritis (OA) that were maintained for 4 years after completion of treatment. Indeed, the estimated net 4-year savings in health care costs were $648 for each patient with RA and $189 for each patient with OA.

A few investigators have examined the efficacy of CBT interventions developed specifically for patients with OA. Keefe et al. (1990a, 1990b), for example, compared the effects of a CBT-based coping skills training program to the effects of arthritis education and standard medical care among patients with OA of the knee. The CBT intervention, relative to the other treatment conditions, produced significant reductions in patients' ratings of pain and psychological disability. These effects were generally maintained at a 6-month follow-up evaluation. In addition, patients who received the CBT intervention reported significant reductions in physical disability from posttreatment to follow-up.

A new development in CBT interventions for chronic pain is the delivery of treatment by telephone in order to reduce costs. Weinberger and his colleagues recently examined the outcomes produced by a telephone intervention, delivered by lay personnel, for patients with OA (Weinberger, Tierney, Booher, & Katz, 1989; Weinberger, Tierney, Cowper, Katz, & Booher, 1993). The treatment personnel provided education, reviewed medications and clinical problems with the patients, and taught strategies for increasing patient involvement during physician encounters. The telephone intervention produced significant reductions in patients' reports of pain and functional disability (Weinberger et al., 1993). Several reanalyses of the data revealed that the beneficial effects of the telephone intervention could not be attributed to enhanced social support, satisfaction with medical care, medication adherence, morale, or intensified medical treatment (Weinberger, Tierney, Booher, & Katz, 1991; René, Weinberger, Mazzuca, Brandt, & Katz, 1992). Maisiak and his colleagues have replicated these results in a controlled trial of a CBT intervention delivered by telephone to patients with OA and RA (Maisiak, Austin, & Heck, 1994).

MAINTENANCE OF TREATMENT GAINS

I have noted earlier that an important concern for practitioners and investigators of CBT interventions for chronic pain is the extent to which patients may maintain their improvements after the completion of therapy. This is a critical issue, given that it is becoming increasingly important for health care providers to justify the costs of their services. Indeed, there are unique problems associated with maintenance of CBT treatment gains among patients with rheumatological disorders, because the natural history of these disorders includes declines in health status over time (Pincus & Callahan, 1992).

Keefe and Van Horn (1993) have recently provided a model for preventing relapse of treatment gains among patients with RA that can also be applied to persons with diverse chronic pain syndromes. This model suggests that relapse tends to occur when patients' symptoms increase in intensity, their perceived abilities to control symptoms are compromised, and their psychological distress is magnified (Keefe & Van Horn, 1993; Schiaffino, Revenson, & Gibofsky, 1991). If patients stop their coping efforts in response to these events, they are likely to experience a major decline in pain control, functional ability, or psychological status. Therefore, Keefe and Van Horn have suggested that CBT interventions may produce better maintenance of treatment gains if they include components designed to help patients cope with potential relapse. Specifically, all phases of treatment should include (1) practice in identifying high-risk situations that are likely to tax patients' coping resources; (2) practice in identifying the early signs of relapse, such as increases in pain or depression; (3) rehearsal of cognitive and behavioral skills for responding to these early relapse signs; and (4) training in self-reinforcement for effective displays of coping with possible relapse.

It should be noted that nearly all CBT interventions for patients with RA (e.g., Bradley et al., 1987) include some elements of relapse prevention training. However, this training is primarily provided during the final treatment sessions or in telephone contacts during follow-up. Thus, important goals for practitioners and investigators will be to implement relapse prevention training early in treatment, to emphasize this training throughout the course of therapy, and to evaluate patients' maintenance of treatment gains for a minimum period of 1 year.

SUMMARY

CBT is based on the premise that perceptions and observable displays of pain are influenced by complex interactions between environmental events and individuals' emotional, physiological, behavioral, and cognitive responses. Therefore, effective interventions for chronic pain must address the emotional, cognitive, and behavioral dimensions of pain, and must also help patients become active participants in learning new methods of responding to their problems. Numerous CBT interventions have been developed for patients with a variety of chronic pain syndromes. However, they all share four components: education, skills acquisition, cognitive and behavioral rehearsal, and generalization and treatment maintenance.

The CBT interventions developed for patients with rheumatological disorders such as RA have produced outcomes representative of those associated with CBT for other chronic pain syndromes. It has been shown that these interventions generate reliable reductions in patients' self-reports of pain, observable pain behaviors, and disease activity. However, two important and related issues concerning CBT interventions must be addressed by practitioners and investigators. The first issue is the need to develop therapies that are cost-effective; one promising attempt to confront this issue has been the development of telephone-based interventions that may be delivered by trained lay personnel.

The second issue is the need to demonstrate that CBT interventions produce improvements that patients can maintain following completion of treatment. It has been especially difficult to show that CBT interventions generate long-term benefits for patients with rheumatological disorders, since the natural history of these disorders usually involves deterioration in health status. Effort is now being devoted to providing patients with relapse prevention training throughout the course of CBT. If it can be shown that CBT interventions reliably produce long-term reductions in pain perceptions and behaviors, it is likely that policy planners will advocate continued financial support for these interventions during the reorganization of the U.S. health care delivery system.

REFERENCES

Achterberg, J., McGraw, P., & Lawlis, C. F. (1981). Rheumatoid arthritis: A study of relaxation and temperature biofeedback training as an adjunctive therapy. *Biofeedback and Self-Regulation*, *6*, 207–223

Anderson, K. O., Bradley, L. A., Young, L. D., McDaniel, L. K., & Wise, C. M. (1985). Rheumatoid arthritis: Review of psychological factors related to etiology, effects, and treatment. *Psychological Bulletin*, *98*, 358–387.

Applebaum, K. A., Blanchard, E. B., Hickling, E. J., & Alfonso, M. (1988). Cognitive-behavioral treatment of a veteran population with moderate to severe rheumatoid arthritis. *Behavior Therapy*, *19*, 489–502.

Bradley, L. A. (1993). Psychosocial factors and arthritis. In H.R. Schumacher, J.H. Klippel, & W.J. Koopman (Eds.), *Primer on the rheumatic diseases* (10th ed., pp. 319–322). Atlanta: Arthritis Foundation.

Bradley, L. A., & Kay, R. (1985). The role of cognition in behavioral medicine. In P.C. Kendall (Ed.), *Advances in cognitive-behavioral research and therapy* (Vol. 4, pp. 137–213). New York: Academic Press.

Bradley, L. A., Richter, J. E., Pulliam, T. J., McDonald-Haile, J., Scarinci, I. C., Schan, C. A., Dalton, C. B., & Salley, A. N. (1993). The relationship between stress and symptoms of gastroesophageal reflux: The influence of psychological factors. *American Journal of Gastroenterology*, *88*, 11–19.

Bradley, L. A., Young, L. D., Anderson, K. O., Turner, R. A., Agudelo, C. A., McDaniel, L. K., Pisko, E. J., Semble, E. L., & Morgan, T. M. (1987). Effects of psychological therapy on pain behavior of rheumatoid arthritis patients: Treatment outcome and six-month follow-up. *Arthritis and Rheumatism*, *30*, 1105–1114.

Bradley, L. A., Young, L. D., Anderson, K. O., Turner, R. A., Agudelo, C. A., McDaniel, L. K., & Semble, E. L. (1988). Effects of cognitive-behavioral therapy on rheumatoid arthritis pain behavior: One-year follow-up. In R. Dubner, G.F. Gebhart, & M.R. Bond (Eds.), *Proceedings of the Vth World Congress on Pain* (pp. 310–314). Amsterdam: Elsevier.

Burish, T. G., & Bradley, L. A. (1983). Coping with chronic disease: Definitions and issues. In T.G. Burish & L.A. Bradley (Eds.), *Coping with chronic disease: Research and applications* (pp. 3–12). New York: Academic Press.

Holzman, A. D., Turk, D. C., & Kerns, R. D. (1986). The cognitive-behavioral approach to the management of chronic pain. In A.D. Holzman & D.C. Turk (Eds.), *Pain management: A handbook of psychological treatment approaches* (pp. 31–50). Elmsford, NY: Pergamon Press.

Jacobson, E. (1938). *Progressive relaxation* (2nd ed.). Chicago: University of Chicago Press.

Keefe, F. J., Caldwell, D. S., Williams, D. A., Gil, K. M., Mitchell, D., Robertson, C., Martinez, S., Nunley, J., Beckham, J. C., Crisson, J. E., & Helms, M. (1990a). Pain coping skills training in the management of osteoarthritic knee pain: A comparative study. *Behavior Therapy*, *21*, 49–62.

Keefe, F. J., Caldwell, D. S., Williams, D. A., Gil, K., Mitchell, D., Robertson, C., Martinez, S., Nunley, J., Beckham, J. C., Crisson, J. E., & Helms, M. (1990b). Pain coping skills training in the management of osteoarthritic knee pain: II. Follow-up results. *Behavior Therapy*, *21*, 435–447.

Keefe, F. J., & Van Horn, Y. (1993). Cognitive-behavioral treatment of rheumatoid arthritis pain: Maintaining treatment gains. *Arthritis Care and Research, 6,* 213–222.

Linton, S. J. (1982). Applied relaxation as a method of coping with chronic pain: A therapist's guide. *Scandinavian Journal of Behavior Therapy, 11,* 161–174.

Linton, S. J., Bradley, L. A., Jensen, I., Spangfort, E., & Sundell, L. (1989). The secondary prevention of low back pain: A controlled study with follow-up. *Pain, 36,* 197–207.

Lorig, K. R., Mazonson, P. D., & Holman, H. R. (1993). Evidence suggesting that health education for self-management in patients with chronic arthritis has sustained health benefits while reducing health care costs. *Arthritis and Rheumatism, 38,* 439–446.

Maisiak, R., Austin, J., & Heck, L. (1994). Health status improvement in arthritis patients produced by a telephone counseling intervention: A controlled clinical trial. *Arthritis and Rheumatism, 37,* S289. (Abstract)

McDonald-Haile, J., Bradley, L. A., Bailey, M. A., Schan, C. A., & Richter, J. E. (1994). Relaxation training reduces symptom reports and acid exposure in patients with gastroesophageal reflux disease. *Gastroenterology, 107,* 61–69.

Melzack, R., & Wall, P. D. (1965). Pain mechanisms: A new theory. *Science, 50,* 971–979.

Nielson, W., Walker, C., & McCain, G. A. (1992). Cognitive behavioral treatment of fibromyalgia syndrome: Preliminary findings. *Journal of Rheumatology, 19,* 98–103.

O'Leary, A., Shoor, S., Lorig, K., & Holman, H. R. (1988). A cognitive-behavioral treatment for rheumatoid arthritis. *Health Psychology, 7,* 527–544.

Parker, J. C., Frank, R. G., Beck, N. C., Smarr, K. L., Buescher, K. L., Phillips, L. R., Smith, E. I., Anderson, S. K., & Walker, S. R. (1988). Pain management in rheumatoid arthritis patients: A cognitive-behavioral approach. *Arthritis and Rheumatism, 31,* 593–601.

Pincus, T., & Callahan, L. F. (1992). Rheumatology function tests: Grip strength, walking time, button test and questionnaires document and predict long-term morbidity and mortality in rheumatoid arthritis. *Journal of Rheumatology, 19,* 1051–1057.

Radojevic, V., Nicassio, P. M., & Weisman, M. H. (1992). Behavioral intervention with and without family support for rheumatoid arthritis. *Behavior Therapy, 23,* 13–30.

René, J., Weinberger, M., Mazzuca, S. A., Brandt, K. D., & Katz, B. P. (1992). Reduction of joint pain in patients with knee osteoarthritis who have received monthly telephone calls from lay personnel and whose medical treatment regimens have remained stable. *Arthritis and Rheumatism, 35,* 511–515.

Schiaffino, K. M., Revenson, T. A., & Gibofsky, A. (1991). Assessing the impact of self-efficacy beliefs on adaptation to rheumatoid arthritis. *Arthritis Care and Research, 4,* 150–157.

Thorndike, E. L. (1913). *The psychology of learning.* New York: Teachers College Press.

Turk, D. C., Meichenbaum, D. H., & Genest, M. (1983). *Pain and behavioral medicine: A cognitive-behavioral perspective.* New York: Guilford Press.

Turk, D. C., & Rudy, T. E. (1989). A cognitive-behavioral perspective on chronic pain: Beyond the scalpel and syringe. In C. D. Tollison (Ed.), *Handbook of chronic pain management* (pp. 222–236). Baltimore: Williams & Wilkins.

Weinberger, M., Tierney, W. M., Booher, P., & Katz, B. P. (1989). Can the provision of information to patients with osteoarthritis improve functional status? A randomized, controlled trial. *Arthritis and Rheumatism, 32,* 1577–1583.

Weinberger, M., Tierney, W. M., Booher, P., & Katz, B. P. (1991). The impact of increased contact on psychosocial outcomes in patients with osteoarthritis: A randomized, controlled trial. *Journal of Rheumatology, 18,* 849–854.

Weinberger, M., Tierney, W. M., Cowper, P. A., Katz, B. P., & Booher, P. A. (1993). Cost-effectiveness of increased telephone contact for patients with osteoarthritis: A randomized controlled trial. *Arthritis and Rheumatism, 36,* 243–246.

CHAPTER 7

Psychodynamic Psychotherapy with Chronic Pain Patients

Roy C. Grzesiak
Gregg M. Ury
Robert H. Dworkin

> *The activist therapeutic posture, epitomized in the injunction "Don't just stand there, do something!" has its place in medical practice, but that place is not in the management of chronic pain in the absence of demonstrable bodily disease. Faced with that problem, both sufferers and their would-be helpers might profit from inverting that phrase and trying to heed the injunction, "Don't just do something, stand there."*
>
> —Szasz (1975, p. vii)

Many chronic pain patients derive substantial benefits from the psychological interventions described in the other chapters of this volume. Our focus in this chapter is on the treatment of chronic pain patients who either have not responded adequately to these treatments, or who have been evaluated at the outset as unlikely to respond to such interventions. Unfortunately, because of the great variability among samples of patients in the very different settings in which chronic pain is evaluated and treated, it is not possible to provide an estimate of the percentage of chronic pain patients who are in this category. However, as is generally appreciated, for every existing treatment for chronic pain—no matter how efficacious it may be—there is an appreciable subgroup of patients who fail to respond, or who respond initially and then return to pretreatment levels of pain, suffering, and disability. Moreover, as we argue below, recent research suggests that psychosocial factors play a role in the development of chronic pain, and some of the psychological factors that have been so implicated are unlikely to respond to the relatively short-term psychological interventions that now constitute the accepted standard of care for chronic pain patients.

Elsewhere, we have described an integrative psychotherapeutic approach to the individual with chronic pain (Dworkin & Grzesiak, 1993). This approach emphasizes the importance of integrating behavioral strategies and cognitive techniques within a psychodynamic perspective that values the importance of developmental history, intrapsychic conflict, interpersonal difficulties, and failure to adapt to chronic illness and persisting pain. In this chapter, we focus on the psychodynamic foundation of this integrative approach to psychotherapy with chronic pain patients. To the best of our knowledge, there have been no prospective, controlled studies of psychodynamic psychotherapy with chronic pain patients (a study by Pilowsky & Barrow, 1990, compared the efficacy of dynamic psychotherapy with amitriptyline in chronic pain). Our presentation therefore combines what is extant in the clinical literature with our clinical experience as psychologists who have worked in a number of pain management programs and clinics.

We do not believe that psychodynamic psychotherapy is the treatment of choice for all individuals suffering from chronic pain. Because pain is a subjective experience involving complex biopsychosocial processes, the array of potential psychological interventions varies from none at all to long-term intensive psychoanalytic psychotherapy. Turk (1990) has emphasized the importance of customizing treatment for the chronic pain patient; he has noted that pain management professionals often hold "patient uniformity myths" as well as "treatment uniformity myths." In describing this tendency to view all patients as essentially the same and all treatments as having the same effect, Turk has stressed the importance of examining the biological, psychological, and social processes at work for each individual pain patient, and then designing a treatment program to address the salient problem areas that have been identified.

Fordyce (1976) also described an "illusion of homogeneity"—the unfortunate tendency to look at all chronic pain patients as if they have similar histories, personalities, and premorbid experiences. Such is clearly not the case. In fact, individuals suffering from persistent pain bring to the clinical situation a vast array of individual differences, including personality, character, premorbid level of adaptation, capacity to cope with adversity, and varying degrees of resourcefulness and resilience. Among other such demonstrations, Sternbach (1974), in a retrospective review of psychometric findings and program outcomes, and Bradley and associates (Bradley, Prokop, Gentry, Van der Heide, & Prieto, 1981; Bradley, Prokop, Margolis, & Gentry, 1978), in a series of sophisticated multivariate studies with the Minnesota Multiphasic Personality Inventory (MMPI), have noted the substantial differences in personality to be found among samples of chronic pain patients. These differences in personality should form part of the foundation for customizing psychological treatment. As psychotherapists, we do not treat individuals with different disorders in the same manner. If they happen to have persistent pain, the unique cognitive and perceptual features of their premorbid personalities will color both their perception of and their adaptation to pain. Although such attempts have been made in other areas of clinical psychology and psychiatry (e.g., Guidano & Liotti, 1983; Frances, Clarkin, & Perry, 1984; Horowitz et al., 1984), we have yet to see the systematic application of differential psychological treatment planning in multidisciplinary pain management.

Before we can address psychodynamic psychotherapeutic approaches to the psychological treatment of people in pain, there are a number of introductory issues that need clarification. First, we review the literature on psychosocial risk factors for the development of chronic pain, focusing on Engel's (1959) approach to pain and studies that have addressed his hypotheses. We then discuss the place of psychodynamic psychotherapy among the diverse psychological interventions that are currently available for chronic pain patients. Next, we review some early as well as more recent descriptions of important psychodynamic aspects of the experience of pain and suffering. Rather than presenting an overview of psychodynamic approaches to pain, we emphasize what we believe are some key themes in the psychodynamics of chronic pain patients. Following this, we discuss the central aspects of psychodynamic psychotherapy that we have found most helpful in our work with chronic pain patients. Throughout, we provide clinical examples from our work with pain patients, as well as references to the work of others.

THE ROLE OF PSYCHOSOCIAL FACTORS IN THE
DEVELOPMENT OF CHRONIC PAIN

As Turk and Rudy (1990, 1991) have noted, most studies of chronic pain base their results on select samples; the majority of chronic pain patients attending tertiary and multidisciplinary pain management centers and clinics are not representative of the population at large suffering from ongoing pain. As such, much of the empirical and clinical research is based on a very small subset of individuals with pain. Furthermore, clinicians working with chronic pain patients may find it relatively easy to lose sight of the fact that the world is full of people with persistent pain and chronic illness. The vast majority of these people do not become chronic pain patients, and they do not engage in inappropriate illness behavior (Crook, Rideout, & Browne, 1984). They continue to work, love, bring up their children, and play without succumbing to their pain in a maladaptive way. What is it that accounts for the differences between these "silent sufferers" (Brena & Koch, 1975) or "adaptive copers" (Turk & Rudy, 1988) and those who become chronic pain patients or chronic sufferers?

Although the suffering caused by chronic pain is difficult to quantify, there is a consensus, based on research and clinical experience, that "in addition to depression, patients develop associated chronic invalid behaviors. . . . [They curtail their] social activity . . . become increasingly homebound, and their chief interaction with others, in the home as well as out of it, is via the sick role" (Sternbach, 1989, p. 244). These social and psychological consequences of chronic pain are substantial, but very little is known regarding the mechanisms by which such pain develops. The major reason for this is that studies of patients who are already suffering from chronic pain and its deleterious effects cannot differentiate the antecedents of chronic pain from its consequences. The confounding of potential antecedents of the development of chronic pain with its negative consequences is most obvious in considerations of the psychological aspects of such pain. For example, it has frequently been reported that a substantial proportion of chronic pain patients suffer from depression (Dworkin & Gitlin, 1991), but studies of chronic pain and depression have not resolved whether the stress of living with chronic pain causes patients to develop a depressive disorder or whether depression causes an experience of chronic pain. It is likely that neither one of these sequences completely explains the relationship between pain and depression. However, research on patients already suffering from chronic pain does not allow the relative contributions of these two different processes to the comorbidity of chronic pain and depression to be assessed.

Additional examples of the difficulty of identifying antecedents of chronic pain are provided by the large number of studies that have used retrospective and cross-sectional methods to examine various psychological and social factors hypothesized to play a causal role in the development of such pain. The shortcomings of such methods are well known and include several problematic assumptions. Not surprisingly, it has been impossible to satisfactorily distinguish antecedents from consequences of chronic pain when retrospective and cross-sectional methods are used (Dworkin, 1991; Gamsa, 1994a, 1994b). Although such studies provide a valuable source of hypotheses, they cannot satisfactorily identify factors that predispose individuals to the development of chronic pain, because the characteristics of chronic pain patients may be consequences of their pain. In order to identify causal antecedents of chronic pain, it is necessary to conduct prospective research in which the investigation of a sample of individuals begins before they have developed chronic pain and then continues while their chronic pain syndromes unfold. The importance of such prospective research with respect to understanding the processes by which chronic pain syndromes develop and individuals become chronic pain patients has been evident for some time, but until recently, studying patients before and after the onset of chronic pain was considered "an obviously impractical task" (Sternbach & Timmermans, 1975, p. 177).

In the past several years, several prospective studies have been reported in which hypothesized antecedents of acute and chronic pain have been examined. The results of these studies have suggested that various psychosocial factors—especially symptoms of depression—may be risk factors for the later development of pain (Bigos et al., 1991; Dworkin et al., 1992; Leino & Magni, 1993; Magni, Moreschi, Rigatti-Luchini, & Merskey, 1994; Pietri-Taleb, Riihimaki, Viikari-Juntura, & Lindstrom, 1994; Turner & Noh, 1988; Von Korff, Le Resche, & Dworkin, 1993; Weickgenant, Slater, & Atkinson, 1994).

The results of these prospective studies have important implications for understanding the development of chronic pain. In suggesting that psychosocial factors are risk factors for chronic pain, these studies provide a basis for further considerations of the nature of the psychological processes that play a role in the etiology of chronic pain and in the psychological development of chronic pain patients. One approach to the development of chronic pain is the concept of "pain-proneness" introduced by Engel (1951, 1959). Grzesiak (1991, 1992a, 1994a, 1994b) has attempted to resurrect this somewhat neglected concept as germane to psychotherapeutic work with many chronic pain patients. Because we believe that the concept of pain-proneness or vulnerability to suffering is important to understanding the potential role of psychodynamically oriented psychotherapy in the management of chronic pain, we would like to expand on this in some detail and provide some examples from the literature suggesting its importance.

Engel (1951, 1959), an internist with psychoanalytic training, used the anamnestic interview in an attempt to identify the early developmental or psychosocial determinants of pain-proneness in patients who either were unresponsive to what appeared to be appropriate treatment, or had no identifiable somatic pathology to account for their chronic pain. He found that these patients shared a number of features with respect to their early life histories. These included physically or verbally abusive parents; harsh or punitive parents who overcompensated with rare displays of affection; cold or emotionally distant parents who were only warm and solicitous when a child was ill; a parent who suffered from chronic illness or pain; and various other parent–child interactions involving guilt, aggression, or pain (Grzesiak, 1994a). Engel labeled these individuals "pain-prone personalities." An unfortunate occurrence in the psychological and pain management literature was the tendency to misinterpret Engel's work as suggesting that there was a single pain-prone personality. That is not what he said and not what he meant. He suggested that an unconscious propensity to pain-proneness and suffering is more common in individuals with hypochondriacal, hysterical, depressive, or schizophrenic personality organizations. Thus, there is no single personality type predisposed to pain-proneness and suffering, but many.

In analyzing the experience of chronic pain, Engel (1959) divided the pain complaint into two parts, which he called "signatures." He spoke of the "peripheral signature" as the part of the pain complaint that has good concordance with what the physician knows about anatomy, physiology, and disease processes. In other words, the patient's complaint makes sense, and the location, pattern, and description of the pain sensation permit proper diagnosis and subsequent appropriate treatment. Engel also spoke of the "individual psychic signature." This term refers to those aspects of the pain experience that do not fit with anatomy and physiology, but instead reflect the private, idiosyncratic meanings the individual attaches to disease, pain, and suffering. The kinds of untoward early life experiences that Engel (1959) identified in his patients were the (usually unconscious) contents of the individual psychic signature. As Engel saw it, the hidden, usually either repressed or dissociated, early experience with suffering, guilt, and anger is what forms the foundation for a vulnerability to suffering later in life.

In a recent paper, Grzesiak (1994b) has combined Engel's concepts of the peripheral and individual psychic signatures with Melzack's work on the neurobiology of pain (Melzack, 1989, 1991, 1992; Melzack & Loeser, 1978). Grzesiak has argued that, at least theoretically, it is possible to integrate psychodynamic concepts within a neurobiological model; such a model makes it possible to understand how a vulnerability to suffering can be integrated with what is known of the neural processes involved in chronic pain.

Until recently, one could find little in the literature to support the concept of pain-proneness or vulnerability to suffering. However, in recent years a few studies, none of them prospective, have made a relatively strong argument for re-evaluating the concept of pain-proneness. In a clinical case report, Harness and Donlon (1988) addressed what they called "cryptotrauma" or hidden trauma. They discussed two cases of facial pain that were unresponsive to treatment until each patient had developed a solid therapeutic alliance with the treating therapist (in these cases, a biofeedback therapist). When rapport and trust were strong, each admitted to having been physically abused; following these admissions, their facial pain abated. A controlled but retrospective study was reported by Adler, Zlot, Hurny, and Minder (1989), in which the investigators compared a psychogenic pain group with three other groups: groups with organic pain, psychogenic bodily symptoms, and organic disease. They found that the psychogenic pain group was significantly different from the other groups on the following variables: (1) parents who were verbally or physically abusive of each other, (2) parents who were physically abusive of a child, (3) a child who deflected aggression from one parent to the other onto himself or herself, (4) parents who suffered from illnesses or pain, (5) an ill parent of the same gender as the patient suffering from pain, (6) pain of patient and parent in the same location, (7) number of surgeries in adulthood, (8) disturbance in interpersonal relationships, and (9) disturbance in work life.

With respect to the last category, disturbance in work life, Blumer and Heilbronn (1989) have described a characteristic of their chronic pain patients that they have labeled "ergomania." Ergomania is a conflicted work ethic that they believe is an important characteristic of many chronic pain patients. These authors suggest that ergomanic pain patients have a history of excessive work performance, relentless activity, self-sacrifice, and the precocious assumption of adult responsibilities. They also have marked difficulty trusting caretakers, including health care providers. Parkes (1973) termed a similar constellation of personality characteristics "pathological self-reliance," and VanHoudenove and associates have referred to these tendencies toward excessive activity as "premorbid hyperactivity" (VanHoudenove, 1986) and "action-proneness" (VanHoudenove, Stans, & Verstraeten, 1987). In a recent study designed to examine a number of Engel's (1959) proposed antecedents of chronic pain, Gamsa (Gamsa, 1990; Gamsa & Vikis-Freibergs, 1991) found that ergomania was one of only two psychological variables that were consistently associated with pain (the other was emotional repression). As clinicians, it has been our observation that many chronic pain patients have the premorbid characteristics of ergomania. In a preliminary study, Ciccone and Grzesiak (1990) compared chronic back and neck pain patients with controls, and found significantly greater levels of this ergomanic trait in the pain patients. In a recent critical review of psychosocial risk factors for vulnerability to chronic pain, Ciccone and Lenzi (1994) concluded that the evidence regarding excessive premorbid activity suggests it is a risk factor for chronic pain, but that more research is necessary.

Also consistent with Engel's (1959) observations were the results of a study of childhood psychological trauma and outcome of spinal surgery conducted by Schofferman, Anderson, Hines, Smith, and White (1992). These investigators, a team of psychiatrists and spinal surgeons, examined the relationship between an operationally defined set of risk factors (based on Engel's work) and the outcome of spinal surgery. The following were considered risk factors: (1) physical abuse by a primary caregiver, (2) sexual abuse by a primary caregiver or other adult, (3) alcohol or drug abuse in one or both caregivers, (4) abandonment (loss of a primary caregiver), and (5) emotional neglect/abuse by primary caregivers. The authors investigated 100 consecutive patients who had undergone spinal surgery and correlated physical outcomes with these risk factors. They found that 95% of the patients who recalled none of these traumas had successful postsurgical outcomes. On the other hand, those patients who recalled three or more of the risk factors as having been part of their developmental history had a successful postsurgical outcome of only 15%. This relationship was linear, such that the addition of each risk factor added to the likelihood of poor outcome. The same group of investigators followed up these observations with another retrospective study correlating the incidence of childhood psychological trauma with chronic low back pain; their results again suggested that early trauma of the sort described by Engel may predispose an individual to the development of low back pain (Schofferman, Anderson, Hines, Smith, & Keane, 1993).

The vulnerabilities to the development of chronic pain that we have discussed to this point involve various psychological processes and risk factors. But the results of research on personality disorders in chronic pain patients are also consistent with the findings reviewed in this section. Personality disorders typically begin in adolescence and continue through adulthood, and reflect a long-standing pattern of poor adaptation to life and its stresses. These disorders appear to be quite common among chronic pain patients: A review of studies examining *Diagnostic and Statistical Manual of Mental Disorders*, third edition (DSM-III) diagnoses in chronic pain patients found that from 18% to 59% of patients received a personality disorder diagnosis (Dworkin & Caligor, 1988). Many personality disorders are notoriously refractory to treatment, and when chronic pain occurs in the context of one of these disorders, behavioral, cognitive-behavioral, and psychopharmacological treatment approaches are unlikely to be very effective. Although psychodynamic psychotherapy with such patients is by no means straightforward, it does provide an approach within which the treatment of personality disorders has received a great deal of attention.

We are by no means suggesting that the research findings reviewed in this section provide evidence that chronic pain can have a "psychogenic" origin. Rather, we believe that the sources of chronic pain are almost always combinations of biological, psychological, and social factors. From this perspective, the findings we have reviewed suggest that individuals who have suffered from early trauma of various sorts are more likely to develop a chronic pain syndrome in response to physical pathology. Early developmental trauma and the personality traits that are associated with it provide a vulnerability to pain and suffering that, in the presence of current disease or injury, compromises the patient's ability to adapt to the sick role, to rely appropriately on health care providers, and to regain health or make a reasonable adjustment to changes in physical functioning.

THE ROLE OF PSYCHODYNAMIC PSYCHOTHERAPY
IN CHRONIC PAIN TREATMENT

As suggested above, a psychodynamically based psychotherapy is certainly not the treatment of choice for all chronic pain patients. However, we believe that psychodynamic psychotherapy is beneficial for many pain patients, because the experience of pain and suffering can be exacerbated or maintained by psychodynamic processes long after tissues have healed. Before considering psychodynamic psychotherapy in more detail, we would like to acknowledge the very important role that other psychological interventions play in the management of the chronic pain patient, and to try to place psychodynamic psychotherapy within this context. The application by Fordyce of learning theory principles to the problem of chronic pain behavior first enabled psychologists to become important members of the multidisciplinary pain management team (Fordyce, 1976; Fordyce, Fowler, & DeLateur, 1968a; Fordyce, Fowler, Lehmann, & Delateur, 1968b). To paraphrase Fordyce, an individual's pain behavior becomes chronic when it is reinforced, especially if the individual's efforts to engage in healthful behaviors are also either tacitly or explicitly discouraged. Therefore, elimination of pain behavior requires reversing the contingencies so that the individual is rewarded for well behavior. Major behaviorally oriented chronic pain programs have successfully utilized this treatment approach (e.g., Fordyce et al., 1973; Gil, Ross, & Keefe, 1988; see Sanders, Chapter 5, this volume). Gil et al. (1988) have suggested that the operant approach to chronic pain behavior may be most appropriate when the patient demonstrates little or no relationship between his or her pain behavior and the underlying disease or illness.

Many pain patients have the resources to control their own behavioral and psychological responses to persisting pain. According to Gil et al. (1988), these individuals may not need an operant program; they may be better suited for interventions that focus on self-control and self-regulation. These patients can benefit from strategies such as relaxation training, biofeedback, self-hypnosis, or cognitive coping skills training. Over the last decade, the most widely used form of psychological intervention for chronic pain has been cognitive-behavioral therapy (Turk, Meichenbaum, & Genest, 1983). This approach is explored in depth by Bradley in Chapter 6 of this volume. A more strictly cognitive therapy has been suggested by Ciccone and Grzesiak (1984, 1988). This approach places thought processes—specifically, irrational ideas about pain and suffering—at the forefront, and suggests that the modification of irrational beliefs about pain and illness is the central ingredient for a more appropriate adaptation to persistent pain. From the perspective of this chapter, we would like to note that in both cognitive-behavioral and cognitive approaches, what patients think about their illness and pain is a central concern of treatment. Patients often maintain an inner dialogue with themselves, and have automatic thoughts, self-statements, and private conceptualizations that add to their symptomatic distress. Although these cognitions are among the targets of intervention in these approaches, little attention is paid to the origins and persistence of these thoughts and beliefs.

There is a subset of chronic pain patients who do not benefit from either behavioral or cognitive-behavioral approaches. They are intractable and prove to be unresponsive to either medical or psychological interventions. These are the patients for whom we believe a more traditional psychodynamic psychotherapy is the treatment of choice. These are the patients who have been called "pain-prone" or "suffering" individuals in the early literature (Engel, 1951, 1959). Following on the work of both Engel (1951, 1959) and Blumer and Heilbronn (1989), Grzesiak (1992a, 1992b, 1994b) has suggested that pain-proneness is an unconscious process that has its origins in untoward early life experiences. These early experiences (trauma, loss, abandonment) lay a foundation of vulnerability to pain-proneness and psychic suffering. In many cases this matrix of unconscious factors lies dormant, encapsulating the consequences of early childhood trauma until life events—usually physical or psychic trauma or illness—provide a theater for the expression of these long-hidden conflicts in chronic suffering. In clinical work with chronic pain patients, it is often suffering, not pain, that poses the primary problem.

PSYCHODYNAMIC THEMES
IN THE EXPERIENCE OF CHRONIC PAIN

Although Freud never systematically discussed physical pain, references to differences between psychic and physical pain can be found throughout his writing. His earliest reference to physical pain is in *Project for a Scientific Psychology* (Freud, 1895/1966), where he began formulating the concept of the "protective barrier"; penetration of the protective barrier by physical sensations leads to the experience of unpleasure by relating the sensation to earlier memory traces. Freud expanded on this notion in *Inhibitions, Symptoms and Anxiety* (Freud, 1926/1959). Although the concept of the protective barrier has not remained a vital concept in psychoanalytic theory, its importance lies in the fact that it acknowledges the role of memory of past pain in the overall clinical picture. Interestingly, Freud addressed diagnostic dilemmas that continue to plague us today. In *Studies on Hysteria*, while discussing the origins of Elisabeth von R's pain, he and Breuer stated: "The circumstances indicate that this somatic pain was not *created* by the neurosis but merely used, increased, and maintained by it. . . . There has always been a genuine, organically-founded pain present at the start. It is the commonest and most widespread human pains that seem to be most often chosen to play a part in hysteria" (Breuer & Freud, 1893–1895/1955, p. 174). In *Fragment of an Analysis of a Case of Hysteria*, Freud noted that the motivation for maintaining a physical symptom may have little to do with the mechanisms that caused the initial medical problem (Freud, 1905/1959). In this short vignette, Freud made an important point that is often ignored by contemporary diagnosticians—namely, that intractable physical symptoms can be divorced from their original biological sources.

Over the years, a number of psychoanalytic theorists have addressed the problem of pain and suffering. It is well known that there is neither a unified theory of psychoanalysis nor a standard approach to conducting psychodynamic psychotherapy. Rather than providing an overview of psychoanalytic principles, we have chosen in this section to highlight some of the psychodynamic themes that we have found useful in our work as psychotherapists with chronic pain patients.

Childhood Development and Early Experiences
with Pain and Illness

One of the central themes of this chapter is the importance of early developmental experiences in influencing the patient's experience of pain and illness and his or her adaptation to these conditions. It is important to recognize that these significant early developmental experiences include not only the traumatic experiences discussed above, but also the behavior of significant others, especially family members, and their influences on the growing child. The following three clinical vignettes illustrate the importance of early memories, identifications, and traumas with respect to the current functioning of chronic pain patients.

A 36-year-old married male was seen in psychotherapy as part of the multidisciplinary management of back pain of recent onset. His pain was of approximately 6 months' duration, associated with a non-work-related lifting injury, and unresponsive to conservative orthopedic care. The patient had been valedictorian of his graduating class at an Ivy League college, but had dropped out of a prestigious dental school after only one semester. By his own admission, dental school itself was not unusually difficult, but the pressure to succeed that he imposed on himself was literally paralyzing. After leaving dental school, he had obtained a master's degree at a local college and had worked for years as a high school biology teacher. In psychotherapy, he reported the following dream: "I was walking with my father; he was getting further and further in front of me and I couldn't keep up. I said to myself: 'I cannot even keep up with my father, and my father is a cripple!'" Further inquiry revealed that his father had a bad leg, ambulated with a marginally functional gait, and was constantly falling behind during family walks. This was the first the psychotherapist had heard of the father's physical disability, and of its possible psychic meanings for the patient's early identifications with his father, which included both fear of success and failure. Particularly noteworthy was the fact that the patient was markedly ambivalent about outdistancing his father. Physical therapy in combination with psychotherapy—which resulted in an increased awareness of the conflictual aspects of his relationship with his father—enabled the patient to return to his work as a high school teacher.

A 51-year-old divorced female was seen for psychotherapy as part of her multidisciplinary pain management program. She had had spinal surgery for a ruptured disc; although she had felt much better during the immediate postoperative period, while she was still in the hospital a nurse had inadvertently spilled urine from a bedpan onto her bed linen. The patient developed an infection at the incision site, and her pain returned and did not remit. The psychotherapist initially focused on her depression, but from the perspective of the pain management team there were other issues as well. She had a compliance problem with respect to medications, frequently refusing to take both the analgesic and the anti-inflammatory medications prescribed for her. She also presented major problems in terms of learning to pace her activities: On a good day she would overexert herself, and then she would fall back into a pattern of inactivity.

In psychotherapy one day, she recalled the following incident. In early adolescence she had lived near a favorite aunt who had chronic back pain. One day after school the patient received a frantic phone call from her aunt, who implored her to come over immediately because her back pain was severe; she had already summoned her physician to make a house call. The patient raced around the corner to her aunt's house and was dumbfounded to be met at the door by her aunt, all smiles and cheer. The patient was confused by this behavior, but before she could question her aunt about the marked change in spirits and behavior, the doorbell rang—it was the doctor. In a flash, the aunt transformed herself into a suffering person. Her face took on the expression of someone in terrible pain, her gait became antalgic, and she limped into the bedroom, where she slid under the covers and then received her physician. He inquired about her pain, did a cursory physical examination, reassured her, wrote her a prescription for "painkillers," and promised to visit the next day. This was all very confusing, and the patient inquired of her aunt as to what exactly was going on. The aunt replied: "When you have a pain like mine, sometimes people don't believe you. You have to make them believe you to get help." The favorite aunt subsequently died, apparently from an overdose of narcotic analgesics. The patient's current refusal to take prescribed medications was understandable; from a psychodynamic perspective, she may have identified with or internalized much of her favorite aunt's pain behavior, and feared that she too would become both addicted and ultimately self-destructive.

A 30-year-old single male with a 10-month history of pain was referred for psychological evaluation and treatment by his physiatrist. The pain had begun after a serious motor vehicle accident in which his vehicle had been rear-ended by a fully loaded dump truck. At the time of initial consultation with the psychologist, the patient complained of back, neck, and temporomandibular joint pain, as well as headaches, fatigue, and dizziness. He had a diagnosis of fibromyalgia and had been minimally responsive to previous treatment, which had included both physical therapy and chiropractic manipulation. Mental status examination did not reveal appreciable cognitive difficulties, although the examiner did note some difficulties with attention and concentration, which appeared to be secondary to the patient's persisting pain and emotional state. There was no evidence of psychiatric illness. He did display significant anger, frustration, and depression. What was particularly important about this man's current state of mind was that previously resolved matters involving early psychological trauma appeared to have been reactivated and now had the potential to significantly confound his rehabilitation outcome. In his own words, he had grown up in a "dysfunctional family." His mother had a psychiatric history that included paranoid schizophrenia and alcoholism. When he was aged 3 his parents divorced, and the mother received custody of the three children. The patient could recall physical, emotional, and sexual abuse at the hands of his mother, who frequently threatened to kill all of her children. She was ultimately hospitalized at a state psychiatric facility.

Years earlier, the patient had sought psychotherapy for the sequelae of his childhood abuse; he had been of the opinion that he had successfully resolved these matters, including his tendency toward excessive alcohol use and a pattern of passive dependency in his relationships with women. A couple of years earlier, he had successfully extricated himself from a relationship with an abusive, manipulative, demeaning woman, with whom he appeared to be re-enacting the masochistic pattern he had learned in relation to his abusive mother. However, what was important in understanding this patient's response to clinical intervention was that his problem-solving style was that of an inhibited coper; he chose to solve problems on his own, did not like to share his difficulties with others, and had a great deal of emotional difficulty in allowing others to be helpful to him.

As we have pointed out above, such self-reliance, whether or not it is defined as "pathological," can often be a deterrent to successful rehabilitation. The adult consequence of the patient's childhood abuse appeared to be that he was prevented from allowing himself to be helped by the health care workers involved in his care. He was spiraling downward into a deeper state of helplessness and depression. The psychological approach used in the treatment of this patient was an integrative one, beginning with history and training in relaxation and self-hypnotic imagery, and then followed by brief psychotherapy to forestall any further interaction of early psychodynamic patterns with current pain and illness-related experiences. This man did very well, became relatively pain-free, and resumed a full schedule of work and activity.

Both clinical observations and retrospective research have suggested that social modeling (Craig, 1978) and early identifications with ill or disabled family members (Engel, 1951, 1959; Adler et al., 1989) may play a role in the later development of a chronic pain syndrome. Such internalized relationships with parents and significant others are often not immediately accessible to conscious recall, but sometimes the experience and behavior of a chronic pain patient can be associated with early experiences and exposure to the ways in which significant others have coped with pain and illness.

Childhood Sexual and Physical Abuse

Childhood physical and sexual abuse is an aspect of childhood experience that has diverse and far-reaching effects on personality and adult psychopathology (e.g., Wolf & Alpert, 1991). Because there is evidence that chronic pain, somatoform disorders, and abnormal illness behavior are associated with both child and adult sexual and physical abuse, it has been recommended that clinicians evaluating and treating chronic pain patients should routinely inquire about such experiences (e.g., Haber & Roos, 1985; Walker et al., 1988, 1992a). Failure to recover after injury or illness may reflect early trauma and a coping mechanism of dissociation (Walker, Katon, Neraas, Jemelka, & Massoth, 1992b). For this reason, proper psychotherapeutic treatment may require empathy and reconstruction of experience at archaic levels of experience, where meaning is not representationally organized and feelings provide the only guidelines (Grzesiak, 1992a).

A 56-year-old father of two developed left-sided arm and leg pain, which remained undiagnosed for several years. At the time of referral he had recently been given a diagnosis of rheumatoid arthritis, and it was thought that this might account for much of his pain. Initial psychological evaluation found him to be moderately depressed, and psychotherapy and antidepressant medication were begun. After several weeks of relaxation training, instruction in hypnosis and self-hypnosis was started, and the patient reported that all of these techniques were moderately helpful in managing his chronic pain but that he remained depressed. His feelings about his rheumatoid arthritis were explored, as was his relationship with his wife, who had been diagnosed with "borderline schizophrenia" many years before and was maintained on a low dose of neuroleptic medication. After several months of weekly sessions of psychotherapy, the patient discovered that his son had become engaged to a woman of a different religion. He reported a dramatic worsening of his depression, accompanied by prominent suicidal ideation and an effective suicide plan. His psychotherapy sessions were increased to twice weekly, and a "contract" was initiated regarding mandatory telephone contact when he was feeling suicidal. The patient now revealed that he had been preoccupied with suicide since his childhood, had kept a large amount of barbiturate medication readily available for this purpose for many years, and had suicidal ruminations on an almost daily basis.

The patient had been sexually and emotionally abused as a child and adolescent by both parents, in a home where both his mother and his paternal grandmother had spent most of his childhood bedridden with ill-defined illnesses. He himself was considered an embarrassment to the family, and all aspects of his appearance and behavior were criticized and devalued (e.g., after he received an award in high school, the only comment made by his father and brother was that the way he walked down the auditorium aisle was "peculiar"). Not surprisingly, he had a very disturbed adolescence, with multiple suicide attempts, a course of electroconvulsive therapy, and one brief psychiatric hospitalization.

The patient complained of having felt at least moderately depressed for much of his life, and also felt hopeless about the possibility of any change in a marriage that brought him no gratification. He reported chronic insomnia and lifelong feelings of guilt, sinfulness, and low self-esteem. Finally, he was, and still is, severely intropunitive; maintains an impressive array of depressogenic self-statements; and has marked fears of interpersonal closeness (which he experiences as "infantile dependency") and abandonment, within the therapy as well as in other relationships.

In psychotherapy, the patient has focused his attention on the traumas of his past and on his extremely poor self-image. In addition, much of the therapeutic work has consisted of exploration of his feelings about the therapist, who has alternately been experienced as the violent and incestuous father, the intrusive yet neglecting mother, and the brutally critical brother. After 6 years of twice-weekly therapy, the patient's self-esteem has increased somewhat; his relationships with friends have become more numerous and deeper; and he is much more able to see connections between the way he experiences himself (and his therapist) and the toxic relationships he had with his family (both parents were dead when the patient began treatment, and after about 3 years of therapy he curtailed contact with his abusive brother). However, he continues to suffer from intermittent episodes of severe dysphoria, which have decreased in frequency but are still accompanied by marked suicidality and feelings of profound worthlessness and depersonalization.

After the onset of his chronic pain, the patient continued to work part-time as a graphic designer, but he has been unable to return to full-time employment because of his pain. He continues to find self-hypnosis effective in managing his pain, which fluctuates in intensity and varies in quality and location, but which has not seemed closely linked to his psychological state. The patient has used self-hypnosis to retrieve memories of his childhood, which are then discussed in therapy, but he has become increasingly convinced that he has repressed the most traumatic events of his past.

Anger, Helplessness, Depression, and Loss

The appropriate acceptance and management of anger constitute one of the central issues in psychotherapeutic work with chronic pain patients. Whale (1992) described a focal, short-term psychotherapeutic approach to the treatment of chronic pain; although she described a small number of cases, all of her patients had to come to terms with their unadmitted and unaccepted anger over various losses in their lives. One source of this anger is often the profound sense of helplessness that many patients feel in the wake of their persisting pain and physical limitations. With respect to adaptation to such physical symptoms as persistent pain, it is the patient's intolerance of the affective experience of helplessness that needs to be addressed in psychotherapy (Levine, Brooks, Irving, & Fishman, 1993).

Depression often accompanies feelings of helplessness, and the relationship between depression and chronic pain has received a great deal of attention. Perhaps the initial successes in treating chronic pain patients with tricyclic antidepressants contributed to some investigators' proposing that chronic pain is a form of depression (e.g., Blumer & Heilbronn, 1989; Lesse, 1974). The relationship between pain and depression is undoubtedly more complex than this (Dworkin & Gitlin, 1991). As Krishnan, France, and Davidson (1988) have suggested, on the basis of the existing research literature, at least four possible relationships between pain and depression can be proposed: "1) pain may be a symptom of depression; 2) depression may be a complication of chronic pain; 3) pain and depression may be inextricably linked; and 4) pain and depression can coexist but may not be related" (p. 195). With respect to individual patients, however, a thorough assessment often makes it possible to determine the temporal sequence between the development of a patient's chronic pain and his or her depression.

Experiences of loss and mourning are often integral aspects of depression in chronic pain patients. In the studies by Schofferman et al. (1992, 1993) discussed above, mourning and dealing appropriately with losses were important components of adaptation or pain relief; in the extensive clinical examples provided by Engel (1951, 1959), dealing with the loss of loved ones was frequently an important psychodynamic consideration.

Indeed, in reviewing Engel's case summaries, one can see that the internalized loss of an ill parent often led to a similar pain and illness picture in the survivor. Whale (1992) has also noted that inappropriate or blocked grieving can play an important role in chronic pain, and that the identification and resolution of losses can lead to diminished pain and improved adaptation.

Pain as an Affect

The idea that pain could be conceived of as an affect was first addressed by Fenichel (1945). The affective experience of pain is as universal as that of anxiety, but it has not received sufficient attention (Szasz, 1957). From a psychoanalytic perspective, the body is the ego's first object (Hoffer, 1950). As Grzesiak (1974) has pointed out, there is agreement within psychoanalytic theory that the concept of affect is inextricably related to the concept of ego. It is impossible to make a statement about pain relative to the adult ego without using the body as a reference point.

Discussing pain as an affect, Bellissimo and Tunks (1984) have stated: "But here we mean the dimension of bodily pain experience involving suffering: The pain itself is a disturbed affect" (p. 28). They go on to note that "Pain suffering must be dealt with in its own right. The affect of pain, like any other affect, is a function of the dynamic relationship between the individual and the environment. It reflects the status of the battle for control and coping, and is not linked in a static way to the state of the lesion only" (p. 32).

More than any other theorist, Szasz (1957, 1975) has explored the idea of pain as an affect. In his first treatise (Szasz, 1957), he used a relatively early version of object relations theory to suggest that pain is a warning about a bodily state. When pain is considered as an affect, it can be viewed in much the same way as anxiety (Swanson, 1984). Anxiety is viewed as a response to a real or imagined threat to the integrity of the self; analogously, pain can be viewed as signaling a threat of the loss of a body part or of bodily function (Szasz, 1957). For the psychotherapist working with pain patients, such a perspective allows for exploration and interpretation of personal meanings related to pain and the functions that the emotion of pain may be serving for the individual. Such psychotherapeutic explorations of the meaning of pain are relevant, regardless of the relative roles played by organic and psychosocial factors in accounting for the patient's experience of pain.

Alexithymia

Alexithymia is often cited as one of the reasons why chronic pain patients do not respond well to a dynamic psychotherapy. The concept of "alexithymia" was introduced by Sifneos (1973), who suggested that the ability to label and/or communicate affective experience may be restricted in patients with chronic pain or other psychosomatic illness. According to Moore and Fine (1990), alexithymia is a cognitive and affective disturbance commonly found in patients suffering from psychosomatic, addictive, or posttraumatic conditions. From a psychoanalytic perspective, McDougall (1985, 1989) has defined alexithymia as a group of developmental defenses, closely allied with denial and splitting. She cautions the psychotherapist about moving too quickly to penetrate these defenses, because the very nature of their existence implies that the patient is unconsciously terrified of his or her affective world and has no symbols to which to attach affective meaning. In psychotherapeutic work with chronic pain patients, it is important to proceed slowly, allowing the patient to become aware of heretofore unavailable feelings. In a recent article, Bromberg (1994) has discussed the laborious analytic process through which previously dissociated material first acquires symbols, then becomes experienced, and ultimately is integrated into a more cohesive sense of self.

Pain and Punishment

A chronic pain syndrome consists of both pain and suffering. Not surprisingly, many patients experience their pain and the suffering it causes as punishment for a past transgression. Some individuals can identify the event for which they believe they are being punished; others cannot, but have a strong belief that such things as chronic pain and chronic illness only happen when people deserve them.

A 32-year-old woman with chronic, progressive multiple sclerosis was referred for psychotherapy and pain management. Both of her parents had survived the Holocaust, and her father had become a very successful businessman who was able to provide the best for his family. The patient's family was unable to comprehend that her illness was continuing to progress in spite of the expert medical evaluation and treatment she had received. In psychotherapy, the patient agonized over the limitations imposed by her disability, and struggled to figure out the reason why she had become ill. Her parents had been saved, but it seemed as though she was being punished. Because she could not identify a specific wrongdoing that warranted such punishment, the feeling of being punished alternated with a numbing despair that her illness (and the impact that it had on her life) was senseless.

A married but childless woman in her early 50s was seen for psychotherapy as part of her multidisciplinary pain management. She came to the pain management center with a 30-year history of abdominal pain, and, in addition, now suffered from chronic low back pain. She entered psychotherapy reluctantly, but ultimately developed a strong alliance with the psychotherapist. A number of medical interventions had not ameliorated her pain, and the pain management team was at a relative loss in terms of suggesting further medical interventions to deal with her persisting pain problems. In psychotherapy, she dealt with the helplessness that she was experiencing in connection with her pain. She had significant depression for which she was receiving tricyclic antidepressants. Finally, after many months of weekly psychotherapy, she "confessed" to the therapist that she had had an illegal abortion when she was in her late teens, and that the complications ensuing from this abortion had led to multiple abdominal complaints, including adhesions and pain. Actually, her overall abdominal status was extremely complicated, including the inoperable mass that continued to grow with no hope of a meaningful medical intervention. The important point is that this woman had held on to this "secret" (her abortion) for over 30 years and had experienced tremendous guilt over the consequences of her behavior for her health. Of course, sharing her secret with the psychotherapist did not relieve her of her persistent abdominal pain, but it did allow her to feel better about herself; to develop a better relationship with her husband, who had been supportive for decades; and to share her story with her elderly mother, from whom she had been estranged for many years.

Pain as a Crystallized Dynamic Conflict

We consider the phenomenon of pain as a crystallized dynamic conflict to be one of the most important of the psychodynamic themes that are relevant to psychotherapy with chronic pain patients. We have borrowed this particular categorization from Bellissimo and Tunks (1984). According to these authors, "the most common configuration of pain

within psychic structure is that the problem of pain, which may have arisen coinciden-
tally from some injury or pathology, has become entangled in personality dynamics that
to some extent [existed before] the painful illness" (p. 106).

Breuer and Freud (1893–1895/1955) suggested that the most common of painful conditions are those that are often chosen for hysterical conversion; they are very real pains
that have then become divorced from their physical origins. Purely psychogenic pain is very
rare. However, pain that continues long after tissues have healed is a frequent occurrence.
Chronic pain often reflects the superimposition of psychodynamic issues on sensory memories to prolong the clinical symptom, encapsulating a conflict that would otherwise reach
awareness and cause anxiety. One of the major reasons we advocate psychodynamic psychotherapy in the treatment of chronic pain patients is the crystallization of conflict often
seen in these patients. Psychodynamic exploration is often necessary, not because the origin
of a patient's experience of pain is psychogenic, but because the additional personal and
private meanings that contribute to and elaborate the experience of the physical sensation
require psychotherapeutic exploration and interpretation.

Other Themes

In this section, we have focused on several psychodynamic themes that we believe often
play a role in the experience of chronic pain. Other important issues that may become a
focus of the psychotherapist's attention include somatization (Potamianou, 1990; Schur,
1955); conversion (Deutsch, 1959; Rangell, 1959); depression and individuation (Joffe &
Sandler, 1965); narcissism (Spiegel, 1966); negativity (Lane, Hull, & Foehrenbach, 1991);
masochism (Berliner, 1958; Katz, 1990); fear and anxiety (Ramzy & Wallerstein, 1958/
1975); avoidance of psychic conflict (Coen & Sarno, 1989); the psychoanalytic understanding of trauma (Rothstein, 1986; van der Kolk, 1987; van der Kolk & van der Hart, 1991);
and psychological consequences of rape, incest, and abuse (Bernstein, 1989; Davis &
Frawley, 1992; Katan, 1973; Rachman, 1989).

PSYCHODYNAMIC PSYCHOTHERAPEUTIC
APPROACHES TO CHRONIC PAIN PATIENTS

There have been few extended discussions of the role of psychotherapy in the treatment
of chronic pain patients. Bellissimo and Tunks (1984) provided such a book over a decade ago. In their text, they define psychodynamic psychotherapy as

> concerned primarily with the analysis and reorganization of thoughts and feelings
> through the medium of conversation, in the context of an ongoing therapeutic rela-
> tionship. It presupposes the reality and the primacy of the patient's inner world, with
> the belief that symptomatic and behavioral change will follow the reorganization of belief
> and feeling. Behavior is not ignored, but it is not the primary focus for the therapeutic
> endeavor. (Bellissimo & Tunks, 1984, p. 97)

They continue by noting that the successful application of behavioral approaches to
chronic pain can "lead to an overshadowing of insight by the behavior-oriented approaches. Polarizing behavior- versus insight-oriented approaches is, however, not in the
best interests of helping patients, nor is it realistic with regard to a complete understanding of patienthood and helping" (Bellissimo & Tunks, 1984, p. 100).

Over the years, the practice of psychodynamic psychotherapy has changed significantly. The stereotype of the aloof and distant, nonresponding psychoanalyst who acts as a "blank screen" is much less appropriate than it has been in the past. Greenson (1965) has pointed out that the view of the psychoanalyst as a "blank screen" onto whom totally idiosyncratic needs and impulses are projected was inappropriate for understanding psychodynamic change from the very beginnings of psychoanalysis. There have been important changes in conceptualizations of the psychoanalytic process. Today, as much emphasis is placed on the nature of the therapeutic relationship as on the interpretation of conflict and insight. In addition to the focus on what the patient brings to the treatment, there is an emphasis on the "intersubjective" reality created between patient and therapist. In other words, there has been a movement away from the historic toward the hermeneutic. However, central to any psychodynamic psychotherapy is the importance of influences on behavior of which the patient may not be aware. The therapeutic process involves gaining understanding of the patient's inner world, and this may be accomplished through clarification of the evolving relationship between the patient and the therapist—the patient's transference and the therapist's countertransference.

Before discussing the aspects of psychodynamic psychotherapy that we believe are most relevant to working with chronic pain patients, we describe the way we initiate such treatment and the content of the first few sessions with patients. Our approach in these important early sessions is different from the less directive approaches that are characteristic of psychodynamic psychotherapy; we believe these modifications are necessary because of the particular ways in which pain patients come to psychological treatment and the expectations (and misconceptions) that they bring with them.

The Early Sessions

Individuals suffering from chronic pain do not come to pain management clinics for psychotherapy; they come for pain relief. The mere idea of seeing a psychologist or a psychiatrist often causes negative reactions, such as "You think it's all in my head!" Therefore, the patient must be educated as to how psychological factors are important components of the pain experience. There are no clear guidelines available for educating patients about the importance of the multidisciplinary approach to chronic pain, which often includes an evaluation by a psychologist, a psychiatrist, or both. DeGood (1983) and Grzesiak (1989) have made suggestions concerning how to introduce psychological concepts gently within the context of multidisciplinary pain management. Psychological factors such as coping with the stress of chronic pain must be depathologized; the normal continuum of coping skills must be emphasized; and, above all, the pain must always be appreciated as real. Oxman (1986) has suggested that not reassuring the patient about the possibility of pain relief often has the paradoxical effect of increasing rapport and fostering a therapeutic alliance. This paradoxical effect may occur because by the time most chronic pain patients have entered treatment, they are very skeptical about the possibility of obtaining pain relief; a therapist may be viewed as more trustworthy if he or she does not make promises that the patient has learned are not likely to be kept. Goldsmith (1983–1984) has noted that the therapist can join the patient's resistance to psychological inquiry by downplaying the potential role of psychological factors during initial evaluation. This often enables chronic pain patients to feel more comfortable about revealing possible psychological contributions to their chronic pain syndromes.

There is a simple approach to describing the role of psychosocial factors in chronic pain that we have found useful with the great majority of patients and that can also be used effectively by physicians attempting to make referrals for psychological treatment.

In this approach, we begin by emphasizing that the reason the patient has been asked to see a psychologist is not because the pain is lacking a physical basis and "is all in the patient's head" (we add that we are not sure we have ever seen such a thing). We continue by saying that psychologists are involved in the treatment of chronic pain for two reasons: because there are effective treatments for chronic pain (such as relaxation training and hypnosis) that psychologists have been trained to administer; and because patients who are suffering from chronic pain often find themselves in a vicious cycle, which it is sometimes helpful to discuss with someone who is familiar with chronic pain. We then describe this vicious cycle, in which pain causes stress and tension (and, depending on what the patient has already revealed, depression, anxiety, or anger), which cause more pain, which causes more stress and tension, and so on. In our experience, most chronic pain patients not only agree with this characterization of their current life, but also then furnish examples of pain causing stress or stress causing more pain. Depending on the patient and the context of the referral, we may refer to this aspect of the psychological intervention as "counseling," in order to minimize the resistance that is very common among chronic pain patients at this early stage of treatment.

With most chronic pain patients, we find it useful to begin psychotherapy by asking the patients to tell us about themselves, beginning with their childhood. When giving a patient an overview of the treatment, we say that this typically takes about two sessions, and that the medical history should be described in detail beginning at the point in the patient's life at which health became problematic. We tell patients that even if we were present when their medical history was taken by the physician, hearing medical problems within the context provided by a narrative of one's life story is very helpful and gives us a much richer appreciation of what they have been going through. Typically, there is little resistance to this endeavor, although some patients race through their premorbid lives, asserting that these have little to do with their chronic pain. There are few chronic pain patients, however, who are averse to describing in detail what their lives have been like since the onset of their pain or illness, and the patients' responses to the open-endedness of these initial sessions provide a wealth of information. Nevertheless, we want to emphasize the importance of the guideline that the psychotherapist working with chronic pain patients should not focus the inquiry on pain. This is not a new idea. Sternbach and Rusk (1973), in a discussion of psychotherapeutic work with chronic pain patients, are quite explicit in suggesting that the psychotherapist not inquire about pain, but rather should focus on other aspects of the patient's life and adaptation. As we hope to demonstrate throughout this chapter, we think it is essential to examine all aspects of a patient's developmental history, relationships, and overall psychological functioning that may contribute to increased pain or excessive suffering.

During these initial sessions, the therapist must be alert to the possibility that the patient is suffering from a psychiatric disorder—for example, major depression, posttraumatic stress disorder, or panic disorder (Dworkin & Caligor, 1988; Dworkin & Gitlin, 1991). A substantial percentage of chronic pain patients have a psychiatric disorder, and this possibility must be evaluated with all patients. Many chronic pain patients, in resisting psychological evaluation and intervention, argue that their psychological distress would disappear if only their pain syndromes were treated effectively. Successful treatment of chronic pain may alleviate a psychiatric disorder in some instances (Maruta, Vatterott, & McHardy, 1989), but when a pain syndrome and a psychiatric disorder occur together, it is usually necessary to treat these disorders concurrently for any lasting relief from chronic pain to occur.

Sometimes patients become defensive about discussing the symptoms of psychiatric disorders, believing that an acknowledgment of such symptoms would suggest that their pain is caused by psychological factors. In some instances, this perception is based on previous evaluations. Although few health professionals would say to a patient, "The pain is all in your head," many do say such things as "We can't find a physical cause for your pain, so it must all be caused by stress or anxiety." Since almost no chronic pain patients want to be told their pain is a result of such factors, they learn to be defensive about psychological symptoms and stress, sometimes denying them entirely. We typically do not conduct a formal psychiatric evaluation, and believe that the symptoms of potential psychiatric disorders can be evaluated within these initial sessions with tact and sensitivity (Dworkin & Grzesiak, 1993).

Relational Issues in Psychodynamic Psychotherapy

Anderson and Hines (1994) have discussed the importance of disturbed attachment bonds in chronic pain patients. In research described in more detail earlier, they found that individuals with a history of significant psychosocial trauma were more likely to have unsuccessful surgery, to have a higher incidence of chronicity, and to be less amenable to psychological interventions (Schofferman et al., 1992, 1993). They interpreted these results as suggesting that

> an individual's capacity to be consoled (i.e., recover from the pain-inducing injury) is directly related to his or her attachment security. The more insecure the attachment, the less consolable the person will be and, as a result, the more vulnerable to chronic pain. Thus, the inability to tolerate and accommodate to pain can be predicted by a lack of a secure base in childhood with its resultant insecure attachment. (Anderson & Hines, 1994, p. 137)

Anderson and Hines (1994) suggest that it is the job of the multidisciplinary team to form a consoling relationship with the patient. This consolation may involve either the entire team or the individual psychotherapist. The patient must learn to be able to depend on, and be consoled by, important figures who essentially undo the negative effects of untoward developmental experiences; insecure attachments are replaced by more secure ones. As we have pointed out above, one of the changes in conceptualizing the process of psychodynamic psychotherapy has been a much greater reliance on the patient–therapist relationship as the arena where mutative change takes place, as is illustrated by the following detailed case history.

> The patient was a single woman in her late 30s who had been referred for "anxiety management" by her orthopedic surgeon. Initially, this appeared to be a straightforward behavioral medicine consultation requiring only short-term treatment. The orthopedist who referred her was concerned that she did not appear to be coping adequately with her pain, and all clinical findings suggested that surgery was indicated. Specifically, the incident that cued the orthopedist to her anxiety was her reaction to a diagnostic procedure. She had a discogram to evaluate intervertebral disc herniation and developed mild complications; instead of the planned 1-day stay, she was required to spend several days in the hospital. Furthermore, she was required to remain as physically still as possible. On the 4th day of her stay, she had what appeared to be a full-blown panic attack.
>   She presented for her initial psychological consultation as a bright, cooperative woman of above-average intelligence. In spite of her efforts to be cooperative, she was obviously anxious and quite guarded. She explained away some of this anxiety

by telling the therapist that she had had many problems with men over the course of her life and that she was therefore uncomfortable with him. The therapist's initial plan was to do a behavioral medicine intervention, using relaxation training as the foundation for training in anxiety and pain management (e.g., see Grzesiak, 1977; and Grzesiak & Ciccone, 1988). However, the therapist's initial effort to induce a relaxed state met with failure. The minute the therapist told her to make herself comfortable and close her eyes, she became hypervigilant. The "dot on the wall" strategy, which is sometimes useful in inducing either a relaxed or a dissociated state, was attempted, but that too was not possible. The patient appeared unable to relinquish even a modicum of control. Paradoxically, she was quite eager for further appointments with the therapist and wanted to discuss matters of personal concern.

The patient had spinal surgery, and began a slow and tortuous convalescence that included thrice-weekly physical therapy and twice-weekly psychotherapy. Nevertheless, she did not appear to be on track for successful recovery. Because she had many of the hard-driving, rigid, and workaholic traits that Blumer and Heilbronn (1989) described as "ergomanic" and predictive of a poor adaptation to pain, and because she was clearly made more anxious by her prolonged convalescence, her therapist suggested to her orthopedist that he recommend that she return to work on a partial basis in order to "take her mind off things." Instead of reassuring her, this advice made her acutely anxious. That very night she dreamed that while she was running away from her mother, her mother shot her in the back. In her session the next day, her associations to the dream brought forth the following memories. When she was in the seventh grade, she had suffered from an increasingly severe stomachache. Her mother gave her daughter's complaints no credence and insisted on her attending school anyway. After approximately 2 weeks of increasingly severe abdominal pain and growing physical debility, and at her father's insistence, the girl was rushed to the local hospital; she was diagnosed as having an appendix near rupture, and immediate surgery was performed.

She also remembered other times when her physical symptoms were disregarded by the mother. It was the therarpist's impression that her growing anxiety in the face of the orthopedist's apparent disregard of her pain was what led to a reactivation of earlier, repressed memories of her mother's disregard for her physical complaints. With her permission, the therapist discussed this with the orthopedist; however, the doctor–patient relationship was never re-established, and the orthopedist remained a so-called "bad object." She changed physicians for follow-up care and increased her psychotherapy sessions to three or four times per week. The patient's tendency to regress and dissociate was easily triggered and only marginally manageable in and between sessions. It was clear that her mother was emotionally abusive, but there were also other areas of physical abuse.

The initial psychodynamic speculation was that the experience of severe spinal pain was what served as the trigger for the releasing of memories of early abuse. This was not so. Approximately 4 years before the onset of her back pain, her mother had died suddenly; 2 weeks after the funeral, the patient's fiancé of several years had announced that he was being transferred to a different part of the country and that he would take this as his opportunity to begin a new life without her. She rebounded into a new relationship that was extremely sadomasochistic and in which she was tortured and humiliated in numerous ways. Because she and the man she was involved with worked together, she was literally and figuratively never out of his sight. From what she told her therapist, it appeared that she had been date-raped on their first date.

It took the patient almost a year to extricate herself from this relationship; during this year of abuse, she developed gastric ulcers, irritable bowel syndrome, recurrent pelvic pain, and finally low back pain. During physical therapy with a male therapist, she developed a marked aversion (both psychological and with psychophysiological concomitants) to the therapist's physically manipulating her. Her physical therapy sessions were followed by periods of increased anxiety and tension, and then by recurrent dreams of being in one particular room of her childhood home where "something happened" when she was about 3 years of age. She had a vague sense of having been abused by an older cousin who had been allowed to stay in the house.

These memories became clearer over the months of psychotherapy that followed: finally, in a daydream, she remembered the physical sensation of penetration and awakened with intense pelvic pain. After each recollected memory, the psychotherapeutic process would consist of long, silent, shaky, tearful periods in which the patient would say little. At times she stated, "This proves that I'm bad." Without attempting a discussion of psychoanalytic theory here, we would like to note that such comments may reflect the internalized sadistic mother, as well as an identification with her cousin, the aggressor. In the psychodynamic process, the therapist has chosen thus far not to interpret, but instead attempts to maintain an empathic connection and simply provides a space for the healing process to continue.

This particular clinical presentation reveals an adult survivor of childhood physical, emotional, and sexual abuse who also has back pain. We would speculate that her failure to recover from her back pain is a manifestation of psychological vulnerability. To use a concept discussed earlier, her physical symptoms have allowed for a crystallization of intrapsychic conflict in what remain very real physical symptoms. This woman's history and treatment illustrate the role of psychodynamic processes in the understanding and treatment of chronic pain patients. She presented with a reactivation of trauma (the recollected memories of physical abuse in connection with issues of her physical illness and its treatment), a re-enactment of trauma (the relationship with the rebound boyfriend), and the crystallization of intrapsychic conflict in physical symptoms (persistence of her pain following medical interventions and beyond the time in which remission of her symptoms would be expected to occur).

We would like to present one more facet of this case. After a long period of silence during a psychotherapy session following her surgery, the patient asked whether she could try to get some things out in the open by writing the psychotherapist a story. In her story, a little girl in a torn, dirty pastel dress was hiding in an abandoned, ruined shack. The landscape was wasted and barren. Amid all this emptiness and destruction, the psychotherapist noticed her and appeared different from the few other passers-by, from whom she had hidden. This story, provided by the patient, illustrates the essence of our approach to psychodynamic psychotherapy with patients such as this one, who have been abused and whose experience of pain reflects that abuse. Our goal with these individuals is to establish a relationship in which patients come to understand the consequences of their abuse by examining these consequences in their current relationships, especially their relationship with the therapist. Despite persisting pain, this patient has returned to work, has learned to pace herself appropriately, and is now involved in what appears to be a meaningful and healthy relationship.

Transference and Therapeutic Change

Relational theorists of psychodynamic psychotherapy (e.g., Atwood & Stolorow, 1984; Mitchel, 1988) have advocated a model of therapy in which the therapeutic relationship is viewed as a context for understanding internalized representations of self and others; intrapsychic processes, such as fixation and regression, are de-emphasized in this approach to psychodynamic psychotherapy. This approach can help guide a clinician in establishing and sustaining a therapeutic relationship that enables chronic pain patients to utilize the therapist in changing their adaptation to physical pain, and thereby ameliorating their psychological suffering.

This newer framework for psychodynamic psychotherapy provides a different orientation to therapy from that based on classical psychoanalysis. Possibly influenced by Heisenberg's uncertainty principle in physics, which calls attention to the role of the observer, the idea that a therapist could be an objective and neutral observer of a patient's behavior came to be questioned. Common assumptions within psychoanalytic thought were challenged by relational theorists, who emphasize the "relational matrix" that a patient mutually constructs with the therapist and other people in his or her life (Mitchell, 1988). The therapist is transformed from one who is supposed to maintain neutrality to foster objective observation into an individual for whom silence may simply be one of many different ways of bringing his or her own subjective reality into the room with the patient.

From this perspective, transference is not only seen as the patient's pathological projections of, for example, an unresolved Oedipal conflict; it is also more broadly defined as the patterns of expectation that the patient has developed through earlier experiences and unconsciously attributes to the therapist, who, as a participant, in turn influences what is being projected (Basch, 1980). These distorted expectations are triggered by conditions resembling the original situation that created the pattern. The triggers are often generated by aspects of the psychotherapist's personality and style of relating that remind the patient of earlier relationships. The projections that follow generally have some basis in reality, but distorted perception leads to a conclusion that is based on a past interactional pattern. It is when these schemas or expectational sets begin to shift through the therapist's therapeutic intervention that change begins to occur. As Frank (1990) has noted,

> All relational approaches agree on the importance of the treatment relationship as a new and positive one. That is, interpersonal patterns formed in infancy and early childhood are perpetuated and can be transformed as they are reenacted in the therapeutic relationship. A central therapeutic element of each involves the therapist's efforts to reach the patient meaningfully, emphathically, or reparatively as [one] who strives to identify and understand, rather than to repeat with him or her the patient's pathological relational patterns. (pp. 739–740)

Since transferential phenomena exist in all relationships, a positive feedback loop develops in which progress made in therapy alters transactional patterns and interpersonal relationships outside the therapeutic relationship. These improvements reinforce the therapeutic alliance and promote further exploration of transferential phenomena that were initially too threatening to the patient's self-concept. The new level of intimacy reached in the therapy improves relations outside treatment, and the cycle repeats itself.

Initially, many patients are not capable of or interested in directly examining the therapeutic relationship, but this does not necessarily inhibit therapeutic growth or a transferential reaction from emerging. Frequently, a distorted perception of the therapist known as a "positive transference" develops. This positive transference is an idealization of the therapist, which often represents a critical initial stage of treatment; when properly managed, positive transference can promote profound changes by enabling patients to suspend fears and doubts surrounding the therapy and to begin revealing their inner world. Such transferential feelings influence the individual's motivation to change, as the analyst becomes parent-like in creating an environment where the patient can bring both success and defeat. Because of its important role in creating a climate that supports change, the initial positive transference must be given an opportunity to mature before it becomes a subject of analysis and interpretation.

The positive transference is most likely to develop when the patient does not feel pathologized or judged by the therapist. This is when Goldsmith's (1983–1984) recommendation to downplay the role of psychological factors in the beginning stages of treatment (and thereby "join" the resistance) can be especially helpful. Relational notions of resistance understand the patient's desire to ignore exploration and insight as a self-protective mechanism preventing a loss of self-esteem or disintegration of the individual's identity. The patient's resistance must be respected and understood for trust to expand and progress to be made.

Many chronic pain patients feel that they (and their pain) are not respected, but are rejected and dismissed by family, friends, and clinicians. The abuse and neglect reported by many patients have left them at greater risk for "negative transferences," which can be destructive to the treatment. A negative transference may be initiated by the expectation that the therapist will act in an unempathic, unsupportive, and ultimately destructive manner, as other individuals have done in the past. These largely unconscious expectations can negatively influence the course of therapy and become self-fulfilling prophecies, which leave the patient feeling reinforced in his or her original mistrust and more deeply isolated. As Basch (1980) notes, the patient can begin to act "as if the therapist were an enemy and the treatment situation may become a battle from which only one participant emerges alive. In this case, the task of treatment is to help the patient to see what his assumptions are, and then to explore what fears lead him to behave so defensively" (p. 36).

For many patients, this negative reaction occurs much later in the therapy and only after the idealization from the positive transference wears thin. In these cases, a strong therapeutic relationship has already developed and these negative feelings can be worked through, bringing about profound alterations of patients' transferential distortions and maladaptive interpersonal behaviors. For other patients, the negative transferential reaction can be immediate, intense, and prolonged. In such very difficult cases (often diagnosed as cases of borderline personality disorder), patients see the therapist as depriving and unconcerned, and pull for a re-enactment of the sadomasochistic dynamics that marked previous attachment patterns. The goal of therapy with this type of patient is to minimize the tendency of the therapist to become the destructive parental figure, and instead to empathically assist the patient in understanding the origins of his or her negative response. Clarifying the self-protective assumptions made by the patient allows the therapist to link them with their developmental history—a process that can be very beneficial.

A 40-year-old, married, childless woman was referred for treatment by her internist to help her more effectively manage severe head pain that appeared to be the result of inadequately performed brain surgery. The patient has assorted other endocrine and immunological problems in relation to the brain tumor that was removed, and had had numerous negative encounters with physicians (including psychiatrists), which left her guarded, angry, and suspicious of the medical community. She had received previous cognitive-behavioral treatment for her head pain, but experienced only minimal improvement in her capacity to cope. She found that an "ergomanic," hard-working lifestyle was the most effective way to escape her pain. Her high-energy existence eventually broke down as medical complications emerged. She was left feeling helpless in her predicament, and this was when she sought further psychological treatment.

From the outset, her mistrust of doctors was palpable. She spent a good part of many sessions "bashing" the medical community and reporting the history of her mistreatment. At one point, she sent the therapist an insurance form with a cartoon added to it that said, "How do you keep three doctors away? . . . Eat an apple every eight hours," reflecting her desire to keep at a distance as many doctors as possible (including the therapist). In one session, she pronounced, "Doctors fall into two categories: those who are only interested in your money, and those who are only interested in your money but act like they're genuinely interested in your welfare." At that point, her therapist said to her, "Well, into which category do I fall?" All her criticisms had been indirect and full of sarcasm. The pointedness of this question stunned her and brought her attacks into the here and now of the therapeutic relationship. She responded in a mildly conciliatory manner, but from that point on, there was an important change in the tone and the affect of the psychotherapy sessions.

As the therapy took a new turn, she began to speak about her problematic marriage, social isolation, and abusive upbringing. She described how her mother would scream at her for no apparent reason, hit her, and complain about the terrible life she now led because of her daughter. The father was intrusive and emotionally unavailable to her, and would deny and avoid the abusive behavior of his wife. As the patient explored the impact of her parents' destructive behavior on her life, she began to recognize patterns within her own marriage: She would criticize and attack her husband; he, in turn, would tell her how happy he was being married to her, while doing his best to steer clear of her.

As the therapeutic alliance became more intimate, aspects of her toxic style of relating resurfaced in the treatment, but this time the efforts to explore and understand these disruptions resulted in a deepened therapeutic bond. Eventually, she became less isolated and reached out to friends with whom she had lost contact because of her anger and depression. The communication within her marriage improved; through increased understanding of the influences of her past experiences on her present behavior, she was able to see how her rage fed her husband's need to lock conflict safely away and escape through the back door. The pain that had been unremittingly plaguing her diminished slightly; more significantly, she no longer felt as victimized or helpless in her capacity to respond to the distress. Imagery and relaxation techniques were introduced into the treatment, and she was able to utilize these much more effectively than she had done in her previous treatment. She stated, "I am starting to turn what would have been bad days of pain into good days."

In this case, an initially negative transferential relationship was diffused, allowing a positive transference and ultimately an undistorted genuine therapeutic alliance to develop. The intensity of the patient's negative transference was based on a combination of factors, including her injurious relationships with her parents, the damage inflicted by the doctor during her operation, the abandonment by her husband, and her failure to respond to previous psychological treatment for her pain. She had little reason to expect or hope that the latest psychotherapeutic relationship would be any different. Her faith in therapy emerged not just because of the therapist's question about which category he fell into, but because at that point, something critical in the pattern of the psychotherapeutic interaction shifted.

Until that session, her attacks had left the therapist feeling impotent; he had not looked forward to the therapy sessions and did not mind when she canceled a session. This pattern of responding was one she typically encountered, and it was a repetition of the disaffection and helplessness she had once felt in her interactions with her parents. The therapist finally stopped re-enacting his part in her drama and provided a new experience for her by addressing her aggression. Through the continual clarification of her rage and disappointment, the therapist was no longer passive and avoidant in relating to her, as her husband and many others were or had been. The patient's willingness to respond to the change in the pattern of relating was also essential. The openness she developed toward probing her developmental history and searching for the multiple levels of repetition in her relations inside and outside the treatment was the most mutative aspect of the psychotherapeutic relationship. The heightened quality of her relationships extended beyond interpersonal interactions and included the way she related to and interpreted her chronic pain.

It is in the working through of such crystallized dynamic conflicts represented by pain that a patient's "relationship" with his or her pain can also improve. In a sense, pain patients have developed a transferential relationship with their pain, which can be transformed through the altering of the transferential relationship they establish with their therapist. Many patients respond to their pain in the same way that they reacted to abusive or neglectful authority figures in their past. Many different transferential responses to pain exist, ranging from patients' feeling oppressed (pain as punishment), abandoned (pain as loss), victimized, and helpless, to a tendency to deny symptoms, push on, and berate themselves for letting the pain inhibit them. As we have discussed above, the latter responses have been described as "ergomanic." The defenses of such individuals often break down because their bodies cannot sustain the abuse and neglect. This is exemplified by the patient presented above, who disregarded her doctors' warnings to slow down until the stress on her body seriously compromised her physical health.

Countertransference and Therapeutic Dialogue

The patient is not the only participant in the therapy who brings his or her transferential perceptions of pain, love, and sadness into the consulting room. Because of the possibility—indeed, inevitability—of the therapist's countertransference distortions, a "therapist must continuously monitor her participation in the therapeutic process with the patient and attempt to understand the contribution of her own history and vulnerabilities to what is happening and to how she understands it" (Wachtel, 1993, p. 13). This perspective differs from the classical psychoanalytic conceptualization of countertransference as the destructive intrusion into the treatment of the therapist's unresolved infantile developmental conflicts, which have no place in the analytic setting and should be expunged immediately. According to relational theorists, this would be a pointless impossibility that would impair the patient's and therapist's capacity to appreciate how they are mutually constructing their relationship (Greenberg & Mitchell, 1983).

Clearly, countertransference distortions have the potential to be very harmful if they are unrecognized by the therapist, and they can drastically limit the therapist's ability to play a reparative role in the patient's life. The most effective way of preventing this from happening is for the therapist not to assume that it is possible to be an impartial observer of a patient's transference, but rather to use his or her own reactions as a means of obtaining a deeper understanding of the patient.

In the case just presented of the 40-year-old woman with head pain, change in the therapeutic dialogue occurred as the therapist became increasingly aware of how his own previous struggles with aggression blocked his capacity to alter the re-enactment of the negative-transference-based pattern of communication that had been established with the patient. As the patient expressed her impotence and anger with doctors and herself, the therapist absorbed and identified with these aggressive projections, and experienced the guilt of being another doctor who failed to help her. In turn, the therapist's sense of futility was projected back onto the patient, and as she identified with his helplessness, the cycle recurred.

This common clinical manifestation is known to psychoanalytic clinicians as "projective identification," which refers to an individual's tendency to split off a part of the self and project it onto another (Greenberg & Mitchell, 1983). The other, by containing the externalized part of the patient's self, enables the patient to outwardly identify what was internal. This notion is substantially more relational than Freud's concepts of "projection" and "identification" (Greenberg & Mitchell, 1983). Projective identification is not limited to psychodynamic treatment and exists in any type of therapy setting—or, it could be said, in any human relationship.

CONCLUSIONS

In this chapter, we have attempted to demonstrate the importance of certain psychodynamic themes in the perpetuation and exacerbation of chronic pain. We have distinguished pain that persists from the development of a chronic pain syndrome, which often involves unremitting suffering with origins in untoward early developmental experiences. Although we have focused quite extensively on psychodynamic issues that can complicate chronic pain and ultimately require a psychodynamically oriented psychotherapy, most of the case material we have presented has had an integrative flavor, in that prior to psychodynamic inquiry the patients were often taught relaxation, imagery, self-hypnosis, or other self-regulatory skills (Dworkin & Grzesiak, 1993). In many cases, such skills are enough to enable appropriate adaptation and the resumption of a meaningful life. However, for vulnerable (or "pain-prone") individuals, a psychodynamic orientation to psychotherapy is needed; these patients bring unique psychological meanings to their pain, which compromise their efforts at adaptation and forestall the possibility of physical rehabilitation.

Although there is increasing interest among psychoanalytically oriented psychotherapists in the contributions that cognitive-behavioral approaches can make to psychodynamic psychotherapy (e.g., Frank, 1990; Wachtel, 1977), cognitive-behavioral therapists unfortunately have not shown a commensurate level of interest in the contribution that psychodynamic perspectives can make to their approach to treatment. Certainly, cognitive-behavioral therapists attend to the idiosyncratic beliefs, maladaptive schemas, dysfunctional thoughts, and dysphoric moods of their patients. However, as we hope to have demonstrated in this chapter, we believe that attention to the more traditional psychodynamic aspects of psychotherapy—including developmental conflicts, resistance, and especially the transference and countertransference aspects of the therapeutic relationship—will substantially increase the effectiveness of cognitive-behavioral therapy.

Psychodynamic approaches to psychotherapy that are relational in orientation can be especially helpful to clinicians working with pain patients, because they allow for the application of cognitive-behavioral techniques without interfering with or minimizing the importance of exploring the meaning of a patient's pain and suffering. Indeed, we believe that psychodynamic and relational issues play an important role in all psychological interventions—not just in psychodynamic psychotherapy—and that an increased understanding of these issues can assist therapists in working with resistant, noncompliant, and unresponsive patients. As we view it, the essence of a psychodynamic approach is attention to three sets of relationships: developmental relationships, especially with parents and siblings; ongoing relationships, especially with family members and friends; and the relationship that is established between the patient and the therapist. An increased awareness of these aspects of the patient's life deepens the therapist's capacity to understand the patient's interpersonal needs and conflicts, and in so doing creates a context that can facilitate the implementation of cognitive-behavioral interventions.

As we have argued throughout this chapter, we conceptualize the chronic pain experience as the result of a complex combination of factors, reflecting processes of both the body and the mind. In reviewing our cases, we have become aware that in the successful treatment of patients with pain and suffering, the individual comes to accept his or her pain. By this we mean that pain and illness are accepted as important but not self-defining parts of the person's life, and as unfortunate and only partially controllable aspects of the human condition. We cannot specify how psychodynamic psychotherapy, either alone or in combination with cognitive-behavioral intervention, contributes to this process whereby the mind no longer disavows the body's pain and illness. However, we do know that when this process occurs, the chronic pain patient becomes an individual with persistent pain—one who is no longer disabled, but able to remove pain from the center of awareness and to replace suffering with meaning.

REFERENCES

Atwood, G., & Stolorow, R. (1984). *Structures of intersubjectivity*. Hillsdale, NJ: Analytic Press.
Adler, R. H., Zlot, S., Hurny, C., & Minder, C. (1989). Engel's "'Psychogenic' pain and the pain-prone patient": A retrospective, controlled clinical study. *Psychosomatic Medicine, 51*, 87–101.
Anderson, D. A., & Hines, R. H. (1994). Attachment and pain. In R. C. Grzesiak & D. S. Ciccone (Eds.), *Psychological vulnerability to chronic pain* (pp. 137–152). New York: Springer.
Basch, M. F. (1980). *Doing psychotherapy*. New York: Basic Books.
Bellissimo, A., & Tunks, E. (1984). *Chronic pain: The psychotherapeutic spectrum*. New York: Praeger.
Berliner, B. (1958). The role of object relations in moral masochism. *Psychoanalytic Quarterly, 27*, 38–56.
Bernstein, A. E. (1989). Analysis of two adult female patients who had been victims of incest in childhood. *Journal of the American Academy of Psychoanalysis, 17*, 207–221.
Bigos, S. J., Battie, M. C., Spengler, D. M., Fisher, L. D., Fordyce, W. E., Hansson, T. H., Nachenson, A. L., & Wortley, M. D. (1991). A prospective study of work perceptions and psychosocial factors affecting the report of back injury. *Spine, 16*, 1–6.
Blumer, D., & Heilbronn, M. (1989). Dysthymic pain disorder: The treatment of chronic pain as a variant of depression. In C. D. Tollison (Ed.), *Handbook of chronic pain management* (pp. 197–209). Baltimore: Williams & Wilkins.
Bradley, L. A., Prokop, C. K., Gentry, W. D., Van der Heide, L. H., & Prieto, E. J. (1981). Assessment of chronic pain. In C. K. Prokop & L. A. Bradley (Eds.), *Medical psychology: Contributions to behavioral medicine* (pp. 91–117). New York: Academic Press.
Bradley, L. A., Prokop, C. K., Margolis, R., & Gentry, W. D. (1978). Multivariate analysis of the MMPI profiles of low back pain patients. *Journal of Behavioral Medicine, 1*, 253–272.
Brena, S. F., & Koch, D. L. (1975). "Pain estimate" model for quantification and classification of chronic pain states. *Anesthesiology Reviews, 2*, 8–13.
Breuer, J., & Freud, S. (1955). Studies on hysteria. In J. Strachey (Ed. and Trans.), *The standard edition of the complete psychological works of Sigmund Freud* (Vol. 2, pp. 1–305). London: Hogarth Press. (Original work published 1893–1895)
Bromberg, P. M. (1994). "Speak! That I may see you": Some reflections on dissociation, reality, and psychoanalytic listening. *Psychoanalytic Dialogues, 4*, 517–547.
Ciccone, D. S., & Grzesiak, R. C. (1984). Cognitive dimensions of chronic pain. *Social Science and Medicine, 19*, 1339–1345.

Ciccone, D. S., & Grzesiak, R. C. (1988). Cognitive therapy: An overview of theory and practice. In N. T. Lynch & S. V. Vasudevan (Eds.), *Persistent pain: Psychosocial assessment and intervention* (pp. 133–161). Boston: Kluwer.

Ciccone, D. S., & Grzesiak, R. C. (1990, October). *Psychological vulnerability to chronic back and neck pain.* Paper presented at the meeting of the American Pain Society, St. Louis, MO.

Ciccone, D. S., & Lenzi, V. (1994). Psychosocial vulnerability to chronic dysfunctional pain: A critical review. In R. C. Grzesiak & D. S. Ciccone (Eds.), *Psychological vulnerability to chronic pain* (pp. 153–178). New York: Springer.

Coen, S. J., & Sarno, J. E. (1989). Psychosomatic avoidance of conflict in back pain. *Journal of the American Academy of Psychoanalysis, 17,* 359–376.

Craig, K. D. (1978). Social modeling influences on pain. In R. A. Sternbach (Ed.), *The psychology of pain* (pp. 73–109). New York: Raven Press.

Crook, J. Rideout, E., & Browne, G. (1984). The prevalence of pain complaints in the general population. *Pain, 18,* 299–314.

Davis, J. M., & Frawley, M. G. (1992). Dissociative processes and transference–countertransference paradigms in the psychoanalytically oriented treatment of adult survivors of childhood sexual abuse. *Psychoanalytic Dialogues, 2,* 5–36.

DeGood, D. E. (1983). Reducing medical patients' reluctance to participate in psychological therapies: The initial session. *Professional Psychology: Research and Practice, 14,* 570–579.

Deutsch, F. (Ed.). (1959). *On the mysterious leap from the mind to the body.* New York: International Universities Press.

Dworkin, R. H. (1991). What do we really know about the psychological origins of chronic pain? *American Pain Society Bulletin, 1*(5), 7–11.

Dworkin, R. H., & Caligor, E. (1988). Psychiatric diagnosis and chronic pain: DSM-III-R and beyond. *Journal of Pain and Symptom Management, 3,* 87–98.

Dworkin, R. H., & Gitlin, M. J. (1991). Clinical aspects of depression in chronic pain patients. *Clinical Journal of Pain, 7,* 79–94.

Dworkin, R. H., & Grzesiak, R. C. (1993). Chronic pain: On the integration of psyche and soma. In G. Stricker & J. R. Gold (Eds.), *Comprehensive handbook of psychotherapy integration* (pp. 365–384). New York: Plenum Press.

Dworkin, R. H., Hartstein, G., Rosner, H. L., Walther, R. R., Sweeney, E. W., & Brand, L. (1992). A high-risk method for studying psychosocial antecedents of chronic pain: The prospective investigation of herpes zoster. *Journal of Abnormal Psychology, 101,* 200–205.

Engel, G. L. (1951). Primary atypical facial neuralgia: An hysterical conversion symptom. *Psychosomatic Medicine, 13,* 375–396.

Engel, G. L. (1959). "Psychogenic" pain and the pain-prone patient. *American Journal of Medicine, 26,* 899–918.

Fenichel, O. (1945). *The psychoanalytic theory of neurosis.* New York: Norton.

Fordyce, W. E. (1976). *Behavioral methods for chronic pain and illness.* St. Louis, MO: C. V. Mosby.

Fordyce, W. E., Fowler, R. S., & DeLateur, B. J. (1968a). An application of behaviour modification technique to a problem of chronic pain. *Behaviour Research and Therapy, 6,* 105–107.

Fordyce, W. E., Fowler, R. S., Lehmann, J., & DeLateur, B. J. (1968b). Some implications of learning in problems of chronic pain. *Journal of Chronic Diseases, 21,* 179–190.

Fordyce, W. E., Fowler, R. S., Lehmann, J., DeLateur, B. J., Sand, P., & Trieschmann, R. B. (1973). Operant conditioning in the treatment of chronic pain. *Archives of Physical Medicine and Rehabilitation, 54,* 399–408.

Frances, A., Clarkin, J., & Perry, S. (1984). *Differential therapeutics in psychiatry: The art and science of treatment selection.* New York: Brunner/Mazel.

Frank, F. A. (1990). Action techniques in psychoanalysis. *Contemporary Psychoanalysis, 26,* 732–756.

Freud, S. (1966). Project for a scientific psychology. In J. Strachey (Ed. and Trans.), *The standard edition of the complete psychological works of Sigmund Freud* (Vol. 1, pp. 281–397). London: Hogarth Press. (Original work published 1895)

Freud, S. (1959). Fragment of an analysis of a case of hysteria. In E. Jones (Ed.), _Sigmund Freud: Collected papers_ (Vol. 3, pp. 13–145). New York: Basic Books. (Original work published 1905)

Freud, S. (1959). Inhibitions, symptoms and anxiety. In J. Strachey (Ed. and Trans.), _The standard edition of the complete psychological works of Sigmund Freud_ (Vol. 20, pp. 75–175). London: Hogarth Press. (Original work published 1926)

Gamsa, A. (1990). Is emotional disturbance a precipitator or a consequence of chronic pain? _Pain, 42_, 183–195.

Gamsa, A. (1994a). The role of psychological factors in chronic pain: I. A half century of study. _Pain, 47_, 5–15.

Gamsa, A. (1994b). The role of psychological factors in chronic pain: II. A critical appraisal. _Pain, 57_, 17–29.

Gamsa, A., & Vikis-Freibergs, V. (1991). Psychological events are both risk factors in, and consequences of, chronic pain. _Pain, 44_, 271–277.

Gil, K. M., Ross, S. L., & Keefe, F. J. (1988). Behavioral treatment of chronic pain: Four pain management protocols. In R. D. France & K. R. R. Krishnan (Eds.), _Chronic pain_ (pp. 376–413). Washington, DC: American Psychiatric Press.

Goldsmith, S. (1983–1984). A strategy for evaluating "psychogenic" symptoms. _International Journal of Psychiatry in Medicine, 13_, 167–171.

Greenberg, J. R., & Mitchell, S. A. (1983). _Object relations in psychoanalytic thought_. Cambridge, MA: Harvard University Press.

Greenson, R. R. (1965). The working alliance and the transference neurosis. _Psychoanalytic Quarterly, 34_, 155–181.

Grzesiak, R. C. (1974). The psychology of pain. In A. B. Cobb (Ed.), _Special problems in rehabilitation_ (pp. 311–345). Springfield, IL: Charles C Thomas.

Grzesiak, R. C. (1977). Relaxation techniques in treatment of chronic pain. _Archives of Physical Medicine and Rehabilitation, 58_, 270–272.

Grzesiak, R. C. (1989). Strategies for multidisciplinary pain management. _Compendium of Continuing Education in Dentistry, 10_, 444–448.

Grzesiak, R. C. (1991). Psychologic considerations in temporomandibular dysfunction: A biopsychosocial view of symptom formation. _Dental Clinics of North America, 35_, 209–226.

Grzesiak, R. C. (1992a, August). _Unconscious processes and chronic pain: On the foundations of pain-proneness._ Paper presented at the annual meeting of the American Psychological Association, Washington, DC.

Grzesiak, R. C. (1992b). Psychological aspects of chronic orofacial pain: Theory, assessment and management. _Pain Digest_, 100–119.

Grzesiak, R. C. (1994a). Psychological considerations in myofascial pain, fibromyalgia, and related musculoskeletal pain. In E. S. Rachlin (Ed.), _Myofascial pain and fibromyalgia: Trigger point management_ (pp. 61–90). St. Louis, MO: C. V. Mosby.

Grzesiak, R. C. (1994b). The matrix of vulnerability. In R. C. Grzesiak & D. S. Ciccone (Eds.), _Psychological vulnerability to chronic pain_ (pp. 1–27). New York: Springer.

Grzesiak, R. C., & Ciccone, D. S. (1988). Relaxation, biofeedback, and hypnosis in the management of pain. In N. T. Lynch & S. V. Vasudevan (Eds.), _Persistent pain: Psychosocial assessment and intervention_ (pp. 163–188). Boston: Kluwer.

Guidano, V. F., & Liotti, G. (1983). _Cognitive processes and emotional disorders_. New York: Guilford Press.

Haber, J. D., & Roos, C. (1985). Effects of spouse abuse and/or sexual abuse in the development and maintenance of chronic pain in women. In H. L. Fields, R. Dubner, & F. Cervero (Eds.), _Advances in pain research and therapy: Vol. 9. Proceedings of the Fourth World Congress on Pain_ (pp. 889–895). New York: Raven Press.

Harness, D. M., & Donlon, W. C. (1988). Cryptotrauma: The hidden wound. _Clinical Journal of Pain, 4_, 257–260.

Hoffer, W. (1950). Development of the body ego. _Psychoanalytic Study of the Child, 5_, 18–24.

Horowitz, M., Marmar, C., Krupnick, J., Wilner, N., Kaltreider, N., & Wallerstein, R. (1984). _Personality styles and brief psychotherapy_. New York: Basic Books.

Joffe, W. G., & Sandler, J. (1965). Notes on pain, depression, and individuation. *Psychoanalytic Study of the Child, 20,* 394–424.

Katan, A. (1973). Children who were raped. *Psychoanalytic Study of the Child, 28,* 208–224.

Katz, A. W. (1990). Paradoxes of masochism. *Psychoanalytic Psychology, 7*(2), 225–241.

Krishnan, K. R. R., France, R. D., & Davidson, J. (1988). Depression as a psychopathological disorder in chronic pain. In R. D. France & K. R. R. Krishnan (Eds.), *Chronic pain* (pp. 195–218). Washington, DC: American Psychiatric Press.

Lane, R. C., Hull, J. W., & Foehrenbach, L. M. (1991). The addiction to negativity. *Psychoanalytic Review, 78,* 391–410.

Leino, P., & Magni, G. (1993). Depressive and distress symptoms as predictors of low back pain, neck–shoulder pain, and other musculoskeletal morbidity: A 10 year follow-up of metal industry employees. *Pain, 54,* 89–94.

Lesse, S. (Ed.). (1974). *Masked depression.* New York: Jason Aronson.

Levine, J. B., Brooks, J. D., Irving, K. K., & Fishman, G. G. (1993). Group therapy and the somatoform patient: An integration. *Psychotherapy, 30,* 625–634.

Magni, G., Moreschi, C., Rigatti-Luchini, S., & Merskey, H. (1994). Prospective study on the relationship between depressive symptoms and chronic musculoskeletal pain. *Pain, 56,* 289–297.

Maruta, T., Vatterott, M. K., & McHardy, M. J. (1989). Pain management as an antidepressant: Long-term resolution of pain-associated depression. *Pain, 36,* 335–337.

McDougall, J. (1985). *Theaters of the mind: Illusion and truth on the psychoanalytic stage.* New York: Basic Book.

McDougall, J. (1989). *Theaters of the body: A psychoanalytic approach to psychosomatic illness.* New York: Norton.

Melzack, R. (1989). Phantom limbs. *Regional Anesthesia, 14,* 208–211.

Melzack, R. (1991). Central pain syndromes and theories of pain. In K. L. Casey (Ed.), *Pain and central nervous system disease: The central pain syndromes* (pp. 195–210). New York: Raven Press.

Melzack, R. (1992). Phantom limbs. *Scientific American,* 120–126.

Melzack, R., & Loeser, J. D. (1978). Phantom body pain in paraplegics: Evidence for a central "pattern generating mechanism" for pain. *Pain, 4,* 195–210.

Mitchell, S. A. (1988). *Relational concepts in psychoanalysis.* Cambridge, MA: Harvard University Press.

Moore, B. E., & Fine, B. D. (1990). *Psychoanalytic terms and concepts.* New Haven, CT: Yale University Press.

Oxman, T. (1986). Psychotherapy. In R. P. Raj (Ed.), *Practical management of pain* (pp. 821–828). Chicago: Year Book Medical.

Parkes, C. M. (1973). Factors determining the persistence of phantom limb pain in the amputee. *Journal of Psychosomatic Research, 17,* 97–108.

Pietri-Taleb, F., Riihimaki, H., Viikari-Juntura, E., & Lindstrom, K. (1994). Longitudinal study on the role of personality characteristics and psychological distress in neck trouble among working men. *Pain, 58,* 261–267.

Pilowsky, I., & Barrow, C. G. (1990). A controlled study of psychotherapy and emitriptyline used individually and in combination in the treatment of chronic intractable "psychogenic" pain. *Pain, 40,* 3–19.

Potamianou, A. (1990). Somatization and dream work. *Psychoanalytic Study of the Child, 45,* 273–292.

Rachman, A. W. (1989). Confusion of tongues: The Ferenczian metaphor for childhood seduction and emotional trauma. *Journal of the American Academy of Psychoanalysis, 17,* 181–205.

Ramzy, I., & Wallerstein, R. S. (1975). Pain, fear, and anxiety. In R. S. Wallerstein (Ed.), *Psychotherapy and psychoanalysis* (pp. 223–263). New York: International Universities Press. (Original work published 1958)

Rangell, L. (1959). On the nature of conversion. *Journal of the American Psychoanalytic Association, 114,* 173–181.

Rothstein, A. (Ed.). (1986). *Reconstruction of trauma.* Madison, CT: International Universities Press.

Schofferman, J., Anderson, D., Hines, R., Smith, G., & Keane, G. (1993). Childhood psychological trauma and chronic refractory low-back pain. *Clinical Journal of Pain, 9,* 260–265.

Schofferman, J., Anderson, D., Hines, R., Smith, G., & White, A. (1992). Childhood psychological trauma correlates with unsuccessful lumbar spine surgery. *Spine, 17*(Suppl.), S138–S144.

Schur, M. (1955). Comments on the metapsychology of somatization. *Psychoanalytic Study of the Child, 10*, 119–164.

Sifneos, P. E. (1973). The prevalence of "alexithymic" characteristics in psychosomatic patients. *Psychotherapy and Psychosomatics, 22*, 255–262.

Spiegel, L. A. (1966). Affects in relation to self and object: A model for the derivation of desire, longing, pain, anxiety, humiliation, and shame. *Psychoanalytic Study of the Child, 22*, 69–92. New York: International Universities Press.

Sternbach, R. A. (1974). *Pain patients: Traits and treatment.* New York: Academic Press.

Sternbach, R. A. (1989). Acute versus chronic pain. In P. D. Wall & R. Melzack (Eds.), *Textbook of pain* (2nd ed., pp. 173–177). Edinburgh: Churchill Livingstone.

Sternbach, R. A., & Rusk, T. N. (1973). Alternatives to the pain career. *Psychotherapy: Theory, Research, and Practice, 10*, 321–324.

Sternbach, R. A., & Timmermans, G. (1975). Personality changes associated with reduction of pain. *Pain, 1*, 177–181.

Swanson, D. W. (1984). Chronic pain as a third pathologic emotion. *American Journal of Psychiatry, 141*, 210–214.

Szasz, T. S. (1957). *Pain and pleasure: A study of bodily feelings.* New York: Basic Books.

Szasz, T. S. (1975). *Pain and pleasure: A study of bodily feelings* (2nd ed). New York: Basic Books.

Turk, D. C. (1990). Customizing treatment for chronic pain patients: Who, what and why? *Clinical Journal of Pain, 6*, 255–270.

Turk, D. C., Meichenbaum, D., & Genest, M. (1983). *Pain and behavioral medicine: A cognitive-behavioral perspective.* New York: Guilford Press.

Turk, D. C., & Rudy, T. E. (1988). Toward an empirically derived taxonomy of chronic pain patients: Integration of psychological assessment data. *Journal of Consulting and Clinical Psychology, 56*, 233–238.

Turk, D. C., & Rudy, T. E. (1990). Neglected factors in chronic pain treatment outcome studies—referral patterns, failure to enter treatment, and attrition. *Pain, 43*, 7–25.

Turk, D. C., & Rudy, T. E. (1991). Neglected topics in the treatment of chronic pain patients—relapse, noncompliance, and adherence enhancement. *Pain, 44*, 3–28.

Turner, R. J., & Noh, S. (1988). Physical disability and depression: A longitudinal analysis. *Journal of Health and Social Behavior, 29*, 23–37.

van der Kolk, B. A. (1987). *Psychological trauma.* Washington, DC: American Psychiatric Press.

van der Kolk, B. A. (1989). The compulsion to repeat the trauma: Re-enactment, revictimization, and masochism. *Psychiatric Clinics of North America, 12*, 389–409.

van der Kolk, B. A., & van der Hart, O. (1991). The intrusive past: The flexibility of memory and the engraving of trauma. *American Imago, 48*, 425–454.

VanHoudenove, B. (1986). Prevalence and psychodynamic interpretation of premorbid hyperactivity in patients with chronic pain. *Psychotherapy and Psychosomatics, 45*, 195–200.

VanHoudenove, B., Stans, L., & Verstraeten, D. (1987). Is there a link between "pain-proneness" and "act-proneness?" *Pain, 29*, 113–117.

Von Korff, M., Le Resche, L, & Dworkin, S. F. (1993). First onset of common pain symptoms: A prospective study of depression as a risk factor. *Pain, 55*, 251–258.

Wachtel, P. L. (1977). *Psychoanalysis and behavior therapy.* New York: Basic Books.

Wachtel, P. L. (1993). *Therapeutic communication.* New York: Guilford Press.

Walker, E. A., Katon, W., Hansom, J., Harrop-Griffiths, J., Holm, L, Jones, M. L., Hickok, L., & Jemelka, R. P. (1992a). Medical and psychiatric symptoms in women with childhood sexual abuse. *Psychosomatic Medicine, 54*, 658–664.

Walker, E. A., Katon, W., Harrop-Griffiths, J., Holm, L., Russo, J., & Hickok, L. R. (1988). Relationship of chronic pelvic pain to psychiatric diagnoses and childhood sexual abuse. *American Journal of Psychiatry, 145*, 75–80.

Walker, E. A., Katon, W., Neraas, K., Jemelka, R. P., & Massoth, D., (1992b). Dissociation in women with chronic pelvic pain. *American Journal of Psychiatry, 149*, 534–537.

Weickgenant, A. L., Slater, M. A., & Atkinson, J. H. (1994, April). *A longitudinal analysis of coping and the development of chronic low back pain.* Paper presented at the meeting of the Society of Behavioral Medicine, Boston.

Whale, J. (1992). The use of brief focal psychotherapy in the treatment of chronic pain. *Psychoanalytic Psychotherapy, 6*, 61–72.

Wolf, E. K., & Alpert, J. L. (1991). Psychoanalysis and child sexual abuse: A review of post-Freudian literature. *Psychoanalytic Psychology, 8*, 305–327.

CHAPTER 8

Biofeedback and Relaxation Therapy for Chronic Pain Disorders

John G. Arena
Edward B. Blanchard

Psychological interventions in traditionally medical realms have increased at an exponential rate in the past three decades. One of the principal reasons why such interventions have become widely accepted by the medical community is their effectiveness in dealing with traditionally refractory medical problems such as chronic pain. Chronic pain is the most frequent cause of visits to primary care health settings (Sobel, 1993), and is probably the most frustrating challenge for traditional medically oriented health care providers to deal with. Cousins (1995) reports that estimates are that the health care costs of chronic pain exceed the costs of cancer, coronary artery disease, and AIDS combined. The two psychological techniques generally believed to have proven the most effective with individuals suffering from chronic pain syndromes are biofeedback and various forms of relaxation therapy; such treatments have usually been classified under the rubric of "psychophysiological interventions" (Craig & Weiss, 1990; Gatchel & Blanchard, 1993; Costa & Vandenbas, 1990; Shumaker, Schron, & Ockene, 1990).

In this chapter, we present a "how-to" guide for clinicians interested in using psychophysiological techniques with chronic pain patients. We deal with the three major types of chronic pain in which psychophysiological interventions have been used most often—namely, chronic tension headache, chronic vascular headache, and low back pain. For each, we first describe the chronic pain disorder, review briefly the current epidemiology and etiology data, and then describe in detail how to conduct biofeedback and relaxation therapy for patients suffering from that syndrome. We purposely assume that the clinician has little knowledge about biofeedback or relaxation therapy. In addition, we emphasize four special groups of headache sufferers: the elderly headache patient, the pediatric headache patient, the headache sufferer with high medication usage, and the patient with chronic, daily headache. Finally, in our concluding remarks, we describe how the procedures used with the pain disorders discussed here can be extrapolated to most other pain problems. It is our intention to make the chapter as clinically useful as possible; we thus include as many "clinical hints" as practicable, and, rather than reviewing the treatment literature in depth, in most instances we refer the reader to recent reviews.

WHAT ARE BIOFEEDBACK
AND RELAXATION THERAPY?

"Biofeedback," as it is commonly employed, is a procedure in which the therapist monitors through a machine the patient's bodily responses (such as muscle tension, surface skin temperature, heart rate, blood flow, and/or electrodermal response) and then feeds back this information to the patient, generally through either an auditory modality (a tone that goes higher or lower depending on, say, muscle tension's going higher or lower) or a visual modality (now usually a computer screen, where, for example, surface skin temperature is graphed on a second-by-second basis during each minute). Through this physiological feedback, it is hoped that a patient will be able to learn how to control his or her bodily responses. A more formal definition of biofeedback is "any technique which increases the ability of a person to control voluntarily physiological activities by providing information about those activities" (Olton & Noonberg, 1980, p. 4). Probably the simplest example of the use of a biofeedback device is a child's looking at himself or herself in a mirror, trying to find the best way to smile or frown.

"Relaxation therapy" is a systematic approach to teaching people to gain awareness of their physiological responses and achieve both a cognitive and a physiological sense of tranquility without the use of the machinery employed in biofeedback. There are various forms of relaxation therapy (see Lichstein, 1988, or Smith, 1990, for excellent reviews of the various types of relaxation therapy). The major forms, however, are progressive muscle relaxation therapy (Jacobson, 1929), meditation (Lichstein, 1988), autogenic training (Luthe, 1969–1973), and guided imagery (Bellack, 1973). By far the most widely used relaxation procedures in chronic pain disorders are variants of Jacobsonian progressive muscle relaxation therapy, and we primarily emphasize these procedures in this chapter.

TENSION HEADACHE

What Is Tension Headache?

Tension headache is generally described as a bilateral "dull ache," "pressure," or "cap-like pain" that is usually located in the forehead, neck, and shoulder regions. The headache typically occurs from 2 to 7 days a week and can last from 1 hour to all day; a small proportion of tension headache sufferers have continuous headache.

Most investigators who work in the area of headache would define chronic tension headache as having lasted for at least 1 year; most would also want patients to characterize the headache as significantly interfering in their lives. Clinicians who deal with headache patients should use a standardized set of inclusion and exclusion criteria for diagnosis, such as those of the Ad Hoc Committee on the Classification of Headache (1962) or the newer Headache Classification Committee of the International Headache Society (1988).

Epidemiology of Tension Headache

When all forms of headache are combined together, headache is the most common pain complaint (Peatfield, 1986), and some investigators speculate that it is the medical problem most frequently seen in medical clinics (Bakal, 1992). Most experts believe that the majority of headaches are tension-related. Rasmussen, Jensen, Schroll, and Olesen (1991), using the diagnostic criteria of the International Headache Society, found that lifetime prevalence for episodic or chronic tension-type headache was 78% for men and women combined, 69% for men, and 88% for women. In that study, the prevalence of tension headache in the previous month was 48% overall. Interestingly, among subjects with migraine in the previous month, 62% had coexisting tension headache. This study is extremely important because it is the first investigation to include a representative random population, to use operational diagnostic criteria, and to include a clinical interview as well as a general physical and neurological examination of all participants. It suggests that the incidence and prevalence of chronic tension headache are much higher than previously believed. Thus, it seems apparent that tension headache is a significant health problem.

Etiology of Tension Headache

Although traditional views on the etiology of chronic tension headache attribute the disorder to sustained contraction of skeletal muscles in the forehead, neck, and shoulder regions, recent psychophysiological investigations that have empirically tested this theory have arrived at conflicting, and for the most part negative, results; the majority of studies have not demonstrated any difference between controls and tension headache sufferers in forehead or neck electromyographic (EMG) activity (see, e.g., Andrasik, Blanchard, Arena, Saunders, & Barron, 1982; Haynes, 1980). Indeed, our own research has at times demonstrated that there are no differences in this activity, regardless of whether a headache is present or absent (Arena, Blanchard, Andrasik, Appelbaum, & Myers, 1985; Arena, Hannah, Bruno, Smith, & Meador, 1991b), while at other times it has shown that there are differences (Arena, Bruno, Brucks, Hanna, & Meador, 1995a).

A second major theory of the etiology of tension headache is that tension and migraine headache are variants of the same disorder and that the headache is attributed to a dysfunctional vasomotor system (Blanchard & Andrasik, 1987; Haynes, 1980; Tunnis & Wolff, 1954; Wolff, 1963). There has been a surprising paucity of research into this theory in recent years, however. The vascular theory of tension headache appears to have fallen out of favor because of two simultaneously occurring factors. First, Wolff, the father of headache research and main advocate of the blood flow abnormality theory in tension headache, stopped publishing in the early 1960s. Second, in 1962 the Ad Hoc Committee on the Classification of Headache published inclusion and exclusion criteria that attributed tension headache solely to muscle tension. Given the research findings that appear to call into question the theory of sustained muscle contraction, it would appear that the vascular theory of tension headache warrants further research.

Psychophysiological Interventions for Chronic Tension
Headache and a Proposed Mechanism of Treatment

Psychophysiological treatments for chronic tension headache have been found to be as effective as pharmacological interventions (Blanchard, 1992). The two primary kinds of psychophysiological interventions used for tension headache are some form of relaxation therapy, generally progressive muscle relaxation therapy, and EMG biofeedback. A number of review articles (Andrasik & Blanchard, 1987; Blanchard, 1992; Blanchard & Andrasik, 1982; Holroyd & Penzien, 1986) have demonstrated that approximately 50%

of tension headache sufferers are significantly improved both statistically (significant pre–post group differences) and clinically (50% or greater reduction in headache activity) through either of these techniques, and most studies find that there is no difference in outcome when the two treatments are directly compared.

The failure (described above) to demonstrate support for the theory that sustained levels of muscle tension cause tension headache is especially troubling for biofeedback clinicians. The rationale for biofeedback treatment is that since these headaches are caused by elevated levels of muscle tension, when tension headache sufferers are taught to decrease their muscle tension levels, there will be a corresponding decrease in their headache activity. This lack of support for a straightforward psychophysiological etiology means that clinicians and researchers must look for mechanisms other than, or in addition to, psychophysiological ones that are responsible for improvements in their tension headache sufferers.

In our opinion, the most sophisticated and methodologically elegant study to date that has examined alternative change mechanisms underlying improvements in tension headache was conducted by Holroyd et al. (1984). In that study, 43 college students who suffered from tension headache were randomly assigned to one of four possible biofeedback conditions in a 2 × 2 factorial design. In the first factor, although all subjects were led to believe that they were decreasing their forehead EMG levels, only half the subjects were given feedback contingent on decreased EMG activity; the other half were given feedback contingent on increasing EMG activity. The second factor consisted of a high-success group (bogus video displays demonstrating high success compared to the rest of the subjects in the experiment) or a moderate-success group (bogus video displays indicating moderate success compared to the rest of the group). Results indicated that it made no difference whether subjects learned to increase or decrease their muscle tension levels; the high-success feedback group showed substantially greater improvements in headache activity (53%) than the moderate-success group (26%).

Blanchard, Kim, Hermann, and Steffek (1993) gave progressive muscle relaxation therapy to 14 tension headache sufferers. At the end of each session, they were also given computerized bogus feedback regarding their performance: six were led to believe that they were highly successful in the relaxation task, whereas eight were informed that they were only moderately successful. Patients who perceived themselves as highly successful at relaxation reported a greater amount of improvement in their headache activity, as measured by the daily headache diary, than those with perceptions of moderate success. These findings extend the results of the Holroyd et al. (1984) study, since they were obtained on a treatment-seeking sample of adults who were in their mid-30s and who had suffered from headaches an average of over 10 years.

The Holroyd et al. (1984) study demonstrated the importance of cognitive mediating factors such as perceived success and self-efficacy in biofeedback training, and the Blanchard et al. (1993) study essentially replicated the Holroyd et al. study's conclusions with relaxation therapy, using a treatment-seeking, nonanalogue population. These findings also suggest that clinicians who work with tension headache patients should attempt to put their patients' results in the best light possible: They should be as optimistic as they can be, de-emphasizing the patients' difficulty in grasping the response, and magnifying even small successes. In effect, a therapist should act somewhat as a public relations person or a political "spin doctor" does. From an ethical perspective, however, we would certainly not recommend that clinicians "fake" data to lead patients to believe they are being successful.

EMG Biofeedback Training for Chronic Tension Headache

EMG Biofeedback Hookup

There is not sufficient space here to describe in detail the complexities of the EMG signal or basic biofeedback instrumentation and safety issues. Prior to conducting biofeedback on any patient, however, the clinician should familiarize himself or herself with such basics by reading a standard text such as Schwartz and Associates (1995) or Basmajian and DeLuca (1985), or the chapter on biofeedback instrumentation in the Association for Applied Psychophysiology and Biofeedback's *Standards and Guidelines* volume (Sherman et al., 1992). It is strongly urged that the novice biofeedback therapist, prior to attempting biofeedback therapy, receive training from a licensed health care provider familiar with biofeedback or become certified in biofeedback by the Biofeedback Certification Institute of America.

The immediate question that the clinician must deal with is this: On which muscle group should the sensors be placed (forehead, neck, shoulder, etc.)? Unfortunately, the research is rather vague here. One approach to answering this question would be to conduct a psychophysiological assessment, measuring the major muscle groups purported to be implicated in tension headache, and then placing the sensors during biofeedback training in the region that exhibits the most elevated muscle tension. There are a number of problems with this strategy, however. First, to our knowledge, there have been no studies demonstrating the clinical utility of this type of psychophysiological assessment. Second, one immediately runs into technical questions such as these: Does the clinician conduct the psychophysiological assessment during baseline (resting) conditions or during stressful conditions? What exactly constitutes the baseline conditions (reclining or standing, eyes open or eyes closed, etc.)? Similarly, what stressful condition does one use— mental arithmetic, stressful imagery, electric shock, an exercise step-up test, ischemic pain, or a cold-pressor task? What happens if neck muscles show elevated tension during mental arithmetic, but not during baseline or the cold-pressor task? Third, what if the patient tells the clinician that the pain is located in the neck and shoulders, but the psychophysiological assessment indicates that there are muscle activity elevations only in the forehead? (We do not have space in this chapter, unfortunately, to provide answers to these rhetorical questions.) Finally, nearly all of the biofeedback tension headache outcome research is conducted with the sensors placed on the forehead region.

Recording from the frontal region has become standard (Budzynski, 1978), in spite of the fact that the vast majority of tension headache sufferers also have involvement in the neck and shoulder regions, and a good many of them state that their headaches emanate from the neck and shoulders. A search of the research literature could find only five studies examining other site placements (Hart & Cichanski, 1981; Hudzinski, 1983; Martin & Mathews, 1978; Philips, 1977; Philips & Hunter, 1981). The only direct comparison of frontal and neck EMG has been the 1981 study by Hart and Cichanski. In that study, 20 tension headache subjects were split into two groups and given up to 15 sessions (average = 7) of either frontal EMG biofeedback training or EMG biofeedback from the back-of-the-neck region (sternocleidomastoid). Results indicated that the individuals in the neck biofeedback group had greater mean reductions in their overall headache activity (57% vs. 43% in the frontal biofeedback group), but the difference was not statistically significant.

Arena, Bruno, Hannah, and Meador (1995b) have conducted the first systematic examination of a trapezius (neck and shoulder region) EMG biofeedback training regimen with tension headache sufferers. It evaluated the differential effects of three psychophysiological treatments for tension headache: (1) a 12-session upper trapezius EMG biofeedback training regimen (n = 10); (2) a standard 12-session frontal EMG biofeedback training regimen (n = 8); and (3) a standard 7-session progressive muscle relaxation therapy regimen (n = 8). Posttreatment assessment at 3 months revealed clinically significant (50% or greater) decreases in overall headache activity in 50% of subjects in the frontal biofeedback group, 100% in the trapezius biofeedback group, and 37.5% in the relaxation therapy group. Chi-square analyses indicated that trapezius biofeedback was more effective in producing significant clinical improvement than were frontal biofeedback and relaxation therapy (which did not differ from each other). Thus, these tentative results, coupled with the limited research, suggest that neck and shoulder placement is at least as effective as forehead placement, and may actually be more efficacious. For now, we feel that clinicians may be justified in using either or both placements; perhaps it should be left up to patients to decide which they should attempt to learn first.

For exact sensor placements for muscle groups, clinicians should refer to standard texts such as Lippold (1967). For clinical purposes, however, we generally just swab the forehead with alcohol (during which time the eyes are closed); then, instructing the patient to stare straight forward, we place the two active sensors on the forehead, in line with the pupil of each eye. The reference (ground) sensor is placed in the center of the forehead, between the two active sensors. For upper trapezius (neck and shoulder) placement, we have the patient shrug his or her shoulder(s) and place the active leads over the belly of the muscle between the spine and the shoulder joint, approximately 1½ inches apart; the reference sensor is placed between the two active ones. Figure 8.1 graphically depicts the upper trapezius muscle site placement.

Clinical hints: Three things are important to note regarding electrode placement. First, following Sherman et al. (1992), we use only disposable EMG sensors to ensure against infection. Second, to decrease anxiety, we call electrodes by the more innocuous term "sensors." Third, also to decrease anxiety, we inform our patients that there is no danger of being harmed during EMG biofeedback training and that the sensors are not sending any electricity into the body; they are only picking up the muscles' electronic patterns.

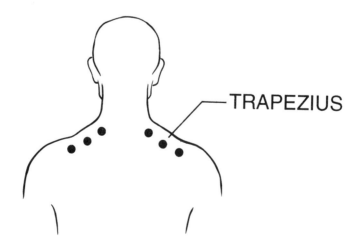

FIGURE 8.1. Electrode placement for bilateral upper trapezius EMG biofeedback training.

Rationale and Strategies Given during Initial Session

As stated above, we believe that with tension headache sufferers, the rationale, strategies, and therapist–patient interactions are paramount in achieving positive treatment outcome. We would advise strongly against attempting to describe a complex rationale such as self-efficacy to patients; rather, we describe the theory of sustained levels of muscle tension. We say something like this:

> "It's traditionally been assumed that the type of headache you have—tension headache—is caused by very high levels of muscle tension in your forehead, neck, and shoulder areas. These muscles have been tense for a long time. Through biofeedback training, you will learn to decrease your muscle tension levels. When you do this, it's hoped that you will get a decrease in your headaches."

We inform patients that stress plays a role in their headaches by leading to elevated muscle tension, and that it is essential to deal with their stress as well as their muscle tension, as these are interrelated. (We routinely provide a number of cognitive-behavioral strategies regarding stress; see Bradley, Chapter 6, this volume, on cognitive-behavioral approaches to pain.)

We emphasize that these techniques are self-regulation skills that will allow the patients to prevent a headache from occurring. We stress to them that they need to incorporate these skills into their lifestyle—that they are making a lifestyle change, rather than receiving a "treatment" from a therapist. In this way, something is not being done to them; they are learning how to employ these skills for themselves. Again, this increases the likelihood of enhancing self-efficacy.

We next give the patients a number of possible strategies from which to choose. We emphasize that learning the biofeedback response is purely an idiosyncratic process and that what works for others may not work for them. We customarily describe seven possible biofeedback strategies:

1. *Relaxing imagery.* The patient imagines a pleasant scene, such as walking through the woods on an autumn evening and listening to the leaves crunch with each step, or lying on a beach listening to the waves as they roll in and roll back out again (a detailed description of a beach scene is given in the section on relaxation therapy for tension headache, below). We routinely tell patients to avoid any possible sexually stimulating imagery, because this is arousing rather than relaxing, and to switch to another image if they are having trouble decreasing their muscle tension with a particular image. We also tell them not to imagine themselves engaging in any vigorous physical activity, and to try to feel as if they are actually in the scene, rather than just imagining a movie playing in front of them (here we also suggest that they try to get every sensory modality involved, such as smell, sound, and touch). Finally, we tell them that, if at all possible, it is best to be by oneself in the image.

2. *Relaxing (autogenic) phrases.* Relaxing phrases, repeated over and over again, can be a very effective strategy. Although there are standardized phrase lists (e.g., Blanchard & Andrasik, 1985), we have found that relaxing phrases are most effective with biofeedback training when the patients think of their own phrases. We emphasize to them that they have to repeat these phrases numerous times (50–100), rather than just once or twice. We also instruct them that sometimes these procedures do not work initially, but may work over repeated sessions. (See the section on thermal biofeedback for vascular headache, below, for additional details on autogenic phrases.)

3. *Deep breathing procedures.* The patient, with eyes closed, concentrates on diaphragmatic breathing (breathing by expanding the lungs fully while keeping the shoulders and chest relaxed, allowing the abdomen to expand) and repeats a relaxing word such as "relax," "calm," or peaceful" when exhaling. We tell patients to limit the pace of breathing to no more than 12 breaths a minute, and preferably to keep it to between 6 and 8 breaths per minute. We have found that for a substantial minority of patients words that have nothing to do with relaxation, such as "plum," "amber," or "stream," are often effective. Some individuals like to pair this with relaxing imagery—for example if they are imagining a beach scene, to pace their breathing with the rhythm of the waves (inhalation with wave coming in, exhalation with wave going out). It is important to inform patients—especially those whose breathing is faster than 30 breaths per minute—that they may feel quite strange when they get their breathing down into the relaxed range. We tell them that this will pass as time goes on, and that they will actually begin to enjoy the novel feelings of relaxation (e.g., heaviness, floating, etc.).

Clinical hint: Research has demonstrated (MacHose & Peper, 1991) that is nearly impossible to breath diaphragmatically if one is wearing tight jeans or clothing (belts, ties, etc.); we remind patients to wear loose-fitting pants or jeans.

4. *Awareness of sensations.* Some individuals are able to lower their forehead muscle tension levels by simply concentrating on and becoming aware of the sensations of tightness and tension in their forehead, neck, and shoulders—in other words, by focusing on what it is like when those muscles relax, loosen up, and unwind. We tell them that as the muscles become relaxed, they may feel warmth, heaviness, and looseness in the muscles that they have not felt before.

5. *Nothingness.* Some patients report that if they can make their minds blank and think of nothing—actually stop thinking—they can relax and lower their muscle tension. This is indeed very difficult for most people to do, and fewer than 2% of individuals can achieve this. However, if some patients can enter into a state of nothingness, it will probably lower their muscle tension levels.

6. *Mental games.* Some patients find that focusing on a color ("warm" colors, such as yellow, green, or brown, seem to work best) helps to relax them and decrease their muscle tension levels. Others actually play a game in their mind, such as tic-tac-toe, bowling, cards, or basketball.

7. *Concentrating on the auditory feedback.* Some individuals just ignore all of the preceding strategies and simply concentrate on the feedback tone. They even report imagining the tone going down when they practice in their everyday environment without a portable biofeedback device.

At the first session, we usually tell a patient to pick only one strategy and stick with it throughout the entire session. We keep the initial session short—a 3- to 5-minute adaptation period ("Just sit quietly with your eyes closed") and a maximum of 12 minutes of biofeedback. (In later sessions, we increase the biofeedback portion to a maximum of 25 minutes.) We emphasize to patients that this is a difficult response to learn and that it will take some time before they can lower their muscle tension reliably; we tell them not to get discouraged if they cannot control their EMG levels immediately. Often, we tell patients that during the first few sessions they should expect to do exactly the opposite of what they are striving for—that in all likelihood they will increase, rather than decrease their muscle tension. This gives us as therapists a rare opportunity for a "no-lose" situation, and potentially a great chance to enhance feelings of self-efficacy and success. If the patients increase their muscle tension, then we say, "That was to be expected for a first session." If they stay the same or actually decrease their muscle tension, then we praise them for succeeding during the first session: "It's very rare to do as well as you've done today; that's a great sign."

During the first session, we instruct each patient to let the response occur, rather than make it occur—to be passive, rather than try to force the forehead or neck muscles to relax. We tell patients that when people have difficulty with biofeedback, it's often because they are trying too hard to obtain the response ("I want you to try very hard not to try very hard"). We go through the various forms of feedback and let them choose which type of visual and auditory feedback they like. Finally, although we restrict our research protocols to 12–16 sessions, it is not unusual for our clinical patients to run up to 24 sessions. In some few instances, we have gone up to 36 sessions; these instances have generally involved advancing to another muscle group (if starting with the forehead, then going to neck and shoulder biofeedback training, or vice versa), and special generalization training.

Coaching and Therapist Attitude

The first and most important thing for a therapist to determine about coaching is whether a patient wants and can benefit from it. This is truly idiosyncratic. From our clinical experience, about 25% of patients do not want to be coached at all. These patients are usually easily identified, as they will most likely tell us that "I can do it better if you just leave me alone," or we can infer that attitude from nonverbal cues. Some very few patients (about 5%) want us to give them constant coaching. The vast majority of patients want and need some coaching, but not all the time. For these individuals, we usually coach a lot during the first biofeedback session; then, during successive biofeedback sessions, we coach a bit at the beginning of each biofeedback phase and then once every 5 minutes or as necessary (e.g., the patient is doing the opposite of the desired response, or has suddenly had an "Ah ha" experience and has learned how to control the response).

Therapists who have ever coached anything already know two important things: the way to coach a biofeedback session, and the fact that a coach's verbal repertoire is extremely limited (especially when the coach cannot use expletives!). A therapist should be prepared for three general situations:

1. The patient has decreased his or her muscle tension levels. Here are some possible responses: (a) "That's fantastic! Keep up the good work." (b) "I want you to remember what you are doing now, so you can tell me later at the end of the session." (c) "Real good! Try to allow it to go even lower."

2. The patient has not been able to decrease his or her muscle tension levels. Possible responses include these: (a) "That's OK. It's as important to find out what makes your muscle tension go up as it is to find out what makes it go down." (b) "I want you to remember what you're doing now, so you can tell me later at the end of the session." (c) "That's OK. You can only go up so far before you have to start going down." (d) "You seem to be at an impasse; you might want to switch to a different strategy."

3. The patient seems frustrated or appears to be trying too hard. Possible responses are as follows: (a) "That's to be expected. Remember, I told you that this is a very difficult response to get. If it was easy, you wouldn't need me or the machines." (b) "Let's take a break. Sometimes all you need is a few minutes to clear your mind, and then you come back like gangbusters." (c) "Remember, this is a skill like learning to drive. At first it's difficult, but with practice and time you become more skilled. Pretty soon, the response

will become automatic, just as driving becomes automatic." (d) "You may want to think of yourself as a scientist, who in a somewhat detached manner tests theories and tosses them in or out, depending upon whether or not they work."

Interestingly, the limited research on coaching and therapist presence during a bio-feedback session indicates that learning is retarded when there is a great deal of coaching (Borgeat, Hadd, Larouche, & Bedwani, 1980). As a rule, we would suggest that coaching be done on a limited basis, as this will help to generalize the response to the "real world," for in everyday situations patients do not have a therapist accompanying them. This will also prevent patients from becoming dependent on the therapist.

Some individuals, especially the elderly who have vision or hearing problems, can benefit from tactile stimulation as coaching. Usually this takes the form of a slight pressure on the wrist or hand, or a slight pat on the back.

The importance of coaching, and especially of therapist attitude, cannot be overemphasized. As Holroyd et al. (1984) demonstrated, imparting to the patient the perception of success is perhaps the essential change mechanism underlying improvement in biofeedback training for tension headache. It is imperative for the therapist to convey enthusiastically to each patient that he or she is doing well in the biofeedback training. A number of researchers have emphasized the importance of other therapist factors, such as perceived warmth and competence, as being essential in biofeedback training (Taub & School, 1978). However, the empirical evidence does not support these assumptions (Blanchard et al., 1983), possibly because the therapists in that study were nearly all rated as warm and competent. We would certainly urge therapists to try to be perceived as positive, warm, and competent.

Postsession Feedback

At the end of each session, we always ask patients what strategy they found to be the most effective (if any were effective), as well as to rate (on either a 0–10 or a 0–5 scale) their degree of relaxation and their level of overall body tension now as compared to the beginning of the session. At both the beginning and end of each session, it is important to explore any situationally stressful events that may have been occurring recently in a patient's life, especially any that have occurred just prior to the onset of the training session (e.g., argument with spouse, difficulty at work, upcoming test or deadlines). If patients are unable during the training session to decrease their muscle tension levels, we frequently point out at the end of the session that these factors may have contributed to their inability to relax that day. It is always useful to have patients rate their headache level (on either a 0–10 or a 0–5 scale) prior to and following the biofeedback training. This can then be used to help give the patients some understanding of how they were performing (i.e., to relate headache activity level to ability to decrease muscle tension levels during biofeedback, as well as to contrast baseline levels from session to session with pain levels from session to session). Moreover, frequently patients are unable to control their muscle tension levels effectively, but their headache activity decreases during the session. When this happens, it can be used to give the patients a perceived sense of self-control over their pain and to enhance self-efficacy.

Homework

Home practice has traditionally been considered an essential element of all psychophysiological interventions for chronic headache (Blanchard & Andrasik, 1985; Blanchard et al., 1991a). We usually begin home practice for biofeedback once patients have demonstrated that they can reliably produce the desired biofeedback response in the office setting. Home practice can be conducted in many ways. The simplest form of homework is to instruct the patients to practice the office strategy that seems to work the best at home and in other real-world locations, such as the job, the supermarket, and so forth (we usually instruct them to do so at least 10 times a day). We want them to practice it when they are brushing their teeth, waiting for a traffic light to change, taking a coffee break, or the like. We tell the patients that the biggest problem they will have in the beginning is simply to remember to practice the biofeedback during the day ("If you can remember to practice, you've got 95% of the problem licked"). We ask them to choose something they do 10–20 times a day and allow that to be the cue to remind them to practice. Some of our patients have practiced every time they look at themselves in a mirror, open and close a door, answer the telephone, or see a specific color. If this proves too troublesome, we ask them to buy colorful "stick-ons" and place these in strategic areas as reminders to practice their biofeedback skills. In other instances, we ask patients to obtain a wristwatch that beeps every 30 or 60 minutes, and let the beep be a reminder to practice.

We sometimes ask patients to use a small pocket mirror during home practice as a biofeedback aid ("Try to smooth out your forehead as much as you can"). Small portable biofeedback devices are available for less than $300, and we routinely lend these to our patients during the course of treatment. It is important to note, however, that there has been no research examining the utility of biofeedback home practice for chronic tension headache, and only one study (Blanchard et al., 1991b) has compared home practice versus no home practice for relaxation therapy (this study found only a trend for relaxation therapy to be more effective with home practice than without). In spite of this paucity of data on the usefulness of homework in biofeedback training for tension headache, for the face validity alone, we would still urge clinicians to place great emphasis on home practice.

Generalization of the Biofeedback Response to the "Real World"

Generalization involves preparing a patient to, or determining whether or not the patient can, carry the learning that may have occurred during the biofeedback session into the "real world." There are many ways to test or prepare for generalization. The most common by far is a "self-control" condition, which is interspersed between a baseline and a feedback condition. The self-control condition involves asking the patient to control the desired psychophysiological response (e.g., "Please try to lower your forehead muscle tension") without any feedback. If the patient can control the response, the clinician may infer that between-session learning (i.e., generalization) has occurred. We routinely add such a condition to our biofeedback training after the second or third session. Another method of testing for generalization is to present the same stressor to the patient before and after treatment; if there is less arousal during and after a stressor at the posttreatment presentation, the clinician may infer that generalization has occurred. (Except in special circumstances, we do not use this method.) A third, and potentially the most useful, way of preparing the patient to generalize the biofeedback response is to attempt to make the office biofeedback training simulate real-world situations. For example, in Augusta, we initially have each patient sit in a reclining chair. Once the patient has mastered the rudiments of biofeedback, we then routinely progress to a comfortable office chair (with arms), an uncomfortable office chair (without arms), and lastly a standing position. Finally, giving patients homework assignments to practice the biofeedback response in the "real world" is, of course, an excellent way of preparing them for generalization.

Problems That Arise in Both Biofeedback and Relaxation Therapy

Intrusive Thoughts

One major problem that patients seem to have with both biofeedback and relaxation therapy procedures is the occurrence of intrusive ("busy") thoughts. We alert patients prior to the initial session that they may initially have problems with such thoughts entering their minds. We tell them simply to expect that these thoughts will occur. Some thoughts will be productive, such as "Oh, how relaxed I am feeling," "I'm feeling more relaxed this time than before," and "My headache has definitely lessened and my neck feels less tense." Other thoughts will be unproductive, such as worries about problems at work, tasks that need to be finished, meals that have to be cooked, and so on. We then tell patients that it is essential that they do *not* attempt to stop those unproductive thoughts, because trying to stop them will only exacerbate the problem. We inform the patients that as they get better at the relaxation/biofeedback procedures, the problem will lessen. We also tell them when they are practicing at home not to get frustrated when the thoughts occur, to let them play themselves out, and always to return to the relaxation/biofeedback response when the thoughts are over.

These suggestions usually work with most people. With those individuals who are having severe intrusive thoughts after numerous sessions, we suggest a mild form of thought stopping:

> "Imagine that these thoughts are like a freight train, and at the first thought they become chained or linked together. In order to stop them, try to imagine a stop light that flashes, and in your mind say, 'STOP!' Immediately replace that unproductive thought with a more productive thought, such as 'I am learning to relax myself more quickly,' or 'I am feeling the relaxation spreading throughout my muscles.'"

Panic Attacks and Relaxation-Induced Anxiety

Although it is not frequently discussed, there is a subset of patients who experience increased tension and anxiety during relaxation therapy and biofeedback. In a few individuals, this may take the form of a panic attack. (For an excellent theoretical discussion of relaxation-induced anxiety, please see Heide & Borkovec, 1983.) Our clinical experience and the limited research available suggest that individuals who suffer from generalized anxiety or panic disorders, or those who are very anxious during the preliminaries to the first session of relaxation therapy and/or who report increased tension as a result of the relaxation or biofeedback, are at increased risk for relaxation-induced anxiety and panic attack. Since relaxation-induced anxiety can lead to patients' dropping out of treatment, it should be carefully assessed. For these subjects at high risk, we have them focus more on the somatic aspects of the biofeedback or relaxation training, instead of focusing on cognitive factors (i.e., stress how the muscles feel rather than how quiet their minds are, etc.). We also emphasize that they are always in control during the biofeedback or relaxation therapy; they will always be aware of what is going on around them, what they are doing, and what we are saying.

In spite of all preparations, panic attacks may occur occasionally. These usually take the form of patients' opening their eyes during the relaxation procedure, crying, stating that they feel very nervous, and/or attempting to leave the therapist's office. There are three things a therapist should do in this situation: stay calm; reassure the patient, "I understand what you are going through, and these feelings will soon pass"; and try not to act as a dynamic, insight-oriented therapist (even if the therapist is one).

The essential thing for the therapist to do during a panic attack is to assume a calm demeanor. Novice therapists especially seem to have trouble with this; they often pick up on the intense affect of these patients and contribute to it with their own fears and concerns. It is important to remember that (to the best of our knowledge) no one has ever died from a panic attack, although they are quite frightening. The worst that could happen from the therapist's perspective is that he or she will have to take the patient to the local emergency room (and we have never heard of any therapists actually having to do this). Therefore the therapist should stay calm, speak in a slow and low voice with a relaxed tone, and act as if things are going to be fine. Even if he or she is extremely concerned and anxious, this should not be conveyed to the patient.

Next, before the patient can say what he or she is experiencing, the therapist should state what the patient is feeling. This lets the patient know that the therapist is understanding and competent, and that whatever else the therapist says will be accurate as well. We say something like this:

> "Right now you're feeling really nervous, like something terrible is going to happen to you. You maybe even feel as if you are going to die. Your heart is pounding, your thoughts are racing, you are breathing very rapidly and shallowly, your mouth is dry, you're sweating a lot, you can't catch your breath, your hands and feet are very cold, and you just want to get out of here. Don't worry; nothing that you feel now is permanent. It will all be over in a few minutes."

We usually get the patient a glass of water and a tissue and then wait for him or her to calm down. We then say: "Remember how you did the diaphragmatic breathing? Let's do it right now. I want you to breathe at the same rate that I am and notice how quickly you are starting to feel more calm and relaxed. Notice that your heart is now slowing down and you feel more in control." If at all possible, the patient should be prevented from fleeing the office, because this can lead to avoidance of relaxation and to a pairing of relaxation or biofeedback with becoming anxious.

It is important for a therapist, especially an insight-oriented psychotherapist, not to try to act as "Supertherapist" and give the patient insight into why he or she is having these feelings. This is not to say that those questions and insights are not important, but during or immediately following a panic attack is not the time to gather such information or impart such interpretations. They are best left for subsequent sessions. At this time, the therapist's main goal should be to calm the patient and demonstrate how even though the patient was very anxious and felt that he or she was going to die, it did not happen, and the patient was able to calm down. From our experiences as supervisors of doctoral candidates in clinical psychology, we have found that questions such as, "Have you ever felt these feelings before at any time in your life?" "During your childhood, were you ever in situations where you felt a loss of control similar to these feelings today?" or "Did any images come to mind when you became very nervous that reminded you of things when you were growing up?" are especially resented by patients experiencing a panic attack.

Usually, when the suggestions above are followed, the patient will calm down and feel well enough to leave the office or continue discussion (we strongly recommend *not* continuing the biofeedback or relaxation therapy during that session). The next session, we spend some time discussing with the patient how he or she felt and whether he or she wishes to continue with the biofeedback or relaxation therapy. Most patients who do not drop out of therapy will continue with the regimen. A small subset of patients—usually those in relaxation therapy—will not wish to continue the psychophysiological intervention, and for those individuals we offer cognitive-behavioral therapy for pain (see Bradley, Chapter 6, this volume) or the other psychophysiological intervention.

Relaxation Therapy for Chronic Tension Headache

It is important to remember that although nearly all of the headache literature treats biofeedback and relaxation therapy as separate interventions, most clinicians combine the two procedures when treating tension headache. With tension headache, however, we generally choose first to give an entire regimen of one intervention; should a patient prove refractory to that treatment, we offer him or her a course of the other psychophysiological procedure. We have previously asserted that relaxation therapy, because it generally entails fewer sessions and does not require machinery, should be administered before biofeedback training; we have employed this strategy in our research (Blanchard et al., 1982b, 1982c, 1985c). There have unfortunately been no direct comparisons of this strategy with that of using EMG biofeedback first, followed by relaxation therapy for those refractory to biofeedback. Therefore, there are no empirical data at the present time to confirm the validity of our assertion.

There are excellent references available for relaxation therapy in general (Bernstein & Borkovec, 1973; Lichstein, 1988; Smith, 1990), as well as for its specific application with tension headache (Blanchard & Andrasik, 1985). In this section, we outline a nine-session relaxation therapy regimen that we have successfully used with tension headache patients (Arena, Hightower, & Chang, 1988; Blanchard et al., 1982b, 1985c). Although we base our relaxation therapy on an abbreviated form of Jacobsonian progressive muscle relaxation therapy (tension–release exercises), we also routinely incorporate other forms of relaxation into the procedure (relaxing imagery, relaxation by recall, cue-controlled relaxation techniques).

Rationale

We usually explain the rationale for relaxation therapy with tension headache to our patients like this:

> "Relaxation therapy involves learning how to achieve a mental and physical state of tranquility in a very brief period of time, as well as how to apply these relaxation skills to your daily living. A lot of people in your life may have told you at one time or another that you needed to relax or that you appeared tense, but none of those people instructing you to calm down or 'chill out' actually showed you how to do so. This procedure will teach you how to achieve a state of relaxation and peacefulness, eventually enabling you to relax in a short period of time. By 'relaxation training,' we mean a very systematic set of procedures, rather than merely trying to relax on your own. After concentrated practice, it is likely that you will experience a significant reduction in headache activity.
>
> "It is generally believed that tension headache is related to your body's reaction to everyday stressful events, such as hassles at work, arguments with your spouse,

child-rearing problems, and so on. You may have noticed that when you are under stress, your body reacts in different ways. Perhaps your neck muscles tighten up and feel stiff and sore. Perhaps you begin to sweat a lot or have a queasy feeling in your stomach, or maybe you feel your heart race, your breathing become short and shallow, or your hands get cold and clammy. These are all indicators that your body is experiencing stress. It's believed that the bodies of tension headache patients react to stressful life situations primarily in the muscles of the upper torso—usually the forehead, jaw, neck, and shoulders. Through relaxation therapy, you will learn how to decrease the amount of muscle tension in those and other areas of your body. If you have other bodily symptoms during stress, such as shallow breathing or rapid heart rate, it will also help control them. You see, the sympathetic nervous system, which is the part of the body necessary to enable you to function at work or gear you up for action-oriented tasks such as sports, controls these bodily responses when you are under stress. We will teach you to recognize these symptoms within yourself as signs of stress or tension, and to apply the relaxation procedures to break up the muscle tension throughout the day that would otherwise cause head pain, as well as to energize the part of the nervous system that will enable you to relax and heal.

"For this training to be of the most benefit to you, you should go through the exercises for about 15 to 20 minutes, as often as you can during a day. A minimum number of practices is twice daily. We want you to practice the relaxation therapy as much as possible, because we want you to get a head start on a major lifestyle change. You see, incorporating relaxation into your daily living is as important as other activities, such as brushing you teeth or washing your hands. You want to practice it as much as possible until it becomes an automatic habit. When you are learning to drive a car, it is necessary to think about each step before you do it—put on the seat belt, turn on the ignition, look in the rear view mirror, and so forth. After driving for a short period of time, you do not have to think about the steps; you just do it. Relaxation therapy should become just as automatic after a period of time. Although some patients become very relaxed after only one or two practice sessions and notice almost immediate relief, the overwhelming majority of patients do not show substantial reductions in their stress levels and do not seem to show a great deal of headache improvement until they have completed the entire course of relaxation training. Therefore, please do not get discouraged if you do not appear to be getting immediate results.

"Remember, relaxation is a self-regulation and prevention skill. By this we mean that you are learning how to recognize signs of tension in your body and reduce them before they reach the level of painful, stiff muscles and headache. Once you are actually experiencing a headache, these techniques may not be as effective as they would be if used prior to a headache's onset. Along the same line of thinking, we suggest that you try to use these exercises as soon as you begin to notice a headache coming on, rather than waiting for a full-blown headache to occur.

"Achieving a deep state of relaxation is a very pleasant experience. In addition to reducing stress and headaches, relaxation has numerous other positive benefits. Many people report feeling a greater degree of self-control, less difficulty falling asleep, decreased blood pressure, less irritability, and a more positive outlook on life following relaxation training. Unlike medication, there are no negative side effects with this form of treatment."

First Session

The first session of relaxation therapy is designed to teach patients to become more aware of the feelings in their muscles and to relax their muscles to allow them to enter a deep state of relaxation. We emphasize that it is imperative for patients to pay special attention to what it feels like when their muscles are tense and when they are relaxed. We tell them that it is essential to be able to label that feeling in the muscles as tense or relaxed, so they can recognize the feelings at times when they are not formally practicing the procedure.

We say something like this to our patients:

> "Relaxation training consists of methodically tensing and then relaxing the major muscle groups of your body. By tensing your muscles in a special way, you are *forcing* them to become relaxed; many individuals with headache need to do this, as they have been so tense for so long that they have forgotten what it feels like to be deeply relaxed. While tensing your muscles, you should pay special attention to the feelings in your muscles and become aware of what it feels like for your muscles to be tense. While relaxing your muscles, you should also pay attention to the muscle sensations and become aware of what it feels like for your muscles to be relaxed. Pay special attention to the contrast between a tense and a relaxed muscle state. After going through this series of tension–release exercises or cycles, you will feel quite relaxed. With repeated practice, you'll be able to relax much more quickly and deeply in situations that are not as conducive to relaxation as this office is."

Before beginning the relaxation procedure, we instruct each patient to remove eyeglasses or hard contact lenses, shoes (especially high heels), and cap or hat, as well as to loosen belt, collar, or tie. We also instruct the patient as to proper body posture: Arms should be resting on the arms of the recliner or by the patient's side if he or she is reclining on a couch; feet should be uncrossed, and, if the patient is sitting in an easy chair, legs should be supported by another chair or (preferably) an ottoman; head and neck should be supported by a pillow if the patient is lying down on a couch or sitting in an easy chair. Room temperature should be comfortable. We suggest that the room temperature be somewhat on the warm side (74–78°F). Lighting should be subdued, phone calls should be transferred, and a "Do not disturb" sign should be placed on the door. Most importantly, the therapist should always remember to turn off his or her beeper.

Introduction of Muscle Groups. Although we frequently use 14 muscle groups in our first session, it is imperative that the therapist determine whether the patient needs or can benefit from such intense training. For example, individuals who have poor concentration skills may become quite bored with such a long procedure and may terminate treatment prematurely as a result. Individuals with mild, episodic tension headache may also not need such intensive training. For these individuals we usually begin with an initial session of 6 or even 4 muscle groups (see the discussion of the fourth and fifth sessions, below). It is important that the therapist not become a slave to the relaxation regimen, but tailor the relaxation procedure to each individual. Many novice therapists have this problem. For example, if the patient has had a life crisis between the present session and the preceding one, it is fine to skip the regularly scheduled relaxation procedure and concentrate on the life crisis.

The therapist should then go over the various muscle groups to be tensed, modeling the exercises to ensure that the patient knows how to tense each muscle group correctly. The 14 muscle groups we usually begin with, and our statements as we go through them with patients, are as follows:

1. *Lower arms and hands.* "Please hold both arms out over your lap and make a fist with each hand."

After a few seconds, we instruct the patient to relax his or her arms. If the patient relaxes quickly, we say, "That was fine. The major goal of a first session of relaxation therapy is to understand the difference between a relaxed and a tense state, and you understand this difference better by increasing the contrast between the two states—that is, by relaxing quickly." If the patient relaxes slowly, we correct him or her using a similar rationale. We then ask patients whether they were able to feel tightness or tension when they tensed the muscle group, and relaxation when they released the tension. If they state that they were unable to feel any tension, we give them an alternative way of tensing the group ("Press your arms and hands down into the chair [bed] as hard as you can"). When we ask them what they felt when they relaxed the muscles, they will frequently state that they felt heaviness or a tingling feeling. We instruct them to label those feelings as the presence of relaxation.

2. *Upper arms.* "Please bring both arms to your shoulders, and apply pressure at each elbow as if you were making muscles."

Alternative tensing strategy: "Please press your elbows into the back of the chair [down into the couch]."

3. *Calves.* "Please point your toes toward your knees."

Clinical hint: At this point, some individuals may express a concern about the possibilities of cramps occurring in their legs, back, shoulders, or neck. We tell them that the relaxation should never hurt; that they do not need to tense so much that it will cause a cramp; and that if they do feel any pain or cramps, it is an indication that they are tensing too much. In our experience, it is very rare for cramps to occur. The therapist can usually predict who may have a high probability of cramping by looking for individuals who brace or guard in their posture, and should be especially careful in instructing such individuals not to tense too intensely.

4. *Lower legs.* "Please point your toes away from your knees."

Alternative tensing strategy for lower legs and calves: "Please press your lower legs down into the chair [couch]."

5. *Thighs.* "Please press your thighs together tightly."

Alternative tensing strategy: "Please press your thighs down into the chair [bed]."

6. *Stomach.* "Please draw your stomach in tightly."

Alternative tensing strategy: "Please push your stomach out as far as it will go."

7. *Chest.* "Please take a deep breath and hold it in."

Alternative tensing strategy: "Holding your hands in front of you, press your palms together as tight as you can."

At this point, it is useful to bring up the importance of diaphragmatic breathing. (Many therapists teach diaphragmatic breathing prior to beginning progressive muscle relaxation therapy; doing so at this point is simply a preference on our part.) We tell patients that learning to breathe correctly is the most important relaxation technique they can master, and that if they become proficient in proper breathing techniques, they have half the relaxation battle won. We instruct them that most adults do not breathe diaphramatically, and that to do so they need to take deep, slow, relaxing breaths and push the air down into the chest—expanding the belly, not the thoracic cavity and shoulders. We tell them that with each deep breath they will feel more relaxed. Breathing in this way will trigger the relaxation response at other times during the day when they do not have time to do the entire procedure.

We instruct the patients that it is difficult to become very anxious if they are breathing correctly. We ask whether they have ever had a panic attack or ever seen someone become very nervous. (Nearly everyone has had one of these experiences.) We point out that the first thing that occurs during a panic attack is that breathing becomes very rapid and shallow, which physiologists term "hyperventilation." We then proceed to instruct the patients that they can prevent high levels of anxiety by breathing diaphragmatically. We tell them: "When you are practicing relaxation at home, put a large phone book on your belly right over your navel, and a smaller book on your chest. Practice making the phone book rise and the smaller book remain still while breathing." We inform them that breathing is so important that we will be including some special breathing exercises at the end of the session.

Note that a therapist who prefers to do so can spend the first session of relaxation simply giving the rationale and stressing diaphragmatic breathing techniques much more than we do above. If so, the therapist should say something like this:

"Diaphragmatic breathing is a technique you can use to control tension in your body. First, place one hand on your chest and one on your abdomen. Take a breath in and notice which hand moves more. If you see the chest move out more, you are breathing in a tense manner. The chest is constructed such that the lungs are in the upper chest and a muscle (the diaphragm) separates the stomach from them. This muscle is used to gain a greater volume of air as you breathe in. If you have ever played a wind instrument, sung in a choir, or done underwater swimming, you probably have learned this technique. Also, this is the way you breathe immediately before going to sleep as you become deeply relaxed. If you have children, you can watch them because they have not learned to breathe in a tense manner. Again, take a long deep breath in, and try to push your stomach out so that it pushes against your belt. If you do this slowly, you will feel the air expand in your lungs, and your stomach will naturally extend outward. This is not a fashion statement, but until you learn to breathe in this way it is helpful.

"Close your eyes and take a deep breath. Feel the coolness of the air as it passes into your nose and expands into your lungs. Feel your stomach expand as you breathe in as the chest becomes full and tight. Breathe out very slowly and easily. Take a second deep breath. Slowly breathe out. With each breath you can feel yourself becoming more relaxed. Concentrate on your breathing. . . . Allow your breathing to become smooth and rhythmic. Practice this breathing exercise 5 to 10 times a day."

8. *Shoulders*. "Please draw your shoulders up toward your ears."

Alternative tensing strategies: (a) "Please press your shoulders firmly back into the chair [couch]." (b) "Holding both arms out in front of you, please roll your shoulders." (c) "Holding your arms at your side, please pull your shoulders down."

9. *Neck*. "Please press your head tightly backward against the chair [pillow]."

Alternative tensing strategy: "Please try to touch your chest with your chin, going as close as you possibly can, but never actually doing so." (This is an isometric exercise; it involves two opposing muscle groups, pressing down and up at the same time. It is actually the best exercise for the neck but many patients cannot do this.)

10. *Lips*. "Please press your lips together tightly without clamping down with your jaw or biting down on your teeth."

11. *Eyes*. "Please close your eyes somewhat tightly."

Here, we tell patients that we do not want them to tense too much, as they will bring into play other muscle groups (particularly the lower forehead) if they do so; they may also bring on or exacerbate a headache. We tell them that their eyes should always be closed during relaxation, but in a quiet, relaxed, easygoing sort of way. The only time we want them to put any pressure on the eyes is when they deliberately tense them.

Clinical hint: Some individuals will be reluctant to close their eyes. This is an important clue to the clinician that such a patient is frightened of the relaxation procedure or the possibility of losing control; it means that the therapist should prepare the patient for the relaxation procedure more thoroughly than usual (perhaps even putting off the first session until next time). The therapist should ensure that statements concerning the patient's always being in control during relaxation are included in the relaxation patter (see below). If the patient is adamant about not closing his or her eyes, the therapist should not force the patient to keep his or her eyes closed, but rather should request the patient to find a spot on the ceiling and stare at it. Almost always, the patient's eyes will close as the session goes on. If this does not occur, we have found this to be nearly a pathogonomic sign of paranoid personality or severe paranoid tendencies. Needless to say, this is a highly reliable sign of poor treatment outcome.

12. *Jaw.* "Please open your mouth as wide as possible."

Alternative tensing strategy: "Please press your teeth together gently."

Clinical hint: Before the jaw is tensed, the therapist should ask the patient whether his or her jaws have ever locked open. If they have, the alternative jaw-tensing exercise should be used instead of the first strategy. Sometimes when a patient opens his or her mouth wide, this makes a very loud popping sound. Although many people will have some clicking or popping sound when they tense their jaws, a very loud sound may be indicative of temporomandibular joint dysfunction and should be evaluated by a physician or dentist.

13. *Lower forehead.* "Now I would like you to frown and try to lower your eyebrows."

14. *Upper forehead.* "Please try to wrinkle your forehead and raise your eyebrows."

Following the tensing of the upper forehead, we tell patients that we will do a deepening procedure, in which we will count from 1 to 5 and tell them that they are becoming more relaxed as we do so (some patients prefer to count from 1 to 10 or from 1 to 3; still others prefer the therapist to count down toward relaxation; whatever a patient prefers is fine). Finally, we will have them do some special breathing exercises that we have alluded to during the instructions on tensing the chest muscles.

Clinical hint: One question that frequently comes up at this point is "How is this going to help me in the real world?" Often, of course, patients cannot stop what they are doing in a stressful situation and tense their arms, legs, and so on. We agree with such patients that the relaxation at this point is not an active coping strategy that they can carry around with them and use in everyday situations; we explain that they have to learn the rudiments of relaxation before they can graduate to more advanced types of relaxation, which are quite quick, portable, and inconspicuous.

Actual Relaxation Procedure. At this point, we begin the actual relaxation procedure. Although there has been a surprising paucity of research concerning this, we feel that it is essential that the therapist talk in a slow, low-pitched, monotonous voice. It is a good idea for novice therapists to tape-record their voices and experiment with different voices prior to actually seeing patients. It is also a good idea for novice therapists to time themselves. If they take less than 1 minute for the tensing and the relaxation of any muscle group (including the "relaxation patter"), they are going too fast. Novice therapists should always have a written version of the relaxation procedure in front of them, to keep them from skipping muscle groups, becoming anxious, or forgetting the sequence or correct phrasing of the exercises (the last of which happens even to experienced therapists all too often).

Our standard format is to ask a patient to tense each muscle group as follows: "Now I want you to tense the muscles of your [respective muscle group] by [respective tensing instructions]. (*Pause to make sure that the patient has tensed the muscle group in question and has not fallen asleep or tensed all muscles.*) Study the tensions in your [respective muscle

group]. Study those tensions. Now relax the muscles of your [respective muscle group]."
It is important to remember that although we use the logic of starting with the muscles
that appear less implicated in headache first and building up to the neck, shoulders, and
facial muscle groups, there is no hard-and-fast rule about the order of muscle group presentation. If a therapist prefers to start at the legs and work upward, that is fine.

Alternative tensing strategy: "Now bring on tension in the muscles of your [respec-
tive muscle group]. Notice the feelings in the muscles as you bring on the tension. Label
that feeling as the presence of tension. (*Pause 5 seconds.*) Now let go of the tension, and as
you relax, label that feeling as the presence of relaxation."

Following each muscle group's tensing, we include 20 seconds or so of "relaxation
patter" in which we suggest to the patient how relaxed he or she is becoming in a general
sense (in some instances, instead of the relaxation patter, we simply have 20 seconds of
silence). Usually the patter includes suggestions of lightness, heaviness, floating, sinking,
warmth, or tingling. In the first session, we always include a statement about the patient's
always being in control. We say something like this: "You will always be clearly aware of
what I am saying and what you are doing as your muscles become more relaxed." The
more anxious a patient seems to be about the relaxation procedure, the more a therapist
should include statements such as this. For very anxious individuals, we include a statement such as this following every other muscle group. We have previously published a
number of relaxation patter statements (Blanchard & Andrasik, 1985). Two such examples
are "Just let yourself become more and more relaxed," and "Just let the relaxation flow
into all the areas of your body."

Following relaxation of the upper forehead, we then induce a deepening procedure
(Blanchard & Andrasik, 1985):

> "Now I want you to relax all the muscles of your body. Just let them become more
> and more relaxed. I'm going to help you to achieve a deeper state of relaxation by
> counting from 1 to 5. As I count, you will feel yourself becoming more and more
> deeply relaxed, going further and further down into a deep, restful state of deep
> relaxation. One—you are going to become more deeply relaxed. Two—down, down
> into a very relaxed state. Three—deeper and deeper. Four—more and more relaxed.
> Five—completely relaxed, a deep, restful state of deep relaxation."

The deepening procedure is always included following the last muscle group of every
relaxation exercise.

We then wait 45–60 seconds and begin a breathing exercise (Blanchard & Andrasik,
1985):

> "Now I want you to remain in your very relaxed state. I want you to begin to concen-
> trate only on your breathing. Breathe through your nose. Notice the cool air as you
> breathe in (*pair this with inhalation*) . . . and the warm, moist air as you breathe out
> (*pair this with exhalation*). (*Wait 20 seconds.*) Just concentrate on your breathing, tak-
> ing deep, slow, relaxing breaths. (*Wait 30 seconds.*) Now, each time you breathe out,
> in your mind repeat the word 'relax.' Breathe in (*pair this with inhalation*). . . . Breathe
> out (*pair this with exhalation*). (*Wait 30–60 seconds.*) Just continue to concentrate on
> your breathing, taking deep, slow, relaxing breaths, and mentally repeating the word
> 'relax' each time you breathe out."

The breathing procedure is always included following the deepening procedure of every
relaxation exercise.

After 45–60 seconds, we begin an alerting procedure (Blanchard & Andrasik, 1985):

"Now I am going to help you to return to your normal state of alertness. In a little while, I am going to begin counting backward from 5 to 1. You will gradually become more alert. When I reach 2, I want you to open your eyes. When I get to 1, you will be entirely roused up in your normal state of alertness, feeling quite refreshed. OK now. Five. Four. You are becoming more and more alert; you feel very refreshed and renewed. Three. Two. Now your eyes are open and you begin to feel very alert, returning completely to your normal state. One. (*Wait 10 seconds.*) When you feel like it, you may sit up and stretch."

The alerting procedure is always the last procedure of every relaxation exercise.

Clinical hint: Sometimes a patient will fall asleep during the relaxation. If the therapist becomes aware of this prior to the alerting procedure, the therapist can simply increase the volume of his or her voice until the patient awakens. At this point, the relaxation should be continued at the point where the therapist became aware that the patient was sleeping. If the patient does not open his or her eyes at the end of the alerting procedure, the therapist should continue to repeat numbers 2 and 1 of the alerting procedure in a successively higher voice until the patient awakens. The therapist should never call the patient's name or touch the patient to awaken him or her; this is terribly frightening to most individuals. After the patient awakens and the normal questions in the postsession inquiry are asked (see below), the therapist should remind the patient that although sleeping indicates a state of great relaxation, the patient should try not to fall asleep, as that will interfere with his or her ability to obtain full benefits from the relaxation procedure.

Postprocedure Inquiry. Upon completion of the procedure, we always ask a number of questions. First, we ask patients to rate how relaxed they were at the beginning of the session, at their most relaxed point in the session, and right now (at the end of the session), on a scale of 1 ("not at all relaxed") to 10 ("as relaxed as I ever was"). (With some individuals who may not be able to place an accurate numerical representation on their relaxation, we ask whether they were able to get somewhat relaxed during the procedure.) If they tell us they were able to achieve any degree of relaxation, we encourage them as much as possible. If they report that they were unable to relax, we relate to them that with practice they will become more able to relax themselves—that relaxing is a skill just like riding a bicycle, and that with more practice they will get better at doing it.

We also ask patients whether they were able to relax one or two muscle groups to a much greater degree or a much lesser degree than others. If they were able to relax a muscle group more than others, we note this and use that as one of the muscle groups that we combine with others or eliminate when reducing the number of muscle groups in the fourth and fifth sessions (see below). If they inform us that they had difficulty with one group, we tell them that many people have a muscle group that is more difficult to relax than others. We advise them to tense that muscle group longer when they practice the relaxation at home, rather than tensing it repeatedly. In addition, if they are having difficulty with a muscle group that has an alternative tensing strategy or strategies, we have them use all the tensing strategies to tense that muscle group. (E.g., see the four ways of tensing the shoulders, above.) We also inquire as to whether patients experienced increased tension or anxiety at any time during the relaxation (see the discussion of relaxation-induced anxiety earlier in the chapter).

Furthermore, we ask the patients what feelings or sensations they experienced during the relaxation procedure. Many patients experience sensations of heaviness, floating, sinking, drowsiness, warmth, lightness, tingling in the arms and hands, the therapist's voice being far away, and so on. Patients should be encouraged that these are all signs of entering a deeply relaxed state. Sometimes patients will tell us that they felt as if they were being hypnotized, as if they were going to cry or laugh, or other uncomfortable feelings. We inform the patients that feelings and sensations such as these are quite common; that they indicate that the patients are becoming very relaxed; and that often when people become relaxed, it is such an unusual feeling that it may actually be uncomfortable at first. With these patients, we make certain in subsequent sessions that we include many statements as to being in control in the relaxation patter (usually after every other muscle group).

Lastly, we ask patients to rate their pain level on a 0–10 scale at the beginning and end of the relaxation. As in biofeedback, we try to relate their pain levels to the stress in their lives, as well as their ability to become deeply relaxed. If they are able to reduce the pain, we reinforce their gaining a sense of self-control over what has been previously perceived as uncontrollable.

Homework. As in biofeedback (see above), homework is very important in relaxation therapy. We instruct our patients to practice the diaphragmatic breathing as frequently as possible and the tension–relaxation exercises at least twice a day. There are some essential differences, however, in the home practice of relaxation therapy as compared to biofeedback. First, it is important to instruct patients that when they have finished the relaxation procedure, they should slowly become more alert. With older patients who are on hypertensive medication, this is especially important because of the increased possibility of orthostatic hypotension (a dramatic drop in blood pressure whenever they go from sitting or lying positions to standing). We stress to patients that they should sit up slowly and wait a few minutes before standing: "Do not stand up suddenly."

We also suggest that patients practice once in the morning and once in the evening. If they are having trouble falling asleep, we tell them that one of these practices can take place just before they go to bed. If they are having no difficulty falling asleep, we stress that it is best *not* to practice just before bedtime, as we do not want them to associate the relaxation with sleep. After each practice, we always have patients fill out a new version of the headache diary (indicating the time they began practicing, the level of relaxation on a 1–10 scale prior to and following the relaxation session, the time practice ended, and of course their headache levels).

Finally, we make an audiotape during the first session and give it to the patient for home practice. This is very useful for most people. We tell them that it is important to practice the relaxation exercises as many times as possible, but to use the tape only once a day. We instruct them that if they can only do the procedure once on a particular day, it is best not to use the tape; this prevents them from becoming too dependent on it. We inform them that they will eventually be weaning themselves off the tape—again because they must not become too dependent on it, as the goal of relaxation is to use the procedures in the "real world" and they will not have the opportunity to play a tape if, for example, a child is "talking back" to them.

Second Session

If it is possible, the second session of relaxation therapy should be scheduled for later during the same week. This will give maximum benefit. If this is impossible, as in many private practice situations, a 1-week interval between sessions is fine. For the second session of relaxation (as for all subsequent sessions), we always begin by asking about home practice. We inquire about whether patients actually practiced the relaxation procedures, whether any problems were encountered, how often they practiced, and so on. If individuals state that they did not have the time to practice as much as needed, we work on basic time management skills. If patients appear not to have practiced, or state that they practiced but did not fill out their diaries, then issues of motivation as well as control may need to be addressed. Therapists should reinforce patients for practicing, especially if they were able to achieve an increase in their level of relaxation from pre- to postexercise, or a decrease in their pain levels. It is imperative that a therapist do everything possible to enhance feelings of self-efficacy, especially in light of the Holroyd et al. (1984) and Blanchard et al. (1993) studies.

There is only one change in the relaxation procedure from the first session to the second session: the addition of a relaxing scene after the attention-to-breathing procedure. We usually ask each patient to describe such a scene prior to the start of the relaxation procedure. For the most part, patients will give everyday scenes. The most common is a beach scene, an example of which we give below. Other popular scenes are waterfalls, walking through the woods on an autumn evening listening to the leaves crunch with every step, being in a cabin in the woods with a warm fire during a snowstorm, mountain streams, and the like. It is essential not to use a "stock" scene, but rather to elicit personal preferences from the patient. With that in mind, here is a sample relaxing scene:

> "Now I want you to imagine that it is a very, very warm summer evening, and you're lying on a blanket on a beach in Florida [Barbados, California, etc.]. You can feel a warm breeze flow across your body and through your hair. And you can smell the salty air of the sea. The sky and the sea are a perfectly clear blue . . . and the sun is just about to set. It's a beautiful, burnt orange color. And you can feel the warmth of the sun pouring down into every muscle of your body. In the distance, you can hear the seagulls . . . and you can see the waves as they roll in and roll back out again. You can see a sailboat on the horizon. You can feel the warmth of the sand from beneath the blanket . . . and you can hear the waves as they roll in, and roll back out again . . . roll in, and roll back out again. . . ."

We tell our patients not to get frustrated if they cannot imagine the pleasant scene as well as they would like; this will come with practice. From now on at every session we include a relaxing scene just before the alerting procedure, with this exception: Some people are simply very poor imaginers and report that they get very discouraged because they are unable to imagine the pleasant scene at all, even after repeated home practice. In this instance, we tell the patients not to use this strategy during home practice, and we eliminate it from the in-session relaxation procedures. We often make a tape of this session to give to each patient, with the same instructions as in the first session.

Third Session

The third session of relaxation therapy involves the introduction of a technique known as "muscle discrimination training." We use this procedure during the session on two muscle groups, the neck and the eye muscles. In muscle discrimination training, we teach the patients to distinguish between the different levels of muscle tension in their bodies. We first have them tense their muscles to full strength (just as they normally do in the relaxation training procedure), then to 50% tension, and finally to 25% tension.

We say something like this:

"Now I want you to tense the muscles of your [muscle area] by [tensing instructions]. Study the tensions located in your [tension location]. Study those tensions. (*After subject has tensed the muscle group for 7–10 seconds:*) Now I want you to tense the muscles of your [muscle area] half as much as the time before. Concentrate on the sensations of tension and how they differ from level to level. (*After subject has tensed the muscle group for 7–10 seconds:*) Now I want you to tense the muscles of your [muscle area] half as much as the time before, or one-quarter the amount of the usual level of tension. Concentrate on the sensations of tension and how they differ from level to level. (*After subject has tensed the muscle group for 7–10 seconds:*) Now relax the muscles of your [muscle area], and study the difference between the tension and the relaxation."

This procedure is extremely important for a sizable subset of tension headache individuals. Some people cannot discriminate between the various levels of muscle tension; they characterize any muscle tension as intense tension. Others refuse to characterize any state of muscle tension as tension unless it is tension near a cramping level. Both types of patients need to be able to label their physiological levels accurately.

After the discrimination training task is conducted, and the normal relaxation queries are over, it is important to ask patients whether they were able to differentiate between the various levels of tension. If they were unable, it is useful for them to practice this task on all of the muscle groups, rather than just the eyes and neck. We tell our patients that we want them to practice the discrimination procedure for the next week formally at least once a day, and that they should begin to use this discrimination procedure on their neck and shoulder muscles prior to perceived stressful situations.

Fourth Session

The fourth session of relaxation therapy is geared toward one goal: decreasing the number of muscle groups used from 14 to 6. We tell the patients something like this.

"The goal of relaxation training is to give you a procedure that is portable—that you can carry around with you and use in the 'real world' as a transferable coping skill. To do this, we must do two things. First, the relaxation must be shorter, and we are going to begin to do that today by reducing the number of muscle groups from 14 to 6. The second thing that we must do is make the relaxation inconspicuous; that is, no one must be able to tell that you are doing the relaxation by looking at you. We are not going to work on this second essential element of the relaxation for a while yet. Today we are just going to reduce the muscle groups to 6. Shortening the number of muscle groups should be just as effective at helping you to achieve a deep state of relaxation as the more lengthy version was."

The muscle groups and the statements we use are as follows:

1. *Arms and hands.* "Bring both arms to your shoulders, applying pressure at the elbows (as if you were making muscles), and making fists."
2. *Legs and thighs.* "Point your toes toward your face, and press your thighs together tightly."
3. *Stomach and chest.* "Draw your stomach in tightly, take a deep breath, and hold them both in."

4. *Shoulders and neck.* "Draw your shoulders up toward your ears (shrug your shoulders). At the same time, press your head tightly backwards against the chair or bed."

5. *Lips and eyes.* "Press your lips tightly together, without biting down or clamping your jaw. At the same time, close your eyes somewhat tightly—that is, try to have them 'squinted' shut. (Do not tense your eyes too much or you could bring on a headache.)"

6. *Jaw and forehead.* "Open your mouth wide, wrinkle your forehead, and try to raise your eyebrows upward."

For alternative tensing strategies, see the list of 14 muscle groups given earlier.

In making this change in the relaxation procedure, the therapist should tailor the relaxation to the needs of the individual patient. The number of muscle groups and the muscles chosen are not written in stone. If a patient has problems with both the neck and shoulder muscles, the therapist may decide to combine the arms and legs into a single group and keep the neck and shoulders separate. Or the patient can continue to relax the two groups separately, simply adding a seventh muscle group. The therapist should be flexible and creative.

Fifth Session

The fifth session of relaxation therapy is also geared toward one goal: decreasing the number of muscle groups used from 6 to 4.

The muscle groups and the statements we use are as follows:

1. *Arms and legs together.* "Bring both arms to your shoulders, applying pressure at the elbows (as if you were making muscles), and making fists. At the same time, point your toes toward your face, and press your thighs together tightly."

2. *Stomach and chest.* "Draw your stomach in tightly, take a deep breath, and hold them both in."

3. *Shoulders and neck.* "Draw your shoulders up toward your ears (shrug your shoulders). At the same time, press your head tightly backward against the chair or bed."

4. *Face.* "Press your lips tightly together, without biting down or clamping your jaw, and close your eyes somewhat tightly. At the same time, wrinkle your forehead and try to raise your eyebrows upward. (Do not tense your eyes too much or you could bring on a headache.)"

Sixth Session

The sixth session of relaxation therapy is probably the most important of all the sessions. In this session, we introduce the concept of portability through a technique known as "relaxation by recall," and we begin to stress the importance of daily practice in the everyday world. We begin by saying something like this:

"The first of two very important goals for this session is to practice becoming relaxed without actually tensing your muscles. This is called 'relaxation by recall.' In the past five sessions you have learned what it feels like for your muscles to be tense, as well as what it feels like for your muscles to be relaxed. During the relaxation-by-recall exercises, you will be focusing your attention on the muscle groups in your body, paying particularly close attention to the muscle tension in six muscle groups: your arms and hands, your legs and thighs, your stomach and chest (which you will always do by tension–release), your shoulders and neck, your eyes and lips, and your jaw and forehead. As you focus on each muscle group, you should try to determine whether your muscles are relaxed or whether there is some tightness or tension present. In relaxing by recall, if you notice that a particular muscle group is tense, you just 'let go' of the muscle tension present and recall what it feels like for that muscle group to relax. In other words, to relax your muscles by recall, simply remember what the muscles feel like when they are relaxed by 'letting go' of whatever tension is present in the muscle.

"As I have just said, your chest muscles are never relaxed through relaxation by recall, but always through the tension–release exercise. There are two reasons for this: The first and main reason is that the chest is a muscle you can tense without anyone knowing you are tensing it. It is therefore already inconspicuous and 'portable.' No one knows when you are tensing your chest. The second reason is that the chest is the most important muscle group in your body. Your breathing is very closely related to your nervous system and to your cardiovascular (heart and blood flow) system, and these bodily systems are most relaxed when the chest is relaxed by tension–release exercises.

"Most people are able to learn how to relax their muscles by recall fairly quickly. Learning the skill will take practice, just as learning the tension–release exercises took practice on your part. It is a very important skill, since you will probably not want to go around all day actually tensing your muscles in order to relax them. You might also feel rather foolish tensing them when other people are present. Relaxation by recall is the main step toward making the relaxation therapy a 'coping skill,' since it is now 'portable' and you can easily use it in your everyday living. You should try to formally practice the relaxation-by-recall exercises at least twice a day."

We strongly suggest that the therapist make a tape of the sixth session to give to each patient for home practice. For this session, we use the six muscle groups outlined above for the fourth session. The actual instructions for relaxation by recall are as follows:

"Now I want you to focus all of your attention on the muscles of your [muscle area], and very carefully identify any feelings of tightness or tension that may be present. Notice where the tightness and the tension are. Notice what they feel like. Focus on the tightness and the tension. (*Wait 5 seconds.*) Now relax the muscles of your [muscle area] by just recalling what it was like when you released the muscles of your [muscle area]. Just let them go and allow them to become more and more deeply relaxed, more and more completely relaxed. Just let the muscles of your [muscle area] go, and notice how they feel now compared to before. (Choose one of the following:) (1) Notice how those muscles feel when they're so completely relaxed. (2) Notice how good those muscles feel as they loosen up, smooth out, unwind, and relax more and more deeply, more and more completely. (3) Notice how those muscles feel when they're so completely relaxed. So very, very calm, tranquil, and relaxed."

After we conduct the relaxation-by-recall procedure, we ask our normal postrelaxation questions. In addition, we always ask patients to contrast the degree of relaxation obtained through this procedure versus the tension–release procedure. If the patients state that they were more relaxed than, or about as relaxed as, they were during tension–release, we inform them enthusiastically that that is a good sign (again, we always attempt to enhance self-efficacy). If the patients state that they were not as relaxed during the recall procedure than during the tension–release, we tell them not to become discouraged; with practice, the recall procedure will become just as effective as the tension–release exercises.

Following the relaxation-by-recall postrelaxation inquiry, we begin the second major component of the sixth session: stressing the importance of practice in the everyday world. We say something like this:

"The second very important component of today's session is to begin to practice applying the relaxation strategies to your daily living. Learning these skills successfully will help you reduce daily stress and prevent headaches. You will gain awareness of increased muscle tension and will be able to relax muscles before they develop painful cramping, which can lead to headaches; this is your ultimate goal.

"In order to apply the relaxation strategies to your daily living, the first thing you must do is to *think about your muscle state throughout the day*. Every so often, it must come into your awareness to think about your muscle tension. Only when you are aware of the state of your muscles can you determine whether or not they are tense and apply the relaxation techniques. You must learn to think about your muscles often enough to prevent muscle contraction from occurring for a long period of time, and therefore to cope better with stress and prevent a headache. Learning to think about the state of your muscle tension, like anything else, just takes time, effort, and practice. Once you think about your tension, try to apply the relaxation-by-recall procedure, relax yourself, and then continue with what you were doing. If you are having trouble thinking about your muscle state, here are some strategies that have helped others: (1) setting and resetting the alarm on your wrist watch every 45 minutes and checking your muscle tension when it goes off; (2) buying 'smiley face' or other stick-on labels, putting them in strategic places, and checking your tension whenever you see one; and (3) checking your tension every time you open and close a door, see yourself in a mirror, or answer a telephone."

Seventh Session

In the seventh session, we do two things: (1) We reduce the number of muscle groups during the relaxation-by-recall procedure to four (just as we do for the tension–release procedure in the fifth session); and (2) following the relaxation by recall, we introduce a number of different strategies that may make the relaxation even shorter—in particular, a strategy called "cue-controlled relaxation."

We say something like this:

"In the second part of this session, you will learn a number of strategies for applying the relaxation techniques into daily living. Some of these strategies come right from the relaxation exercises that you have been doing. The first strategy is called 'cue-controlled relaxation.' It consists of the following steps: First take a deep breath, hold it for a second or two, then breathe out. As you breathe out, repeat the word 'relax' to yourself. Next, quickly scan your muscles and find any muscle tension that may be present. If you find any muscle tension, just allow the tension to drain out so that your muscles feel relaxed. Then focus on your breathing again, taking several more deep breaths to become more relaxed. Once your breathing is deep and relaxed, pair the word 'relax' with breathing out for a minute or so.

"Whenever you do these relaxation exercises, remember to use your diaphragm muscles to draw in the air and to breathe it out (that is, take 'belly breaths'). This prevents tension from building up in your chest and shoulder muscles. To know whether you are using your diaphragm muscles while breathing, place a large book on your stomach and a small book on your chest while you are lying down. As you breathe, the large book should move up and down and the small book should remain still. You should make sure that your stomach is rising a good deal and that you are breathing out all of the air. You should also be sure that your breathing is in one motion; you should not be taking short, choppy breaths or holding your breath.

"Using the cue-controlled relaxation strategy, you will be able to become relaxed in a very short period of time. After some practice, it should take less than 5 minutes to perform. When you get very good at it, you will be able to get very relaxed in just about a minute, but this will take further time and practice. When you apply this skill in your daily living, you may not become as relaxed as you do when you are lying down in a bed or reclining on a comfortable chair. But the cue-controlled relaxation will allow you to relax quickly in the real world."

In addition to these instructions for the basic cue-controlled relaxation procedure, we tell our patients that there are other things they can do to help themselves become more relaxed in their daily living. Such strategies include imagining their relaxing scene; tensing briefly some of the muscle groups that they may be having difficulty in relaxing by using the recall procedure; using the "deepening exercise" that is part of the relaxation procedure by itself; or repeating relaxing (autogenic) phrases to themselves (these phrases are described later in this chapter).

Eighth Session

The eighth session is essentially the same as the seventh session. We conduct relaxation by recall on the four muscle groups of the seventh session; we also practice the cue-controlled relaxation procedure. Emphasis is placed on doing the relaxation exercises in the everyday world. At this point, we suggest that patients stop using the relaxation tapes except on a very infrequent basis (i.e., once or twice a week), and that they begin to practice the exercises in situations that they would not normally think of as being conducive to relaxation (e.g., standing up, sitting in a hard-backed chair, driving a car, attending meetings, etc.). We discuss with each patient which of the brief strategies seem to work best for him or her; if one appears to be substantially better than the others, we have the patient concentrate on that strategy. It is essential to inculcate patients with the perception that these are their own abilities rather than the therapist's—that they are discovering what works for them and healing themselves. The patients must also understand that these are preventative rather than abortive techniques. They must scan their muscles periodically throughout the day, identify any muscle tension that may be there, and relax it away by using the techniques they have learned. We tell patients to imagine a prior stressful event, feel the increased muscle tension (and other bodily responses, such as increased respiration, heart rate, sweat gland activity, etc.), perform their relaxation exercises, and notice how quickly they can return to a state of relaxation and peacefulness. The patients should always be encouraged as much as possible.

Last (Ninth) Session

The last session of relaxation therapy is generally a brief one, spent primarily in reviewing what the patient has learned in the previous sessions. If necessary, we will have a patient spend some time practicing the cue-controlled relaxation procedure or will conduct a 15-minute session of autogenic relaxation phrases. We remind our patients that they always need to practice the relaxation procedures—that this should now be part of their everyday lives, just as brushing their teeth and combing their hair is. We tell them that in order to learn this skill it was essential for them to practice it a lot at first, and now that they have learned it they must continue to practice it, but at a less intense pace. We instruct them to practice the tension–release exercises at least once a week, the relaxation-by-recall procedures once a day or more often, and the procedures for applying the relaxation to their everyday living (cue-controlled relaxation, imagery, deepening procedures, diaphragmatic breathing, etc.) as frequently as possible, but at least 10–20 times a day. We remind them how the three main relaxation procedures are built on one another. That is, cue-controlled relaxation is a variant of relaxation by recall, and relaxation by recall is based on the tension–release exercises.

We tell patients that if they find their headaches returning after a while, they should immediately contact us. We then instruct them that if the character of the pain changes or is accompanied by other unusual symptoms (e.g., weakness in a limb, blurred vision, loss of bladder or bowel control), they should contact their physician. We then schedule "booster sessions" for each patient. For the first year, we do this every 3 months. After the first year, a "booster session" once every 6 or 12 months is generally fine.

Clinical hint: If headaches do return to pretreatment levels, there are usually a number of possible reasons:

1. The patients have stopped doing the relaxation. The answer to this is obvious—return to the relaxation exercises.
2. There is more stress in their lives than there previously was. If this is the case, they should intensify the relaxation exercises.
3. The relaxation-by-recall procedures seem to be ineffective in relaxing the patients, even though they practice fairly regularly. In most cases, this can be attributed to patients' failing to practice the tension–release exercises. Many times, patients fail to understand that the relaxation-by-recall procedures are built on the tension–release foundation. If they fail to practice the tension–release exercises, they will not have a good memory of what the muscles felt like when they were tense and when they were relaxed, and the relaxation by recall will be ineffective. The answer here is to return to the tension–release exercises on a daily basis for at least 2 weeks before returning to a normal once-a-week schedule. (For some patients, doing the tension–release exercises on a weekly basis, as suggested, is not enough. In this case, twice or even three times a week may be required.)

VASCULAR HEADACHE

There are two primary headache disorders that are vascular in origin: migraine headache and cluster headache. The latter is a smaller problem in terms of prevalence and in terms of research from a psychophysiological viewpoint. We discuss it briefly before devoting the bulk of this section to migraine headache and its treatment with thermal biofeedback. In addition to both migraine and cluster headaches being vascular in nature, they share to some extent a proximal pain mechanism (see below): Both types of headaches tend to be episodic. Thus, the vast majority of sufferers go from being headache-free to having a headache of some duration (with intensity building fairly rapidly—in minutes to an hour or two) to again being headache-free.

Pain Mechanisms in Vascular Headache

At present, our best understanding of the proximal pain mechanism in vascular headache centers around the dilation of extracranial, and probably intracranial, arteries. These blood vessels are surrounded by tiny neural pain fibers, so that as a vessel dilates abnormally the pain fibers are stretched and activated, sending pain signals centrally. The pulsating or "throbbing" quality of vascular headache pain arises because with each beat of the heart, a pressure wave is transmitted along each artery (hence a person can feel his or her pulse at the wrist or carotid because of these pressure waves). These additional dilations cause additional, intermittent stretching of the pain fibers as the pressure wave passes.

What causes these dilations to begin is not clearly understood and is the subject of ongoing research and debate. A discussion of this topic is beyond the scope of this chapter; for an overview, see Dalessio (1987). Two causal factors for the chain of events that culminates in vasodilation are especially relevant for psychologists and other nonphysician therapists: Psychosocial stress seems to play a role, as do food sensitivities or allergies. The role of exacerbational stress, however, seems more tonic than phasic. That is, single stressful events do not seem to lead to vascular headaches; instead, cumulating stressful events seem to set the stage for headaches.

Clinical hint: This distinction between a tonic and a phasic role for stress in vascular headache has profound treatment implications. Psychophysiological treatments such as thermal biofeedback should be presented to patients as "stress management" or prophylactic procedures, designed to prevent or reduce the overall level of headache. They are generally not useful as abortive or palliative (i.e., phasic) treatments once a headache has begun.

Cluster Headache

Symptoms

Cluster headache tends to be much rarer than migraine (perhaps up to 10% as prevalent; Kudrow, 1980) and tends to be found predominantly in males. It is generally diagnosed by its very distinctive temporal pattern. Most patients with cluster headache have episodic cluster headache; 5–10% have chronic continuous cluster headache. (See Kudrow, 1980, for an excellent monograph on cluster headache.) In episodic cluster headache, the patient is headache-free for months to years and then enters a so-called "cluster bout." During the cluster bout, the one-sided headaches appear fairly regularly, once or twice per day to every other day. The headaches are described as intense, excruciating pain; they last from 15–30 minutes to 2–3 hours. Many patients are so debilitated by this type of headache that it can take hours for them to return to a normal level of functioning. The cluster bout lasts several weeks to several months and then disappears. For some patients, there is a seasonal regularity to the onset of the cluster bout. This has led some to suspect that cluster headache is part of an allergic reaction, but research has not borne this out (Kudrow, 1980).

Clinical hint: During a cluster bout patients seem especially sensitive to alcohol, such that a single drink can trigger a headache. A therapist can thus try to help a patient become abstinent during the cluster bout. This sensitivity does not seem present between cluster bouts.

Psychophysiological Treatments

There is only a limited literature on the psychosocial treatment of cluster headache, with most reports presenting data on one to five cases (see Blanchard & Andrasik, 1987, for a summary). A report by Blanchard, Andrasik, Jurish, and Teders (1982a) has probably the largest series ($n = 11$). Only 2 of the 11 (19%) were helped somewhat, based on follow-ups of 20 to 30 months. For these two patients, the headaches were sometimes less intense and of shorter duration after treatment than before treatment. Subsequent cluster bouts were perhaps of shorter duration.

The treatment regimen responsible for these meager results was fairly intensive, involving 10 sessions of relaxation training over 8 weeks, followed by 12 sessions of thermal biofeedback over 6 weeks. (The treatment protocols were very much like those described for those procedures in this chapter.)

Clinical hint: Given Blanchard et al.'s (1982a) relatively poor results, we no longer take cluster headache patients, and we would advise the reader to be cautious about offering the procedures described in this chapter to the cluster headache sufferer.

There have been isolated case reports of the apparently successful treatment of chronic cluster headache (cluster headache without the usual regular remission of the cluster bout; the headaches are there continuously) with psychosocial procedures. For example, King and Arena (1984) successfully treated a 69-year-old male with chronic cluster headache with a combination of thermal biofeedback, relaxation home practice, and marital therapy. At a 15-month follow-up, his medication consumption was markedly reduced and his headaches were improved.

Migraine Headache

Symptoms

As mentioned above, migraine headache is episodic: The typical attack lasts from 2–3 hours to 2–3 days, and is usually accompanied by sensations of nausea (and sometimes vomiting) and sensitivity to light and sound. A typical migraine headache starts as a one-sided headache but usually progresses so that the whole head is involved. Headache frequency varies from one to two headaches per year to three to four headaches per month. In our experience patients seeking treatment usually have one or two headaches per month or more.

Up to half of patients with migraine headache also meet the criteria for tension headache. These unfortunate individuals have been labeled as having "mixed migraine and tension headache" or "combined migraine and tension headache." We have typically lumped both pure migraine and mixed migraine and tension headaches together under the label of "vascular headache" and treated them in the same fashion.

Epidemiology

Migraine headache is predominantly a disorder of women during the childbearing years. In prepubertal children, migraine is approximately equally distributed across the sexes. With the onset of menarche, females begin to outnumber males by about two or three to one. An outstanding recent epidemiological survey (Stewart, Lipton, Celentano, & Reed, 1992) involving over 20,000 subjects across the United States found that 17.6% of females and 5.7% of males had one or more migraine headaches per year, with almost 4.5 million adults suffering from one or more migraine headaches *per month.* (In our experience, women outnumber men by four or five to one in terms of seeking psychosocial treatment for migraine headaches.)

Clinical hint: A key question to ask in diagnosing mixed headaches is this: "Do you have more than one kind of headache?" If the answer is "yes," we advise taking a separate description of each type of headache. One occasionally finds that the difference is primarily in intensity but that the phenomenology and temporal factors are the same. In this case, a diagnosis of mixed headache is not appropriate.

Treatment for Vascular Headache

Several generalizations seem warranted about the treatment of vascular headache (see Blanchard, 1993, for a more detailed summary). For mixed headache, both thermal biofeedback and relaxation training are generally needed. Mixed headache sufferers, as a group, respond relatively poorly to relaxation training alone: In one study, just 22% of subjects with mixed headaches receiving only relaxation therapy met our criterion for clinically significant improvement, which we have defined as at least a 50% reduction in headache activity as documented by a daily headache diary (Blanchard et al., 1982b). Moreover, mixed headache sufferers in another study did not do as well as pure migraine sufferers with thermal biofeedback alone (Blanchard et al., 1991a); they required additional treatment with relaxation.

Our "standard" treatment for vascular headache has been a combination of relaxation training (as described earlier in the chapter) and thermal biofeedback (to be described below). Across three separate samples of 50 or more patients each, treated with this combination over a 10-year period in Albany, Blanchard and his colleagues found that 52% of each sample met the success criterion of 50% reduction in headache activity (Blanchard et al., 1982b, 1985a, 1990a). This replicability is impressive to us.

Thus either relaxation alone or biofeedback alone seems poor for mixed headache and fair for migraine. Thermal biofeedback alone is adequate for migraine and for mixed headache but the combination of relaxation and thermal biofeedback seems to work best for vascular headache.

One other point needs to be made about psychosocial treatments of primary headache disorders. The addition of a cognitive therapy component, especially cognitive stress coping therapy modeled after the work of Holroyd (Holroyd & Andrasik, 1982), does *not* seem to improve overall outcome with vascular headache (Blanchard et al., 1990c) (even with samples of 30 per condition), but it does seem to make a difference when added to a relaxation regimen with tension headache (Blanchard et al., 1990b). Discussion of cognitive therapies for chronic pain are found in Chapter 6.

Thermal Biofeedback

Thermal biofeedback as a treatment for migraine headache was initially described over 20 years ago by Sargent, Green, and Walters (1972). The essence of this treatment is to teach patients to warm their hands with the assistance of relatively immediate sensory feedback. It is reasonably well established that this treatment involving volitional peripheral vasodilation is beneficial to sufferers of migraine headache. For a somewhat dated comprehensive review, see Blanchard and Andrasik (1987).

This treatment has been found to be beneficial in other pain problems, such as rheumatoid arthritis (Appelbaum, Blanchard, Hickling, & Alfonso, 1988), irritable bowel syndrome (Neff & Blanchard, 1987), and reflex sympathetic dystrophy (Blanchard, 1979). It has also been used with great success in the treatment of Raynaud's disease (Freedman, 1987, 1993) and with mixed success in the treatment of essential hypertension (Fahrion, Norris, Green, Green, & Snarr, 1986; Blanchard et al., 1986, 1988).

Practical Concerns

Treatment Duration and Spacing. When we treat migraine headache (and also mixed headache), treatment length is usually 8 to 12 sessions, once or twice per week. Our recommendation is for twice-per-week sessions, at least for the first 2 weeks. There is an apparent skill-like component in learning peripheral vasodilation, so that relatively massed training sessions seem to help early on. (This point has not, to the best of our knowledge, been empirically tested.)

Duration of Sessions. The actual feedback portion of the session should be relatively brief, in the range of 15–20 minutes. Sustained hand warming is subjectively difficult for patients. Patients who are beginning to show control tend to trail off or lose the control after about 15 minutes.

We do know that for acquisition of the vasodilation response and subsequent headache relief, a sustained or continuous trial of 15–20 minutes is superior to 10–20 brief 1- to 2-minute trials with 30-second breaks (Andrasik, Pallmeyer, Blanchard, & Attanasio, 1984).

Feedback Instruments. The actual biofeedback instrument is a fancy thermometer; the brand does not seem to matter very much. The thermal biofeedback instrument consists of a temperature-sensitive probe or sensor, a thermistor, and an electronic device that converts the temperature signal to a feedback display. It seems that a fairly high degree of sensitivity is needed; the device should register changes of 0.1°F or 0.1°C.

We routinely let patients sample both visual and auditory (a tone changing in pitch) feedback signals. Over 80% of patients receiving thermal biofeedback choose the visual display. The feedback display can be the pen on a voltmeter, a digital output, or bars on a video screen. The actual form of the visual feedback display does not seem to matter (Evans, 1988).

Thermistor Placement. The thermistor placement is somewhat arbitrary. We have routinely used the ventral pad of the last digit on the index finger of the nondominant hand. No empirical research of which we are aware shows an advantage for one placement over another. The thermistor should be held in close contact with the skin by either a Velcro band or paper tape. Care should be taken when tape is used not to encircle the finger fully and create a tourniquet.

Room Temperature. The patient should be comfortably seated in a relaxed posture. However, a recliner with a head rest is not necessary, as it is for good relaxation training. The room should be reasonably warm, at least 72°F and preferably 75–78°F. It is very hard for a patient to warm his or her hands in a cool or cold room. In this latter circumstance, the patient is fighting a very strong reflex (heat conservation by peripheral vasoconstriction).

Timing of Phases within the Session. We recommend that routine sessions (those after the first one or two) should begin with at least 10 minutes devoted to adaptation and in-session baseline. (In Albany, New York, in the winter, Blanchard and colleagues use a longer adaptation period if a patient is freshly arrived from outdoors.) Next, we recommend a 3- to 5-minute self-control phase in which the patient is asked to warm his or her hands without the assistance of the feedback display. Data from this portion of the session enable the therapist to monitor progress toward the eventual goal of treatment—true volitional control of hand temperature without the assistance of external feedback.

Home Practice. We strongly urge headache patients to practice the hand-warming procedures at home on a regular basis between clinic training sessions. Our normal recommendation is for at least 20 minutes of practice per day, preferably in a single session (but we also encourage two 10-minute sessions as an alternative). We routinely give patients a small alcohol-in-glass thermometer as a home practice device; it can be read accurately to within 2°F, and possibly 1°F. Alternatively, we have used electronic home trainers with digital output; however, they cost $50 to $125, as compared to 50¢ for the thermometer. We ask patients to record beginning and ending temperatures as well as length of home practice sessions, as a way of checking on compliance and progress.

Evidence in support of the value of regular home practice is scant. We (Blanchard et al., 1983) reported that a low level of continued home practice (vs. no practice) was associated with better maintenance of headache reduction and with other symptomatic improvement.

In an empirical test of the role of home practice, Blanchard et al. (1991a) gave 46 vascular headache sufferers 12 sessions (2 per week) of thermal biofeedback alone (with *no* adjunctive relaxation training). For half of the subjects, instruction for regular home practice were included (and followed fairly well); for the other half, no mention was made of home practice, and patients' inquiries were politely rebuffed. There was no difference between the groups in headache relief, either statistically or in terms of the proportion of the sample who improved significantly. The major difference was in the temperature control data: Those patients practicing regularly appeared to master the volitional vasodilation response by about the sixth or seventh session, whereas those without regular home practice appeared to need 9 or 10 sessions to reach the same level of proficiency. Thus home practice seems to improve the efficiency of thermal biofeedback training, but not the overall efficacy if enough treatment is provided.

Initial Session Instruction and Rationale

We believe that the initial instructions and rationale given to the patient are very important. Summarized here is the information we try to convey to migraine patients at the first treatment session. We begin by telling patients we want them to learn to warm their hands with the assistance of the biofeedback training, and then by acknowledging that the connection between hand warming and migraine relief is not obvious. We go on to say that to warm one's hands, the tiny blood vessels in the periphery must open up or dilate. This vasodilation is under the control of the autonomic nervous system—the branch of the nervous system that controls involuntary functions, such as how fast the heart beats. In particular, the sympathetic nervous system, the part of the autonomic nervous system that controls the "fight-or-flight" response, controls peripheral vasoconstriction and vasodilation. When there is sympathetic nervous system activity, or "sympathetic outflow," the blood vessels constrict. (We should note that it is not clear whether this is truly the mechanism involved; the evidence is mixed. McCoy et al., 1988, found contrary evidence.) Thus patients are told that, in essence, we are attempting to reduce sympathetic nervous system activity (outflow) and monitoring it by measuring hand temperature.

We also stress that this treatment is designed to bring about a "tonic charge," or generalized reduction in sympathetic activity. Thus regular daily practice is important. The treatment is not especially designed as a phasic or short-term coping strategy. The overall goal is to reduce the frequency and intensity of headache (a prophylactic or preventative strategy), not to abort headaches or reduce their discomfort once they have begun.

An immediate question many patients have is how they are supposed to do this. It is good to anticipate this question by acknowledging it and admitting that no strategy is universally successful. Instead, we explain to the patients that the biofeedback setup or "loop" allows them to explore various strategies to find one that will work for them. It is thus a trial-and-error (or trial-and-success) process. Strategies that some people have used successfully include mental images of warm sun at the beach, watching the meter directly and trying to control it, or attending to the feeling of blood pulsations in the fingertips.

Clinical hints: We believe that it is useful if the therapist has tried to warm his or her own hands with the assistance of biofeedback, so as to be able to speak more authoritatively on this point.

Two other points need to be mentioned. First, the patients need to relax to make this work. We mention that this treatment is not just a way to teach relaxation, but that relaxation is necessary and facilitative, but not sufficient, to achieve the hand warming. Second, we emphasize that the patients should *not try too hard* to warm their hands because the active striving elicits a sympathetic nervous system response and defeats the whole experience. Instead, they should try to use *passive volition*, allowing the response to occur rather than trying to force it to occur.

Finally, patients should be warned that some people find the task very difficult and frustrating at first. Thus, they should try not to be discouraged if it takes several sessions to begin to succeed. This forewarning can help prevent early discouragement and premature termination.

Autogenic Phrases

The initial description of thermal biofeedback training for migraine headache by Sargent et al. (1972) included the use of limited autogenic training (Schultz & Luthe, 1969)—in particular, training in relaxation, heaviness, and warmth. "Autogenic training" is a meditational form of relaxation that focuses on very specific self-instructions.

We have routinely introduced limited autogenic phrases during the first two thermal biofeedback training sessions by describing them to our patients as one possible strategy to generate hand warming. Patients are cautioned that the phrases may or may not help them, but they are offered as one strategy within the trial-and-success framework. The actual relaxation phrases are listed in Table 8.1.

Our recommendation for how to conduct this part of the training is for therapists to tell patients that the therapists will be giving them a series of phrases in the first person (see Table 8.1). The patients are to repeat the phrase verbatim (hence the use of the first person) to themselves; as the patients give themselves these self-instructions, they should try to have the experience described and notice the peripheral sensations. We routinely give each patient a copy of the phrases to use at home as he or she chooses.

Clinical hint: Pacing, or timing, of the presentation of the phrases is very important. There needs to be enough time for a patient to repeat the phrase mentally and try to generate the response. The therapist can measure the time roughly by repeating the phrase silently to himself or herself.

TABLE 8.1. Autogenic Phrases

1. I feel quite quiet.
2. I am beginning to feel quite relaxed.
3. My feet feel heavy and relaxed.
4. My ankles, my knees, and my hips feel heavy, relaxed, and comfortable.
5. My solar plexus, and the whole central portion of my body, feel relaxed and quiet.
6. My hands, my arms, and my shoulders feel heavy, relaxed, and comfortable.
7. My neck, my jaw, and my forehead feel relaxed. They feel comfortable and smooth.
8. My whole body feels quiet, heavy, comfortable, and relaxed.
9. (Now go back through the sequence on your own.)
10. I am quite relaxed.
11. My arms and hands are heavy and warm.
12. I feel quite quiet.
13. My whole body is relaxed and my hands are warm, relaxed and warm.
14. My hands are warm.
15. Warmth is flowing into my hands, they are warm, warm.
16. I can feel the warmth flowing down my arms into my hands.
17. My hands are warm, relaxed and warm.
18. (Now go back through the sequence on your own.)

Presence of Therapist

A decision needs to be made on whether the therapist is in the room with the patient or not (this assumes an office arrangement that allows such a choice). In the work in Albany, a therapist was routinely in the same room with the subject for the first two sessions (when the autogenic phrases were used) and then in a separate room, but in voice contact, during the remainder. The only empirical research (Borgeat et al., 1980) suggests that leaving the subject alone with the feedback display promotes learning (or that the therapist's presence is a hindrance or distractor).

Training to a Temperature Criterion

It has long been advocated by clinicians involved in the development of thermal biofeedback (especially Fahrion, 1977) that patients be trained to a specific temperature criterion. The recommended temperature is 95°F; the empirical basis for this temperature is not clear. There is some limited empirical evidence (Libo & Arnold, 1983) that patients trained to the 95°F criterion did better during a long-term (1-year) follow-up than those who did not reach this level.

Another criterion suggested by Sargent et al. (1972) is that the patient be able to produce a 1.5°F rise in hand temperature within 2 minutes. Again, the empirical basis for this criterion is unclear.

In our own work, the strongest overall correlation between temperature training parameters and headache reduction is with the number of sessions on which any temperature rise above in-session baseline is noted (Blanchard et al., 1983). We have also observed a discontinuity in outcome for patients who achieve 96°F or higher at any point during training. Those who reach this level have a significantly higher likelihood of experiencing a clinically meaningful reduction in headache activity (at least 50%) than those who reach lower maximum levels (Blanchard et al., 1983). This apparent threshold was replicated in a later study on a new cohort of vascular headache patients (Morrill & Blanchard, 1989).

Manipulation of Attributional Responses

Given the powerful results of Holroyd et al. (1984) in showing that manipulation of the attributions made by tension headache sufferers profoundly affected headache reduction in EMG biofeedback, it was logical to see whether similar results would be obtained with vascular headache patients receiving thermal biofeedback.

In a study on 28 vascular headache patients receiving 12 sessions of thermal biofeedback with no home practice, Blanchard et al. (1994) tried an attributional manipulation similar to Holroyd et al.'s. It was not universally successful in leading patients to believe that they were either highly successful or modestly successful at the hand-warming task. For the patients for whom the manipulation succeeded, the expected effects on headache relief were found: Patients who believed they were highly successful experienced greater headache relief than those who believed they were only moderately successful.

Limited-Contact, Home-Based Treatments

The availability of relatively low-cost, high-precision thermal biofeedback training devices lends itself to the possibility of a limited-therapist-contact, largely home-based treatment regimen. Blanchard and colleagues have published three separate studies (Blanchard et al., 1985a, 1990a; Jurish et al., 1983) evaluating a treatment regimen of three sessions (over 2 months) combining thermal biofeedback and progressive relaxation training. In all three instances, very positive results were found for this attenuated form of treatment. Similar results were reported by Tobin, Holroyd, Baker, Reynolds, and Holms (1988).

We believe that some limited therapist contact is necessary, so that patients understand the rationale for the treatment and that problems (trying too hard, thermistor misplacement, etc.) can be caught and corrected early. We also believe that detailed manuals to guide the home training, and telephone consultation to troubleshoot problems, are crucial in this approach. Given the national push for improving the efficiency of treatments, this approach has much to recommend it. We should also note that this home-based approach was not as successful as office-based treatment of essential hypertension with thermal biofeedback (Blanchard et al., 1987).

SPECIAL HEADACHE POPULATIONS

Most of what has been described thus far in this chapter is based on research and clinical treatment with the general adult headache population. There are, however, several special headache populations to which relaxation and biofeedback have been applied. These populations, and changes in standard treatment procedures that should be made for them, are described in this section.

Pediatric Headache

Migraine headache affects approximately 2.5% of the child and adolescent population of the United States, with the prevalence and incidence progressively higher with older cohorts within this attenuated age range (Stang et al., 1992).

There is now a sizable body of research attesting to the efficacy of thermal biofeedback with pediatric migraine (see Blanchard, 1992, Table 2, for a concise narrative summary). A meta-analysis by Hermann, Kim, and Blanchard (1993) comparing drug and nondrug treatments revealed that thermal biofeedback and propranolol appeared to be the treatments of choice, with both yielding high levels of headache relief. The average percentage of improvement in studies of thermal biofeedback with pediatric migraine is about 70%—substantially better than one finds with adults.

In adapting thermal biofeedback to a pediatric population, certain ideas seem relevant:

1. *Length of training session.* The attention span of pediatric patients, especially pre-adolescents, is somewhat limited. For that reason we recommend a 30-minute total session length, with the baseline and self-control phases reduced to about 2–3 minutes and the feedback portion reduced to about 12 minutes. Home practice should probably be monitored by parents of younger children, who seem not to remember this task readily.

2. *Feedback display.* The feedback display needs to sustain the pediatric patient's attention. Many patients in this age range are very familiar with video games and computerized graphics; thus their expectations may be high. We recommend, in the absence of empirical data, that the therapist stay in the room with the patient to act as a coach.

3. *Home-based treatment.* Hermann (1994) has recently shown that a limited-contact thermal biofeedback regimen (four sessions over 8 weeks) is very effective with a pediatric population. Sixty-nine percent of her 32 subjects showed clinically significant reductions in headache activity as documented by headache diaries.

Headaches of the Elderly

Almost everyone reading this chapter is aware of the rapid growth of the older segment of the U.S. population. Although headaches are often thought of as disorders that afflict the young or middle-aged, epidemiological data show that over 9% of adults over the age of 65 have moderate to severe headaches from benign (i.e., migraine or tension-type headaches) causes (Cook et al., 1989).

In the mid-1980s, conventional clinical wisdom held that older headache patients did not respond well to the pain treatment procedures discussed in this chapter, relaxation and biofeedback training. This view was reinforced by an uncontrolled series of cases from Albany (Blanchard, Andrasik, Evans, & Hillhouse, 1985b) that presented the data from 11 headache patients over the age of 60 who had been treated with various combinations of biofeedback and relaxation therapies. Only 2 of 11 (19%) showed clinically meaningful reductions in headache activity.

Uncontrolled studies by Arena and colleagues (Arena et al., 1988; Arena, Hannah, Bruno, & Meador, 1991a) on elderly tension headache patients successfully challenged this conventional wisdom by showing very high levels of success with relaxation training (70% success in Arena et al., 1988) and frontal EMG biofeedback training (50% success in Arena et al., 1991a). The key to this success by Arena and colleagues was adapting the treatments to the information-processing capacities of an older population. Instructions were repeated as necessary and presented more slowly; more handouts, often in larger type, were made available to guide home practice; and other alterations to make the treatments more age-relevant were made.

The Albany group profited from Arena's advice and incorporated these changes into the treatment protocols. A new uncontrolled series of elderly headache patients in Albany (Kabela, Blanchard, Appelbaum, & Nicholson, 1989) showed that 4 of 8 (50%) tension headache patients improved and 6 of 8 (75%) of vascular headache patients improved. Interestingly, 5 of 16 patients eliminated all or almost all (80%+) of their headache medications. This alone is a major benefit for the elderly, who are often taking several medications chronically.

Finally, in a controlled study, Nicholson and Blanchard (1993) showed a significant advantage for treatment combining relaxation and biofeedback over headache monitoring in a population of older (age range = 61 to 80) headache sufferers when the treatments were tailored to the population and its information-processing capacities. With such changes, older headache patients readily respond to biofeedback and relaxation.

Chronic, Daily High-Intensity Headache

Blanchard and colleagues (Blanchard, Appelbaum, Radnitz, Jaccard, & Dentinger, 1989) have identified a relatively refractory headache type that they have labeled "chronic, daily high-intensity headache." Individuals with this type of headache account for about 6% of patients seen at university-based headache clinics; they describe their headache as present essentially all of the time (at least 27 out of 28 days) at a moderately severe to severe level of pain and distress. Thus, although these patients usually meet the nominal criteria for tension-type headache, their severity ratings are like those of migraine patients and show little variability. In a retrospective case–control analysis, Blanchard et al. (1989) found that only 13% of patients with chronic, daily high-intensity headache responded favorably to combinations of biofeedback, relaxation, and cognitive therapy. Moreover, this group of patients shows a higher degree of distress in standard psychological tests than gender- and diagnosis-matched controls who had more variability to their headaches but who received similar treatments.

Thus far, we have not developed successful treatments for this subset of patients. Our impression, in the absence of conclusive data, is that longer treatment regimens including a large dose of cognitive therapy may be needed.

High-Medication-Consumption Headache

Kudrow (1982) first called attention to a phenomenon he labeled "analgesic rebound headache." In a pioneering but poorly controlled study, he found that those patients who continued on high levels of regular analgesic medication responded much more poorly to amitriptyline than did comparable patients who were able to discontinue most of the analgesic. This relative refractoriness of patients who take high levels of all medications was also found to be associated with poor response to behavioral treatments and a very high dropout rate by Mathew, Kurman, and Perez (1990).

Michultka, Blanchard, Appelbaum, Jaccard, and Dentinger (1989) have identified a group of headache patients as having what they have termed "high-medication-consumption headache." This group was identified on the basis of daily records of medication consumption. Using the medication-scaling procedures of Coyne, Sargent, Segerson, and Obourn (1976) (over-the-counter analgesics such as aspirin and acetaminophen are scaled as 1, Fiorinal as 2, etc.), Michultka et al. identified patients with average weekly scores of 40 or greater across 4 consecutive weeks (this translates into roughly six aspirin per day, three Fiorinal per day, etc.). About 12% of headache patients met this criterion. Using retrospective case–control analysis, the authors found that high-medication-consumption headache sufferers did significantly poorer than diagnosis-matched patients taking lower levels of medication who received comparable behavioral treatments; only about 29% of the high-medication patients responded favorably.

In an uncontrolled case series, Blanchard, Taylor, and Dentinger (1992) developed a special protocol for 10 high-medication-consumption patients. After baseline headache and medication recording, a consulting neurologist gave the patients individually tailored schedules for discontinuing their medication. As the patients tried to decrease the medication, they were simultaneously given relaxation training and a great deal of psychological support (phone consultations, at least two office visits per week, etc.) to assist in the detoxification process. Patients had also been carefully warned about the possibility of rebound headache.

After patients had decreased their medication as far as possible, they received standard biofeedback, relaxation, and/or cognitive therapy. Of the 10 patients, 8 had substantial decreases in medication, and 6 had clinically significant decreases in headache activity that were maintained at follow-ups of up to 1 year. Two patients experienced complete failure, despite two (and in one case three) attempts to reduce medication. Moreover, in two cases patients dropped out of treatment after successfully eliminating their medication. They were apparently content to tolerate their continued headaches.

Clinical hints: It thus seems clear that high-medication-consumption headache cases can be helped, primarily by focusing first on reducing or eliminating the medications and then on treating the patients' residual headache. The key to the medication reduction step is a high level of support for the patients as they go through this process, especially during the period of increased headache severity and duration that is very likely to occur.

CHRONIC LOW BACK PAIN

Incidence, Prevalence, and Psychophysiology of Chronic Low Back Pain

Chronic low back pain (LBP), with the exception of the common cold, is the most frequent cause of visits to physicians' offices (Borenstein & Wiesel, 1989; Cavanaugh & Weinstein, 1994). Estimates are that from 12% to 45% of the adult population will suffer from LBP, at any one time, and that 60–80% of the population will at some point in their lives experience LBP (Andersson & McNeill, 1989). Twelve percent of all sick leave is taken because of LBP, and the average sick leave period is 30 days (Borenstein & Wiesel, 1989). LBP also accounts for 25% of all compensatable disabilities in the workplace (Cavanaugh & Weinstein, 1994). Estimates are that on any given day, 0.5% of the work force has been disabled for more than 6 months as a result of LBP (Wood & Bradley, 1980), and that 2% of all workers injure their backs on the job each year (Teasell & White, 1994). In the United States each year, 115,000 laminectomies and 34,000 other lumbar spine operations are performed (Andersson & McNeill, 1989), and the rate of surgeries in the United States for herniated disks is four to nine times higher than that of other industrialized countries (Cavanaugh & Weinstein, 1994). Although females report LBP symptoms just as frequently as men, men have twice the surgery rate (Cavanaugh & Weinstein, 1994). LBP is responsible for at least $16 billion a year in the United States in *direct medical costs* (such as surgeries, hospital/physician visits, and disability insurance payouts) (Borenstein & Wiesel, 1989), with some estimates going up to $60 billion (Frymoyer, Akeson, Brandt, Goldenberg, & Spencer, 1989), and the indirect medical costs (such as sickness absence and lost productivity) are much higher. The personal pain and suffering of the chronic LBP sufferer are incalculable—how can one put a price on time missed from family and friends? Clearly, LBP is the most common and significant nonfatal medical problem in the United States.

Although most LBP is temporary and alleviated within a month or two, a considerably large minority of individuals suffer from chronic LBP. This segment of the LBP population has been increasing greatly in recent years, in spite of the fact that the percentage of Americans who suffer from LBP has remained the same. Unfortunately, our ability to treat these chronic LBP patients successfully, or even to predict who will be a successful treatment candidate, is at best fair. Even more troubling, our understanding of the factors involved in the etiology and maintenance of chronic LBP is remarkably limited. Only 10–15% of patients with LBP have demonstrated pathology or a clear-cut cause for their symptoms (Frymoyer et al., 1989).

In spite of the fact that we know so little about the etiology of chronic LBP, Arena and his colleagues have argued (Arena, Sherman, Bruno, & Young, 1989, 1990, 1991c; Sherman & Arena, 1992) that some diagnostic schema needs to be incorporated in both LBP research and clinical work if clinicians are ever to understand LBP and improve on current treatments. They have used the criteria and diagnostic schema set forth by the American Academy of Orthopedic Surgery (1986). Their orthopedists and neurosurgeons have broken LBP down into five types.

First, "spondylarthritis" is a disorder characterized by inflammation of the surfaces of the segments of the spinal vertebral column. This type can include patients both with radiculopathy (i.e., pain caused by compression of the spinal cord or nerve roots) and without radiculopathy (i.e., pain caused by lumbar or lumbosacral arthritis). "Radiculopathy" means pain that can be referred from the back into other areas, such as the hip and the legs.

Second, "intervertebral disk disorders" are characterized by problems with the disks between each of the spinal vertebrae. As in spondylarthritis, we include in this type patients with and without radiculopathy. Disk space narrowing, facet joint hyperextension, anterior traction spurs, vacuum sign, and/or disk calcification should be documented in patients' medical history from X-rays or other medical tests. This is the category in which we place those patients with herniated disks (i.e., cases in which a disk protrudes out of its normal space because of injury or collapse) or ruptured disks (i.e., cases in which the disk covering is torn and the disk fluid has escaped into the surrounding tissue, so the vertebrae are sitting on top of each other with no cushion and can be compressing the nerves). Only 1–3% of chronic LBP is the result of intervertebral disk disorders.

Third, "unspecified musculoskeletal backache" is back pain that is attributal to muscle tension, lumbosacral sprain/strain, myofascial (soft tissue) sprain/strain, or "mechanical" pain (a catch-all term for those individuals with suspected muscle abnormalities). The vast majority of LBP falls into this category (Cavanaugh & Weinstein, 1994).

A fourth group ("combined back pain") includes individuals with some combination of the first three diagnoses. Finally, a fifth group includes patients with other types of back pain ("other back pain"), including pain of unknown origin, pain resulting from scoliosis (a congenital deformity of the spinal column, which causes an abnormal curvature of the spine) and "psychogenic" pain (this, we believe, is extremely rare).

There are a number of theories concerning the relationship between muscle tension and chronic LBP (Dolce & Raczynski, 1985; Nouwen & Bush, 1984). These can be broken down into two major models. The first of these is the "biomechanical theory," according to which the paraspinal muscles of the lower back are unduly lower than normal, or there is a left–right asymmetry in the lower back (in this case, one side of the back musculature is abnormally lower or higher than the other). This is presumed to be the result of some mechanical or physical pathology, such as lesions, trauma, abnormal gait, poor posture, or the like. The second major model is the "stress causality theory" or "psychosocial stressor theory," in which back pain is presumed to be the result of increased paraspinal muscle activity caused by ineffective stress coping skills. There is limited evidence to support either of these two theories (Arena et al., 1989; Dolce & Raczynski, 1985; Nouwen & Bush, 1984). With LBP patients, biofeedback has been used as a general relaxation and stress reduction technique, as well as a specific strategy to correct muscle tension abnormalities.

Psychophysiological Intervention with Chronic Low Back Pain

There is one major difference in the psychophysiological treatment of chronic LBP and chronic headache: Whereas with chronic headache, treatments such as biofeedback and relaxation training can be the primary or even sole therapy, with chronic LBP we feel that psychophysiological intervention should never be used alone. There are data to support this assertion. In 1992, Sherman and Arena exhaustively reviewed the biofeedback treatment of chronic LBP (this review was limited to biofeedback as the *sole* treatment). They found that most of the studies suffered from a number of critical methodological and conceptual limitations, including small sample sizes ($n \leq 10$), unspecified diagnosis, lack of inclusion and exclusion criteria, lack of adequate control groups, the mingling of acute and chronic LBP, inadequate description of the biofeedback procedures, lack of clinical significance (i.e., what percentage of subjects were significantly helped?), and no or limited follow-up. Sherman and Arena concluded that biofeedback in and of itself had not been adequately demonstrated to reduce back pain sufficiently to the point where no further treatment was necessary. (We had planned in this chapter to perform a similar critique of the relaxation therapy literature for chronic LBP. However, after an exhaustive review, we felt that the literature was so methodologically flawed that it would preclude any meaningful conclusions.)

Psychophysiological interventions are essential components of nonsurgical chronic LBP treatment. However, instead of being used by themselves, they should be included in an overall multidisciplinary treatment program that can encompass such services as physical therapy, pharmacological management, kinesthetic therapy, recreational therapy, behavioral and cognitive-behavioral treatments, social work, nursing, vocational counseling, orthopedic/neurosurgical/anesthesiological treatment, and so forth. Indeed, when biofeedback and relaxation procedures are combined with such interventions, treatment effects are maximized (Deardroff, Rubin, & Scott, 1991; Flor, Fydrich, & Turk, 1992; Pearce & Tunks, 1990).

As with a headache patient, it is essential for the nonphysician therapist to have a chronic LBP patient medically screened prior to the onset of treatment and to coordinate treatment with the physician who is managing the patient. Indeed, the latter may be even more important with LBP than with headache patients: In general, headaches do not change over the course of treatment, whereas LBP can change drastically (as a result of age, trauma, disease, etc.) and may require medical intervention.

Clinical hint: If while under treatment a patient reports recent loss of bladder or bowel control, the therapist should notify the referring physician immediately. This may be a result of nerve root compression, which can cause paralysis, and usually requires surgical intervention.

It is important to familiarize oneself with basic anatomy and physiology prior to working with LBP patients. Any therapist who works with the lower back needs to have a text handy that has anatomical drawings of the bones, nerves, and muscles of the back. We use *Grant's Atlas of Anatomy* (Agur, 1991), as well as Clemente's *Anatomy* (Clemente, 1987). It is not possible in the space allocated to review all but the essentials. The spinal column runs from the skull to the coccyx and is divided into a number of regions: cervical (neck region), thoracic (upper back), lumbar (lower back), and sacral (hip region). Most back surgeries are done in or near the fourth and fifth lumbar vertebrae (L_4–L_5).

From the two major theories concerning the relationship of muscle tension and LBP (see above), one could hypothesize two psychophysiological strategies with EMG biofeedback. The first would be to conduct a psychophysiological assessment, in which paraspinal and other muscles presumed to be involved in LBP (upper trapezius, biceps femoris, etc.) would be measured. The therapist would then attempt through EMG biofeedback to correct any abnormality found (e.g., if abnormally low or high muscle tension was present, the therapist would teach the patient to increase or decrease the muscle tension to normal levels; if a left–right asymmetry was noted, the therapist would teach the patient to increase or decrease the muscle tension in the abnormal side). The second strategy would be to conduct frontal EMG biofeedback training as a general technique for enhancing muscle tension awareness, stress reduction, and relaxation training. In the review of the literature described earlier, Sherman and Arena (1992) concluded, "There is no evidence that use of biofeedback from muscle groups (to correct demonstrated muscle tension pattern abnormalities) is more effective than use of biofeedback from the frontal or general upper trunk regions (as part of general muscle tension awareness and relaxation training)" (p. 189). The studies that have been published since that review have not changed these conclusions.

In Georgia, Arena and his colleagues in Augusta use a combination of both strategies with LBP patients, based upon clinical experience as well as assessment research (Arena et al., 1989). In that research, surface EMG recordings of bilateral paraspinal muscle tension were made on 207 subjects from the five LBP groups described above, and 29 nonpain controls, during six positions: standing, bending from the waist, rising, sitting with back unsupported, sitting with back supported, and prone. Results of both individual and group analyses revealed controls to have significantly lower overall EMG levels than the groups with intervertebral disk disorders and unspecified musculoskeletal backache. Control subjects during the standing position had significantly lower EMG levels than all LBP groups, and subjects with intervertebral disk disorders had significantly higher EMG levels than all other groups during the supported sitting position. It is especially important to note that the diagnostic groups did not differ from one another in the prone position. It is in this position that LBP subjects and normals are measured in the majority of surface EMG studies. Another study (Arena et al., 1991c) found that the paraspinal muscle tension levels of LBP subjects did not change as a function of low or high pain levels (the above-described assessment was conducted twice—once in a low-pain state and once in a high-pain state—on 21 individuals with intervertebral disk disorders and 25 subjects with unspecified musculoskeletal backache). This later study demonstrated that EMG levels alone are not substantially connected with the maintenance of chronic LBP.

On the basis of this research and their clinical experiences, Arena and his colleagues use the following psychophysiological protocol with chronic LBP patients. They first give a regimen of frontal EMG biofeedback, followed by upper trapezius EMG biofeedback, using a strategy of general relaxation therapy and muscle tension awareness. With chronic LBP, Arena and his colleagues always teach patients to generalize the biofeedback response (in an attempt to make the office biofeedback training simulate real-world situations) after initially training the patients on a recliner or couch. Once they have mastered the rudiments of biofeedback, they then routinely progress to a comfortable office chair (with arms), an uncomfortable office chair (without arms), and finally a standing position. This strategy is followed for both frontal and upper trapezius training. This generally takes 12 to 16 sessions.

If significant relief is achieved with frontal and upper trapezius EMG biofeedback, at this point they terminate therapy. When insufficient relief occurs, Arena and his colleagues follow one of two treatment courses. If some reduction in pain has been obtained through frontal and upper trapezius biofeedback, they continue with the general relaxation strategy by beginning relaxation therapy (see the discussion of relaxation training for tension headache patients, above). Their relaxation regimen for LBP is essentially the same as that for tension headache, with one exception: For all LBP patients, except those suffering from interverteberal disk disorder, they include a back muscle group after the legs. ("Please press your lower, middle, and upper back against the back of the chair." Alternative tensing strategy: "Please arch your back.") In addition, they sometimes have patients tense the hips and buttocks. ("Please tighten the muscles of your buttocks." Alternative tensing strategy: "Please push your hips and buttocks down into the chair [couch].") During the muscle discrimination task, they have LBP patients practice this task on their back and neck muscle groups, rather than their eyes and neck as with headache.

Clinical hint: With LBP patients who are having trouble discriminating between the different levels of muscle tension in their back, the therapist can conduct a muscle discrimination task using biofeedback, in which sensors are connected to the paraspinal muscles in the L_4–L_5 region. Simply instruct patients to tense full strength, 50%, and then 25%, giving them feedback on their muscle discrimination ability.

With those individuals who fail to achieve any relief with frontal and upper trapezius EMG biofeedback, or with those individuals who do not get sufficient relief from relaxation therapy, Arena and his colleagues then conduct a psychophysiological assessment, following the logic of the biomechanical theory of LBP. This assessment consists of bilateral paraspinal (L_4–L_5) and biceps femoris (back of thigh) muscle tension readings in at least two positions: sitting with back supported in a recliner or other comfortable chair, and standing with arms by sides. They use biceps femoris for the leg measure, because in their clinical work they have found more abnormalities in this region than in other leg sites, such as quadriceps femoris (front of thigh) or gastrocnemius (back of calf). The back of the leg is enervated by the sciatic nerve, and is usually the area where most patients say that their pain is referred from the lower back. For exact sensor placement for the paraspinal and biceps femoris muscles, please see Basmajian and DeLuca (1985) or Lippold (1967). Figure 8.2 graphically depicts the paraspinal muscle site placement, as well as the biceps femoris muscle site placement.

The Aususta group looks for three possible muscle tension abnormalities in both the paraspinal and biceps femoris muscle groups: (1) unusually low muscle tension levels (this usually occurs only with nerve damage and resultant muscle atrophy); (2) unusually high muscle tension levels (this is the abnormality most frequently found); or (3) a left–right asymmetry, in which one side of the back or thigh muscles has normal muscle tension levels, while the other side has unusually low or high readings. (Unfortunately, normative values are based on the equipment used. Readers should refer to their equipment reference manuals or run some nonpain controls to obtain their own norms.) In the first instance, they teach patients through biofeedback to increase their muscle tension levels

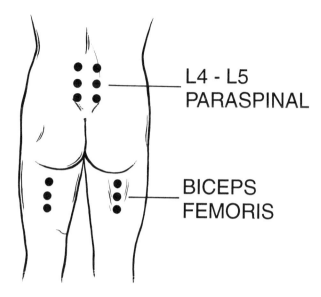

L4 - L5
PARASPINAL

BICEPS
FEMORIS

FIGURE 8.2. Electrode placements for bilateral paraspinal and biceps femoris EMG biofeedback training.

in the respective muscle group(s); in the second instance, they teach them through biofeedback to decrease their muscle tension levels in the respective muscle group(s). When no asymmetry is found, as in these two instances, they usually give feedback from a single side during the biofeedback sessions. If an asymmetry is found (the third instance), they use biofeedback to increase or decrease the abnormal side. The goal is to bring both sides into the normal range.

Clinical hints: It is essential to look at the gait and posture of every LBP patient. Nearly all will have the neck forward, the gait slowed, and weight usually borne on the unaffected side. The therapist should have the patient walk, without making it obvious that the patient is being observed. Gait and posture abnormalities should be corrected through education, as well as through biofeedback. A full-length mirror used as a biofeedback device to correct exaggerated posture is very helpful. In many instances of severe gait and posture abnormalities, a physical therapist referral is quite helpful.

Finally, with LBP, it is imperative to deal with the cognitive-behavioral component as well as the psychophysiological one. Again, readers should refer to Bradley, Chapter 6, this volume, for assistance in this area.

CONCLUSIONS

It has been our intent in writing this chapter to present the novice clinician with a reasonably detailed "how-to" guide for conducting psychophysiological interventions with chronic headache and LBP, as well as to provide the more advanced reader with an understanding of how two fairly experienced clinician-researchers approach some of the major pitfalls and questions that arise when relaxation therapy and biofeedback procedures are employed with chronic pain patients. We hope we have succeeded in our goal.

It is an additional hope of ours that the reader will modify the relaxation and bio-feedback procedures we use with chronic headache and LBP for application to other pain disorders. This does not mean that the reader should charge blindly ahead and imple-ment these procedures with every patient who presents with chronic pain; that would be neither ethical nor prudent. Rather, we anticipate that the procedures outlined in this chapter, *coupled with a careful reading of the available psychophysiological intervention litera-ture* on the pain disorder in question, should enable the clinician to approach the pain problem with some level of expertise and comfort. It is important to scrutinize the exist-ing literature carefully, both to avoid making obvious mistakes (e.g., treating a vascular disorder such as Raynaud's disease with EMG biofeedback rather than thermal) and to avoid repeating the failure of others (e.g., attempting to treat cluster headache with psy-chophysiological interventions or mixed headache with only relaxation therapy).

Although we have repeatedly stressed a common theme throughout this chapter, it bears repeating: It is impossible to overemphasize the importance of tailoring any psy-chophysiological treatment to the needs of the individual patient. It is the clinician's job to be creative and flexible. For example, if a patient has trouble relaxing when caught in rush hour traffic, the therapist can make an audiotape or videotape of the stressful event and have the patient practice the relaxation or biofeedback exercises while the tape is playing. If a patient generally gets headaches after working on a computer, the therapist can connect the EMG sensors to the forehead and trapezius muscles, have the patient use a computer, and see whether the patient is inadvertently tensing those muscles or has poor posture while working at the task.

Although we have had both the novice and the experienced clinician of various dis-ciplines in mind during the writing of this chapter, the prototypical audience has been our students—doctoral-level graduate students and interns in clinical psychology. We are well aware that many students (and indeed many psychologists), having dealt only with conventional psychological problems such as depression and anxiety, feel somewhat un-comfortable in applying their behavioral science principles and skills to a traditionally medical domain such as chronic pain. We hope we have demonstrated to them through-out this chapter that psychology's sound theories and techniques are readily transferable to problems such as chronic pain. We hope we have also demonstrated to these clini-cians that they should not put their basic clinical and common-sense skills "on the shelf" when they are using psychophysiological interventions. Too often, we have heard from both students and experienced clinicians that they "feel like technicians" when they per-form procedures such as biofeedback and relaxation therapy. It is our experience that if such feelings occur, they are often an indication that a clinician has failed to grasp the complexities and nuances of a patient or a pain disorder. Although we have been search-ing now for quite some time, we have yet to see the "textbook" chronic pain patient. The fact that every patient is different from the others is what makes clinical work both en-gaging and rewarding.

ACKNOWLEDGMENTS

This chapter was supported by a Department of Veterans Affairs Merit Review awarded to John G. Arena, and by National Institute of Mental Health Grant No. MH-41341 awarded to Edward B. Blanchard. John G. Arena gratefully acknowledges the assistance of Glenda Bruno, RN, MS, in the preparation of this chapter. Thanks to her invaluable help, sections of the chapter—especially the discussion of diaphragmatic breathing—are much more readable and considerably more use-ful to clinicians.

REFERENCES

Ad Hoc Committee on the Classification of Headache. (1962). Classification of headache. *Journal of the American Medical Association, 179*, 127–128.

Agur, A. M. R. (1991). *Grant's atlas of anatomy* (9th ed.). Baltimore: Williams & Wilkins.

American Academy of Orthopedic Surgery. (1986). *Common orthopedic procedures and codes: A reference guide.* New York: Authors.

Andersson, G. B. J., & McNeill, T. W. (1989). *Lumbar spine syndromes: Evaluation and treatment.* New York: Springer-Verlag.

Andrasik, F., & Blanchard, E. B. (1987). Biofeedback treatment of muscle contraction headache. In J. P. Hatch, J. G. Fisher, & J. D. Rugh (Eds.), *Biofeedback: Studies in clinical efficacy* (pp. 281–315). New York: Plenum Press.

Andrasik, F., Blanchard, E. B., Arena, J. G., Saunders, N. L., & Barron, K. D. (1982). Psychophysiology of recurrent head pain: Methodological issues and new empirical findings. *Behavior Therapy, 13*, 407–429.

Andrasik, F., Pallmeyer, T. P., Blanchard, E. B., & Attanasio, V. (1984). Continuous versus interrupted schedules of thermal biofeedback: An exploratory analysis with clinical subjects. *Biofeedback and Self-Regulation, 9*, 291–298.

Appelbaum, K. A., Blanchard, E. B., Hickling, E. J., & Alfonso, M. (1988). Cognitive-behavioral treatment of a veteran population with moderate to sever rheumatoid arthritis. *Behavior Therapy, 19*, 489–502.

Arena, J. G., Blanchard, E. B., Andrasik, F., Appelbaum, K., & Myers, P. E. (1985). Psychophysiological comparisons of three kinds of headache sufferers during and between headache states: Analysis of post-stress adaptation periods. *Journal of Psychosomatic Research, 29*, 427–441.

Arena, J. G., Bruno, G. M., Brucks, A. G., Hannah, S. L., & Meador, K. J. (1995a). *Psychophysiological comparisons of tension headache sufferers during headache and non-headache states: Effect of multiple movements and positions.* Manuscript submitted for publication.

Arena, J. G., Bruno, G. M., Hannah, S. L., & Meador, K. J. (1995b). A comparison of frontal electromyographic biofeedback training, trapezius electromyographic biofeedback training, and progressive muscle relaxation therapy in the treatment of tension headache. *Headache, 35*, 411–419.

Arena, J. G., Hannah, S. L., Bruno, G. M., & Meador, K. J. (1991a). Electromyographic biofeedback training for tension headache in the elderly: A prospective study. *Biofeedback and Self-Regulation, 16*, 379–390.

Arena, J. G., Hannah, S. L., Bruno, G. M., Smith, J. D., & Meador, K. J. (1991b). Effect of movement and position on muscle activity in tension headache sufferers during and between headaches. *Journal of Psychosomatic Research, 35*, 187–195.

Arena, J. G., Hightower, N. E., & Chang, G. C. (1988). Relaxation therapy for tension headache in the elderly: A prospective study. *Psychology and Aging, 3*, 96–98.

Arena, J. G., Sherman, R. A., Bruno, G. M., & Young, T. R. (1989). Electromyographic recordings of five types of low back pain subjects and non-pain controls in different positions. *Pain, 37*, 57–65.

Arena, J. G., Sherman, R. A., Bruno, G. M., & Young, T. R. (1990). Temporal stability of paraspinal electromyographic recordings in low back and non-pain subjects. *International Journal of Psychophysiology, 9*, 31–37.

Arena, J. G., Sherman, R. A., Bruno, G. M., & Young, T. R. (1991c). Electromyographic recordings of five types of low back pain subjects and non-pain controls in different positions: Effect of pain state. *Pain, 45*, 23–28.

Bakal, D. (1992). *Psychology and health* (2nd ed.). New York: Springer.

Basmajian, J. V., & DeLuca, C. J. (1985). *Muscles alive: Their functions revealed by electromyography.* Baltimore: Williams & Wilkins.

Bellack, A. (1973). Reciprocal inhibition of a laboratory conditioned fear. *Behaviour Research and Therapy, 11*, 11–18.

Bernstein, D. A., & Borkovec, T. D. (1973). *Progressive relaxation training*. Champaign, IL: Research Press.

Blanchard, E. B. (1979). A case study of the use of temperature biofeedback in the treatment of chronic pain due to causalgia. *Biofeedback and Self-Regulation, 4*, 183–188.

Blanchard, E. B. (1992). Psychological treatment of benign headache disorders. *Journal of Consulting and Clinical Psychology, 60*, 537–551.

Blanchard, E. B. (1993). Behavioral therapies in the treatment of headache. *Headache Quarterly, 3*, 53–56.

Blanchard, E. B., & Andrasik, F. (1982). Psychological assessment and treatment of headache: Recent developments and emerging issues. *Journal of Consulting and Clinical Psychology, 50*, 859–879.

Blanchard, E. B., & Andrasik, F. (1985). *Management of chronic headache: A psychological approach*. Elmsford, NY: Pergamon Press.

Blanchard, E. B., & Andrasik, F. (1987). Biofeedback treatment of vascular headache. In J. P. Hatch, J. D. Rugh, & J. G. Fisher (Eds.), Biofeedback: Studies in clinical efficacy (pp. 1–79). New York: Plenum Press.

Blanchard, E. B., Andrasik, F., Appelbaum, K. A., Evans, D. D., Jurish, S. E., Teders, S. J., Rodichok, L. D., & Barron, K. D. (1985a). The efficacy and cost-effectiveness of minimal-therapist-contact, non-drug treatments of chronic migraine and tension headache. *Headache, 25*, 214–220.

Blanchard, E. B., Andrasik, F., Evans, D. D., & Hillhouse, J. (1985b). Biofeedback and relaxation treatments for headache in the elderly: A caution and a challenge. *Biofeedback and Self-Regulation, 10*, 69–73.

Blanchard, E. B., Andrasik, F., Evans, D. D., Neff, D. F., Appelbaum, K. A., & Rodichok, L. D. (1985c). Behavioral treatment of 250 chronic headache patients: A clinical replication series. *Behavior Therapy, 16*, 308–327.

Blanchard, E. B., Andrasik, F., Jurish, S. E., & Teders, S. J. (1982a). The treatment of cluster headache with relaxation and thermal biofeedback. *Biofeedback and Self-Regulation, 7*, 185–191.

Blanchard, E. B., Andrasik, F., Neff, D. F., Arena, J. G., Ahles, T. A., Jurish, S. E., Pallmeyer, T. P., Saunders, N. L., Teders, S. J., Barron, K. D., & Rodichok, L. D. (1982b). Biofeedback and relaxation training with three kinds of headache: Treatment effects and their prediction. *Journal of Consulting and Clinical Psychology, 50*, 562–575.

Blanchard, E. B., Andrasik, F., Neff, D. F., Saunders, N. L., Arena, J. G., Pallmeyer, T. P., Teders, S. J., Jurish, S. E., & Rodichok, L. D. (1983). Four process studies in the behavioral treatment of chronic headache. *Behaviour Research and Therapy, 21*, 209–220.

Blanchard, E. B., Andrasik, F., Neff, D. F., Teders, S. J., Pallmeyer, T. P., Arena, J. G. Jurish, S. E., Saunders, N. L., & Rodichok, L. D. (1982c). Sequential comparisons of relaxation training and biofeedback in the treatment of three kinds of headache, or the machines may be necessary some of the time. *Behaviour Research and Therapy, 20*, 469–482.

Blanchard, E. B., Appelbaum, K. A., Nicholson, N. L., Radnitz, C. L., Morrill, B., Michultka, D., Kirsch, C., Hillhouse, J. Dentinger, M. P. (1990a). A controlled evaluation of the addition of cognitive therapy to a home-based biofeedback and relaxation treatment of vascular headache. *Headache, 30*, 371–376.

Blanchard, E. B., Appelbaum, K. A., Radnitz, C. L., Jaccard, J. Dentinger, & M. P. (1989). The refractory headache patient: I. Chronic, daily, high intensity headache. *Behaviour Research and Therapy, 27*, 403–410.

Blanchard, E. B., Appelbaum, K. A., Radnitz, C. L., Michultka, D. M., Morrill, B., Kirsch, C., Hillhouse, J., Evans, D. D., Guarnieri, P., Attanasio, V., Andrasik, F., Jaccard, J., & Dentinger, M. P. (1990b). A placebo-controlled evaluation of abbreviated progressive muscle relaxation and relaxation combined with cognitive therapy in the treatment of tension headache. *Journal of Consulting and Clinical Psychology, 58*, 210–215.

Blanchard, E. B., Appelbaum, K. A., Radnitz, C. L., Morrill, B., Michultka, D., Kirsch, C., Guarnieri, P., Hillhouse, J., Evans, D. D., Jaccard, J., & Barron, K. D. (1990c). A controlled evaluation of thermal biofeedback and thermal biofeedback combined with cognitive therapy in the treatment of vascular headache. *Journal of Consulting and Clinical Psychology, 58,* 216–224.

Blanchard, E. B., Kim, M., Hermann, C., & Steffek, B. D. (1993). Preliminary results of the effects on headache relief of perception of success among tension headache patients receiving relaxation. *Headache Quarterly, 4,* 249–253.

Blanchard, E. B., Kim, M., Hermann, C., & Steffek, B. D. (1994). The role of perception of success in the thermal biofeedback treatment of vascular headache. *Headache Quarterly, 5,* 231–236.

Blanchard, E. B., McCoy, G. C., McCaffrey, R. J., Berger, M., Musso, A. J., Wittrock, D. A., Gerardi, M. A., Halpern, M., & Pangburn, L. (1987). Evaluation of a minimal-therapist-contact thermal biofeedback treatment program for essential hypertension. *Biofeedback and Self-Regulation, 12,* 93–103.

Blanchard, E. B., McCoy, G. C., McCaffrey, R. J., Musso, A., Wittrock, D. A., Berger, M., Gerardi, M. A., Pangburn, L., Khramelashvili, V. V., Aivasyan, T. A., & Salenko, B. B. (1988). The USSR–USA collaborative cross-cultural comparison of autogenic training and thermal biofeedback in the treatment of mild hypertension. *Health Psychology, 7,* 19–33.

Blanchard, E. B., McCoy, G. C., Musso, A., Gerardi, R. J., Cotch, P. A., Siracusa, K., & Andrasik, F. (1986). A controlled comparison of thermal biofeedback and relaxation training in the treatment of essential hypertension: I. Short-term and long-term outcome. *Behavior Therapy, 17,* 563–579.

Blanchard, E. B., Nicholson, N. L., Radnitz, C. L., Steffek, B. D., Appelbaum, K. A., & Dentinger, M. P. (1991a). The role of home practice in thermal biofeedback. *Journal of Consulting and Clinical Psychology, 59,* 507–512.

Blanchard, E. B., Nicholson, N. L., Taylor, A. E., Steffek, B. D., Radnitz, C. L., & Appelbaum, K. A. (1991b). The role of regular home practice in the relaxation treatment of tension headache. *Journal of Consulting and Clinical Psychology, 59,* 467–470.

Blanchard, E. B., Taylor, A. E., & Dentinger, M. P. (1992). Preliminary results from the self-regulatory treatment of high medication consumption headache. *Biofeedback and Self-Regulation, 17,* 179–202.

Borenstein, D. G., & Wiesel, S. W. (1989). *Low back pain: Medical diagnosis and comprehensive management.* Philadelphia: W.B. Saunders.

Borgeat, F., Hade, B., Larouche, L. N., & Bedwani, C. N. (1980). Effects of therapist active presence on EMG biofeedback training of headache patients. *Biofeedback and Self-Regulation, 5,* 275–282.

Budzynski, T. (1978). Biofeedback in the treatment of muscle-contraction (tension) headache. *Biofeedback and Self-Regulation, 3,* 409–434.

Cavanaugh, J. & Weinstein, J. (1994). Low back pain: Epidemiology, anatomy, and neurophysiology. In P. Wall & R. Melzack (Eds.), *Textbook of pain* (3rd ed., pp. 441–445). New York: Churchill Livingstone.

Clemente, C. D. (1987). *Anatomy: A regional atlas of the human body* (3rd ed.). Baltimore: Urban & Schwarzenberg.

Cook, N. R., Evans, D. A., Funkenstein, H., Scherr, P. A. Ostfeld, A. M., Taylor, J. O., & Hennekens, C. H. (1989). Correlates of headache in a population-based cohort of elderly. *Archives of Neurology, 46,* 1338–1344.

Costa, P. T., & Vandenbos, G. R. (Eds.). (1990). Psychological aspects of serious illness: Chronic conditions, fatal diseases, and clinical care. Washington, DC: American Psychological Association.

Cousins, M. J. (1995). Foreword. In W. E. Fordyce (Ed.), *Back pain in the workplace: Management of disability in nonspecific conditions. A report of the Task Force on Pain in the Workplace of the International Association for the Study of Pain.* Seattle, WA: International Association for the Study of Pain.

Coyne, L., Sargent, J., Segerson, J., & Obourn, R. (1976). Relative potency scale for analgesic drugs: Use of psychophysical procedures with clinical judgments. *Headache, 16,* 70–71

Craig, K. D., & Weiss, S. M. (Eds.). (1990). *Health enhancement, disease prevention and early intervention: Biobehavioral strategies.* New York: Springer.

Dalessio, D. J. (Ed.). (1987). *Wolff's headache and other pain* (5th ed.). New York: Oxford University Press.

Deardroff, W., Rubin, H., & Scott, D. (1991). Comprehensive multidisciplinary treatment of chronic pain: A follow-up study of treated and non-treated groups. *Pain, 45,* 35–43.

Dolce, J. J., & Raczynski, J. M. (1985). Neuromuscular activity and electromyography in painful backs: Psychological and biomechanical models in assessment and treatment. *Psychological Bulletin, 97,* 502–520.

Evans, D. D. (1988). *A comparison of two computerized thermal biofeedback displays in migraine headache patients and controls.* Unpublished dissertation, State University of New York, Albany.

Fahrion, S. L. (1977) Autogenic biofeedback treatment for migraine. *Mayo Clinic Proceedings, 52,* 776–784.

Fahrion, S. L., Norris, P., Green, A., Green, E., & Snarr, C. (1986). Biobehavioral treatment of essential hypertension: A group outcome study. *Biofeedback and Self-Regulation, 11,* 257–278.

Flor, H., Fydrich, T., & Turk, D. C. (1992). Efficacy of multidisciplinary pain treatment centers: A meta-analytic review. *Pain, 49,* 221–230.

Freedman, R. R. (1987). Long-term effectiveness of behavioral treatments for Raynaud's disease. *Behavior Therapy, 18,* 387–399.

Freedman, R. R. (1993). Raynaud's disease and phenomenon. In R. J. Gatchel & E. B. Blanchard (Eds.), *Psychophysiological disorders: Research in clinical applications* (pp. 245–267). Washington, DC: American Psychological Association.

Frymoyer, J. W., Akeson, W., Brandt, K., Goldenberg, D., & Spencer, D. (1989). Postural support structures: Part A. Clinical perspective. In J. W. Frymoyer & S. L. Gordon (Eds.), *New perspectives in low back pain* (pp. 217–248). Park Ridge, IL: American Academy of Orthopedic Surgeons.

Gatchel, R. J., & Blanchard, E. B. (Eds.). (1993). *Psychophysiological disorders: Research and clinical applications.* Washington, DC: American Psychological Association.

Hart, J. D., & Cichanski, K. A. (1981). A comparison of frontal EMG biofeedback and neck EMG biofeedback in the treatment of muscle-contraction headache. *Biofeedback and Self-Regulation, 6,* 63–74.

Haynes, S. N. (1980). Muscle contraction headache: A psychophysiological perspective of etiology and treatment. In S. N. Haynes & L. R. Gannon (Eds.), *Psychosomatic disorders: A psychophysiological approach to etiology and treatment* (pp. 447–484). New York: Gardner Press.

Headache Classification Committee of the International Headache Society. (1988). Classification and diagnostic criteria for headache disorders, cranial neuralgias and facial pain. *Cephalgia, 8*(Suppl. 7), 29–34.

Heide, F. J., & Borkovec, T. D. (1983). Relaxation-induced anxiety: Paradoxical anxiety enhancement due to relaxation training. *Journal of Consulting and Clinical Psychology, 51,* 171–182.

Hermann, C. U. (1994). Pediatric migraine: A comprehensive assessment and treatment study. Unpublished doctoral dissertation, University of Tubigen, Tubigen, Germany.

Hermann, C. U., Kim, M., & Blanchard, E. B. (1993). The efficacy of behavioral intervention in the treatment of pediatric migraine: A meta-analytic review. In *Proceedings of the 24th Annual Meeting of the Association for Applied Psychophysiology and Biofeedback, March 25–30, 1993* (pp. 149–154). Wheatridge, CO: Association for Applied Psychophysiology and Biofeedback.

Holroyd, K. A., & Andrasik, F. (1982). A cognitive-behavioral approach to recurrent tension and migraine headache. In P. E. Kendall (Ed.), *Advances in cognitive-behavioral research and therapy* (Vol. 1, pp. 275–320). New York: Academic Press.

Holroyd, K. A., & Penzien, D. B. (1986). Client variables and the behavioral treatment of recurrent tension headache: A meta-analytic review. *Journal of Behavioral Medicine, 9,* 515–536.

Holroyd, K. A., Penzien, D. B., Hursey, K. G., Tobin, L. R., Holm, J. E., Marcille, P. J., Hall, J. R., & Chila, A. G. (1984). Change mechanisms in EMG biofeedback training: Cognitive changes underlying improvements in tension headache. *Journal of Consulting and Clinical Psychology*, 52, 1039–1053.

Hudzinski, L. G. (1983). Neck musculature and EMG biofeedback in treatment of muscle contraction headache. *Headache*, 23, 86–90.

Jacobson, E. (1929). *Progressive relaxation*. Chicago: University of Chicago Press.

Jurish, S. E., Blanchard, E. B., Andrasik, F., Teders, S. J., Neff, D. F., & Arena, J. G. (1983). Home versus clinic-based treatment of vascular headache. *Journal of Consulting and Clinical Psychology*, 51, 743–751.

Kabela, E., Blanchard, E. B., Appelbaum, K. A., & Nicholson, N. (1989). Self-regulatory treatment of headache in the elderly. *Biofeedback and Self-Regulation*, 14, 219–228.

King, A. C., & Arena, J. G. (1984). Behavioral treatment of chronic cluster headache in geriatric patients. *Biofeedback and Self-Regulation*, 9, 201–208.

Kudrow, L. (1980). *Cluster headache: Mechanisms and management*. New York: Oxford University Press.

Kudrow, L. (1982). Paradoxical effects of frequent analgesic use. In M. Critchley, A. P. Friedman, S. Gorini, & F. Sicuteri (Eds.), *Advances in neurology: Vol. 33. Headache: Physiopathological and clinical concepts* (pp. 335–341). New York: Raven Press.

Libo, L. M., & Arnold, G. E. (1983). Does training to criterion influence improvement? A follow-up study of EMG and thermal biofeedback. *Journal of Behavioral Medicine*, 6, 397–404.

Lichstein, K. L. (1988). *Clinical relaxation strategies*. New York: Wiley.

Lippold, D. C. J. (1967). Electromyography. In P. H. Venables & I. Martin (Eds.), *Manual of psychophysiological methods* (pp. 245–297). New York: Wiley.

Luthe, W. (Ed.). (1969–1973). *Autogenic therapy* (6 vols.). New York: Grune & Stratton.

MacHose, M., & Peper, E. (1991). The effects of clothing on inhalation volume. *Biofeedback and Self-Regulation*, 16, 261–265.

Martin, P. R., & Mathews, A. M. (1978). Tension headaches: Psychophysiological investigation and treatment. *Journal of Psychosomatic Research*, 22, 389–399.

Mathew, N. T., Kurman, R., & Perez, F. (1990). Drug induced refractory headache: Clinical features and management. *Headache*, 30, 634–638.

McCoy, G. C., Blanchard, E. B., Wittrock, D. A., Morrison, S., Pangburn, L., Siracusa, K., & Pallmeyer, T. P. (1988). Biochemical changes associated with thermal biofeedback treatment of hypertension. *Biofeedback and Self-Regulation*, 13, 139–150.

Michultka, D. M., Blanchard, E. B., Appelbaum, K. A., Jaccard, J., & Dentinger, M. P. (1989). The refractory headache patient: II. High medication consumption (analgesic rebound) headache. *Behaviour Research and Therapy*, 27, 411–420.

Morrill, B., & Blanchard, E. B. (1989). Two studies of the potential mechanisms of action in the thermal biofeedback treatment of vascular headache. *Headache*, 29, 169–176

Neff, D. F., & Blanchard, E. B. (1987). A multi-component treatment of irritable bowel syndrome. *Behavior Therapy*, 18, 70–83.

Nicholson, N. L., & Blanchard, E. B. (1993). A controlled evaluation of behavioral treatment of chronic headache in the elderly. *Behavior Therapy*, 25, 395–408.

Nouwen, A., & Bush, C. (1984). The relationship between paraspinal EMG and chronic low back pain. *Pain*, 20, 109–123.

Olton, D. S., & Noonberg, A. R. (1980). *Biofeedback: Clinical applications in behavioral medicine*. Englewood Cliffs, NJ: Prentice Hall.

Pearce, T., & Tunks, E. (1990). Mulimodal treatment for chronic pain. In E. Tunks, A. Bellissimo, & R. Roy (Eds.), *Chronic pain: Psychological factors in rehabilitation* (pp. 255–270). Malabar, FL: Robert E.

Peatfield, R. (1986). *Headache*. New York: Springer.

Philips, C. (1977). The modification of tension headache pain using EMG biofeedback. *Behaviour Research and Therapy*, 15, 119–129.

Philips, C., & Hunter, M. (1981). The treatment of tension headache: II. Muscular abnormality and biofeedback. *Behaviour Research and Therapy*, 19, 859–489.

Rasmussen, B. K., Jensen, R., Schroll, M., & Olesen, J. (1991). Epidemiology of headache in a general population: A prevalence study. *Journal of Clinical Epidemiology, 44*, 1147–1157.

Sargent, J. D., Green, E. E., & Walters, E. D. (1972). The use of autogenic feedback training in a pilot study of migraine and tension headaches. *Headache, 12*, 120–124.

Schultz, J. H., & Luthe, W. (1969). Authogenic methods. In W. Luthe (Ed.), *Autogenic threapy* (Vol. 1, pp. 1–245). New York: Grune & Stratton.

Schwartz, M. S., & Associates. (1995). *Biofeedback: A practitioner's guide* (2nd ed.). New York: Guilford Press.

Sherman, R. A., & Arena, J. G. (1992). Biofeedback in the assessment and treatment of low back pain. In J. Bazmajian & R. Nyberg (Eds.), *Spinal manipulative therapies* (pp. 177–197). Baltimore: Williams & Wilkins.

Sherman, R. A., Arena, J. G., DeGood, D. E., Glaros, A. G., Marrero, M. V., & Pope, A. T. (1992). Instrumentation and safety. In Applications Standards Committee of the Association for Applied Psychophysiology and Biofeedback (Ed.), *Standards and guidelines for biofeedback applications in psychophysiological self-regulation* (pp. 50–80). Wheatridge, CO: Association for Applied Psychophysiology and Biofeedback.

Shumaker, S. A., Schron, E. B., & Ockene, J. K. (Eds.). (1990). *The handbook of health behavior change.* New York: Springer.

Smith, J. C. (1990). *Cognitive-behavioral relaxation training: A new system of strategies for treatment and assessment.* New York: Springer.

Sobel, D. S. (1993). Mind matters, money matters: The cost-effectiveness of clinical behavioral medicine. *Mental Medicine Update, 2*, 1–8.

Stang, P. E., Yanagihara, T., Swanson, J. W., Beard, C. M., O'Fallon, W. M., Guess, H. A., & Melton L. J. (1992). Incidents of migraine headache: A population-based study in Olmstead County, Minnesota. *Neurology, 42*, 1657–1662.

Stewart, W. F., Lipton, R. B., Celentano, D. D., & Reed, M. L. (1992). Prevalence of migraine headache in the United States. *Journal of the American Medical Association, 267*, 64–69.

Taub, E., & School, P. J. (1978). Some methodological considerations in thermal biofeedback training. *Behavior Research Methods and Instrumentation, 10*, 617–622.

Teasell, R. W., & White, K. (1994). Clinical approaches to low back pain: Part 1. Epidemiology, diagnosis, and prevention. *Canadian Family Physician, 40*, 481–486.

Tobin, D. L., Holroyd, K. A., Baker, A., Reynolds, R. V. C., & Holms, J. E. (1988). Development and clinical trial of a minimal contact, cognitive-behavioral treatment for tension headache. *Cognitive Therapy and Research, 12*, 325–339.

Tunnis, M. M., & Wolff, H. G. (1954). Studies on headache: Cranial artery vasoconstriction and muscle contraction headache. *Archives of Neurology and Psychiatry, 71*, 425–434.

Wolff, J. G. (1963). *Headache and other head pain.* New York: Oxford University Press.

Wood, P. H. N., & Bradley, E. M. (1980). Epidemiology of low back pain. In M. I. Jayson (Ed.), *The lumbar spine and back pain* (pp. 13–17). London: Pitman.

CHAPTER 9

Hypnosis and Imagery in the Treatment of Pain

Karen L. Syrjala
Janet R. Abrams

Hypnosis and imagery have captured the interest of the public, the mass media, health care professionals, and patients with pain that is unrelieved by medical treatments. Inquiries into the potential efficacy of hypnosis as a pain treatment usually stem from either fears of the side effects of medical treatments or the lack of efficacy of medical treatments attempted. The fact that medical care does not alleviate all pain without undesired side effects makes hypnosis and other imagery strategies worth pursuing and worthy of scientific inquiry. This chapter describes the practical application of mental imaging strategies to assist patients with unrelieved pain.

WHAT ARE HYPNOSIS AND IMAGERY?

The distinctions among various terms used to describe mental transformations in pain perception are largely hypothetical. "Hypnosis" and "imagery" are widely agreed to be states of highly focused attention during which alteration of sensations, awareness, and perceptions can occur. More in dispute are the questions of whether hypnosis is an altered state of consciousness requiring a trance, and whether it is distinct from imagery because of this. Hypnosis has been hypothesized to reduce pain by mechanisms including attention control and dissociation (E. R. Hilgard & Hilgard, 1983; Orne, 1959; H. Spiegel & Spiegel, 1978). Many other strategies may have more commonalities with than differences from hypnosis; in addition to imagery induction, these include deep breathing, progressive muscle relaxation, passive (autogenic) relaxation, and meditation. We incorporate all of these into our practice, basing our choice of which method or methods to use on the characteristics of the individual patient and the particular situation. We also employ modifications of formal hypnosis and imagery strategies as these appear warranted (e.g., brief imagery for transforming acute, short-duration pain; metaphors and suggestions outside of formal inductions; and storytelling, especially involving the patient in telling the story).

"Imagery" and "visualization" are synonymous in our use of the terms and generally indicate incorporation of visual images, whereas "hypnosis" may or may not include visual imagery. Although imagery implies the use of "mental pictures," there has been no scientific demonstration to indicate that these pictures are essential to effective use of the strategy for pain control. In other words, a patient who says that he or she does not actually picture an image, but rather hears sounds or has a particularly soothing thought or feels the warmth of a light moving through his or her body, may receive as much benefit as the patient who can describe visual images in great detail. On the other hand, hypnosis implies an effort to achieve a state of highly focused attention, during which time the patient is more susceptible to suggestion. Suggestion is an integral part of hypnosis, whereas suggestion may or may not be offered in imagery, relaxation, or meditation strategies.

WHAT IS THE ROLE OF SUGGESTION?

For the purposes of pain relief, suggestion is a central component of what we consider the clinical efficacy of these methods. As such, the concept of "suggestion" may be much more important for the practitioner to understand than the concept of "trance." In essence, suggestion is, as it sounds, a way of conveying to a patient that something will be accomplished or experienced; this can be explicit or implied. In other words, patient and clinician may simply act as though pain relief will be accomplished with treatment, and this can be a powerful suggestion. Alternatively, the clinician can suggest comfort and mastery over physical well-being. As a rule, we find positive suggestion (i.e., the indication of what *is* felt) more broadly powerful than negative suggestion (e.g., "The pain will disappear"). Similarly, for many acute pain situations, where long-term coping with pain is not necessary, analgesic or sensory transformation suggestions are not even needed. Relief is obtained by actively moving the patient's mind to comfort and pleasure unrelated to symptoms. The suggestion is implicit, since both patient and clinician know that comfort is the goal.

Although suggested analgesia may be more powerful in the hypnotic state than without hypnosis (McGlashan, Evans, & Orne, 1969), suggestion is an extremely powerful tool in any state. It may account in large measure for what we call the "placebo effect," which is increasingly recognized as an effect that we should maximize (Turner, Deyo, Loeser, VonKorff, & Fordyce, 1994). Cognitive-behavioral strategies such as reframing or distraction, which involve music or other mental transformation strategies, may actually incorporate suggestion along with images or highly focused mental processing; in their mechanism of effect, they may thus be difficult to distinguish from hypnosis or imagery. Regardless of the choice of terminology or method selected, effects will almost certainly be stronger if clinicians actively use suggestion to increase patients' comfort and sense of control over their well-being.

DOES HYPNOTIZABILITY MATTER?

"Hypnotic susceptibility" is defined as the degree of responsiveness to suggestions following a hypnotic induction. Susceptibility can be measured by performance on standardized tests (Shor & Orne, 1962; Weitzenhoffer & Hilgard, 1959) or less formally, by methods described below. Responsivity to hypnosis on standard instruments is relatively stable, and some believe that this is a trait—in other words, that there is little one can do to enable a low-susceptibility person to have a hypnotic experience (E. R. Hilgard & Hilgard, 1965; D. Spiegel, 1985). Data do concur that highly hypnotizable subjects reduce pain more than less hypnotizable subjects in laboratory studies (Spanos, Kennedy, & Gwynn, 1984; Spanos, Radtke-Bodorik, Ferguson, & Jones, 1979), but even in this case hypnotizability is not the best predictor of response (Price & Barber, 1987). For clinical patients, with stronger motivating factors, response on standard measures seems even less useful as a predictor of ability to benefit from these strategies (J. Barber, 1980; Frischholz, Spiegel, Spiegel, Balma, & Markell, 1981).

Although there are conflicting and inconsistent clinical and laboratory reports on who is or is not a good candidate for hypnosis, our clinical experience is that almost any patient can benefit from individualized treatment, as long as the patient wants to use hypnosis or imagery. Diamond (1984) suggests that some capacity for hypnotic trance resides within most people. He believes that teaching can increase responsiveness to hypnosis. This is compatible with the work of Spanos and colleagues, who have explored cognitive skills training to increase hypnotic responsiveness (Spanos, Robertson, Menary, & Brett, 1986). With the same outcome, J. Barber encourages a different method for increasing the percentage of patients able to respond to hypnosis. He recommends that with an indirect approach, as used in his rapid-induction analgesia, nearly all patients can benefit from hypnosis (J. Barber, 1977, 1980). We agree that with some motivation on the part of the patient and with individualization of the methods, nearly any patient can benefit from these techniques, although the patient with more responsivity will probably respond more readily to any approach.

WHO BENEFITS FROM WHAT METHOD?

The goal of treatment is less to selectively apply these techniques than to blend the methods as needed to be as effective as possible in the individual situation. In practice, we avoid distinguishing among different terms, and adapt the method to the presentation of the patient. Some people feel uncomfortable being "hypnotized" because of their fear that the clinician or an evil force may take control of their minds (Hendler & Redd, 1986). For others, the implied "magic" is a powerful component. Clinical trial data indicate that use of the term "relaxation with imagery" is as effective as the term "hypnosis" when the terms are applied to nearly identical procedures (Syrjala, Cummings, & Donaldson, 1992a; Syrjala, Donaldson, Davis, Kippes, & Carr, 1995). For the practical purpose of reducing pain, we use an individualized approach with labels and language that fit the patient's request and personal style. We generally use the term "imagery" unless a patient specifically requests "hypnosis" or seems to have a strong avoidance of taking control. For patients who request hypnosis, the perceived magic of the method and the wish to see the clinician as in control seem to help the patients attribute more power to the method.

WHEN IS IMAGERY OR HYPNOSIS HELPFUL?

Numerous studies have indicated that imagery and hypnosis can significantly reduce many types of pain. Since World War II, clinicians have described hypnosis to help medically ill patients (Erickson, 1959; Sacerdote, 1965, 1970) and have reviewed the area of clinical hypnosis in analgesia and anesthesia (Crasilneck & Hall, 1985; E. R. Hilgard & Hilgard, 1983; Wadden & Anderton, 1982). In regard to chronic pain, several writers have suggested that hypnosis is effective in changing the pain experience by shifting attention away from bodily sensations (Crasilneck, 1979; Sachs, Feuerstein, & Vitale, 1977).

In a meta-analysis of the efficacy of cognitive-behavioral methods for pain control, Fernandez and Turk (1989) reported that imagery was the most powerful component, demonstrating significant effects across numerous studies with various types of pain. Other research has incorporated relaxation with imagery into multimodality cognitive-behavioral interventions and found that the package is only as helpful as relaxation with imagery alone (Syrjala et al., 1995; Turner & Jensen, 1993). Thus imagery strategies have repeatedly demonstrated the greatest effect size of all cognitive-behavioral strategies tested for efficacy in pain control.

To date, there have been few controlled clinical trials using hypnosis or imagery for pain control with continuous pain. D. Spiegel and Bloom (1983) randomly assigned breast cancer patients to three groups: no treatment, support group, and support group with brief hypnosis. At 1 year, those in the hypnosis group reported the lowest pain levels, although these were not significantly lower than those in the support-only group. Syrjala and colleagues have completed two clinical trials testing the efficacy of cognitive-behavioral skills for pain related to bone marrow transplantation (Syrjala et al., 1992a, 1995). These studies showed that patients could learn and apply hypnosis to pain management with two sessions of training followed by brief "booster" sessions. With chronic benign pain, hypnosis, meditation, imagery, and relaxation have all demonstrated efficacy in providing relief; however, no studies indicate that one method is superior to others (Kabat-Zinn, Lipworth, & Burney, 1985; McCauley, Thelen, Frank, Willard, & Callen, 1983; Turner & Jensen, 1993). Burn pain, migraine, and phantom limb pain have also responded to hypnosis (Olness, MacDonald, & Uden, 1987; Patterson, Everett, Burns, & Marvin, 1992; Patterson, Questad, & DeLateur, 1989; Sthalekar, 1993).

HOW CAN ASSESSMENT IMPROVE CHOICE OF METHOD AND OUTCOME?

Before a clinician can responsibly develop a psychological treatment plan incorporating hypnosis or imagery, a patient needs to have a medical evaluation for diagnosis and determination of appropriate medical treatments. Although additional psychological assessment is valuable, the depth of this assessment depends in part on the duration of pain relief being sought. Very brief imagery for a procedural pain may require only a brief assessment. Designing a strategy for management of chronic pain, whether benign or cancer-related, takes a more thorough assessment and reassessment. The assessment needs to be updated as the patient's needs change, depending, for instance, on the course of the illness, cognitive shifts, and input from others such as family members. Further details on assessment of pain are available from other sources (Cleeland & Syrjala, 1992; Turner & Romano, 1990). In addition to a standard psychological assessment for pain, certain factors need to be considered when a clinician is developing a pain treatment plan that includes hypnosis or imagery. These are summarized in Table 9.1.

Pain Assessment

A good description of the pain will help in developing hypnotic strategies and suggestions that can be tailored to the individual needs of the patient.

Etiology and Location

An understanding of the etiology and location of the pain is necessary. Is the pain a result of a procedure, surgery, chemotherapy, radiation, disease progression, an accident, or an injury, or is it of unknown origin? Location refers not just to body part, but also to organ or tissue type. For instance, in the case of knee pain, is the pain in the joint, soft tissue, or specific nerves? The answers to these questions not only tell the practitioner

TABLE 9.1. Assessment Components That Influence Selection of Hypnosis or Imagery Strategy

1. Routine pain assessment
   Etiology and location
   Pain severity
   Pain quality and temporal pattern
   Meaning of the pain
   Treatments used to manage the pain and their efficacy
   Concurrent medical illnesses, symptoms, and treatments
2. Coping style of the patient
   Active coping
   Avoidance
   Catastrophizing
   Support seeking
3. Mental and psychiatric status
   Alertness/concentration
   Cognitive capacity and style
   Affective state
4. Other factors that may interact with use of hypnosis/imagery
   Motivation and expectation
   Control need and self-efficacy specific to the pain
   Family attitudes and involvement
   Religious and cultural factors
   Hypnotizability

Note. Depth and length of assessment depend on goals of treatment, as well as on duration and severity of pain. More thorough assessment is required when the effect must extend over time.

about the targets and goals of treatment; they also provide some information about the potential meaning of the pain to the patient and secondary goals that may be achieved with hypnosis.

Pain Severity

The severity or intensity of the pain is easily measured with a scale from 0 ("no pain") to 10 ("pain as bad as can be"). A baseline assessment and reassessment after the use of imagery can assist both the patient and clinician in evaluating the efficacy of treatment. In itself, this can act as a suggestion and motivator, reminding the patient that the time spent using the technique has had a measurable effect even if the pain has not disappeared altogether.

Pain Quality

In the use of analgesic imagery, the patient's description of the qualities of the pain is essential, along with a clear understanding of the pain pattern. Is the pain brief, continuous, or intermittent? Is it expected to remain as it is indefinitely, or to progress in severity? For instance, with a brief pain, imagery can focus on active distraction of the patient away from the setting for the duration of pain. For a continuous or progressive pain, mere distraction will not be as effective in treating the pain (Suls & Fletcher, 1985; McCaul & Malott, 1984); a method is needed to integrate the pain perception into the patient's ongoing life. For continuous pain that is moderate to severe, the sensory transformation strategies described below may be more helpful.

Descriptions of the pain (e.g., stabbing, burning, pressing) can be incorporated into the sensory transformation experience. For example, for a burning or hot pain, we often use images of blowing freezing Arctic air through the sensation. During analgesic suggestions, we may use strategies that acknowledge the pain and then take the patient through a process to transform the pain. We may have the patient imagine what the pain looks like and then modify the image—sometimes in surprising ways, as in this example:

> "What shape is the headache? Notice the tightness (*pause*). Now just picture it getting bigger and bigger (*pause*). Notice how the feeling changes, what that is like (*pause*). It may become so big you can't see or feel where it starts and stops. Just let it expand until it is like the air, impossible to see where it is, so just let it go."

In a similar way, the pain perception can be changed through the description of the color or texture of a pain.

Meaning of the Pain

What is the meaning of the pain to the patient? Does the person want the symptom diminished? Is the pain a sign of frustration, helplessness, or loss to the patient, or is it a cause for anxiety and questions about whether a disease is progressing? In a life-threatening illness, patients sometimes see the pain as a signal of their health status and may be reluctant to give it up altogether. In other cases, patients may receive special care or attention because of the pain. Possible secondary gains may need to be evaluated. In understanding the meaning of the pain, it is helpful to ask patients what they believe is causing the pain, what will happen to the pain over time (whether it will get better, get worse, or stay the same forever), and what would happen to them if the pain went away (what would change in their lives, what activities would change).

Previous Treatments and Their Efficacy

It is important to identify treatments that have been attempted to this point, as well as their efficacy. What increased the patient's discomfort and distress? What reduced discomfort or distress? This inquiry should include both medical and cognitive or behavioral methods. The evaluation should result not only in a plan for using imagery, but also in improvement of medical treatment if possible.

Concurrent Medical Illness

What other treatments or symptoms is the patient experiencing? Pain often is not an isolated problem. For instance, a cancer patient may have pain along with severe fatigue from the disease, nausea from treatment, and sleep disruption from medications or anxiety. Another patient may have low back pain, but also may be suffering from arthritis. These symptoms and concurrent illnesses need to be considered, both for how they may influence response to hypnosis and whether these problems may benefit from being integrated into the treatment plan.

Coping Style

The way a person copes with pain or stress is useful to understand in selecting a methodology. "Active copers" want to gather information, to solve problems, and in particular to find something to do about the pain. "Avoiders" prefer not to think about problems, especially the pain problem. "Catastrophizers" tend to have extreme thoughts in response to the pain, such as "This is so terrible, I can't stand it. What if it just gets worse and worse? It's never going to stop." Finally, it is useful to understand the extent to which a person uses "support-seeking" coping.

Active copers tend more readily to use imagery strategies in which they can participate. Avoiders and catastrophizers are less likely to seek these methods, although they often respond well if the clinician uses hypnosis and is willing to take somewhat more control and be more directive in the methods. Avoiders particularly like to use images involving pleasant places and means of escape. We use this approach initially with these patients; as confidence builds, we then incorporate more sensory transformation and mastery images as described below. Patients who have some ability to use support seeking as a coping style may be more willing to allow the clinician to be helpful.

As important as understanding the patient's primary coping style is understanding the patient's flexibility in using this style. Those with more flexibility will probably be easier to work with. Even active copers, who in general are ready to participate in their pain relief, can require more care if they are concrete, inflexible, or very biologically minded in their use of this coping strategy. These are more often males who initially see imagery or hypnosis as too nonspecific and intangible. We find that this type of person responds very well to initial training with tension–release progressive muscle relaxation followed by brief imagery. The physical experience of the contrast between tension and relaxation is instructive to such patients, and they then have greater confidence in using imagery without the formal relaxation.

Mental and Psychiatric Status

Alertness and Concentration

A critical question is this: How alert is the patient? A sedated patient is more likely to fall asleep during the induction. Also, is the patient able to focus attention, and is fatigue or agitation manageable? A patient with limited attention or concentration will need brief methods, is more likely to need the clinician to be actively involved (vs. self-hypnosis), and may benefit from more active imagery or storytelling that involves the patient's providing some of the images. Patients with delirium are generally poorer candidates for these methods.

Cognitive Capacity and Style

Language needs to be tailored to the comprehension of the patient. A highly elaborate induction may be ineffective in a patient with limited vocabulary or verbal skills, whereas it may be ideal for a vigilant, highly verbal, cognitively oriented patient. Patients also have dispositions toward being visual, auditory, or tactile in their experiences. Using natural dispositions in the images or suggestions offered will certainly make things easier for everyone.

Affective State

The emotional state of the patient is as important to assess prior to employing hypnosis as it is prior to implementing any psychological method. The actively distressed patient may have difficulty focusing on imagery until the distress is discussed and explored at least briefly. The depressed patient may seem to bring little motivation to the process. With these patients, it is important to distinguish (to the extent possible) between depression resulting from poor pain control and broader clinical depression. The sense of helplessness that accompanies depression can be assisted with imagery that re-establishes mastery and a sense of control. However, clinical depression should be treated psychologically and/or pharmacologically along with the imagery for pain control. Similarly, the anxious or extremely tense patient may have difficulty with focusing attention. Shorter methods may be needed for the anxious person. We find tension–release progressive muscle relaxation a very effective beginning strategy for patients who benefit from first taking control of the tension and then noticing the physical change to relaxation. This is also helpful with patients who are not aware of the amount of tension they carry.

The phobic patient or the patient with panic attacks needs different considerations. If catastrophizing and anxiety reach a level of diagnosable panic, it is rarely necessary or possible to provide an induction. We move directly into breathing control, imagery, and suggestion, and evaluate by response whether this benefits the patient. The content of imagery and suggestion is shaped to counter the content of thoughts and images during the panic attack. Pharmacological methods should be considered if panic recurs and imagery does not readily reduce symptoms. We also see phobias develop, particularly in relation to procedures that must be repeated and during which a patient experiences uncontrolled pain and an extreme feeling of loss of control. In such a situation, we closely review the patient's recollections of the procedure, particularly the most difficult or painful parts. We then provide systematic desensitization, using imagery to assist the patient in gaining control over the procedure and his or her thoughts and emotions during the procedure.

Other Factors That May Interact with Use of Hypnosis/Imagery

Motivation and Expectation

How invested is the patient in these methods' working? How important is symptom reduction for the patient? What are the patient's expectations for pain reduction? Usually someone in acute pain is highly motivated. By contrast, those with chronic pain may have exhausted their positive expectations; this can reduce their motivation to attempt new treatments that require their participation. Before a clinician begins an intervention, it is important to ask about previous experience with hypnosis and current expectations of treatment. Sometimes patients request hypnosis because they believe it will relieve them of personal responsibility for a role in alleviating symptoms. For other patients, anything but total pain relief is seen as a failure. With treatment, symptoms may not be eliminated, but they may be reduced or better managed.

Control Need and Self-Efficacy

A sense of the patient's need or preference for control is useful in anticipating likely responses and in tailoring the intervention to these individual needs. Patients with a very strong need for control will respond well to being left in control. This may be achieved both through indirect methods (discussed below) that allow them to determine their experience, and often through the use of a skills training model (i.e., teaching them to do imagery or self-hypnosis). Some of these patients are so vigilant during inductions that it is helpful to explain the steps before beginning an induction.

At the other extreme are patients who want no control or active participation. Directive approaches may work better and save time with these people. A clinician should be especially alert to a patient who seems passive, but in fact is quite in need of control.

We also consider the patient's level of self-efficacy specific to the pain (Bandura, 1982). That is, we are interested in the person's confidence that he or she can successfully implement mental strategies to produce pain relief. The clinician will assist self-efficacy by expressing confidence in the patient and the method, and by individualizing interventions to match the capabilities of the patient. Self-efficacy can be enhanced by success. Often, beginning with a simple exercise that demonstrates to the patient that his or her mind can influence perceived sensation can build confidence. We focus on developing a sense of control over what can be controlled, when there may be much that is outside of control for many medical patients.

Some fear of being controlled by hypnosis is normal. Fears can be reduced with clear, simple explanations. A clinician can explain that no one can force someone to concentrate or relax. It is the patient who decides whether he or she wants to enter a state of focused attention. We tell patients who are quite worried about being "controlled" that they can stop the experience at any time by merely opening their eyes, and we encourage them to experiment with this. Hypnosis or imagery can help one *gain* a sense of control over problems rather than *lose* control. The more control a patient needs, the more helpful it can be to be indirect—not specifying images the patient will see, but offering options and the suggestion that the patient will know what will make him or her most comfortable. For example: "You may notice your right hand, or it may be your left hand, or it may be neither. What's important is that you are experiencing what's happening right now—that's right, exactly as you are doing."

Family Involvement and Attitudes

If family members are active in the patient's pain problem, their beliefs and attitudes may need to be considered. They can assist or hinder the process of hypnosis or imagery. Ideally, family members support the use of these methods, but leave the responsibility for their use with the patient. Some families may actively discourage interested patients or may convey all of their own fears about these approaches. Alternatively, families may be so invested in the use and success of the method that they badger the patients or leave the patients feeling like failures if enough "success" is not achieved.

When family members are supportive and available, they may be good "coaches" for patients, helping them to use the method when pain escalates and the clinician is not available. We have taught patients and their family members together and assisted the family members in coaching. Scripts can be helpful to ease family members' performance anxiety. Frequently, they are initially quite hesitant, believing that there is something special in the voice or experience of the hypnotherapist. Gentle support and encouragement can often overcome this reluctance.

Religion and Culture

It is important to understand the role of religion and culture in the person's life. If religion is a central determinant of the patient's perspective, it is helpful to ask how the patient imagines God or whether there are religious phrases or images that are particularly soothing for the person. For patients who do incorporate strong positive beliefs into their lives, we readily bring God into the imagery to assist the patients.

Religion can be a powerful facilitator or inhibitor in hypnotic work. In our own and others' experience, some patients reject hypnosis because of their religious beliefs or cultural perspectives (Schafer, 1976). Frequently this rejection includes all forms of imagery and relaxation, because the religion or culture teaches that these methods allow evil forces to take control of the patient's mind (Vandeman, 1973). We have had numerous patients ask members of the clergy whether these methods are safe to use. With these people, we are most likely to suggest that God or their spiritual beliefs be incorporated into the imagery to help them. We never dispute a patient's beliefs, nor do we try to convince people to try these methods if they are uncomfortable for any reason.

Hypnotizability

In the clinical setting, hypnotic susceptibility is rarely directly tested. We actually do not recommend use of a standardized measure, because this can cause a person who scores in the low-hypnotizability range to expect not to benefit from hypnosis. If training is planned for a continuous pain problem, however, it may be useful to have some sense of the patient's susceptibility. Simple questions about absorption provide some clues. For instance, how readily does the patient become deeply absorbed in movies? (Does the patient often forget he or she is in a theater?) Is he or she able to picture favorite places or fantasies easily? Similar questions are available in the absorption test developed by Tellegen and Atkinson (1974). The goal of assessment in this area is to establish the best approach for a patient, rather than to set expectations or to determine whom to treat.

Reassessment

As with any treatment, it is important to reassess the pain and the patient's experience. This should be done very briefly immediately after each session and before the start of each new session until the patient and clinician are comfortable with the patient's response and with the efficacy of the method selected. It is helpful to assess pain level and any observations, discomforts, or preferences of the patient. Once patient and practitioner are assured that the method is appropriate, it is usually best not to reassess pain immediately after a session; this is because assessment brings the patient's attention back to the pain, which the imagery or hypnosis has most likely drawn the person's mind away from. This can decrease comfort and make the patient understandably irritated.

WHAT IS THE INFLUENCE OF THERAPEUTIC RELATIONSHIP AND CLINICIAN STYLE?

Any successful treatment requires a trusting environment. In addition, the clinician must present a calm and confident demeanor, with the expectation that suggestions will be effective. The practitioner communicates this in a caring manner: "I'm not afraid of your pain; I'm here to relieve your pain. Your pain will be relieved." The clinician becomes the guide in whom the patient can confide doubts or fears, without transferring these doubts and fears to the clinician. This is not always easy. Among the most common reasons why practitioners trained in hypnosis do not use the technique more often are their own doubts and fears about whether the method will work. The burden on the clinician to make it work seems very heavy. One way to ease this burden is to adopt all of the confidence expressed above within the framework of an experimenting approach to the problem, without reducing the potential for a "magic" or unexplainable effect. We may say to a patient, "I'm sure we will find something that helps you to be more comfortable. Let's try this and see how it is for you. There are lots of things we can do and ways we can do them, but you might be surprised at how well these can work for you." Thus we suggest that the patient take an experimental attitude, that there is more than one method, but that something will work. We leave room for the patient to decide and tell us what works.

HOW TO CONDUCT HYPNOSIS
OR IMAGERY SESSIONS

Technique is similar across most imagery and hypnosis methods, although the time spent in each step may vary greatly, depending on the needs of the patient and the situation. The first full training session for a continuous or repeated problem usually takes about 90 minutes, including introduction and assessment. For future sessions, less than 30 minutes is adequate for analgesic work unless one is also doing psychotherapy.

The basic framework for conducting hypnosis or imagery is outlined in Table 9.2. We adapt this framework to the duration and intensity of pain, as well as the individual characteristics of a patient. When pain is chronic but mild to moderate, we select a method that teaches self-hypnosis, or we use a skills training model as described below. If pain is severe, concentration is always more of a problem. We are then more likely to use brief inductions and relatively more direct suggestions. Alternatively, we may actively engage the patient in talking with us during the imagery, to keep his or her focus away from the pain more completely. If pain is unpredictable but brief (e.g., severe cramps or a postherpetic neuralgia with intermittent shooting pain), we have the patient describe the quality of the pain, and we select an image with the patient that counters the painful sensation. The patient uses this along with controlled breathing. For procedural pain with significant anxiety, we prefer time to work with the patient prior to the procedure. We can then provide some desensitization, establish rapport, and create trust that the method will help. Next we rehearse a pleasant but physically challenging activity that both counters the pain sensations and maintains active engagement of attention.

Direct versus Indirect Language

Direct approaches instruct the patient in what to do and how to feel (e.g., "Close your eyes and take a deep breath. Let it out slowly and notice . . ."). Indirect methods offer the patient choices from which he or she selects experiences (e.g., "I wonder whether you will notice your right arm feeling heavy, or perhaps it is your left. Perhaps both arms feel heavy. Or is it a feeling of lightness? It really doesn't matter; however it is for you is fine. Just notice how relaxed you can feel"). Indirect wording works when patients might otherwise be saying to themselves, "No, that's not what is happening." These approaches do not rely on the clinician's knowing exactly what the patient experiences.

Data indicate that indirect approaches, both in inductions and analgesic suggestions, are effective for more people than direct suggestions are (Alman & Carney, 1980; J. Barber, 1977, 1980; T. X. Barber, 1969; Fricton & Roth, 1985). On the other hand, with a highly responsive patient, direct suggestions may provide greater effect and can be quicker

TABLE 9.2. Basic Elements of Imagery or Hypnosis

Preliminary requirements:
    Some attention capacity.
    Limited disruptions in the setting (or incorporation of these into induction/imagery).
    Some interest and motivation on the part of the patient.
Step 1: Capture patient's attention.
    Have patient close or focus eyes.
    Have patient focus in the mind, using:
        Breathing
        Simple, repeated image or words
Step 2: Deepen the focus of attention (dissociate focus from the outside world).
    Induce relaxation.
    Count to deepen relaxation with each number.
    Move patient into images of another place.
    Change sensory awareness.
    Maintain intense interest.
Step 3: Recreate patient's pleasant place.
    Represent a situation with words and images.
    Involve all senses:
        Sight (color, shape, light)
        Smell
        Sounds
        Taste
        Touch (texture, softness, warmth)
Step 4: Suggest.
    Suggest images that accomplish goals:
        Comfort, well-being
        Mastery, participation in health
        Numbness, change in sensations
    Make posthypnotic suggestions:
        "You can accomplish these goals any time you choose to."
        Use breathing or another image to anchor this suggestion (e.g., "Take three deep breaths
            and picture this image when you wish to return to this feeling of comfort").
Step 5: Return patient to alertness.
    Count in reverse to return patient to being alert and refreshed.

to administer (Lynn, Neufeld, & Matyi, 1987). We tend to use indirect approaches when we have the time and a patient is not clearly highly responsive. When symptoms are severe or when the patient seems quite responsive and motivated, we use more direct, rapid measures, such as those included in a brief induction (see Appendix 9.2).

Physical Surroundings

For the purposes of teaching a patient hypnosis, the physical surroundings can enhance the experience. Ideally, one teaches the technique in a quiet area, uninterrupted, with the telephone turned off and with the patient in a comfortable chair that supports the head and shoulders. Realistically, it is possible to do very successful hypnosis with the patient in a regular chair or lying in bed. Although quiet is always preferred during the training experiences, in hospital settings interruptions are frequent. If these are incorporated into the induction and imagery, the patient can continue to remain deeply relaxed. For example: "And just allow any sounds to drift by and away, reminding you that it is possible to be so comfortable and far away that it really doesn't matter."

Introducing Hypnosis or Imagery

The clinician must convey the message that the pain is real. We explicitly say this to patients, while briefly and simply explaining the gate control theory (Melzack & Wall, 1965). For instance:

> "Even though the pain message starts in your leg, you won't feel pain unless your brain gets the pain message. The pain message moves along nerves from where the injury is located to the brain. These nerves enter the spinal cord, where they connect to other nerves, which send the information up the spinal cord to the brain. The connections in the spinal cord and brain act like gates. The gates help you to not have to pay attention to all the messages in your body all the time. For example, right now as you are listening, you do not notice the feelings in your legs, although those feelings are there if you choose to notice them. If you are walking, you might notice feelings in your legs but not in your mouth. One way we block the gates to pain is with medications. Or we can block the gates by filling them with other messages. You do this if you hit your elbow and then rub it hard. The rubbing fills the gate with other messages, and you feel less pain. You've done the same thing if you've ever had a headache and you get busy doing something that takes a lot of concentration. You forget about the headache because the gates are full of other messages. Imagery is one way to fill the gate. You can choose to feel the pain if you need to, but any time you like you can fill the gate with certain thoughts or images. Our goal is to find the best gate fillers for you."

Next we continue with the assessment as described above. Finally, we explore patients' most enjoyable places—where they feel safe, calm, perhaps even energized. We ask them what it is about each place that they find most enjoyable. We have had many surprises in identifying pleasant places. It is always important for clinicians to check out any assumptions they might plan to incorporate. For instance, some people are afraid of water; some people have never been to a beach or mountain. Using their own places always allows patients to bring much more of their own imagination to the experience, which makes it more authentic for them.

When we are ready to begin the induction, we explain:

> "What we are about to do is very much like things that happen to all of us all the time when we daydream or focus intently on something. For example, driving from one place to another while you are lost in thought, you don't notice any of the familiar route, yet you arrive safely. If you needed to pay attention, you could bring your mind right back to driving, but in the meantime your mind is far away. In the same way, some people can get so absorbed in a movie that everything around them fades away. It's as if, for a little while, the movie is all that is real. This is like deep relaxation or hypnosis. When you are intensely absorbed in an experience, it is also easier to find relief from pain. Any experience that concentrates your attention away from the body can bring comfort."

We then briefly review the steps the patient can anticipate, as described in Table 9.2.

Induction

The induction phase is a way to establish the attention necessary to shift the patient's focus away from bodily sensations or to transform his or her sensations. The length of this phase depends on how long it takes the patient to enter into a focused state or trance. As we have emphasized throughout this chapter, the unique characteristics and attitudes of the patient should be in large part the determining factors in the clinician's decision about what kind of induction would be most beneficial. Inductions can be as long as 30 minutes, and these are used when the patient is new to the experience (see the script in Appendix 9.1 for an example of a longer induction). Short inductions, which can be as brief as 1 minute, are used when a patient has severe pain. As patients become comfortable with the method and familiar with the trance state, they prefer shorter inductions. Brief inductions are also more effective when a patient does not have the attention span to maintain longer imagery, or if the patient believes in the "magic" of hypnosis, seems relatively high in hypnotizability, and gives a lot of power to the clinician. (See Appendix 9.2.)

Early in the induction, most clinicians suggest that patients may find it easier to close their eyes, if this has not already happened. Closed eyes help patients stay absorbed in their mental experiences. Patients who do not wish to close their eyes may focus on an object or fixed place in the room. Most inductions then have the patients focus on deep, rhythmic breathing. This slows autonomic arousal and begins to reduce tension.

An important component of the induction is "pacing." The clinician needs to attend closely to the patient's responses. The clinician can begin by making a suggestion such as this one:"Just become aware of your breathing . . . you might enjoy taking a deep breath and just noticing how it is to breathe deeply and then let it out slowly." We know that all people breathe, so the clinician is suggesting something the patient is already doing; this is pacing with the patient. Next, the clinician makes a suggestion to take a deep breath, and observes whether or not the patient is following along. The goal, particularly with indirect methods, is to stay with the patient and give suggestions with which the patient cannot disagree or that are close to what the patient is already doing, so that the patient does not think, "Oh, no, that's not what I feel; I must not be hypnotized." Any sharp discordance during the induction between what the clinician says and what the patient experiences will leave a patient less deeply focused. For this reason, indirect permissive methods that provide options but do not dictate experience can be useful.

In a patient's first session, we often teach progressive muscle relaxation as part of the induction (Bernstein & Borkovec, 1973; Schultz & Luthe, 1969). We explain to the patient that a natural response during pain or stress is to tense the muscles around the pain or stress. During the relaxation, warm images that are relaxing, such as the sun or a warm bath or shower, may be added to the relaxation. We next deepen the relaxation and focus, often with counting and an image that begins to move the patient toward his or her favorite place: "You may float on a cloud, or you may go down a staircase, or you may find a special way to get there, or you may simply find yourself there. The important thing is to find yourself in a place that is safe, where you can be entirely at ease." The patient is then ready for any imagery and analgesic suggestions.

For the imagery phase, we most often use patients' favorite places. Sometimes we use places patients have already explained to us, but if we are relatively sure that a patient is comfortable with the procedure, we may leave the location open to the patient's choice at the time. If we wish to make sure patients are still with us, we suggest they lift a finger to signal when they are in this favorite place. For patients with moderate to severe continuous pain, the escape to a comfortable, safe place, as time out from the pain, is as important as direct analgesic suggestions. We find that patients immensely enjoy this time out, and this pleasure makes them more ready to use the method again. When we use only analgesic suggestions, the mental concentration required, without the pleasure, can leave some patients reluctant to use the methods when they feel pain but are also fatigued.

We encourage a patient to move into a pleasant place as follows:

"As you are feeling more relaxed, just allow your mind to go to a very special place—a place where you feel peaceful, tranquil, and safe. It may be a new place, one you have never been to before, or it may be a favorite place going back as far as when you were a child. What's important is that you go to this special place and begin to notice what is around you."

We then make suggestions to facilitate deepening this experience. Suggestions include noticing all the surrounding details; seeing shapes, color, and light; hearing sounds; feeling the air and sun against the face; smelling whatever is in the air; and touching things nearby. We have the patient walk in this place to feel his or her own body as healthy, whole, and knowing how to move and take care of itself even without conscious thought. To take the mind away from moderate to severe pain, we suggest physical activity within the imagery. Often we bring someone else into the imagery. Thus we ask patients whether they can see someone else, someone coming toward them. We suggest they listen to see whether that person has something to say to them that can be helpful—something that can give them what they most need to hear right now.

This entire process can be conducted out loud as a conversation between a patient and a clinician, with the clinician asking questions and the patient filling in the details. This keeps the clinician aware of and able to immediately respond to the patient's experience, while the patient is required to stay deeply involved in the imagery to be able to respond to the questions. We are most likely to use this oral method with patients who have difficulty in creating their own images, or in concentrating on images without tangential thoughts' disrupting their focus. But this method can be effective for anyone.

Analgesic Suggestions

Once patients have enjoyed being in their special place, we bring in analgesic suggestions developed during the assessment of pain qualities. Most often, we use an image of ice placed on the painful area. As the ice melts, the cold is absorbed into the place that hurts until that area is numb or just tingles. Ice works well for several reasons: It is familiar to most people, and ice can be brought into many different pleasant places. In the mountains, snow can be used; at the beach or in a warm cozy house, an ice-cold, refreshing drink can be used, with the ice taken out of the drink and placed where it will help the most. Many other analgesic suggestions are available, as described in Table 9.3. Selecting several of these options and becoming comfortable with using them is far more important than knowing them all. No data indicate that any particular image is more valuable than any other.

Posthypnotic Suggestion

Once comfort has been achieved, posthypnotic suggestions are built into the imagery. We suggest that patients take a picture of their place—both a visual picture and a "feeling" picture of just how they are now. Any time they would like to recapture this feeling of comfort, they need only take a deep, slow breath and take out their mental picture; they can once again feel their bodies relax as the tension flows out and the comfort flows in. And whenever they need it, they can bring in the analgesic image and increase their comfort even more.

TABLE 9.3. Hypnotic Suggestions for Pain Control

Most frequently used:
1. Create escape or distraction by having patient go to a favorite place.
   a. Include action for added intensity or involvement.
   b. Metaphors for dissociation may include flying above or away from the physical sensations.
   Advantages
      Most enjoyable.
      Takes the least effort from an energy-depleted patient.
   Disadvantage
      May provide shorter duration of pain relief.
2. Block pain through suggestions of anesthesia or analgesia.
   a. Use numbness via cold or anesthetic.
   b. Use "flipping switches" in the brain or spinal cord to disconnect pain messages or switch channels.
   Advantages
      Includes a cognitive component the patient can use outside of hypnosis.
      Has potential to extend pain relief past the duration of hypnosis.
   Disadvantages
      Takes more active participation and concentration ability from the patient.
      May require higher hypnotizability to be effective.
3. Sensory transformations.
   a. Have patient go to the pain location and explore it; "open to the pain" instead of pushing it away; and watch as the pain changes (usually it diminishes greatly).
   b. Take the pain description and have patient use an image that can change as pain changes:
      Find the color of pain and change the color.
      Change the intensity of pain (e.g., reduce an "8" to a "3").
      Blow cold Arctic air through a hot burning pain.
      Take a knotted, cramping pain, gather the knot into the fist, and throw it away; or unknot the pain, soften it, and smooth it.
   Advantages
      Takes less energy and goes with the patient's focus of attention instead of fighting it.
      Can be done quickly without lengthy induction, especially for patients with acute-onset, severe pain.
      Can be very effective.
   Disadvantages
      Does not seem to "get rid of the pain."
      Pain may initially seem worse, scaring the patient.

Less often used:
4. Move pain to a smaller or less vulnerable area (e.g., hand).
5. Substitute another feeling for the pain (e.g., itch or pressure).
6. Alter the meaning of the pain to make it less fearful or debilitating (e.g., itch, pressure, or burning is a sign of treatment working; sensations are indications of healing).
7. Increase tolerance of pain or decrease perceived intensity of pain (e.g., use metaphor of dessert: "With each bite you are less aware of the taste. By the 68th taste it isn't bad; you just don't care about the flavor any more. It's just there, but you don't notice").
8. Dissociate the body from the patient's awareness or move the mind out and away from the body.
9. Distort time so it seems to go by very quickly.
10. Suggest amnesia to forget pain and reduce fear of painful recurrences.

Finally, we count patients back to being alert and refreshed. Usually we do this by counting from 5 to 1, with the patients becoming more alert and aware of the present with each number.

Skills Training Model

In cases where patients have a relatively inflexible, vigilant cognitive style, or in situations where pain is long-term and patients need to develop methods for using imagery or hypnosis on their own, we use a skills training model. Patients receive explanations about why the methods work, and they go through an individualized induction with the clinician. They are then given a printed handout (see Appendix 9.3), provided with an audiotape of the session induction, and asked to practice at home. A second session is provided within a week. Problems are considered and addressed, and a second induction is offered and audiotaped. The second session usually has less relaxation and more imagery and suggestion. Again, patients are encouraged to practice on their own, both in quiet and (more briefly) during activities when discomfort may occur. From this point on, sessions are highly individual; the number of sessions and content of suggestions are tailored to the needs of the patient and the circumstances.

Mastery is an important component of any imagery. We always include reminders that these are patients' own experiences; they are the one who have done it, and now that they see how easily it can be done, they will be able to do it again.

In essence, most of our work is "self-hypnosis." We not only conduct hypnosis; we teach the patients to do so as well, so that they can utilize the intervention without the direct guidance of the clinician. This helps medically ill patients gain back some control, when, so often, much control has been taken away from them. Patients are empowered by experiencing their own internal resources—ones they may not have known they had.

HOW CAN INTERVENTIONS BE ADAPTED TO SPECIFIC PATIENT CHARACTERISTICS?

Throughout this chapter, we have talked about the need to adapt interventions to specific needs and other characteristics of the patient. Certain factors are common enough that some planning for how to accommodate them is possible (see Table 9.4 for details). We have already discussed the importance of assessing pain, coping style, control needs, fatigue, and distress, and adapting methods to these features. Age is an important factor that should also be considered. We discuss the use of hypnosis and imagery in work with children here, as an example of how to adapt these interventions to a specific age group.

The controlled clinical trial data on the use of hypnosis or imagery with children confirm that these are successful strategies for assisting with pain control (Broome, Lillis, McGahee, & Bates, 1992). However, most of this efficacy has been demonstrated with acute, procedural pain rather than chronic pain (Jay, Varni, & Elliott, 1987; Katz, Kellerman, & Ellenberg, 1987; Kuttner, 1988). Nonetheless, these methods can be readily adapted to children's chronic pain problems and to self-hypnosis training (Kohen & Olness, 1993). Children often have an easier time than adults do in responding to hypnosis, most likely because of their ready access to imagination and fantasy (T. X. Barber & Calverley, 1963; Olness & Gardner, 1988). Children lack distinct boundaries between fantasy and reality, and consequently can go into hypnosis without formal induction (Kohen & Olness, 1993). Strategies include telling a favorite story or acting out through

TABLE 9.4. Adapting to Specific Patient Characteristics

Characteristic	Suggestions/adaptations
Coping style	
Avoidant	Start with escape images.
Biologically minded	May help to start with progressive muscle relaxation to enhance awareness of physical change.
Support-seeking	Patients may need talk first.
Intense need for control	These patients have most difficulty. Give choice to them for what will work. Use very permissive, indirect approaches.
Action-focused	These patients do well. Extremely action-oriented patients may respond well to progressive muscle relaxation as a first step, so they "feel like they're doing something."
Age	
Elderly	Elderly patients may use fewer coping strategies. They may be less accustomed to using imagination. They may be more open to turning over control to medical providers; therefore, they may respond well to "hypnosis."
Children	Children use imagination easily. They need action, not passive images. Use less formal inductions. Storytelling may be ideal. Children may not close eyes, but still may be very responsive.
Fatigue or severe pain	
First:	Use medications for better pain control. Consider medication options for fatigue/depression.
Then:	Use brief images; little induction is needed. *As appropriate*, use touch on the hand, foot, or shoulder to help the patient focus, to anchor the patient away from the location of the pain, and to provide a competing sensation to the pain. Begin simply; do only what is possible (e.g., breathing with an image of pain description changing; see Table 9.3, "Sensory transformation").
High distress	Patients have difficulty concentrating. They may become more anxious. They need to talk out feelings first. If patients are feeling out of control, give signs that you are in control and believe the situation is manageable. Let them know they can relax because you are in control and will make sure they are OK.

play, then incorporating hypnotic and posthypnotic suggestions for mastery, comfort, and analgesia, always at a language and image level appropriate for the child (Kuttner, 1988). Any child with the ability to attend to and enjoy books or stories is able to respond to imagery. If a child cannot think of a story, the clinician can make one up, or can adapt a child's favorite TV show. Furthermore, the child can help tell the story, and can learn to use analgesic suggestions such as glove analgesia or "pain switches," like light switches, that they can flip off. Children may initially disconcert the clinician because they tend to keep their eyes open and yet can be fully involved in the process. The use of hypnosis for pain control in children is discussed in detail by J. R. Hilgard and LeBaron (1984) and Olness and Gardner (1988).

HOW SHOULD PROBLEMS BE DEALT WITH?

Unanticipated responses can leave a clinician fearful of using hypnosis or imagery again. However, many problems can be solved if a practitioner is ready to adapt to them. In Table 9.5 we list difficulties we have faced more than once, and some solutions that have worked well. Some of these we have already discussed above. Others, such as patients' not using imagery on their own when they have chronic pain problems, are complex issues that need individual evaluation. Sometimes pain improves simply as a result of the sessions with the clinician, and use of self-hypnosis is unnecessary. At other times, methods do not seem effective to patients when they carry them out on their own, or they are reluctant to practice them (as they would be with any homework assignment). Addressing and agreeing on a plan will help both patient and practitioner set realistic expectations.

We have never seen an instance of a patient's crying or becoming agitated that could not be readily resolved with discussion. It is usually possible to check with such patients during the imagery, to see whether they can share their experience and whether they would like to stop or continue. Sometimes patients indicate that crying is simply a release and does not bother them; in this case, we continue with the process and then review the event after completing imagery. Even if patients elect to stop the imagery, they may benefit from sorting out the thoughts or images related to the emotion. A decision can then be made about whether to use the imagery again. It is most important for the clinician to calmly let the patients know that sometimes crying or agitation does occur; it is fine; and the clinician is prepared to deal with it.

Some of the following fears and concerns have also been expressed to us by clinicians:

• "What if a patient falls asleep while in trance?" Many people with chronic pain have sleep disturbances; hypnosis can provide the relaxation needed so that they can have restful sleep. Patients in the hospital or using the methods at home can be instructed simply to continue with a deep, restoring sleep. They can then awaken in the same way they awaken from a nap or a regular night's sleep. For patients who fall asleep in the office or who complain that they always fall asleep when trying to practice at home, and therefore are not benefiting from the analgesic suggestions, several approaches are possible. In the office, it can help for the clinician to raise the tone of his or her voice, and to continue with imagery that is less focused on relaxation and requires more attention or mental action from the patient. For at-home practice, we usually instruct patients to sit up instead of lying down and to select a time of day when they are not too tired. As they are learning to use these methods, we want them to be able to focus without falling asleep.

TABLE 9.5. Problems Encountered in Clinical Practice, and Solutions

Problem	Solutions
Lack of concentration	Use brief images.
	If patient is preoccupied, talk about preoccupations.
	Perhaps try at a later time.
Unsupportive family	Talk to the family.
	Involve the family in helping the patient.
	Help the patient solve the problem.
Not practicing	Review what gets in the way.
	Problem-solve.
	Try to remove guilt or "homework" associations so patient can "claim" the activity, not see it as externally imposed.
Skeptical patient	Encourage an experimenting attitude—"See what happens."
Religious patient	Discuss, but be prepared to defer to patient's beliefs.
	Assure that patient is always in control, can stop at any time.
	Offer an option to observe first.
	Explore whether faith or help of God can be incorporated as a focus of imagery.
Crying, increased anxiety, or other negative effects	Ask whether patient is OK and wants to stop or continue.
	Talk about it; start again if patient is comfortable.
	Have patient open eyes if this feels safer.
Falling asleep	For patients in severe pain with sleep deprivation, encourage to continue with a deep, restful sleep.
	Raise the tone of voice and incorporate suggestions for more active imagery.
	If patients complain of falling asleep during home practice, suggest that they practice sitting up and at a time of day when they are more alert.
Unresponsive patient	Explore whether the patient has control fears.
	Discuss what was experienced.
	Decide if it is worth trying again or if change in method is indicated.
	Reassure the patient that successful hypnosis/imagery often takes practice and gets easier with practice, or that you may need to try several approaches to find the one that works best for him or her.

• "What if the patient does not come out of trance?" This is extremely rare, but it is the clinician's responsibility to ensure that each patient is alert and fully out of hypnosis prior to allowing the patient to leave the office. For highly hypnotizable patients, it is helpful to directly state to them: "You are no longer hypnotized; you are completely alert and out of hypnosis."

• "What if the patient has an extreme reaction?" In rare instances, traumatic material will surface without a lot of warning. This needs to be discussed and worked through, at least to the point at which the patient feels in control of his or her emotions, before the patient leaves. Working through intense emotional material is an important process that can be done through hypnosis, but it is beyond the scope of this chapter to elaborate on that process.

- "What if I can't get the patient hypnotized? That is, what if nothing happens?" These fears lessen as a clinician sets realistic goals and does not promise instant and total relief. Rather, the clinician should express a commitment to do everything possible to relieve the problem, together with a readiness to listen to the patient, to adapt interventions to the patient's style, and to try different approaches until something is helpful.
- "How do I know whether or not the patient was hypnotized?" This is an easy fear to erase if a clinician simply does not care or worry about the state, and instead stays focused on the goal of pain relief.

Clinicians should use the psychological techniques described in this chapter after they have some training and understand the basics of how and why they work and how to respond to some of the common problems discussed above. At the same time, continued practice is the only way to become skilled with these methods. Supervision or consultation can be very helpful when practitioners are learning clinical applications of these techniques.

APPENDIX 9.1. COMFORT AND ANALGESIA SCRIPT

When you are ready to begin, adjust your body so that you can feel as comfortable as possible, as you get ready to become even more relaxed and at ease. At any time you wish, you can make any adjustments or changes to help you feel even more comfortable. All that's important is for you to become as relaxed as you are ready to feel, letting go of any unnecessary tension as we go along, remembering that there is nowhere else you need to be right now, nothing you need to be doing, that this is your time to be here right now. To experience whatever you experience and perhaps to enjoy that experience in whatever way you feel it right now. You may find that at times your mind may wander. If it does, that's fine; just gently bring back your attention to the sound of my voice, knowing that right now there's nothing to bother you and nothing to disturb you, that all you need to do is to listen to the sound of my voice and allow yourself to become as comfortable as you would like to feel right now.

Begin then to focus on your breathing. Really pay attention to what it feels like to breathe in and out, breathing in easily and deeply, holding the breath for a moment and then exhaling fully. And perhaps imagining that as you breathe in, you breathe in comfort and calmness, and as you breathe out, you breathe out discomfort and tension. And you might imagine that with each breath your body becomes twice as relaxed, just breathing in and out, twice as relaxed. And at times you may hear some sounds from outside, and that's all right. You may notice that they don't really make any difference; they are just passing by, becoming part of your whole experience as you continue to focus inward, on your breathing and on the growing sense of comfort and calmness, just breathing in comfort and calmness, breathing out tension and discomfort, allowing yourself to be soothed by the steady rhythm of your breathing, in and out, with nothing to bother you and nothing to disturb you.

And as you enjoy this increasing sense of comfort, you may want to imagine a pleasant warmth beginning to spread through your body. Perhaps it's the warmth of a bath, or the sun, or another warmth you enjoy. Soaking that warmth into your muscles as you soften all the parts of your body, one after another. First the warmth over the top of your head, softening the muscles of your scalp, moving down through your forehead into all the small muscles of your eyes. Feeling all those small muscles as they soften and relax in the warmth. Allowing that feeling to absorb and relax the muscles of the cheeks and jaw and even the tongue. Feeling that flow of warmth moving down through your neck and into your shoulders, smoothing the muscles and increasing your sense of comfort . . . the warmth continuing down into the right arm into the palm and through each finger. Then the left arm into the palm of the hand and fingers, feeling as the tension just flows away, as the warmth takes its place. And now the warmth spreading into your upper body, through your chest and abdomen and down through your back, soothing and comforting all the muscles there.

That warmth flowing freely and easily down through the top of your legs, through your lower legs and into the feet and toes. Enjoying that warmth as it fills your whole body now, soothing and calming. Letting all the tension flow away, leaving only a feeling of comfort. Take a moment now to notice if there is any part of your body that you want to be more comfortable . . . and if there is, go to that area and focus your breathing on it, imagining breathing through that place, the breath moving through each cell, gently blowing away tightness and discomfort, just watching as the sensations change, finding all the nooks and crannies of concern or tension and watching as the peacefulness takes their place.

As you continue to enjoy this pleasant sense of ease, begin counting to yourself from 100 to 99, seeing each number in front of you, and with each number feeling twice as relaxed as before, seeing 98 and 97, twice as relaxed, 96, perhaps the numbers hardly matter any more, finding yourself comfortable and as deeply relaxed as you'd like to feel right now, with an increased sense of peace and well-being that you feel when your body and mind are in tune and at ease, when you feel in charge of your own well-being.

And as you enjoy this feeling of deep comfort and well-being, allow yourself to begin to create a special place of your choosing. A place where you feel safe and secure and content. It may be a place you've been before, it may be a place you'd like to go now, or a place only in your imagination. All that matters is that you find a place for you right now. And begin to notice that place. Notice if it is indoors or out. Observe what is all around you now. Take it in. Notice the colors, the different hues and tones of color. Perhaps there are reds or yellows, I'm certain somewhere there may be greens, and notice how many different greens are still green. The light and the dark shades, the light around you as it moves and changes.

Explore the shapes in your surroundings . . . perhaps you can reach out and touch things, notice what they feel like . . . are they soft or hard, rough or smooth, warm or cool? Making it all real for you now, enjoying being in this pleasant, safe place, experiencing it fully. And I wonder if you might be surprised by any of the smells in the air . . . perhaps the smells of life or energy or freshness, just taking a moment to smell the air and feel the air against your skin . . . notice if it is cool or warm or perhaps a bit of both . . . warmth from the sun or something else cool from the fresh air. It doesn't really matter what it is; whatever is there is just fine. And maybe you can allow yourself to enjoy this fresh air as it refreshes your face and body. Taking in a deep cleansing breath, feeling the comforting coolness. And notice whether you can find something icy cold nearby. You may need to move around or look about you. It may be a refreshing drink with ice, or perhaps even the cold of snow or a different cold.

But wherever it is, however it is for you, just explore that feeling of cold in your hand. As you hold it, notice how the sensations change. First cold, then perhaps tingly or maybe numb, no feeling at all. You might even be curious to put that icy cold on a part of your body where you sometimes feel discomfort and notice how the feelings change. Gradually the coldness seeps in . . . a tingling feeling, perhaps . . . and then the feelings become less intense, perhaps even becoming numb or no feeling at all. However it is for you, just less noticeable or less bothersome, just cool sensations around the edges perhaps, but soothing cool.

And you can hold this coolness there for as long as you like. And know that whenever you would like to come back to this comfort or numbness, you need only to close your eyes, take a deep breath, see this place in your mind, and bring back the feeling of fresh air in your face. Then you can bring this icy cool to any place on your body as you allow the sensations to change and you become more and more comfortable. And you might even be surprised at how easy this becomes for you.

And you can continue now to carry these feelings of comfort and ease with you as you move through the next hours or even the next days. Knowing that they are of your own creation, that these abilities to find greater comfort and health are within yourself. Realizing perhaps your own abilities to create or to change your experience. You might even notice that you are sometimes surprised with your own strength and competence, how much you can do with very little thought, and how easy it can be to stay comfortable. Take a moment now to remind yourself of what your body needs to be as healthy as possible. And then begin once again to focus on your breathing, bringing with you these feelings of increased peacefulness and comfort and strength.

And in a moment I will begin to count from 5 to 1. And as I do, you can gradually come back to being aware of your surroundings, preparing to feel alert and refreshed and energized. Still relaxed, but ready to continue with what you choose to do with this day. So when you open your eyes, you can feel refreshed and comfortable . . . fully alert. And now, 5, 4, beginning to be more alert, aware of the sounds of the world around you, 3, taking in a deep refreshing breath, 2, moving your muscles to feel the blood flow, stretching your arms, legs, feet, feeling aware of your body again, and 1, opening your eyes when you are fully ready, alert, refreshed, energized. Make sure that you are fully alert and awake now as you continue with the rest of your day.

APPENDIX 9.2. BRIEF INDUCTION

Brief induction is for patients who are (1) responsive to hypnosis; (2) highly motivated with moderate to severe symptoms, and/or (3) experienced and wish to have more rapid inductions to the hypnotic state. Numerous methods are available; these share similarities of focusing on the eyes, breathing, brief counting and letting the hand float or become heavy. The entire session can take a few minutes. This method can be taught to patients as an induction to self-hypnosis, or can be used by the clinician prior to introducing suggestions for comfort and analgesia.

Induction: We will count from 1 to 3. One, look up with your eyes as far as you can without moving your head. Up, up, that's right. Two, slowly close your eyelids, keep your eyes up, while you take a deep breath. Good. Three, as you let the breath out, let your eyes relax and let your body feel twice as relaxed. Fine. Now I will raise your hand. [Hold the hand about a foot off the lap. If self-hypnosis is being taught, patient can raise his or her own hand.] Let your hand feel very heavy, as if bricks are attached to it. That's right, very heavy. [Wait until the arm and hand loosen and relax. Give more suggestion if needed: "Very heavy, as if it's just too much trouble to hold it up, as if a huge weight is on it."] Now, as your arm drops to your lap you can feel twice as relaxed as before, deeply comfortable and relaxed.

Next, add imagery or suggestions to accomplish goals.

APPENDIX 9.3. INSTRUCTIONS FOR LEARNING
RELAXATION WITH IMAGERY

These printed instructions may be given to patients along with audiotapes for home practice.

You can relax and take your mind to an enjoyable, comfortable place. This is an extremely powerful way of reducing pain, tension, anger, fear, and frustration. Emotions often accompany physical discomforts and make them worse.

Deep relaxation is a skill that needs *practice*. With practice now, you will be able to relax when and where you want to. You might even be surprised at how well you can use relaxation to increase feelings of well-being and comfort at any time.

A Three-Step Method of Relaxation

A three-step method of deep relaxation is described below. Patients tell us that the individual steps can each be helpful at different times, so you will want to practice each one. When you wish to really take a break and feel better, you can put all three steps together.

Step 1—Deep Breathing

Deep breathing quickly sends a signal to your entire body to relax. Whenever you notice some tension in your body, or your emotions are in turmoil, you can use these steps:

    a. Make your *position* (sitting, lying or standing) as comfortable as you can.

    b. Deeply *inhale* through your nose while counting slowly to 4.

    c. As you inhale, pull the oxygen into your abdomen, then through your entire chest and upward to your shoulders. Notice your chest moving up and your shoulders moving back as you breathe in deeply.

    d. *Hold your breath* for a few moments.

    e. *Exhale* through your mouth, making a relaxing, whooshing sound like the wind as you blow out to a slow count of 4.

    f. As you exhale, let your breath go from the bottom of your abdomen up through your chest and all the way up to your shoulders. Notice your chest moving down and your shoulders moving forward as you breathe out all the air.

    g. Imagine all the tension from your body being pulled into your lungs and being exhaled with your breath.

    h. Continue breathing deeply for several minutes.

    i. Scan your body for any area that may remain tense. Focus on this area and imagine breathing directly in and out of this area.

    j. When you have learned to relax yourself using deep breathing, practice it whenever and wherever you feel yourself getting tense.

Step 2—Muscle Relaxation

By relaxing your muscles one group at a time, you can relax your whole body. This is usually easier than trying to relax your whole body all at once. When you relax your muscles, start at the top of your head and move your attention to each muscle group. For example, you might relax in the following order:

    Forehead, eyes, cheeks, and tongue
    Neck
    Shoulders
    Right arm and hand
    Left arm and hand
    Chest
    Abdomen
    Right leg and foot
    Left leg and foot

There are two common ways to relax these muscles:

    a. Tense the muscle (not so much that it hurts, but enough to feel the tension). Let the tension go and feel the relaxation move in.

    b. Bring your attention to the muscle and relax it while imagining tension draining away. Imagine the muscle as heavy and warm, or use another image that substitutes relaxation for tension.

Step 3—Imagery

Imagery is simply picturing something in your mind, using shapes, colors, sounds, thoughts—anything that helps you to feel like you are there. In a relaxed state, your mind is most open to imagery. Imagery can also be a fun way to relax. You can use it just to take your mind away from its worries for a while, and even to feel more in charge of what is happening to your body. Imagery can last just long enough to give you a clear, positive picture in your mind, or it can last for 30 minutes of deep relaxation. There are lots of ways to do imagery. There is no right or wrong way.

Here are a few tips from people who have used imagery successfully:

a. Don't put any pressure on yourself to come up with images. Instead, just let your mind wander across memories of places you've enjoyed or places that seem like they would be enjoyable, safe, and relaxing.

b. Allow yourself to experiment with all your senses—sight, smell, taste, touch, and sound. Allow the imagery to be as real and involving as you can. See the shapes, colors, light. Feel the air. Touch objects and notice if they are smooth, hard, soft, fuzzy, warm. Notice if there are any tastes or scents. Is anything moving? Are other people there, or do you prefer to be alone? Listen to the sounds. Change any parts you would like to be different.

c. Allow yourself to develop images to use at different times. You might see yourself going through something difficult, doing well and feeling calm. You might see yourself finished with something difficult, feeling strong and looking back on how well you did.

d. It's normal for your mind to wander. Sometimes it is just a sign that you are relaxing. Gently bring your mind back to the imagery. Do whatever works for you, and don't be afraid to try a new idea if you find something isn't working.

e. When you are ready to stop, give yourself time to become alert, take a deep breath, and stretch your muscles.

Images that I will try:

_____

_____

A Few More Thoughts about Relaxing and Using Imagery

With practice, you will be able to relax quickly even in difficult situations. Practice at least once a day with a tape or on your own. Find a comfortable, quiet place and go through your relaxation with imagery.

Here are the steps for doing relaxation and imagery on your own:

1. Breathe deeply to start relaxing and to focus your attention.
2. Allow your muscles to relax, from the top of your head to the bottom of your feet.
3. Take your mind to a favorite place, using all your senses. Feel your body as comfortable, strong, and healthy in that place.
4. Take a few deep breaths and stretch to bring your attention back to the present.

This is a special time for you, a time out from all of your usual responsibilities and concerns. Give yourself that 20 minutes each day.

ACKNOWLEDGMENTS

This work was supported by the following grants from the National Cancer Institute: No. CA38552, No. CA57807, and No. CA63030.

REFERENCES

Alman, B. M., & Carney, R. E. (1980). Consequences of direct and indirect suggestions on success of posthypnotic behavior. *American Journal of Clinical Hypnosis, 23,* 112–118.

Bandura, A. (1982). Self-efficacy mechanism in human agency. *American Psychologist, 37,* 122–147.

Barber, J. (1977). Rapid induction analgesia: A clinical report. *American Journal of Clinical Hypnosis, 19,* 138–147.

Barber, J. (1980). Hypnosis and the unhypnotizable. *American Journal of Clinical Hypnosis, 23,* 4–9.

Barber, T. X. (1969). *Hypnosis: A scientific approach.* New York: Van Nostrand Reinhold.

Barber, T. X., & Calverley, D. S. (1963). "Hypnotic-like" suggestibility in children. *Journal of Abnormal and Social Psychology, 66,* 589–597.

Bernstein, D. A., & Borkovec, T. D. (1973). *Progressive relaxation training: A manual for the helping professions.* Champaign, IL: Research Press.

Broome, M. E., Lillis, P. P., McGahee, T. W., & Bates, T. (1992). The use of distraction and imagery with children during painful procedures. *Oncology Nursing Forum, 19,* 499–502.

Cleeland, C. S., & Syrjala, K. L. (1992). How to assess cancer pain. In D. C. Turk & R. Melzack (Eds.), *Handbook of pain assessment* (pp. 362–387). New York: Guilford Press.

Crasilneck, H. B. (1979). Hypnosis in control of chronic low back pain. *American Journal of Clinical Hypnosis, 22,* 71–78.

Crasilneck, H. B., & Hall, T. A. (1985). *Clinical hypnosis: Principles and applications* (2nd ed.). New York: Grune & Stratton.

Diamond, M. (1984). It takes two to tango: The neglected importance of the hypnotic relationship. *American Journal of Clinical Hypnosis, 26,* 1–13.

Erickson, M. H. (1959). Hypnosis in painful terminal illness. *American Journal of Clinical Hypnosis, 1,* 117–122.

Fernandez, E., & Turk, D. C. (1989). The utility of cognitive coping strategies for altering pain perception: A meta-analysis. *Pain, 38,* 123–135.

Fricton, J. R., & Roth, P. (1985). The effects of direct and indirect hypnotic suggestions for analgesia in high and low susceptible subjects. *American Journal of Clinical Hypnosis, 27,* 226–231.

Frischholz, E. J., Spiegel, D., Spiegel, H., Balma, D. L., & Markell, C. S. (1981). Differential hypnotic responsivity of smokers, phobics, and chronic pain. *Journal of Abnormal Psychology, 91,* 269–272.

Hendler, C. S., & Redd, W. H. (1986). Fear of hypnosis: The role of labeling in patients' acceptance of behavioral interventions. *Behavior Therapy, 17,* 2–13.

Hilgard, E. R., & Hilgard, J. R. (1965). *Hypnotic susceptibility.* New York: Harcourt, Brace & World.

Hilgard, E. R., & Hilgard, J. R. (1983). *Hypnosis in the relief of pain* (rev. ed.). Los Altos, CA: William Kaufmann.

Hilgard, J. R., & LeBaron, S. (1984). *Hypnotherapy of pain in children with cancer.* Los Altos, CA: William Kaufmann.

Jay, S. M., Varni, J. W., & Elliott, C. (1987). Acute and chronic pain in adults and children with cancer. *Journal of Consulting and Clinical Psychology, 54,* 601–607.

Kabat-Zinn, J., Lipworth, L., & Burney, R. (1985). The clinical use of mindfulness meditation for the self-regulation of chronic pain. *Journal of Behavioral Medicine, 8,* 163–190.

Katz, E. R., Kellerman, J., & Ellenberg, L. (1987). Hypnosis in the reduction of acute pain and distress in children with cancer. *Journal of Pediatric Psychology, 12,* 379–394.

Kohen, D. P., & Olness, K. (1993). Hypnotherapy with children. In J. W. Rhue, S. J. Lynn, & I. Kirsch (Eds.), *Handbook of clinical hypnosis* (pp. 357–381). Washington, DC: American Psychological Association.

Kuttner, L. (1988). Favorite stories: A hypnotic pain-reduction technique for children in acute pain. *American Journal of Clinical Hypnosis, 30,* 289–295.

Lynn, S. J., Neufeld, V., & Matyi, C. L. (1987). Inductions versus suggestions: Effects of direct and indirect wording on hypnotic responding and experience. *Journal of Abnormal Psychology, 96,* 76–79.

McCaul, K. D., & Malott, J. M. (1984). Distraction and coping with pain. *Psychological Bulletin, 95,* 516–533.

McCauley, J. D., Thelen, M. H., Frank, R., Willard, R., & Callen, K. (1983). Hypnosis compared to relaxation in the outpatient management of chronic low back pain. *Archives of Physical Medicine and Rehabilitation, 64,* 548–552.

McGlashan, T. H., Evans, F. J., & Orne, M. T. (1969). The nature of hypnotic analgesia and the placebo response to experimental pain. *Psychosomatic Medicine, 31,* 227–246.

Melzack, R., & Wall, P. D. (1965). Pain mechanisms: A new theory. *Science, 50,* 971–979.

Olness, K., & Gardner, G. G. (1988). *Hypnosis and hypnotherapy with children* (2nd ed.). New York: Grune & Stratton.

Olness, K., MacDonald, J., & Uden, D. (1987). Prospective study comparing propanolol, placebo, and hypnosis in the management of juvenile migraine. *Pediatrics, 79,* 593–597.

Orne, M. T. (1959). The nature of hypnosis: Artifact and essence. *Journal of Abnormal and Social Psychology, 58,* 277–299.

Patterson, D. R., Everett, J. J., Burns, G. L., & Marvin, J. A. (1992). Hypnosis for the treatment of burn pain. *Journal of Consulting and Clinical Psychology, 60,* 713–717.

Patterson, D. R., Questad, K. A., & DeLateur, B. J. (1989). Hypnotherapy as an adjunct to narcotic analgesia for the treatment of pain for burn debridement. *American Journal of Clinical Hypnosis, 31,* 156–163.

Price, D. D., & Barber, J. (1987). An analysis of factors that contribute to the efficacy of hypnotic analgesia. *Journal of Abnormal Psychology, 96,* 46–51.

Sacerdote, P. (1965). Additional contributions to the hypnotherapy of the advanced cancer patient. *American Journal of Clinical Hypnosis, 7,* 308–319.

Sacerdote, P. (1970). Theory and practice of pain control in malignancy and other protracted or recurring painful illnesses. *International Journal of Clinical and Experimental Hypnosis, 18,* 160–180.

Sachs, L. B., Feuerstein, M., & Vitale, J. H. (1977). Hypnotic self-regulation of chronic pain. *American Journal of Clinical Hypnosis, 20,* 106–113.

Schafer, D. W. (1976). Patients' reactions to hypnosis on a burn unit. In F. H. Frankel & H. S. Zamansky (Eds.), *Hypnosis at its bicentennial: Selected papers* (pp. 229–235). New York: Plenum Press.

Schultz, J. H., & Luthe, W. (1969). *Autogenic therapy* (Vol. 1). New York: Grune & Stratton.

Shor, R. E., & Orne, E. C. (1962). *The Harvard Group Scale of Hypnotic Susceptibility, Form A.* Palo Alto, CA: Consulting Psychologists Press.

Spanos, N. P., Kennedy, S. K., & Gwynn, M. I. (1984). Moderating effects of contextual variables on the relationship between hypnotic susceptibility and suggested analgesia. *Journal of Abnormal Psychology, 93,* 285–294.

Spanos, N. P., Radtke-Bodorik, H. L., Ferguson, J. D., & Jones, B. (1979). The effects of hypnotic susceptibility, suggestions for analgesia, and the utilization of cognitive strategies on the reduction of pain. *Journal of Abnormal Psychology, 88,* 282–292.

Spanos, N. P., Radtke, H. L., Hodgins, D. C., Stam, H. J., & Bertrand, L (1983). The Carleton University Responsiveness to Suggestion Scale: Normative data and psychometric properties. *Psychological Reports, 53,* 523–535.

Spanos, N. P., Robertson, L. A., Menary, E. P., & Brett, P. J. (1986). Component analysis of cognitive skill training for the enhancement of hypnotic susceptibility. *Journal of Abnormal Psychology, 95,* 350–357.

Spiegel, D. (1985). The use of hypnosis in controlling cancer pain. *CA: A Cancer Journal for Clinicians, 35,* 221–231.

Spiegel, D., & Bloom, J. R. (1983). Group therapy and hypnosis reduce metastatic breast carcinoma pain. *Psychosomatic Medicine, 45,* 333–339.

Spiegel, H., & Spiegel, D. (1978). *Trance and treatment: Clinical uses of hypnosis.* New York: Basic Books.

Sthalekar, H. A. (1993). Hypnosis for relief of chronic phantom pain in a paralysed limb: A case study. *Australian Journal of Clinical Hypnotherapy and Hypnosis, 14,* 75–80.

Suls, J., & Fletcher, B. (1985). The relative efficacy of avoidant and nonavoidant coping strategies: A meta-analysis. *Health Psychology, 4,* 249–288.

Syrjala, K. L., Cummings, C., & Donaldson, G. (1992a). Hypnosis or cognitive behavioral training for the reduction of pain and nausea during cancer treatment: A controlled clinical trial. *Pain, 48,* 137–146.

Syrjala, K. L., Danis, B., Abrams, J. R., & Keenan, R. (1992b). *Coping skills for bone marrow transplantation.* Seattle, WA: Fred Hutchinson Cancer Research Center.

Syrjala, K. L., Donaldson, G. W., Davis, M. W., Kippes, M. E., & Carr, J. E. (1995). Relaxation and imagery and cognitive-behavioral training reduce pain during cancer treatment: A controlled clinical trial. *Pain, 63*(2), 189–198.

Tellegen, A., & Atkinson, G. (1974). Openness to absorbing and self-altering experiences ("absorption"), a trait related to hypnotic susceptibility. *Journal of Abnormal Psychology, 83,* 268–277.

Turner, J. A., Deyo, R. A., Loeser, J. D., VonKorff, M., & Fordyce, W. E. (1994). The importance of placebo effects in pain treatment and research. *Journal of the American Medical Association, 271,* 1609–1614.

Turner, J. A., & Jensen, M. P. (1993). Efficacy of cognitive therapy for chronic low back pain. *Pain, 52,* 169–177.

Turner, J. A., & Romano, J. M. (1990). Psychologic and psychosocial evaluation. In J. J. Bonica (Ed.), *The management of pain* (2nd ed., pp. 595–609). Philadelphia: Lea & Febiger.

Vandeman, G. E. (1973). *Psychic roulette.* Mountain View, CA: Pacific Press.

Wadden, T. A., & Anderton, C. H. (1982). The clinical use of hypnosis. *Psychological Bulletin, 91,* 215–243.

Weitzenhoffer, A. M., & Hilgard, E. R. (1959). *Stanford Hypnotic Susceptibility Scale, Forms A and B.* Palo Alto, CA: Consulting Psychologists Press.

CHAPTER 10

Group Therapy for Patients with Chronic Pain

Francis J. Keefe
Pat M. Beaupré
Karen M. Gil

Pain is a private experience that has important social consequences. Knowing that someone is experiencing pain changes the way others treat and respond to that person. The social responses to pain, in turn, can affect how the individual copes with pain. Individuals who receive support and encouragement for their attempts to remain active and involved in life despite persistent pain often have less severe pain and a better ability to tolerate pain. Conversely, individuals whose access to support and attention is limited only to the times they are having difficulty coping with pain often have high levels of pain and are much more disabled.

Given that pain occurs in a social context, it is not surprising that psychologists have emphasized the utility of group therapy approaches in helping patients learn to cope with persistent and disabling pain. Group therapy approaches have many advantages. First, a group provides a setting in which chronic pain patients can be exposed to other individuals with similar problems, and can learn that they are not alone in experiencing behavioral and psychological problems. Second, group therapy can help patients gain a much better understanding of pain and the role that their own behavior, thoughts, and feelings can play in influencing pain. Finally, group therapy can teach patients more effective coping skills and provide concrete demonstrations of how one can use these skills to deal with difficult situations such as pain flare-ups.

Over the past decade, group therapy has emerged as one of the major forms of psychological treatment for persistent pain. Controlled research studies evaluating the efficacy of group therapy interventions have been conducted with patients suffering from low back pain (Turner & Clancy, 1988; Nicholas, Wilson, & Goyen, 1991), rheumatoid arthritis (Bradley et al., 1987; Parker et al., 1988), and osteoarthritis (Keefe et al., 1990). These studies have demonstrated that group therapy can significantly reduce pain and improve the functioning of many patients with chronic pain.

Although there is an emerging research literature on the efficacy of group therapy for pain patients, practical information on how to conduct such groups is not widely available. The purpose of this chapter is to address this need. The chapter is divided into three sections. The first section discusses three types of group therapy used in the management of chronic pain: behavior change groups, patient education groups, and social support groups. The second section provides an overview of the methods used in a cognitive-behavioral pain management group. This section addresses such practical topics as providing a rationale for group therapy, training in pain coping skills, and methods for helping patients maintain treatment gains. The third section of this chapter focuses on important clinical issues in conducting group therapy with patients having chronic pain.

BASIC APPROACHES TO GROUP THERAPY
FOR CHRONIC PAIN

Group therapy approaches for chronic pain typically focus on one of three major goals: (1) fostering behavior change, (2) educating patients about their pain or disease, or (3) providing social support. The specific goal is important in determining the basic format and structure of the group, the types of patients treated, and the level of training required for group therapists.

Behavior Change Groups

Behavior change groups are based on the assumption that with instruction and practice, patients will be able to acquire and maintain a new set of coping behaviors that will help them reduce their pain and improve their day-to-day functioning. The groups are structured to facilitate the learning of these behaviors. They are typically small (six to nine patients) and provide patients with many opportunities for practice and feedback. Behavior change groups are usually scheduled so that all patients start and end treatment together. Treatment is short-term (8 to 10 weeks) and focuses on acquisition of a variety of behavioral and cognitive pain coping skills. The format is structured and emphasizes instruction, rehearsal, and practice with pain coping skills. Therapists usually follow a treatment manual that provides details on the methods to be used in each session.

Patients who are most appropriate for therapy groups focused on behavior change are those who accept the fact that their pain is likely to persist, and who are willing to learn new pain management skills. Since most groups use written materials and require patients to keep home diary records of practice, an ability to read and write is necessary. Patients who lack formal education can also benefit from these groups if arrangements are made to assist them with written assignments. Behavior change groups are often made up of individuals having a similar duration of pain (e.g., chronic) and a similar type of pain problem (e.g., back pain or headaches). This increases the likelihood that patients will share common problems and issues in managing pain.

Behavioral and cognitive-behavioral group therapy interventions are typically led by PhD-level psychologists with a background in pain management. This high level of training is necessary because of the fact that many of the interventions focus on changing long-standing behaviors and beliefs, which may be tied to complex and emotionally difficult issues.

Evidence for the effectiveness of cognitive-behavioral and behavioral group therapy interventions for chronic pain is strong. Studies have shown that these group therapy approaches can reduce pain and improve functional status significantly, compared to control conditions (Turner & Clancy, 1988; Bradley et al., 1987; Keefe et al., 1990). Recent studies suggest that patients who show the greatest increases in the use and perceived effectiveness of cognitive and behavioral pain coping skills over the course of group therapy are likely to have the best outcomes (Keefe et al., 1990; Parker et al., 1989).

Patient Education Groups

Group therapy interventions can also focus primarily on educating patients about their pain or disease. The basic assumption underlying this approach is that information can lead to improved knowledge and a much better adjustment to persistent pain. A good example of group therapy approaches to patient education is Lorig and colleagues' early research on arthritis pain (Lorig, Lubeck, Kraines, Seleznick, & Holman, 1985). Lorig et al. developed a six-session educational course, called the Arthritis Self-Help Group, designed to provide basic information about arthritis and its treatment. The course used a small-group format. Each session included a didactic lecture presentation and opportunities for group discussion. Visual aids and handouts were used to supplement the lecture material. The course leaders included not only nurses and other health professionals, but also laypersons who themselves suffered from arthritis. Topics covered in the course included the nature of arthritis, methods of diagnosis, medical and surgical treatments, and home remedies. Participants were given tests before and after the completion of the group sessions, to evaluate improvements in their knowledge about arthritis. The Arthritis Self-Help Group materials are available through the Arthritis Foundation and have been widely used to set up educational groups in community settings.

Patient education groups are used with a wide range of patients. Patient education interventions are often used with patients whose pain is related to a disease such as arthritis or cancer. Since the focus is on information rather than behavior change, a lower level of patient motivation may be required. Patients must, however, be willing to attend sessions on a regular basis.

Patient education interventions have traditionally been conducted by nurses. As noted above, Lorig et al. (1985) successfully used laypeople suffering from arthritis as educational group therapists. Research is needed to assess the relative effectiveness of trained nurses and laypersons as therapists leading patient education groups.

Patient education groups are widely employed in medical settings. Evidence for the efficacy of these groups is limited. Most studies show that although they are effective in increasing patients' knowledge, the improvements in knowledge that are achieved often fail to correspond to improvements in pain and functional status (Daltroy & Liang, 1988; Goeppinger, Arthur, Baglioni, Brunk, & Brunner, 1989). On the basis of these findings, Lorig and her colleagues have begun incorporating behavioral and cognitive-behavioral interventions into their patient education courses (Holman, Mazonson, & Lorig, 1989). These more comprehensive group therapy protocols appear to be more effective than patient information group sessions alone.

Social Support Groups

Group therapy interventions for chronic pain may also have increasing social support as their primary goal. Social support groups are based on the idea that many individuals having chronic pain feel isolated and alone in coping with pain, and may benefit from the support and encouragement of others in the same situation.

Informal social support groups for chronic pain sufferers are available in many communities. The format for these groups varies widely, but typically it is much less structured than that for cognitive-behavioral or educational group therapy approaches. Although there may be a brief didactic component, most of each group session is devoted to discussion of participants' experiences in coping with pain. Group leaders are typically individuals with chronic pain. Their role is often intentionally limited to administrative issues (e.g., identifying a meeting place, scheduling sessions), in order that they can still participate as regular group members. Leadership of the group may change from session to session, so that one individual does not have primary responsibility for the group. Support group sessions may be scheduled weekly or monthly, with the number of sessions varying widely across groups. The group sessions are typically open, with patients free to participate in as many or as few sessions as they like.

There are two national self-help organizations that provide materials to individuals wishing to start their own support group for chronic pain: (1) the American Chronic Pain Association (P.O. Box 850, Rocklin, California 95677), and (2) the National Chronic Pain Outreach Association (7979 Old Georgetown Road, Suite 100, Bethesda, Maryland 20814).

The research literature on social support groups for chronic pain is sparse. One of the few controlled treatment outcome studies to include a social support therapy condition noted that this therapy did reduce psychological distress in chronic pain patients (Bradley et al., 1987). The efficacy of social support groups in reducing pain and disability in chronic pain patients has yet to be determined, however.

A PRACTICAL GUIDE TO COGNITIVE-BEHAVIORAL
GROUP THERAPY FOR PAIN MANAGEMENT

A number of practical issues need to be addressed in carrying out group therapy for patients with chronic pain. These issues include getting the group started, helping patients cope with their pain, and developing a plan to help patients maintain progress once group therapy has ended. In this section, we draw on our experience with cognitive-behavioral group therapy to address these practical issues.

Screening Patients for Group Therapy

Patients with chronic pain differ in terms of their ability to benefit from group therapy. It is important to interview patients to determine whether they are appropriate candidates for group therapy. Patients who do best in cognitive-behavioral group therapy are those who are willing to attend group sessions regularly and to take an active role in their own pain management. Those who have behavioral problems (e.g., inactivity, excessive dependence on others) or emotional problems (e.g., anxiety, depression) that can serve as targets for group therapy efforts also tend to respond well. Patients who are extremely angry and hostile are inappropriate for group therapy. These patients often ruminate about their negative experiences with medical personnel and can monopolize group sessions. They often fail to respond to corrective feedback from therapists or group members. Severely depressed patients are also poor candidates for group therapy. These individuals are often so withdrawn that they are unable to interact in the group setting. Some chronic pain patients have extreme fears of social situations, particularly groups, and are thus better treated through individual therapy. Patients with low levels of intelligence have difficulty with the cognitive therapy components of group therapy. Nevertheless, we have found that many individuals with limited formal education benefit substantially from cognitive-behavioral group therapy. These individuals sometimes require additional assistance during and after the group sessions to maximize their response, but when they are provided with such assistance, they often respond quite positively.

During the initial screening interview, a careful behavioral assessment of the patient's pain problems should be carried out. Keefe (1988) has previously discussed the basic elements of cognitive-behavioral interviewing for patients having persistent pain. These elements include (1) an assessment of the intensity, location, and quality of the patient's pain; (2) identification of factors that increase or decrease pain; (3) a review of the patient's family and work activities, to examine patterns of pain and well behaviors; (4) an assessment of cognitive factors, such as beliefs about pain (e.g., "My pain is a punishment for my actions"), irrational cognitions (e.g., "Because I have pain, I am a worthless individual"), and negative expectations (e.g., "The future is hopeless"); and (5) an analysis of affective responses that may be contributing to pain (e.g., depression, anxiety, or guilt). The behavioral interview provides the group therapist with an indication of the cognitive and behavioral problems experienced by the patient. These problems can then be targeted for intervention in group therapy.

As part of the screening process, each patient should be provided with a basic description of the group. Information should be given on the number of participants, frequency of sessions, and basic goals of the group. In addition, the therapist should highlight how the group can help the patient with his or her specific problems in coping with pain.

Structure of the Group

Cognitive-behavioral group therapy can be structured in a variety of ways. When setting up a group, one is faced with decisions about the number, length, and timing of sessions; the size of the group; whether the group is to be open to new members or closed; and the training of therapists.

Most cognitive-behavioral groups are relatively short in duration (e.g., 6 to 12 sessions). Sessions are usually 1½ to 2 hours in duration. We typically schedule sessions once a week for outpatients and once a day for inpatients or outpatients who are enrolled in intensive daily treatment programs. We recommend running the sessions late in the day (e.g., 4 to 6 P.M.), because it provides group leaders with an opportunity to review how patients have applied pain coping methods earlier in the day. We typically conduct groups of four to eight patients. When fewer than four patients are enrolled, the cohesiveness of the group may be threatened if a patient misses a session; when there are more than eight patients in a group, it is usually difficult to provide enough time for individualized skills rehearsal and feedback.

Cognitive-behavioral group therapy typically uses a closed-group format, in which all patients start and complete the group together. The description of group therapy methods below is based on such a format. However, we have also found that this type of group therapy can be carried out in an open format, in which participants may start and complete the group at different time points. An open-group format is particularly well suited to an inpatient setting in which patients may have varying lengths of stay. In an open group, pain coping skills are taught in modules that can be introduced at any point in treatment. In these groups we typically begin each session by reviewing each patient's status, in order to target particular cognitive problems (e.g., excessive worry) or behavioral problems (e.g., excessive tension evident in pain avoidant posturing) that need intervention. We then introduce a module (e.g., relaxation training) designed to address a problem shared by several group members. Invariably, in an open group there are some patients who have been in the group for a while and who have been exposed to a particular module already. These "veteran" participants can be asked to describe how the methods worked for them. The modeling provided by these more experienced patients can play a key role in prompting newer group members to get involved in treatment.

We usually use two cotherapists to run group therapy sessions. At least one of the therapists should be a PhD-level clinical psychologist with thorough training and experience in cognitive-behavioral approaches to pain management. A psychology trainee or other mental health specialist (e.g., social worker, psychiatric nurse) can serve as a cotherapist.

The First Group Session

The first session of cognitive-behavioral group therapy is focused on establishing the basic structure and rationale for treatment. An effort is made to help group members become acquainted, and ground rules for the group are discussed. Patients are also given a chance to discuss their adaptations to persistent pain. Finally, a rationale for group therapy is presented that emphasizes how coping skills training can be used to control and decrease pain.

Warm-Up and Ground Rules of the Group

The first therapy session begins with the therapists' introducing themselves and describing their roles in the group. To help group members get acquainted, it is often helpful to use a warm-up exercise. We usually ask each patient to pair off with another patient and spend 10 minutes becoming acquainted (i.e., learning something about each other's pain, family situation, and general interests). At the end of 10 minutes, the patients return to the group and introduce their partners rather than themselves. After everyone is introduced, the participants' reactions to the warm-up exercise are discussed. The warm-up exercise is a good way to get participants talking and helps them realize that they share much in common with other group members. The exercise also invariably engenders some good-natured joking when participants are making introductions and find that they have forgotten some information about their partners.

Basic information about the group, and general group rules and expectations, are also discussed with patients. The patients are told that each group session deals with a different topic, and a list of each of the topics is typically reviewed. The therapists will start and end each group session on time, so it is important that patients come to every group session and be on time. In the event that a patient knows he or she will miss a session, the patient is asked to announce this in the group session the week preceding the absence. Patients are given phone numbers where therapists may be reached if there is an emergency or if they unexpectedly need to miss a group session. In order to protect confidentiality, the participants are also requested not to discuss personal matters raised during the group sessions outside of the group.

Adaptation to Pain

To help group members understand how pain has changed their lives, we use an adaptation model. A simple diagram, such as Figure 10.1, is drawn on the board to illustrate this model. The model starts with the basic assumption that every group member has a pain problem that has gone on for some time. As pain has persisted, patients' lives have changed in some important ways. Some of these adjustments to pain have been helpful; others have not been. To focus the discussion on issues relevant to cognitive-behavioral intervention, group members are asked to discuss life changes they have noted in three major areas: (1) daily activities (e.g., how active they are overall, what they are able to do

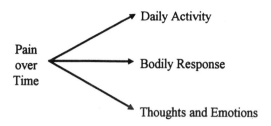

FIGURE 10.1. Adaptation model.

and not able to do), (2) bodily responses (e.g., sleep disruption, muscle weakness), and (3) thoughts and emotions (e.g., negative thoughts about themselves or others, feelings of depression/anger/guilt). This discussion gives patients a chance to talk about their pain history and learn that they have much in common with other group members. It also serves to increase patients' level of comfort about talking in a group setting.

We begin the discussion of the adaptation model by having group members talk about how their activities have changed in response to persistent pain. This is a good topic to start with, because it is relatively nonthreatening and is a problem area for most patients. Group members can easily identify specific changes that have occurred in their lives, such as a decrease in time spent up and out of bed, an inability to work or carry our household chores, and an increase in pain-related behaviors (such as taking medications, going to the doctor, or talking about pain). Typically, there are patients in the group who are able to recognize that changes that they have made to avoid pain (e.g., reclining in bed) can in turn have long-term negative consequences for pain coping (e.g., a decreased tolerance for activity).

After discussing changes in activity, the group members are asked to discuss changes in bodily responses that have developed as pain has persisted. Group members often report being bothered by a low energy level and difficulty sleeping. These changes may be attributable to the physical deconditioning that occurs when patients spend excessive time in bed. The group therapists try to help patients become aware of how adaptations to pain in one area (e.g., activities) can affect other major areas (e.g., bodily responses).

We typically delay a discussion of the impact of chronic pain on thoughts and emotions until the latter part of the discussion about adjustment to pain. Some patients are reluctant to share their negative feelings and thoughts with others. They may fear that they will be seen as emotionally disturbed or that their pain will not be taken seriously. Delaying discussion of this topic helps overcome this problem by giving patients an opportunity to become more comfortable with one another. In addition, reports of changes in feelings and thoughts often emerge spontaneously during discussion of changes in activities and bodily responses. We have found that once one or two group members open up and discuss changes in their thoughts and feelings, other group members are usually willing to share their own experiences. Occasionally, there are a few patients who have difficulty identifying changes in their thoughts and feelings. To deal with this problem, we typically prompt the participants to review the changes that have occurred in their daily activities, and ask them to reflect on what they think and feel about these changes.

In closing the discussion of the adaptation model, the group leaders point out that a major goal of cognitive-behavioral therapy is to alter patients' adaptations to pain. Patients will learn new coping strategies to help them better adapt to pain.

Rationale for Coping Skills Training

Helping patients reconceptualize their pain and their own ability to control pain is one of the most important goals of cognitive-behavioral group therapy (Turk, Meichenbaum, & Genest, 1983). To accomplish this goal, we typically use a simplified version of the gate control theory (Melzack & Wall, 1965). A simple diagram, such as Figure 10.2, is drawn on the board to begin a discussion of this model. The diagram includes a representation of the basic elements of the traditional pain pathway, including (1) special nerves that pick up pain signals in the periphery at the site of injury; (2) spinal nerves that carry pain signals to the brain; and (3) sensory areas of the brain, where pain is experienced. Not only is the traditional pain pathway described, but its limitations are also discussed. For example, the pain pathway concept fails to explain phenomena such as the presence of pain following limb amputation (phantom limb pain). Group members are encouraged to share puzzling experiences that they or others have had with pain. Many patients, for example, report having been surprised in the past when they had little or no pain following a sports injury suffered during an important game. Other patients have friends or family members who have suffered from phantom limb pain or other unusual pain phenomena.

The gate control model is presented as an alternative to the pain pathway model. To illustrate this model, a schematic depiction of a gate is added to the pain pathway diagram, as shown in Figure 10.3. Patients are told that the gate can be fully or partially opened or closed, determining the intensity of pain that is experienced. The role that thoughts and emotions can play in opening and closing the gate is described. Group

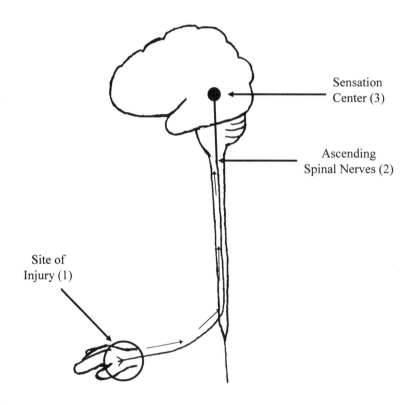

Sensation
Center (3)

Ascending
Spinal Nerves (2)

Site of
Injury (1)

FIGURE 10.2. Pain pathway.

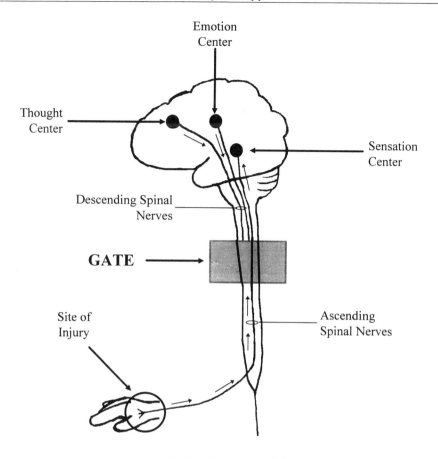

Emotion
Center

Thought
Center

Sensation
Center

Descending Spinal
Nerves

GATE

Site of
Injury

Ascending
Spinal Nerves

FIGURE 10.3. Gate control theory.

members are asked to identify specific thoughts and emotions that they have noticed influence their pain and that may affect the gate control mechanism. Patients often mention guilt, anger, depression, and anxiety as emotions that may open the gate, and happiness and feeling calm as emotions that may close the gate. Negative thoughts that may increase pain often include "I can't deal with this any more," or "No one really cares about or understands my pain." Patients often recognize that distracting activities (e.g., reading a favorite book, listening to music) can change their negative thinking and reduce pain. If group members have difficulty identifying factors that influence pain, it is often helpful to prompt them by referring back to the thoughts and feelings that were identified in the earlier group discussion of adaptations to pain.

Patients are told that the purpose of group therapy is to help them learn skills for controlling pain by changing the thoughts and emotions that affect pain. Patients are told that they will be exposed in subsequent group sessions to a "menu" of pain coping skills. The coping skills menu is compared to a menu in any fine restaurant. Each skill item on the menu is designed to be consistently high in quality, and on certain days or in specific situations, one skill from the menu may be preferred over the others. Emphasizing that group members have choices and control over coping is important, because research has shown that these factors can influence perceived pain (Litt, 1988). The importance of regular home practice in the development of effective coping skills is also emphasized, and patients are told that they will be given home assignments that will be reviewed at the start of each group therapy session.

It is important to discuss patients' reactions to the rationale presented above. Often, the gate control model validates an experience with pain that a group member has had (e.g., increased pain when feeling depressed or angry), but has been reluctant to discuss with others. Group members generally respond quite favorably to this rationale. After the rationale is presented, group members often report that this is the first time they believe they might be able to develop some control over their pain.

Comment

Getting a group started is in many ways the most important phase of group therapy. If the group leaders are perceived as competent and willing to help the patients, patients are more apt to develop positive expectations and to be motivated to participate actively in treatment. The first therapy session provides an opportunity for the group members to discuss their pain in a nonthreatening environment. In hearing others' stories, the participants develop a realization that they are not alone in their pain experiences.

The first session of cognitive-behavioral group therapy also gives many patients their first exposure to an alternative to the medical model of pain management. Conceptualizing pain in terms of Melzack and Wall's (1965) model assists patients in seeing their pain differently. It also helps focus them on the importance of learning new pain coping skills.

Training in Pain Coping Skills

The second phase of cognitive-behavioral group therapy is devoted to training in pain coping skills. To illustrate this phase of treatment, we discuss the basic format of pain coping skills training sessions and the methods used for training patients in relaxation, activity–rest cycling, and attention diversion strategies.

Basic Format of Coping Skills Training Sessions

The coping skills training phase typically begins with the second group therapy session and continues for 6 to 10 sessions. Each session begins with a review of group members' home practice over the past week. We ask participants to keep home diary records of practice. The therapists review the records and reinforce those patients who have been able to practice regularly. Problem-solving methods are used to assist patients who have had difficulty with their practice. Specific obstacles to practice (e.g., lack of free time, frequent interruptions during relaxation practice) are identified, and the group as a whole is asked to identify potential ways to overcome these obstacles. Group members often come up with innovative solutions to problems in practicing. Having patients share these solutions with one another is a good way to model problem-solving skills.

During the review of home practice, group members are asked to discuss how they have applied pain coping skills in real-life situations in which pain is likely to be a problem. In particular, patients are asked to share information about any situations in which they were able to use pain coping skills to control or decrease their pain. The emphasis is on people who have had successes, in order to model adaptive coping for others. This sharing is beneficial in two ways. First, a patient who has experienced success has an opportunity to get encouragement and positive feedback from other group members. Second, reports of success often motivate other group members to continue with their practice.

Behavioral rehearsal is one of the most effective ways to structure pain coping skills practice sessions in group therapy. Behavioral rehearsal involves therapist instruction in a coping skill, patient rehearsal, and therapist feedback. Before beginning behavioral rehearsal, we assess baseline pain level by having patients perform an activity for 15 to 30 seconds that will increase their pain somewhat (e.g., walking, going from a sitting to a standing position). Care is taken to assure that each group member is able to perform the activity he or she has chosen without causing too much of an increase in pain. At the end of the activity, each group member rates the pain he or she experienced on a 0–100 scale on which 0 = "no pain" and 100 = "pain as bad as it can be." The therapists then teach the group members a specific pain coping skill (e.g., relaxation) and model how this might be applied during the specific activities chosen by group members. The group members are then asked to apply the coping skill while they perform the pain-inducing activity. During rehearsal, the therapist provides feedback on performance, along with suggestions about how best to use the coping skill. After the group members discuss their reactions, they are asked to rehearse using the pain coping skill on their own while engaging in the pain-inducing activity. The group members then rate their pain on the 0–100 scale, and these pain ratings are compared to those taken at baseline. Many patients are surprised to find that when they apply the pain coping skill, they are able to reduce their pain by 25% to 40%. Reasons for reductions in pain (e.g., distraction from pain, relaxation of tense muscles) are discussed in the group. The therapists also encourage patients who failed to achieve pain relief to discuss their reactions to the exercise. Possible explanations for a lack of change in pain include individual differences in responsiveness to different coping skills and the need for additional practice to achieve mastery of the skill. Most patients report an increased sense of self-efficacy after going through the behavioral rehearsal exercise. Behavioral rehearsal can even be helpful for those patients who do not experience immediate pain relief. These patients benefit from the positive modeling provided by other patients, and often report being more optimistic about the outcome of coping skills training.

Home practice assignments are reviewed at the end of each coping skills training session. The assignments are written down and are very specific (e.g., listening to the relaxation tape once a day). They are also graduated in terms of difficulty, with earlier assignments being easier and later assignments requiring more time and skill. This graduated approach to home practice is important for two reasons. First, it helps patients phase the coping skills into their daily routine more easily. Second, it challenges patients to gradually extend the application of coping skills to a much broader range of daily activities and events.

Readings and handouts can provide useful adjuncts to group therapy. For each coping skills training session, we typically give patients a one- to two-page handout that provides a brief review of the rationale and recommended home practice procedures. Patients are encouraged to read the information on the handout between sessions. The handouts also serve as reference material after the group ends.

Relaxation Training

Relaxation training is probably the most widely used cognitive-behavioral coping skill. Relaxation training can be easily carried out in group therapy sessions. Because patients respond so readily to relaxation training, we usually introduce it early in the course of pain coping skills training.

Conceptual Background. From a conceptual standpoint, there are a variety of reasons why relaxation training is helpful in pain control. First, relaxation methods can help break the link between stressful events and pain. Severe stressors can produce autonomic arousal and emotional reactions that can exacerbate pain (Keefe & Gil, 1986). Research has shown that stressors such as family conflict and job disruption are related to increased pain in patients with chronic low back pain (Feuerstein, Sult, & Houle, 1985). Second, relaxation methods can reduce muscle spasm and tension, which have long been thought to be important causes of chronic pain (Travell, Rinzler, & Herman, 1943). Through relaxation training, patients can learn to control spasm and excessive tension in specific muscle groups that are contributing to their pain (e.g., the upper trapezius muscles for a patient who is having neck pain following a whiplash injury). Third, relaxation training may be useful in altering abnormal patterns of muscle activity that contribute to pain. Patients who engage in abnormal pain-avoidant posturing when walking or shifting from one position to another often report increased pain and fatigue. By applying relaxation methods such as biofeedback training, these patients can learn to reduce pain by decreasing excessive tension and normalizing their movements (Wolf, Nacht, & Kelly, 1982). Finally, relaxation training can reduce emotional responding during pain episodes. The gate control theory (Melzack & Wall, 1965) highlights the role that emotional responses such as depression and anger can play in exacerbating pain. After going through relaxation training, patients often report that they can maintain a calmer emotional disposition during episodes of increased pain. As a result, the intensity and duration of the pain are reduced.

Before relaxation training is begun, it is important to discuss patients' beliefs and concerns about relaxation methods. Most patients readily grasp the role that relaxation training can play in pain control. Some patients, however, may be worried about using relaxation methods. A common concern is that the therapists, not the patients, will be in control during relaxation. It is important to acknowledge such fears and to point out that they are common (Bernstein & Borkovec, 1973). Patients can be reassured that they will be in control of both the timing and level of tension and relaxation during the relaxation practice sessions. Allowing patients to keep their eyes open during relaxation practice can be helpful in overcoming concerns about loss of control.

Progressive Relaxation Training. When teaching relaxation training in group therapy, we use a protocol developed by Surwit (1979) that is a modified version of Jacobson's (1938) original progressive muscle relaxation method. This protocol consists of a series of exercises in which the individual tenses and slowly relaxes muscle groups, starting with muscles in the feet and legs and progressing to muscles in the face and head. The group therapists briefly demonstrate each of the relaxation exercises and then have the patients repeat these exercises. This demonstration and rehearsal of the tension–relaxation exercises helps the therapists identify patients who may misunderstand the instructions or who may have increased pain or difficulty with particular exercises. To prevent increased pain, patients are urged to use caution when tensing muscle groups surrounding a painful area. If patients are unable because of physical limitations to tense a muscle group, they are simply told to eliminate this particular exercise.

After demonstrating the exercises, the therapists guide the group members through a 20-minute relaxation session. During the session, patients are instructed to focus systematically on sensations of muscle tension as they tense and relax their muscles. The therapists emphasize the importance of gradually building up and then slowly releasing tension. Patients are asked to pay particular attention to the way their muscles feel when they are tense, and, by contrast, when they are relaxed.

At the end of the relaxation session, group members are asked to discuss their reactions. Patients often report that they have less pain and feel much more calm and relaxed. The therapists encourage patients to share any problems that they may have had during the relaxation sessions, such as muscle cramping, sleepiness, or difficulty concentrating. Bernstein and Borkovec (1973) have given a number of practical suggestions for overcoming such problems. Cramping, for example, can be avoided by using lower levels of tension during the exercises and holding the tension for shorter periods. Falling asleep can be minimized by having patients keep their eyes open during the session or by reducing the length of practice periods. Concentration typically becomes less of a problem as patients develop a regular practice schedule. Involving the group members in identifying and solving problems with relaxation training is a useful way to overcome obstacles to practice and prevent setbacks in coping (Keefe & Van Horn, 1993).

To facilitate home practice, each member of the group can be provided with a relaxation audiotape. The tape that we use was developed by Surwit (1979) and is available through the Behavioral Physiology Laboratory at Duke University Medical Center, Box 3842, Durham, North Carolina 27710. Patients are instructed to practice with the tape twice a day. It is important that patients practice in a quiet, comfortable place, with no interruptions or time pressures.

Brief Relaxation Methods: The Minipractice Technique. We also use the group therapy setting to teach brief relaxation methods. This training is introduced after patients have practiced with progressive relaxation training for 1 week or more and have developed an ability to relax when in a reclining or seated position. Brief relaxation can provide a means of reducing tension or pain when one is unable to go to a quiet area and do a full progressive relaxation practice session.

The brief relaxation method we use is called the "minipractice" because it takes a very short period of time (20 to 30 seconds). The therapists initially model the minipractice while the group members observe. The therapists then guide the patients through a minipractice with the following instructions:

1. "Stop whatever activity you are doing."
2. "Take a deep breath."
3. "Think the word 'relax.'"
4. "As you exhale, allow sensations of heaviness to flow downward from muscles of the face and neck to those of the arms, trunk, legs, and feet."
5. "Hold that feeling of relaxation for 10 to 15 seconds before returning to your activity."

Through behavioral rehearsal, patients are taught to apply minipractices in a variety of situations. Patients are initially taught to use the minipractices when they are in a quiet, seated position with their eyes closed. Later they are taught to apply this skill during more demanding situations, such as standing, sitting, walking, or conversing. The importance of using minipractices to achieve differential relaxation is stressed. That is, patients are taught to relax unnecessary tension, while maintaining the tension needed to engage in an activity. For example, it is necessary to have some tension in the leg muscles while standing, but muscles in the neck, shoulders, lower back, and face can be relaxed.

The group setting is an ideal one for training in brief relaxation methods. Patients often serve as effective models for one another, pointing out the situations in which they have been able to use a minipractice to reduce their pain or tension. Patients are encouraged to identify a variety of real-life situations in which they might have difficulty using minipractices, such as sitting in meetings at work, bending down to pick something up from the floor, or standing in line at the grocery store. The group is then given the task of developing a strategy for using the minipractice in these situations and then rehearsing that strategy in the group itself.

Patients are initially given the goal of doing five minipractices a day as part of their home practice. This goal is gradually increased until patients reach 20 minipractices per day. Patients are encouraged to use physiological cues (e.g., increase in pain or tension) and environmental cues (e.g., sitting at a traffic light, waiting for an elevator) as reminders to do a minipractice. In the group sessions, a list of potential cues for doing minipractices is compiled weekly.

Activity–Rest Cycling

Activity–rest cycling (Gil, Ross, & Keefe, 1988) is a method to help patients control pain by learning to pace and then gradually increase their activity level.

Conceptual Background. As people in pain attempt to perform activities, they often persist until severe pain forces them to stop and rest. Activities that formerly could be performed pain-free now become associated with increased pain. We typically use a simple figure such as that in Figure 10.4 to illustrate the pain cycle. With repetition, the pain cycle (i.e., overactivity leading to extreme pain leading to prolonged rest) becomes an entrenched and maladaptive habit. The negative consequences of this pain cycle include increased fear of activity, fatigue, muscle tension, and avoidance of activity (Fordyce, 1976; Gil et al., 1988). Ultimately, patients in the pain cycle can adopt an overly sedentary lifestyle in which they spend only minimal amounts of time up and out of the reclining position.

Training in Activity–Rest Cycling. The activity–rest cycle represents an adaptive alternative to the pain cycle. To introduce the activity–rest cycle, we first draw a simple diagram of the pain cycle (Figure 10.4) and ask group members to discuss the relevance of

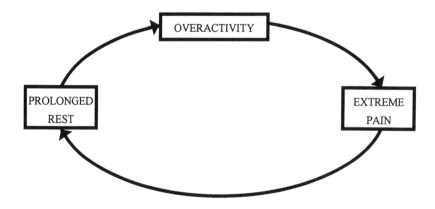

FIGURE 10.4. Pain cycle.

this cycle for their own pain. Most patients with chronic pain recognize this cycle as having a major influence on their lives. We usually ask patients to identify the reasons for getting stuck at different points in the cycle (e.g., overdoing activity or resting excessively). Many patients report that external factors (e.g., financial problems, the need to care for young children) are important. Internal factors (e.g., depression, anger, or guilt) can also play a role. Group members frequently report that they have made unsuccessful attempts to break out of the cycle. Patients can also often identify the negative impact that the pain cycle has had on their own lives and the lives of their family and friends. We then draw a diagram of the activity–rest cycle (see Figure 10.5) to illustrate a more adaptive way to perform activity.

The activity–rest cycle works by making activity levels contingent on time, not pain (Fordyce, 1976; Gil et al., 1988). Patients set a goal to engage in a period of moderate activity followed by limited rest. As patients repeat this cycle throughout the day, they often find that their pain is reduced and their tolerance for activity is increased. Over the course of weeks, patients are able to gradually increase their level of activity and decrease the amount of time they spend resting.

Group members are asked to use brainstorming to generate a list of the potential benefits and limitations of activity–rest cycling. Benefits that are often mentioned include the avoidance of extreme pain, fewer and shorter pain episodes, an increase in productivity, a more stable level of activity, and less tension and fatigue. Limitations of the activity–rest cycle are that it requires record keeping, tends to structure the day, and can interrupt ongoing activities. Before implementing the activity–rest cycle, group members are asked to weigh its potential benefits against its limitations. Typically, most patients agree that the benefits are well worth the costs involved in acquiring and maintaining this behavioral coping skill.

To implement the activity–rest cycle, a baseline record of current activity patterns is needed. Patients are given a home practice assignment of keeping daily records of the time they spend up and out of a reclining position. Reviewing these records in group sessions can be very revealing. Patients are often surprised to find that they are more active than they thought or more active than many other group members. Patients also

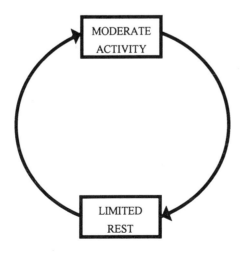

FIGURE 10.5. Activity–rest cycle.

are usually able to identify pain cycling patterns as they review their own records. It is particularly helpful for patients to realize that although the specifics may vary, pain cycling is a very common pattern. Some patients, for example, are very active during the day, and then spend almost all of their time in the evening reclining. Other patients may have 2 or 3 days of overactivity, followed by 4 or 5 days of rest.

The activity–rest cycle involves four basic steps. First, patients set a goal (in minutes or hours) for engaging in a moderate amount of activity. "Moderate activity" is defined as a level of activity that a patient can maintain without increasing his or her pain to a very high level. For some patients, moderate activity may be spending 30 minutes up and out of bed. For other patients, moderate activity may be working at a word processor for 60 minutes. Second, patients set a goal for a limited rest period, which they will take after completing their moderate-activity goal. This rest period should be sufficient to give them some pain relief, but not so long that their total rest each day exceeds their average rest time during baseline recording. A limited rest period for a sedentary patient may be 30 minutes in bed, whereas for a very active patient it may be 5 minutes sitting in a relaxed position. Third, patients are instructed to repeat the cycle of moderate activity followed limited rest (e.g., 45 minutes up and out of bed, 15 minutes of rest) frequently through-out the day. The goal is to use the cycle at least 70% of the waking day. Patients keep a daily record of the number of repetitions of the activity–rest cycle they are able to achieve. This monitoring helps increase awareness of how to use this skill in a variety of situa-tions, and helps reinforce patients for adherence. Fourth, over a period of days to weeks, patients are instructed to gradually increase their goal for moderate activity and decrease their goal for limited rest. The ultimate goal of activity–rest cycling is to enable patients to be able to tolerate up to 1½ to 2 hours of activity, followed by a 5- to 10-minute relax-ation break.

At the start of each group therapy session, patients' home practice with activity–rest cycling is reviewed. Initially, many patients have practical problems with implementing this cycle. Group members are asked to identify obstacles to the use of activity–rest cycling and then to generate ideas about ways to overcome these obstacles. Obstacles frequently mentioned include simply forgetting about the time limit and feeling embar-rassed about the need to rest. Ideas for solving problems are discussed in the group set-ting, and patients are encouraged to think of creative strategies to overcome these prob-lems. For example, several years ago one of our group members who had difficulty following through with the activity–rest cycle brought a digital kitchen timer to one of our group sessions and told group members about how helpful it was in prompting him when to start and stop activity periods. Since this, we have regularly advised patients about this strategy. Another strategy we use is role playing. Role playing is used to help patients become more comfortable about explaining the activity–rest cycle to family, friends, and coworkers. This helps with feelings of embarrassment and with getting support from others during periods of stress.

In working on activity–rest cycling in group therapy, it may be important to discuss patients' thoughts and feelings about resting. Problems may arise when patients fear stop-ping their activity because of the belief that they will not be able to resume the activity. In addition, some patients view changing their activity levels as "giving in" to their pain, and subsequently fight to maintain control by continuing or even increasing their activities. Other patients may believe that resting is a sign of laziness. Reiterating how the pain cycle works, as well as giving these patients permission to rest during their activity, often alle-viates these problems.

Attention Diversion Strategies

Patients vary in their response to attention diversion strategies. Patients may find one attention diversion strategy (e.g., pleasant imagery) quite helpful, but report little benefit from another strategy (e.g., counting backwards). Group therapy provides a good setting for training in attention diversion strategies, because it gives patients an opportunity to sample different strategies and to be exposed to modeling influences. Patients with chronic pain often become much more interested in learning specific attention diversion strategies when they observe that these methods work for other patients.

Conceptual Background. There is a large research literature supporting the effectiveness of attention diversion strategies for pain control (McCaul & Malott, 1984). Diverting attention away from pain by distraction, and refocusing attention on something other than pain, appear to be particularly effective in pain management (Turk et al., 1983).

Training Methods. To introduce attention diversion strategies, it is helpful to review the gate control model (Melzack & Wall, 1965) and emphasize the role that shifting concentration can play in modulating pain perception. We typically instruct patients in three attention diversion techniques: pleasant imagery, use of a focal point, and counting backward. Patients are reminded that they are in control when using these strategies, which require alertness and concentration. The attention diversion techniques can be used to enhance relaxation, and patients are encouraged to use them either after listening to the relaxation tape or while doing a minipractice. Attention diversion training is usually introduced after patients have practiced with relaxation for several weeks.

Pleasant imagery is one of the most common and effective attention diversion strategies (Turk et al., 1983). It involves deliberately shifting attention from an unpleasant situation (e.g., increased pain during prolonged sitting) to an imagined pleasant scene (e.g., reclining on a beach on a warm, sunny day). In teaching pleasant imagery in group therapy, we ask patients to identify and share with the group members pleasant or enjoyable experiences that they have had or would like to have. These experiences might include watching the sun set over a lake, sitting by a brook, walking through a field of flowers on a spring day, or watching a movie with a special friend. Patients are then asked to close their eyes, do a minipractice, focus on a particular pleasant scene, and try to involve all of their senses in the imagery. The group therapists cue patients when to start and stop the pleasant imagery, with practice periods varying between 2 and 10 minutes. After practicing with imagery, patients are encouraged to discuss their reactions. Patients often report that they find pleasant imagery to be very relaxing. We have found that patients vary greatly in the amount of pain relief they initially experience using imagery: Some patients have substantial decreases in pain, while others report little or no change in pain. Although individual differences are evident in response to imagery, with regular practice most patients are able to develop an ability to control pain by using pleasant imagery.

The use of a focal point is a second attention diversion strategy that can be helpful in pain control (Turk et al., 1983). Focal point distraction involves deliberately directing one's attention to objects in the immediate environment (e.g., a picture of a loved one or a floral arrangement) for a 1- to 2-minute period. The focal point has long been used to assist women in coping with labor pain, and has more recently been extended to management of chronic pain (Turk et al., 1983).

Counting techniques represent a third attention diversion strategy that can be used to enhance pain control (Turk et al., 1983). We usually ask patients to count backward slowly from 100 to 1. It is often helpful to think the word "Relax" between numbers. Some patients also imagine the numbers by seeing white numbers superimposed on a black screen, and having each number melt away or flip over to the next number.

We typically introduce attention diversion over the course of several group sessions. Patients are initially guided through use of the strategies by the therapists, and then learn to practice on their own. Behavioral rehearsal, outlined earlier, is used to teach patients how to apply these techniques during activities that increase pain. For problem situations that cannot be rehearsed in the group, therapists can use cognitive rehearsal, in which patients imagine themselves applying the strategies in a step-by-step fashion.

After patients have been exposed to each of the attention diversion strategies, they are encouraged to combine them to cope with difficult pain situations. For example, to reduce severe pain during a flare-up, an arthritis patient might use counting techniques while walking and imagery or focal point distraction techniques while resting.

Preparing Patients for Maintenance of Coping Skills

Regular and continued practice of pain coping skills is essential if patients are to achieve effective control over their pain. To help patients maintain treatment gains, it is important that group therapists plan ahead instead of expecting maintenance to occur automatically. Marlatt and Gordon (1985) have developed a relapse prevention model in the course of their work with patients who are addicted to alcohol and other drugs. They examine the situational, interpersonal, and emotional factors surrounding relapse, as well as patients' thought processes. Keefe and Van Horn (1993) have modified this model for use with patients having chronic pain, and have outlined a number of relapse prevention methods. These methods can be integrated into cognitive-behavioral group therapy sessions.

A discussion of maintenance of pain coping skills should not be left until the last group session. Maintenance issues should be addressed in the initial session and in every session of group therapy. One way to begin a discussion of maintenance issues is to have group members identify obstacles and high-risk situations that might interfere with their practicing and applying pain coping skills on a daily basis. Group discussion often helps patients identify problem situations that they have not considered. To help patients assess their confidence in their ability to cope with these situations, they are asked to provide ratings on a 0–10 scale of their current ability to cope with the situation and the likelihood that the situation might cause them to stop practicing pain coping skills. The ratings are reviewed in the group, and similarities and differences in ratings across patients and situations are discussed.

To help patients cope better with setbacks in coping, and to ensure that these setbacks are minor and temporary, group training is provided in a four-step relapse prevention method (Marlatt & Gordon, 1985). The first step involves stopping and paying attention to the cues that a setback is occurring. The second step is to keep calm, using relaxation or other strategies to prevent overly emotional responding. The third step is to review the situation leading up to the setback. The final step is to make an immediate plan for implementing coping.

Patients have an opportunity in the group therapy session to role-play how they might cope with setbacks and relapse situations. With rehearsal and therapist feedback, patients are often able to develop a higher level of confidence in their ability to cope with high-risk situations.

CLINICAL ISSUES IN GROUP THERAPY

Although the application of group therapy approaches to chronic pain may seem straightforward, it can raise a number of potentially difficult clinical issues. These clinical issues can be divided into three groups: (1) problems related to conducting group therapy itself; (2) issues regarding the involvement of spouses and other family members; and (3) issues relating to integrating group therapy with other pain treatment modalities.

Problems in Conducting Group Therapy with Chronic Pain Patients

Group therapists encounter a number of problems when leading groups of chronic pain patients. Two of the most common and important problems are a mismatch between patients' expectations and the goals of therapy, and dealing with anger and high levels of emotional distress. To illustrate each of these problems, we present a clinical vignette followed by a discussion of strategies for managing the problem.

Dealing with Patients' Expectations

> Mr. Jones came to the group therapy session but was visibly annoyed. The session focused on learning how to cope with pain. Mr. Jones was quiet during the group, speaking up only when asked to do so. When approached by a therapist after the group session, Mr. Jones explained that he wasn't interested in learning how to cope, but only in getting rid of his pain. He stated, "If you can't do anything to take my pain away, I'd rather not waste my time with the sessions."

One of the most important issues in group therapy is dealing with patients' expectations about treatment. These expectations can vary greatly. Some chronic pain patients expect group psychological therapy to fail, because they view their pain as a problem that can only be addressed through medical treatment. Other patients unrealistically expect that group therapy will give them unique insights or powerful techniques that will permanently eliminate their pain. In either case, patients are likely to be dissatisfied when treatment fails to meet their expectations. These patients may fail to become involved in treatment or may prematurely drop out of group therapy.

Several methods can be used before and during group therapy to deal with problems related to patients' expectations. First, a screening interview should be carried out with all patients before they start group therapy. In the interview, patients should be encouraged to discuss their thoughts and beliefs about pain and its treatment. The interviewer should take a supportive, nonjudgmental approach, in order to gather as much information as possible about patients' expectations. Patients may have fears or concerns based on their own or others' experiences with group therapy. At the end of the screening interview, patients should be provided with basic information about the group therapy. Patients often benefit from a discussion that focuses on the nature of pain problems typically experienced by patients undergoing group therapy, the goals of the group, intervention methods, and typical outcomes in terms of pain relief and functional status.

Second, it is important that group therapists directly address patients' expectations early in the course of the group itself. One way of doing is to conduct a brief group exercise in which each patient briefly discusses what he or she hopes to accomplish in the group. Patients are encouraged to discuss both their hopes and their doubts about treatment outcome. This exercise is particularly effective when a new patient is entering an established group. The veterans of the group often frankly discuss their own initial skepticism and concerns about the effectiveness of the group. These veteran patients also can convincingly convey that group therapy is helpful not only in terms of pain relief, but also in terms of increased activity and improved mood.

Third, therapists can meet individually with patients outside of the group to discuss and deal with problems. As noted above, one of the most common and difficult problems is that chronic pain patients often consider pain relief to be the only meaningful index of their improvement. When they fail to achieve substantial reductions in pain, their motivation for treatment may diminish. Diary records can be used to help patients shift their focus away from pain relief per se and toward a broader conceptualization of treatment outcome. For example, patients can keep daily diary records in which they monitor not only their pain level, but also their exercise and activity level, participation in pleasant activities, and mood. The records can be reviewed daily, and simple graphs can be used to display changes in pain and improvements in activity and mood measures. When they review the graphs, patients are able to see that moderate reductions in pain may be accompanied by very substantial increases in the level and range of pleasant activities.

Dealing with Anger and Emotional Distress

> During a group session focusing on negative thinking and pain, Mrs. Edwards vented her angry feelings toward her doctors: "It is all Dr. Smith's fault. He told me the operation would take care of the pain. Now the pain is worse than ever. If he hadn't operated and cut that nerve, this never would have happened." Other group members joined in and shared their anger toward physicians and other health professionals. As the group went on, the level of anger escalated, with some members crying and visibly shaking as they made statements such as these: "The doctors are useless," "None of the people who have treated me understand or believe me," and "I wish they could walk in my shoes for just one day; then they would know what pain is like."

Anger is one of the most common and difficult emotions that chronic pain patients experience. Some psychodynamic pain theorists, such as Engel (1959), believe that unresolved anger is a key factor in the maintenance of chronic pain. Anger and resentment can certainly interfere with group treatment. We have found that having patients engage in a prolonged discussion of their feelings of anger or resentment is not very fruitful. Patients often report that they remain emotionally upset long after these sessions, and that they gain little insight or improvement in coping from a persistent focus on these feelings.

Several strategies can be used to handle high levels of anger and emotional distress in group therapy. First, therapists can help group members calm themselves to the point at which they can cope with anger rationally. One way of doing this is to interrupt discussion for a relaxation break. Patients can be guided through a relaxation exercise designed to help reduce emotional arousal and enable them to cope more effectively. Another method is to intentionally limit the amount of time devoted to discussing anger, or to postpone the discussion to a later session in which the issues can be handled more productively.

Second, therapists can help group members identify the underlying source of their anger. For many patients, anger is related to issues of loss. The loss of the ability to work, in particular, can be associated with high levels of anger and resentment. Loss of the ability to engage in valued recreational or family activities can also fuel angry feelings. For other patients, anger is related to a sense that life has been unfair to them. Identifying sources of anger is an important first step in problem solving. Once the sources of anger have been identified, problem-solving methods can be used to help group members cope better with their feelings. In problem solving, patients develop a plan for coping with anger and then implement it. Problem solving is particularly effective in a group setting, where some patients may have learned to cope with anger while others have not. Patients often suggest coping methods to one another. For example, a patient who is angry with his or her doctor may be encouraged by group members to talk to the doctor. Role playing can be used to teach the patient how to communicate effectively. Patients often encourage group members to focus on acceptance rather than on their anger. This involves shifting their attention away from blaming others for losses, and instead emphasizing what they can do to replace losses.

Third, we have used a "time-out" strategy with patients whose angry feelings are so strong that they are unable to get much out of the group and actually disrupt the group. We typically meet with these patients individually and suggest that they try a "time-out" approach in which they will attend the group, but remain silent for two to three group sessions. These patients are encouraged simply to listen to what other group members are saying. A therapist meets individually with such a patient after each group session to review his or her reactions. With use of the "time-out" method, angry patients often report feeling less resentful, more comfortable with the group, and more optimistic about how it might help them. After several sessions with this procedure, most patients are able to resume a normal role in the group and to work on learning new pain coping methods.

We have found that a combination of the strategies discussed above works most of the time in dealing with patients who are angry. In some instances, however, patients seem "stuck" and do not respond to these interventions. In these cases, we work individually with the patients until they are ready for group therapy.

Involving Spouses and Family Members in Group Therapy

Chronic pain is a problem not only for patients, but also for their spouses and other family members. There is a growing recognition that the responses of spouses and family members to pain can influence patients' ability to cope (Keefe, Dunsmore, & Burnett, 1992). There is also heightened interest in involving spouses and other family members in pain treatment programs.

Group therapy provides an excellent setting in which to work with patients and their families. We often have a patient's spouse and family members sit in on regular group therapy sessions with the patient. This provides the family members with exposure to other individuals with chronic pain, and helps them better understand the patient's own problems in coping. We also conduct special multifamily group therapy sessions that are attended by two or three patients and their families. The multifamily groups have two major goals: (1) reviewing how each patient's difficulties in coping have affected each family, and (2) identifying one or more specific ways that family members can become involved in the patients' pain management program.

We have recently developed a comprehensive spouse training intervention, to be used in the context of a 10-week couples group therapy program for managing osteoarthritic knee pain. The intervention integrates spouse training with training patients in pain coping skills. The intervention has three key components. The first component, "patient–spouse behavioral rehearsal," is used to teach spouses how to prompt and reinforce pain coping skills in problem situations. Patient–spouse rehearsal is particularly useful in teaching spouses to prompt pain control techniques (e.g., relaxation methods) in public situations where patients may be reluctant to use them (e.g., while talking with a store clerk in a mall, or conversing with friends at a party). The second component of spouse training, "joint practice," teaches patients and their spouses how to practice together with relaxation, imagery, and other cognitive coping skills in practice sessions at home or during demanding physical activities (e.g., stair climbing, going from a sitting to a standing position). This joint practice not only familiarizes the spouses with the specifics of coping skills; it also enhance the spouses' confidence in the patients' ability to cope with problem situations. The third component of spouse training, "maintenance enhancement training," teaches couples strategies for maintaining frequent practice of pain coping skills. The couples learn how to identify high-risk situations that may set coping efforts back, how to develop a plan for dealing with pain flares, and how to identify natural cues that may serve to maintain coping efforts.

We have found that most spouses of chronic pain patients are eager to participate and benefit substantially from involvement in group therapy. In some cases, however, there are impediments to involving spouses or family members. Some patients are resistant to the idea of having their spouses attend group sessions. In addition, some spouses may be unwilling to participate in treatment. Often these problems can be overcome by meeting with a patient, his or her spouse, and other family members for a preliminary interview before the group therapy sessions. The meeting can be used to elicit and address concerns about group treatment, and to provide basic information on the structure and nature of the group sessions. Most spouses are reassured by the information provided and agree to participate fully in treatment. A continued refusal to participate is almost invariably a negative prognostic sign.

Integrating Group Therapy with Other Treatments

Group therapy approaches need not, and in most cases should not, be the sole treatment modality for chronic pain. The methods outlined in this chapter typically make up one component of a comprehensive treatment program, which also involves the use of exercise, medications, and other pain management modalities.

Combining group therapy with other pain treatments does raise a number of important clinical issues. The first issue is confidentiality. If patients are to open up in the group, they need to be assured that there are limits on what will be communicated to other members of the treatment team. Typically, therapists provide feedback on the specific treatments provided and the patients' progress. Therapists often use a "need-to-know" rule in determining when to share more confidential information with other treatment team members. That is, detailed information on emotionally sensitive topics is not shared with other team members unless it is likely to have a significant impact on a patient's treatment course.

A second issue is the need for other treatment team members to support and reinforce the goals of group therapy. Patients are more likely to view group treatment as important if the goals and methods used are viewed as valuable by other treatment specialists. Educational efforts are sometimes needed to teach these specialists about group therapy and to identify how they may assist patients in progressing through treatment.

A third issue is how the goals of group therapy fit with those of other treatment modalities. Ideally, treatment team members need to communicate and agree as to the goals of therapy before treatment begins. If inconsistencies arise over the course of treatment, a brief telephone call can often address the problems. Treatments that seem inconsistent may not be so. For example, a group therapy program encouraging patients to become active was seen by one patient as incompatible with a physical therapy regimen emphasizing the use of rest, hot packs, and ultrasound. During a telephone conversation with the physical therapist, the group therapist learned that the physical therapist had instructed the patient to use hot packs and rest after a period of moderate activity and exercise. The physical therapist agreed that activating the patient was important and felt that the hot packs and rest might serve as effective reinforcers for increased activity.

CONCLUSIONS

Although further research is needed to evaluate its effectiveness, group therapy does appear to represent a viable treatment option for many patients with chronic pain. As pointed out in this chapter, successful group therapy requires attention to a number of important practical and therapeutic issues. It is our hope that this chapter will stimulate a broader use of group therapy and will lead to heightened recognition of the benefits of this psychological treatment approach.

REFERENCES

Bernstein, D. A., & Borkovec, T. D. (1973). *Progressive relaxation training: A manual for the helping professions.* Champaign, IL: Research Press.

Bradley, L. A., Young, L. D., Anderson, J. O., Turner, R. A., Agudelo, C. A., McDaniel, L. K., Pisko, E. J., Semble, E. J., & Morgan, T. M. (1987). Effects of psychological therapy on pain behavior of rheumatoid arthritis patients: Treatment outcome and six-month follow-up. *Arthritis and Rheumatism, 30,* 1105–1114.

Daltroy, L. H., & Liang, M. H. (1988). Patient education in the rheumatic diseases: A research agenda. *Arthritis Care and Research, 1,* 161–169.

Engel, G. (1959). "Psychogenic" pain and the pain-prone patient. *American Journal of Medicine, 26,* 899–918.

Feuerstein, M., Sult, S., & Houle, M. (1985). Environmental stressors and chronic low back pain: Life events, family, and work environment. *Pain, 22,* 295–307.

Fordyce, W. E. (1976). *Behavioral methods for chronic pain and illness.* St. Louis, MO: C.V. Mosby.

Gil, K. M., Ross, S. L., & Keefe, F. J. (1988). Behavioral treatment of chronic pain: Four pain management protocols. In R. D. France & K. R. R. Krishnan (Eds.), *Chronic pain* (pp. 317–413). Washington, DC: American Psychiatric Press.

Goeppinger, J., Arthur, M. W., Baglioni, A. J., Jr., Brunk, S. E., & Brunner, C. M. (1989). A reexamination of the effectiveness of self-care education for persons with arthritis. *Arthritis and Rheumatism, 32,* 706–717.

Holman, H., Mazonson, P., & Lorig, K. (1989). Health education for self-management has significant early and sustained benefits in chronic arthritis. *Transactions of the Association of American Physicians, 102,* 204–208.

Jacobson, E. (1938). *Progressive relaxation* (2nd ed.). Chicago: University of Chicago Press.

Keefe, F. J. (1988). Behavioral assessment methods for chronic pain. In R. D. France & K. R. R. Krishnan (Eds.), *Chronic pain* (pp. 299–320). Washington, DC: American Psychiatric Press.

Keefe, F. J., Caldwell, D. S., Williams, D. A., Gil, K. M., Mitchell, D., Robertson, D., Robertson, C., Martinez, S., Nunley, J., Beckham, J. C., & Helms, M. (1990). Pain coping skills training in the management of osteoarthritic knee pain: A comparative study. *Behavior Therapy, 21,* 49–62.

Keefe, F. J., Dunsmore, J., & Burnett, R. (1992). Behavioral and cognitive-behavioral approaches to chronic pain: Recent advances and future directions. *Journal of Consulting and Clinical Psychology, 60,* 528–536.

Keefe, F. J., & Gil, K. M. (1986). Behavioral concepts in the analysis of chronic pain syndromes. *Journal of Consulting and Clinical Psychology, 54,* 776–783.

Keefe, F. J., & Van Horn, Y. V. (1993). Cognitive-behavioral treatment of rheumatoid arthritis pain: Maintaining treatment gains. *Arthritis Care and Research, 6,* 213–222.

Litt, M. D. (1988). Self-efficacy and perceived control: Cognitive mediators of pain tolerance. *Journal of Personality and Social Psychology, 54,* 149–160.

Lorig, K., Lubeck, D., Kraines, R. G., Seleznick, M., & Holman, H. R. (1985). Outcomes of self-help education for patients with arthritis. *Arthritis and Rheumatism, 28,* 680–685.

Marlatt, G. A., & Gordon, J. R. (Eds.). (1985). *Relapse prevention.* New York: Guilford Press.

McCaul, D., & Malott, J. M. (1984). Distraction and coping with pain. *Psychological Bulletin, 95,* 516–533.

Melzack, R., & Wall, P. (1965). Pain mechanisms: A new theory. *Science, 50,* 971–979.

Nicholas, M. K., Wilson, P. H., & Goyen, J. (1991). Comparison of operant-behavioural and cognitive-behavioural group treatment, with and without relaxation training for chronic low back pain. *Behaviour Research and Therapy, 29,* 225–238.

Parker, J. C., Frank, R. G., Beck, N. C., Smarr, K. L., Buescher, K. L., Phillips, L. R., Smith, E. I., Anderson, S. K., & Walker, S. E. (1988). Pain management in rheumatoid arthritis patients: A cognitive-behavioral approach. *Arthritis and Rheumatism, 31,* 591–601.

Parker, J. C., Smarr, K. L., Buescher, K. L., Phillips, L. R., Frank, R. G., Beck, N. C., Anderson, S. K., & Walker, S. E. (1989). Pain control and rational thinking: Implications for rheumatoid arthritis. *Arthritis and Rheumatism, 32,* 984–990.

Surwit, R. S. (1979). *Progressive relaxation training manual.* Durham, NC: Duke University Medical Center.

Travell, J., Rinzler, S., & Herman, M. (1943). Pain and disability of the shoulder and arm: Treatment by intramuscular infiltration with procaine hydrochloride. *Journal of the American Medical Association, 120,* 209–233.

Turk, D. C., Meichenbaum, D., & Genest, M. (1983). *Pain and behavioral medicine: A cognitive-behavioral perspective.* New York: Guilford Press.

Turner, J. A., & Clancy, S. (1988). Comparison of operant-behavioral and cognitive-behavioral group treatment for chronic low back pain. *Journal of Consulting and Clinical Psychology, 58,* 573–579.

Wolf, S. L., Nacht, M., & Kelly, J. L. (1982). EMG feedback training during dynamic movement for low back pain patients. *Behavior Therapy, 13,* 395–406.

CHAPTER 11

Treating Families
of Chronic Pain Patients

Robert D. Kerns
Annette Payne

There has been a persistent call in the chronic pain literature to attend to (if not actually to emphasize) the social context, particularly the role of the family, in the analysis of the problem (Flor, Turk, & Rudy, 1987b; 1987c; Karoly, 1985; Roy, 1992). Encouragement for this perspective lies in contemporary multidimensional theoretical models of chronic pain (e.g., Flor, Birbaumer, & Turk, 1990; Fordyce, 1976, 1988; Turk, Meichenbaum, & Genest, 1983; Kerns & Jacob, in press), systems perspectives on health and illness issues (e.g., Ramsey, 1989; Schwartz, 1982), and specific calls for attention to the role of the family in chronic illness (e.g., Kerns, 1994a, in press; Turk & Kerns, 1985a). Reports of clinical observations, and a substantial and growing empirical base that describes the impact of chronic pain and the family on each other, similarly encourage this approach to the problem.

Recently, this family perspective has led to initial efforts to propose and develop clinical assessment and treatment strategies with a family focus. Particularly exciting are ongoing studies designed to evaluate theory-driven family-based, or at least couple-based, treatment approaches to pain management. These studies have the potential to significantly advance both theory development and clinical efficacy, and generally to encourage continued evolution of a family perspective on chronic pain and pain management.

This chapter begins by presenting three integrative theoretical perspectives that can help to organize information about the family of an individual with chronic pain and provide a framework for refinements in the treatment and management of such a family. In particular, an integrative family-focused cognitive-behavioral transactional model is emphasized as a framework for further discussion. A second section briefly reviews some of the most relevant empirical literature that informs this model. A third section describes a clinical perspective based on this model and includes two case presentations that serve to highlight important aspects of the clinical approach. The chapter closes with a brief discussion of future directions for theory building, research, and refinements in the clinical arena.

THEORETICAL FOUNDATIONS

Biopsychosocial Perspective

The emergence of the field of behavioral medicine—the interdisciplinary field developed to foster improved understanding of a full range of physical health and illness issues via the integration of the behavioral and social sciences and medical science—was informed importantly by systems theory, and in particular by a biopsychosocial perspective (Schwartz, 1982). The biopsychosocial model articulated the importance of the social domain, in addition to emphasizing the dynamic and reciprocal relationships between the domain and the biological and psychological spheres of the physical health problem. Consistent with more general systems theories, the model noted that a change in one sphere (e.g., the biological sphere in the case of a chronic painful condition) necessarily results in changes in the psychological and social spheres. Ultimately, the biopsychosocial system is driven to restore homeostasis within the system.

The model's specific influence on the chronic pain field has been limited, however. The model has been commended for emphasizing that the social domain should be attended to in terms of the impact of the experience of chronic pain (Kerns & Jacob, in press). In this context, the negative effects of pain and disability on the family (e.g., shifting roles, lost income, and increased family and marital distress and dysfunction) have been noted. The model has failed, however, to contribute to specific theoretical refinements concerning mechanisms of transaction, particularly the potential influence of the social (and family) domain on the development and perpetuation of the chronic pain condition or its associated problems.

Family Adjustment and Adaptation Response Model

Family systems and family stress theories have emerged as potentially influential frameworks for understanding the role of the family with a chronically ill individual, including the individual with persistent pain (Patterson & Garwick, 1994). These perspectives have been important in hypothesizing mechanisms (or at least factors) that may influence the response of the family to the chronic pain condition, and, via circular and continuous feedback, may influence the adjustment and adaptation of the individual with chronic pain. One family systems framework that has been advanced for understanding the role of the family in chronic illness is the "family adjustment and adaptation response" (FAAR) model (Patterson, 1988, 1989; Patterson & Garwick, 1994).

The FAAR model hypothesizes that the family attempts to maintain homeostasis or a balance in functioning by using its capabilities—that is, its resources and coping capacities—in an effort to meet the demands and stressors associated with a chronic illness. The model further notes that the meanings (e.g., attributions, beliefs) that the family ascribes to the demands of the illness and to its own capabilities are what ultimately influence the balance in functioning. The model articulates a dynamic process of adjustment, a period in which the family makes use of existing capabilities to resist change in the face of acute demands and stressors. In the face of a chronic condition such as persistent pain in a family member, the family is likely to experience a longer period of adaptation, during which it attempts to restore homeostasis by developing new resources and coping behaviors, by reducing the challenges of the condition, and by altering its appraisals of the situation and the family.

The FAAR model appears to have important strengths that enhance its potential utility in the field of chronic pain. The specification of the primary hypothesized constructs of the model (i.e., stress, coping, adaptation, and adjustment), and the articulation of the critical mediating role of cognitive appraisal, are advances of the FAAR model over the more general biopsychosocial perspective and other family systems and family stress theories. The fact that these constructs already play a central role in the field of behavioral medicine is a key asset. A much-cited shortcoming of previous family medicine perspectives has been the absence of reliable measurement strategies for constructs of interest. An advantage of the FAAR model is the fact that psychometrically sound measures have been developed for many of the constructs central to the model. Finally, the model is important to the extent that it emphasizes that the family system, rather than the individual, should be the primary target of clinical analysis and intervention.

The FAAR model is not without its shortcomings. As is true of other family systems models, the FAAR model's scope and complexity may be too cumbersome for it to be practically applied in empirical research. Considerable overlap or ambiguity has also been noted among the definitions of some of the key constructs and their measurement. Although there have been important advances in the assessment of key constructs, the implications of the model for family intervention have not yet been well articulated. Finally, the model has not yet been specifically refined or elaborated for the problem of chronic pain.

Operant Behavioral Perspective

Wilbert Fordyce (1976) is credited with the elaboration of a specific operant behavioral formulation of the development and maintenance of chronic pain, and with the further refinement of a learning-theory-based perspective on this complex clinical problem (see Sanders, Chapter 4, this volume). Central to the model is the notion that observable "pain behaviors" (e.g., complaining, grimacing, bracing, taking medications, reducing activity, etc.) may be maintained via contingent social reinforcement (e.g., the sympathetic response of significant others), even in the absence of continued nociception. Family members, as well as health care providers, have been specifically noted to play potentially critical roles as primary sources of social reinforcement for pain behaviors, to the detriment of alternative "well behaviors" (e.g., continued productive activity, exercise, and other health-promoting behaviors).

Interest in testing the model with clinical samples contributed to the development of intensive inpatient treatment environments. Such controlled environments were viewed as necessary in order to alter these contingencies and improve outcomes. Although these inpatient programs were successful, enthusiasm for them was tempered by their high costs and questionable maintenance of improved outcomes once the patients returned to their home environments. Unfortunately, more detailed elaboration of the hypothesized role of the family, empirical examinations of the importance of pain-related family interactions, and the development of family-based outpatient interventions consistent with the model have been slow in coming.

Cognitive-Behavioral Transactional Model

Consistent with its roots in cognitive/social learning theory and in behaviorism, a cognitive-behavioral transactional model of the role of families in the course of chronic illness has been elaborated (Kerns, in press; Kerns & Weiss, 1994; Turk & Kerns, 1985b). The model shares important features with the FAAR model just described, with Reiss's (1989) family paradigm model, and with contemporary models of stress and coping (Friedman, 1992; Lazarus & Folkman, 1984). In addition, this model for understanding the role of the family in chronic pain, with its implications for family assessment and treatment, can be viewed as a specific extension of a diathesis–stress model of chronic pain that has also been recently elaborated (Kerns & Jacob, in press). Central to this integrative model is the emphasis on the social context in general, and the family context in particular, as the key environment in which adaptation or maladaptation occurs in the face of a chronically painful condition. Figure 11.1 illustrates this diathesis–stress framework.

As can be seen in Figure 11.1, the family context is highlighted as the central environment in which complex interactions occur between the individual's prior vulnerabilities in biological (i.e., central nervous system neurobiological), behavioral, cognitive, and affective domains and the specific challenges or stresses of the painful condition. The model suggests that these interactions take place within a social (family) learning environment that selectively reinforces coping attempts and outcomes in terms of optimal pain management, continued constructive activity, and emotional well-being, or, conversely, heightened pain, unnecessary impairment and disability, and affective distress. As such, the model has advantages over previous models by specifying a salient role of social and particularly family interactions as important influences on the course of the chronic pain condition. Consistent with a cognitive-behavioral perspective on chronic pain (Turk et al., 1983), this transactional family model hypothesizes that the family plays an active role in seeking out and evaluating information about the painful condition itself and the specific challenges it poses, as well as in making judgments about the family's (and its members') capacities and vulnerabilities in meeting the challenges. It is on the basis of these appraisals that the family and its members make active decisions about alternative responses, act upon their decisions, and evaluate the adequacy of the response.

Also consistent with cognitive theory and with Reiss's (1989) description of family paradigms is the notion that the family and its members develop "schemas" or a relatively fixed set of beliefs about the world, and, even more directly relevant, about concepts such as illness, pain, disability, and emotional responding. The family's more specific appraisals of its ongoing experiences in living with the individual with the painful condition are based in part on these more enduring schemas. These more specific

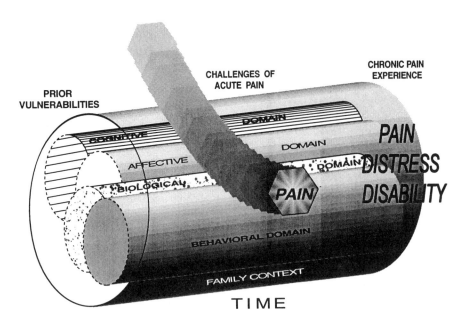

FIGURE 11.1. Diathesis–stress model of chronic pain. From Kerns and Jacob (in press). Copyright by Plenum Press. Adapted by permission.

appraisals of its present experiences are hypothesized to influence both the individual's and the family's responses to the challenges perceived, and ultimately to determine their level of adaptation. The family also maintains beliefs about its available resources to cope with the challenges posed by the painful condition. The family's flexibility versus rigidity in adopting new strategies for coping with the challenges of chronic pain, together with its more characteristic patterns of responding to stress and challenges, further mediates the response.

Finally, the family's appraisals of its success in mastering the challenges and in promoting optimal outcomes contribute to future responding. This later step in the appraisal–coping process—that is, the family's and its members' evaluations of the success of the response—will determine whether the response is repeated or not.

Central to the transactional model is the additional notion that the family's response and its perceived effects in turn shape future appraisals of stress and challenge in a dynamic and reciprocal fashion. Perceptions of failed efforts to manage the painful condition will probably enhance the intensity of the perceived threat of the condition, perhaps contributing to a heightened level of perceived pain, increased disability, and affective distress. Conversely, perceptions of success in coping will probably moderate the experience of pain, increase confidence in the family's ability to respond effectively in the future, and reinforce the repeated use of similar strategies.

One final point should be emphasized with regard to the integrative diathesis–stress and transactional family models. The diathesis–stress model represented in Figure 11.1 emphasizes the importance of several domains of the chronic pain condition—namely, the condition itself, and the experiences of pain, disability, and emotional distress. Consistent with Fordyce's (1976) operant analysis of chronic pain, the cognitive-behavioral transactional model places its emphasis on the family's appraisals of discrete observable behaviors. As such, the family's response to behaviors representing one domain may be quite different from its response to behaviors representing another domain. Furthermore, the family's response to one set of behaviors, such as the individual's complaints of pain, may have unexpected direct and indirect effects on another aspect of the individual's overall experience. This specification of the model may help to explain observations that a family's response may have positive effects on one domain but negative effects on another—for example, the observation that positive support from the spouse for the individual's expressions of pain may buffer the individual from depression, while inadvertently contributing to reports of heightened pain and increased pain behavior frequency (Kerns, Haythornthwaite, Southwick, & Giller, 1990). The model argues for behavioral specificity in the family's influence on the course of the chronic pain experience.

EMPIRICAL SUPPORT FOR THE COGNITIVE-BEHAVIORAL TRANSACTIONAL MODEL

Although the model as articulated above is most important in attempting to explain the influence of the family on the chronic pain experience, the model also generally acknowledges the impact of chronic pain on the family and its members. Interestingly, in this regard there is conflicting evidence to support the conclusion that chronic pain commonly has a negative impact on the family and its members. Although it is true that investigators have offered evidence of marital and sexual dysfunction, increased prevalence of psychophysiological disorders, and elevated emotional distress (particularly depression) among the partners of individuals with chronic pain (e.g., Ahern, Adams, & Follick, 1985;

Feuerstein, Sult, & Houle, 1985; Flor, Turk, & Scholz, 1987d; Maruta, Osborne, Swenson, & Holling, 1981; Mohamed, Weisz, & Waring, 1978), these studies have generally been poorly controlled, and it is not clear that families of chronic pain patients experience a higher level of distress or other problems than do families of other chronically ill individuals (e.g., Revenson & Majerovitz, 1990).

An additional shortcoming is that the available literature is largely descriptive rather than explanatory. Theory-driven research based on either family systems or cognitive-behavioral perspectives is just beginning, as investigators attempt to identify patterns of family beliefs or coping that account for variance in negative functioning or distress (e.g., Elliot, Trief, & Stein, 1986; Thomas & Roy, 1989). Such research will be valuable in informing future refinements of the theoretical model, as well as clinical conceptualizations and assessment and intervention planning.

Research on the influence of the family on the individual's adaptation to the chronic pain experience is equally limited. The one area that has drawn attention is an examination of the validity of operant formulations of chronic pain. Consistent with claims by Fordyce and others that spouses may serve particularly influential roles because they serve as a primary source of potential social reinforcement, investigators have focused much of their attention on this dyadic relationship. Results to date generally support the hypothesis that positive attention from a spouse contingent on a patient's expressions of pain is associated with higher reported levels of pain and pain behaviors (e.g., Block, Kremer, & Gaylor, 1980; Kerns et al., 1990), higher frequency of observed pain behaviors (Romano et al., 1992), and reports of greater disability and interference (Flor, Turk, & Rudy, 1989; Turk, Kerns, & Rosenberg, 1992). Conversely, there is evidence that a high frequency of negative responding to pain is reliably associated with depressive symptom severity and other demonstrations of affective distress (e.g., Kerns et al., 1990, 1991b). There is also emerging evidence that level of global marital satisfaction and gender may moderate these findings (e.g., Flor et al., 1989; Turk et al., 1992). Kerns and his colleagues have begun to examine more complex patterns of pain-relevant interactions (Weiss & Kerns, 1995) and the role of cognitive appraisal of these interactions, in an effort to improve the prediction of pain and disability.

Despite extensive encouragement in the literature for the application of family therapy for chronic pain, and the availability of relatively detailed descriptions of family therapy approaches (e.g., Roy, 1986), there have been no reports to date of controlled empirical evaluations of family therapy for chronic pain. There have recently been a few published reports documenting the efficacy of couples therapy for chronic pain (e.g., Moore & Chaney, 1985; Radojevic, Nicassio, & Weisman, 1992; Saarijarvi, 1991). Unfortunately, descriptions of the treatments in these published reports were generally not detailed enough to permit an evaluation of their consistency with any specific theoretical framework that could be applied to the idiosyncrasies of the chronic pain experience. In addition, demonstrations of the effectiveness of the treatments relative to control conditions were weak and inconclusive. It is clear that refinement of the treatment approaches, and additional testing of their efficacy, are needed.

FAMILY THERAPY FOR CHRONIC PAIN

Clinical Implications of the Theoretical Model

Both the FAAR model and the integrative cognitive-behavioral transactional and diathesis–stress model encourage a view of the family system as the primary unit of analysis and (most likely) of intervention. This notion is certainly not new, having been encouraged as the appropriate perspective for health care problems in general (Litman, 1974), as well as for chronic pain more specifically (Karoly, 1985). However, such an orientation is certainly contrary to common clinical practice in the 1990s, which remains primarily focused on the individual.

Consistent with this view of the family as the primary unit of analysis, the cognitive-behavioral transactional and diathesis–stress model places emphasis on the active, reciprocal transactions among family members, including the individual with the chronic pain condition. Although the clinician may, for the sake of parsimony and clarity, focus primarily on one "direction" of the transaction relative to the other at times, or on one dyadic pair (e.g., the marital relationship), the model encourages ongoing reframing of these interactions within a family context.

A hypothesis-generating and hypothesis-testing approach to clinical assessment, treatment planning, and intervention should be encouraged by attention to this theoretical perspective. The model can be used to inform and to guide the development of an integrative conceptualization of the problems experienced by the family and its members, based on theory-driven assessment. Ongoing assessment and empirically based efforts to intervene can be thought of as opportunities to evaluate the validity of the conceptualizations. Outcomes of this approach can be used to refine the specific hypotheses about the problems and factors maintaining them, and ultimately to shape revisions in the treatment plan and delivery of services.

There are several other distinct and important clinical implications of a family theoretical model. The integrative cognitive-behavioral transactional and diathesis–stress model, in particular, emphasizes that a comprehensive and multimodal approach to assessment is critical. The model identifies several specific targets for assessment, such as the domains of the chronic pain experience; the specific aspects of the chronic painful condition and the experience of pain that represent challenges or problems for the family and its members; and historical information about the available resources and supports for coping with or solving these problems or challenges. The model encourages efforts to develop a "time line" of information that evaluates dynamic interactions between the challenges of the pain problem and the individual's and family's efforts to master the challenges, including, but not limited to, the current relevant transactions. Finally, the model highlights the importance of assessing the family's attitudes, beliefs, and attributions concerning the pain experience, as well as its behavioral and affective responses to this experience.

Consistent with treatment recommendations based on a cognitive-behavioral perspective (Turk et al., 1983), treatment should be time-limited, goal-oriented, and learning-based. Broadly, family therapy should first encourage the development of an adaptive problem-solving perspective to the problems of chronic pain. Increasing the effective use of available family resources, teaching family members new skills, and helping them to draw upon available external resources are important areas of intervention. Efforts to help family members reduce the stress and challenge of the painful condition and/or reconceptualize the problems and challenges as less threatening constitute a second general goal. Reduction of the negative impact of the pain problem on the family and its members (including the individual with the chronic pain condition), and promotion of adaptive family functioning and well-being, are the overarching or higher-order goals of the therapeutic approach.

On the basis of a comprehensive assessment, the clinician should be able to generate specific hypotheses about the nature of the problems being experienced and the mechanisms (or at least the factors) that may be contributing to their maintenance over time. It is on the basis of this conceptualization that a multidimensional and frequently multimodal plan for treatment can be developed. Despite a paucity of empirical research evaluating the effectiveness of family treatment for chronic pain, the models presented can be used to guide relatively "prescriptive" treatment planning (Kerns, 1994b). Ultimately, the clinician, in collaboration with the family, can develop a plan for treatment that specifically targets identified problems and hypothesized contributing mechanisms. For example, treatment of one family may focus primarily on patterns of solicitous pain-relevant communication, whereas treatment of a second family may specifically target the family's pervasive depressogenic cognition. Given the complexity of the experience of chronic pain, and the multidimensional model that is used to inform hypotheses about the functioning of an individual family, the intervention plan commonly incorporates multiple treatment targets and strategies. Optimally, the plan and its implementation emphasize continuous efforts to remain integrative and internally consistent with the model and the goals of the family for treatment.

In the following sections, two case examples of family therapy for chronic pain are described. In each instance, the case is first briefly introduced; the case description is then followed by a more detailed discussion of the assessment and treatment of the family.

The Case of the Family of Mr. G

Mr. G was a 48-year-old married Caucasian male who was originally referred by the Neurosurgery Service for a clinical neuropsychological evaluation of his competence to have his left arm amputated, in order to relieve severe chronic pain. He reported that the pain, although increasing in severity in recent years, had been present for 16 years. He attributed his present pain to a series of surgeries, and only through extensive interviewing was the original organic cause of his pain uncovered—a fractured bone in his wrist that had occurred nearly 30 years earlier. Obviously, by the very nature of the referral question, one can assume the severe distress of a man who would literally "give an arm" to experience relief from pain. At the time of the evaluation, the only medical treatments were occasional nerve blocks and 5 mg Valium three times a day, which the patient described as only minimally effective in reducing pain.

Assessment

In response to the referral, an initial screening appointment with the patient and his wife was scheduled. It was in this meeting that the spouses acknowledged that they were concerned about the psychological impact of the pain problem on their two adolescent sons, and that their own relationship was threatened. It was decided to include the two sons (an older married daughter who did not live with them was not included) in subsequent assessment meetings. A comprehensive evaluation was planned. Several strategies were used in the assessment process, including a semistructured pain assessment interview involving the family during three 1-hour meetings; the administration of several questionnaires, inventories, and psychological tests; the patient's self-monitoring of his daily pain intensity, as well as situational antecedents and consequences of periods of peak pain; and daily "pain diaries" kept by the spouse and sons. A similar assessment format was conducted immediately after treatment and at 3- and 6-month follow-up intervals.

Care was taken from the initial visit to establish expectations that the family members were "in this together" and that the assessment and treatment process would best involve each of the family members as equally important participants. The family members were encouraged to take a "family view" of the problems they were experiencing, and to accept the idea that solutions would necessarily require a family effort. All members were reassured that each of their concerns and views about the problems would be heard, and that efforts would be made to help each of them feel better about the current situation and the future.

Interviewing began by discovering the family members' views of the pain problem, including a description of the problem (e.g., site, changes over time, medical history, intensity, fluctuations), attributions of causality, and expectations for recovery or rehabilitation. Care was taken to involve each family member in the discussion and to reflect when there appeared to be a shared "family view" and when there appeared to be individual differences in perspectives. For example, it was clear that the patient and his children generally held a medical view of the cause of the pain problem and believed that doctors should be able to do something about it. The sons believed that their father was experiencing an extremely high level of pain, and they reported a high level of worry and sadness about their father. On the other hand, it was clear that Mrs. G believed that her husband exaggerated his pain and should be able to be more active around the home, despite his pain. She verbalized a high degree of frustration, irritability, and frank anger toward her husband, and a high level of worry about her sons. All felt relatively helpless and hopeless about finding a solution to the problem.

A second major focus of the interview related to perceived impact of the pain problem on the patient's and the family's functioning. In this area, there was a strong consensus that the pain condition was associated with a significant decline in family-related activities, in other activities around the home, and in social and recreational activities on the part of Mr. G. He did, however, continue to work full-time as an accounting assistant, although he was frequently absent or left work early secondary to complaints of pain. It should be added that Mr. G expressed dissatisfaction with his level of employment, independent of his pain condition. The family reported that Mr. G typically withdrew into his bedroom or lay on the couch upon returning home from work. He was reported to do few household chores, rarely participated in any activities with his sons, and even less frequently left home for any family-related activity. Mr. G became tearful when describing his limited involvement with his sons. His younger son, in particular, acknowledged his disappointment that his father was not involved in activities. His wife acknowledged that she and her husband were never sexual with each other and that he rarely showed any affection toward her. Mr. G believed that he was unable to do any more than he was already doing, given his current pain condition. His sons generally agreed. As already noted, Mrs. G thought that he was unnecessarily restricting his activities, and that his major problems were that he was depressed and avoidant of responsibility.

Mr. G demonstrated markedly depressed mood and frequently became tearful during the interview, and remained generally quiet and withdrawn throughout. His wife's affect was notably angry. The younger son appeared to be quite sad and also frequently became tearful, while the older son remained generally tense and reserved. The family members reported that their current distress had been building over a few years. Overall, the family evidenced a high level of affective distress throughout the interview process. They agreed that each of the family members was depressed and that they all wanted help to feel better.

The family members were also interviewed regarding their views of the family's and Mr. G's functioning prior to the onset of pain, the challenges represented by the pain problem, and their efforts to cope with the pain condition and to help Mr. G. All agreed that there had been a time when the family had been very happy and "did a lot together." Mrs. G reported that her husband was a good provider for her and her family, but that she had always "been the strong one" when it came to coping with problems or challenges. She also said that he had never been very involved with household chores or in parenting roles. The family members agreed that pain had always been an issue, but thought that Mr. G had "given up" over the last 3 years. Mrs. G was outspoken in her criticism of Mr. G's inability to "live with the pain" and stated that she thought that he was "weak." This conflict in views between Mr. and Mrs. G was clearly a source of considerable distress for the children. The sons stated that they were "tired of the fighting" and "wished that Dad could get well."

In addition to the interview, questionnaires and diaries were used to gather information and to engage the family in the therapeutic process outside of the formal sessions with the clinician. The cornerstones of the questionnaire battery were the Patient and Significant Other versions of the West Haven–Yale Multidimensional Pain Inventory (WHYMPI; Kerns, Turk, & Rudy, 1985; Kerns & Rosenberg, 1995). These measures are based in cognitive-behavioral theory, are brief, and together provide a comprehensive view of the experience of chronic pain. The first section of the Patient version of the WHYMPI has several subscales that provide a view of the patient's pain experience as well as his or her own affective and behavioral responses. The second section is a set of three subscales reporting on the significant other's frequency of responding to the patient's pain with either solicitous (e.g., expressing sympathy), distracting (e.g., cuing adaptive coping), or negative (e.g., expressing irritation) responses. Two nearly identical sets of items make up the Significant Other version of the measure. The items of the second section of the Significant Other version are presented in Table 11.1. A third section of the Patient version provides indices of the patient's activity level.

On the Patient version of the WHYMPI, Mr. G reported a high level of pain, a high degree of interference of pain in his life, a low level of activity, a low level of self-control in relation to his pain, a high level of depressed mood, and a low level of support from

TABLE 11.1. Item Content of the Significant Other Version of the Pain-Relevant Response Scales of the WHYMPI

Solicitous responses
    Ask what I can do to help.
    Express sympathy.
    Give him/her a massage.
    Take over his/her jobs or duties.
    Try to get him/her to rest.
    Get him/her some medication.
    Get him/her something to eat or drink.
    Try to comfort him/her by listening to his/her complaints.
    Tell him/her not to exert himself/herself.
    Turn on the TV to take his/her mind off the pain.
Distracting responses
    Talk to him/her about something else to take his/her mind off the pain.
    Try to involve him/her in some activity.
    Encourage him/her to work on a hobby.
Negative responses
    Leave the room.
    Express irritation at him/her.
    Express my frustration at him/her.
    Express anger at him/her.

Note. From Kerns and Rosenberg (1995). Copyright 1995 by the International Association for the Study of Pain. Reprinted by permission.

significant others. He also reported a high level of responses from significant others, including each of the categories of solicitous, distracting, and negative responses. Mrs. G and their children generally corroborated his report. However, Mrs. G reported a significantly lower level of positive responses to her husband's pain, while the children reported few negative responses. Mrs. G and their younger son reported high levels of personal distress in response to Mr. G's pain. Not surprisingly, Mrs. G and both the children viewed Mr. G as highly dependent on others.

Other questionnaires revealed Mr. G to experience a severe level of depressive symptoms and anxiety, and a moderately low level of marital satisfaction. He also acknowledged poor perceptions of personal control and problem-solving abilities. Mrs. G reported a mild level of depression and a high level of marital dysfunction. Both sons acknowledged a mild level of depressive symptoms.

Mr. G also completed a pain intensity self-monitoring procedure (Kerns, Finn, & Haythornthwaite, 1988), which demonstrated an overall high level of pain intensity with nearly daily exacerbations in the late afternoon and evening. Mrs. G and her sons were trained in a diary procedure that is displayed in Figure 11.2 (Flor, Kerns, & Turk, 1987a). Each was trained to make entries in the diary when they observed Mr. G to be exhibiting pain (e.g., rubbing his forearm or grimacing). They were to record the behavior indicating pain, what they thought, what they felt, what they tried to do to help (if anything), and a rating of how effective they felt that they had been. These recordings were discussed extensively during the assessment process and continued to be a focus of discussion throughout the treatment phase. In particular, a pattern of solicitousness on the part of the sons, and frequently Mrs. G, in response to the patient's displays of pain was noted to be associated with feelings of helplessness and frustration and with ratings of limited effectiveness. There was very little evidence of efforts to cue adaptive coping, activity, or verbal interaction. Figure 11.2 displays examples of Mrs. G's diary entries.

Conceptualization

By the end of the third assessment session, a more focused discussion took place that articulated several specific problem domains and hypothesized contributors to these problems. Highlighted were Mr. G's low level of pleasurable and constructive activity, including a very low level of pleasurable interaction among the family members, and an associated high level of affective distress experienced by each of the family members. Contributors to these difficulties included the family's beliefs that it was helpless to do anything to promote positive change and that withdrawal/avoidance was an effective strategy in lowering Mr. G's pain and suffering.

Treatment

After this conceptual framework was discussed, the family agreed to remain involved in treatment. A plan was established that called for both individual and family therapy. Weekly individual sessions were planned; these sessions were intended to help Mr. G develop improved pain coping strategies and reduce his depressive cognitions. Goals for increasing physical activity and exercising, and decreasing absenteeism from work, were established and became additional targets in the individual therapy sessions. Monthly family therapy sessions were also scheduled. Primary goals of the family work included altering patterns of pain-relevant communication within the family, increasing time spent in non-pain-related conversation among the family members, and increasing pleasurable

Instructions: To help us learn more about the nature of your spouse's pain, it is important that you keep careful records. The Spouse Diary is designed to provide detailed information about periods when your spouse's pain is most severe, how you respond to your spouse when he or she is experiencing severe pain, and how effective your response is in reducing the pain. It is particularly important that we obtain this information, so that we can design the most appropriate treatment program for your spouse.

Specifically, we would like you to keep a record of the times when you were aware that your spouse's pain was particularly severe. Note the date, the time, and your location (for example, home, in the car, etc.). Next we would like you to record how you recognized your spouse's pain (for example, he or she told you, lay down, asked you to bring him or her some medications, looked very distressed and was moaning, etc.). Then note what you thought and how you felt at the time when you noted your spouse's pain was severe (for example, distressed, helpless, thought "Why can't the doctors find some way to help?", frustrated, etc.). Then indicate what you tried to do to reduce the pain or discomfort (for example, gave him or her some pain medication, tried to talk to him or her, gave him or her a massage, tried not to bother him or her). We would also like you to indicate how effective your attempt to reduce the pain was. That is, rate how much you think your action helped, using a scale ranging from 0, "did not help at all," to 5, "seemed to completely eliminate the pain." (0, "did not help at all"; 1, "helped very little"; 2, "helped somewhat"; 3, "helped a lot"; 4, "helped very much"; 5, "seemed to completely eliminate the pain.") Using the numbers listed, try to rate how effective any of your attempts were to reduce your spouse's pain. To illustrate what we would like you to do, we have included a sample below. Use as much paper as you want to complete this diary between now and our next appointment. Thank you for your help.

Name: _____   **Date:** _____

Time	Location	How you recognized spouse's pain	What you thought	How you felt	How you tried to help	Your effectiveness (0–5)
2:00 P.M.	At home, in living room	He was lying down, face looked drawn, heard him breathing, moaning.	"It seems hopeless."	Frustrated Angry at doctors	I asked him if I could get him some painkillers or make some tea.	0
					I rubbed his shoulder.	4
					I made some tea.	1
11:00 P.M.	In bed, at home	Husband got out of bed, was pacing the floor and took some medicine.		Frustrated Helpless	I didn't know what to do, so I turned over and cried myself to sleep.	0

FIGURE 11.2. Spouse Diary.

activities with the children and pleasurable spousal activities. In addition, Mr. G agreed to a referral for vocational/educational counseling related to his interest in improving his vocational skills, in order to increase his marketability for higher-level positions.

Ultimately, active treatment lasted for 3 months and involved 12 individual and 3 family sessions. A didactic/problem-solving orientation was employed in each session. For example, Mr. G and the family were taught to distinguish the experiences of pain, disability, and distress, and to consider discrete ways to reduce pain, increase functioning, and improve mood. In this context, for example, the family was encouraged to set activity goals and to work toward them, regardless of Mr. G's reports of pain or other family members' perceptions of his pain. Family activities that had previously been viewed as pleasurable were particularly encouraged. Obstacles to goal accomplishment were specifically discussed, and ways to continue to work toward the goals despite pain or other perceived barriers were discovered. Again, a collaborative process that placed value on each family member's input was employed.

Therapeutic efforts consistently attempted to reinforce the patient's sense of control or mastery of his pain and to reduce his feelings of helplessness and depression. Similarly, the family members were encouraged to appreciate that there were important ways to change their patterns of interaction with Mr. G that would be effective in helping him in his efforts to improve his management of pain and to improve his functioning. The important role of thoughts as mediators of each family member's behavior and emotional response was emphasized. All members were made aware that their beliefs that they were helpless with regard to Mr. G's pain problem were inaccurate, and that maintenance of such beliefs was contributing to their own distress and to the family's generally inactive, passive, or avoidant approach to the problem. For example, diaries were used throughout the treatment process to reinforce the idea that one individual's appraisals (e.g., the wife's belief that her husband was using his pain as an excuse for avoiding doing the dishes) of another's behavior (e.g., Mr. G's lying on the couch and moaning) contributes to the individual's emotional and behavioral response (e.g., Mrs. G's expressing irritation). Alternative ways of framing the situation (e.g, viewing it as an opportunity to cue adaptive behavior, such as an activity with the children) were encouraged and consistently reinforced.

Specific skills (i.e., autogenic relaxation and other attention diversion strategies) were presented, and practice of the skills was expected to occur at home. Although Mr. G was taught a relaxation exercise in his individual sessions, he agreed to teach his sons the exercise, and together they practiced at home throughout the remainder of the therapy. In the family sessions, the family was engaged in discussions about alternative strategies. It was in this context that Mr. G's older son related that his father was particularly good at mental arithmetic and other mathematical manipulations. Mr. G became enthusiastic about the idea of using mental arithmetic (in fact, performing mathematical proofs in his head!) as an effective attention diversion strategy.

The family was taught to encourage and reward Mr. G's involvement in pleasurable activities; weekly activity goals were established, and progress was monitored. The family also chose to institute a family exercise program at home, and the patient decided to stop smoking as a function of family and individual discussions about increasing "well behaviors." Through his vocational counseling, Mr. G was able to obtain financial assistance to take college courses in order to improve his employability.

Posttreatment Assessment

At the time of termination of treatment, all goals that had been established prior to treatment and many other positive behavioral changes had been achieved. Mr. G's self-report of pain intensity had dramatically decreased. Quantifiable indices of depression, somatization, anxiety, and overall psychological distress had returned to levels within the normal range. The family reported a high level of satisfaction with the patient's changes. However, a mild degree of marital dissatisfaction reported at pretreatment was still present. No change in Mr. G's vocational status had yet occurred, although substantial progress toward enrollment at an area college had been achieved. Maintenance of most of these positive changes was reported at both the 3- and 6-month follow-up intervals. The only concern was a linear and mild increase in depressed mood over this period. The mild level of depression reported was not judged to be a significant problem at the 6-month follow-up, but Mr. G was encouraged to recontact our program should he so desire.

The Case of the Family of Mr. F

Mr. F, a 64-year-old widowed male with a 12-year history of chronic neck pain, was referred by Oncology for a chronic pain evaluation. Mr. F was interviewed with his adult daughter, with whom he lived.

Assessment

As in the case of Mr. G, a comprehensive evaluation was conducted; this included a semistructured pain assessment interview, administration of several questionnaires, and self-monitoring of daily pain intensity and situational antecedents and consequences of periods of peak pain. In the first assessment session, Mr. F and his daughter were encouraged to adopt a perspective of a shared responsibility for the pain problem and for finding solutions for it. Consistent with this view, the clinician attempted to involve Mr. F and his daughter equally in all aspects of the assessment and treatment process, and emphasized the importance of each of their perspectives.

As the assessment process started, it was clear that Mr. F and his daughter had different beliefs about the nature of the pain experience. Mr. F generally held a medical or biological perspective of the cause of the pain problem, and stated that "The doctors should be able to figure out why I have pain." In contrast, Mr. F's daughter believed that the situational events in the last 2 years (i.e., Mr. F's wife's death and the loss of his employment) were playing a significant role in the current pain experience. Both agreed they felt helpless in their attempts to reduce pain and hopeless about potential treatment efficacy.

Both Mr. F and his daughter described significant changes in their lives because of the pain experience. Mr. F described reductions in his activity level because "I am worried that something else is going to happen to me if I am not careful about what I do." Mr. F avoided most of his previously enjoyed activities, such as golf, walking, yardwork, woodworking, and remodeling; he believed that these activities might increase the damage to his neck and limit his abilities "even more." He also noted that he didn't participate in social activities (visiting friends, going to the senior citizen center's activities, etc.), because "I don't feel like it" and "I don't want people feeling sorry for me because of my pain." Mr. F's daughter confirmed that her father's social and physical activities had decreased, and added that she was concerned about his lack of activity.

Besides changes in his physical and social activities, Mr. F described changes in his mood and thoughts. He stated that he had been feeling depressed and frustrated when he thought about his pain. Mr. F reported that he felt "like an old decrepit man" when he couldn't perform household chores. He described getting down on himself and saying things like "I'm useless" and "I am a burden to my daughter." Mr. F and his daughter both noted that when Mr. F was "in a bad mood," he often reported that his pain was more severe and he stayed in bed. He also expressed feelings of uselessness and dependency, which may have contributed to his depressed mood. Despite Mr. F's depressed mood, his daughter denied symptoms of depressed mood and noted that "I have to be strong enough for both of us."

On further evaluation, Mr. F and his daughter completed 1 week of hourly pain ratings with a structured rating system (Kerns et al., 1988). Mr. F's ratings were varied, ranging (on a scale of 0 to 5) from 1 to 4, with higher ratings (e.g., 3 to 4) in the morning and late afternoon and lower ratings (e.g., 1 to 2) at midday and evening. These ratings tended to correspond with Mr. F's medication use. Mr. F's daughter rated the patient's pain as showing little variability across or within days, and she consistently rated his pain higher than he did.

Mr. F and his daughter also completed questionnaire packets for patients and family members that were similar to those administered to Mr. G and his family. To evaluate pain severity, Mr. F's WHYMPI (Kerns et al., 1985) scores and McGill Pain Questionnaire (Melzack, 1975) ratings revealed a low level of reported pain severity when compared with levels in a clinical sample (i.e., other pain patients). In contrast, Mr. F's daughter reported on the Significant Other version of the WHYMPI (Kerns & Rosenberg, 1995) that she rated Mr. F's pain severity higher than he did, and her ratings were in the average range compared with ratings in other clinical samples. Mr. F's WHYMPI subscales revealed a high level of solicitous responding by his daughter; this was consistent with the daughter's rating. Mr. F's and his daughter's scores were relatively low for punishing and distracting responses.

On the Pain Behavior Check List (PBCL; Kerns et al., 1991a), Mr. F reported few pain behaviors (e.g., affect, distorted ambulation, facial distortion). In contrast, his daughter reported that she frequently noticed pain behaviors exhibited by her father. The daughter's reports were consistent with the clinician's ratings of pain behavior on the PBCL: Both the daughter and the clinician reported high levels of overt pain behavior, while Mr. F reported lower levels.

Mr. F completed several measures of affective distress, including the Beck Depression Inventory (BDI; Beck, Ward, Mendelson, Mock, & Erbaugh, 1961) and the State–Trait Anxiety Inventory (STAI; Spielberger, Gorsuch, & Lushene, 1976). Most striking was Mr. F's acknowledgment of a mild level of depressive symptoms. Mr. F's daughter denied significant depressive symptoms for herself.

Mr. F and his daughter established four specific behavioral goals for Mr. F in treatment: (1) to attend activities at the senior center more often, (2) to golf with his brother, (3) to return to woodworking as a hobby, and (4) to assist the daughter with light housework. These goals were developed with the patient's physical limitations and current medical status in mind. He and his daughter negotiated a step-by-step process for completing these goals and decided which of these steps were realistically attainable.

Conceptualization

Conceptualization of the pain experience was an important next step. During the assessment, Mr. F and his daughter provided information about the pain experience based on their previous attempts to understand the pain and to figure out what to do about it. These preconceived beliefs and expectations about the pain experience affected how Mr. F and his daughter viewed potential treatments, and during the conceptualization phase these beliefs and expectations were addressed.

Mr. F described a 12–year history of chronic neck pain, but neither he nor his daughter could identify an event that corresponded with the onset of pain. However, Mr. F stated that he believed his neck pain might have been caused by "overuse" of his neck and upper back muscles over the course of his vocational career, and that 2 years ago "something happened in my neck." He reported that probably "getting older" was also contributing to his pain. However, Mr. F's daughter stated that prior to 2 years ago, she had known relatively little about her father's pain complaints and in fact had not realized the extent of his chronic pain problem. She stated her belief that Mr. F's neck pain was related to the death of her mother (the patient's wife). She stated that his pain had begun after her mother was diagnosed with breast cancer and had markedly increased since her mother's death 14 months ago. She believed that he had "not dealt with" the loss of his wife, and she wondered whether this might have contributed to or caused his difficulties with pain.

During conceptualization, the clinician developed a clear understanding of both the patient's and his daughter's beliefs and expectations about the chronic pain problem. Once these beliefs and expectations had been outlined, the next step involved assisting Mr. F. and his daughter in reconceptualizing the chronic pain problem. Specifically, the clinician redefined it as a series of specific problems that had potential solutions (i.e., treatment), rather than as a generalized and vague problem.

Mr. F and his daughter agreed that there might well be other ways to view the pain problem, and they agreed to discuss some of these. After some discussion, Mr. F and his daughter agreed that anxiety and fear about injury, rather than actual physical limitation, were major contributors to Mr. F's inactivity. Mr. F had described "not being able" to perform activities in the past, but he concluded that both his and his daughter's concern about injury currently kept him inactive. Since this was one of Mr. F's primary concerns, anxiety and fear about injury were viewed as one area targeted within his treatment.

Mr. F's daughter encouraged Mr. F to think about the impact of his wife's death and how this related to pain. Previously, Mr. F had denied any significant relationship between his wife's death and his increased pain reports. The patient was encouraged to think broadly about depressed mood, anxiety, and anger, and about the impact of these emotions on his pain. Mr. F and his daughter decided that anxiety and depressed mood played a big role in how the patient described his pain, and that strategies to manage his mood might reduce his experience of pain.

Through discussion of Mr. F's day-to-day activities, a pattern of increased pain appeared. Because of chronic pain, Mr. F rested for long periods of time. This lack of activity caused Mr. F to lose strength and flexibility; thus, he felt as though he couldn't do anything. This lack of activity made him feel frustrated and depressed, as if he was not productive or living up to expectations. Thus, when he experienced lower pain he tended to push himself too hard, and then his pain symptoms returned and he couldn't finish what he started. Mr. F and his daughter described this as a common cycle of pain, depressed mood, and inactivity. This cycle of overexertion and inactivity was agreed upon as a target for treatment.

Finally, Mr. F and his daughter were involved in a pattern of communication that actually reinforced Mr. F's pain complaints. Mr. F's daughter clearly wanted to "help" her father, and often asked him how he was feeling and what she could do for him. In fact, she stated that she tried to do everything she could for him, so that he wouldn't have to be in pain. However, Mr. F stated that the more she did for him the less he did, and that he actually felt less active and more depressed as a result. So, in performing most of the housework and routinely asking about Mr. F's pain, Mr. F's daughter inadvertently increased his pain. This pattern of communication between them was also targeted for treatment.

Treatment

Treatment for Mr. F's chronic pain focused on several areas. First, there were specific skills the patient and his daughter could learn, such as relaxation training, identification of distorted cognitive and behavioral patterns, distraction techniques, and problem solving. Second, cognitive and behavioral practice of these skills was incorporated into the patient's repertoire via out-of-session homework assignments. Treatment goals focused primarily on increasing activity (i.e., social activities) and altering distorted thinking and behavioral patterns. Third, the patient and his daughter were encouraged to play an active role in this process of developing strategies for pain management. This process of active involvement increased their confidence that they would learn strategies to manage Mr. F's pain effectively.

A strategy for altering distorted thinking patterns was addressed first. Mr. F and his daughter monitored thoughts, behaviors, feelings, situations, and reports of pain. Mr. F's and his daughter's diaries revealed a pattern of "all-or-nothing" or "black-and-white" thinking that dominated the way Mr. F thought and behaved in multiple situations and responded to pain. For example, Mr. F decided he would perform some light housework (e.g., dusting the living room). However, shortly after he started to dust, Mr. F noticed that he was thinking, "I can't do anything important around the house" and "I'm useless." Once Mr. F started having these thoughts, he decided to quit dusting because "It isn't really going to help anyway." During treatment, the clinician encouraged Mr. F and his daughter to discuss the negative thought patterns and to develop alternative thoughts Mr. F could use while performing housework, such as "I am doing something to help" and "I am glad I can help around the house." In conjunction with these different thoughts, Mr. F's daughter stated that she would reinforce these thoughts by making positive comments on her father's work, such as "the dusting looks great." Over time, Mr. F and his daughter concluded that his assisting with chores in the house was helpful, no matter how small the chores appeared, and that altering Mr. F's thought patterns made him feel he was contributing to the household.

Mr. F and his daughter also wanted to increase activity in several areas of Mr. F's life. After some discussion, it became clear that one reason Mr. F had decreased his activities was that his wife was the person who planned activities for him; after she died, no one planned activities for him, so he didn't have things to do. Mr. F and his daughter discussed how this problem could be addressed for multiple activities.

Mr. F had significantly decreased how often he went to the senior center in his town, despite the fact that he had many friends who routinely attended the center. He expressed a strong interest in increasing his attendance and participation in activities at the center. Mr. F started by calling a friend from the center and asking the friend to give him a ride to several chosen activities during the course of the week. Mr. F stated that this "forced me to go," and that once he got there, he had a good time and was glad he went. Mr. F's daughter agreed to ask routinely about the activities her father participated in at the center and to support his attendance there.

Furthermore, Mr. F used to golf regularly with his brother, but had stopped going with him. During goal setting, Mr. F decided to contact his physician to determine whether he could resume golfing safely to some extent. His physician stated that Mr. F could play golf, but should limit himself to nine holes a day, take frequent breaks, and stop if he felt any "new" pain, discomfort, or weakness. Mr. F started to golf by first riding in the cart and then putting only; eventually, he moved up to playing several holes a day. Mr. F reported feeling pleased with himself for golfing and "figuring out" how to accomplish this goal.

Also, Mr. F had been involved with woodworking and carpentry around the house, but in the past years had gotten away from this work. He stated that he wanted to increase his involvement with this, and decided to make projects for people in the neighborhood (e.g., wooden reindeers for neighbors' yards at Christmas). He scheduled 30 minutes a day to work on projects in three 10-minute blocks of time during the day.

As Mr. F discussed some of his goals, his daughter stated that she was nervous about his increasing his activity, because he might get hurt; she thought he should spend more time resting. She also stated that she was performing much of the housework so that the patient wouldn't have to "do things that could hurt him." As the discussion continued, it became clear that the daughter's concerns played a large role in supporting the patient's inactivity. After reassurance from the patient's primary physician, Mr. F's daughter agreed to support and encourage her father in pursuing his increased activity goals.

One of the specific skills Mr. F and his daughter focused on learning was a relaxation exercise. Although Mr. F and his daughter stated that Mr. F already used relaxation training, this was described as using "one of those tapes" once and trying to say to himself, "You should relax more." During the assessment, both Mr. F and his daughter described themselves as having a high level of general arousal, "feeling worried and nervous most of the time." Mr. F and his daughter decided that relaxation training would be helpful for both of them, so they would perform the training together. During the treatment, a relaxation training session was audiotaped, and they used these tapes at home several times a week. Interestingly, Mr. F's daughter reported that the tapes assisted her in developing a "more relaxed attitude" toward many everyday issues, including the pain experience.

Finally, Mr. F and his daughter were involved in a pattern of communication that actually reinforced Mr. F's pain complaints. Mr. F and his daughter agreed that both of them knew that Mr. F had chronic pain and that his daughter would like to help him, so she didn't need to ask questions about how he was feeling or whether he was in pain. In fact, when Mr. F exhibited pain behavior (e.g., grimacing, moaning, taking pain medications), his daughter wouldn't comment. Instead, she would focus comments on what activities he was performing, and would provide support and encouragement for his "well behaviors."

Posttreatment Assessment

Two weeks after treatment was concluded, Mr. F and his daughter returned for a follow-up session. Both Mr. F and his daughter reported that each had completed the behavioral, social, and personal goals set prior to treatment. Furthermore, Mr. F stated that he wanted to continue setting goals for himself to support the changes he had accomplished. Mr. F was particularly pleased with his daughter's efforts to support his increased activity, and openly shared his feelings with her. Mr. F's daughter reported that the relationship between her and her father had greatly improved in quality over the course of treatment, and that one future goal for her was to do something with her father once a week. In describing pain reports, Mr. F and his daughter reported a decreased level of pain intensity and episodes of flare-ups. Overall, the posttreatment questionnaires revealed a general decrease in psychological distress; specifically, Mr. F's depression ratings were significantly lowered.

Comments on the Cases

These two cases provide clinical details of how the transactional model for family treatment for chronic pain may be applied. The first example of a couple and their children exemplifies how the chronic pain experience can have an impact on everyone in a family and how multiple areas of functioning for a family are affected. Conversely, it exemplifies how other family members' beliefs contribute to patterns of interaction with a patient that may serve to reinforce pain, disability, and distress. Treatment in this case was focused on involvement of the whole family in discussing, understanding, and developing strategies for the pain problem. With this emphasis on the family context, and specific engagement of the family in a process of reinforcing changes that the "patient" was making during treatment, multiple outcomes were enhanced. Ultimately, all family members experienced important benefits associated with their perceptions of contributing to a solution to the problem. The family's overall experience of helplessness and discouragement was replaced by one of accomplishment and optimism. The second case, a dyad, is probably more typical of those seen in clinical practice. Usually the dyad consists of a patient and significant other (e.g., spouse). However, the impact of the pain problem on a dyad is similar to its impact on a family, as can be seen in the case summary.

CONCLUSIONS AND FUTURE DIRECTIONS

The cognitive-behavioral transactional model of family functioning has important implications for understanding the complexities of functioning within the family of an individual with a chronic painful condition. The model, and the empirical data available to support it, offer a specific, testable framework for assessing family functioning—specifically, for examining the role of the family's influence on the ongoing adaptation and adjustment of the individual with chronic pain. Particularly important is the development of methodologies that encourage examination of illness-specific family interactions in the context of more general patterns of family exchanges. Using these methods allows tests of specific learning-based hypotheses—an approach that has largely been lacking in literatures based on family systems perspectives or more traditional models of family functioning.

Critical to empirical efforts to evaluate the relevance of the model is the continued development of reliable measures of family cognition, particularly the family's beliefs, attributions, and meanings concerning both the individual with the painful condition and pain-related interactions among family members. It is important to continue to respect the relatively independent domains of the experience of chronic pain (i.e., pain, disability, and distress) and the patterns of verbal and nonverbal interaction that are specific to these domains. To complement available measures of spousal interaction, measures relevant to interactions with younger children, as well as adult children or others not living with the patient, should be evaluated. Efforts should be directed toward evaluating the predictive validity of aggregated scores versus individual family members' scores for behavioral and cognitive measures of pain-relevant interaction. Finally, given the obvious difficulties and limitations inherent in conducting longitudinal, naturalistic studies of family interaction that could test the model, treatment outcome studies that examine the efficacy of specific theory-driven family interventions are strongly encouraged.

Future directions in the clinical domain are similar to those outlined for research efforts. Of primary importance is the continued elaboration of truly family-focused models of clinical assessment and intervention with families of individuals experiencing persistent pain. This means equal attention to each member of the family, as well as attention to their composite family functioning. Increased use of available measures (such as several of those utilized in the case examples presented in this chapter), as well as of newly developed family-oriented measures consistent with the FAAR model, is encouraged. Theory-driven conceptualization of the functioning of the family and the development of a family treatment plan should be based on a hypothesis-testing approach to assessment. Further specification of truly family-focused treatment strategies that are consistent with the cognitive-behavioral transactional model is the ultimate goal. This will require creativity and probably some risk taking, in order to break from the present tradition of individually oriented clinical efforts.

REFERENCES

Ahern, D., Adams, A., & Follick, M. (1985). Emotional and marital disturbance in spouses of chronic low back pain patients. *Clinical Journal of Pain*, *1*, 69–74.

Beck, A. T., Ward, C. H., Mendelson, M., Mock, J., & Erbaugh, J. (1961). An inventory for measuring depression. *Archives of General Psychiatry*, *4*, 561–571.

Block, A., Kremer, E., & Gaylor, M. (1980). Behavioral treatment of chronic pain: The spouse as a discriminative cue for pain behavior. *Pain*, *9*, 243–252.

Elliot, D. J., Trief, P. M., & Stein, N. (1986). Mastery, stress, and coping in marriage among chronic pain patients. *Journal of Behavioral Medicine*, *9*, 549–558.

Feuerstein, M., Sult, S., & Houle, M. (1985). Environmental stressors and chronic low back pain: life events, family and work environment. *Pain*, *22*, 295–307.

Flor, H., Birbaumer, N., & Turk, D. C. (1990). The psychobiology of chronic pain. *Advances in Behavioral Research and Therapy*, *12*, 47–84.

Flor, H., Kerns, R. D., & Turk, D. C. (1987a). The role of spouse reinforcement, perceived pain, and activity levels of chronic pain patients. *Journal of Psychosomatic Research*, *31*, 251–259.

Flor, H., Turk, D. C., & Rudy, T. E. (1987b). Pain and families: I. Etiology, maintenance and psychosocial impact. *Pain*, *30*, 3–27.

Flor, H., Turk, D. C., & Rudy, T. E. (1987c). Pain and families: II. Assessment and treatment. *Pain*, *30*, 29–45.

Flor, H., Turk, D. C., & Rudy, T. E. (1989). Relationship of pain impact and significant other reinforcement of pain behaviors: The mediating role of gender, marital status and marital satisfaction. *Pain*, *38*, 45–50.

Flor, H. Turk, D. C., & Scholz, O. B. (1987d). Impact of chronic pain on the spouse: Marital, emotional, and physical consequences. *Journal of Psychosomatic Research*, *31*, 63–71.

Fordyce, W. E. (1976). *Behavioral methods for chronic pain and illness*. St. Louis, MO: C.V. Mosby.

Fordyce, W. E. (1988). Pain and suffering: A reappraisal. *American Psychologist*, *43*, 276–283.

Friedman, H. (1992). *Hostility, coping, and health*. Washington, DC: American Psychological Association.

Karoly, P. (1985). The assessment of pain: Concepts and procedures. In P. Karoly (Ed.), *Measurement strategies in health psychology* (pp. 461–516). New York: Wiley.

Kerns, R. D. (1994a). Families and chronic illness. *Annals of Behavioral Medicine*, *16*, 107–108.

Kerns, R. D. (1994b). Pain management. In M. Hersen & R. T. Ammerman (Eds.), *Handbook of prescriptive treatments for adults* (pp. 443–462). New York: Plenum Press.

Kerns, R. D. (in press). Family assessment and intervention in chronic illness. In P. Nicassio & T. Smith (Eds.), *Psychosocial adjustment to chronic illness*. Washington, DC: American Psychological Association.

Kerns, R. D., Finn, P. E., & Haythornthwaite, J. (1988). Self-monitored pain intensity: Psychometric properties and clinical utility. *Journal of Behavioral Medicine*, *11*, 71–72.

Kerns, R. D., Haythornthwaite, J., Rosenberg, R., Southwick, S., Giller, E. L., & Jacob, M. C. (1991a). The Pain Behavior Check List (PBCL): Factor structure and psychometric properties. *Journal of Behavioral Medicine*, *14*, 155–167.

Kerns, R. D., Haythornthwaite, J., Southwick, S., & Giller, E. L. (1990). The role of marital interaction in chronic pain and depressive symptom severity. *Journal of Psychosomatic Research*, *34*, 401–408.

Kerns, R. D. & Jacob, M. C. (in press). Toward an integrative diathesis–stress model of chronic pain. In A. J. Goreczny & M. Hersen (Eds.), *Handbook of recent advances in behavioral medicine.* New York: Plenum Press.

Kerns, R. D., & Rosenberg, R. (1995). Pain-relevant responses from significant others: Development of a Significant Other version of the WHYMPI Scales. *Pain, 61,* 245–250.

Kerns, R. D., Southwick, S., Giller, E. L., Haythornthwaite, J., Jacob, M. C., & Rosenberg, R. (1991b). The relationship between reports of pain-related social interactions and expressions of pain and affective distress. *Behavior Therapy, 22,* 101–111.

Kerns, R. D., Turk, D. C., & Rudy, T. E. (1985). The West Haven–Yale Multidimensional Pain Inventory (WHYMPI). *Pain, 23,* 345–356.

Kerns, R. D., & Weiss, L. H. (1994). Family influences on the course of chronic illness: A cognitive-behavioral transactional model. *Annals of Behavioral Medicine, 16,* 116–130.

Lazarus, R. S., & Folkman, S. (1984). *Stress, appraisal, and coping.* New York: Springer.

Litman, T. J. (1974). The family as basic unit in health and medical care: A social-behavioral overview. *Social Science and Medicine, 8,* 495–519.

Maruta, T., Osborne, D., Swenson, D. W., & Holling, J. M. (1981). Chronic pain patients and spouses: Marital and sexual adjustment. *Mayo Clinic Proceedings, 56,* 307–310.

Melzack, R. (1975). The McGill Pain Questionnaire: Major properties and scoring methods. *Pain, 1,* 277–299.

Mohamed, S. N., Weisz, G. N., & Waring, E. M. (1978). The relationship of chronic pain to depression, marital adjustment, and family dynamics. *Pain, 5,* 285–292.

Moore, J. E., & Chaney, E. F. (1985). Outpatient group treatment of chronic pain: Effects of spouse involvement. *Journal of Consulting and Clinical Psychology, 53,* 326–334.

Patterson, J. M. (1988). Families experiencing stress: The family adjustment and adaptation response model. *Family Systems in Medicine, 5,* 202–237.

Patterson, J. M. (1989). A family stress model: The family adjustment and adaptation response. In C. N. Ramsey, Jr. (Ed.), *Family systems in medicine* (pp. 95–118). New York: Guilford Press.

Patterson, J. M., & Garwick, A. W. (1994). The impact of chronic illness on families: A family systems perspective. *Annals of Behavioral Medicine, 16,* 131–142.

Radojevic, V., Nicassio, P. M., & Weisman, M. H. (1992). Behavioral intervention with and without family support for rheumatoid arthritis. *Behavior Therapy, 23,* 13–30.

Ramsey, C. N., Jr. (Ed.). (1989). *Family systems in medicine.* New York: Guilford Press.

Reiss, D. (1989). Families and their paradigms: An ecologic approach to understanding the family and its social world. In C. N. Ramsey, Jr. (Ed.), *Family systems in medicine* (pp. 119–134). New York: Guilford Press.

Revenson, T. A., & Majerovitz, S. D. (1990). Spouses' support provision to chronically ill patients. *Journal of Social and Personal Relationships, 7,* 575–586.

Romano, J. M., Turner, J. A., Friedman, L. S., Bulcroft, R. A., Jensen, M. P., Hops, H., & Wright, S. F. (1992). Sequential analysis of chronic pain behaviors and spouse responses. *Journal of Consulting and Clinical Psychology, 60,* 777–782.

Roy, R. (1986). A problem-centered family systems approach in treating intractable pain. In A. D. Holzman & D. C. Turk (Eds.), *Pain management: A handbook of psychological treatment approaches* (pp. 113–130). Elmsford, NY: Pergamon Press.

Roy, R. (1992). *The social context of the chronic pain sufferer.* Toronto: University of Toronto Press.

Saarijarvi, S. (1991). A controlled study of couple therapy in chronic low back pain patients: Effects on marital satisfaction, psychological distress and health attitudes. *Journal of Psychosomatic Research, 35,* 265–272.

Schwartz, G. E. (1982). Testing the biopsychosocial model: The ultimate challenge facing behavioral medicine. *Journal of Consulting and Clinical Psychology, 50,* 1040–1053.

Spielberger, C., Gorsuch, R., & Lushene, N. (1976). *Manual for the State–Trait Anxiety Inventory.* Palo Alto, CA: Consulting Psychologists Press.

Thomas, M., & Roy, R. (1989). Pain patients and marital relations. *Clinical Journal of Pain, 5,* 255–259.

Turk, D. C., & Kerns, R. D. (Eds.). (1985a). *Health, illness and families: A life span perspective*. New York: Wiley.

Turk, D. C., & Kerns, R. D. (1985b). The family in health and illness. In D. C.Turk & R. D. Kerns (Eds.), *Health, illness and families: A life span perspective* (pp. 1–22). New York: Wiley.

Turk, D. C., Kerns, R. D., & Rosenberg, R. (1992). Effects of marital interaction on chronic pain and disability: Examining the down side of social support. *Rehabilitation Psychology, 37,* 259–274.

Turk, D. C., Meichenbaum, D., & Genest, M. (1983). *Pain and behavioral medicine: A cognitive-behavioral perspective*. New York: Guilford Press.

Weiss, L. H., & Kerns, R. D. (1995). Patterns of pain-relevant social interactions. *International Journal of Behavioral Medicine, 2,* 157–171.

CHAPTER 12

Integration of Pharmacotherapy with Psychological Treatment of Chronic Pain

Peter B. Polatin

Pain is a dramatic symptom, and one of the easiest and most successful ways of relieving it is with a pill or an injection. In medicine today, there are many classes of drugs with documented efficacy in controlling pain. Early or acute pain is treated aggressively, with agents that act directly either on the anatomical sites of the pain or on the central receptors. The initial focus is on reducing the intensity of the primary nociceptive symptom.

The longer the pain lasts, the more complicated the treatment process becomes. This is certainly true in the pharmacological approach to pain. As the pain process continues, other pharmacological agents may be employed that act on the transmission or augmentation of the nociceptive signal in the nervous system, and on the secondary symptoms that may develop with chronicity. The psychotropic agents, particularly the antidepressants, have a well-documented role in the management of chronic pain, although it is sometimes unclear whether their primary effects are on the nociception or the emotional distress (Atkinson, 1989).

Issues of tolerance, withdrawal, dependence, and abuse are concerns with some pharmacological agents used to treat pain, particularly the opioids, the stimulants, and the minor tranquilizers (anxiolytics). "Tolerance," which is physiological and receptor-specific, refers to the need to increase the dose of a drug over time to achieve the same effects as originally desired. "Withdrawal" is a physiological syndrome of symptoms precipitated by the cessation of a particular drug, and ranges from mild restlessness to severe manifestations such as seizures or coma. "Dependence" is a behavioral syndrome characterized by repetitive use of a drug, with intoxication and withdrawal, the development of tolerance, preoccupation with procurement and usage, and ambivalence about usage, with social and occupational impairment. Similarly, "abuse" is a maladaptive pattern of psychoactive substance usage of a month or more, in spite of awareness of impairment and exposure to physical hazards. In addition to these very serious physiological and behavioral syndromes, other side effects of a particular agent may limit its usefulness for the long-term control of chronic pain. Regulatory measures from outside the medical profession, instituted to minimize such risks, now influence prescribing practices.

Pharmacotherapy is an important treatment approach for chronic pain, but it is best utilized in a multidisciplinary context along with other biobehavioral interventions aimed at decreasing suffering and increasing functional and personal autonomy. This team effort requires interdisciplinary planning, communication, monitoring, and feedback. To assume that medication alone will resolve the complex psychosocioeconomic stressors with which the chronic pain patient is attempting to cope is both naive and simplistic. Therefore, because the treatment of chronic pain is a process of collaboration among health care disciplines, it is important not only for physicians but also for allied health professionals to be knowledgeable about choices of medication to control pain, efficacy of specific drugs in various chronic pain syndromes, dosage ranges, and side effects. Later in this chapter, I provide some examples of this interdisciplinary approach in the treatment of some common chronic pain profiles.

NOCICEPTIVE AND PSYCHOLOGICAL SYMPTOMS IN CHRONIC PAIN

The experience of pain in chronic pain states may differ, depending on the site and nature of the pathology. Cluster headaches are descriptively different from migraine or muscle tension headaches. Low back pain secondary to degenerative disk disease is different from low back pain secondary to a herniated disk with nerve root irritation. This primary nociceptive difference is associated with variations in efficacy of different drugs. Although the opioids are the most universally effective pain medications, they are less successful with neuropathic syndromes and bone pain (Twycross, 1994). Psychotropic agents, which do not have any recognized analgesic properties, nevertheless dramatically alleviate certain pain syndromes. For example, lithium carbonate, used to treat bipolar affective disorder, controls pain in some cases of migraine and cluster headaches (Kudrow, 1977; Mathew, 1978). Carbamazepine (Tegretol), an antiepileptic and psychotropic, is the drug of choice to relieve the pain of trigeminal neuralgia (Delfino, 1983).

Secondary symptoms of emotional distress are frequently seen in patients with chronic pain (Kinney, Gatchel, Polatin, Fogarty, & Mayer, 1993; Polatin, Kinney, Gatchel, Lillo, & Mayer, 1993), and will worsen the prognosis unless they are adequately treated. In some cases, the onset of these symptoms follows and is a result of the pain. In other instances, emotional symptoms may have preceded pain onset but either resolved or became less troublesome, and then may have been exacerbated by the duration of the pain syndrome. Maladaptive coping styles, commonly associated with personality disorders or with previous experiences of physical and psychic trauma, may become more clinically evident as a result of chronic pain. Studies have repeatedly documented high prevalence rates of major depression, anxiety syndromes, substance and alcohol abuse, and personality disorders in this group of patients (Brandt, Celantano, Stewart, Linet, & Polstein, 1990; Fishbain, Goldberg, Meagher, Steele, & Rosomoff, 1986; Katon, Egan, & Miller, 1985; Polatin et al., 1993). In addition, the worsening of pre-existing biological illnesses such as schizophrenia and bipolar affective disorder, or increasing psychotic or dysfunctional symptoms in borderline or antisocial personality disorders, may require management with psychotropic medication. Therefore, the full range of clinical psychopharmacology is required to treat secondary symptoms of emotional distress in the chronic pain population.

PHARMACOLOGICAL AGENTS USED
TO TREAT CHRONIC PAIN

Opioids

The opioids are unquestionably the most useful agents for the relief of pain, because of their primary agonistic effects on μ opioid receptors in the brain and spinal cord. Peripheral opioid receptors in primary afferent nociceptive neurons, when stimulated, may raise the pain threshold and inhibit the release of pain-producing inflammatory substances from these neurons. There are mediating receptors in the spinal cord, midbrain, brainstem, and thalamus, as well as in the limbic system and cortex, all of which may be affected by both endogenous and exogenous opiates.

Concerns about psychological dependence, including aberrant drug-seeking behavior, have greatly restricted the use of the opioids, except in treating the group of patients with the worst prognosis (i.e., patients with cancer pain). Even in acute pain patients, surveys have shown that physicians underprescribe the opioids (Cooper, Czechowicz, Petersen, & Molinan, 1992; Gourlak & Cousins, 1984; Marks & Sacher, 1973; McCaffey & Hart, 1976), with doses that are suboptimal, are too infrequent, or last for inadequate periods of time. Fortunately, studies on the use of long-term opioids to treat chronic pain have demonstrated that the risk of addiction in patients with opioid-responsive pain is very low in the absence of such factors as a past history of substance abuse, severe personality disorder, or experience of childhood traumatic events (Portnoy & Foley, 1986; Taub, 1982).

Concern about respiratory depression has also limited the use of opioids in chronic pain. However, experience and research have demonstrated that though this side effect is readily seen in the addict or control subject without clinical pain, pain physiologically antagonizes central nervous system (CNS) depressant effects of the opioids (Twycross, 1994; Walsh, Baxter, Bowman, & Leber, 1981), and even high doses of potent narcotics may be used with careful medical monitoring in chronic pain patients.

Guidelines have been proposed for providing opioid maintenance therapy to patients with chronic nonmalignant pain. These include prior trials of alternative analgesia (covered later in this chapter), exclusion of patients with risk factors for dependence, and primary medication responsibility by a single physician. The pain syndrome must be documented as responsive to opioids by clinical trial. Goals for functional improvement should be stipulated and agreed upon to justify the regimen. Careful monitoring and documentation of degree of analgesia, side effects, functional status, and evidence of aberrant drug-related behavior should be carried out on a regular basis (Portnoy, 1994).

It should be emphasized that these guidelines are largely empirical and not supported by large clinical trials. For example, it has not been unequivocally established that prior addiction or personality disorder is always contraindicative for opioid treatment of chronic nonmalignant pain. And, conversely, following all the guidelines does not protect the practitioner from exposing some patients to addiction. However, in spite of the tentative nature of the concept of long-term opioid maintenance for nonmalignant pain, guidelines are becoming institutionalized. Recently, the state of California has drafted a position paper for the treatment of chronic pain with opioids according to "principles of responsible professional practice," including a history, physical examination, formulated treatment plan, informed consent from the patient, periodic review, consultation as necessary, accurate record keeping, and compliance with controlled substance regulations (Medical Board of California, 1994). Similar guidelines are being explored in other states.

The most convenient route of administration is oral, but delivery by rectum, parenterally (subcutaneously, intramuscularly, or intravenously), or by interspinal injection has also been described. The oral or rectal dose is generally two to three times higher than that administered by the parenteral routes. For maximum comfort, dosing intervals should not be "as needed"; by the time pain re-emerges, the patient will have an interval of discomfort prior to the therapeutic onset of the next dose. Rather, patients should be dosed on a time-contingent basis according to the half-life of the particular medication, which may range from 2 hours for meperidine (Demerol) to 8 hours for methadone (France & Krishnan, 1988). It should be noted that opioids with shorter half-lives, such as meperidine and pentazocine, require more frequent dosing and are less desirable for the treatment of chronic pain.

The choice of particular medication should proceed from a weaker to a stronger agent, depending on the clinical response. Obviously, an increase in dose or potency proceeds from the need to control the pain, but may be reflective of tolerance. In opioid-responsive pain, patients will typically "plateau" at a particular dose, beyond which further increases will not be required to control pain. Thus, an initial trial with a nonsteroidal anti-inflammatory drug (NSAID; see below) with poor response would proceed to a weak opioid such as codeine or hydrocodone, and then—if necessary—to a strong opioid such as morphine, oxycodone, or methadone (Twycross, 1994) (see Table 12.1).

Side effects of opioids must be monitored carefully (see Table 12.2). Constipation is quite common, but can be controlled easily with laxatives. Respiratory depression is rarely seen in chronic pain patients, and only when pain is relieved (e.g., after surgery or a neural ablative procedure) and the opioid dosage is not adjusted downward thereafter (Hanks, Twycross, & Lloyd, 1981). Geriatric patients are at greater risk for oversedation, hypotension, and urinary retention, but with careful monitoring of dosage and side effects, opioids may still be effectively given to these patients for chronic pain complaints.

Non-Narcotic Analgesics

The non-narcotic analgesics include aspirin, acetaminophen (Tylenol), and the NSAIDs. The major analgesic effect of the non-narcotic analgesics is at the tissue site of the pain, although there may be centrally mediated analgesic effects as well (Dubas & Parker, 1971; Malmberg & Yaksh, 1992). Although these drugs are used quite frequently for chronic pain, their efficacy is proven only in those syndromes associated with inflammatory processes, such as rheumatoid arthritis and osteoarthritis. They may also be useful for the short-term management of musculoskeletal pain and headaches, and are a good initial

TABLE 12.1. Opioid and Centrally Acting Analgesic Dosages (Compared to Morphine)

Drug	Dose (mg), oral	Dose (mg), i.m.	Duration (hours)
Morphine	30	10	4
Codeine	30–60		4–6
Hydrocodone (Lortab)	5–10	–	4–8
Methadone (Dolophine)	20	10	5
Oxycodone (Percodan)	30		4
Meperidine (Demerol)	300	75	1–3
Pentazocine (Talwin)	50	30–60	2–3
Hamadol (Ultram)	50–100		4–6

TABLE 12.2. Side Effects of Opioids

CNS	*Gastrointestinal*
Mental clouding	Constipation
Mood changes	Abdominal pain
Drowsiness	Nausea, vomiting
Miosis	
Respiratory depression	*Other*
Suppressed cough	Urinary retention
	Sweating, itching, flushing
Cardiovascular	Tolerance, addiction, withdrawal
Orthostatic hypotension	

choice for the control of mild to moderate acute pain. In chronic pain syndromes of central or peripheral origin, their utility is far more controversial, and they are not effective in chronic pain syndromes with secondary symptoms of emotional distress.

Dosage varies, depending on the agent (see Table 12.3). Certain of these medications may be given once a day, making them more convenient for responsive patients. Because these drugs have a ceiling effect, increasing the dosage beyond a certain threshold does not increase analgesia, although it may increase duration of pain relief. Analgesia results from the blocking of stimulation of primary afferent nociceptors (Fields, 1987) through inhibition of the cyclo-oxygenase enzyme, thereby preventing prostaglandin biosynthesis and inflammatory response. Other, less prominent peripheral effects include direct spinal blockade of hyperalgesia (Malmberg & Yaksh, 1992) and prevention of release of certain inflammatory secretions from white blood cells (Abramson, 1991).

Side effects are frequent, particularly in the gastrointestinal tract. Irritation of the stomach, lower esophagus, and colon may cause symptoms of indigestion, heartburn, and diarrhea, progressing to passage of blood in vomitus or stool. With prolonged therapy,

TABLE 12.3. NSAIDs: Chemical Groupings and Dosages

Drug	Dose (mg)	Times per day	Maximum daily dose (mg.)
Propionic acids			
Fenoprofen (Nalfon)	200–600	2–4	3200
Flurbiprofen (Ansaid)	100	2–3	300
Ibuprofen (Motrin)	400–800	2–6	3200
Ketoprofen (Orudis, Oruvail)	50–200	1–3	300
Naproxen sodium (Anaprox)	275–550	2–4	1375
Naproxen (Naprosyn)	350–500	2–3	1500
Acetic acids			
Diclofenac (Voltaren)	50–75	2–3	200
Etodolac (Lodine)	300–400	2–3	1200
Indomethacin (Indocin)	25–75	2–4	200
Ketorolac (Toradol)	10	2–4	40
Sulindac (Clinoril)	200	2	400
Tolmetin (Tolectin)	200–600	2–4	2000
Fenamates (anthranilic acids)			
Meclofenamate (Meclomen)	50–100	2–6	400
Mefenamic acid (Ponstel)	250	4	100
Oxicams			
Piroxicam (Feldene)	10–20	1–2	20

elevation of liver function tests may occur, although rarely does this progress to tissue damage. Impaired kidney function, prolonged bleeding time, easy bruising, broncho-spasm, worsening asthma, skin rashes, photosensitivity, and occasional CNS effects (tinnitus, hearing loss, headache) may be seen with these drugs. Therefore, careful medical monitoring is essential. One side effect not seen, however, is dependence or addiction, making these agents more popular for the treatment of chronic pain than their documented clinical efficacy would justify.

There is no good way of choosing which NSAID to use, but if one drug does not work, the next choice should be from a different chemical group (see Table 12.3). Before the NSAIDs are rejected, trials of at least four different agents should be attempted, with 2 weeks on each drug and administration on a regularly scheduled basis (time-contingent dosage). While these agents are being used, patients should be periodically questioned about side effects and should have tests of bleeding time and of liver and kidney function performed at some regular interval.

Antidepressants

There is a documented role for the antidepressants in the treatment of chronic pain syndromes—particularly headache and neuropathic pain, but less so in arthritis and low back pain, where they are most commonly employed (Atkinson, 1989; Monks, 1994; Onghena & Van Houdenhove, 1992). It is frequently not clear whether these agents promote improvement in chronic pain by direct antinociceptive effect or by mitigation of the secondary symptom of depression, so commonly seen in these patients (France & Krishnan, 1988). However, there have been several studies documenting that these agents have direct analgesic properties (Spiegel, Kalb, & Pasternak, 1983). Clinical trials in groups of chronic arthritis and migraine patients without clinical depression have documented pain relief (Gomersall & Stewart, 1973; Gringas, 1976; McDonald-Scott, 1969). Other research has been able to differentiate pain relief without improvement of depression in chronic pain patients treated with antidepressants (Couch, Ziegler, & Hassanein, 1976; Lance & Curran, 1964; Watson et al., 1982). It should be noted that although the use of antidepressants for chronic pain syndromes has been clinically recognized, a recent review of clinical studies has suggested that most such studies are unsatisfactory because of lack of design and protocol criteria, and therefore that the use of heterocyclic antidepressants for syndromes other than chronic headache remains unproven (Goodkin & Gullion, 1989).

Antidepressants may be divided into two general categories: the heterocyclics and the monoamine oxidase (MAO) inhibitors. The heterocyclics exert their therapeutic effect by blockading the reuptake of biogenic amines at interneuronal synaptic junctions in the CNS and spinal cord. The amines most critically involved in depression and chronic pain are norepinephrine and serotonin, and the heterocyclics vary in their specificity for one or both of these amines (see Table 12.4).

The MAO inhibitors act on a different metabolic pathway: As the category name suggests, they inhibit the enzyme MAO in the brain, and therefore block degradation of the biogenic amines. In clinical practice, these agents are less desirable than the heterocyclics because of the risk of potentially severe hypertension caused by the effect of certain foods and pharmacological agents on the MAO-inhibited patient. Individuals on MAO inhibitors must be on a tyramine-free diet and must also avoid a number of prescription and over-the-counter medications. The MAO inhibitors have nevertheless been demonstrated to relieve migraine headache and atypical facial pain (Anthony & Lance, 1969; Lascelles, 1966), as well as the symptoms of depression.

TABLE 12.4. Specificity of Serotonin versus Norepinephrine Reuptake Blockade of the Heterocyclics

Serotonin only		Serotonin and norepinephrine equally	Norepinephrine only
Trazodone (Desyrel)	Clomipramine	Doxepin (Sinequan)	Maprotiline (Ludiomil)
Fluoxetine (Prozac)	(Anafranil)	Imipramine (Tofranil)	Desipramine (Norpramin)
Paroxetine (Paxil)	Amitriptyline	Vanlafaxine (Effexor)	Nortriptyline (Pamelor)
Sertraline (Zoloft)	(Elavil)	Bupropion (Wellbutrin)	
Nefazodone (Serzone)		Amoxapine (Asendin)	
Fluvoxamine (Luvox)			

Heterocyclic Antidepressants

Dosages of the various heterocyclic agents are noted in Table 12.5. These drugs have two different dosage ranges, depending on whether pain or depression is the symptom being treated. Pain responds at a lower dose and at a shorter time after initiation of therapy than does depression. This is particularly important when one is treating a chronic pain patient without depression, where the lower dose will be used. It is less relevant when both symptoms are present, because the antidepressant dosage will be used.

It follows that evaluation for depression should occur before antidepressant therapy is initiated. All heterocyclics have demonstrated antidepressant effects, but some have more of a mitigating effect on chronic pain than others. These include amitriptyline, desipramine, doxepin, imipramine, and clomipramine (Alcoff, Jones, Rust, & Newman, 1982; Couch & Hassanein, 1979; France, Houpt, & Ellinwood, 1984; France & Krishnan, 1988; Hameroff et al., 1982, 1984; Onghena & Van Houdenhove, 1992; Pilowsky, Hallett, Bassett, Thomas, & Penhall, 1982; Tollison & Kriegel, 1984; Ward, Bloom, & Friedel, 1979). Documentation of a primary analgesic affect is less clear with newer agents, such

TABLE 12.5. Dosages of Heterocyclic Antidepressants

Drug	Dose for pain (mg)	Dose for depression (mg)
Desipramine (Norpramin)	75	75–200
Nortriptyline (Pamelor)	50–100	75–150
Maprotiline (Ludiomil)	?	75–300
Doxepin (Sinequan)	50–100	150–300
Imipramine (Tofranil)	50–75	150–300
Amitriptyline (Elavil)	75–150	150–300
Trazodone (Desyrel)	?	150–400
Fluoxetine (Prozac)	?	20–80
Sertraline (Zoloft)	?	50–200
Paroxetine (Paxil)	?	20–80
Venlafaxine (Effexor)	?	75–375
Clomipramine (Anafranil)	?	100–250
Bupropion (Wellbutrin)	?	200–450
Amoxapine (Asendin)	?	200–300
Nefazodone (Serzone)	?	300–600
Fluvoxamine (Luvox)	?	100–300

as trazodone, fluoxetine, paroxetine, and sertraline (Petitto, Mundle, Nagy, Evans, & Golden, 1992; Theeson & Marsch, 1989).

The choice of heterocyclic agent will be based on degree of sedation desired, side effect profile, and specificity of biogenic amine reuptake blockade. Patients with agitation, anxiety, and insomnia will generally benefit from a more sedating heterocyclic, such as doxepin, amitriptyline, or trazodone. Those with anergia and psychomotor retardation will usually do better on a drug with a more energizing profile, such as nortriptyline, fluoxetine, or paroxetine.

The issue of which biogenic amine is primarily affected by the heterocyclic agent has both conceptual and clinical applications. Heterocyclic agents with the best-documented nociceptive effects appear to be those agents that cause both serotonin and norepinephrine reuptake blockade, although primary serotonin and primary norepinephrine reuptake blockers have also demonstrated analgesia in chronic pain (Ward et al., 1979).

Beyond this conceptual consideration, the degree of norepinephrine versus serotonin reuptake blockade of any individual heterocyclic will influence its side effect profile (see Table 12.4). Heterocyclics with a high degree of noradrenergic activity are associated with primary autonomic, cardiac, and ocular side effects, which may be particularly problematic for older patients with heart disease, glaucoma, prostatic hypertrophy, or cognitive impairment. Primarily serotonergic agents may be preferable in this age group, as well as in patients who have had a particularly refractory reaction to a previously tried heterocyclic, such as increased appetite, sedation, or intolerable dry mouth. However, the serotonergic agents are more frequently associated with headaches, gastric symptoms, and agitation, and may not be helpful in patients with a high level of anxiety.

Side effects of the heterocyclic antidepressants are common and require careful clinical monitoring (Table 12.6). Doses of all heterocyclics are started low and titrated upward, guided by improvement in pain or depression and by emergence of side effects. With several of the older tricyclics (amitriptyline, doxepin, imipramine), a therapeutic blood level is associated with some dry mouth or morning "hangover." However, any side effect that is associated with distress or impaired functioning will require dosage modification or a change of medication.

The drawing of blood levels to monitor clinical response is useful when (1) an agent with a "therapeutic window" is being prescribed, such as imipramine; (2) the clinical response is ambiguous, raising the questions of absorption and compliance; and/or (3) an older or more medically complicated patient is being treated. The routine use of blood levels is, however, not essential for a safe and effective administration of these antidepressant medications.

The heterocyclic antidepressants have also been used as adjuncts to narcotic analgesics in the treatment of chronic pain (France, Urban, & Keefe, 1984b; Urban, France, Steinberger, Scott, & Maltbie, 1986). Patients on this combined regimen tend to tolerate a lower narcotic maintenance dosage without dependence or abuse. Pain syndromes previously refractory to narcotics alone may be more responsive to combined therapy.

MAO Inhibitors

The use of the MAO inhibitors to treat chronic pain with or without depression has documented efficacy (Anthony & Lance, 1969; Lascelles, 1966), but the precautions required by this group of agents make it a less desirable choice than the heterocyclic antidepressants. Before an MAO inhibitor is initiated, the patient must be fully educated about a tyramine-free diet and the avoidance of certain medications (meperidine, sympathomi-

TABLE 12.6. Side Effects of Heterocyclic Antidepressants

Autonomic
   *Dry mouth
   Retarded ejaculation or orgasm
   *Decreased intestinal mobility
   *Urinary retention
   Pathological sweating
   Anorexia
   Insomnia
   Psychomotor stimulation
CNS
   *Sedation, psychomotor slowing
   Muscle weakness
   Nervousness
   *Headaches
   *Agitation
   Vertigo
   Tremor, ataxia
   Dysarthria
   Nystagmus
   Lowered seizure threshold
   Toxic delerium (central anticholinergic syndrome)
   *Withdrawal syndrome
Cardiac
   *Postural hypotension
   Tachycardia
   Arrhythmia
   EKG changes (flattened T waves, prolonged QT intervals,
      depressed ST segments)

Ocular
   *Blurred vision
   Worsening of narrow angle
   Glaucoma
Gastric
   *Constipation
   Heartburn
   Nausea
Hematologic
   Leukocytic effects
   Purpura
   Agranulocytosis
Skin
   Rash, petechiae
   Photosensitivity
   Urticaria
Miscellaneous
   Priapism (trazodone)
   Tinnitus
   Increased appetite
   Edema
   Alopecia

*Commonly seen.

metic amines, and heterocyclic antidepressants). Pretreatment evaluation should include a blood count, liver function tests, and an electrocardiogram (EKG) and blood pressure determination, particularly in the elderly.

Available MAO inhibitors and their dosage ranges are listed in Table 12.7. Phenelzine (Nardil) is the most commonly used; it is started at a low dose and titrated up gradually while side effects and clinical response are monitored. Periodic blood assessment of degree of platelet MAO inhibition gives information about adequacy of therapeutic level. Pain inhibition has been found with platelet MAO inhibition of 80% (Raft, Davidson, Wassik, & Maddox, 1981).

The difference between an antinociceptive and an antidepressant dosage is not as striking as with the heterocyclics. Maintenance dose should be at the same level as the initial dose. Side effects include dizziness, nausea, drowsiness, orthostatic hypotension, headache, difficulty urinating, inhibition of ejaculation, weakness, fatigue, dry mouth, blurred vision, and skin rashes. Some patients report tremor, insomnia, and increased sweating. There is some risk of liver toxicity. The most serious toxic effect is hypertensive crisis, caused by the interaction of ingested tyramine, sympathomimetic amines, or certain drugs in a patient on an MAO inhibitor. This abrupt and severe elevation of blood pressure is a medical emergency. Because of this high-toxicity profile, these agents, in spite of significant antidepressant and antinociceptive effect, are used only if there have been previous trials of heterocyclics with documented poor response.

TABLE 12.7. MAO Inhibitors and Their Dosages

Drug	Dose for pain (mg)	Dose for depression (mg)
Phenelzine (Nardil)	15–45	15–60
Isocarboxazid (Marplan)	10–20	10–40
Tranylcypromine (Parnate)	10–40	10–40

Anticonvulsants

Certain anticonvulsive agents have documented efficacy in mitigating chronic pain syndromes of neurogenic origin. The pathophysiological etiology of epilepsy and de-afferentation pain are similar (Loeser & Ward, 1967). These agents stabilize the hyper-excitable neural membranes of pain-transmitting cells (Glaser, Penry, & Woodbury, 1980; Hisbani, Pincus, & Lee, 1974) and reduce repetitive discharge of stimulated second-order neurons (Fromm & Killiam, 1967).

The anticonvulsants that have been found to be most helpful in chronic pain, and their therapeutic dosages, are recorded in Table 12.8. The responsive pain syndromes include trigeminal neuralgia, diabetic neuropathy, central thalamic pain syndrome, migraine headaches, postherpetic neuralgia, and postsympathectomy neuralgia. Carbamazepine and diphenylhydantoin are the first-line anticonvulsants used with neuropathic pain syndromes, either alone or adjunctively with antidepressants. Valproic acid has also been found to be useful in some clinical trials (Hering & Kuritzky, 1989, 1992). Clonazepam, a benzodiazepine with anticonvulsant properties, may also be useful for neuropathic pain (Smirne & Scarlato, 1977) and has a lower side effect profile.

These drugs are started at a low dose and titrated upward at set intervals, with monitoring of therapeutic response and/or emergence of side effects. Blood levels are checked periodically. The total daily dose depends on therapeutic response or intolerable side effects; side effects can be severe and can limit the usefulness of these agents. CNS symptoms, such as nystagmus, ataxia, slurred speech, confusion, and drowsiness, are common and dose-related. Gastrointestinal effects include nausea, vomiting, and constipation. There is a risk of hepatitis or liver damage, particularly with diphenylhydantoin. The most severe side effects may be on the hematopoietic system and include anemia and bone marrow suppression. Therefore, patients need to be monitored very carefully, with full medical evaluation prior to the initiation of therapy, and interval assessment of blood count and liver functions. Clonazepam, although more benign in its side effect profile, does have the potential for dependence and addiction.

TABLE 12.8. Dosages of Anticonvulsants for Chronic Pain

Drug	Dosage (mg/day)
Diphenyhyldantoin (Dilantin)	150–400 (av. 300)
Carbamazepine (Tegretol)	100–1600 (av. 400–600)
Clonazepam (Klonopin)	1.5–6
Valproic acid (Depakene)	250–1000

Lithium

Lithium, a psychotropic agent used to treat bipolar affective disorder, has been found to mitigate pain in some cases of cluster headache (Domasio & Lyon, 1980; Ekbom, 1981; Kudrow, 1977; Medina, Fareed, & Diamond, 1978) and migraine (Medina & Diamond, 1981). Although its exact mechanism of action is unknown, lithium appears to affect serotonin and dopamine, and to have a particular benefit in cyclical disorders. However, given the facts that controlled trials are lacking and that relapse and lack of response are also documented in the few current studies, lithium should be considered a second-order agent in the treatment of these chronic pain syndromes.

Lithium is commonly administered two or three times a day, with initial regular monitoring of serum blood level. The dosage range for pain control is between 300 mg and 1200 mg per day, which is significantly lower than its psychiatric dosage (900–2400 mg per day). The desirable blood level is within the range of 0.4 to 0.8 meq/liter.

Pretreatment patient evaluation should include a cardiovascular history, an EKG, a blood count, electrolyte levels, and kidney and thyroid function tests. Common side effects include diarrhea, nausea, fine motor tremor, and somnolence. Patients should be monitored for more severe toxic reactions, such as polyurea, polydipsia, edema, hypothyroidism, rigidity, tremor, and EKG changes. Lithium toxicity, which may occur even with a moderate lithium blood level, manifests itself as vomiting, diarrhea, tremor, weakness, vertigo, ataxia, hyperreflexia, and somnolence. Lithium has adverse interactions with certain NSAIDs, sedatives, and diuretics. However, lithium is an effective and safe psychotropic agent with careful medical monitoring, and may be a reasonable choice for cluster headaches or migraine syndromes that have not responded to other measures.

Muscle Relaxants

The term "muscle relaxants" is a misnomer, since these drugs have no peripheral action on "tight muscles"; rather, they act on the CNS, as do the benzodiazepines (e.g., diazepam) that are also prescribed for "muscle spasm." The so-called "muscle relaxants" include cyclobenzaprine (Flexeril), carisoprodol (Soma), baclofen (Lioresal), methocarbamol (Robaxin), chlorzoxazone (Parafon Forte), and orphenadrine (Norflex). They are sedating, have addictive potential and a withdrawal syndrome, and generally provide very little therapeutic benefit for chronic pain (Schoefferman, 1994). They may, however, be useful in the early treatment of acute musculoskeletal pain. In addition, baclofen has been found to be effective in relieving the pain of trigeminal neuralgia (Fromm & Killiam, 1967) and may have usefulness in the control of other chronic neuropathic pain syndromes (Steardo, Leo, & Marano, 1984), primarily through central facilitation of gamma-aminobutyric acid (GABA) transmission. Baclofen is initiated at a low dose and titrated upward to a range of 50 to 60 mg per day, in divided doses. Side effects include drowsiness, dizziness, ataxia, confusion, and epigastric distress. After prolonged use, it should be tapered slowly, to avoid hallucinations, anxiety, and tachycardia.

Antianxiety and Sedative Agents

A number of pharmacological agents are useful in controlling core symptoms of anxiety and insomnia (see Table 12.9). To treat these secondary symptoms in chronic pain patients, physicians will certainly utilize antianxiety and sedative medications. Although some clinical studies have suggested that these medications have an antinociceptive

TABLE 12.9. Antianxiety and Sedative Agents

Benzodiazepine anxiolytics	Other antianxiety agents	Sedatives
Lorazepam (Ativan)	Buspirone (BuSpar)	Benzodiazepines
Oxazepam (Serax)	Propranolol (Inderal)	Flurazepam (Dalmane)
Alprazolam (Xanax)	Meprobamate (Equanil)	Temazepam (Restoril)
Clordiazepoxide (Librium)	Barbiturates	Triazolam (Halcion)
Clorazepate (Tranxene)	Antihistamines	Barbiturates
Diazepam (Valium)		Chloral derivatives
Prazepam (Centrax)		Antihistamines
		Zolpidem (Ambien)

Note. Sedatives no longer recommended: glutethimide (Doriden), methyprylon (Noludar), methaqualone (Quaalude), ethchlorvyne (Placidyl).

effect in acute pain because of decreased emotional response (Chapman & Feather, 1973; Gracely, McGrath, & Dubner, 1978), there has been only equivocal documentation of such an effect in chronic pain states (Lance, Curran, & Anthony, 1965; Yosselson-Superstine, Lipman, & Sanders, 1985).

The benzodiazepines are the major class of psychotropics employed for the control of anxiety and insomnia in chronic pain. They are used frequently in acute pain to decrease muscle spasm, or to reduce anticipatory anxiety prior to a procedure. Their mechanism of action is through alteration of metabolism of biogenic amines in the brain, particularly by increasing release of the inhibitory neurotransmitter GABA (Polatin, 1991). Various benzodiazepines are useful for the short-term treatment of anxiety (see Table 12.9). They are best used over a period of a few weeks or months to control initial symptoms, in conjunction with other biobehavioral interventions, and then tapered slowly as the patient stabilizes with nonpharmacological cognitive-behavioral techniques. Side effects such as drowsiness or ataxia are common. Less frequently seen are psychomotor impairment, short-term memory loss, and behavioral disinhibition. These agents do have addictive potential, with risk for tolerance or dependence, and should be used carefully in patients with a history of drug abuse or predisposing psychopathology. In addition, there is a withdrawal syndrome, requiring a tapering of dosage under medical supervision. This is particularly true with alprazolam: Symptoms of "delayed withdrawal," such as irritability or increased anxiety, may develop 3 or 4 weeks after this medication has been discontinued.

Certain benzodiazepines are considered to be primarily sedatives, and there are several other useful classes of medication for this purpose (see Table 12.9). In choosing an agent to treat insomnia, one should take into consideration any primary etiological diagnoses. A patient with chronic pain and insomnia, with or without depression, should be treated with a sedating antidepressant; these agents may mitigate the sleep-disruptive pain, as well as improve sleep patterns even if depression is not present. In chronic pain, primary sedatives should be reserved for those patients whose insomnia has been refractory to a trial of several antidepressants, or who are unable to tolerate any antidepressants secondary to side effects. Many of the primary sedatives do have potential for oversedation, addiction, dependence, and withdrawal, and should be used cautiously, particularly in patients with risk factors for drug abuse.

Neuroleptics

The neuroleptics are also called "major tranquilizers" or "antipsychotic agents." Table 12.10 lists these agents and their equivalent doses compared to chlorpromazine, which

TABLE 12.10. Antipsychotic Agents

Drug	Equivalent dosage (mg)
Chlorpromazine (Thorazine)	100
Thioridazine (Mellaril)	100
Loxapine (Loxitane)	15
Perphenazine (Trilafon)	10
Molindone (Moban)	10
Trifluoperazine (Stelazine)	5
Haloperidol (Haldol)	2–5
Thiothixene (Navane)	5
Fluphenazine (Prolixin)	2–5
Risperidone (Risperdal)	4–8
Clozapine (Clozaril)	50

was the first of these agents used in clinical psychopharmacology. These medications have a potent effect on psychotic behavior and agitation, primarily through the block-ade of dopamine receptors in various brain pathways. However, there is little evidence for a primary analgesic affect, although the neuroleptics have been used to poten-tiate opioid analgesia postoperatively (Minuck, 1972) and to control some chronic pain syndromes (Maltbie, Cavener, Sullivan, Hammett, & Zung, 1979), with some positive results.

These agents do have significant side effects, including various movement disorders, sedation, cardiac toxicity, and bone marrow suppression. The higher-potency agents are less sedative, but do have more potential for extrapyramidal reactions. Tardive dyskinesia, which is often irreversible, poses a significant risk with long-term continuous use of the neuroleptics. Given the lack of evidence for significant benefit in chronic pain states, the side effect profile of neuroleptics limits their use in chronic pain, unless a psychosis or a volatile personality disorder necessitates their usage by traditional psychopharmacologi-cal guidelines. This may include the concomitant use of an antiparkinsonian agent to prevent or control extrapyramidal side effects.

Adjuvant Agents

Several types of medications have been found to enhance the analgesic affect of the non-narcotic analgesics and the opioids in chronic pain states. The heterocyclic antidepres-sants, neuroleptics, and anticonvulsants have primary application in chronic pain as described previously, but may also be used as adjuvants with opioids.

Caffeine has been used to enhance NSAID analgesia, and shortens the time to onset of effect (Laska et al., 1984; Schachtel, Filligan, Lane, Thoden, & Barbutt, 1991; Ward, Whitney, Avery, & Dunner, 1991). The usage of antihistamines along with opioids in chronic pain states permits a lower dose of narcotic to be employed and provides addi-tional sedation (Sunshine & Olsen, 1994). Both of these categories of drugs are relatively nontoxic, with minimal side effect profiles. Neuroleptics may have some enhancing effect on opioid analgesia, but at the very least reduce the nausea commonly seen with use of the narcotics.

Psychostimulants such as dextroamphetamine and methylphenidate (Ritalin) augment narcotic analgesia and also counteract sedation seen with the opioids. However, the risk of CNS toxicity and addiction is significant in these agents and must be monitored carefully.

INTEGRATING PHARMACOTHERAPY
AND PSYCHOLOGICAL TREATMENT
OF CHRONIC PAIN: CASE EXAMPLES

General Comments

Physicians evaluating chronic pain patients for pharmacotherapeutic management do not make decisions in a vacuum. Integral to the process is a good medical history, including an inquiry of previous psychiatric or psychological treatment and prior response to medications. A comprehensive physical examination should be performed, including an assessment of general health and of cardiovascular, pulmonary, gastrointestinal, genitourinary, and neuromuscular function. Psychological assessment—including behavioral observations and the results of initial psychometric tests, such as the Beck Depressive Inventory (BDI), the Hamilton Rating Scale for Depression (HRSD), and the Minnesota Multiphasic Personality Inventory (MMPI)—indicates severity of depression, somatization, and other relevant psychopathology (see Gatchel, Chapter 2, this volume). The use of the self-report BDI to screen for depression is helpful, but the HRSD, which is a clinician-administered questionnaire, can confirm the diagnosis. Symptoms requiring medication control, and contraindications to certain pharmacotherapeutic approaches (e.g., long-term opiate maintenance), will be delineated on psychological assessment. Socioeconomic stressors affecting a patient's presentation may be provided to the treatment team by a social worker or disability case manager.

Symptoms and behaviors initially observed by the physical and occupational therapists in the rehabilitation setting, such as noncompliance with exercise routines, lack of attendance, pain sensitivity, functional and physical capacity deficits, decreased level of alertness, inability to retain instruction, or poor interpersonal skills, are important pieces of information for the managing physician in monitoring clinical response to medications and detecting side effects such as oversedation or obtundation. The most effective form in which such an exchange of information can take place is an interdisciplinary staff meeting, which should occur on at least a weekly basis while a patient is in rehabilitation.

Chronic pain remains a clinical challenge. Because pain is a subjective symptom, it is frequently difficult to assess and monitor, and the clinician must depend on the self-reports of patients whose complex psychosociodemographic issues may unpredictably augment their pain complaints. Therefore, there is no single way to treat chronic pain, and the most successful therapies integrate the best efforts of many disciplines.

The following cases are presented to illustrate the importance of an interdisciplinary approach to chronic pain. Each example illustrates a particular patient profile. None of these could be adequately treated solely with pharmacotherapy. As emphasized earlier (see also Turk, Chapter 1, and Gatchel, Chapter 2, this volume), chronic pain is associated with a complex array of psychosocioeconomic stressors that need to be appropriately managed by behavioral psychological methods.

The Somatic Patient

A 50-year-old married female was seeking treatment because of a recent "flare-up" of intense neck and shoulder pain, which had first occurred following an automobile accident 10 years earlier. There were no litigation issues outstanding on this case. The patient described this pain as "paralyzing" to her during the day while doing housework. She also had a history of chronic headaches, as well as joint pain, which she attributed to arthritis. Her complaints of intense pain did not appear to be congruent with her actual observed movement and impairment during therapy. She regularly complained of pain, but would often complete a required task, although it was a struggle and the therapist had to urge her on constantly. She would also often request rest breaks and passive means of pain relief (medication, massage, ice, etc.).

Her initial injury 10 years previously had caused severe neck and shoulder pain that lasted for 3 years and resolved over a period of 6 months after the case was litigated successfully. Six months ago, her husband had sustained a back injury at work and had been disabled since that time. On initial psychological testing, she presented with a BDI score of 16, an HRSD score of 15, and an MMPI presenting with elevations above 70 on Scales 1 and 3. She was reluctant to discuss psychological issues, but did not demonstrate marked elevations on indices of depression.

This patient was currently being treated in an interdisciplinary setting, and her case was presented in a staff meeting. Physical therapists working with her were instructed to take a very supportive approach with her pain complaints, but to emphasize the importance of adequate stretching and strengthening exercises, using passive modalities as a reinforcement for hard work in rehabilitation exercises. In addition, it was decided to give her instruction on the interrelationship between pain and emotional distress, and to encourage her in psychological counseling to discuss her feelings about her husband's recent disability and the demands placed upon her because of this. She was also evaluated by the physician on the team, who recommended, in spite of the absence of significant depression, a trial of a somewhat sedating antidepressant at a low dose because of complaints of ongoing pain, some increased anxiety, and a primary and secondary sleep disturbance.

The patient was placed on amitriptyline (Elavil), starting at 25 mg before bedtime. She reported some dry mouth and slight morning hangover, but these side effects resolved after the first 2 days, such that she was able to increase the dose to 50 mg. At this dosage, she noted that she was sleeping through the night; some dry mouth recurred, but this decreased after an additional week on this dose. She began to voice somewhat lesser intensity of her pain, which allowed her to continue to work more easily in the pain management setting. After 2 weeks on this medication, she was perceived as significantly improved: She participated more easily in the physical rehabilitation exercises, and was beginning to demonstrate an interest in some of the educational interpretations offered to her. She continued on Elavil at a dose of 50 mg before bedtime. She noted, on one occasion when she ran out of the medication over a weekend, that she had an immediate recurrence of sleep disturbance and increased perception of pain; these resolved after 2 days back on the medication.

The patient completed rehabilitation after 4 weeks, but was maintained on the Elavil for an additional 4 months, after which it was discontinued. She noticed some transitory sleep disturbance and increased irritability for 1 week after stopping the Elavil, but then improved, and continued to do well without medication.

The Depressed Patient

A 45-year-old assembly-line worker and divorced mother of two developed neck and shoulder pain after falling at work. She was referred for physical therapy after this pain continued for 6 weeks. She had had an orthopedic evaluation with negative workup for cervical disk herniation, radiculopathy, or shoulder impingement. She had some initial response to an NSAID, but then continued to experience pain. She had been unable to return to work, and there had been some concern about progressive physical deconditioning. In initial rehabilitation, she was quite passive and lethargic, and had to be constantly pushed to exert maximal effort during therapy. She also did not seem to be following through with recommended home exercises, and complained that she could never find the time or energy to do the exercises. She admitted to difficulty with sleep, loss of appetite, low energy, and recent headaches. Whenever she was confronted by her physical therapist, she became tearful and depressed, and promised to try to do better in the future.

On further questioning, she admitted to a feeling of sadness most of the day every day for the past month. She had had thoughts of death (but no suicidal ideation), had lost interest in things that previously engaged her in her life, was socially isolating herself, and had a triphasic sleep disturbance and anergia. She had been divorced 3 years previously; at that time she had been hospitalized for 3 weeks with depression and treated with trazodone (Desyrel). She had stayed on that medication for 6 months and then tapered it with no recurrence of depression.

She currently had a BDI score of 30 and an HRSD score of 26. Her MMPI demonstrated elevations above 70 on Scales 1, 2 and 3. On interview, she presented as a somewhat disheveled, downcast middle-aged woman. Her mood was clearly depressed, with some tearfulness during the interview and blunting of her affect. She was oriented to time, place, and person, with an adequate fund of knowledge suggestive of average intelligence. She demonstrated no pressured speech, flight of ideas, ideas of reference, loosening of association, or any other abnormality of thought process. She did seem somewhat ruminative and pessimistic.

This patient was discussed in an interdisciplinary staffing conference. It was decided to continue her physical therapy, with additional supportive encouragement to be provided by her therapist. She was referred to a psychologist for implementation of brief cognitive therapy for her depression, education about the interrelation of pain and emotional distress, and relaxation training to assist her in decreasing the severity of her pain experience. A vocational specialist was called in to meet with her employer and to help her construct a return-to-work plan, with a transitional part-time, light-duty, "phase-in" period while she was still in treatment. She was placed back on Desyrel because of her previous good response, initially at a dose of 50 mg before bedtime, and progressed over a 1-week period to 150 mg before bedtime. She slept much better almost immediately, and also reported lessening of her pain within 1 week after starting the Desyrel. Although she had some initial morning hangover at the 150-mg dose, this side effect diminished when she began taking the medication 2 hours earlier.

After a period of 3 weeks, the patient began to note a lessening of her depression and was visibly brighter. She returned to work with light-duty restrictions for limited hours, but continued in interdisciplinary treatment. Over the next 4 weeks, she progressed to full-time, full-duty work. Although she still had pain, she was more comfortable applying specific learned techniques to reduce it and was able to continue working. She became more depressed when the Desyrel was tapered at 6 months, but improved when it was restarted at the same dose. It was decided to continue the Desyrel at the full antidepressant dose, with periodic medical follow-up over the next 12 months.

The Psychotic Patient

A 32-year-old woman was referred for hand therapy 4 weeks after a right carpal tunnel release. She had developed symptoms in her right wrist while at work as an assembler, and was fearful that she would not be able to return to that job. She reported that the pain had not improved at all since surgery. She had been compliant with initial postsurgical treatment. She demonstrated residual tenderness over the operated wrist, but no evidence of nerve compression; her pinch and grip strength were markedly decreased bilaterally. She attended therapy regularly, appeared compliant, and actually demonstrated gradual improvement, but was still at suboptimal functional capacity after another 3 weeks of therapy. The pain complaint continued unchanged. She expressed discouragement and was noted to be tearful at times.

She admitted to a suicide attempt 5 years ago, followed by a 1-month hospitalization. At that time, she had been treated with an antidepressant and a neuroleptic; she reported that she had been hearing voices prior to her suicide attempt. Twelve years ago, she had had a prior brief psychiatric hospitalization, but did not recall much about it.

The patient's BDI score was 40; her HRSD score was 30; and her MMPI demonstrated elevations on Scales 1, 2, 3, and 8. On interview, she presented as a somewhat unkempt, agitated middle-aged woman. Her mood was clearly anxious. She was oriented, but demonstrated some pressured speech and paranoid ideation, and admitted to hearing voices again. She also reported that she was isolating herself at home, staying in bed most of the day when she was not in therapy.

The patient's case was presented at an interdisciplinary staff meeting, where problems of compliance, motivation, somatization, depression, and psychosis were identified. She was placed in a structured tertiary care setting. Attendance and compliance with prescribed routines were closely monitored by the physical and occupational therapists. A psychologist encouraged her to acknowledge her depression and to understand that she was experiencing hallucinations related to depression. She was also given education about the effects of her current emotional distress on her pain levels.

The patient was seen by the physician, and venlafaxine (Effexor), a new antidepressant, was prescribed, as well as thiothixene (Navane), a neuroleptic. She progressed slowly from 37.5 mg of Effexor twice a day to 75 mg twice a day, increasing the dose by 37.5 mg every other day. At the initial dose, she had some nausea and sedation, but could tolerate these side effects. The Navane was begun at 2 mg twice a day; she was closely observed for any extrapyramidal and other side effects, but tolerated this medication as well. Within 2 days of being placed on the neuroleptic, she reported significant diminution of the auditory hallucinations, and within 1 week was no longer hearing the voices at all.

The patient had a visible brightening of affect and decrease in her agitation by the end of the first week, and by the end of the second week she was clearly less depressed and working more easily in rehabilitation. At that time, a vocational specialist became involved to meet with her employer and to implement a return-to-work plan. She completed rehabilitation after 6 weeks and returned to work. She continued in once-a-week psychotherapy for another 3 months. After 1 month, her Navane was discontinued with no recurrent psychosis. However, she was kept on Effexor at a dose of 75 mg twice a day with bimonthly medical monitoring for an additional extended period of time.

The Anxious Patient

A 40-year-old man was referred for physical therapy with a complaint of neck pain, which had developed after a motor vehicle accident 3 weeks previously. He had marked tenderness in the paracervical areas bilaterally with tightness and some spasm, and with marked restriction of cervical mobility. On initial presentation, he spent some time describing his symptoms, and was fearful of being examined. He attended physical therapy regularly, practiced his exercises at home, and expressed motivation to recover, but continued to complain of pain and muscle tension and was not progressing. He admitted to previously being treated for "nerves" with alprazolam (Xanax), but was not taking it now. On careful questioning, he admitted to having panic attacks every other day. He had a BDI score of 20, an HRSD score of 24, and an MMPI demonstrating elevations of Scales 1, 2, and 3.

His case was presented at an interdisciplinary staff meeting, at which it was decided to continue physical therapy for mobilization and strengthening, but also to initiate psychological consultation. The patient was educated on the interrelationship of muscle tension, anxiety, and pain severity; in addition, relaxation training was initiated, resulting in dramatic relief of neck pain. He was also seen in consultation by a physician, who started him on imipramine (Tofranil) at a dose of 25 mg once a day, progressing to a dose of 25 mg three times a day. Initially, the patient noticed dry mouth and jitteriness, which gradually resolved. At the same time, he was placed back on Xanax at a dose of 0.5 mg twice a day. His panic attacks were immediately relieved. After a period of 10 days, when the Tofranil was up to a dose of 75 mg a day, the patient was able to taper his Xanax with no worsening of panic attacks. He was visibly more relaxed and began to improve significantly in physical therapy, with decrease in his pain complaint, improved range of motion of the cervical spine, and markedly decreased spasm. After a period of 1 month, he was essentially pain-free. He continued on the Tofranil, but was able to discontinue his physical therapy, and continues with home stretching, strengthening, and relaxation exercises. The Tofranil was tapered after 6 months by 25 mg per week, with no recurrence of panic attacks or pain.

The Intellectually Disadvantaged Patient

A 32-year-old man presented with low back pain after a work-related injury. He had been disabled since his injury and was referred for work hardening. On initial testing, he demonstrated low functional capacity, with poor effort on testing and some inconsistency in the test results. On physical examination, there was marked superficial tenderness, stocking anesthesia, and exclamations of pain suggestive of symptom magnification. He subsequently demonstrated poor attendance in therapy and failed to progress. The therapist noted some confusion in his ability to follow directions, with mistakes being made each time, even after explanation. He moved slowly, hardly spoke, and did not appear to establish any relationships with either therapists or peers. Other patients ignored or avoided him because of his poor personal hygiene. He did not talk about his work, and did not even know whether his job was still available.

He had dropped out of school in the eighth grade, had held a number of manual labor jobs, and was unmarried. He lived in a trailer in his mother's backyard. He had a Wechsler Adult Intelligence Scale (WAIS) Full Scale IQ of 70, a BDI score of 20, and an HRSD score of 15. His MMPI was invalid, with many incomplete items. He did admit to a sleep disturbance, primarily because of pain at night.

This patient's case was presented at an interdisciplinary staff meeting, at which time it was decided to transfer him to a tertiary functional restoration program. He was assigned physical and occupational therapists, who spent extra time monitoring compliance, with positive reinforcement of praise for regular attendance and good performance. His exercise progression was closely supervised, and he was repeatedly instructed as necessary in the use of the exercise equipment. A case manager was assigned to establish a return-to-work plan, with some involvement of a vocational retraining facility, since it was found that his old job would not be available. Relaxation training to improve sleep and to assist in decreasing reactivity to pain was initiated, as well as basic education on pain and stress. He was assessed by a physician, and started on fluoxetine (Prozac) at a dose of 20 mg per day, for his mild depression and to mitigate pain.

There was some visible brightening of the patient's affect within a period of 10 days. He began to speak with other patients and to act more appropriately in social situations, with less frequent complaints of pain. He was given some basic social and hygiene instructional information, to which he responded, and he gradually began to progress in therapy. Upon completion of the program, he entered job retraining; he completed this in 3 more months and then had a trial placement. His Prozac was continued for 4 months and then discontinued, with no adverse affect.

The Highly Stressed Patient

A 45-year-old man presented with pain in the right upper extremity. He had been injured at work as a press operator when he sustained a crush injury to the index and middle fingers of the right hand. He was initially treated with reconstructive surgery to the hand, but thereafter his pain progressively increased, extending up the entire extremity into the neck. He subsequently had several decompressive procedures (including a right carpal tunnel release and a right cubital tunnel release), with some temporary relief of pain, but recurrence within a period of 2 months and progressive worsening of the extremity pain. On presentation, he had almost no function of his right upper extremity, with some generalized wasting of the musculature and a coolness and dryness of the limb. A diagnosis of reflex sympathetic dystrophy had been made. He had been referred for rehabilitation therapy in the past, but had not been able to progress because of worsening of his pain. In addition, he reported that he had become more irritable at home, and was fearful of harming his wife or one of his children because of temper outbursts. He had a very prominent sleep disturbance, admitted to feeling hopeless, and had thoughts of suicide.

This patient had been on military combat duty 20 years ago. He reported that he had not been wounded, but had witnessed a number of violent events. When he returned to the United States after discharge, he did receive therapy at the Veterans Administration for what was then diagnosed as "stress syndrome." He reported that although he was markedly improved after a number of years, he still had occasional "flashbacks" and nightmares. However, he had been able to hold a job and lead a fairly normal life. His symptoms had gotten worse after his current injury. He had a BDI score of 40 and an HRSD score of 28. His MMPI demonstrated elevations on Scales 1, 2, 3, 4, 7, and 8.

This patient was discussed in an interdisciplinary staff meeting. Identified problems appeared to be extreme pain sensitivity, refusal to use his right upper extremity, emotional lability, insomnia, and depression. Because of his outbursts, he was a management problem in the rehabilitation milieu, and the therapists were afraid of him. In addition, his residual deficits would limit his employability, and although he had indicated a preference to continue working, he had also applied for long-term disability benefits.

The patient was placed in a tertiary interdisciplinary functional restoration program. A psychologist immediately initiated a suicide contract and began supportive psychotherapy in which coping strategies were emphasized. Relaxation training helped to reduce his anxiety and decrease his emotional outbursts, and he was very receptive to education about the relationship between emotional distress and pain. At the same time, the psychologist emphasized the importance of regular attendance and participation in the rehabilitation program, and was "on call" for the physical and occupational therapists if the patient's irritability became problematic in the rehabilitation setting.

Concurrently, this patient was evaluated by a physician who placed him on amoxapine

(Asendin), a sedating antidepressant with additional dopamine receptor selectivity, and clonazepam (Klonopin), a benzodiazepine and anticonvulsant. He progressed on the Asendin from 25 mg before bedtime to 150 mg over a period of 2 weeks, raising the dose by 25 mg every other day. Initially, he experienced light-headedness, dry mouth, and constipation. Because of his underlying anxiety and suspiciousness, he initially refused to continue the medication, but after the physician spent additional time explaining the rationale for treatment and the side effects, he agreed to continue. Although dry mouth and postural hypotension persisted, the patient accepted these side effects and did note improved sleep, decreased irritability, and decreasing depressed mood.

He became easier to work with in the rehabilitation program, following through on his exercises and progressing well. He underwent vocational evaluation and was referred for job retraining after he completed functional restoration.

The Asendin was continued for 6 months at full dosage. The Klonopin was tapered from 0.5 mg three times a day after 1 month, with no increase in irritability or anxiety but with some increase in pain, so that it was reinstituted at 0.5 mg twice a day. After 6 months, the Asendin was tapered by 25 mg every other day with no adverse affect.

A Patient for Narcotic Maintenance

A 60-year-old man presented with chronic low back pain radiating to the right foot. He had been aware of this pain for the past 10 years. He had had a lumbar diskectomy and then a posterior lumbar interbody fusion, with some initial relief of pain but subsequent recurrence. A lumbar magnetic resonance imaging scan demonstrated lumbar epidural fibrosis (i.e., fibrous adhesions around the spinal nerve roots). He had been through intensive rehabilitation with improvement after his last surgery. He reported that although he had severe pain, he continued to work full-time as an attorney, sometimes putting in as many as 70 or 80 hours a week. He remained active, playing racquetball and working out regularly at his health club. His pain sometimes was so severe that he had to spend a day or two in bed, and occasionally he had gone to a hospital emergency room for a "pain shot." He had used NSAIDs intermittently with some control of the pain. His BDI score was 15, and his HRSD score was 10. His MMPI demonstrated no abnormal scales. He appeared younger than his stated age, well conditioned, and in no acute distress. He was very focused on the problem of intermittent pain, which interfered with his ability to perform his daily activities.

This patient was referred to a pain program. He indicated, however, that he did not wish rehabilitation or pain management therapy, but wanted to have medication available to him when his pain became unbearable. His case was reviewed in a staff meeting. He did not demonstrate significant psychopathology; he was active and oriented toward functioning; he appeared to be coping well with his pain; and he was very clear about his needs. He was thus placed on a low dose of doxepin (Sinequan, 25 mg at bedtime), and reported that at this low dose he had some lessening of his pain, but continued to be symptomatic. He intermittently used naproxen (Naprosyn), an NSAID, but still requested some "backup" pain medication. After careful discussion with him, his managing physician agreed to prescribe a low-dose narcotic, hydrocodone (Lortab, 5 mg), not to exceed three pills a day and with careful monitoring of the refillable prescription. He was also referred to a psychologist for biofeedback to reduce muscle tension and thereby more effectively control his pain. Over a period of 2 months, the patient reported that he was able to further limit his usage of Lortab, although he still found it useful to have some available for particularly severe pain episodes.

SUMMARY

Pharmacological treatment of chronic pain has as its goals analgesia and the relief of emotional distress, and utilizes medications at doses and for applications that may not be always readily recognized by the medical community. This is particularly true for the antidepressants, the anticonvulsants, lithium, and baclofen. Moreover, the use of narcotics for the long-term treatment of chronic nonmalignant pain is still considered controversial. It is therefore important that clinicians treating chronic pain patients be familiar with these pharmacological approaches and be prepared to educate colleagues, who may challenge some of these prescriptions.

Because of the clinical complexities of chronic pain syndromes, it is not uncommon to see patients on a number of different pharmacological agents, progressing from the most directly analgesic agents to psychotropics for control of emotional distress. The utilization of an NSAID, an opioid, an antidepressant, and an anticonvulsant concomitantly is not uncommon. Optimal communication among treatment disciplines is essential and can only be achieved through frequent interdisciplinary staff meetings in which clinical and behavioral observations, medical assessment, and treatment planning are shared responsibilities.

REFERENCES

Abramson, S. (1991). Therapy and mechanisms of nonsteroidal anti-inflammatory drugs. *Current Opinion in Rheumatology, 3*, 336–340.

Alcoff, J., Jones, E., Rust, P., & Newman, R. (1982). Controlled trial of imipramine for chronic low back pain. *Journal of Family Practice, 14*(5), 841–846.

Anthony, M., & Lance, J. (1969). Monoamine oxidase inhibition in the treatment of migraine. *Archives of Neurology, 21*, 263–268.

Atkinson, J. (1989). Psychopharmacological agents in the treatment of pain syndromes. In D. Tollison (Ed.), *Handbook of chronic pain management* (pp. 69–102). Baltimore: Williams & Wilkins.

Brandt, J., Celentano, D., Stewart, W., Linet, M., & Polstein, M. (1990). Personality and emotional disorder in a community sample of migraine headache sufferers. *American Journal of Psychology, 147*(3), 5.

Chapman, C., & Feather, B. (1973). Effects of diazepam on human pain tolerance and pain sensitivity. *Psychosomatic Medicine, 35*, 330–340.

Cooper, J., Czechowicz, D., Petersen, R., & Molinan, S. (1992). Prescription drug diversion control and medical practice. *Journal of the American Medical Association, 268*, 1306–1310.

Couch, J., & Hassanein, R. (1979). Amitriptyline in migraine prophylaxis. *Archives of Neurology, 36*, 695–699.

Couch, J., Ziegler, D., & Hassanein, R. (1976). Amitriptyline in the prophylaxis of migraine. *Neurology, 26*, 121–127.

Delfino, U. (1983). An advance in trigeminal therapy. In S. Lipton & J. Miles (Eds.), *Persistent pain: Vol. 4. Modern methods of treatment.* London: Grune & Stratton.

Domasio, H., & Lyon, L. (1980). Lithium carbonate in the treatment of cluster headaches. *Journal of Neurology, 224*, 1–8.

Dubas, T., & Parker, J. (1971). A central component in the analgesic action of sodium salicylate. *Archives of International Pharmacodynamic Therapeutics, 194*, 117–122.

Ekbom, K. (1981). Lithium for cluster headache: Review of the literature and preliminary results of long-term treatment. *Headache, 21*, 132–139.

Fields, H. (1987). The peripheral pain sensory system. In H. Fields (Ed.), *Pain* (pp. 13–40). New York: McGraw-Hill.

Fishbain, D., Goldberg, M., Meagher, R., Steele, R., & Rosomoff, H. (1986). Male and female chronic pain patients categorized by DSM-III psychiatric diagnostic criteria. *Pain, 26*, 181–197.

France, R., Houpt, J., & Ellinwood, E. (1984a). Therapeutic effects of antidepressants in chronic pain. *General Hospital Psychiatry, 6*, 55–63.

France, R., & Krishnan, K. (1988). Psychotropic drugs in chronic pain. In R. France & K. Krishnan (Eds.), *Chronic pain* (pp. 323–374). Washington, DC: American Psychiatric Press.

France, R., Urban, B., & Keefe, F. (1984b). Long-term use of narcotic analgesics and chronic pain. *Social Science and Medicine, 19*, 1379–1382.

Fromm, G., & Killiam, J. (1967). Effect of some anticonvulsant drugs on the spinal trigeminal nucleus. *Neurology, 17*, 275–280.

Glaser, G., Penry, J., & Woodbury, D. (1980). *Antiepileptic drugs: Mechanism of action.* New York: Raven Press.

Gomersall, J., & Stewart, A. (1973). Amitriptyline in migraine prophylaxis. *Journal of Neurology, Neurosurgery and Psychiatry, 36*, 684–690.

Goodkin, K., & Gullion, C. (1989). A critical review of clinical trials using heterocyclic antidepressants for the relief of chronic pain syndromes with a focus on chronic low back pain. *Annals of Behavioral Medicine, 11*(3), 83–101.

Gourlak, G., & Cousins, M. (1984). Strong analgesics in severe pain. *Drugs, 28*, 79.

Gracely, R., McGrath, P., & Dubner, R. (1978). Validity and sensitivity of sensory and affective verbal pain descriptors: Manipulation of affect by diazepam. *Pain, 5*, 19–29.

Gringas, M. (1976). A clinical trial of Tofranil in rheumatic pain in general practice. *Journal of Internal Medicine Research, 4*, 41–49.

Hanks, G., Twycross, R., & Lloyd, J. (1981). Unexpected complication of successful nerve block. *Anesthesia, 36*, 37–39.

Hameroff, S., Weiss, J., Lerman, J., Cork, R., Watts, K., Crago, G., Newman, C., Womble, J., & Davis, T. (1984). Doxepin's effects on chronic pain and depression: A controlled study. *Journal of Clinical Psychiatry, 45*, 47–53.

Hameroff., S., Cork, R., Scherer, K., Crago, B., Newman, C., Womble, J., & Davis, T. (1982). Doxepin effects on chronic pain, depression, and plasma opioids. *Journal of Clinical Psychiatry, 43*, 22–27.

Hering, R., & Kuritzky, A. (1989). Sodium valproate in the treatment of cluster headache: An open clinical study. *Cephalalgia, 9*, 195–198.

Hering, R., & Kuritzky, A. (1992). Sodium valproate in the prophylactic treatment of migraine: A double blind study versus placebo. *Cephalalgia, 12*, 81–84.

Hisbani, M., Pincus, J., & Lee, S. (1974). Diphenylhydantoin and calcium movement in lobster nerves. *Archives of Neurology, 31*, 250–254.

Katon, W., Egan, K., & Miller, D. (1985). Chronic pain: Lifetime psychiatric diagnoses and family history. *American Journal of Psychiatry, 142*(10), 1156–1160.

Kinney, R., Gatchel, R., Polatin, P., Fogarty, W., & Mayer, T. (1993). Prevalence of psychopathology in acute and chronic low back pain patients. *Journal of Occupational Rehabilitation, 3*, 95–103.

Kudrow, L. (1977). Lithium prophylaxis for chronic cluster headache. *Headache, 17*, 15–18.

Lance, J., & Curran, D. (1964). Treatment of chronic tension headache. *Lancet, i*, 1236–1239.

Lance, J., Curran, D., & Anthony, M. (1965). Investigations into the mechanism and treatment of chronic headaches. *Medical Journal of Australia, ii*, 909–914.

Lascelles, R. (1966). Atypical facial pain and depression. *British Journal of Psychiatry, 112*, 651–659.

Laska, E., Sunshine, A., Mueller, R., Elvers, W., Siegel, C., & Rubin, A. (1984). Caffeine as an analgesic adjuvant. *Journal of the American Medical Association, 251*, 1711–1718.

Loeser, J., & Ward, A. (1967). Some effects of deafferentation on neurons of the cut spinal cord. *Archives of Neurology, 17*, 629–636.

Malmberg, A., & Yaksh, T. (1992). Hyperalgesia mediated by spinal glutemate or substance receptor blocked by spinal cyclo-oxygenase inhibition. *Science, 257*, 1277–1280.

Maltbie, A., Cavener, J., Sullivan, J., Hammett, E., & Zung, W. (1979). Analgesia and haloperidol: A hypothesis. *Journal of Clinical Psychiatry, 40,* 323–326.

Marks, R., & Sacher, E. (1973). Undertreatment of medical inpatients with narcotic analgesics. *Annals of Internal Medicine, 78,* 173.

Mathew, N. (1978). Clinical subtypes of cluster headaches and response to lithium therapy. *Headache, 18,* 26–30.

McCaffey, M., & Hart, L. (1976). Undertreatment of acute pain with narcotics. *American Journal of Nursing, 10,* 1586.

McDonald-Scott, W. (1969). The relief of pain with an antidepressant in arthritis. *The Practitioner, 202,* 802–897.

Medical Board of California. (1994). *Guidelines for prescribing controlled substances for intractable pain.* Sacramento: Author.

Medina, J., & Diamond, S. (1981). Cyclical migraine. *Archives of Neurology, 38,* 343–344.

Medina, J., Fareed, J., & Diamond, S. (1978). Blood amines and platelet changes during treatment of cluster headache with lithium and other drugs. *Headache, 18,* 112.

Minuck, R. (1972). Postoperative analgesia: Comparison of methotrimeprazine and meperidine as postoperative analgesia agents. *Canadian Anesthesiological Society Journal, 19,* 87–96.

Monks, R. (1994). Psychotropic drugs. In P. Wall & R. Melzack (Eds.), *Textbook of pain* (3rd ed., pp. 963–989). New York: Churchill Livingstone.

Onghena, P., & Van Houdenhove, B. (1992). Antidepressant-induced analgesia in chronic nonmalignant pain: A meta-analysis of 39 placebo-controlled studies. *Pain, 40,* 205–219.

Petitto, J., Mundle L., Nagy, B., Evans, D., & Golden, R. (1992). Improvement of arthritis with fluoxetine. *Psychosomatics, 33*(3), 338–341.

Pilowsky, I., Hallett, E., Bassett, D., Thomas, P., & Penhall, R. (1982). Controlled study of amitriptyline in the treatment of chronic pain. *Pain, 14,* 169–179.

Polatin, P. (1991). Psychoactive medications as adjuncts in functional restoration. In T. Mayer, V. Mooney, & R. Gatchel (Eds.), *Contemporary conservative care for painful spinal disorders* (pp. 465–472). Philadelphia: Lea & Febiger.

Polatin, P., Kinney, R., Gatchel, R., Lillo, E., & Mayer, T. (1993). Psychiatric illness and chronic low back pain: The mind and the spine—Which goes first? *Spine, 18,* 66–71.

Portnoy, R. (1994). Opioid therapy for chronic nonmalignant pain: Current status. In H. Fields & J. Liebeskind (Eds.), *Progress in pain research and management* (Vol. 1, pp. 247–287). Seattle, WA: International Association for the Study of Pain Press.

Portnoy, R., & Foley, K. (1986). Chronic use of opioid analgesics in nonmalignant pain: Report of 38 cases. *Pain, 25,* 171–186.

Raft, D., Davidson, J., Wasik, J., & Mattox, A. (1981). Relationship between response to phenelzine and MAO inhibition in a clinical trial of phenelzine, amitriptyline, and placebo. *Neuropsychobiology, 7,* 122–126.

Schactel, B., Fillingim, J., Lane, A., Thoden, W., & Barbutt, R. (1991). Caffeine as an analgesic adjuvant: A double-blind study comparing aspirin with caffeine to aspirin and placebo in patients with sore throat. *Archives of Internal Medicine, 151,* 733–737.

Schoefferman, J. (1994, February). *The use of medications for pain of spinal origin.* Paper presented at "The Final Link to Therapeutic Success" course, Seton Medical Center, San Francisco, CA.

Smirne, S., & Scarlato, G. (1977). Clonazepam in cranial neuralgias. *Medical Journal of Australia, i,* 93–94.

Spiegel, K., Kalb, R., & Pasternak, G. (1983). Analgesic activity of tricyclic antidepressants. *Annals of Neurology, 13,* 462–465.

Steardo, L., Leo, A., & Marano, E. (1984). Efficacy of baclofen in trigeminal neuralgia and some other painful conditions: A clinical trial. *European Neurology, 23,* 51–55.

Sunshine, A., & Olson, N. (1994). Non-narcotic analgesics. In P. Wall & R. Melzack (Eds.), *Textbook of pain* (3rd ed., pp. 923–942). New York: Churchill Livingstone.

Taub, A. (1982). Opioid analgesics in the treatment of chronic intractable pain of non-neoplastic origin. In L. Kitahata & J. Collins (Eds.), *Narcotics, analgesics in anesthesiology* (pp. 199–208). Baltimore: Williams & Wilkins.

Theeson, K., & Marsch, R. (1989). Relief of diabetic neuropathy with fluoxetine. *Drug Intelligence and Clinical Pharmacy, 23*, 572–574.

Tollison, C., & Kriegel, M. (1984). Selected tricyclic antidepressants in the management of chronic benign pain. *Southern Medical Journal, 81*(5), 562–564.

Twycross, R. (1994). Opioids. In P. Wall & R. Melzack (Eds.), *Textbook of pain* (3rd ed, pp. 943–962). New York: Churchill Livingstone.

Urban, B., France, R., Steinberger, E., Scott, D., & Maltbie, A. (1986). Long-term use of narcotic/antidepressant medication in the management of phantom limb pain. *Pain, 24*, 191–196.

Walsh, T., Baxter, R., Bowman, K., & Leber, B. (1981). High dose morphine and respiratory function in chronic cancer pain. [Abstract] *Pain* (Suppl. 1), *39*, 539.

Ward, N., Bloom, V., & Friedel, R. (1979). The effectiveness of tricyclic antidepressants in the treatment of coexisting pain and depression. *Pain, 7*, 331–341.

Ward, N., Whitney, C., Avery, D., & Dunner, D. (1991). The analgesic effects of caffeine in headache. *Pain, 44*, 151–155.

Watson, C., Evans, R., Reed, K., Merskey, H., Goldsmith, L., & Warsh, J. (1982). Amitriptyline versus placebo in postherpetic neuralgia. *Neurology, 32*, 671–673.

Yosselson-Superstine, S., Lipman, A., & Sanders, S. (1985). Adjunctive antianxiety agents in the management of chronic pain. *Israeli Journal of Medical Science, 21*, 113–117.

PART III

SPECIAL
POPULATIONS
AND TOPICS

Controlling Children's Pain

Patricia A. McGrath

Loretta M. Hillier

During the past decade, unprecedented attention has been focused on the special pain problems of infants, children, and adolescents, so that there have been enormous advances in our understanding of children's pain perception and in our ability to alleviate their suffering (for reviews, see Barr, 1994; Bush & Harkins, 1991; Houck, Troshynski, & Berde, 1994; P. A. McGrath, 1990, 1994; P. J. McGrath & Unruh, 1987; Pichard-Leandri & Gauvain-Piquard, 1989; Ross & Ross, 1988; Schechter, Berde, & Yaster, 1993; Tyler & Krane, 1990). Many of the myths underlying our past treatment of children's pain have been refuted. We now know that children, like adults, can experience many different types of acute, recurrent, and persistent pain. We recognize that infants perceive pain at birth and that the failure to alleviate their pain has adverse physiological effects, in addition to the suffering that they experience. We know that children in severe pain require potent analgesics for pain relief, and that the fear that they will become addicted has been unduly exaggerated. We know that children can describe their pain qualitatively, using language that reflects their own experiences, and that they can rate their pain quantitatively on a variety of standardized scales. Yet one of the most remarkable advances—because of its important implications for pain management—has been our gradual realization that the system that mediates children's pain perceptions is a marvel of subtlety and complexity.

Like adults, children can experience pain without tissue injury or any apparent injury at all. They can also sustain injury without experiencing pain, and can experience very different pains from the same type of tissue damage. Children's nociceptive systems are plastic, in that they have the capacity to respond differently to the same amount of tissue damage. We now know that children's pain perception depends upon complex neural interactions: Impulses generated by tissue damage are modified both by ascending systems activated by innocuous stimuli (e.g., touch) and by descending pain-suppressing systems activated by various situational factors, such as a child's expectations about what he or she will feel (for reviews, see P. A. McGrath, 1990; Price, 1988; Wall & Melzack, 1994; Willis, 1985). Since pain is not simply and directly related to the level of tissue damage, we now know that we cannot completely control a child's pain by gearing our interventions solely to the source of tissue damage. We must also modify the factors that affect nociceptive processing.

Thus, controlling children's pain requires a dual emphasis on administering appropriate analgesics and on selectively modifying the factors that exacerbate their pain. The common factors that exacerbate children's acute, recurrent, and persistent pain are summarized in this chapter. Case studies from our pain clinic are presented to illustrate a practical approach for obtaining accurate information about the sensory characteristics of children's pain and about the relevant factors that modify their pain perception. The cognitive, behavioral, and physical interventions that address these factors and lessen children's pain provide the foundation for practical and effective treatment programs for children.

THE NATURE OF CHILDREN'S PAIN

Like adults, most children experience a wide variety of pains that differ in intensity, quality, location, and duration. All children's diverse pain experiences are categorized generally as "acute," "recurrent," or "persistent" pain. Acute pain is caused by a well-defined noxious or tissue-damaging stimulus (e.g., an injection or superficial skin injury). Recurrent pain syndromes, repeated episodes of headaches, abdominal pains, or limb pains, constitute special pain problems for many otherwise healthy and pain-free children. The recurring pains in such a case are not symptomatic of an underlying disease that requires medical treatment. Instead, the pain syndrome itself is the disorder, and the multiple factors responsible for the pains must be identified and managed. Persistent pain is any prolonged pain. The pain may be caused by a disease, such as cancer or arthritis, or may continue beyond the usual time period required for healing injuries. In addition, children may experience persistent pain without any clear evidence of injury or tissue damage. Although we do not yet know the specific prevalence and incidence of children's pains, we do know that they experience many different types of acute, recurrent, and persistent pain.

Children's perceptions of pain are not simply and directly related to the extent of their physical injuries or to the severity of their diseases. Tissue damage initiates a sequence of neural events that may lead to pain, but many factors can intervene to alter the sequence of neural transmission and thereby modify a child's pain perception, as shown by the model illustrated in Figure 13.1. Some factors are relatively stable for a child, such as age, gender, cognitive level, previous pain experience, family learning, and cultural background (shown in the open box in the figure). These characteristics shape how children generally interpret and experience the various sensations caused by tissue damage. In contrast, the cognitive, behavioral, and emotional factors (shown in the shaded boxes) are not stable. They represent a unique interaction between the child experiencing pain and the context in which the pain is experienced (P. A. McGrath, 1990; Ross & Ross, 1988). These situational factors can vary dynamically, depending on the specific circumstances in which children experience pain. Even though the pain source may remain constant, the particular set of situational factors is unique for each occurrence of pain. Moreover, unlike the stable child characteristics listed in Figure 13.1, situational factors can be changed by health professionals so as to lessen children's pain dramatically.

What children understand, what they do, and how they feel have a profound impact on their pain experience. Differences in situational factors may account for why the same tissue damage can evoke pains that vary in intensity, and may partially explain why proven analgesics can vary in effectiveness for different children and for the same child at different times. In addition, some situational factors are the primary causes of certain recurrent and persistent pains in otherwise healthy and pain-free children.

Cognitive factors include children's understanding about the pain source; their ability to control what will happen; their expectations regarding the quality and strength of

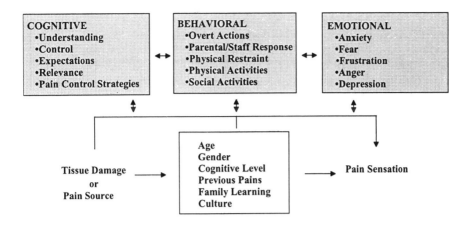

FIGURE 13.1. A model depicting the situational factors that modify children's pain perception.

pain sensations that they will experience; their primary focus of attention (i.e., whether they are distracted away from the pain or focused on what is happening); the relevance or meaning of the situation; and their knowledge of simple pain control strategies. In general, the following will all lessen children's pain: providing accurate, age-appropriate information about pain, particularly the specific sensations that children will experience (e.g., the stinging quality of an injection); increasing control by giving children simple choices (e.g., choosing which arm for an injection, deciding whether to participate actively); explaining the rationale for what is happening and what can be done to reduce pain; and teaching simple pain-reducing strategies (Beales, 1983; Beales, Keen, & Holt, 1983; Kavanagh et al., 1991; P. A. McGrath, 1993; Peterson & Shigetomi, 1981; Ross & Ross, 1982).

Behavioral factors include children's overt physical behaviors (e.g., crying, using a pain control strategy); parents' and health care workers' behavioral responses to them (e.g., displaying frustration, calmly providing encouragement for children to use pain control strategies); the extent to which children are physically restrained during invasive procedures; and the broader behavioral effects of recurrent or persistent pain on children's lives, including their ability to attend school, participate in sports and social activities with peers, and assume typical family and household responsibilities. Some behaviors reduce pain and promote a healthy recovery, whereas distress behaviors or altered behavioral patterns may initiate, exacerbate, or maintain children's pain. In general, as children's physical activity increases, as children use coping and pain control methods, as their distress and disability behaviors decrease, and as staff/parental responses become more consistent in encouraging them to use pain control methods, their pain should lessen (Cataldo, Jacobs, & Rogers, 1982; Melamed, Robbins, & Graves, 1982; P. A. McGrath, 1990, 1994; Varni, Katz, & Dash, 1982).

Children's emotions affect their ability to understand what is happening, their ability to cope, their behavioral responses, and their pain experiences. Children's immediate emotional reactions to pain may vary from a relatively neutral acceptance to annoyance, anxiety, fear, frustration, anger, or sadness. The specific emotions depend on the nature of the pain and on children's beliefs about its immediate and eventual impact on their lives. In general, the more emotionally distressed children are, the stronger or more unpleasant their pain. When children do not understand what is happening, when they lack control, and when they do not know simple pain control strategies, their emotional distress increases and their pain intensifies. Similarly, when children's behaviors are restricted, when they are physically restrained during medical procedures, or when their usual sports and peer activities are disrupted, their emotional distress and pain can intensify. Thus, there are dynamic interactions among cognitive, behavioral, and emotional factors. Although the causal relationship between an injury and a consequent pain sensation seems direct and obvious, the things children know, do, and feel all affect their pain. It is essential to recognize and evaluate the impact of these factors in order to relieve any type of pain that children experience.

ASSESSING CHILDREN'S PAIN

The most effective treatment programs for children begin with a careful and thorough assessment to determine the causative and contributing factors for their pain. A medical examination and pain assessment provide the foundation for an accurate differential diagnosis of children's pain complaints, in relation to both the underlying physical trauma/ condition initiating activity in nociceptive afferents and the relevant factors that modulate nociceptive activity. When all initiating and contributing pain sources are identified, an effective treatment plan can be designed to manage children's medical condition and alleviate their pain adequately. The most appropriate pharmacological and nonpharmacological interventions are selected to address all the responsible factors, as outlined by the treatment algorithm in Figure 13.2 (P. A. McGrath, 1992). A primary pharmacological intervention, consisting of either analgesics or anesthetics, is usually selected to attenuate nociceptive activity. However, cognitive, physical, or behavioral interventions must also be used to mitigate the pain-exacerbating impact of situational factors.

Many pain measures are now available for children (for reviews, see Beyer & Wells, 1989; Matthews, McGrath, & Pigeon, 1993; P. A. McGrath, 1990; P. A. McGrath & Brigham, 1992). The criteria for an accurate pain measure for children are similar to those required for any measuring instrument—validity, reliability, and minimal response bias. A pain measure must be valid, in that it unequivocally measures a specific aspect of pain (e.g., intensity), so that changes in children's pain ratings represent meaningful differences in their pain experiences. The measure must be reliable, in that it provides consistent ratings that do not vary over time (unless the child's pain changes). The measure must be relatively free from response bias, in that children use it appropriately regardless of how they may wish to please adults or how adults may administer it. In addition, pain measures should be practical for assessing different types of pain and versatile for use in diverse clinical settings.

Like those for adults, children's pain measures are classified generally as behavioral, physiological, or self-report, depending on the type of response that is measured—overt distress (e.g., grimaces, cries, protective guarding gestures), physical state (e.g., heart rate, sweat index, blood pressure, cortisol level), or self-report (e.g., words, numerical ratings, drawings). Behavioral and physiological measures must be used for infants and for children who are unable to communicate verbally (for reviews of the pain measures available for infants, see Craig & Grunau, 1993; Porter, 1993.) These measures provide indirect estimates of children's pain, because we can only infer the presence or strength of their pain from the type and magnitude of their distress behaviors or physical states. In

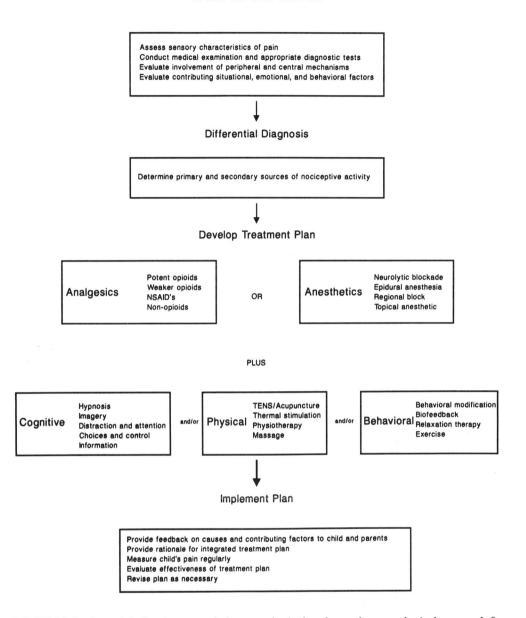

FIGURE 13.2. A model of an integrated pharmacological and nonpharmacological approach for controlling children's pain. NSAID, nonsteroidal anti-inflammatory drug; TENS, transcutaneous electrical nerve stimulation. From McGrath (1992). Copyright 1992 by Paul M. Deutsch Press. Reprinted by permission.

contrast, self-report measures provide direct information about many aspects of children's pain: the sensory characteristics, the aversive components, and the contributing cognitive, behavioral, and emotional factors. At present, self-report measures represent the "gold standard" for assessing children's pain.

Children learn specific words to describe the various aspects of all their perceptions—words to denote different sounds, colors, and tastes. Similarly, they learn a vocabulary to describe their pain so that they can communicate meaningful information about its unique attributes. Children's understanding and descriptions of pain reflect their age, cognitive level, and pain experiences. Children first begin to verbalize the hurting aspect of pain as toddlers. As they mature, they begin to describe their pain according to both its unpleasant hurting aspect and its sensory attributes—the quality (aching, burning, stinging, throbbing, sharp, or dull), intensity (weak to strong), duration (a few seconds to years), location (various body regions), and frequency (constant or episodic). Children's descriptions provide the richest source of pain information for clinicians. Children can express what they feel, describe what they do, record prospectively how often pain occurs on diaries, and use pain intensity scales to rate its severity.

Children's interviews are ideally suited for obtaining concise information about children's pain problems, pain histories, and the factors that influence their pain. When psychologists are treating many children with similar pain problems (e.g., recurrent headaches), they should conduct structured interviews by asking all children a set of standard questions in a similar manner. This format ensures that they will obtain the same information from all children, so that they can gradually learn to identify which children will respond best to which treatments. The essential topics covered in a pain interview are listed in Table 13.1. As in any clinical session, interviewers must listen carefully and pursue children's hesitant or superficial responses by asking children to provide concrete examples of specific situations in which they had pain, in order to elicit the most accurate and thorough information about their pain experience.

TABLE 13.1. Principal Topics Covered in Pain Interviews

Sensory characteristics	*Clinical factors*
History	Environment features
Location	Roles of medical and health staff
Intensity	Nature of interventions
Quality	Documentation of pain
Duration	Criteria for determining analgesic efficacy
Frequency	
Accompanying symptoms	*Behavioral factors*
Seasonal/temporal variations	General coping style
	Learned pain behaviors
Cognitive factors	Overt distress
Understanding of pain source	Parents' behaviors
Understanding of diagnosis,	Physical activities and limitations
treatment, and prognosis	Social activities and limitations
Expectations	
Perceived control	*Emotional factors*
Relevance of disease or	Frustration
pain-inducing stimuli	Anger
Knowledge of pain control	Sadness
	Fear
	Anxiety

Many pain intensity rating scales have been validated for children above 5 years of age. Children choose a level on the scale that best matches the strength of their own pain (i.e., a level on a thermometer varying from 0 to 100, or a position on a visual analogue scale or colored analogue scale). These scales are easy to administer, requiring only a few minutes for children to rate their pain intensity. Visual analogue scales are a simple and versatile method for assessing pain intensity. These are usually 10-cm lines with endpoints marked "No pain" and "Strongest pain possible." Visual analogue scales can also be used to assess many different aspects of pain, such as sadness and perceived control. As a consequence, they are a useful component of many structured interviews, diaries, and questionnaires for children with recurrent or persistent pain. Some clinicians also use separate measures of pain affect, such as a facial affective scale, to evaluate the unpleasantness aspect of children's pain (P. A. McGrath, 1990).

When such recording is possible, children should complete pain diaries (e.g., a calendar on which they record the days on which they experience pain) and pain logs on which they record their pain experiences in a more detailed manner (e.g., onset, duration, child's behaviors, interventions used). Prospective records enable therapists to identify any temporal patterns and pain triggers, as well as to monitor children's pain control strategies to select the most effective interventions. A pain log for a child with recurrent headaches is shown in Figure 13.3.

HEADACHE LOG FOR PAIN PROGRAM

Name: _7-year-old girl_   Session: ___1___

COMPLETE A SEPARATE SHEET FOR EACH HEADACHE THAT YOU HAVE FROM NOW UNTIL YOUR NEXT TREATMENT SESSION.

1. Day _thrusday_   Date _1994 10 13_   When (what time) did it start? _7:30_

2. Did the headache start slowly and get stronger? (Yes) No   Or, did it start suddenly at a strong level? Yes   No

3. What were you doing when you started to get the pain? _going in the tub._

4. How were you feeling emotionally? _tired._

5. At its strongest, how much did it hurt? (Use the red pain scale.) Pain Scale Number _6_

6. At its strongest, how much did it bother you? (Draw a circle around the best words.)

    not at all   a little   between a little and a lot   (a lot)   very much

7. Which face shows me how you felt deep inside when you had this headache? (Use the face scale.) _.75_

8. What methods did you use to stop the headache? When (what times) did you do this? How much did it help? (Note: If you took medicine, please list what you took and how much.)

What I tried	Time	How much did it help?			
read a book	8:30	not at all	(a little)	a lot	it took it away
listen to a tape	8:00	not at all	a little	(a lot)	it took it away
a hotwaterbottle	8:15	not at all	(a little)	a lot	it took it away
		not at all	a little	a lot	it took it away

9. When/what time did the headache end? _9:00_

10. Did the headache end gradually? (Yes) No   Or, did it end suddenly?   Yes   No

11. What did you do then? _I went to sleep._

12. What do you think caused this headache? _I don't know._

13. What was the worst part of this headache for you? _having it._

FIGURE 13.3. A pain log completed by a 7-year-old girl with recurrent headaches.

AN INTEGRATED APPROACH
FOR CONTROLLING CHILDREN'S PAIN

Controlling children's pain requires an integrated approach, because many factors are responsible, no matter how seemingly clear-cut the etiology. Adequate analgesic prescriptions administered at regular dosing intervals must be complemented by a practical cognitive-behavioral approach to ensure optimal pain relief.

Pharmacological Interventions

We have made enormous progress in controlling children's pain pharmacologically since Swafford and Allan's (1968) postoperative survey, in which they stated, "Pediatric patients seldom need medication for relief of pain. They tolerate discomfort well" (p. 133). Regrettably, though, many hospitalized children still suffer pain needlessly. Several articles in the 1970s and 1980s highlighted the special problem of undermedication for children and raised serious questions as to the scope of the problem. Retrospective chart reviews were conducted, in which the prescription and administration of drugs (type of drug, dosage, administration route, and efficacy, as assessed by voiced pain complaints) were compared for adults and children who had similar medical problems and presumably similar pain experiences. Investigators reported major discrepancies between adults and children in the prescription or subsequent administration of analgesics, with children receiving minimal pain control (Anand & Aynsley-Green, 1988; Anand & Hickey, 1987; Beyer, DeGood, Ashley, & Russell, 1983; Eland, 1974; Mather & Mackie, 1983; Schechter, Allen, & Hanson, 1986). Information about analgesic efficacy for children has been complicated by our failure to document children's pain routinely. Hospital chart notations may include general statements such as "voiced pain complaints," "crying and fussing," or "irritable," along with appropriate documentation for prescribed and administered drugs. However, the notations are not ordinarily standardized as to terminology, recording frequency, and criteria for evaluating pain. Wide variation in pain documentation is common within a single ward. Consequently, little prospective information about the extent of pain reduction can be obtained from our current charting systems.

Further difficulties arise because the responsibility for providing pain control is often diffused among various professionals, so that no one individual ensures that a child has received adequate pain relief. Basic guidelines for selecting and administering analgesic interventions are not consistently followed, so that children do not always receive appropriate analgesics in adequate doses and at required dosing intervals. Thus, psychologists who specialize in pain assessment and management should have a working knowledge of the main categories of analgesic and adjuvant drugs administered to children, as well as of the major types of anesthetic techniques available for children. Data about what types of drugs children receive, how much, and how often are essential components of their pain assessment, particularly for children who are hospitalized.

Four simple concepts should be followed when administering analgesics to children: "by the ladder," "by the clock," "by the mouth," and "by the child." "By the ladder" refers to a three-step approach for selecting progressively stronger analgesic drugs (acetaminophen, codeine, or morphine) based on a child's pain level (mild, moderate, or strong). If pain persists despite use of the appropriate drug, recommended dose, and recommended dosing schedule, the child should receive the next most potent analgesic. This ladder approach was initially developed by the World Health Organization (1986, in press). Even when children require opioid analgesics, they should continue to receive acetaminophen (and nonsteroidal anti-inflammatory drugs if appropriate) as supplemental analgesics. (For reviews of analgesic and anesthetic interventions for children, see Cohen, 1993; Houck et al., 1994; Maunuksela, 1993; Miser, 1993; Schechter, 1993; Yaster & Maxwell, 1993; Yaster, Tobin, & Maxwell, 1993.)

"By the clock" refers to the timing for administering analgesic medications. Analgesics should be administered on a regular schedule (e.g., every 4 or 6 hours) based on the drug's duration of action and the child's pain severity, not on an "as-needed" (*pro re nata* or p.r.n.) basis—unless children's pain episodes are truly intermittent and unpredictable. On a p.r.n. basis, children must first experience pain before they can obtain pain relief. These "breakthrough" pain episodes can cause serious problems for children, who fear that their pain cannot be controlled. As a result, they may become progressively frightened and upset, so that their pain increases. Moreover, the doses of opioids required to relieve existing or breakthrough pain are higher than those required to prevent the recurrence of pain. Children should receive analgesics at regular times, by the clock, to provide consistent pain relief and prevent breakthrough pain.

"By the mouth" refers to the route of drug administration. Medications should be administered to children by the simplest effective route, usually by mouth. Since children are afraid of painful injections, they may deny that they have pain or may not request medication. When possible, children should receive medications through routes that do not cause additional pain. Although no detailed surveys have been conducted, anecdotal information suggests that the route and schedule of drug administration are common causes of pain problems for children receiving analgesics. For example, an order for an intramuscular injection of codeine ("codeine i.m.") may be written for nurses to control children's postoperative pain on hospital wards, even though children may have existing intravenous lines through which analgesics could be administered. (Note: Licensing regulations may prohibit members of the nursing staff from administering opioids intravenously, so that medical personnel may be required for basic analgesic administration.) In other situations, children's intravenous lines are withdrawn when they leave the recovery room instead of capped, so that they would be able to receive additional drugs on the floor by a relatively painless route.

Finally, "by the child" refers to the need to base analgesic doses on each individual child's circumstances. No one analgesic dose will necessarily relieve pain for all children with a similar medical condition or similar level of pain. Instead, children vary with respect to how much of a drug (and what type of a drug) is required to control their pain. It is essential to monitor a child's pain regularly and adjust analgesic doses as necessary to control pain.

Cognitive, Physical, and Behavioral Interventions

Nonpharmacological interventions are classified generally according to whether the interventions modify thoughts and coping abilities, the peripheral or central nervous systems, or behaviors. The specific cognitive, physical, and behavioral interventions listed in Figure 13.2 are ranked in an order similar to the analgesic ladder, in which the different methods required to control progressively stronger or more prolonged pains are listed in an ascending order. Although each method is listed within a main category, most methods vary in the particular combination of cognitive, physical, and behavioral modulation involved. For example, hypnosis is considered primarily a cognitive intervention because children learn to reduce pain by their mental focus through intense concentration, even though a hypnotic induction process often includes a behavioral component of progressive muscle relaxation.

Cognitive interventions are the most powerful and versatile nonpharmacological pain therapies for children. When health professionals provide age-appropriate information about a pain source to children or teach them how to use a simple coping strategy, they are administering a basic cognitive intervention. Accurate information about what will happen and what children may feel can improve their understanding, increase their control, lessen their distress, and reduce their pain (Anderson, Zeltzer, & Fanurik, 1993; Carr, Osgood, & Szyfelbein, 1993; Fowler-Kerry & Lander, 1987; Hilgard & LeBaron, 1984; Kavanagh et al., 1991; Kuttner, 1993; Manne & Andersen, 1991; Maron & Bush, 1991; P. A. McGrath & deVeber, 1986; Olness, 1981; Routh & Sanfilippo, 1991; Siegel & Peterson, 1981; Zeltzer & LeBaron, 1982). Additional information about pain gates and the simple strategies children can use to close these gates can further reduce their pain (P. A. McGrath, 1994). The extent of detailed information that a child receives should be based on the child's individual needs, interests, and developmental level (and not the parents'). For example, some children benefit from very detailed information about a painful procedure and should attend carefully to the sensations that they experience; other children should receive general information about what will happen, but should be helped to divert their attention away from what they are feeling during the procedure.

Distraction and attention, as well as guided imagery, are practical tools that health professionals and parents can routinely use when children experience pain. Unfortunately, distraction is often not used appropriately because it has been incorrectly perceived as a simple diversionary tactic, in which a child's attention is passively diverted away from pain. The implication is that the pain is still there, but that the child is momentarily focused elsewhere. However, genuine distraction and attention—when the child's attention is fully absorbed by an activity or topic other than his or her pain—is a very active process that can lessen the neuronal responses evoked by tissue damage. In this case, the child does not simply ignore the pain, but is actually reducing it. Parents and staff members can assist children to concentrate fully on something else besides their pain. Music, lights, colored objects, tactile toys, sweet tastes, and other children are effective "attention-grabbing" stimuli for infants and young children. Conversation, games, computers, and interesting movies are effective distractors for older children and adolescents. Guided imagery is a specific method of distraction and attention, in which health professionals or parents guide children to remember and vividly describe some previous positive experience; a story that they have seen, read, or written; or relaxing pain-free sensations associated with pleasurable activities. The more vividly children imagine their positive experiences, the less pain they experience.

Physical interventions reduce pain by activating peripheral non-nociceptive nerves, which subsequently inhibit the effects of nociceptive nerves, and by activating central pain-inhibiting systems. The physical intervention most familiar to children is simple massage or rubbing of painful areas. Children learn quickly that rubbing painful areas after injuries can relieve pain. Health professionals should adopt physical interventions more routinely in clinical practice. For example, children receiving finger pricks and intramuscular injections report less pain when they rub the site of the injection deeply, immediately before and after the invasive procedure.

Massage, as well as physiotherapy and simple stretching/conditioning exercises, can be an effective adjunct therapy for children with persistent pain or any disease that prevents them from participating in normal activities. Children may gradually lose flexibility as they withdraw from their usual physical activities. Other sources of pain may develop from resulting abnormal sensory input. Simple stretching exercises for 10–20 minutes, prescribed four times a week, can help children maintain their flexibility. The goal of physical therapy is to return all systems, including the pain system, to normal or optimal functioning. The specific physical interventions selected are individualized for each child and based on diagnosis, physical findings, and chronicity of the pain (for a review, see Allen, Jedlinsky, Wilson, & McCarthy, 1993). Children who receive physical interventions participate actively in their own pain management programs, rather than depend solely on medications, professionals, or parents for pain relief.

Behavioral interventions are designed to change either children's own behaviors or the behaviors of the adults who interact with them. The therapeutic objective is to lessen behaviors that can increase children's pain and distress, while increasing behaviors that can reduce pain. Progressive muscle relaxation and simple repetitive physical exercises (depending on children's preference) are convenient methods for most children to use during painful medical treatments. During stressful treatments, many children seem naturally to tense their muscles and hold their breath. Some children can learn to relax by alternately tightening and loosening their fists, by rhythmically moving a leg, or by deep, paced breathing. These simple methods can dramatically lessen their pain. General exercise regimens are an important component of pain management for children experiencing recurrent or persistent pain, as well as for children requiring multiple and repeated painful treatments. The objective is to restore as many of children's normal activities as possible, in order to provide them with enjoyment, increase their participation in social events, increase their independent pain management, and help them to reduce their stress. An exercise program should be based on the sports and activities that are enjoyable and physically possible for children. With such a program, children's mental and social well-being improve; they become more involved in the world and less preoccupied with their health and pain.

Most cognitive and behavioral methods for alleviating children's pain are used in conjunction with one another, rather than independently. The term "cognitive-behavioral" has evolved as the most appropriate description for a comprehensive approach to pain management, in which the objectives are to provide children with accurate information and realistic expectations about their pain; to improve their control by teaching them specific pain-reducing strategies; to modify any behaviors (the children's or the staff's) that intensify pain; and to lessen their emotional distress.

PAIN MANAGEMENT PROGRAMS FOR CHILDREN

As previously noted, pain management begins with a careful and thorough assessment to determine the pain source, to evaluate contributing situational factors, and to select the most appropriate pharmacological and nonpharmacological interventions. Since the inception of our Paediatric Pain Program (an integrated research program and pain clinic for children) at the University of Western Ontario in 1983, we have conducted pain assessments and designed treatment programs from the theoretical perspective depicted in Figure 13.2. Although each child with pain has a unique set of causative and contributing factors, the many pain assessments conducted during these years have revealed some situational factors that are common for children experiencing similar types of pain, as shown in Table 13.2. After brief descriptions of these factors, case studies are presented

TABLE 13.2. Situational Factors That Increase Children's Pain

Factor	Acute treatment-induced pain	Recurrent pain syndrome	Persistent pain
Cognitive			
Inaccurate information regarding			
cause/sensations/treatment effectiveness	S	A	U
Little perceived control	U	U	S
Few independent pain-reducing strategies	U	U	S
Aversive significance	U	S	A
Learned pain triggers	S	A	R
Behavioral			
Overt distress behaviors	U	S	S
Inconsistent parental responses	S	U	S
Prolonged physical distress	R	S	U
Limited physical activity	S	S	U
Limited peer and social activities	S	S	U
Emotional			
Specific anxiety and fear regarding:			
Diagnosis/treatment	S	A	U
Future implications	S	U	U
General anxiety/stress	S	U	S
Inability to identify and resolve stress	R	U	R
Inability to identify and express emotions	R	U	R
High expectations for achievement	R	U	R

Note. A, always present; U, usually present; S, sometimes present, R, rarely present. From McGrath (1993). Copyright 1993 by Williams & Wilkins. Adapted by permission.

to illustrate how to modify these factors to achieve optimal control over acute treatment-induced pain, recurrent pain syndromes, and persistent pain. (Pseudonyms are used in the case studies.)

Acute Treatment-Induced Pain

Situational Factors That Modify Children's Acute Pain

The majority of acute pains children experience are caused by minor injuries during normal activities. These pains provide children with unequivocal warning signals to teach them about potentially harmful activities. There are no prolonged emotional consequences from these "protective" acute pains, and the pains lessen progressively as injuries heal. Children develop effective pain-reducing strategies, such as seeking a parent for a special hug, cleansing and bandaging an injured area, or swallowing medication. They quickly learn that the cause of their pain is physical damage, often easily visible; that their pain is relatively brief; and that many interventions can alleviate their discomfort. Thus, children usually have accurate age-appropriate information about acute pain and positive expectations for pain relief. The aversive significance is determined by the actual pain intensity and by any disruption in children's normal activities, rather than by children's concerns about continued pain and disability. As a result, children perceive acute pain more as the occasionally inevitable result of daily activities than as something to fear.

However, the situational factors associated with acute pain caused by invasive medical treatments are usually quite different (Anderson et al., 1993; P. A. McGrath, 1990). Children often are uncertain about what to expect; they may not understand the need for a treatment that will hurt, particularly if they do not feel sick; they may not be offered any choices or participate in any health care decisions; and they may not know any pain-reducing strategies that they can use during their treatments. Children may be physically restrained or told how to behave during a painful treatment in a manner that makes the procedure easier for the adults administering the treatment, but more difficult for the children. As a result, children often believe that they have no control. Lack of understanding about pain, expectations for continued pain, uncertainty about obtaining eventual pain relief, and lack of control over the pain are common factors that can increase pain for children requiring repeated medical treatments, such as blood sampling, injections, and lumbar punctures.

Children are often visibly distressed during painful treatments. Generally, the more overtly distressed a child is, the greater his or her pain (Fowler-Kerry & Lander, 1987; Jay, Ozolins, Elliott, & Caldwell, 1983; Jay, Elliott, Ozolins, Olson, & Pruitt, 1985; Katz, Kellerman, & Siegel, 1980; Kuttner, Bowman, & Teasdale, 1988; P. A. McGrath & deVeber, 1986; Russo & Varni, 1982). Children with diseases or injuries requiring long-term medical management are at risk for developing progressively more pain-exacerbating behaviors throughout the course of their treatment, including overt distress behaviors during procedures (e.g., crying, tensing muscles) and more subtle changes in their daily activities (e.g., acting more aggressively toward siblings, withdrawing socially). Some distress behaviors during invasive procedures may reflect a child's underlying emotional distress, whereas other behaviors, particularly stalling, may represent a simple conditioned response. If parents or staff members inadvertently reinforce children by delaying treatment or by inconsistently coaching, reassuring, or coercing, then children will exhibit increasing distress to continue to delay aversive procedures.

All children experience some anxiety, fear, and sadness incidental to their pain. Yet children requiring repeated medical treatments are at risk for developing heightened fear and anxiety. Children and their families can experience prolonged emotional distress (Jay et al., 1985; Peterson, Harbeck, Chaney, & Muir Thomas, 1990; P. A. McGrath, 1990; Zeltzer, Jay, & Fisher, 1989). Usually young children are affected more adversely by the immediate effects of the diagnosis, medical tests, treatments, hospitalization, and separation from family members than by the future consequences of the disease. Older children are distressed both by the immediate effects and by the future implications for a normal, healthy childhood and life. Parents may be overwhelmed with fear about the disease or injury, particularly the possibility of more severe complications or death. Parents' emotional distress as they adjust to their children's diagnosis can exacerbate children's own anxiety, and subsequently their pain.

Case Study: Acute Treatment-Related Pain

A 6-year-old boy, John, was referred to the pain clinic because he began to experience severe pain and exhibit extreme behavioral distress during the finger pricks, venous blood sampling, and injections he required to manage his diabetes. John had been diagnosed with juvenile diabetes when he was 2 years old; his pain during treatments had increased gradually since then, and he was exhibiting numerous distress behaviors (stalling, crying, screaming, kicking, etc.). John's pain assessment included structured individual interviews with him and his parents at the clinic, and a home visit to observe how his finger pricks and injections were conducted.

Although much attention has been focused on pain problems for children who require repeated medical treatments, the emphasis has been primarily on children receiving treatments in hospitals. The unique problems parents experience when administering painful treatments to their children have not been documented fully. Thus, whenever possible, our pain therapists conduct home visits analogous to their observations of children receiving invasive treatments in the hospital. These visits are an integral component of pain assessments, because they enable therapists to directly observe children and their families and to assess the situational factors that contribute to the children's pain problems. Table 13.3 lists the relevant information that should be obtained. When a home visit is not possible, this information must be obtained indirectly through a clinical interview. A therapist must emphasize that he or she needs to know exactly what happens at home, with the same richness and detail as if he or she were actually present. Since what parents and children believe happens during treatment is not always what actually happens, therapists must interview parents and children in a thorough manner. Subtle but relevant information may be overlooked unless a therapist carefully obtains information about all the situational factors that can affect pain.

The information obtained in the clinical interview about John's distress contrasted sharply with John's actual behaviors during the home visit. Although a therapist's arrival usually (but not always) adds a more positive significance to a treatment, the therapist had a special significance in John's case. Not only did she make it a more special occasion, but her arrival gave a definite signal about the onset of treatment. After he greeted the therapist, John knew that his treatment would begin soon. Usually John's mother

TABLE 13.3. Information about Relevant Situational Factors during Parental Administration of Treatments

- Are procedures conducted at regular times and in a consistent manner?
- Where is the child before treatment, and what is he or she doing (fully absorbed in a positive activity, or anxiously waiting)?
- Do parents interact with the child in a manner that lessens his or her anxiety?
- Who calls the child for treatment (parent or clock)?
- How does the child respond (stall, refuse, comply) to treatment? Subsequently, how does the parent respond (reward, frustration, coercion, reason) to child?
- Is the location of the treatment (chaotic, distraction-filled, quiet) conducive to the child's using some independent pain control strategies?
- Which parent performs the treatment? Is he or she prepared, or does the child wait while the parent prepares materials?
- What are the roles of the other parent/siblings?
- To what extent is the child actively involved in the preparation of treatment materials or equipment, and in the administration of treatment?
- Is the child restrained? If so, how?
- What do the parent and child do and say during treatment?
- Do parents inadvertently reward distress behaviors?
- Does the child have choices or receive any additional information during the procedures?
- When other people are present, how do they affect the child's distress?
- When there is a time lag between invasive treatments (e.g., between a finger prick and an insulin injection), what do the child and parent do during this period?
- How long does the procedure take?
- How does the child react following the treatment (calms quickly, continues to be distressed)?
- Is this a typical treatment? If not, how is it different?
- In general, what are the child's and parents' perception of how well the observed procedure went?
- Which aspects of the observed procedure were the easiest and most difficult?
- How much did it hurt?

prepared all the equipment in the kitchen at some point near dinnertime and then called him for his finger prick, but the time of the procedure varied substantially. When John's mother called him during the therapist's visit, he (atypically) responded immediately and did not resist or cry. As the mother always did, she chose the finger for his prick, operated the glucose monitor, and evaluated the results. John returned to the playroom while she waited for his glucose reading. Approximately 3 minutes later, John was called back to the kitchen for his "boo-boo," the term used for his injection; again, he responded immediately. The mother prepared the syringe, and she selected and prepared the site for injection. John stayed calm throughout the injection and then returned to the playroom.

Although John's calm behavior at home was atypical, the therapist observed treatment aspects that could have adversely affected John. The procedures were not consistently timed, either according to the clock or according to John's activities. Thus, he had no regular preparation time for himself before treatment and was generally anxious throughout a 2-hour period near dinnertime. The dramatic change in his demeanor and distress during the home visit suggested that he would benefit greatly from more predictability and more active participation. At the end of the visit, his parents also indicated that the two of them usually conducted the procedures differently: His mother preferred that John wait with her between the finger prick and injection, while his father allowed him to return to his playroom. The home visit, combined with the clinic interview, revealed that several situational factors were responsible for John's pain and distress. He misunderstood the rationale for his treatments, their procedural aspects, and the equipment; he had inadequate control during treatments; and he lacked effective pain control methods. His stalling and distress during procedures reflected inconsistent parental responses and his family's increasing frustration. Thus, the therapist recommended a simple pain management program consisting of four ~45-minute weekly sessions.

The focus of John's first session was educational. First, although he had a good understanding about diabetes and why he required insulin injections, John did not understand the need for daily injections. He believed that injections were just one available treatment option, and that if he had "a new pancreas," he would not need insulin injections. Since John naturally preferred this "painless" option, the therapist focused on helping him understand that the only treatment available was insulin injections, because a pancreas transplant was only a possible future treatment option. Second, since John seemed frightened by the equipment used, he actively participated in practice sessions where he conducted injections on puppets. He also reviewed a photo album detailing treatment equipment, with pictures of children of various ages receiving finger pricks and injections. Some photographs were of children prior to their pain management programs, when they were very distressed; others showed the same children after their programs, when they used pain control methods and were not visibly distressed. Initially, John demonstrated his anxiety by trying to change the subject and distract his therapist. His therapist persisted and taught John about his pain gating system. She also told him about methods to "close his gate," including selecting a finger for his finger prick; assisting his mother by opening the alcohol swab packet; rubbing the injection site before and after the injection; and distracting himself by counting, singing, talking to his brother, and/or squeezing his brother's hand. To encourage him to use these strategies, a behavioral program was designed in which he earned a sticker for each treatment during which he assisted his mother with the preparations and used a strategy from his list. (Note: Many behavioral programs are not effective because the emphasis is solely on minimizing the child's distress behavior, rather than on increasing his or her active pain control. For example, children earn a sticker when they do not show distress, rather than when they try to reduce their pain.)

At his second session, John had already earned a sticker for most of the injections he had received. His stalling, resisting and screaming had lessened considerably. However, his parents were frustrated because John would often cooperate and remain calm during one treatment, but then would be distressed during the next treatment. They did not know what to do, and required assistance to develop some consistent methods of responding to him—regardless of how inconsistently he behaved or who conducted the procedures. For example, there was a delay of 3 minutes after John's finger prick until his glucose levels were ready. John's mother often forced him to remain with her throughout this time, even though he argued with her about returning to the playroom. In contrast, John's father allowed him to return to the playroom, but he had great difficulty getting John to return for his injection. After a discussion of alternative approaches, both parents were asked to encourage John to participate actively during the interim period. The emphasis was shifted from his parents' forcing treatments onto John (as a passive recipient) to John's and his parents' working as an active team to treat his diabetes. He helped his parents to read the glucose monitor results, to determine how much insulin was required, and to prepare the syringe. Even when he felt anxious, attempted to leave the room, or tried to distract his parents, they were asked to continue the preparations while engaging John in conversation about upcoming events (e.g., what was for dinner, what was on TV). In addition, they agreed to stop calling John's injections "boo-boos" and to begin using the phrase "getting insulin." After injections, he helped to store the equipment and discard the swabs.

John also began to select the sites for his injections. The selection of injection sites is a common problem for children with diabetes who are referred to our clinic. Children often develop favorite sites while excluding others (particularly the abdomen site). Yet children eventually must use all sites. The therapist can develop some simple methods for site selection to improve children's control and increase their choices without increasing their anxiety. For example, the therapist can mark all the required sites for injections on a body outline. The outline is photocopied and cut so that there is a sufficient number of each injection site to provide a week's treatment sites. Prior to each injection, children can then pull a cutout from an envelope and use the site chosen. In this manner, children are not excessively worried because they eventually have to choose a particular aversive site; instead, the site is randomly selected. After a short time of randomly selecting cutouts, children usually begin to rotate their injection sites independently. Another effective approach is to have children select stickers (representing the different sites) and place them on calendars or in a diabetes diary ahead of the scheduled treatments, so that on the day of treatment, site selection is regulated by the calendar. In this way, site selection does not lead to major confrontations between parents and children. John chose a sticker for his treatment calendar each day, to ensure that he was alternating sites appropriately.

By John's fourth session, he had earned a sticker for all of his injections. He used simple attention and distraction strategies from his pain control list. He no longer screamed, cried, or refused his injections. He actively participated in all procedures. As a result, his parents were no longer frustrated or anxious; they felt confident that they could be consistent even if he had a difficult day.

Recurrent Pain Syndromes

Situational Factors That Modify Children's Recurrent Pains

When children are diagnosed with a recurrent pain syndrome, it is usually the first time that they and their families have encountered pains that are not symptoms of an injury or condition that requires medical treatment. Instead, the frequent headaches, abdominal pains, or limb pains experienced by these otherwise healthy and pain-free children actually constitute the disorder, and the multiple factors responsible for triggering their pains must be identified and controlled (Apley, MacKeith, & Meadow, 1978; Barr, 1981, 1983; Chutorian, 1978; Fenichel, 1981; P. A. McGrath, 1987, 1990; Rappaport & Leichtner, 1993; Rothner, 1993; Schechter, 1984; Shinnar & D'Souza, 1981). As a consequence, there is usually much uncertainty about the syndrome, because almost all other pains that the children have experienced have been linked directly to tissue damage. When parents often seek medical attention, they receive explicit reassurances that the pains are not related to a particular disease or disorder, and may receive implicit messages that no further treatments are required. Yet the pains continue, and they do not know what to do for their children. The parents may thus remain apprehensive about the cause and seek additional diagnostic tests.

Parents and children usually do not receive a rationale for how recurrent pains can be triggered by a variety of external and internal factors, particularly events that provoke stress. Parents usually have considered whether any environmental stimuli that may have been associated with at least one painful episode can cause their children's pains. They tentatively identify certain foods, certain weather conditions, and some of their children's normal activities as probable causes. Children can then become so anxious that these neutral events might cause pain that their increasing anxiety eventually evokes a painful episode as a conditioned response to that event (Andrasik, Blake, & McCarran, 1986; Joffe, Bakal, & Kaganov, 1983; P. A. McGrath, 1990). The longer children endure the apparently unpredictable pain episodes and the more their parents search for environmental causes, the greater the risk becomes that children will develop "learned" or "conditioned" pain triggers.

The uncertainty of a recurrent pain syndrome is exacerbated because parents and children do not usually receive a firm diagnosis, recommendations for identifying potential triggers, suggestions for controlling pain episodes, and a clear prognosis. As a result, when painful episodes persist, parents' and children's anxiety increases while their expectations for a clear-cut etiology and a favorable outcome decrease (P. A. McGrath, 1990). Thus, children who experience recurrent pains usually have extremely low expectations that any treatment will alleviate their pain and suffering. They lack practical, independent strategies for reducing the painfulness of individual episodes and for coping with the syndrome. Children may adopt an increasingly passive role—depending primarily on parents, rest, or medication, rather than learning how to actively modify the circumstances that evoke pains. The unpredictability of pains, the uncertainty of eventual pain relief, a progressive tendency to assume a passive patient role, and an increasing number of conditioned pain triggers create ideal circumstances for initiating new pain episodes and exacerbating pain intensity (P. A. McGrath, 1990).

What parents say and do in response to their children's recurring pain experiences have a profound impact both on the children's ability to cope during painful episodes and on their ability to alleviate pain triggers. Parents may respond inconsistently to children's pain complaints, providing excessive emotional and physical support during some pain episodes, but suggesting that the children manage independently during other episodes. As a result, the children may gradually exaggerate their complaints or develop new symptoms to obtain their parents' attention. Parents may also increase children's pains inadvertently when they allow the children to stay at home instead of attending school, encourage them to withdraw from potentially stressful sports or social situations, and relieve them from routine responsibilities. These secondary gains may prolong pain episodes or contribute to the development of new episodes when children are stressed. In addition, some children may tense specific muscle groups for extended periods, alter their usual sitting or standing posture, or progressively restrict their physical activities because they are concerned that their normal physical movements or sports could trigger additional pain. Yet the abnormal sensory input from these altered behaviors may actually increase their pain.

Children with recurrent pain syndromes are usually extremely anxious about the true etiology for their pain, the effectiveness of different drugs for alleviating painful episodes, and the future implications for living normally without unpredictable episodes of debilitating pain. Many children with recurrent headaches develop painful episodes in response to stressful situations (academic, athletic, or social)—stress that they fail to recognize and are unable to resolve effectively (Apley, 1975). Their pains remove them temporarily from the source of stress and may even lead to some positive benefits through increased parental attention and decreased expectations for achievement. As a result, their bodies' pain responses to stress are gradually reinforced, so that they become involuntary protective reactions that may recur in potentially stressful or aversive situations. As shown in Table 13.2, the inability either to identify or to express emotions is rarely present as a pain-exacerbating factor for children with acute treatment-induced pain or for children with persistent pain, but is usually present for children with recurrent pain syndromes. These children are generally unable to identify typical stress-inducing situations and unable to recognize their bodies' reactions to stress. As an example, children with recurrent headaches do not differ in actual stress levels from children without headaches (Andrasik et al., 1988), but they seem to respond differently to typical everyday stressors (Andrasik et al., 1986). Many children with recurrent pains have not learned effective and practical responses that truly alleviate the source of anxiety. Instead, their anxiety is suppressed and eventually released in real pain episodes. As children learn to recognize and express their feelings, the frequency and intensity of their recurrent pain episodes decrease (P. A. McGrath, 1987, 1990).

Treatment Programs for Recurrent Pain Syndromes

Each year approximately 200 children and adolescents with recurrent pain syndromes are referred to our Paediatric Pain Program. A multistrategy treatment program, combining cognitive, behavioral, and physical interventions, was designed for these children in 1987 and has been refined recently after rigorous evaluation. The program is kept flexible in order to allow different treatment emphases (e.g., behavioral or cognitive) and to provide different strategies (e.g., concrete or abstract), according to the primary factors responsible for each child's pains and the unique needs of each child and family.

The program begins with a pain assessment consisting of independent structured interviews with children and their parents and completion of the Children's Comprehensive Pain Questionnaire (CCPQ). The CCPQ provides quantitative and qualitative information about the sensory characteristics of children's pain and about contributing situational, familial, and social factors that may contribute to recurrent or persistent pains.

At the assessment, children receive a pain diary and pain logs, and are asked to monitor their pains for 1 month. This time period enables the pain therapist to obtain an accurate record of the frequency, intensity, length, and time of onset for painful episodes, as well as of children's and their families' behaviors during these episodes. Approximately a month after the pain assessment, parents and children attend a feedback appointment in which the therapist provides general information about the recurrent pain syndrome in question, specific feedback about the causative and contributing factors he or she has identified for children (from the assessment measures and from reviewing the completed pain diaries), and practical recommendations for treatment. (Note: All pain assessment measures are available from us.)

During the feedback appointment, parents are first asked whether any of the common contributing factors (shown in Table 13.2) are relevant for their children, in order to initiate discussion about the specific results of the assessment. The therapist then describes the primary causative and secondary contributing factors he or she has identified as relevant. The upper section of Figure 13.4 provides an example of this; it lists all the cognitive, behavioral, and emotional factors playing a part in the recurrent headaches of a 10-year-old girl named Kate (whose case is discussed in more detail later). After reviewing these factors thoroughly, the therapist presents specific treatment objectives that should address each of these factors, and outlines the multistrategy treatment program to the parents and children. (The lower section of Figure 13.4 lists the treatment recommendations made for Kate.) After the recommendations are reviewed, the parents receive a copy of the feedback summary. A feedback session is generally all that is required to treat children with a mild problem, as defined by pain frequency (approximately one pain episode per month), by syndrome duration (approximately 6 months or less), and by accompanying disability (slight). Individual treatment programs, varying from two to six sessions, are required to treat children with moderate or severe problems. (Note: The therapist does not always attempt to identify the factors that initiated the syndrome, because pain onset is not usually clearly linked to a single traumatic event. It is more therapeutic to focus on the current maintaining factors, so that the therapist can address these factors in the subsequent treatment program. Even when pain onset is clearly related to a specific incident [e.g., the death of a family member, a parental separation or divorce, the birth of a new baby, or the start of school], so that the initial cause is known, the focus of the program continues to be on the current factors responsible for maintaining pain.)

During the first treatment session, the therapist helps children to develop their own treatment goals in a "Pain Control Program" or "Get Well Plan" (for younger children), allowing children to think about possible causes and how to address these causes, not just cope with the painful episodes. The template shown in Figure 13.5 is used with all children. With guidance from the therapist, children select the overall goal of their treatment program and then the smaller goals that, once achieved, will lead to the completion of their overall goal. Children who participate in planning their treatment programs seem to understand the rationale for their treatment better and to become more motivated to work toward their goals than children who are passive recipients of a program planned without their involvement.

The therapist then begins to implement the specific treatment objectives, spending part of each session separately with children and parents. The therapist teaches children independent and practical strategies to reduce pain and to alleviate stress. The focus of parent involvement varies according to children's specific programs, but may include guidance in behavioral management or counseling. For example, parents may learn that

Factors Involved in Kate's Pain: Summary Sheet

Cognitive Factors	Behavioral Factors	Emotional Factors
• Inaccurate understanding of headache syndrome	• Strong secondary gains from temporary stress reduction	• Anxiety related to unrealistic expectations for her academic performance
• Poor independent control	• Withdrawal from social and physical activities	• Anxiety related to unrealistic expectations for her and her friends' behaviors
• Expectations for continuing pain and disability	• Passive approach to pain control	• Parental anxiety regarding the cause of her headaches
• Aversive relevance	• Multiple learned triggers	• High frustration levels
• Few pain control strategies	• Positive family history of headaches	• Anxiety related to her peer relationships
• Failure to identify and resolve stress	• Inappropriate use of analgesics	• Increasing stress because of her failure to resolve stressful issues effectively

HEADACHES ⟶
- Age
- Gender
- Cognitive Level
- Previous Pains
- Family Learning
- Culture

PAIN SENSATION

Treatment Recommendations:

1. Assist Kate in identifying and resolving stressful situations.

2. Teach Kate to cope more effectively with routine frustrations.

3. Teach Mrs. K and Kate about pain systems, recurrent pain syndromes, and true vs. learned headache triggers.

4. Reduce secondary gains associated with Kate's pain by providing consistent and nonmaladaptive responses to her pain complaints.

5. Teach Kate nonpharmacological methods of pain control, such as muscle relaxation through biofeedback and nonstressful exercise.

FIGURE 13.4. The pain summary sheet for a 10-year-old girl with recurrent headaches. The therapist used this summary to discuss the causative and contributing factors with parents and to provide the rationale for the treatment recommendations.

they may have inadvertently placed excessive demands on their children for high performance, for intensive emotional support, or for excessively good behavior. If so, then the therapist assists parents in establishing more reasonable expectations for children's achievements. If family members do not generally express their emotions openly, they are counseled about the potential adverse consequences of this behavior for their children, and helped to recognize that their children need acceptable emotional outlets. Physical activities and exercise regimens may be modified for children who have reduced

Pain Control Program for Lindsay

Main Goal: To have fewer headaches and have them hurt less.

Goal 1:   To learn how pain works.
  • *We have pain "gates."*
  • *What I think, feel, and do can increase or decrease pain.*

Goal 2:   To learn ways to make pain hurt less.
  • *Change what I think, feel, and do.*
  • *Use my pain control list.*

Goal 3:   Figure out what causes my headaches.
  • *What is the problem?*
  • *How can I stop this from happening again?*

Goal 4:   To solve the problems that could give me headaches.
  • *Use my problem-solving skills.*
  • *Talk to Mom and Dad about my feelings.*

FIGURE 13.5. The template for a pain control program for a 10-year-old girl. The italicized text represents the therapist's achievement of these goals in her sessions with this child.

their exercise levels to avoid pain, or for children who are so physically active that sports and exercise have become a source of stress.

Children complete pain logs between appointments, to enable the therapist to monitor whether they are using any of the pain control strategies that they have learned during treatment sessions. Using the logs, the therapist teaches children how to identify possible triggers. Some parents complete an event diary in which they monitor their children's daily activities, emotional states, pain episode onset and duration, and use of pain interventions. This information enables the therapist to help parents and children to understand the relationships among stressful events, emotions, and pain onset, and to guide them to use analgesic interventions (both pharmacological and nonpharmacological) more effectively. The diary enables parents to record their actual responses to their children's pain complaints; parents may believe that they respond in a certain manner, but may not recognize how they truly respond when their children complain about pain.

Since children with recurrent pain syndromes are often unable to resolve problems to the extent necessary to completely alleviate the stress associated with those problems, the therapist teaches children how to modify stressful situations and their reactions so as to minimize painful episodes. A problem-solving worksheet is used to discuss problem ownership and solutions, using incidents from the children's lives. The focus is on gradually changing the emphasis from the therapist's assisting children to parents' and children's applying the principles of pain control, problem resolution, and emotional expression that they have learned to new situations that will naturally arise within the family, peer and social groups, scholastics, and sports.

Case Studies: Recurrent Headaches

Treatment programs for children with mild, moderate, and severe pain problems are described in the following case studies. These represent the most common pain problems referred to our outpatient clinic—recurrent migraine and tension headaches. The causative and contributing factors for each child's pain problem, and the strategies designed to address them, are detailed.

Mild Problem. A 6-year-old girl, Jean, had experienced monthly headaches for 2 years. Her parents decided to seek additional treatment to alleviate her headaches when it appeared that they had become a long-term problem. Her headaches had begun abruptly after her family moved from a small community to a large city. However, her parents did not consider that the move was stressful for her, even though she had been separated from her extended family. Her headaches usually developed in the late afternoon and lasted approximately 5 hours. Her pain was localized in her forehead and frontal regions, with some pain spreading behind her left eye. The pain intensity was variable, described as ranging from "quite low" to "very bad"; numerical ratings ranged from 4 to 6.5 on the 0–10 Coloured Analogue Scale (P. A. McGrath et al., in press). She described the quality of her pain as aching, pounding, and hot. Jean experienced nausea and vomiting during some headaches. She lay down, rested with cold compresses, and received hugs from her mother to obtain pain relief for mild headaches, but took acetaminophen to relieve strong headaches. She was quite distressed during headaches because she felt sick, anxious, and frightened.

Jean was an intense, serious, and quiet child, who was the eldest of three children. She was in Grade 1 in a regular program. She had a neutral attitude toward school and performed at an average level. At the beginning of the school year, her teacher had been concerned about Jean's lack of concentration and her inability to complete tasks. Jean had several hobbies and activities, but was described as a follower rather than a leader.

The results of the assessment revealed that Jean had a mild pain problem consistent with recurrent pain syndrome. The primary factors responsible for her headaches were unresolved stress, initially associated with the family's move to the new city and now related to school and peer pressures, and anxiety related to her concerns about new experiences. The secondary factors were anxiety reduction resulting from the special attention and reassurance she received during headaches, and her family's consistent focus on multiple environmental triggers.

At the feedback session, the therapist provided basic information about recurrent pain syndromes and headache triggers. She used the model shown in Figure 13.1 to explain how situation-specific stress and behavioral factors were maintaining Jean's headaches, so that a practical approach of stress management, combined with teaching Jean simple problem-solving techniques and consistently managing her behaviors during headaches, should lessen her pain and distress and reduce headache onset. The therapist then discussed how Jean's mother could help her to identify and resolve stress—both current stressors at school and in social situations, and future stressors related to new experiences. The therapist helped Jean's mother to understand the difference between conditioned environmental triggers and true headache triggers. Jean's mother was very insightful and indicated that she could work with Jean to help her identify and resolve stressors and manage her headaches with active, stress-reducing strategies (e.g., coloring, playing outside, inviting a friend to visit). When Jean complained about pain, her mother would reward her for using these strategies to relieve her pain, instead of inadvertently rewarding her for adopting a dependent, sick role orientation. In addition, the therapist provided Jean's mother with suggestions for how to assist Jean in coping with new situations, which included planning activities in advance, role playing so that she could learn more social skills, and praising her increasing independence from her parents. The therapist determined that the feedback session with specific recommendations was the only treatment Jean required. Jean's headaches stopped, and she had not experienced any other headaches at follow-up 3 months later.

When Is a Headache Really Just a Pain Complaint? The majority of children with recurrent headache syndrome suffer discrete episodes of moderate to strong pain. However, a few children can complain of pain when they do not have a headache. They may report pain when they experience normal somatic sensations, because they are overly concerned about their health. Some children's pain complaints gradually increase because they have received special attention and support during painful episodes; because previous pains enabled them to withdraw from stressful or unpleasant situations; or because there are reduced expectations for their performance in school, sports, or social activities when they have pain. These secondary gains, as well as strong behavioral or emotional factors, can occasionally maintain a child's pain complaints in the absence of actual pain experiences.

For example, Anne, an 11-year-old girl, was referred to the pain clinic for assessment and management of persistent headaches. Her pain history was quite unusual. Her first headache had occurred when she hit her head in a bicycle accident 1 year earlier. At that time, she was admitted to a hospital for observation. Although all medical tests and examinations were normal, her headache lasted 1 week, and she suffered from nausea and vomiting throughout this period. Anne subsequently began experiencing intermittent, moderately strong headaches that lasted only about 5 minutes.

The assessment revealed that Anne's initial head injury and her subsequent hospitalization had been extremely stressful. At that time, she was quite frightened that she would be punished because she did not have permission to go bike riding and she did not wear a helmet. Since then, her headaches often developed after minor head injuries (e.g., mild bumps sustained during play activities). As a result of her anxiety about her head injury, whenever she subsequently bumped her head, she was excessively concerned about it and labeled it as a major pain problem. The pain therapist taught Anne the difference between true headaches and her head pains—specifically, how her pains were related to mild traumas that were the normal and relatively benign injuries of childhood.

Moreover, the severe anxiety associated with Anne's injury, and the nausea and vomiting accompanying her first headache, were intensified when her medical examinations revealed no abnormalities. Anne and her parents feared that an as-yet-undiagnosed medical problem was the cause. Any subsequent pains in her head—even those attributable to normal bumps—were causes for the family's concern. Thus, her headaches reflected her anxious attention to normal somatic sensations. The therapist taught Anne and her family that she could learn to manage these pains independently by distracting herself in other activities. Anne did not require an individualized treatment program and was discharged from our service after she and her mother received feedback about the assessment results and our recommendations. She had not experienced any additional headaches at follow-up 5 months later.

Moderate Problems. Ian, a 10-year-old boy, had experienced recurrent headaches for 5 years. His first headache had occurred suddenly while his parents were away competing in a volleyball tournament. Ian was playing with other children when he suddenly complained of a headache and vomited. Since then, he had experienced only occasional headaches until the past year, when they increased to approximately two per month. His pain lasted 5 hours and was localized to his forehead region. He described the pain as moderate, with a numerical rating of 5.6 (Coloured Analogue Scale). The quality of the pain was atypical—hot and burning, as well as dull and pounding. Ian always told his parents when he had a headache. He ignored his headaches for as long as possible so that he could continue his regular activities, but was very frustrated because he sometimes had to stop his activities. Ian then used acetaminophen, applied a cold cloth, and tried to sleep. Both Ian and his mother endorsed many environmental (e.g., noise, weather, nitrates) and internal (e.g., hunger, overexertion) triggers for his headaches. In addition, his mother indicated that excitement, anger, and worry caused his headaches. Ian believed that most of his headaches occurred on summer evenings, usually on busy days. Although they often coincided with sports and parties, he attributed these headaches to heat and fatigue.

Ian lived at home with his parents and an older sister, aged 13. There were many conflicts between him and his sister; they often resorted to physical fighting during disagreements. Ian was in Grade 4 and was an average student. However, he was so popular and easygoing that his teachers paired him with more challenging pupils. Ian had expressed frustration about this situation to his mother. He also had occasional conflicts with his friends, particularly during sports. More recently, he was having trouble unwinding at night and difficulty going to sleep.

The results of Ian's assessment revealed that he had a moderate pain problem consistent with a recurrent pain syndrome. Several cognitive, behavioral, and emotional factors were identified as triggering and maintaining his headaches. Situation-specific stress related to performance issues, compounded by his focus on external pain triggers and by his anxiety and frustration during headaches, maintained his headaches. The primary factors responsible for Ian's headaches were his inability to identify and appropriately express emotions; his failure to resolve situation-specific stress related to his athletic performance and to typical preadolescent concerns (conflicts with his sister, teachers, and peers); and his lack of understanding about the relationship between his emotional reactions and his headaches. The secondary factors were his overreliance on medication for pain management; his primary focus on environmental triggers, which precluded him from identifying and resolving stressors; his frustration and anxiety during headache episodes; and his absence of stress-reducing activities prior to bedtime.

In a 2-hour feedback session, the therapist provided Ian's parents with detailed assessment results and specific recommendations for pain management. She defined "recurrent pain syndrome" and "headache triggers"; she also emphasized the need to continually identify and resolve stressors, and to include Ian in problem solving, in order for him eventually to become more independent in resolving issues. His parents needed to assist him in expressing and discussing his feelings. Using the pain model, the therapist then discussed the factors relevant to Ian, introducing specific treatment recommendations to address each factor. In an individual session with Ian, the therapist explained that Ian needed to do the following:

- To identify and resolve stressors specifically related to his performance, by developing more independent problem-solving abilities and by discussing his feelings.
- To increase his independent control over his pain and reduce his frustration during pain episodes by developing a repertoire of simple, nonpharmacological pain

control strategies (e.g., a combination of relaxation time and participation in socially, physically, and mentally distracting activities).

- To use analgesic medication more effectively by learning to use clear and consistent criteria for taking analgesics (i.e., at a particular pain intensity and a particular point during a headache).
- To reduce general stress naturally by expanding his noncompetitive physical activities (e.g., bike riding, roller skating, in-line skating).

The therapist focused on teaching Ian how to identify problems by the presence of strong uncomfortable emotional reactions, to consider problem ownership (i.e., "Whose problem is this, really?"), to brainstorm various solutions, and to think about their outcomes. Ian's real-life problems (e.g., athletic performance anxiety, concern regarding his ill grandmother) were used to introduce these basic problem-solving strategies. The therapist decided that the information received in the feedback session should be sufficient to enable Ian and his parents to begin to reduce the causative factors and to begin to manage his headaches more independently and effectively. Thus, he did not begin a treatment program. At a 3-month follow-up, Ian's pain diaries revealed that his headaches had decreased in frequency by 66%, to only one headache every 6 weeks. They also decreased in intensity by ~30% (from 5.6 to 4) and in length (from 5 to 2 hours). He used active pain reducing activities and no longer relied solely on medication.

In contrast to Ian, many children with moderate problems require individualized treatment programs. The therapist should consider several criteria in deciding whether a child requires only feedback or a more intensive pain management program. Parents and children who readily understand the relationship between stress and somatic complaints, who have independently demonstrated an ability to identify true pain triggers, and who have made appropriate attempts to resolve these triggers will benefit most from a feedback session that supports and extends their efforts by providing additional recommendations to assist them. Children who are minimally disabled by their headaches, and who already have some understanding that active strategies (e.g., distraction, physical activity) provide effective pain control, will benefit from information that explains why these strategies are effective and from the therapist's encouragement to continue to intervene actively. Often children and parents will benefit from written material addressing specific issues, such as preparing for the birth of a sibling or changing schools, learning how to cope with stress, communicating more effectively with parents and peers, and adjusting to adolescence. Many magazines, books, and pamphlets on such topics are readily available in local bookstores and health-oriented publishers. Our pain clinic is continually adding to our library of resources regarding parenting, child development, and typical life issues. These resources are available for parents and children to read in the waiting room, and for them to sign out for use at home. Although much new and sometimes overwhelming information is provided at the feedback session, this information begins a learning process that some parents and children can continue independently and effectively.

However, other children require more intensive assistance. These include children who are very disabled by their pain, who adopt primarily passive approaches to pain control, or who have typically had minimal success at achieving pain control independently. Unlike Ian, Kate, a 10-year-old girl, required more intensive pain management. She had experienced approximately one headache every 3 months since she was 7 years old. About 6 months prior to her pain assessment, the frequency had gradually increased to a headache every other day. Her mother was unable to identify any specific triggers for the increased frequency. Her pain was atypical, in that it was localized to the top of her head. The quality was pounding, described "like a hammer on my head." Her headaches were quite variable in duration, lasting from 3 to 8 hours. Pain intensity ratings varied widely, from 5 to 9 (Coloured Analogue Scale). Kate experienced stomachaches and some dizziness coincident with her headaches. She had tried ergotamine or acetaminophen for pain relief, but neither medication was effective. She usually attempted to attend school when she had a headache, but she withdrew from social and physical activities. Kate believed that a variety of weather conditions, anxiety regarding schoolwork, and certain physical activities triggered her headaches. Her parents had sought the opinion of several physicians and specialists, because they were worried that the headaches were caused by an undiagnosed disorder.

Kate was the younger of two children. She and her older brother (aged 12) had a typical sibling relationship. Kate was in Grade 5 in a regular school program. She had a very positive attitude toward school and achieved at an above-average level. Although her family had recently moved to a new area, Kate had not changed schools. However, she was having some difficulty interacting with the children in her new neighborhood. She believed that these children played unfairly, and she could not tolerate their injustice. Her mother described her as a happy, likeable child who was sensitive about what others thought about her, as well as sensitive to others' feelings. However, she described Kate as a perfectionist in all that she did; Kate had high expectations for her own and for other people's behavior. Kate also required a predictable schedule and was easily frustrated when her routine was disrupted. Kate had recently developed stomachaches and was having trouble sleeping.

The results of the assessment showed that Kate had a moderate problem consistent with a recurrent pain syndrome, and that she required a pain management program. Kate's accompanying stomachaches and difficulty sleeping at night indicated that stress was a significant factor contributing to her headaches. Her lack of insight into the relationship between stress and somatic complaints resulted in her focusing on external stimuli as pain triggers, increasing the likelihood that she had already developed some learned headache triggers. The primary factors responsible for her headaches were stress related to excessively high expectations for her academic performance, for her behavior, and for the behavior of others; an inability to resolve the frustration resulting from her irritation and the perceived unfairness of others' actions; and a failure to identify and truly resolve stressful situations. The secondary factors were the temporary stress reduction she received from her headaches, because of the reduced expectations for her to participate in stressful and anxiety-producing activities (particularly social and physical activities); recent parental anxiety about her headaches, which increased her own anxiety and distress during painful episodes; her inability to obtain consistent pain control; and a family history of headaches, which provided an environment wherein Kate's pain complaints, in part, represented a modeled response to stress. (The factors identified for Kate are summarized in Figure 13.4, above.)

At the feedback appointment, Kate's mother expressed much frustration with her own inability to reduce Kate's pain, and indicated that she needed to continue seeking opinions and/or treatment from other specialists to ensure that all potential medical conditions had been excluded. The therapist emphasized that Kate had a recurrent pain syndrome. She explained that pharmacological interventions relieved the pain of individual headaches, but that a broad, multistrategy approach was required to address all the causative factors and thereby to alleviate the syndrome. Even though the focus of Kate's pain control program was similar to that of Ian's feedback session, Kate's mother required more active assistance from the therapist. Kate's frequent headaches had been reinforced inadvertently by parents, teachers, and coaches, so that she received extensive behavioral and emotional "pain rewards." She had regular breaks (almost every other day) during stressful or frustrating periods. Kate and her mother had little insight into how these stress breaks were maintaining her headaches. Thus, Kate was enrolled in a pain management program.

Kate's parents had difficulty understanding how she could be healthy and still experience headaches. In similar cases, parents require time and assistance to learn about recurrent pain syndromes, particularly parents who have maintained inaccurate beliefs about their children's headaches for a long period of time. Because of their erroneous beliefs, these parents may have inadvertently adopted maladaptive responses to their children's pain complaints. Thus, they will require more intensive assistance in implementing the treatment recommendations. A pain management program provides parents with the opportunity to receive ongoing assistance by resolving any concerns or questions that arise as they begin to manage their children's pains in a more adaptive manner.

The goals of Kate's program were to teach Kate and her mother about pain systems, recurrent pain syndromes, and the differences between true and learned headache triggers; to help Kate to identify and resolve stressful situations; to assist Kate in coping more effectively with routine frustrations; to reduce secondary gains associated with her pain, by ensuring that adults would respond consistently in a manner that would encourage her to actively reduce her headaches; and to teach Kate nonpharmacological methods of pain control, such as muscle relaxation through biofeedback and nonstressful exercises. (These are also summarized in Figure 13.4.)

During her first session, the therapist worked with Kate to develop her own treatment goals. To encourage more independence immediately, the therapist helped Kate to generate a list of pain control strategies for use at home and at school. After learning how tension could physiologically cause her headaches, and how the various situational (e.g., low control, high expectations), behavioral (e.g., distress, maladaptive coping strategies), and emotional (e.g., frustration, sadness) factors could exacerbate her pain, Kate worked with the therapist in selecting pain control strategies to modify her physiological responses (e.g., to help her relax) and to modify the exacerbating factors. Kate's list consisted of a variety of active and relaxing pain control strategies: lying down with a cold cloth on her head, rubbing her head, fixing her hair, coloring or drawing, reading, watching TV, taking medicine, drinking or snacking, taking a short break at school by putting her head down on the desk for a few minutes, and ensuring that she was not holding her pencil too tight. This list was used as a "prescription" for pain control. Her parents were instructed to direct Kate to her list whenever she complained of pain, so that they were acknowledging that Kate had a legitimate pain that required intervention, but emphasizing that the interventions should be implemented independently and actively.

The strategies that children are encouraged to generate depend on the specific factors that contribute to their headaches, the treatment methods (active vs. passive, adaptive vs. disabling) they are presently using, and the efficacy of these methods. Children who tend to adopt a passive, sick role orientation are encouraged to generate more active, "get better" strategies, by engaging in distracting physical, social, and mental activities. Children who typically sleep or isolate themselves to rest for all their headaches are encouraged to be more selective about when they use this strategy—perhaps reserving it for more severe headache episodes or for times when they are unable to obtain relief through more active strategies. Early in Kate's treatment program, the abstract concept of control was made more concrete for her by using biofeedback to show how emotional reactions affect muscle tension and thus can result in tension headaches. The biofeedback session, with progressive muscle relaxation exercises and visual imagery, was tape-recorded and added to her list of pain control strategies.

The strategies children use should not be arbitrary, but should be selected and refined by the therapist in consideration of the severity of the headache, the likelihood that a particular strategy will be successful, and knowledge of the factors causing the headaches. Resolving the causative factors is the best strategy for fully alleviating headaches. For example, many children can readily acknowledge that when a headache is caused by worrying about completing homework, the pain control strategy "Engage in a socially distracting activity" will not reduce the anxiety and the headache pain as effectively as will completing the homework (i.e., resolving the real problem and headache trigger). Children are also taught to base the selection of strategies on their understanding of how the strategies function to reduce pain. For example, children learn that medication will reduce (or block) some of their pain, but that it will have a minimal effect on reducing the muscle tension created within a stressful situation. Thus, a combination of pharmacological and nonpharmacological approaches is required, in which they take medication but also use another strategy from their list.

Throughout her program, Kate used pain diaries to monitor her headaches. Two weeks after the feedback session, her pain complaints had decreased slightly to three per week, and her pain intensity had decreased so that her strongest headaches were ~5 (Coloured Analogue Scale). Like Ian, Kate learned to identify and resolve stressful situations and to cope more effectively with routine frustrations. The therapist reviewed and analyzed her pain diary with her, to highlight that she had a consistent pattern of headaches starting at school, and to begin brainstorming about what factors (specifically, her emotional reactions) in school situations triggered her headaches. With assistance, Kate described and discussed her concerns about her academic performance; her fear of not meeting her goals and expectations; and her eagerness to please others and to gain their approval. She was also able to understand how her inability to cope with routine frustration (e.g., changes in plans, friends' not meeting her expectations for their behavior) stemmed from her need to be in control and to keep her life well organized and predictable. The following steps summarize the problem-solving strategies the therapist used to assist Kate in resolving the stressors identified in her pain diary.

Steps to Solve Problems

1. How do you feel?
2. What is the problem?
3. Whose problem is it?
4. What is your goal?
5. Stop and think. Brainstorm solutions.
6. What are the consequences of these solutions?
7. Throw out the bad ideas and keep the good ones.
8. Try one of the good ideas.
9. How well did it work? Is the problem solved? How do you feel?

To respond consistently and adaptively to Kate's pain complaints, her parents were encouraged to minimize the attention they paid to her pain complaints, to focus her attention on independently making decisions about what to do when in pain, and to praise her attempts at active pain management. In addition, her parents were instructed to help her to use problem-solving skills and to be more independent in resolving the stressors that were contributing to her headaches. The therapist emphasized that resolution rather than avoidance of stress was necessary, because Kate had a tendency to remove herself from anxiety-provoking situations (usually social and physical activities). The temporary stress reduction she gained when she was anxious was not an effective long-term solution for the specific situation or for headache pain control. The continued lack of resolution would intensify Kate's anxiety and pains. As her parents began to understand the nature of Kate's headaches, assisted her in resolving problems, and responded differently to her pain complaints, their sense of competence and control over the pain problem increased and their anxiety about her headaches lessened. Subsequently, Kate's anxiety and disability behaviors also decreased.

Severe Problem. George, a 16-year-old boy, had a severe pain problem. George had experienced intermittent headaches since he was 10 years of age. However, approximately 18 months prior to the assessment, he had an abrupt onset of daily headaches. His pain was localized in the occipital region, with some pain spreading into his shoulders. Although the headaches were described as daily, the pain lasted from 1 to 3 days. He described the pain as intense, with a numerical rating of 8 on the Coloured Analogue Scale. The pain had an atypical burning and aching quality; he experienced some accompanying dizziness and fatigue. George was unable to achieve satisfactory pain relief, despite trying many medications, sleep, and massage therapy. As a result of the intense pain, he missed approximately 60 days of school during the spring term. Because his parents realized that his attending school was important, they were frustrated by their inability to make him attend classes. Once school ended, his headaches decreased to approximately two per week throughout the summer. George attributed his headaches to stress related to school, family, and occasionally sports.

George was the youngest of four children; his older sisters and brothers were in their early 30s, so he lived at home alone with his parents. His parents believed that his older siblings were envious of George's advantages as the youngest child. They described George as a perfectionist with regard to his schoolwork and as an overachiever. Despite his recent school absences, he passed all his courses and completed Grade 10 with the help of a tutor. However, George had more difficulties socially. His closest friend was his 30-year-old sister's boyfriend. He had few same-age peer relationships and participated in only a few social activities.

The results of the pain assessment showed that George's headache pattern was not consistent with a moderate problem or a typical recurrent pain syndrome. The abrupt onset of daily headaches, atypical pain characteristics, lengthy school absences, unrealistic expectations for achievement, and increasing withdrawal from social activities indicated that his pain was attributable primarily to underlying emotional factors. His headaches would not resolve unless he received more specialized psychological counseling to address the real cause for his pain and relieve his emotional distress.

The results of the pain assessment were reviewed independently with George and his parents. The therapist emphasized that his headaches were a symptom of underlying emotional distress and that he should receive psychological counseling. (Note: Our pain clinic does not provide the specialized counseling required to treat children and adolescents with pain related to depression, anxiety, or abuse. Thus, we refer these young people to our hospital psychology and psychiatry services or to specialized private practitioners.) The therapist recommended that George use a combined pharmacological and nonpharmacological treatment regimen. He should be reintegrated into school, and his parents should not allow him to remain home as his major pain control strategy. George also needed to participate in more social, physical, and mentally challenging activities. In a separate session with George, the therapist described the relationship between general emotional suppression and his headaches; discussed how long-standing anxiety stemming from high expectations for performance can lead to self-esteem and emotional difficulties; and explained her rationale for referring George for specialized counseling. However, George was hesitant to accept a referral, indicating that he was uncomfortable discussing emotional issues with other people. (Note: This is a common reaction among adolescents with daily headaches referred to our clinic, who typically deny or suppress emotional reactions, and who strive to behave outwardly in a manner that they perceive is socially acceptable.)

George did not accept our recommendation for counseling, despite the therapist's strong belief that his headaches would continue unless the emotional factors responsible were resolved. His headaches decreased after the feedback appointment, coincident with the summer school break. However, by mid-September his headaches increased. Prior to his first exam, he had a severe headache that lasted 3 days and that necessitated a 5-day recuperation period. He became concerned that he was beginning the pain-and-absenteeism pattern of the previous school year, so he began counseling.

Comment. These case studies illustrate that recurrent pain syndromes have both common and unique causative factors. Regardless of the similarity in pain characteristics among children, there are still certain factors that may be primary causes for one child's pain, but almost negligible as causes for another child's pain. Thus, treatment emphasis must include a general approach to address the common factors, and an individual approach to address the uniquely relevant factors for each child. The extent to which cognitive, emotional, behavioral, and familial factors are the primary causes for recurrent pain will determine the particular composition of a multistrategy treatment. Because pharmacological methods relieve the painfulness of an episode, but do not generally alleviate the syndrome, an integrated flexible approach for combining physical, behavioral, and cognitive methods should be used.

Persistent Pain

Situational Factors That Modify Children's Persistent Pain

Children can experience many types of persistent pain caused by disease, injury, and emotional distress (P. A. McGrath, 1990; P. J. McGrath & Unruh, 1987; Ross & Ross, 1988; Schechter et al., 1993). Although many of the situational factors described previously for acute and recurrent pain can intensify children's persistent pain, the most salient situational factor is probably the relevance or aversive significance of the prolonged pain and any accompanying disability. All aspects of children's lives are adversely affected by the pain. Children may endure a prolonged period of physical disability, continuing pain, and varied medical treatments. Parents are distressed by the pain itself, its implications for their children's future, its life-threatening potential (if any), and the prospect of progressive pain and disability. Parents tend to emphasize the future consequences of the children's physical condition and their pain, whereas the children themselves are more preoccupied by the immediate consequences. The dynamics within the family inevitably change as persistent pain prevents children from pursuing their normal activities and as each family member adjusts to the altered circumstances.

Although most children receive accurate information about their disease and required treatments, few receive concrete information about their pain, the factors that attenuate or exacerbate it, and effective nonpharmacological pain-reducing strategies. Thus, most children do not know simple interventions that they can incorporate into their daily activities to complement the medical management of their disease. Also, they do not know that prescribed pain control treatments may vary in efficacy at different times throughout their treatment, because of variations in disease activity or in situational factors. Without this knowledge, children's and parents' confidence in certain therapies can decrease, even though these therapies may effectively alleviate pain at another time. Children's expectations that they will experience persistent pain, that they must rely exclusively on potent analgesic medication for partial pain relief, and that they will always live their lives differently from other children can create enormous emotional distress, which can exacerbate their pain and disability. Children's persistent pain is further complicated by decreased independence, reduced control, and an uncertain prognosis.

Children's usual behaviors are restricted by the disability caused by their condition or injury. Children may gradually withdraw from social activities with peers and from most physical sports. As children's general physical activity and normal exercise decrease, abnormal sensory input may increase, producing concomitant increases in pain. This problem can be confounded by the responses of children's parents and siblings. Parents who encourage children to adopt passive patient roles, to behave differently from other children, and to depend primarily on others for pain control will undoubtedly create a situation wherein children's pain is maximized. Parents who encourage children to resume as many of their normal activities as possible create a situation wherein children's pain should be minimized.

Children with persistent pain feel anxious and distressed by their prolonged suffering and altered lives. Medications may cause various adverse physical effects, such as hair loss and bloating. Children can become overly self-conscious about their physical appearance and about their inability to participate in daily activities, so that they become ill at ease with their peers. They may withdraw socially because they anticipate negative reactions from their friends. Increased withdrawal and social isolation can exacerbate their pain. When their prognosis is uncertain, they may feel extremely anxious and frightened. Some children may become increasingly irritable and may act out by provoking arguments, disobeying parents, and not completing assigned schoolwork. Other children may outwardly cope with the pain and accept required treatments, but may actually suppress their true emotional reactions—anger, anxiety, or depression. These children are at risk for developing progressively more somatic complaints as other outlets for their emotional expression diminish.

Two case studies are presented to illustrate how a cognitive-behavioral approach is a necessary component of pain control programs for children with persistent pain.

Case Study: Cancer-Related Pain

Mary, an 11-year-old girl with leukemia, was referred for treatment of severe pain (numerical rate of 8 on the Coloured Analogue Scale) caused by the effects of chemotherapy. At the time of her assessment, she was hospitalized and receiving morphine (3.3 mg/hour) on continuous infusion, plus bolus morphine (2.5 mg every 20 minutes) for pain control. During the 24-hour period preceding the assessment, she had received 26 boluses. Mary's affect was markedly low, and she seemed depressed. She was lying in a darkened room in which there were no personal mementos (which children often bring with them to the hospital), even though Mary had been hospitalized for a few weeks. Mary's mother was always in the room with her. She regularly indicated to the nursing staff that her daughter was in a lot of pain. Nurses reported that Mary had refused to participate when child life specialists entered the room and had not attempted to attend any of the hospital activities available for children, even before her pain had increased to its current level. The pain consultation was requested by the nursing staff, who were concerned about the morphine dose Mary was receiving and wondered whether she was demanding boluses when she really needed attention.

Inpatient pain consultations are conducted by obtaining the information outlined in Figure 13.6, through brief interviews with children, parents, and relevant members of the health care staff. Mary described her pain as a severe burning sensation, localized to her enlarged hemorrhoids and spreading diffusely into a moderate pain sensation throughout her body. After explaining her role, the therapist described pain systems and gates to Mary. She then used the television set in Mary's room and the three attached colored wires to explain that morphine controls pain via one pathway, but that there are other pathways—a physical set activated by sensory stimulation, and a cognitive set activated by mental concentration. The therapist explained that Mary was receiving partial pain control, because she was relying exclusively on only one of these systems. Mary showed much interest, and easily understood that if each of the three cables attached to the television was necessary for it to work well, then two other methods of pain control should complement her morphine so that she would have even less pain.

Mary's mother also listened very attentively to the therapist's explanation. Nurses had informed the therapist that the mother asked Mary repeatedly whether she was in pain, but did not have any other interactions with Mary except for comforting and holding her when she affirmed that she did have pain. Thus, the therapist used another analogy to emphasize why Mary should not monitor her pain too closely: "Imagine that you are going to see a movie and people are sitting near you; they have popcorn and many candies wrapped in crinkly paper. Suppose I ask you to ignore the sounds of people unwrapping and eating their candies, and just pay attention to the movie. But what if every 2 minutes I ask you if you can still hear the crinkling?" Mary smiled and said that the more she paid attention to the noise, the less she would be able to truly ignore it and watch the movie. The therapist then explained that people should not ask her too often about whether she had pain; otherwise, they might accidentally interfere with how the morphine worked. Instead, the nurses and doctors would ensure that she had enough drug and nondrug techniques to lessen her pain, and that the therapist would help her to set up a plan to ensure that all three systems were working to relieve her pain. Her mother's role would change from checking on Mary's pain to actively massaging her at specified times during the day and encouraging Mary to implement the "Get Well Plan," including participating in child life activities (to the extent that it was possible); reminding people entering her room to talk with her about other aspects of her health; and not constantly monitoring her pain. Mary was asked to have her dad bring some pictures from home to display, so that she could let people know about other things in her life and they could talk about more interesting topics. A simple plan was drawn on a poster and mounted on her wall. In order to assist her mother, the therapist further explained why regular periods of massage and increased, varied physical stimulation would be beneficial for Mary. Nurses began to assess and chart Mary's pain level using the Coloured Analogue Scale every 4 hours, rather than relying on Mary's mother to monitor the level.

Name: _____**Date:** _____

Admission Date/Diagnosis: _____

Reason for Referral (note specific behaviors/complaints/difficulties motivating referral):_____

_____

Contact Person on Floor: _____

History of Present Admission:
• Precipitating event
• Complaints
• Additional referrals
• Relevant medical/sociocultural history
Pain Characteristics:
• Onset, quality, intensity
• Temporal pattern (episodic/continuous duration)
• Location, spread to other sites (consistent with neurological pattern)
Medical/Surgical:
• Investigations conducted
• Consultation results
• Lab tests (as related to pain problem)
Analgesic and Adjuvant Medications:
• Type, dose, frequency
• Method of administration
• Evaluative comments by staff or patient
Potential Exacerbating Factors:
• Cognitive
• Behavioral
• Emotional
• Familial/cultural
• Psychiatric
Note other relevant information (e.g., contacts with other health services):

FIGURE 13.6. Form for an inpatient pain consultation.

In addition, the therapist designed a simple behavioral management program. Mary would earn stickers on a calendar for following the recommendations in her "Get Well Plan." Six hours later, when the therapist returned with the calendar and some stickers, Mary was remarkably different. She was sitting up, and her affect was quite positive; she had participated in child life activities for approximately 2 hours; and she had not requested any morphine boluses since the therapist met with her earlier. She and her mother received a star for the day. She was gradually weaned off morphine as her hemorrhoidal inflammation subsided. (Note: Local anesthesia was contraindicated; morphine was the appropriate analgesic.)

Issues Related to Opioid Use

Some issues in Mary's case are pertinent for many children receiving morphine for pain control. Nurses were unsure about how much pain Mary was experiencing and whether her fear and distress might be increasing her morphine requirements. They were also concerned that some of her pain complaints were related to Mary's need to converse with nurses and gain some attention. There was some diffusion of responsibility for ensuring that she had adequate pain control among nurses and physicians, as well as some disagreement as to whether analgesics, sedatives, or some combination of the two categories was most appropriate.

Parents, and occasionally staff members, have misconceptions about the use of potent opioids. Although the sensory characteristics of children's pain should be consistent with the known pattern from the presumed source of tissue injury, the source is not easily identified for all children. This is particularly true for children who have cancer, since there may be multiple sources of noxious stimulation from the disease itself and toxic therapies. Yet children's pain must be controlled, even when the specific etiology is not yet determined. Otherwise, children become increasingly anxious, fearful, and distressed, thus beginning a cycle of increasing pain that will be more difficult to alleviate.

Parents are often anxious about the use of opioids for their children, particularly when children require dose increments. When children receive morphine, therapists must help parents to understand that dependence and tolerance are very different from addiction. Dependence and tolerance are normal drug effects; they do not mean that children with pain have become addicted. Drug dependence occurs when children's bodies become accustomed to a certain level of drug, so that they require the drug on a continuous or periodic basis. This effect is well recognized. When opioids are suddenly withdrawn, children suffer irritability, anxiety, insomnia, diaphoresis, rhinorrhea, nausea, vomiting, abdominal cramps, and diarrhea. These withdrawal symptoms are prevented by gradually tapering doses for all children who have been on opioid therapy for longer than a week. Drug tolerance occurs after repeated opioid administration when children gradually adjust to a drug level, so that they require progressively higher levels of opioids to receive the same pain relief. Even though children with severe pain may require progressively higher and more frequent opioid doses because of drug tolerance, they should receive the doses they need to relieve their pain. However, children who require increased opioids to relieve previously controlled pain should also be assessed carefully to determine whether the disease has progressed, since pain may be the first sign of advancing disease.

In contrast, drug addiction occurs when individuals are overwhelmingly involved in obtaining and using a drug for its euphoric rather than its analgesic effects. Regrettably, though, the fear of opioid addiction remains a common myth preventing many children with severe pain from receiving adequate analgesia.

Therapists can use familiar analogies to explain dependence, tolerance, and addiction. For example, parents are often accustomed to drinking coffee in the morning. They know that they will experience some noticeable effects without their usual caffeine intake, but they also know that they can withdraw from coffee by gradually lowering their daily consumption. The fact that their bodies are used to a certain amount of caffeine at certain times of the day means that they are dependent. Similarly, many people become accustomed to a certain level of salt for a food to taste "salty." After a while they may need to increase their salt intake if they want foods to taste the same, because their bodies have adjusted to or now tolerate the previous amount of salt, so that it no longer has the same effect. In the same way, their children can become tolerant to a morphine dose, so that they require a slightly higher dose to achieve the same pain reduction. These benign examples of a body's normal responses to substances often help parents understand that when opioids are prescribed for their children, the effects of those drugs are well known, are well understood, and will not lead to adverse effects (including addiction).

Case Study: Persistent Pain

Clorissa, a 14-year-old girl, was referred for assessment and treatment of persistent pain in her right shoulder and arm, suggestive of reflex sympathetic dystrophy (RSD). The purposes of her assessment were to evaluate the sensory characteristics of her pain, to identify primary and secondary factors responsible, to determine whether her pain was characteristic of neuropathic pain (specifically RSD), and to recommend appropriate treatment. Her pain assessment was similar to those described previously for children with recurrent pain.

Clorissa's pain had started abruptly 11 months earlier. She experienced a sudden throbbing when she was completing some paperwork at school. Within an hour her arm turned purple and became numb, and she was unable to move it. She was admitted to a hospital; a nerve block restored sensation immediately, but she was still unable to move the arm. Three days prior to pain onset, her family physician had diagnosed muscle spasms in her neck, presumably caused by the strain of carrying roof shingles while helping her father repair their roof. Since her hospitalization, Clorissa had seen several physicians, had received limited physiotherapy (because she viewed it as ineffective), and had used several different pain medications—all without success. She was very frustrated by the lack of a clear diagnosis and effective treatment.

Clorissa's pain was a constant, moderate sensation, usually rated as 5 (Coloured Analogue Scale), but increasing in intensity (to 8) in the evening. Several days a week she awoke with stronger pain. She reported that her pain was weakest when she was concentrating on schoolwork or participating in social activities. She had experienced a few episodes of sudden increases in pain, followed by periods of complete loss of motion in her arm. Although she attended school regularly and attempted to maintain her social life, she was unable to do so completely. She had withdrawn from physical education classes and many activities. She limited most arm movements excessively, even though she could bend her arm at the elbow.

Clorissa was the younger of two children and had a typical sibling relationship with her older brother (aged 16). She was in Grade 9 in a regular school program and had a positive attitude toward school. She was achieving at an above-average level in all her courses. Although her mother described her as a generally happy and positive teenager, her mood had changed since the onset of her pain. She was becoming increasingly depressed and frustrated. In particular, she was very upset that her friends had begun to exclude her from social activities that involved physical activity.

The assessment results indicated that some of Clorissa's pain features were typical of neuropathic pain (specifically RSD), and that she had the potential for long-term disability. The primary factors responsible for her pain were possible accidental trauma or soft-tissue injury leading to RSD; decreased activity and mobility; poor consistency in receiving physiotherapy; and emotional distress regarding the uncertainty of recovery, which impeded her rehabilitation. The secondary factors identified were a protected environment that reduced stress for her; her continuing expectations for limited physical movement; and the special attention she received from peers, parents, and teachers.

At the assessment, the therapist encouraged Clorissa to use her arm as normally as possible. She explained that this type of pain was relieved by restoring and increasing activity, not by reducing it. By the feedback session, Clorissa had attempted to use her arm more often. Although she reported no change in pain levels, she indicated that she no longer took pain medication. When she used it, she had also noticed some changes in the mottled coloring of her arm and experienced some periods of paresthesia and numbness alternating with pain. The therapist discussed these changes as healthy signs that her sensation and function were recovering. The therapist provided Clorissa and her mother with some general feedback about neuropathic pains and RSD. She emphasized that these pains are characterized by great individual variation in physical symptoms and length of disability, thus making it difficult to diagnose the problem initially and to provide a predictable time course for full recovery. However, Clorissa's pain features indicated that she would benefit from an intensive rehabilitation program. The therapist recommended that she should continue to use her arm, minimize any guarding or protective behaviors, receive intensive physiotherapy, and stop using any ineffective analgesic medications. She should continue her regular activities and gradually resume her usual physical activities. Her treatment program included a cognitive-behavioral emphasis, with supportive counseling for Clorissa and her mother to improve their understanding of the complex aspects of neuropathic pain, particularly the need for immediate rehabilitation of her shoulder and arm.

Clorissa experienced an almost immediate improvement in her arm as she followed the therapist's recommendations. She increased her physiotherapy to five sessions per week. During the next 2 months, she had episodes of pain, swelling, and discoloration that were interspersed with progressively longer pain-free periods. She also received a series of stellate ganglion blocks in combination with her physiotherapy and pain management program. She was pain-free and had no symptoms of RSD at follow-up 4 months later.

SUMMARY

Children's pain perception is plastic and complex. The neural responses initiated by tissue damage can be modified by a diverse array of physical and situational factors, so that children can experience very different pains from the same type of tissue damage. Thus, we cannot completely control a child's pain by gearing our interventions solely to the source of tissue damage; instead, we must also control the situational factors that affect the child's nociceptive processing. Only then can we truly alleviate the child's pain and suffering. Pain management for all children begins with a careful and thorough pain assessment to identify the primary source of noxious stimulation, assess the sensory aspects (usually to facilitate diagnosis and monitor treatment efficacy), and determine the extent to which situational factors are exacerbating the pain. The different constellation of cognitive, behavioral, and emotional factors guides our selection of the general treatment approach needed to control children's acute, recurrent, and persistent pain.

The unique perspectives of children, parents, and health care professionals must be considered to identify all the factors affecting children's pain. Then a consistent management program can be developed by selecting the treatments appropriate for modifying not only nociceptive input, but also relevant situational factors. Analgesic or anesthetics attenuate nociceptive activity and are necessary for controlling children's pain, but nonpharmacological interventions are also necessary to mitigate the pain-exacerbating impact of cognitive, behavioral, and emotional factors. Specific nonpharmacological interventions are selected for children according to the type of pain, the children's age or cognitive level, and the contributing factors identified in the pain assessment. Several cognitive, physical, and behavioral interventions should be taught to children, so that they can develop a flexible repertoire of pain-reducing strategies. Since the same strategy will not be consistently effective for all episodes of children's pain, undue emphasis should not be placed on the magical benefits of any one method.

Children with recurrent or persistent pain should learn principles of pain management so that they can naturally evolve their own techniques. In addition, all children with pain and their parents must understand the rationale for controlling the pain, based on a working knowledge of the plasticity and complexity of the pain system. This provides them with a logical framework for administering and evaluating analgesics and for selecting, adapting, and refining practical nonpharmacological interventions. Individual differences among children and their families, as well as relevant situational factors, necessitate that all pain programs be flexible so that they can be adapted to the special needs of each child, family, and pain problem.

REFERENCES

Allen, J., Jedlinsky, B. P., Wilson, T. L., & McCarthy, C. F. (1993). Physical therapy management of pain in children. In N. L. Schechter, C. B. Berde, & M. Yaster (Eds.), *Pain in infants, children, and adolescents* (pp. 317–330). Baltimore: Williams & Wilkins.

Anand, K. J. S., & Aynsley-Green, A. (1988). Does the newborn infant require potent anesthesia during surgery? Answers from a randomized trial of halothane anesthesia. In R. Dubner, G. F. Gebhart, & M. R. Bond (Eds.), *Pain research and clinical management: Vol. 3. Proceedings of the Vth World Congress on Pain* (pp. 329–335). Amsterdam: Elsevier.

Anand, K. J. S., & Hickey, P. R. (1987). Pain and its effects in the human neonate and fetus. *New England Journal of Medicine, 317,* 1321–1329.

Anderson, C. T. M., Zeltzer, L. K., & Fanurik, D. (1993). Procedural pain. In N. L. Schechter, C. B. Berde, & M. Yaster (Eds.), *Pain in infants, children, and adolescents* (pp. 435–457). Baltimore: Williams & Wilkins.

Andrasik, F., Blake, D. D., & McCarran, M. S. (1986). A biobehavioral analysis of pediatric headache. In N. A. Krasnegor, J. D. Arasteh, & M. F. Cataldo (Eds.). *Child health behavior: A behavioral pediatrics perspective* (pp. 394–434). New York: Wiley-Interscience.

Andrasik, F., Kabela, E., Quinn, S., Attanasio, V., Blanchard, E. B., & Rosenblum, E. L. (1988). Psychological functioning of children who have recurrent migraine. *Pain, 34,* 43–52.

Apley, J. (1975). *The child with abdominal pains.* Oxford: Blackwell Scientific.

Apley, J., MacKeith, R., & Meadow, R. (1978). *The child and his symptoms: A comprehensive approach.* Oxford: Blackwell Scientific.

Barr, R. G. (1981). Recurrent abdominal pain. In S. Gabel (Ed.), *Behavioral problems in childhood: A primary care approach* (pp. 229–241). New York: Grune & Stratton.

Barr, R. G. (1983). Recurrent abdominal pain. In M. D. Levine, W. B. Carey, A. C. Crocker, & R. T. Gross (Eds.), *Developmental–behavioral pediatrics* (pp. 521–528). Philadelphia: W. B. Saunders.

Barr, R. G. (1994). Pain experience in children: Developmental and clinical characteristics. In P. D. Wall & R. Melzack (Eds.), *Textbook of pain* (3rd ed., pp. 739–765). Edinburgh: Churchill Livingstone.

Beales, J. G. (1983). Factors influencing the expectation of pain among patients in a children's burn unit. *Burns, 9,* 187–192.

Beales, J. G., Keen, J. H., & Holt, P. J. L. (1983). The child's perception of the disease and the experience of pain in juvenile chronic arthritis. *Journal of Rheumatology, 10,* 61–65.

Beyer, J. E., DeGood, D. E., Ashley, L. C., & Russell, G. A. (1983). Patterns of postoperative analgesic use with adults and children following cardiac surgery. *Pain, 17,* 71–81.

Beyer, J. E., & Wells, N. (1989). The assessment of pain in children. *Pediatric Clinics of North America, 36,* 837–854.

Bush, J. P., & Harkins, S. W. (Eds.). (1991). *Children in pain: Clinical and research issues from a developmental perspective.* New York: Springer-Verlag.

Carr, D. B., Osgood, P. F., & Szyfelbein, S. K. (1993). Treatment of pain in acutely burned children. In N. L. Schechter, C. B. Berde, & M. Yaster (Eds.), *Pain in infants, children, and adolescents* (pp. 495–504). Baltimore: Williams & Wilkins.

Cataldo, M. R., Jacobs, H. E., & Rogers, M. C. (1982). Behavioral/environmental considerations in pediatric inpatient care. In D. C. Russo & J. W. Varni (Eds.), *Behavioral pediatrics: Research and practice* (pp. 271–298). New York: Plenum Press.

Chutorian, A. M. (1978). Migrainous syndromes in children. In R. A. Thompson & J. R. Green (Eds.), *Pediatric neurology and neurosurgery* (pp. 183–204). Jamaica, NY: Spectrum.

Cohen, D. E. (1993). Management of postoperative pain in children. In N. L. Schechter, C. B. Berde, & M. Yaster (Eds.), *Pain in infants, children, and adolescents* (pp. 357–384). Baltimore: Williams & Wilkins.

Craig, K. D., & Grunau, R. V. E. (1993). Neonatal pain perception and behavioral measurement. In K. J. S. Anand & P. J. McGrath (Eds.), *Pain in neonates* (pp. 67–105). Amsterdam: Elsevier.

Eland, J. M. (1974). *Children's communication of pain.* Unpublished master's thesis, University of Iowa.

Fenichel, G. M. (1981). Migraine in children. In A. J. Moss (Ed.), *Pediatrics update: Reviews for physicians* (pp. 25–41). New York: Elsevier.

Fowler-Kerry, S., & Lander, J. R. (1987). Management of injection pain in children. *Pain, 30,* 169–175.

Hilgard, J. R., & LeBaron, S. (1984). *Hypnotherapy of pain in children with cancer.* Los Altos, CA: William Kaufmann.

Houck, C. S., Troshynski, T., & Berde, C. B. (1994). Treatment of pain in children. In P. D. Wall & R. Melzack (Eds.), *Textbook of pain* (3rd ed., pp. 1419–1434). Edinburgh: Churchill Livingstone.

Jay, S. M., Elliott, C. H., Ozolins, M., Olson, R. A., & Pruitt, S. D. (1985). Behavioural management of children's distress during painful medical procedures. *Behaviour Research and Therapy, 23,* 513–552.

Jay, S. M., Ozolins, M., Elliott, C. H., & Caldwell, S. (1983). Assessment of children's distress during painful medical procedures. *Health Psychology, 2,* 133–147.

Joffe, R., Bakal, D. A., & Kaganov, J. (1983). A self-observation study of headache symptoms in children. *Headache, 23,* 20–25.

Katz, E. R., Kellerman, J., & Siegel, S. E. (1980). Behavioral distress in children with cancer undergoing medical procedures: Developmental considerations. *Journal of Consulting and Clinical Psychology, 48*(3), 356–365.

Kavanagh, C. K., Lasoff, E., Eide, Y., Freeman, R., McEttrick, M., Dar, R., Helgerson, R., Remensynder, J., & Kalin, N. (1991). Learned helplessness and the pediatric burn patient: Dressing change behavior and serum cortisol and beta-endorphin. In L. Barness (Ed.), *Advances in pediatrics* (Vol. 38, pp. 335–363). St. Louis, MO: Mosby–Year Book

Kuttner, L. (1993). Hypnotic interventions for children in pain. In N. L. Schechter, C. B. Berde, & M. Yaster (Eds.), *Pain in infants, children, and adolescents* (pp. 229–236). Baltimore: Williams & Wilkins.

Kuttner, L., Bowman, M., & Teasdale, M. (1988). Psychological treatment of distress, pain and anxiety for young children with cancer. *Journal of Developmental and Behavioral Pediatrics, 9,* 374–381.

Manne, S. L., & Andersen, B. L. (1991). Pain and pain-related distress in children with cancer. In J. P. Bush & S. W. Harkins (Eds.), *Children in pain: Clinical and research issues from a developmental perspective* (pp. 337–372). New York: Springer-Verlag.

Maron, M., & Bush, J. P. (1991). Burn injury and treatment pain. In J. P. Bush & S. W. Harkins (Eds.), *Children in pain: Clinical and research issues from a developmental perspective* (pp. 275–296). New York: Springer-Verlag.

Mather, L. E., & Mackie, J. (1983). The incidence of postoperative pain in children. *Pain, 15,* 271–282.

Matthews, J. R., McGrath, P. J., & Pigeon, H. (1993). Assessment and measurement of pain in children. In N. L. Schechter, C. B. Berde, & M. Yaster (Eds.), *Pain in infants, children, and adolescents* (pp. 97–111). Baltimore: Williams & Wilkins.

Maunuksela, E. L. (1993). Nonsteroidal anti-inflammatory drugs in pediatric pain management. In N. L. Schechter, C. B. Berde, & M. Yaster (Eds.), *Pain in infants, children, and adolescents* (pp. 135–144). Baltimore: Williams & Wilkins.

McGrath, P. A. (1987). The multidimensional assessment, and management of recurrent pain syndromes in children and adolescents. *Behaviour Research and Therapy, 25,* 251–262.

McGrath, P. A. (1990). *Pain in children: Nature, assessment, and treatment.* New York: Guilford Press.

McGrath, P. A. (1992). Pain control in children. In R. S. Weiner (Ed.), *Innovations in pain management: A practical guide for clinicians* (pp. 32-1–32-79). Orlando, FL: Paul M. Deutsch Press.

McGrath, P. A. (1993). Psychological aspects of pain perception. In N. L. Schechter, C. B. Berde, & M. Yaster (Eds.), *Pain in infants, children, and adolescents* (pp. 39–63). Baltimore: Williams & Wilkins.

McGrath, P. A. (1994). Alleviating children's pain: A cognitive-behavioural approach. In P. D. Wall & R. Melzack (Eds.), *Textbook of pain* (3rd ed., pp. 1403–1418). Edinburgh: Churchill Livingstone.

McGrath, P. A., & Brigham, M. C. (1992). The assessment of pain in children and adolescents. In D. C. Turk & R. Melzack (Eds.), *Handbook of pain assessment* (pp. 295–314). New York: Guilford Press.

McGrath, P. A., & deVeber, L. L. (1986). The management of acute pain evoked by medical procedures in children with cancer. *Journal of Pain and Symptom Management, 1*(3), 145–150.

McGrath, P. A., Seifert, C. E., Speechley, K. N., Booth, J. C., Stitt, L., & Gibson, M. C. (in press). A new analogue scale for assessing children's pain: An initial validation study. *Pain.*

McGrath, P. J., & Unruh, A. (1987). *Pain in children and adolescents.* Amsterdam: Elsevier.

Melamed, B. G., Robbins, R. L., & Graves, S. (1982). Preparation for surgery and medical procedures. In D. C. Russo & J. W. Varni (Eds.), *Behavioral pediatrics: Research and practice* (pp. 225–267). New York: Plenum Press.

Miser, A. W. (1993). Management of pain associated with childhood cancer. In N. L. Schechter, C. B. Berde, & M. Yaster (Eds.), *Pain in infants, children, and adolescents* (pp. 411–424). Baltimore: Williams & Wilkins.

Olness, K. (1981). Imagery (self-hypnosis) as adjunct therapy in childhood cancer: Clinical experience with 25 patients. *American Journal of Pediatric Hematology/Oncology, 3,* 313–321.

Peterson, L., Harbeck, C., Chaney, J., & Muir Thomas, A. (1990). Children's coping with medical procedures: A conceptual overview and integration. *Behavioral Assessment, 12,* 197–212.

Peterson, L., & Shigetomi, C. (1981). The use of coping techniques to minimize anxiety in hospitalized children. *Behavior Therapy, 12,* 1–14.

Pichard-Leandri, E., & Gauvain-Piquard, A. (Eds.). (1989). *La douleur chez l'enfant.* Paris: Medsi/McGraw Hill.

Porter, F. (1993). Pain assessment in children: Infants. In N. L. Schechter, C. B. Berde, & M. Yaster (Eds.), *Pain in infants, children, and adolescents* (pp. 87–96). Baltimore: Williams & Wilkins.

Price, D. D. (1988). *Psychological and neural mechanisms of pain.* New York: Raven Press.

Rappaport, L. A., & Leichtner, A. M. (1993). Recurrent abdominal pain. In N. L. Schechter, C. B. Berde, & M. Yaster (Eds.), *Pain in infants, children, and adolescents* (pp. 561–569). Baltimore: Williams & Wilkins.

Ross, D. M., & Ross, S. A. (1982). *A study of the pain experience in children* (Final report, Ref. No. 1 RO1 HD13672–01). Bethesda, MD: National Institute of Child Health and Human Development.

Ross, D. M., & Ross, S. A. (1988). *Childhood pain: Current issues, research, and management.* Baltimore: Urban & Schwarzenberg.

Rothner, A. D. (1993). Diagnosis and management of headaches in children and adolescents. In N. L. Schechter, C. B. Berde, & M. Yaster (Eds.), *Pain in infants, children, and adolescents* (pp. 547–554). Baltimore: Williams & Wilkins.

Routh, D. K., & Sanfilippo, M. D. (1991). Helping children cope with painful medical procedures. In J. P. Bush & S. W. Harkins (Eds.), *Children in pain: Clinical and research issues from a developmental perspective* (pp. 397–424). New York: Springer-Verlag.

Russo, D. C., & Varni, J. W. (Eds.). (1982). *Behavioral pediatrics: Research and practice.* New York: Plenum Press.

Schechter, N. L. (1984). Recurrent pains in children: An overview and an approach. *Pediatric Clinics of North America, 31,* 949–968.

Schechter, N. L. (1993). Management of pain associated with acute medical illness. In N. L. Schechter, C. B. Berde, & M. Yaster (Eds.), *Pain in infants, children, and adolescents* (pp. 537–546). Baltimore: Williams & Wilkins.

Schechter, N. L., Allen, D. A., & Hanson, K. (1986). Status of pediatric pain control: A comparison of hospital analgesic usage in children and adults. *Pediatrics, 77,* 11–15.

Schechter, N. L., Berde, C. B., & Yaster, M. (Eds.). (1993). *Pain in infants, children, and adolescents.* Baltimore: Williams & Wilkins.

Shinnar, S., & D'Souza, B. J. (1981). The diagnosis and management of headaches in childhood. *Pediatric Clinics of North America, 29,* 79–94.

Siegel, L. J., & Peterson, L. (1981). Maintenance effects of coping skills and sensory information on young children's response to repeated dental procedures. *Behavior Therapy, 12,* 530–535.

Swafford, L. I., & Allan, D. (1968). Pain relief in the pediatric patient. *Medical Clinics of North America, 52,* 131–136.

Tyler, D. C., & Krane, E. J. (Eds.). (1990). *Advances in pain research and therapy* (Vol. 15). New York: Raven Press.

Varni, J. W., Katz, E. R., & Dash, J. (1982). Behavioral and neurochemical aspects of pediatric pain. In D. C. Russo & J. W. Varni (Eds.), *Behavioral pediatrics: Research and practice* (pp. 177–224). New York: Plenum Press.

Wall, P. D., & Melzack, R. (Eds.). (1994). *Textbook of pain* (3rd ed.) Edinburgh: Churchill Livingstone.

Willis, W. D. (1985). *The pain system: The neural basis of nociceptive transmission in the mammalian nervous system.* Basel: Karger.

World Health Organization. (1986). *Cancer pain relief.* Geneva: Author.

World Health Organization. (in press). *Cancer pain relief and palliative care in children.* Geneva: Author.

Yaster, M., & Maxwell, L. G. (1993). Opioid agonists and antagonists. In N. L. Schechter, C. B. Berde, & M. Yaster (Eds.), *Pain in infants, children, and adolescents* (pp. 145–172). Baltimore: Williams & Wilkins.

Yaster, M., Tobin, J. R., & Maxwell, L. G. (1993). Local anesthetics. In N. L. Schechter, C. B. Berde, & M. Yaster (Eds.), *Pain in infants, children, and adolescents* (pp. 179–194). Baltimore: Williams & Wilkins.

Zeltzer, L. K., Jay, S. M., & Fisher, D. M. (1989). The management of pain associated with pediatric procedures. *Pediatric Clinics of North America, 36,* 941–964.

Zeltzer, L. K., & LeBaron, S. (1982). Hypnosis and nonhypnotic techniques for reduction of pain and anxiety during painful procedures in children and adolescents with cancer. *Journal of Pediatrics, 101*(6), 1032–1035.

CHAPTER 14

Persistent Pain in the Older Patient
Evaluation and Treatment

William G. Kee
Susan J. Middaugh
Kim L. Pawlick

The proportion of the U.S. population aged 65 or older is growing rapidly. At present this age group represents 12% of the population, and it will expand to 20% by the year 2030 (Taeber, 1990). Yet this age group is seriously underrepresented in pain research and in clinical programs. Fewer than 1% of the 400 papers published on pain each year focus on pain in the elderly. The available literature indicates that relatively few individuals over the age of 60 are included in many chronic pain rehabilitation programs (CPRPs), and that older pain patients who are seen in pain treatment centers are offered less treatment and fewer treatment options than their younger counterparts (Melding, 1991; Ortega, Leonard, & Smeltzer, 1988). This is surprising, given that from 73% to 80% of the elderly population reports some degree of pain (Demlow, Liang, & Eaton, 1986; M. R. Thomas & Roy, 1988). The prevalence of chronic pain, for example, increases with age, reaches a maximum at age 55–64, and declines gradually thereafter (Andersson, Ejlertsson, Leden, & Rosenberg, 1993). At least 24% of individuals with serious impairment resulting from low back pain are over age 65 (Wood & Badley, 1980).

Health care professionals are likely to take age into account when developing treatment plans for older patients (Binstock & Post, 1991; Williams, 1988). Age may be considered overtly in the making of clinical decisions. For example, multidisciplinary CPRPs that are vocationally oriented may exclude older individuals (Corey, Etlin, & Miller, 1987; Stark, 1985; Turk & Rudy, 1990). Age may also influence the decision-making process indirectly. It is often assumed, for example, that the older pain patient will be less open to behavioral and other nonpharmacological interventions and less likely to benefit from them. However, research suggests that when older patients are offered behavioral therapies, they are as likely as younger patients to accept and to benefit from them (Carstensen, 1988; Schaie, 1993; Sorkin, Rudy, Hanlon, Turk, & Steig, 1990).

At present, treatment of persistent pain in the older individual appears to rely extensively on pharmacological interventions. This reliance on pain medications is particularly disturbing, given the fact that older patients are more sensitive to pain medications, and also more susceptible to side effects and problems resulting from drug interactions (Kwentus, Harkins, Lignon, & Silverman, 1985; Wilcox, Himmelstein, & Woolhandler, 1994). The older pain patient is thus at risk for health-threatening complications, including falls. These problems are particularly serious with polypharmacy, which is common in the older patient.

Fortunately, both clinicians and clinical investigators are beginning to give serious attention to assessment and treatment of persistent pain in the older individual. This chapter focuses on these issues. The first half of the chapter focuses on information that is now available on treatment outcome for older patients with chronic, nonmalignant pain who are treated in multidisciplinary settings. The second half of the chapter focuses on clinical issues related to evaluation and treatment of the older individual with chronic pain.

CLINICAL OUTCOME IN THE OLDER PAIN PATIENT: A REVIEW OF THE LITERATURE

There is considerable interest in expanding treatment options for the older pain patient. In particular, multidisciplinary CPRPs are beginning to increase services to the older segment of the chronic pain population. At the same time, in an era of increasing health care accountability, it is important to examine the effectiveness of this treatment approach with the elderly members of this population.

An extensive published literature documents favorable treatment outcomes for patients who are admitted to multidisciplinary CPRPs, which are widely recognized as the treatments of choice for chronic, nonmalignant pain (Deardorff, Rubin, & Scott, 1991; Ng, 1981). A recent meta-analysis has reported that these multimodal treatment programs generally achieve clinical gains that are approximately twice those obtained with unimodal treatment approaches (Flor, Fydrich, & Turk, 1992). Unfortunately, older patients are underrepresented and often excluded from outcome studies. The mean age in the clinical outcome studies that have been published to date is typically quite low. Frequently the mean age is 45 years or younger, with few if any participants over the age of 60 years.

The exclusion of older patients from this research leads to the following questions. Do older participants who are admitted to multidisciplinary CPRPs achieve clinically relevant gains? Are these gains equal to, or less than, the gains of younger pain patients treated in the same programs? Until relatively recently, little information has been available to the interested clinician, and some of this information has been misleading. Many outcome studies have been presented at conferences and published only in abstract form. Of the studies that have been published, most were not designed to answer age-related questions; consequently, their findings need to be interpreted with some caution. Selected studies are reviewed below, with the intentions of (1) highlighting the literature on treatment outcomes in older pain patients; (2) discussing problems that are commonly encountered in studies of older pain patients; and (3) raising clinical and research questions that remain to be answered.

Age as a Predictor Variable

A number of clinical outcome studies in the literature, while not specifically investigating treatment outcomes in older participants, have included age as a demographic variable and tested for relationships between age and selected measures of treatment success or failure. Two early studies of clinical outcome of multidisciplinary CPRPs reported data on age as a predictor variable. These two studies illustrate the findings, as well as the limitations, associated with this research approach.

Aronoff and Evans (1982) reported that age was significantly and negatively corre-lated with treatment outcome, as measured by staff ratings of global improvement on a scale of 0–4 obtained at discharge in 104 patients ($r = -.24$, $p < .05$). Aside from the pos-sible role of age-related bias in these staff ratings, the relatively low mean age (43.5 years, $SD = 10.2$ years, no age range provided) indicates that the study actually included very few geriatric individuals (approximately 2.4% aged 64+ years). The "older" patients in this sample were predominantly in their 50s. Correlations between age and outcome variables in a truncated age distribution provide little information on clinical outcome in a geriatric pain population, usually defined as 60 years of age or older. In addition, the correlation coefficient in this study accounted for only 5.7% of the variance in treatment outcome—an amount with questionable clinical relevance. Nevertheless, the authors con-cluded that "With age the significant negative correlations indicate a decline in success rate with older patients" (p. 71).

Another early outcome study (Painter, Seres, & Newman, 1980) obtained follow-up data from 145 patients who responded to extensive self-report questionnaires. The 25 patients who were the most successful were compared with the 25 who were least suc-cessful. A disproportionate number of both younger patients (20–30 years) and older patients (51+ years) were found in the failure group, while those in the age groups 30–40 years and 41–50 years were overrepresented in the success group. These findings approached significance by chi-square ($p < .10$). As in the previous study, the mean age was low (43.5 years, $SD = 10.2$ years), and only 2 of the 50 patients in this study were over the age of 60 (4%, both failures). This study primarily suggests that pain patients in their 50s do not perform as well as those in their 30s and 40s. Incidentally, age in this study was not correlated with outcome, since both the oldest and youngest individuals did less well.

In addition to a truncated age range, the Painter et al. (1980) study raises another important issue—namely, the appropriateness of treatment goals and success criteria for older patients. This treatment program, like many other behaviorally oriented multi-disciplinary CPRPs, was geared toward returning patients to work. It is likely that those patients who were selected as the 25 most successful (the top 17%) had achieved goals related to return to work. These goals may be less realistic for the older injured worker, and also less appropriate if retirement is an option. No information was provided on ages or outcomes for the 95 patients (66% of the sample) who fell between the success and failure extremes. Many of these individuals might have benefited from the pain program and achieved outcomes that could be defined as "successful" by criteria more suitable for evaluating treatment outcome in the older pain patient.

It is unfortunate that these two early studies have been interpreted and cited as pro-viding evidence that behaviorally oriented, multidisciplinary CPRPs are of limited value in treatment of the geriatric pain patient. In reality, studies such as these provide little information on clinical outcome for the older segments of the pain population, particu-larly patients aged 60 or older.

Age-Related Differences in Diagnosis and Treatment

Older patients who seek treatment in multidisciplinary CPRPs often present with a greater variety of pain-related diagnoses than younger patients, as well as a higher incidence of diagnoses such as postherpetic neuralgia (shingles), diabetic neuropathy, and osteoporosis. Differences in pain diagnoses can be a substantial problem in research studies that com-pare outcome data for older versus younger pain patients. Differences in treatment outcome may be attributed to age when they may instead be attributable to differences in medical diagnoses. This problem is further complicated by the evidence that older and younger pain patients seen in the same clinic setting are often provided with different therapeutic modalities. Therefore, differences in treatment outcome may be attributed to age when they may instead be the results of differences in treatment delivery.

Kaplan and Kepes (1989) retrospectively compared clinical information obtained from the charts of 206 patients under age 40 and 192 patients over age 70. Back pain was the most common complaint for both age groups; however, older patients had a higher incidence of postherpetic neuralgia, whereas younger patients had a greater frequency of myofascial pain and reflex sympathetic dystrophy. Narcotic therapy was prescribed more often for the elderly, while transcutaneous electrical nerve stimulation (TENS) and biofeedback were considered "less suitable" for this age group. The authors concluded that older patients showed a "less favorable outcome" (p. 29). An earlier study from the same center (P. S. Thomas, Kepes, & Marcus, 1981) reported similar findings, with a reported success rate of 33% for those over the age of 65 compared with 45% for those under age 65. Clinicians were advised to "screen geriatric patients very carefully before admission" to a pain treatment center, in the interest of "cost-effectiveness" (p. S297). In both of these studies, however, it is impossible to determine whether older pain patients had less favorable treatment responses because of their age or because of differences in diagnoses and treatment options. No outcome data were provided by diagnosis or by treatment modality.

This problem of interpretation, in which differences are attributed to age rather than diagnosis or treatment, can be quite subtle. McCreary, Naliboff, Cohen, and McArthur (1988) retrospectively compared treatment outcome between younger patients (under age 35) and older patients (over age 55) from a total of 1,160 patients seen in three different pain treatment settings. All had chronic low back pain, "reflecting the total range of the types of patients who suffer from chronic back pain" (p. 147). Older women showed less reduction in pain ratings as a result of treatment than did older men or younger patients. The investigators concluded that older woman may be less responsive to treatment because of less social support, as inferred from the high percentage of widows in this group. The authors did not report the etiology or severity of physical findings for their age–gender subgroups, and it is possible that the older women simply had a higher incidence of conditions (e.g., severe osteoporosis) that can be particularly difficult to treat. No information was provided on possible differences in either the amount or type of treatment provided for these subgroups.

A considerably more optimistic report is provided by Hallett and Pilowsky (1982). Clinical outcome was examined in 270 patients seeking treatment in a hospital pain clinic setting for a wide range of diagnoses, including low back pain, headache, postherpetic neuralgia, cancer, and spinal cord injuries. Patients were categorized as either improved (partial or complete relief) or not improved (no change or worse) upon termination of treatment, based on information obtained retrospectively from clinic charts. The results were reported separately for four age groups, and there were no age-related differences in success rates as tested by chi-square. In fact, those in the oldest group (42 patients over age 65; 15.7% of the total sample) had the highest rate of improvement, 50%, as compared to 33–37% for the three younger age groups. No information was provided on possible differences in diagnosis or treatment by age.

Ortega et al. (1988) have provided some thought-provoking data on delivery of pain treatment services to geriatric patients. These authors conducted a chart review of all patients referred to a multidisciplinary pain clinic. Only 11% ($n = 30$) of 263 patients evaluated in their clinic setting were aged 65 or older. These older pain patients had pain of longer duration than those under age 65 (mean = 12.6 vs. 5.1 years, $p < .05$). Stable pain conditions were more common in younger pain patients, whereas progressively deteriorating conditions such as rheumatoid arthritis were more likely in the older patients ($p < .005$). These findings would seem to indicate a substantial need for pain-related therapies in the older group; however, older patients were less likely to receive treatment following initial evaluation (47% vs. 69%, $p < .01$). Furthermore, older patients who were treated received appreciably less service (an average of 11 vs. 34 sessions, $p < .001$). No outcome data were reported.

These studies suggest that there is substantial undertreatment of persistent pain in the elderly—a suggestion that has been made by others as well (Crook, Weir, & Tunks, 1989; Melding, 1991). Older patients are not referred to specialized pain centers in proportion to estimated need. When referred to a pain center for evaluation, older patients are less likely to be treated than younger pain patients seen in the same setting. When treated, the older pain patients are likely to be provided with different therapeutic modalities and fewer treatment sessions. To what extent are these differences in delivery of pain services attributable to differences in medical needs, preferences, and finances? To what extent are they the results of age bias on the part of health care providers? Do such differences in pain service delivery translate into poorer clinical outcomes for older individuals? How do treatment outcomes compare for older and younger pain patients if the comparisons are controlled for these diagnostic and treatment variables? How do treatment outcomes compare for older and younger pain patients if measures of "success" are used that are equally appropriate for both age groups? Research studies, such as those reviewed below, are beginning to provide answers to these questions.

Behavioral Therapies and the Older Pain Patient

A number of studies have used prospective experimental designs to evaluate the effectiveness of specific cognitive and behavioral therapies in relatively homogeneous groups of older pain patients, particularly those with osteoarthritis. These studies have shown very encouraging results.

Miller and LeLievre (1982) used behavioral techniques to increase the level of physical exercise and decrease pain behavior in four nursing home residents aged 56–89. All subjects had chronic pain as a result of osteoarthritis and had similar levels of functioning prior to the start of the study. Attention and verbal praise were used to encourage exercise to preset levels, and extinction procedures were used to discourage pain behaviors. Subjects were unable to increase their exercise tolerance, possibly because all four were participating in an exercise program prior to the start of the study and perhaps had already reached their maximum exercise tolerance. There was also no increase in participation in recreational activities. There were, however, documented decreases in the use of pain medications, frequency of pain behaviors, and scores on the McGill Pain Questionnaire (Melzack, 1987) including decreases in subjective ratings of pain intensity.

Puder (1988) examined the effectiveness of stress inoculation training (SIT) in 69 patients with chronic nonmalignant pain recruited from area pain centers and (by advertisement) from the community. Seventy percent had musculoskeletal pain diagnoses, and there were no age-related differences in diagnostic category. Ages ranged from 27 to 80 years (mean = 52.7 years, $SD = 14.4$ years). The sample sizes within each decade were relatively well balanced, and 32% ($n = 22$) were 60 years of age or older. Half received immediate treatment, and half entered treatment after a delay during which they served as a waiting-list control. The SIT treatment for older as well as younger participants consisted of 10 weekly 2-hour group sessions with instructions on cognitive and behavioral pain management techniques, including progressive muscle relaxation, deep breathing, imagery, cognitive restructuring, and problem solving. As measured by daily diary ratings, SIT was effective in increasing the effectiveness of coping, reducing pain interference with activity, and (to a lesser extent) reducing maximum pain intensity. These changes were maintained at 1-month and 6-month follow-ups. The author concluded that SIT is effective in teaching pain management skills and that older patients with chronic pain benefit from such treatment.

Three recent studies have investigated coping strategies and training designed to improve coping skills in older pain patients. Keefe and Williams (1990) compared four age groups, including a geriatric group with a mean age of 72 years, on the Coping Skills Questionnaire (Rosenstiel & Keefe, 1983), which measures the use and the perceived effectiveness of common cognitive and behavioral strategies for coping with pain. All subjects ($n = 88$, 22 per age group) had chronic nonmalignant pain, predominantly cervical pain, low back pain, and headache. The authors found no age differences, and concluded that individuals who are coping with a similar life event adopt similar coping strategies regardless of age.

Keefe et al. (1990) also evaluated pain coping skills training as a clinical intervention for older patients with persistent pain resulting from osteoarthritis of the knee. A total of 99 patients with a mean age of 64 years ($SD = 11.5$ years) and a mean duration of symptoms of 12 years were randomly assigned to one of three groups. Subjects in a pain coping skills training group and an arthritis education control group each attended 10 weekly sessions; subjects in a standard treatment control group received only routine medical care. Following training, the pain coping skills group had significantly less pain and less psychological disability (but not less physical disability), than the other two groups, as measured by the Arthritis Impact Measurement Scales (Kazis, Meenan, & Anderson, 1983). The authors conclude that training to improve pain coping skills can reduce pain and psychological disability in older patients with osteoarthritis.

A third study, by Fry and Wong (1991), supports the effectiveness of coping skills interventions for reducing pain and emotional distress in homebound elderly patients (aged 63–82) with chronic knee pain. In addition, this study suggest that such intervention may be most effective when coping skills training is matched to the individual patient's preferred coping style, as indicated by the Ways of Coping Scale (Folkman & Lazarus, 1980).

These studies were all specifically designed to evaluate the effectiveness of cognitive and behavioral pain management procedures in treatment of the older pain patient. Taken together, their findings make a very strong case for the suitability and the effectiveness of such procedures for treatment of older patients with chronic musculoskeletal pain. The psychological interventions in these studies placed a strong emphasis on coping and pain management rather than physical rehabilitation. Consequently, it is not surprising that the reported benefits were reductions in pain and emotional distress. There was little reported effect on measures of physical function.

Biofeedback Therapy and the Older Pain Patient

The research literature that examines the effectiveness of biofeedback and related physiological self-regulation therapies in older pain patients is particularly interesting and instructive. Two retrospective clinical outcome studies (Blanchard, Andrasik, Evans, &

Hillhouse, 1985; Diamond & Montrose, 1984) and one meta-analytic study (Holroyd & Penzien, 1986) of biofeedback therapies for treatment of headache reported that older patients had lower success rates than younger patients treated in the same settings. These authors suggested that the problem may lie with the extended duration and presumed refractory nature of pain symptomatology in older headache patients, or with possible differences in psychophysiological responding. On close examination of these studies, however, it is possible to attribute the poor outcome in older headache patients at least in part to the familiar problems of truncated age ranges, use of retrospective data, and possible age-related differences in treatment referral, admission, and delivery, as discussed earlier in this chapter.

Diamond and Montrose (1984) reviewed a total of 395 cases and analyzed multiple outcome variables by chi-square analysis for four age groups (ages 0–21 = 22%, 22–30 = 21%, 31–46 = 41%, 47+ = 16%) and two to four descriptive categories (e.g., "worse," "slight improvement," "moderate improvement," or "excellent improvement"). Neither age range, mean age, or standard deviation was provided, so it is difficult to discern the age composition of the 47+ age group. It is probable that few patients were elderly, since the methods section of this paper states that the Diamond Headache Clinic considered bio-feedback training to be contraindicated for "most patients over the age of 50" (p. 6). Biofeedback therapy included a comprehensive package of thermal and electromyographic (EMG) biofeedback training, imagery, relaxation therapies, and an educational package that included stress management and cognitive techniques. Age was significantly related to most indicators of improvement, such as reported headache frequency, severity, and duration at follow-up. However, in almost every instance this finding was attributable to markedly better performance in the youngest age group, 0–21 years. The 47+ age group, in fact, was very similar to the two intermediate age groups on most outcome measures. On a few measures, each older age group was somewhat less successful than the one preceding it, but on most measures there was no such stepwise change with age. In fact, the authors did not conclude that older patients do poorly; rather, they pointed out the exceptional positive response of the youngest patients. This study thus does not provide evidence of systematically worsening outcome with increasing age, although it has often been cited as doing so.

Holroyd and Penzien (1986) carried out a meta-analytic review of biofeedback and relaxation therapies in treatment of headache. They reported that age was negatively correlated with treatment outcome ($r = -0.55$, $p < .001$) and accounted for a substantial 30% of the variation across 37 studies. Once again, the mean age for all 37 studies was low, 33.1 years ($SD = 7.4$ years), with a range of 19–52 years. This finding indicates that age was a very relevant client variable, but also indicates that factors other than age accounted for 70% of the treatment outcome. This study also provides no information on treatment outcome in headache patients over the age of 52 years; none were included in 37 studies. Nevertheless, the authors concluded that "older clients are less responsive to behavioral intervention" (p. 531), and their age–outcome correlation is often inter-preted as evidence that geriatric headache patients (usually defined as 60 years of age or older) do not benefit from biofeedback and related behavioral therapies.

A number of studies have specifically examined treatment outcome in headache patients aged 60 years or older. Blanchard et al. (1985) retrospectively reviewed clinical outcome for 11 patients aged 60–68 (4.4% of 250 total cases) who completed treatment in this research group's behavioral headache treatment protocols over a period of 5 years. Only 2 of these 11 patients (18%) met the criterion for clinical improvement, which was a 50% reduction in headache activity. A third patient had a 30% reduction. The authors concluded that these poor results can be viewed as a caution against offering behavioral treatments to older headache patients, or as a challenge to develop protocols designed to meet the needs of this age group more effectively.

Three subsequent studies—all with prospective designs and treatment protocols that were adapted for the older headache patient—present very different, positive results. Arena and colleagues reported clinical improvements (a 50% reduction in headache activity) in 50–70% of 18 tension headache patients aged 62–80 years, treated with progressive muscle relaxation procedures (Arena, Hightower, & Chong, 1988) or frontal EMG biofeedback procedures (Arena, Hannah, Bruno, & Meador, 1991). Both studies also had an educational component and homework. The treatment protocols included a number of techniques to ensure that older patients heard and understood the treatment rationale and instructions. The therapist made an effort to talk at a slower rate, to simplify the instructions, and to avoid the use of jargon. Comprehension was checked by asking the subjects to repeat the instructions aloud. In addition, instructions were briefly summarized and repeated in subsequent sessions. An extra 10 minutes was scheduled for each session so that an unhurried atmosphere could be maintained.

Blanchard's research group (Kabela, Blanchard, Appelbaum, & Nicholson, 1989) conducted a prospective study of 16 headache patients aged 60–77 with varied headache diagnoses who were treated with individualized combinations of biofeedback, relaxation therapies, and cognitive techniques. Procedures similar to those suggested by Arena et al. (1991) were included to enhance comprehension and retention of the clinical material. In this study, 63% of patients achieved the clinical goal of 50% reduction in headache activity. This success rate was similar to that of younger headache patients.

The recommended protocol adaptations used in the studies reported above are similar to methods employed by experienced biofeedback clinicians with their older patients. Abrahamson (1987), for example, has observed that older individuals may require more sessions, as well as more time within sessions, to achieve the desired physiological change with biofeedback training. If the clinician is willing to be flexible, the older patient can be treated successfully.

In two studies, Middaugh and colleagues (Middaugh, Woods, Kee, Harden, & Peters, 1991; Middaugh, Kee, King, Peters, & Herman, 1992) compared the performance of older (55–78 years, mean age = 62 and 63 years) and younger (29–48 years, mean age = 37 and 38 years) patients with chronic, nonmalignant pain in learning physiological self-regulation skills as taught in the biofeedback component of a multidisciplinary CPRP. Diagnoses varied, but over 70% were musculoskeletal, cervical, or low back pain for both age groups. Older and younger patients were treated together in a small-group format. The biofeedback component consisted of progressive muscle relaxation with EMG and skin temperature monitoring, diaphragmatic breathing, and EMG biofeedback training to teach improved control of muscles in the areas of pain.

In both of the Middaugh et al. studies, older pain patients were able to learn the physiological self-regulation skills as taught in the biofeedback protocol. Both age groups showed significant and similar increases in digital skin temperature and decreases in respiration rate. Moreover, both age groups showed similar improvements on measures of muscle control. There was no evidence that the pain symptoms of the older patients were more "fixed" or less amenable to change. The older patients also achieved significant reductions in pain ratings in response to the multidisciplinary CPRP as a whole, and these reductions equaled or exceeded those of the younger patients treated in the same program.

These studies are very instructive. The findings demonstrate that biofeedback and related physiological self-regulation therapies can be used effectively with older pain populations. Problems, when they arise, may primarily indicate a need for appropriate modification of treatment protocols to accommodate older individuals.

Chronic Pain Rehabilitation Programs

A number of recent studies from multidisciplinary CPRPs, including our own, are beginning to provide good information on pretreatment status, treatment acceptance, and treatment outcome in older pain patients who are referred to these comprehensive programs. CPRPs offer a structured combination of psychological and physical rehabilitation therapies that are designed to teach the patient how to manage chronic nonmalignant pain. The goals are to minimize pain, increase physical function, and improve psychological well-being, while reducing reliance on health care providers and pain-related medications.

In times of increasing attention to treatment cost, it is valid to consider whether CPRPs are appropriate and effective for the geriatric pain patient. Referring physicians often assume that these relatively comprehensive and rigorous rehabilitation programs will not be effective with older individuals, because older patients are likely to have relatively permanent physical problems (e.g., degenerative joint disease) that may limit their capacity to improve. Physicians may also assume that older individuals will not accept the CPRP approach, but will instead seek a medical solution to their pain.

The studies in this section address these issues. These studies are considered prospective, in that systematic research data were collected as part of planned treatment outcome studies. However, none of these studies were originally designed to compare treatment outcome for older versus younger age groups, which were defined post hoc. Nevertheless, these studies are far more rigorous and informative than the studies discussed earlier in the chapter.

Sorkin et al. (1990) compared older and younger pain patients referred to their multimodal CPRP on pretreatment physical and psychological status, as well as rates of treatment admission and treatment completion. Treatment outcome was not reported. The authors compared 26 consecutive patients aged 65 or older (mean age = 72.5 years) with 26 randomly selected patients aged 35 or younger (mean age = 27.7 years). Since a disproportionate number of patients in the older group were female (19, vs. 7 males), the younger group was also matched for gender. Both groups were heterogeneous with respect to diagnosis. Neuropathic pain syndrome was the most frequent diagnosis in the older group (35%), and myofascial pain syndrome was most frequent for the younger group (42%). All subjects were given the same orientation to the program and the same physical and psychological evaluations. Patients were offered 6–8 weeks of individual therapy that included medication management, physical therapy, and cognitive-behavioral pain management. The study excluded those whose primary need was for alternative treatment, such as surgery or psychotherapy. Older and younger patients were very similar in the proportion who were offered multidisciplinary treatment, the proportion who accepted treatment, and the number who completed this treatment. These findings are in agreement with H. Leventhal, Leventhal, and Schafer's (1992) observation that older patients are as compliant with health care procedures as younger patients, if not more so.

The older group in the Sorkin et al. (1990) study had a significantly higher rate of abnormal physical findings on medical examination, particularly with respect to identified neurological symptoms. No age-related differences were found on psychological examination. The older and younger groups had comparable self-reported levels of pain severity, emotional distress, disability attributable to pain, and general activity, as measured by the West Haven–Yale Multidimensional Pain Inventory (Kerns, Turk, & Rudy, 1985). This study provides clear evidence that older pain patients will accept and complete a multidisciplinary CPRP as often as younger pain patients, when this treatment option is offered. Athough older pain patients may have more pathophysiology than younger patients, this difference may not be as important as the similarities in the intensity of pain and the impact of pain on the individuals' lives.

Treatment outcome data are available from two published studies that have systematically compared groups of older and younger pain patients participating in the same treatment programs (Cutler, Fishbain, Rosomoff, & Rosomoff, 1994; Middaugh, Levin, Kee, Barchiesi, & Roberts, 1988). Both programs included physical therapy, occupational therapy, psychology, vocational counseling, and medication management (including drug detoxification) in a rehabilitation setting.

Cutler et al., (1994) examined pretreatment status and treatment outcome in 470 pain patients treated in their program over a period of years. Patients were divided into three age groups, with 191 (40.4%) aged 21–44 years, 126 (26.6%) aged 45–64 years, and 153 (32.3%) aged 65–79 years. A higher proportion of the oldest (geriatric) subjects were female and had a gradual, rather than a traumatic, onset of pain. Examination of the medical records for a small subsample of each age group showed a higher incidence of physical findings such as spinal stenosis and osteoporosis in the older age group, but these findings are limited by the very small number of cases sampled ($n = 19, 14$, and 11 for the three age groups, respectively). All patients participated, as either inpatients or outpatients, in a 4-week multimodal CPRP.

The data were first examined to determine whether the geriatric group improved with treatment. The oldest age group improved ($p < .05$) on 37 of 43 self-report rating scales obtained at admission and discharge. The data were then examined to determine whether the geriatric group responded as well as the young and middle-aged groups. The age groups were found to differ from one another at admission. Surprisingly, the geriatric group was the least impaired, as indicated by better scores than either the middle-aged or the young group on 62% of the 43 measurement scales at admission. The middle-aged group was the most impaired. Because of this finding, analyses of covariance were used to compare age groups on extent of change from admission to discharge. Only 6 of 43 measures showed significant age-related differences in extent of improvement. The geriatric group showed less improvement in ability to stand without pain and ability to perform three trunk movements. The geriatric group showed greater improvement on two measures of compliance with the exercise program.

The Cutler et al. (1994) study indicates that geriatric pain patients respond well to the CPRP treatment approach. Older patients not only improved, but made gains equal to those of younger patients participating in the same program on most measures. Older patients may also have been more compliant. This study is unusual in two respects: the high percentage of geriatric patients, and their superior performance on the research measures at admission. The authors suggest that these findings may be attributable to the program's location near large retirement communities in Florida. Their geriatric group may not be representative of geriatric pain patients as a whole. On the other hand, the high percentage of geriatric patients treated in this program (32.3%) may be an accurate indicator of the need for pain management services in the geriatric population.

Middaugh et al. (1988) compared pretreatment status and treatment outcome for 17 consecutive older patients (aged 55–78 years, mean = 62.4 years) and 20 consecutive younger patients (aged 29–48 years, mean = 38.5 years) treated in a CPRP. Age 55 was selected as the starting point for the older group, because this is the point at which retirement first becomes socially acceptable and treatment goals begin to change accordingly. It is also the age at which vocationally oriented pain rehabilitation programs tend to exclude many individuals. The age range for the younger group was selected to provide a comparison group that, according to the literature, would be expected to benefit optimally from a CPRP (i.e., patients in their 30s and 40s; Painter et al., 1980). On the basis of an initial evaluation, patients were assigned to an inpatient program for 3–4 weeks or an outpatient program for two mornings a week for 8 weeks. The two treatment formats had the same content, but differed in time frame (condensed vs. extended) and frequency of supervision (daily vs. twice a week). Older and younger patients were treated together in a small-group format (three to four patients per group), which ensured equivalent treatment regardless of age. Patients had varied diagnoses, but over 75% in both age groups had chronic cervical and/or low back pain. A higher proportion of older patients were female (75% vs. 45%) and inpatient (59% vs. 35%). Data were obtained at evaluation and again at follow-up, 6 to 12 months after discharge.

Middaugh et al. (1988) included seven quantitative measures related to treatment goals. These measures were analyzed separately, and also combined into a summary score that was used to place each individual in (1) a clinical impairment category prior to treatment ("marked," "moderate," or "minimal" impairment) and (2) a clinical outcome category following treatment ("failure," "moderate success," or "marked success"). An effort was made to ensure that these measures were applicable to both age groups. For example, "work" was measured as the sum of hours per week spent in housework, yardwork, volunteer work, paid employment, and school.

Comparison of the two age groups at evaluation indicated that the older patients had a higher level of health care utilization ($p < .002$) and averaged nearly four times as many physician visits, emergency room visits, and hospital days in the previous year as the younger group. Given the exploratory nature of the study, two other findings were considered relevant. Older patients worked 44% fewer hours ($p < .07$), indicating a lower level of productive physical activity. Older patients also took 76% more pain-related medications ($p < .06$) than younger patients. This difference in medication was considered to be clinically significant, since older individuals are known to be more sensitive to pain medications and need less medication than younger individuals to achieve equivalent pharmacological effects (Cohen, 1986; Kaiko et al., 1982; Kwentus et al., 1985). Older patients are also more susceptible to negative complications of medication use (Willcox, Himmelstein, & Woolhandler, 1994). The two age groups did not differ on self-reported pain ratings, "uptime" (time spent out of a reclining position), walking tolerance, or Symptom Checklist 90 (SCL-90) scores prior to treatment.

Middaugh et al. (1988) also compared treatment outcome for the two age groups. Both age groups improved ($p < .05$) from evaluation to follow-up on all measures except the SCL-90 (on which neither improved). The only age-related difference in treatment outcome was a larger reduction in health care utilization for the older group ($p < .001$). Since the older group included a high percentage of women, gender was tested, and no differences were found on outcome measures. The most interesting finding was that the older patients were able to decrease their use of pain-related medications by an average of 93%, and, at the same time, to decrease their pain intensity and increase their physical activity. On the basis of the summary score, 82% of older patients were categorized as having marked impairment prior to treatment as compared with 65% of younger patients, suggesting that the older patients were more clinically impaired in this study. Nevertheless, success rates were very similar for the two age groups at a 6- to 12-month follow-up, with 76% of older patients and 70% of younger patients categorized as achieving moderate or marked success.

The findings of the three studies discussed in this section provide substantial evidence that multidisciplinary CPRPs are well accepted by older patients who are offered this treatment option. Two of these studies have documented that older pain patients make clinical gains that are not only substantial, but similar to the clinical gains made by younger pain patients treated in the same program. This was found whether the comparisons were made at discharge (Cutler et al., 1994) or 6–12 months after discharge (Middaugh et al., 1988). These findings are somewhat limited because of differences between age groups on factors such as gender, diagnosis, and inpatient versus outpatient treatment format. These problems need to be addressed in studies that are specifically designed, in advance of data collection, to compare pretreatment status and treatment outcome in older and younger pain patients. Our research group has recently completed such a study, and these data are presented in the second half of this chapter.

ASSESSMENT AND TREATMENT OF THE OLDER PAIN PATIENT: SELECTED CLINICAL ISSUES

In the remainder of this chapter, we focus on selected clinical issues that often arise in the course of evaluation, admission, and treatment of the older pain patient. The information in this section comes primarily from a series of research studies on geriatric chronic pain that have been completed recently at our CPRP and are in preparation for publication. Some of this research has been presented in preliminary form at conferences. This information is supplemented with additional clinical information on assessment and treatment of the older pain patient, based on the experience of our clinical team and others who have worked with this interesting population.

Age Bias as a Factor in Admission

As noted earlier in this chapter, there is considerable research evidence that older patients who are offered a multidisciplinary CPRP accept this treatment option and achieve success rates comparable to those of younger individuals treated in the same program. It is now relevant to raise the following additional questions. How widely available is this treatment option for the older pain patient? How common are age requirements for admission? Is there an age bias that reduces the likelihood of admission for the older pain patient?

In a study designed to address this issue (Kee, Middaugh, Redpath, McCabe, & Brena, 1995), 96 CPRPs accredited in 1991 by the Commission on Accreditation of Rehabilitation Facilities (2500 N. Pantano Road, Tucson, Arizona 85715) were contacted by telephone and provided information on admissions policies. No program reported having admission criteria that excluded individuals above a specific upper age limit. However, 6.3% of programs did exclude patients with no chance of return to work and the same percentage gave the age of their oldest admitted patient as under 60 years. These findings indicate that although age was not used as an overt criterion for exclusion, some programs were effectively unavailable to most geriatric patients because of indirect age-related criteria, such as a requirement for vocational goals.

The same 96 programs were then asked to complete a written questionnaire, and 60 (62.5%) did so. This questionnaire had brief descriptions of eight individual patients that provided information on the medical, psychological, and social status of each patient. On the basis of this information, and under the assumption that funding was available, each of the eight patients was to be rated on two 100-mm visual analogue scales reflecting (1) likelihood of admission ("What is the likelihood that this patient would be admitted to your program?") and (2) prognosis if admitted ("How would you rate this patient's chances for making long-term clinical improvement in your program?"). All eight patients were older chronic pain patients aged 62 to 83 years (mean = 69 years; four males, four females) who had been admitted and treated successfully (with 6- to 12-month follow-up) in our CPRP (Middaugh et al., 1988). However, two descriptions were generated for each patient; these were identical except that one gave the individual's true age while the other gave a younger stated age (36–52 years, mean = 47 years), with a few minor changes in biographical data (e.g., years of marriage) that were needed to correspond to the younger age. Patients were rated as less likely to be admitted and less likely to benefit (by an average of 15%) when their true, older age was given than when a younger age was stated ($p < .0001$). These findings point to a significant age bias and suggest that age, in and of itself, is indeed a factor that limits access to CPRP treatment for older pain patients.

Another factor is likely to limit access to CPRP treatment for older pain patients. Of the 96 programs examined in the Middaugh et al. (1993) study, 41% served only outpatients. We have found, in two separate studies comparing older (aged 55+) and younger patients referred to our CPRP, that older pain patients are more likely to require inpatient treatment. In a study described earlier in this chapter (Middaugh et al., 1988), we found that older pain patients were 1.68 times as likely to be treated on an inpatient basis. That is, 59% of older patients were treated as inpatients, as compared with 35% of younger patients. However, two factors may have encouraged inpatient treatment of the older pain patient: (1) relatively poor Medicare coverage of outpatient treatment and good coverage for inpatient care, and (2) lack of convenient hotel and day program options for out-of-town patients.

These problems were corrected in a second study that is described in more detail below (Pawlick, Middaugh, Kee, & Nicholson, 1995). An effort was made to treat as many patients as possible on an outpatient basis. Low-cost hotel rooms were made available for out-of-town patients; research funds were available to cover gaps in coverage for outpatient treatment; and objective criteria were established for inpatient admission. These criteria were (1) need for 24-hour medical supervision of medication reductions and/or concurrent medical conditions; and (2) low uptime or physical deconditioning to an extent that precluded outpatient participation. Essentially, these were patients who could not be safely treated as outpatients or did not have the physical capacity to attend as outpatients. As a result of these changes, a lower percentage of both age groups were treated as inpatients in our second study (44.4% of older and 26.1% of younger patients aged 30–45). Yet older patients still required inpatient treatment 1.70 times as often as younger patients. This ratio was virtually identical for the two studies.

These two studies suggest that CPRPs that accept only individuals who can participate on an outpatient basis (41% of programs in our survey) will disproportionately reject older pain patients (17 older for every 10 younger). The low availability of inpatient programs is therefore a major factor that currently limits access to CPRP treatment for the older pain patient. This is a matter of serious concern, since national trends are leading toward major reductions in inpatient care. If home-based treatment strategies are developed as a substitute for inpatient care, the older pain patient will require such services almost twice as often. If such substitutes are not as effective, the older pain patient will be disproportionately affected.

Psychological Assessment

CPRPs begin with an evaluation process that typically includes psychological assessment. Accurate assessment is important in matching available treatment options to the individual patient's needs, and thus contributing to successful treatment outcome. It is relevant to consider whether the procedures that are currently used to evaluate younger chronic pain patients are equally valid for older pain patients, and whether additional procedures are needed to screen for problems (e.g., dementia) that may be largely confined to the older pain population.

Most standard psychological tests, including those commonly used to evaluate psychological status in pain patients, are valid for use in older patients. For example, the sample used to develop test norms for the Minnesota Multiphasic Personality Inventory-2 (MMPI-2) includes older individuals (17.4% aged 60+ years), and an examination of subgroups based on age has found that separate norms are not needed for different age groups (Graham, 1990; Keller & Butcher, 1991).

Assessment of pain does not entail different procedures or different interpretation of test results for older individuals. It is a common assumption that pain sensitivity decreases in the elderly, in much the same way that hearing and vision decrease with age. However, this assumption is not supported by the experimental pain literature, which indicates that pain is well preserved in advanced age for healthy individuals. Pain, the suffering associated with pain, and the qualitative properties of pain (e.g., sensations of burning, aching, stabbing) are not demonstrably different in the elderly individual (Harkins & Price, 1992, 1993). Simple subjective measures of pain such as a visual analogue scale (McCormack, Horne, & Sheather, 1988) are valid for older as well as younger pain patients (Price & Harkins, 1992). These findings are also supported by the clinical studies reviewed in this chapter, which report similar pain levels for older and younger chronic pain patients (Middaugh et al., 1988; Sorkin et al., 1990; see also Table 14.2, below).

Assessment of cognitive status is a standard component of psychological evaluation for all ages. For the younger pain patient, cognitive deficits may result from head injuries received, for example, in automobile accidents. The older pain patient may have cognitive impairment as a result of dementia, which occurs with increasing frequency with increasing age. If the psychologal interview suggests problems with mental status, we obtain further information through interview of a family member or friend and mental status testing. The Mini-Mental Status Examination (Folstein, Folstein, & McHugh, 1975) and subtests of the Wechsler Memory Scale—Revised (Lichtenberg & Christensen, 1992) have norms for older individuals and can be administered quickly to determine the need for more detailed neuropsychological or neurological evaluation.

The assessment of cognitive status should also include an appraisal of transient, reversible factors that can impair mental function. Patients who are anxious, agitated, or severely depressed, and those who are overly sedated or mentally confused because of medications such as narcotics, barbiturates, or benzodiazepines, can present as cognitively impaired. The older patient in particular is susceptible to side effects of pain-related medications (Rummans, Davis, Morse, & Ivnik, 1993; Wilcox et al., 1994). Pain and fatigue, aggravated by the rigors of the evaluation process itself, can complicate the problem. These factors make accurate evaluation of cognitive status difficult. When this is the case, and the patient is otherwise an appropriate candidate for a CPRP, our approach is to admit the patient for a 1-week treatment trial, usually on an inpatient basis. The members of the pain team are then able to provide detailed information on the individual patient's ability to learn new information, retain this information, and put behavioral changes into practice. The questionable older pain patient often performs surprisingly well, once ancillary problems (e.g., inappropriate medications) are addressed.

There is a serious risk of overinterpreting mild cognitive problems. Several thought-provoking recent studies illustrate the pitfalls associated with cognitive testing of older pain patients, and strongly caution against routine or simplistic exclusion on the basis of test scores alone.

Bruce et al. (1992) compared the cognitive profiles of 36 elderly patients (aged 60–86 years, mean = 69 years) who were treated in a CPRP at the Mayo Clinic with normative data for individuals aged 55–97 (Peterson, Smith, Kokmen, Ivnik, & Tangelos, 1992). Although 28% of the older pain group tested as mildly cognitively impaired and 11% tested as moderately impaired, most of these patients were able to complete and benefit from the CPRP.

A study of the cognitive effects of drug dependence in the elderly by Rummans et al. (1993) found that older individuals (aged 55+) with benzodiazepine dependence had significant deficits in ability to learn and remember new material on neuropsychological tests administered 6–10 days after detoxification. No such deficit was found in a comparison group undergoing alcohol detoxification or in a drug-free control group. The authors conclude that in older individuals, benzodiazepine use can produce significant memory impairments that extend into a drug-free period. This finding is particularly relevant in light of a recent study by our research group (Redpath, Middaugh, Kee, & Levin, 1992), which examined medication use in 61 older (aged 55–85) and 61 younger (aged 30–50) chronic pain patients. The older patients had a 50% greater use of pain-related medications in general ($p < .01$), and, surprisingly, a 110% greater use of benzodiazepines in particular ($p < .02$).

The assessment of depression also raises an important issue. It is often assumed that depression is an especially prominent feature of chronic pain in older individuals, yet recent research does not support this assumption. Older individuals in the general population do tend to have higher scores on self-report depression scales; however, this appears to be attributable to endorsement of items related to physical symptoms and somatic complaints, rather than to actual differences in mood (Bolla-Wilson & Bleeker, 1989). This finding suggests that older individuals will not necessarily have higher scores on self-report depression scales when testing involves patient groups (e.g., chronic pain patients) in which physical symptoms are prominent in younger as well as older individuals. Indeed, a recent study of depression in chronic pain patients by Haythornthwaite, Sieber, and Kerns (1991) found that depressed pain patients were more likely to be younger. Our research group has noted this as well (see Table 14.2, below).

When the older pain patient is depressed, functional disability is likely to play an important role. Williamson and Schultz (1992) found that physical disability accounted for a greater proportion of the variance in depression in community-dwelling elderly than in nursing home elderly, independent of reported pain, which was prevalent and equivalent in both groups. The authors have hypothesized that those who live in the community are more affected by functional disabilities, since they are more responsible for their own daily activities, including social and recreational events. This suggests that treatments that are designed to improve functional ability in the elderly pain patient, such as a CPRP, may decrease depression even if pain levels remain unchanged.

Measures of Treatment Success

Any attempt to evaluate the effectiveness of CPRPs in treating older pain patients must also address the issue of how to define and measure treatment success. As noted earlier in the literature review, older patients will not appear to be successful if the success criteria are not age-appropriate—for example, if success is based disproportionately on achievement of vocational goals. If the outcome measures are appropriate for older as well as younger participants, then we can proceed to ask, and answer, the clinically relevant question: Do older and younger pain patients differ with respect to the nature, the extent, or the durability of the clinical improvements achieved with treatment?

Our research group has addressed this question in a recently completed prospective study (Pawlick, 1994; Pawlick et al., 1995), using a set of treatment outcome measures that were developed to compare older and younger patients and pilot-tested in an earlier study (Middaugh et al., 1988). These measures are (1) quantitative; (2) closely related to specific treatment goals; and (3) designed to give patients credit for clinically relevant gains in six different pain-related problem areas without overemphasizing any single area of improvement, such as work or pain reduction. This approach acknowledges that individual pain patients (both within and between age groups) can differ widely at admission in the nature and the extent of their pain-related problems, and can take different paths to treatment success as a result. The six outcome measures are described in detail below.

In the present study, only patients with chronic musculoskeletal, cervical, and/or low back pain were included. The older group consisted of 23 consecutive patients aged 55 or older (range 55–84). An equal number of younger patients (aged 30–45) were selected consecutively until the number of outpatients approximated that of the older group; at that point, only those who met the requirements for inpatient treatment (see "Age Bias as a Factor in Admission," above) were added to the study. This process produced two groups that were well balanced by treatment mode and, without additional selection, also balanced by gender (see Table 14.1). As might be expected, the older group had a significantly longer duration of pain symptoms. For the older group, pain was also less likely to have a traumatic onset or to be job-related.

Older and younger patients were admitted and treated together in a small-group format (three to four patients per group), which ensured equivalent treatment regardless of age. Inpatient stays lasted 3–4 weeks. Outpatients participated 5 days a week for 3–4 weeks or three mornings a week for 6 weeks. Treatment content was the same for all three formats and included the following components: cognitive and behavioral psychology, biofeedback, physical therapy, occupational therapy, and medical management. Additional activities, such as vocational counseling and marital therapy, were included as appropriate on an individual basis.

Comparisons of pretreatment status and treatment outcome for the two age groups were based on multiple quantitative measures obtained at evaluation, discharge, 1-month follow-up, and 1-year follow-up. Selected data are presented here and in a later section of this chapter (see "Response to Treatment Components," below). The primary outcome measures are closely related to the clinical goals of our CPRP, which are to increase physical function and to decrease pain, pain-related medication, and emotional distress. These measures all have a quantitative value that can be used for statistical comparisons and to

TABLE 14.1. Patient Characteristics

	Younger group (n = 23)		Older group (n = 23)	
	Mean	SD	Mean	SD
Age (years)	38.5	4.3	66.2[a]	8.1
Education (years)	11.4	2.8	13.3	3.9
Pain duration (months)	33.9	34.9	97.8[a]	102.2
Number of surgeries (pain-related)	0.5	0.9	1.2	1.6
Number of concurrent medical diagnoses	1.1	0.4	1.4	1.1
	Percent		Percent	
Female	47.8%		52.2%	
Traumatic onset	87.0%		30.4%[b]	
Job-related injury	65.2%		13.0%[b]	
Inpatient treatment mode	43.5%		47.8%	

Note. From Pawlick et al. (1995).
[a] $p < .05$ (univariate analysis of variance).
[b] $p < .05$ (chi square).

calculate percentage of change (see Table 14.2, below). In addition, each measure has an objectively defined criterion level that can be used to determine whether an individual patient has met (or has not met) each of six clinical goals. For each measure, the criterion can be met in either one of two ways: (1) by achieving a specified score (e.g., an uptime of 12 hours per day); or (2) by achieving a specified percentage of change, with a required minimum score for some measures. The minimum score is set to allow credit for meaningful increases from very low levels (e.g., a 100% increase in uptime from 4 hours to 8 hours per day), but to exclude gains that are clinically irrelevant (e.g., a 100% increase in uptime from 1 hour to 2 hours per day). In addition, the number of criteria met (out of a possible six) serves as a summary score (0–6) that is used to define pretreatment impairment and posttreatment success for the individual patient and to calculate a success rate for the treatment groups (see Table 14.3, below). This approach provides a method for quantifying both pretreatment status and treatment outcome in terms that

TABLE 14.2. Treatment Outcome Measures

Measure	Younger group (n = 23)			Older group (n = 23)		
	Pre	Post	Change	Pre	Post	Change
Pain rating						
Present	63.1	34.7	45.0%	48.9	33.3	31.9%
Minimum	31.0	20.9	32.6%	27.4	17.1	37.6%
Maximum	86.3	58.7	27.6%	84.7	65.7	22.4%
Medication (MQS score)	9.1	7.8	14.3%	13.8	6.7	51.4%
Emotional Distress (BDI score)	15.9	10.3	35.2%	12.1	7.8	35.5%
Walking tolerance (minutes)	38.3	50.0	30.5%	30.6	54.8	79.1%
Daily uptime (hours)	13.5	15.7	16.3%	13.1	14.9	13.7%
Work, job/home (hours per week)	21.0	29.5	40.5%	16.7	22.0	31.7%

Note. From Pawlick et al. (1995).

TABLE 14.3. Clinical Classification of Patients, Based on Number of Criteria Met

	Pretreatment		
	Marked impairment (0–2 met)	Moderate impairment (3 met)	Mild impairment (4–6 met)
Older	56.5%	21.75%	21.8%
Younger	69.6%	17.4%	13.0%
	Posttreatment		
	Failure (0–2 met)	Partial success (3 met)	Success (4–6 met)
Older	13.1%	21.7%	65.2%
Younger	8.7%	13.0	78.3%
	1-year follow-up		
	Failure (0–2 met)	Partial success (3 met)	Success (4–6 met)
Older	12.5%	31.2%	56.3%
Younger	21.4%	7.2%	71.4%

Note. From Pawlik et al. (1995).

are clinically relevant, directly related to program goals, and equally applicable to older and younger age groups. The six outcome measures and their criterion levels are as follows:

1. *Pain Rating.* Self-reported pain is measured on three 100-mm visual analogue scales representing present pain, minimum pain in the previous week, and maximum pain in the previous week (retrospective report). The criteria are ratings of 30 or less, or decreases of 30%, on two of the three scales.

2. *Medication.* The Medication Quantification Scale (MQS; Steedman et al., 1992) is used to quantify intake of pain-related medications. The criterion is an MQS total score of 5 or less, or a 50% decrease.

3. *Emotional Distress.* The Beck Depression Inventory (BDI; Beck & Steer, 1987; Schuster & Smith, 1994) is used. The criterion is a score of 11 or less, or a 20% decrease.

4. *Walking Tolerance.* The amount of time (up to 120 minutes) the patient reports being able to walk without taking a break is determined. The criterion is 45 minutes or more, or a 50% increase with a 30-minute minimum.

5. *Daily Uptime.* The number of total hours per day spent up, defined as being out of a reclining position, is assessed. The criterion is 12 hours per day or more, or a 100% increase with an 8 hour minimum.

6. *Work.* The total number of hours per week spent in paid employment, housework, yardwork, volunteer work, and school is determined (summed for all categories). The criterion is 25 hours per week or more, or a 100% increase with a 14-hour minimum.

Table 14.2 presents the quantitative values for these six treatment outcome measures at evaluation (pre) and discharge (post) and the corresponding percentages of change for the older and younger groups in our outcome study. For the variable "work," the posttreatment data were obtained 1 month after discharge, since most patients could not work during treatment. Both age groups made significant improvements from evaluation to discharge on all six measures ($p < .01$), with no age-related differences. This indicated a substantial and similar response to treatment for older and younger patients.

Two findings in Table 14.2 are of clinical interest, even though they were not statistically significant. One finding is that the mean BDI score was numerically lower for the older group. This is in agreement with the findings of Haythornthwaite et al. (1991) and indicates that depression is not a greater problem for older than for younger pain patients. The second finding is that the mean MQS score was 51.6% higher for the older group ($p < .10$). This is in agreement with the findings in our earlier study (Middaugh et al., 1988) and points to probable overmedication of older pain patients, since geriatric pharmacologists (Cohen, 1986; Kaiko et al., 1982) recommend that substantially lower doses be prescribed for older individuals because of their lower metabolic rate (i.e., a lower dose provides equal analgesic effects). This interpretation is supported by the success of the older group in markedly reducing medication scores while increasing physical activity and also reducing pain.

Table 14.3 presents the data on the summary measure—the number of criteria met, which provides a score from 0 to 6 for each patient as an index of overall clinical status before and after treatment. Before treatment, the number of criteria met is used to place each subject in one of three impairment categories. The majority of patients in both age groups were in the marked-impairment category prior to treatment. After treatment, the same variable is used to place each subject in one of three treatment outcome categories. The success rates for older (65.2%) and younger (78.3%) patients were very similar. There were no differences in the distribution of older and younger patients within these categories as tested by chi-square.

Table 14.3 also includes treatment outcome data for a subset of these patients (16 older and 14 younger) for whom 1-year follow-up data are now available (Pawlick, Middaugh, Kee, & Nicholson, 1994). This subset ($n = 30$) did not differ from those lost to follow-up with respect to subject characteristics or pretreatment measures. One-year success rates remained high, at 56.3% for older and 71.4% for younger pain patients, with no significant difference in success rates for the two age groups. However, analysis of all six measures across all three time points (admission, discharge, and 1-year follow-up) for this subset did find two significant age-related differences, one in favor of each age group ($p < .05$). Younger patients nearly doubled the number of hours worked per week from discharge to 1-year follow-up, while the older group maintained but did not improve their discharge work levels. However, older patients maintained low scores on the BDI from discharge to 1-year follow-up, while the younger group regressed to pretreatment BDI values.

This controlled, prospective outcome study strongly supports the effectiveness of multidisciplinary CPRPs for older pain patients. Older and younger patients entered and completed treatment at equal rates. At discharge, the two age groups rated their overall improvement as nearly identical (older = 4.1, younger = 4.0 on a 0–6 Likert scale on which 3 = "moderately improved"). When the groups were equated for relevant patient characteristics such as gender, diagnostic category, and inpatient versus outpatient treatment format, older patients were relatively similar to younger patients on measures of pain and pain-related dysfunction prior to treatment. Older and younger patients also showed significant and similar improvements from admission to discharge on commonly used measures of pain, physical function, and psychological distress. Furthermore, this improvement was well maintained by older patients at a 1-year follow-up, indicating that the older pain patient is not necessarily subject to deterioration and decline over time. Younger patients did show greater long-term improvement on our measure of work, whereas older patients achieved more lasting improvement in emotional distress.

Response to Treatment Components

There is now considerable evidence, from the study just discussed and from others reviewed in this chapter, that older individuals with chronic pain respond well to multi-disciplinary CPRPs and enjoy overall success rates similar to those of younger partici-pants. However, a number of questions can still be raised. There is a common percep-tion that the older pain patient is likely to be harder to treat in some way. For example, the older pain patient may respond well to a CPRP as a whole, but may require extra clinician time and effort, may need extensive modification of treatment protocols, or may perform poorly in one or two components of the CPRP.

In an effort to address this issue, we asked each patient in our clinical outcome study (described in the preceding section) and each clinician who treated that patient to com-plete a number of rating scales at discharge, in order to report the benefits and prob-lems they perceived for each treatment component. A number of objective measures were also included in the research protocol, to permit us to evaluate whether older patients had a different response than younger patients to the five major treatment components of our multidisciplinary CPRP. Selected data are presented below.

Rating Scales

For each of the five major treatment components, the appropriate clinician was asked to rate (on a 0–6 Likert scale) each patient at the time of discharge on his or her perfor-mance in that component. The clinician rated the patient on (1) compliance, (2) amount of clinician time and attention required, (3) need for modification of treatment proto-cols, and (4) extent of improvement in that component. There were no differences between the two age groups on these clinician ratings. The patient was asked to rate (also on a 0–6 scale) the extent of benefit he or she derived from each component. As shown in Table 14.4, older patients rated themselves as receiving considerable benefit from each of the five treatment components and did not differ from younger patients in their self-reports.

These findings indicate that the clinicians' experience in treating these older chronic pain patients was a positive one. The older patients responded well and were not harder to treat than younger patients participating in the same component. Furthermore, no single treatment component appeared to pose a special problem for the older patients as a group. From the point of view of the older patients, and also the clinicians treating them, each of the treatment components seemed beneficial, as indicated by a rating of 3.0 (moderate benefit) or higher.

Physical Therapy Component

The physical therapy component included an extensive daily exercise program with stretch-ing and strengthening exercises and aerobic conditioning through walking, stationary cycling, and/or swimming. Figure 14.1 shows the average number of different strength-ening exercises and the average number of repetitions per exercise that were included in the daily exercise program for the two age groups at discharge. Both age groups began at

TABLE 14.4. Clinician and Patient Ratings of Benefit Received from Five Treatment Components

Component	Clinician ratings		Patient ratings	
	Older	Younger	Older	Younger
Physical therapy	4.6	4.7	4.3	3.8
Occupational therapy	3.6	3.6	4.7	4.5
Biofeedback	4.2	4.4	4.5	3.8
Psychology	4.7	3.7	4.5	3.6
Medical management	3.1	2.6	3.0	3.6

Note. On the 0–6 scale used, 0 = "no improvement," 3 = "moderate improvement," 6 = "maximum improvement."

admission with three repetitions of relatively few exercises, and both groups progressed to an extensive daily exercise program by discharge. However, the discharge exercise program of the older patients had significantly fewer exercises ($p < .01$) and somewhat fewer repetitions of each exercise (n.s.). The number of strengthening exercises in the daily program (11.6) multiplied by the number of repetitions of each exercise (16.2) (Figure 14.1) indicates that the older group performed, on average, 188 strengthening repetitions per day. This was 31.4% less than the younger group's average of 274. These findings are in agreement with the exercise physiology literature, which reports both (1) a gradual loss of muscle strength and flexibility with normal aging, particularly after age 60; and (2) a substantial capacity for relative increases in muscle strength, endurance, and range of motion with exercise programs in geriatric individuals (Frontera et al., 1988; Stamford, 1988).

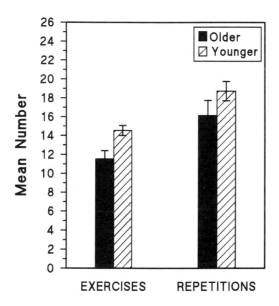

FIGURE 14.1. The mean number of strengthening exercises and repetitions of each exercise in the daily exercise program of older and younger pain patients at discharge.

Our clinical experience has been that older patients make steady progress, but at a slower rate and with a lower ceiling, than younger patients. Older patients are also more prone to pain flare-ups if their exercise program is increased too quickly. We have found that a relatively modest exercise program (as few as 5 repetitions of 10 strengthening exercises and 5 minutes on a stationary bicycle, for some older patients) can produce substantial gains in the ability to perform daily activities.

Occupational Therapy Component

The occupational therapy component focused on the use of correct posture, good body mechanics, and appropriate use of activity–rest cycles (pacing) while performing a wide range of daily activities. The goals were to reduce physical strain, reduce pain flare-ups, and prevent reinjury while increasing daily activities. As shown in Figure 14.2, both age groups showed similar and significant ($p < .01$) improvements in posture from admission to discharge. The posture score is the total number of degrees of postural deviation (in standing), summed for seven quantitative measures included in the Skan-A-Graf Posture Test (available from Reedco Research, 51 N. Fulton St., Auburn, New York 13021). Lower scores indicate better posture (less deviation). The surprising similarity between the two age groups on this measure suggests that a considerable portion of these patients' posture problems were antalgic—that is, adopted by the patients in response to pain. With education and instruction, both age groups were able to resume a more normal posture by discharge (though still far from perfect) without increasing pain.

Clinically, the treatment emphasis in this component was somewhat different for the two age groups. Some of the older patients required detailed and repeated instruction on safe performance of self-care and household activities, with the assistance of

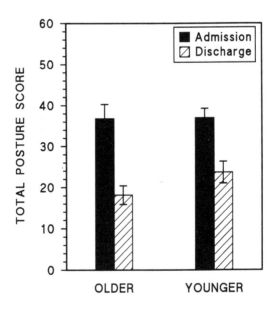

FIGURE 14.2. The mean Skan-A-Graf posture score at admission and discharge for older and younger pain patients. Lower scores indicate improved posture.

adaptive devices. Home visits were often arranged, and the patients' families were educated as well. On the other hand, many of the younger patients needed instruction in work-related activities and methods for correcting poor work station arrangements (ergonomics). Visits to the patients' worksites were arranged if feasible. Usually it was possible to individualize treatment within the small-group format, with added time for home and work visits scheduled separately. Occasionally a group was divided, with one or more members scheduled separately, to meet highly divergent patient needs more effectively.

Biofeedback Component

The biofeedback component was carried out by a physical therapist with certification from the Biofeedback Certification Institute of America (10200 W. 44th Avenue, Suite 304, Wheatridge, Colorado 80033). Patients were taught progressive muscle relaxation and diaphragmatic breathing to reduce widespread muscle bracing. EMG biofeedback was used to correct patterns of muscle overuse and underuse in the areas of pain. These procedures have been described elsewhere (Middaugh & Kee, 1987; Middaugh, Kee, & Nicholson, 1994). The biofeedback performance of older and younger pain patients treated in our multidisciplinary program has been compared in two studies (Middaugh et al., 1991, 1992). In both studies, older patients readily acquired the physiological self-regulation skills that were taught in our biofeedback treatment component.

Figure 14.3 shows data from 59 older and 58 younger pain patients (Middaugh et al., 1992). Digital skin temperature (Figure 14.3A), reflecting peripheral vasodilation, and respiration rate (Figure 14.3B) were recorded in the first and last minute of a 15–minute relaxation practice during the first and last biofeedback session for which these data were available. Both age groups achieved significant ($p < .05$) temperature increases and respiration decreases both within and across sessions. This indicates solid acquisition of the desired physiological responses. The only age-related difference was a higher respiratory rate for the older group across all time points ($p < .05$). That is, the older patients started and ended with a higher respiratory rate than the younger patients, but made equivalent changes during biofeedback training.

We have found that older pain patients also do well in learning improved muscle control. In one subset of patients with chronic cervical pain, for example, 75% of older and 100% of younger patients met EMG training goals for relaxation of the upper trapezius muscle (Middaugh et al., 1991).

Our clinical observations are consistent with the research findings cited above. We find that biofeedback procedures pose no unique problems for older pain patients, who usually enjoy this treatment component. As suggested by the respiration data above, we tend to train for relative change in a desired direction (a slower respiratory rate), rather than to train to a set physiological goal (8–10 breaths per minute), which may be unrealistic for some older patients.

As we have noted in this chapter's review of the literature, hearing loss can be a problem. We find that hearing problems can usually be circumvented with minor adaptations (sitting close to the patient, making good eye contact, speaking slowly) and a little extra time early in the course of treatment. For example, a patient who has difficulty hearing can be provided with a written script to follow while listening to the instructional tape on progressive muscle relaxation. In most cases, once the patient becomes familiar with the script, he or she can hear the tape sufficiently well to carry out homework practice.

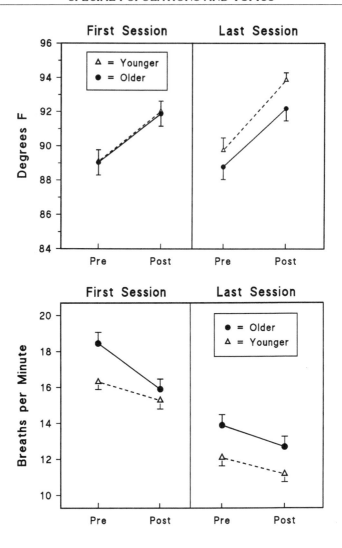

FIGURE 14.3. (A) Digital skin temperature response to biofeedback training in younger and older pain patients. (B) Respiration response to biofeedback training in younger and older pain patients. From Middaugh et al. (1992).

Medical Management Component

The medical management component included diagnostic tests, correction of excessive or inappropriate medication use, and provision of medical interventions as appropriate. The physician also ensured that the pain rehabilitation activities were appropriate for patients with concurrent medical problems such as cardiovascular disease. Patients were encouraged to take control of their treatment and to become less dependent on medical personnel for pain management. As shown in Table 14.1, older and younger patients did not differ significantly at admission on two indicators of medical status: the number of surgeries related to the pain diagnosis, and the number of concurrent medical diagnoses such as diabetes and hypertension.

Response to the medical management component of our CPRP was evaluated in terms of reductions in health care utilization and use of pain-related medications—two factors that are closely related to health care costs. As noted earlier, both older and younger patients were able to reduce their use of pain-related medications from admission to discharge, as measured by the MQS (Table 14.2). Data obtained for 16 older and 14 younger patients at the 1-year follow-up revealed continued low use of pain-related medications, with a mean MQS score of 4.8 for older and 3.9 for younger patients.

Figure 14.4 presents two measures of health care utilization: the number of inpatient hospital days and the number of outpatient visits to health care providers. These data are presented for two time periods—the 12 months preceding evaluation (for 23 older and 23 younger patients), and the 12 months between discharge and 1-year follow-up (for 16 older and 14 younger patients). Older patients did not differ significantly from younger patients at either of the two time periods. Both age groups reported major reductions in health care utilization at the 1-year follow-up, with 71.6% fewer outpatient visits and 84.1% fewer inpatient days for the two age groups combined.

Individuals with chronic pain place a considerable burden on the health care system, and a major outcome goal of treatment programs is to reduce subsequent health care costs. The findings presented above indicate that older as well as younger patients who are treated in CPRPs do learn self-management skills and no longer require extensive assistance from health care providers and medications.

Psychology Component

The psychology component focused on two areas: pain management and communication skills. Pain management included training in appropriate selection and pacing of daily activities, cognitive and behavioral coping strategies, effective problem solving, and

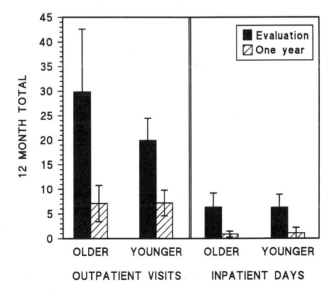

FIGURE 14.4. Mean number of outpatient visits and inpatient days for the 12 months preceding evaluation and the 12 months between discharge and 1-year follow-up. From Pawlick et al. (1994).

stress management. Communication skills included recognition and reduction of pain behaviors and training in assertive communication. Some patients received short-term psychotherapy to address psychological issues that were likely to interfere with treatment progress. The psychologist also met with family members to ensure their good understanding of the treatment program.

The primary age-related difference in psychological status at the time of evaluation was that older patients reported less psychological distress, as defined by a set of intercorrelated variables identified by factor analysis: the BDI; the State Anxiety scale of the State–Trait Anxiety Inventory (Spielberger, Gorsuch, & Lushene, 1970); and the Catastrophizing subscale of the Cognitive Skills Questionnaire (CSQ; Rosenstiel & Keefe, 1983). One potential explanation for this difference in level of psychological distress is the supposed tendency of older patients to bias their reports in a socially desirable manner and to deny psychological distress. This possibility was examined by comparing the two age groups on the MMPI-2 validity subscales. No difference was found ($p > .05$). The older patients were no more likely than younger patients to bias their responses in a socially desirable manner or to deny difficulties. This is an important finding, since many of the assessment and outcome measures in pain research involve self-report.

The differing levels of distress experienced by older and younger patients are most likely related to situational factors, as well as to differences in health care beliefs and attitudes toward illness and pain. E. A. Leventhal and Prohaska (1986), for example, have noted that older persons (aged 60+ years) reported less anger and less fear associated with becoming ill than younger individuals. According to these authors, older patients are more likely than younger patients to anticipate a decline in health, and so are less likely to display emotional distress and self-blame. They are also less likely to seek medical treatment in response to symptoms. In our study, the older group had a much longer duration of pain symptoms, and a high proportion (70% of older vs. 17% of younger) had a gradual onset of pain symptoms (Table 14.1). The emotional impact of pain symptoms and pain-related problems is likely to be very different for those individuals who experience a sudden onset of pain symptoms and have sudden and dramatic changes in life circumstances as a result. In our study, 87% of younger pain patients fell into this category, compared with 30% of older patients. The younger pain patients were therefore more likely to perceive their pain problem as unfair and attributable to unanticipated events that could have been avoided, such as an automobile accident or an injury on the job.

Psychological assessment also included evaluation of two other aspects of chronic pain: coping strategies and social support. We found that older and younger pain patients did not differ on a Coping Skills factor identified by factor analysis (CSQ subtests 1, 2, 3, 4, 5, 7, and 8). This indicates, as suggested earlier by Keefe and Williams (1990), that older and younger patients use similar coping techniques when confronted with a similar stressor, such as chronic pain.

Demographic data and information from the Social Support Questionnaire (SSQ; Sarason, Levine, Basham, & Sarason, 1983) indicated that older pain patients had, on average, fewer persons living in their homes than younger patients did. However, the older patients reported considerable social support from individuals living outside their homes. As a result, the two age groups did not differ with respect to available social support or satisfaction with social support as measured on the SSQ. The SSQ ratings for satisfaction with social support were 5.4 for the older patients and 5.5 for the younger patients. These scores indicate relatively high levels of satisfaction and are comparable to ratings reported by college students. These findings suggest that social support was not a major problem for most older patients in our study population.

Clinically, psychological treatment of the older pain patient often does involve some changes in content and presentation, but does not, on average, involve more clinician time than treatment of the younger pain patient. The psychology sessions, whether carried out on an individual basis or in a small-group format, routinely address the different needs of individual patients. For younger patients, for example, considerable clinical time may be spent dealing with individual problems related to work, legal, or financial issues. For older patients, that clinical time may be used for somewhat slower presentation of information, as well as for review and repetition of pain management principles and their application. We have found that pain management strategies, such as cognitive skills training, guided imagery, and hypnosis, pose no particular problems for the older patients.

Clinical psychology time may also be needed to explore problems the older patient may have with social resources and communication style. For example, older pain patients often have sources of social support available to provide transportation to leisure activities, but may be reluctant to ask for assistance because they do not want to burden others. The therapist should also be alert for any tendency in the older patient to be a "good patient" and minimize pain in order to "please the doctor." The pain team may overlook the "good patient"'s needs because he or she reports doing so well.

Clinical time may also be needed to address the concerns of the older patient and his or her family about the physical and mental changes associated with the aging process. It may be necessary, for example, to counter attitudes such as passive acceptance of pain as an inevitable part of aging. The patient's emotional well-being can be improved substantially by encouraging a more active role in health care, life choices, and daily activities. Family involvement is important for all pain patients, but can be particularly important for older patients. Two or three family sessions over the course of treatment can ensure that a spouse or other family member understands the program principles and can assist the patient with homework assignments and implementation of pain management strategies in the home environment.

CONCLUSIONS

A review of the literature and our own research provide solid evidence that older individuals who have persistent, nonmalignant pain develop multiple pain-related problems that are similar to those of younger individuals faced with this health problem. When offered the opportunity, the older pain patient will accept and benefit from the same psychological therapies that are widely available to the younger pain patient, such as cognitive coping skills training and biofeedback therapy. When admitted to formal, multidisciplinary CPRPs that combine physical rehabilitation with psychological therapies, older patients will perform well in each therapeutic component and will enjoy a program success rate equivalent to that of younger patients with similar diagnoses treated in the same programs. The majority of older patients will maintain good reductions in pain and emotional distress and meaningful improvements in physical function a year after treatment. In addition, older patients will achieve substantial reductions in pain-related health care costs, as indicated by decreases in use of pain-related medications and health care services.

The research presented in this chapter does point to some differences between older and younger pain patients. First, older patients with persistent pain are less likely to be admitted to CPRPs than younger pain patients. Age bias (based on an assumption that older pain patients will not perform well) may reduce the likelihood that older patients will be admitted. In addition, a substantial number of pain programs do not offer treatment formats needed by older pain patients. Programs that do not offer inpatient treatment will disproportionately exclude older pain patients, who, in our two studies, required inpatient treatment considerably more often than younger patients. In addition, outpatient programs that are designed primarily to return patients to work will also exclude many older patients, since few have return-to-work goals.

Second, there is a strong suggestion that older pain patients are overmedicated. Geriatric pharmacologists recommend prescribing substantially lower doses of medications for older individuals, because of their lower metabolic rate (a lower dose provides equal analgesic effects) and higher susceptibility to side effects and drug interactions (Wilcox et al., 1994). Yet we have found in three clinical studies that older pain patients do not take less pain-related medication, but, on average, take 50% more than younger patients. Furthermore, the use of benzodiazepines by older patients appears to be widespread, even though this class of medication is recognized as posing significant hazards for older individuals. Older pain patients can, however, reduce pain-related medications while simultaneously decreasing reported pain and increasing physical function.

Finally, there is evidence from our research and that of Haythornthwaite et al. (1991) that older pain patients tend to be less psychologically distressed than younger pain patients. The gradual onset of symptoms, a lower incidence of work-related injuries (with the attendant financial and legal burdens), and differences in health beliefs may account for the lower levels of distress. Otherwise, older pain patients are very similar to younger pain patients on psychological measures.

In contrast, considerable care must be taken in comparing older and younger pain patients on measures of treatment outcome that are related to physical capacity. Older pain patients perform well on physical aspects of a pain rehabilitation program. They achieve and maintain significant improvements in physical capacity with therapeutic exercise programs. However, they may not attain the same quantitative endpoints as younger patients. We found, for example, that our older patients equaled the younger patients at discharge on two measures that did not reflect strength (i.e., degrees of postural deviation and walking tolerance in minutes). At the same time, younger patients exceeded the older patients on measures related to strength (i.e., the number of strengthening exercises performed at discharge and the hours of work-related activities per week after discharge). Such differences are to be expected, given the decrements in muscle strength and respiratory capacity that occur with normal aging and the optional nature of many work-related activities for many older adults. These differences need to be taken into account when clinicians are measuring treatment outcome and defining treatment success. When this is done, our findings support the observation of Sorkin et al. (1990) that the differences between older and younger chronic pain patients are less important than the similarities.

ACKNOWLEDGMENTS

This research was supported by the National Institute of Disability and Rehabilitation Research (Grant No. H133G90085); by National Institutes of Health Grant No. RR1070 to the Medical University of South Carolina General Clinical Research Center; and by Medical University of South Carolina Institutional Funds for Research (Grant No. 4400).

REFERENCES

Abrahamson, C. F. (1987). Response to the challenge: Effective treatment of the elderly through thermal biofeedback combined with progression relaxation. *Biofeedback and Self-Regulation, 12*, 121–125.

Andersson, H. I., Ejlertsson, G., Leden, I., & Rosenberg, C. (1993). Chronic pain in a geographically defined general population: Studies of differences in age, gender, social class, and pain location. *Clinical Journal of Pain, 9*, 174–182.

Arena, J. G., Hannah, S. L., Bruno, G. M., & Meador, K. J. (1991). Electromyographic biofeedback training for tension headache in the elderly: A prospective study. *Biofeedback and Self-Regulation, 16*, 379–390.

Arena, J. G., Hightower, N. E., & Chang, G. C. (1988). Relaxation therapy for tension headache in the elderly: A prospective study. *Psychology and Aging, 3*, 96–98.

Aronoff, G. M., & Evans, W. O. (1982). The prediction of treatment outcome at a multidisciplinary pain center. *Pain, 14*(1), 67–73.

Beck, A., & Steer, R. (1987). *The Beck Depression Inventory manual.* New York: Harcourt Brace Jovanovich.

Binstock, R. H., & Post, S. G. (1991). Old age and the rationing of health care. In R.H. Binstock & S.G. Post (Eds.), *Too old for health care?* (pp. 1–12). Baltimore: John Hopkins University Press.

Blanchard, E. B., Andrasik, F., Evans, D. D., & Hillhouse, J. (1985). Biofeedback and relaxation treatments for headache in the elderly: A caution and a challenge. *Biofeedback and Self-Regulation, 10*, 69–73.

Bolla-Wilson, K., & Bleeker, M. L. (1989). Absence of depression in elderly adults. *Journal of Gerontology, 44*, 53–55.

Bruce, B. K., Rome, J. D., Malec, J. F., Hodgson, J. E., Suda, K. S., Payne, J. E., & Maruta, T. (1992). *Cognitive impairment: A primary reason for the exclusion of the elderly from chronic pain rehabilitation programs?* Paper presented at the meeting of the American Pain Society, San Diego, CA.

Carstensen, S. L. (1988). The emerging field of behavioral gerontology. *Behavior Therapy, 19*, 259–281.

Cohen, J. L. (1986). Pharmacokinetic changes in ageing. *American Journal of Medicine* (Suppl. 5A), 31–38.

Corey, D. T. Etlin, D., & Miller, P. C. (1987). A home-based pain management and rehabilitation programme: An evaluation. *Pain, 29*, 219–229.

Crook, J., Weir, R., & Tunks, E. (1989). An epidemiological follow-up survey of persistent pain sufferers in a group family practice and specialty pain clinic. *Pain, 36*, 49–61.

Cutler, R. B., Fishbain, D. A., Rosomoff, R. S., & Rosomoff, H. L. (1994). Outcomes in treatment of pain in geriatric and younger age groups. *Archives of Physical Medicine and Rehabilitation, 75*, 457–464.

Deardorff, W. W., Rubin, H. S., & Scott, D. W. (1991). Comprehensive multidisciplinary treatment of chronic pain: A follow-up study of treated and non-treated groups. *Pain, 45*, 35–43.

Demlow, L., Liang, M., & Eaton, H. (1986). Impact of chronic arthritis on the elderly. *Clinics in Rheumatic Disease, 12*, 329–335.

Diamond, S., & Montrose, D. (1984). The value of biofeedback in the treatment of chronic headache: A four-year retrospective study. *Headache, 24*, 5–18.

Flor, H., Fydrich, T., & Turk, D. C. (1992). Efficacy of multidisciplinary pain treatment centers: A meta-analytic review. *Pain, 49*, 221–230.

Folkman, S., & Lazarus, R. S. (1980). An analysis of coping in a middle-aged community sample. *Journal of Health and Social Behavior, 21*, 219–239.

Folstein, M. F., Folstein, S. E., & McHugh, P. R. (1975). "Mini-Mental State": A practical method for grading the cognitive state of patients for the clinician. *Journal of Psychiatric Research, 12*, 189–198.

Frontera, W. R., Meredith, C. N., O'Reilly, K. P., Knuttgen, H. G., & Evans, W. J. (1988). Strength conditioning in older men: Skeletal muscle hypertrophy and improved function. *Journal of Applied Physiology, 64,* 1038–1044.

Fry, P. S., & Wong, P. T. P. (1991). Pain management training in the elderly: Matching interventions with subjects' coping styles. *Stress Medicine, 7,* 93–98.

Graham, J. R. (1990). *MMPI-2: Assessing personality and psychopathology.* New York: Oxford University Press.

Hallett, E. C., & Pilowsky, I. (1982). The response to treatment in a multidisciplinary pain clinic. *Pain, 12,* 365–374.

Harkins, S. W., & Price, D. D. (1992). Assessment of pain in the elderly. In D. C. Turk & R. Melzack (Eds.), *Handbook of pain assessment* (pp. 315–331). New York: Guilford Press.

Harkins, S. W., & Price, D. D. (1993). Are there special needs for pain assessment in the elderly? *American Pain Society Bulletin, 3,* 1, 5–6.

Haythornthwaite, J. A., Sieber, W. J., & Kerns, R. D. (1991). Depression and the chronic pain experience. *Pain, 46,* 177–184.

Holroyd, K. A., & Penzien, D. B. (1986). Client variables and the behavioral treatment of recurrent tension headache: A meta-analytic review. *Journal of Behavioral Medicine, 9,* 515–536.

Kabela, E., Blanchard, E. B., Appelbaum, K. A., & Nicholson, N. (1989). Self-regulatory treatment of headache in the elderly. *Biofeedback and Self-Regulation, 14,* 219–228.

Kaiko, R. F., Wallenstein, S. L., Rogers, A. G., Grabinsky, P. Y., & Houde, R. W. (1982). Narcotics in the elderly. *Medical Clinics of North America, 66,* 1079–1089.

Kaplan, R., & Kepes, E. (1989). *Pain problems over 70 and under 40 years.* Paper presented at the meeting of the American Pain Society, Phoenix, AZ.

Kazis, L. E., Meenan, R. F., & Anderson, J. (1983). Pain in the rheumatic diseases: Investigations of a key health status component. *Arthritis and Rheumatism, 26,* 1017–1022.

Kee, W. G., Middaugh, S. J., Redpath, S., McCabe, K., & Brena, S. (1992). *Age as a factor in likelihood of admission to chronic pain rehabilitation.* Manuscript in preparation.

Keefe, F. J., Caldwell, D. S., Williams, D. A., Gil, K. M., Mitchell, D., Robertson, C., Martinez, S., Nunley, J., Beckham, J. C., Crisson, J. E., & Helms, M. (1990). Pain coping skills training in the management of osteoarthritic knee pain: A comparative study. *Behavior Therapy, 21,* 49–62.

Keefe, F. J., & Williams, D. A. (1990). A comparison of coping strategies in chronic pain patients in different age groups. *Journal of Gerontology, 45,* 161–165.

Keller, L. S., & Butcher, J. N. (1991). *Assessment of chronic pain patients with the MMPI-2.* Minneapolis: University of Minnesota Press.

Kerns, R. D., Turk, D. C., & Rudy, T. E. (1985). The West Haven–Yale Multidimensional Pain Inventory (WHYMPI). *Pain, 23,* 345–356.

Kwentus, J. A., Harkins, S. W., Lignon, N., & Silverman, J. J. (1985). Current concepts in geriatric pain and its treatment. *Geriatrics, 40,* 48–54.

Leventhal, E. A., & Prohaska, T. R. (1986). Age, symptom interpretation, and health behavior. *Journal of the American Geriatrics Society, 34,* 185–191.

Leventhal, H., Leventhal, E. A., & Schafer, P. (1992). Vigilant coping and health behavior: A life span problem. In M. G. Ory, R. P. Abeles, & P. D. Lipman (Eds.), *Aging, health and behavior.* Newbury Park, CA: Sage.

Lichtenberg, P. A., & Christensen, B. (1992). Extended normative data for the Logical Memory subtests of the Wechsler Memory Scale–Revised: Responses from a sample of cognitively intact elderly medical patients. *Psychological Reports, 71,* 745–746.

McCormack, H. M., Horne, D. J., & Sheather, S. (1988). Clinical applications of visual analogue scales: A critical review. *Psychological Medicine, 18,* 1007–1019.

McCreary, C. P., Naliboff, B. D., Cohen, M. J., & McArthur, D. L. (1988). Age differences in patients with chronic low back pain. *Canadian Pain Society and American Pain Society Joint Meeting Abstracts,* 146.

Melding, P. (1991). Is there such a thing as geriatric pain? *Pain, 46,* 119–121.

Melzack, R. (1987). The short-form McGill Pain Questionnaire. *Pain, 30,* 191–197.

Middaugh, S. J., & Kee, W. G. (1987). Advances in electromyographic monitoring and biofeedback in treatment of chronic cervical and low back pain. In M. G. Eisenberg & R. C. Grzesiak (Eds.), *Advances in clinical rehabilitation* (Vol. I, pp. 137–172). New York: Springer.

Middaugh, S. J., Kee, W. G., King, S. R., Peters, J. R., & Herman, K. (1992). Physiological response of older and younger pain patients to biofeedback-assisted relaxation training. *Biofeedback and Self-Regulation, 17*, 304–305.

Middaugh, S. J., Kee, W. G., & Nicholson, J. (1994). Muscle overuse and posture as factors in the development and maintenance of chronic musculoskeletal pain. In R. C. Grzesiak & D. S. Ciccone (Eds.), *Psychological vulnerability to chronic pain* (pp. 55–88). New York: Springer.

Middaugh, S. J., Levin, R. B., Kee, W. G., Barchiesi, F. D., & Roberts, J. M. (1988). Chronic pain: Its treatment in geriatric and younger patients. *Archives of Physical Medicine and Rehabilitation, 69*, 1021–1026.

Middaugh, S. J., Woods, S. E., Kee, W. G., Harden, R. N., & Peters, J. R. (1991). Biofeedback-assisted relaxation training for chronic pain in the aging. *Biofeedback and Relaxation, 16*, 361–377.

Miller, C., & LeLievre, R. B. (1982). Method to reduce chronic pain in elderly nursing home residents. *Gerontologist, 22*, 314–317.

Ng, L. K. Y. (Ed.). (1981). *New approaches to treatment of chronic pain: A review of multidisciplinary pain clinics and pain centers* (NIDA Research Monograph 36). Rockville, MD: National Institute on Drug Abuse.

Ortega, D. F., Leonard, T. D., & Smeltzer, J. D. (1988). *Chronic pain in the geriatric population: Location, duration, and progression.* Paper presented at the Ninth Annual Meeting of the Society of Behavioral Medicine, Boston, Massachusetts.

Painter, J. R., Seres, J. L., & Newman, R. I. (1980). Assessing benefits of the pain center: Why some patients regress. *Pain, 8*(1), 101–113.

Pawlick, K. (1994). *Multidisciplinary treatment of the older chronic pain patient: A comparison of older and younger patients.* Unpublished doctoral dissertation, University of Chicago.

Pawlick, K., Middaugh, S., Kee, W., & Nicholson, J. (1994). *Multidisciplinary treatment of the older pain patient: One year follow-up.* Paper presented at the meeting of the American Pain Society, Miami, FL.

Pawlick, K., Middaugh, S., Kee, W., & Nicholson, J. (1995). *Multidisciplinary treatment of the older chronic pain patient: A comparison of older and younger patients.* Manuscript in preparation.

Peterson, R. C., Smith, G., Kokmen, E., Ivnik, R. J., & Tangalos, E. G. (1992). Memory function in normal aging. *Neurology, 42*, 396–401.

Price, D. D., & Harkins, S. W. (1992). Psychophysical approaches to pain measurement and assessment. In D. C. Turk & R. Melzack (Eds.), *Handbook of pain assessment* (pp. 111–134). New York: Guilford Press.

Puder, R. S. (1988). Age analysis of cognitive-behavioral group therapy for chronic pain outpatients. *Psychology and Aging, 3*, 204–207.

Redpath, S., Middaugh, S. J., Kee, W. G., & Levin, R. (1992). *Medication profiles of older versus younger patients evaluated by a chronic pain rehabilitation program.* Paper presented at the Meeting of the American Pain Society, San Diego, CA.

Rosenstiel, A., & Keefe, F. J. (1983). The use of coping strategies in chronic low back pain patients: Relationship to patient characteristics and current adjustment. *Pain, 17*, 33–44.

Rummans, T. A., Davis, L. J., Jr., Morse, R. M., & Ivnik, R. J. (1993). Learning and memory impairment in older, detoxified, benzodiazepine-dependent patients. *Mayo Clinic Proceedings, 68*, 731–737.

Sarason, I. G., Levine, H. M., Basham, R. B., & Sarason, B. R. (1983). Assessing social support: The Social Support Questionnaire. *Journal of Personality and Social Psychology, 44*, 127–139.

Schaie, K. W. (1993). Ageist language in psychological research. *American Psychologist, 48*, 49–51.

Schuster, J. M., & Smith, S. S. (1994). Brief assessment of depression in chronic pain patients. *American Journal of Pain Management, 4*, 115–117.

Sorkin, B. A., Rudy, T. E., Hanlon, R. B., Turk, D. C., & Stieg, R. L. (1990). Chronic pain in old and young patients: Differences appear less important than similarities. *Journal of Gerontology, 45,* 64–68.

Spielberger, C. D., Gorsuch, R. L., & Lushene, R. E. (1970). *Manual for the State–Trait Anxiety Inventory.* Palo Alto, CA: Counseling Psychologists Press.

Stamford, B. A. (1988). Exercise and the elderly. *Exercise and Sport Sciences Reviews, 16,* 341–379.

Stark, E. (1985). Breaking the pain habit: Chronic sufferers learn to cope with and control their pain by changing their attitudes and behavior. *Psychology Today, 19,* 31–36.

Steedman, S. M., Middaugh, S. J., Kee, W. G., Carson, D. S., Harden, R. N., & Miller, M. C. (1992). Chronic pain medications: Equivalence levels and method of quantifying usage. *Clinical Journal of Pain, 8,* 204–214.

Taeber, C. (1990). Diversity: The dramatic reality. In S. Bass, E. Kutza, & F. Torres-Gil (Eds.), *Diversity in aging: The issues facing the White House Conference on Aging and beyond* (pp. 1–45). Glenview, IL: Scott, Foresman.

Thomas, M. R., & Roy, R. (1988). Age and pain: A comparative study of the younger and older elderly. *Journal of Pain Management, 1,* 174–179.

Thomas, P. S., Kepes, E. R., & Marcus, N. J. (1981). Critical evaluation of 110 geriatric patients in pain treatment center (PTC). *Pain*(Suppl. 1), S297.

Turk, D. C., & Rudy, T. E. (1990). Neglected factors in chronic pain treatment outcome studies: Referral patterns, failure to enter treatment, and attrition. *Pain, 43,* 7–25.

Wilcox, S. M., Himmelstein, D. V., & Woolhandler, S. (1994). Inappropriate drug prescribing for the community-dwelling elderly. *Journal of the American Medical Association, 272,* 292–296.

Williams, T. F. (1988). Rehabilitation: Goals and approaches in older people. In J. W. Rowe & R. W. Besdine (Eds.), *Geriatric medicine* (2nd ed.). Boston: Little, Brown.

Williamson, G. M., & Schulz, R. (1992). Pain, activity, restriction, and symptoms of depression among community-residing elderly adults. *Journal of Gerontology, 47,* 367–372.

Wood, P. H. N., & Badley, E. M. (1980). Back pain in the community. *Clinics in Rheumatic Diseases, 6,* 3–16.

CHAPTER 15

The Psychologist as a Pain Consultant in Outpatient, Inpatient, and Workplace Settings

Douglas E. DeGood
Joseph R. Dane

A "consultant" is defined as one who gives professional advice or services. Of all medical problems, chronic pain may be the problem for which psychological consultation is the most widely sought and readily accepted, because of the degree of frustration it can engender in health care providers (HCPs) and patients alike, as well as the wide recognition among HCPs that pain and coping with pain are readily influenced by psychological factors. Not surprisingly, Hickling, Sison, and Holtz (1985) found that 85.5% of the multidisciplinary pain clinics responding to a survey reported employing at least one psychologist.

People with pain seldom spontaneously seek out assistance from psychologists. Therefore, a psychologist's encounter with pain patients nearly always involves consultation with third-party referral sources—most commonly physicians and other medical therapists, employers, attorneys, and insurance representatives. This chapter focuses on some of the practical issues faced by the pain psychologist in the role of consulting with these various parties. There are several other useful recent works on the general topic of hospital consultation by clinical psychologists (Bieliauskas, 1991; Dane & Kessler, 1994; Huszti & Walker, 1991).

Three key points regarding pain consultation are stressed in this chapter. First of all, effective consultation hinges on a recognition of the critical psychosocial dimensions of pain, as well as an understanding of how these dimensions can influence pain sensation and management. Second, formulations by a consultant must be communicated to all parties in a manner that will facilitate positive therapeutic interaction with a patient. Third, we argue that to meet this goal, effective consultation is not primarily assessment of a patient's mood or behavior; rather, it depends on recognizing and facilitating interactions between a patient and the critical others in his or her environment. These points are elaborated as we discuss the three types of consultation with which we are most familiar: (1) consultation on chronic pain in an outpatient interdisciplinary pain center; (2) consultation on acute pain within inpatient medical and surgical units in a general teaching hospital; and (3) systems consultation to those dealing with workplace injuries.

THE PROCESS AND CONTENTS OF CONSULTATION

The Nested-Matrix Model of Consultation

Our basic conceptual model for the psychological assessment and treatment of both acute and chronic pain characterizes the interacting dimensions of the pain experience as a series of three-dimensional matrices nested one within the other. The somewhat intricate nature of this model reflects the complexity that is often present when HCPs are attempting to treat pain. At the same time, it provides a way for caregivers to organize their thinking and behavior in order to develop appropriate interventions. The broadest and most inclusive of these matrices (see Figure 15.1A) identifies the basic misconceptions and corrective realities about pain that may be operative among both staff and patients, along with potential models of psychological intervention that may be used. Taken together, these vectors constitute a background/context within which the pain experience occurs. Embedded within this context, we posit two further matrices, one embedded within the other. The second matrix (see Figure 15.1B) consists of more or less static moderator vectors or variables, which are unique to each patient's situation but which modulate the third level of vectors—dynamic process variables (see Figure 15.1C), which are also unique to each patient. Static moderator variables include (1) whether the pain is best characterized as acute, chronic, or "chronically acute"; (2) the phase of therapy within which action is being formulated; and (3) a range of individual-difference factors (prior learning, coping style, level of hypnotic capacity, etc.). Individual dynamic process variables include (1) the patient's position within the recovery process, and in particular within the grieving process that can accompany pain and injury; (2) the patient's premorbid and/or current "emotional age" (i.e., "regression" vs. "character disorder"); and (3) the patient's status on the continuum from "victim/blamer" to "manager" stance vis-à-vis his or her pain. These factors constitute a multidimensional, interactive set of matrices within which both patients and caregivers can be placed in a way that clarifies the relationship among numerous complex variables and fosters development of rational treatment decisions that are specific to the individual patient. For details of this nested-matrix model that are immediately relevant to the pain psychologist's role but that are not discussed here, the reader is referred to chapters elsewhere by Dane and Kessler (1994) and by Rowlingson, Kessler, Dane, and Hamill (1994).

Essential Knowledge and Skills

If a psychologist is to function effectively as a pain consultant working within the nested-matrix model, certain types of knowledge about pain and certain skills are critical:

1. *Medical knowledge.* One needs to be familiar with medical facts, diagnoses, usual treatments, and, most importantly, patients' subjective experiences associated with various common types of chronic pain. Beyond the obvious value of such knowledge in fostering understanding of patients' plight, it enhances credibility with patients and consultees.

2. *Systems knowledge.* One needs to understand the environment (or culture) of each patient and everyone concerned with this patient. It can be helpful to have spent some time in a blue-collar job to fully appreciate the typical fears, beliefs, and expectations engendered in such environments, as well as to recognize the common social and famil-

A. Background/Context

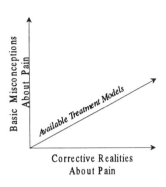

Basic Misconceptions:

-Mind vs. body
-Imaginary vs. "real" pain
-Simplistic understanding
about physiology of pain

Corrective Realities:

-Pain = sensation <u>and</u> suffering
-Only valid index of pain = patients report
-Cognitive and affective principles governing
pain perception
-Distinctions between acute vs. chronic pain
-"Pain" = pain behavior
-Behavior = communication ==> feeling "heard"
==> reduced need to communicate

Treatment Models:

-Levels and types of systems interventions
(nursing, M.D., PT, OT, etc.)
-"Interpersonal influence"
(serving as container for displaced affect)
-Self-regulation training
(biofeedback, self-hypnosis, etc.)

B. Static Patient Moderator Variables

Individual Difference Factors:

-Prior learning/conditioning about pain
-Ethnic/family norms about pain
-Coping style (repressor vs. sensitizer)
-Problem-solving skills
-Personal meaning of pain
-Hypnotic capacity
-Prognostic indicators
-Conflicting agendas about pain behavior
(e.g., lawyers, insurance co., psychologists, etc.)

C. Dynamic Patient Process Variables

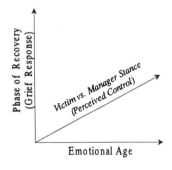

Grief Response:

-Shock/denial
-Anger
-Mourning
-Acceptance
-Arrested grief response

Emotional Age:

-Premorbid vs. current
(=character disorder vs. regression)

Victim vs. Manager Stance:

-Perceived control
(interacts with repressor vs. sensitizer coping style)

FIGURE 15.1. Nested-matrix model for the assessment and treatment of pain. Matrix C is nested within Matrix B, which is nested within Matrix A.

ial interaction patterns of laborers. Similarly, a recognition of the values, decision-making processes, and interaction styles of the medical system and the insurance industry can be essential.

3. *Psychological knowledge.* Most crucial, of course, is knowledge about the psychology of pain. One needs to have a frame of reference for understanding the evolution of coping skills in the life history of the individual, and the interaction of such skills with pain and loss. Likewise, one needs to recognize the interplay between cognition and emotion in response to pain, and the ways in which these internal psychological events influence overt adaptive and maladaptive behavior.

Without the necessary background knowledge and skills, pain consultation can be risky. We have seen psychologists who were ill prepared to enter this murky field soon finding themselves confused and embarrassed, and even becoming the objects of litigation for perceived incompetence and harm. Remember that this is a patient group often involved in litigation.

Consultation and the Assessment Function

The traditional skills of the psychologist in assessment, intervention, and research can be readily adapted to the pain setting. However, if these skills have been honed primarily in psychological or psychiatric mental health settings, some retooling is required. Conducting psychological assessments without adjusting for the norms or unique needs of the new patient population is inappropriate and possibly unethical. The danger of a misapplication of assessment procedures is the greatest in cases where an ill-informed referral source desires to have an equally ill-informed consultant make pseudodeterminations regarding the pseudoissue of whether the pain is real or imaginary.

Psychological consultation involving individuals, however, does remain intimately related to the assessment function. Maloney and Ward (1976) state that effective psychological assessment requires (1) knowing what the referral source is asking, and (2) being familiar with the content of the problem. Both requirements must be met if decisions based on the consultant's recommendations are to be useful, reasonable, and fair.

Beginning about two decades ago, when large numbers of psychologists began moving into the burgeoning field of pain management, assessment was largely keyed to diagnoses of mood state disorders (especially anxiety and depression) coexisting with chronic pain. Other commonplace diagnoses were conversion hysteria, various somatoform disorders, and certain personality disorders (particularly passive–aggressive personality, passive–dependent personality, and inadequate personality). These were of course diagnoses familiar to psychologists from their mental health background. It is noteworthy that attention to depression and anxiety, which both come complete with pharmacological treatments, has always been more prominent than attention to anger, which may be an equally relevant emotion with pain patients (Beutler, Engle, Oro'-Beutler, Daldrup, & Meredith, 1986; Kerns, Rosenberg, & Jacob, 1994). We are not suggesting that traditional psychological assessment has no role in the understanding and treating the pain patient; rather, we are making the point that the mere assignment of a formal diagnosis leaves the task of the consultant incomplete. Even worse, diagnostic labeling may result in the creation of a pseudoportrait of the patient that is simply inadequate to the requirements of the pain management setting.

Psychologists concerned with pain are not alone in shifting assessment paradigms. Most behavioral medicine applications of psychology, with roots primarily in cognitive-behavioral theory, have tended to move away from mental illness models of human functioning toward concepts of maladaptive coping and stress management (e.g., see Gentry, 1984; Malamed & Siegel, 1980). This has led to an often unsystematic, but nevertheless dynamic, emergence of new behavioral and cognitive-behavioral assessment strategies (e.g., relative to pain assessment, see Turk & Melzack, 1992). These strategies are more often based on adaptations of attribution theory (e.g., see Forsterling, 1988), and information-processing approaches to clinical psychology (e.g., see Ingram, 1986) than on classical psychiatric symptom assessment.

The Key Elements (Contents) of the Consultant's Assessment

As we have discussed elsewhere (DeGood, 1988; Dane & Kessler, 1994), a wide variety of patient variables must be addressed in pain consultation, including mood state, grief over loss of abilities, past and current experience with pain and illness, and life history indications of the development of coping skills. However, of greatest interest to the cognitive-behavioral psychologist are the patient's beliefs about the nature of his or her pain and its treatment, and the attitudes tied to these beliefs. These data, we believe, constitute the critical agenda of the patient. If the consultant can identify these beliefs and expectations about the pain and its treatment, and can determine their impact on the patient's behavioral interaction patterns with all other relevant parties, he or she will then be in a strategic position to facilitate all relevant parties' working with rather than against one another.

Patient Stereotyping and Professional Ethics

HCPs can become very frustrated by patients with persistent pain, and may react by being too willing to attribute the problem to psychological factors. Psychologists must avoid falling into the trap of feeling obligated to provide psychosocial explanations of pain by default (i.e., whenever physical finding do not adequately account for the pain). Functional explanations require the presence of positive psychosocial evidence, not merely the absence of physical evidence. Furthermore, psychosocial symptoms frequently appear to emerge only after the onset of pain and seem to reflect a loss of role, upset of daily routine, and resultant concerns about work and economic issues.

A psychologist must always try to maintain respect for the dignity of the individual patient. It is always a temptation for clinicians to see patients, especially those from different cultural, ethnic, and socioeconomic backgrounds, as unlike themselves. Admittedly, chronic pain patients, who may feel victimized or disenfranchised, can be taxing in their displays of anger and general disgruntlement. Psychologists are not immune from feeling overwhelmed, but every effort must be made to maintain a demeanor of concern and respect, whether this comes from spiritual, humanitarian, or scientific inner resources. A positive demeanor alone can reduce the interaction problems that so often characterize these patients' encounters with the health care system. An effective consultant must be perceived by all parties as knowledgeable, objective, and fair. Fairness becomes especially important when the consultant's input may be sought by different parties with contradictory vested interests.

CONSULTATION IN THE OUTPATIENT
MEDICAL SETTING

Different Types of Outpatient Medical Settings

Requests for consultations with pain patients may come from a variety of sources. The psychologist may be part of an interdisciplinary pain center, or may function as a staff person in a surgical or medical specialty clinic. He or she may be a member of a psychiatry or psychology service assigned on a full-time or part-time basis to such clinics, or may see pain patients referred from such clinics within a hospital or private practice. Meeting with patients directly in a nonpsychiatric medical clinic, rather than as referrals to a setting identified as primarily psychological, will often reduce patients' hesitancy about meeting with a psychologist.

Within a given setting, the source of the requested consultation may vary from patient to patient. In our hospital-based outpatient pain center, the most frequent referral sources are the physicians and other staff members within the clinic itself. However, we also receive consultation requests from staffs located in many other departments within the hospital, as well as from outside the hospital.

Preparing the Patient for a Psychological Consultation

Absolutely the worst preparation for a productive consultation is no preparation—that is, when a patient is not informed that the appointment is with a psychologist. Upon arrival, the patient may feel betrayed or tricked to such a degree that establishing rapport is nearly impossible. The encounter can be equally problematic when a patient announces, "My doctor said he would not give me any more medication unless I went to see you." We have seen patients in acute withdrawal, with no clear plan established as to how this crisis is to be handled. When psychologists become involved in pain management, unpredictable things can happen as an outgrowth of how alienated some patients have become from the medical system and how desperate some doctors are to get rid of patients who have become an intolerable burden.

Preferably, the psychologist should clarify in advance what both the referring party and the patient expect from the consultation. Does the referring party want recommendations or treatment, or is he or she simply attempting to transfer the patient? Is the patient expecting an evaluation, advice, and/or some form of ongoing treatment? Even when the consultant feels that expectations have been made clear, he or she should double-check with the patient at the start of the session. Even from patients sent by reliable sources, we have on occasion heard statements such as "I was told that you would help me get my workers' compensation," "My doctor said that you can hypnotize away my pain," or simply "I was told I had to see you; I don't know why."

"Who is in charge?" is a common concern of chronic pain patients. After an injury the patient may initially see a primary care physician, who refers him or her to a specialist (often a surgeon) who after a bout of conservative treatment may send the patient to another specialist, who in turn may pass the patient on to still other specialists. Each specialist may assume that someone else is in charge. When no one will take responsibility for filling out "the forms," the patient feels angry and ignored. The heart of the problem may be that, in fact, no one is clearly in charge. Helping the patient through the hazards of the medical system may sometimes be the most therapeutic service a consultant can provide.

Establishing Rapport with the Patient

The patient's concerns about dealing with a psychologist may go beyond those generated by clumsy referral maneuvers. The reluctance may be part of a generalized passive approach to handling pain, in which the patient seeks only a procedure to "fix" the problem. The concepts of "exaggerated illness behavior" (e.g., Pilowsky & Spence, 1976) and "learned helplessness" (Seligman, 1975) may be useful descriptors of those who use physical suffering to maintain dependency and other emotional needs. However, a more commonplace reason for reluctance to speak with a psychologist is merely that the patient does not understand the reason for the referral. The hidden (or sometimes not so hidden) message perceived by the patient is that "Your pain is all in your head." Resentment and anger are the inevitable consequences. Common signs of this reaction are failure to keep a previously scheduled appointment, guarded answers to questions, lack of spontaneity, exaggerated bewilderment, or simply a generalized hostile manner.

There are some strategies that can be useful in defusing apprehension about the interaction with a psychologist. We introduce ourselves with a statement such as this:

> "I know that if pain lasts a long time, it starts to have serious effects on a person's life. Since I am a psychologist, I will want to learn more about how your life was before the pain, how the pain has changed your life, how you are dealing with those changes, and what you expect will happen to you in the future. Such information, combined with medical information, can help us better understand your struggle with pain."

We try to capitalize on the fact that most patients are eager to be heard and understood, especially patients with chronic pain, who often feel that doctors are always in too much of a hurry to listen. Despite our best efforts, however, there are always occasional patients who are unable to give up the notion that we are trying to brand them as "crazy," or who remain convinced that we are spies for employers, insurance companies, or even the medical system.

Several other general strategies (from DeGood, 1983) for countering patients' reluctance to become involved with a psychologist in pain management include the following:

1. *Attempting immediately to defuse the "organic" versus "functional" myth.* The key here is to encourage patients to think of psychological/behavioral issues as consequences or correlates to pain rather than the cause. Nearly all chronic pain involves some combination of physical and psychosocial factors. A dualistic (either–or) conception of "organic" versus "functional" causes is a myth of no value to either patients or therapists.

2. *Avoiding premature efforts to "psychologize" the patient's problem.* It is essential to establish rapport with a patient before introducing matters that may create discomfort. There is no need to provide instant psychological insight; the patient should simply be encouraged to tell his or her story. Initial rapport building may require allowing the patient to relate to the psychologist via physical complaints.

3. *Listening patiently, without arguing, preaching, or offering quick solutions.* The psychologist should be tolerant of ambiguity, and should not be too quick to offer solutions that will inevitably seem superficial to the patient. The reaching of mutual decisions should be cultivated. If the interaction becomes "adult to child" in manner, the "child" will inevitably find ways to sabotage the "adult's" good advice. For example, it is futile to announce to patients facts they already know (e.g., that they should exercise more, lose weight, or stop smoking). Just being told does not help; they need to be assisted in developing strategies for doing so.

4. *Attempting to move beyond ritualized interactions.* Many chronic patients develop a ritualized pattern of interacting with HCPs. The patient begins with a description of pain and misery, followed by the physician's conducting a perfunctory exam and writing a prescription. Both parties may be polite, but neither one addresses the feeling that the treatment will not help. Rituals allow people to feel comfortable without having to think about underlying emotions. Fortunately, ritualized interactions can often be interrupted by empathetic statements. For example, when a patient presents with an endless litany of physical symptoms, a psychologist can respond by saying, "Your lack of progress must be frustrating for you." He or she can then proceed to ask, "Do you believe things might ever be different?" This type of simple redirection can break up the ritualized interaction and prompt the expression of feelings and beliefs that must be addressed if the interaction is ever to move forward. Likewise, patients who endlessly "doctor-shop" out of the fear that the right doctor has not been found may need to be challenged to consider this: "When might enough be enough?"

There can be diagnostic value in determining whether the psychologist can possibly break through a ritualized encounter and establish rapport with the patient. If the patient cannot go beyond the level of a strict symptom focus, the relationship with all HCPs will probably remain fixated at the same level of unproductive ritual.

5. *Trying to shape adaptive beliefs instead of challenging a patient's misconceptions.* It can be useful to view pre-existing beliefs as "myths" in the fashion often described by family therapists (e.g., Selvini-Palazzoli, Cecchin, Prata, & Boscolo, 1978). For example, many patients with "bad backs" but minimal radiographic or neurological findings will nevertheless insist that they have a pinched nerve, spinal stenosis, bulging disk, lumbalgia, or some equally vague diagnosis. Rather than challenging such beliefs, a psychologist can add that the patients may also have scar tissue, fibromyositis, chronic inflammation, muscle spasm, ischemia, or muscle and ligamentous injuries. Furthermore, people can have any of these common soft-tissue problems without any radiographic evidence.

Such a patient seldom objects to this expansion of the physical myth; it is entirely consistent with his or her preferred belief system. The discussion remains mythical, however, because in the individual case such explanations can seldom be proven true or false. But the advantage of the expanded myth is that it logically relates to a broader range of intervention options than does the original. Physical exercise, weight control, non-narcotic medications, and the learning of self-regulatory skills can now be rationally incorporated as reasonable alternative treatments. Ideally, the consultant has moved the patient away from the belief in a discrete corrective procedure toward a broader rehabilitation perspective, without directly debating the fundamental etiology of the symptoms.

6. *Attempting to get patients to make an active decision to participate in a treatment program.* Commitment to the necessary effort to manage pain may be lacking when medical assistance is sought because of drug dependency, fear of loss of compensation, family or other social pressures, or simply a well-established behavioral pattern of pain and illness. As long as any treatment is simply "prescribed," its falure to help can be readily perceived by the passive patient as the HCP's fault. Commitment can be increased if patients truly provide informed consent based on understanding of options, and feel that critical choices are in their hands.

7. *Fostering realistic expectations by specifying feasible outcome goals.* Individuals with long-standing pain must be urged to look for gradual improvement rather than sudden cures. Success should be reframed as consisting of very small steps, rather than "all or nothing." Furthermore, "ups and downs" must be anticipated; it is important to discourage

catastrophizing over temporary setbacks. The psychologist must strive to replace a "cure" perspective with the "rehabilitation" perspective that it is important for patients to accomplish all they can, while accepting their limitations.

8. *Recalling that the superordinate strategy of the consultant is not to diagnose, but to educate.* The effective psychological consultant must increase the patient's awareness of the interplay among behavior, mood, and physical distress, as well as the patient's understanding of the relationship of these dimensions to his or her social and physical environment. Increasing coping, rather than diagnosing, must be the goal. The patient must be encouraged to appreciate that biological healing is not analogous to auto mechanics. A living organism is seldom restored by repairing or replacing worn-out parts. Only after being challenged to recognize such distinctions can the patient begin to understand how his or her own attitude and behavioral skills are vital elements in coping with pain.

The Recognition of Beliefs and Attitudes

The Importance of Beliefs about Pain and Its Treatment

Once a psychological consultant is attuned to spotting characteristic patient beliefs, the process of gathering such information need not be particularly difficult. Patients wish to be taken seriously and feel understood. Therefore, as long as the psychologist will listen in a nonjudgmental and empathetic manner, patients tend to be quite willing to disclose their views about what is wrong, what they believe doctors should or should not do, how fairly or unfairly they have been treated by others, and what they fear about the future. Important attitudes about the home, work, and treatment situation can be uncovered in this manner. Beliefs do not arise in a vacuum, but emerge from the context of each individual's experience. A pain belief can be true or partially true, and yet can still be maladaptive. A few examples of common problematic beliefs about pain are as follows:

"I do not have a correct diagnosis."
"Doctors should be able to cure me."
"I need an operation."
"I should be on stronger medication."
"I should rest in bed."
"I may become paralyzed if I am physically active."
"I need to wait for a medical breakthrough."
"Nobody understands what I am going through."
"I should not be working."
"My suffering is someone's else's fault."
"My pain is either real (physical) or all in my head."

In a busy office where staff members must move quickly from patient to patient, there is a natural disinclination to attend to what appear to be ill-informed patient opinions. It is easy to dismiss such beliefs as mere artifacts of the chronic pain experience—cognitions that will disappear once a correct diagnosis and treatment has been determined. But such beliefs may constitute the internal reality controlling a patient's pain behavior, and as such may lie at the heart of the patient's persistent lack of response to treatment. The patient is not likely to improve while holding to the belief that his or her medical care reflects others' indifference, ignorance, or misunderstanding (DeGood & Kiernan, in press). There is considerable evidence that beliefs are related to outcomes (e.g., Jensen,

Turner, & Romano, 1994; Shutty, DeGood, & Tuttle, 1990). Although pain beliefs are usually readily discernible from an interview, there are now several experimental self-report questionnaires for measuring these beliefs (see DeGood & Shutty, 1992).

Assessing Beliefs via Interview

Examples of interview questions that can be useful in eliciting relevant pain beliefs and their associated attitudes are as follows:

1. Why are you here today?
2. What do you believe might be causing your pain?
3. What has, and has not, helped in the past? Is there anything you can do that can make a difference?
4. What do you think should be done for your pain? What did you hope [expect] we would do here?
5. What does this pain keep you from doing that you would otherwise be doing?
6. How are you getting along financially since this pain started?
7. What have our doctors here suggested to you? Does it make sense?
8. Do you feel someone else is responsible for your pain and suffering?
9. How do you think this problem is going to turn out for you?

The first of these questions may appear obvious, but it can easily be overlooked. Patients are referred to pain specialists not only because of pain, but because that pain is causing problems in living. There may be a concern (either stated or unstated) about narcotic use, or the patient may have become angry and disillusioned with past medical care. The patient's spouse may have announced that he or she can no longer tolerate the patient's irritability or "inability" to participate in family activities. A lawyer, seeking evidence prior to a forthcoming hearing, may have arranged the visit. An employer may have presented a time ultimatum beyond which a job will no longer be held open, or an insurance company may be demanding the patient's assignment to an undesirable, low-paying job. The possibilities are endless, but the consultation will produce just another form in the patient's record unless the psychologist is able to address the relevant agenda.

Many of the questions above exemplify probes that can facilitate the breaking up of ritualized interactions. Rather than concentrating on endless physical details about the symptoms, it is often more productive to counter with queries like this one: "How do these symptoms affect your daily activities—your job, your recreation, your sex life, your interactions with family members?" Likewise, after listening patiently for a period of time to a patient's account of what has been said by various doctors, the consultant may ask: "What do you think might be wrong? Do you feel something serious has been missed?" Sometimes such shifting of attention will abruptly change the patient's focus to emotionally charged narratives of family members with similar symptoms who died of cancer, heart attack, or a stroke, shortly after a doctor stated the pain was "nothing serious."

Numerous examples could be given illustrating how small adjustments in interview techniques can prompt patients to think, contemplate, speculate, and confide their fears and fantasies. A psychologist faced with an angry recounting of the uncaringness of past doctors can respond in this way: "Do you feel these doctors *would not* or *could not* help you? What do you feel they *should* have done?" Replies to such questions can provide insight into whether the patient is merely frustrated or truly paranoid. In response to a patient's proclamation that the present clinic staff is no better than the others, the psychologist might respond: "I am concerned that when you leave here today, this will have been just another in your long line of wasted efforts at getting help. What had you hoped we might do? How might we have made it different for you today?" Since patients do not have readily rehearsed answers to such unexpected questions, the results can be surprising and informative.

The consultant must try to understand, not simply recognize, beliefs about pain. Recognition alone does not suggest a solution. Further understanding requires a history of the experiences that has led to maladaptive pain beliefs. One must attempt to engage the patient in presenting his or her life story, always remaining observant as to how pain and illness fits into this story. Most of all, how does the patient interpret this story? Out of the story may emerge the keys to understanding the current pain agenda; these may suggest directions to pursue in improving the likelihood of working with, rather than against, the treatment plan.

Common Interaction Problems between Patients and Practitioners

Some patients come for help with a paradox-filled agenda. A patient may wish to experience less pain, yet may feel compelled to demonstrate that his or her pain and suffering has been insufficiently appreciated by others. Or a patient may want to be cooperative, yet may need to prove that he or she cannot be helped. The patient may honestly wish for the best possible medical treatment for pain, but still may have no expectation that treatment will help. Such paradoxical needs and behaviors inevitably lead to conflicts. The psychological consultant must try to identify these problems and suggest possible solutions.

At the core of many doctor–patient interaction problems is a patient's belief that his or her complaint is not being taken seriously. The consequence is an individual who feels compelled to prove the legitimacy of his or her pain experience. This can stimulate pain behaviors that HCPs interpret as amplified, exaggerated, nonanatomical, or indicative of "functional overlay," if not as signs of malingering, low pain tolerance, or weakness of character. Insurance carriers are inclined to see malingering motivated by a sense of entitlement. But this is never a patient's interpretation of pain. Patients invariably believe in the reality of their pain. They experience an unpleasant sensory event, which they believe to be indicative of an underlying physical pathology that must be diagnosed and cured. All of us are taught from early childhood that pain is a warning sign that something is wrong with the body, and that we should go to a doctor to identify and treat the underlying problem—an appropriate response to acute trauma or illness. When expectations for relief are not met, fear soon emerges and often turns to anger and despondency.

The situation can become further complicated as employers, insurance companies, and family members become concerned about the lack of progress. Paranoid ideation can become rampant, to the point that a patient becomes suspicious that everyone is part of a plot to discredit the pain. He or she may interpret discouragement of further diagnostic testing as doctors' giving up; recommendations to reduce narcotic medication as an indication that no one cares how much he or she suffers; suggestions to become more physically active as evidence that no one believes how much he or she really hurts; and efforts to involve work rehabilitation as a trick to get him or her fired or deny benefits. The consultant who understands how these critical cognitive contents shape the patient's interactions with the medical system must then try to deflect these interactions in a more productive direction.

Communicating the Information Obtained in Consultation

The "How" of Feedback in the Medical Culture

Knowing not just *what*, but *how* to communicate is essential to the consultation process. The atmosphere of a medical hospital or clinic can seem militaristic to a psychologist, with those of lessor status presenting information and looking to the more senior members for subsequent "orders." Medical training seems to produces a less speculative individual than does psychological training (Kingsbury, 1987). Medical practitioners, by and large, do not think in terms of theories, paradigm shifts, and probabilities, but are geared toward pragmatic technical (impersonal) solutions to problems. Trained to seek "positive diagnostic findings," the physician may perceive psychological communications as meandering speculations about vague hypothetical constructs. The slow process by which psychologists gather information also does not fit well into the medical environment. The requirement for establishing rapport with patients—the reason why consultation often cannot be reduced to a few minutes—may be poorly understood by many HCPs (Huszti & Walker, 1991). Nevertheless, in medical environments, psychologists must learn to work more efficiently than might be their normal routine. Patient interviews need not be hours long, nor is it unreasonable to be prepared immediately to compress into a 5-minute exchange one's major impressions and recommendations.

Any consideration of the medical culture must again highlight the prominence of diagnosis. Psychologists may fail to appreciate that diagnosis is the essential ingredient of sound medical practice. Implicit in a correct diagnosis of a well-understood condition are a scientifically based etiology and a corresponding treatment regimen with a known prognosis. Unfortunately, psychological diagnoses are unlikely to carry the same implications. Even popular diagnoses, such as pain amplification, somatoform pain disorder, and illness behavior syndrome—all of which are vague descriptive codes that the pain complaint seems excessive—are seldom really useful. The referring HCP typically already knows that the pain is excessive; all that is accomplished by the diagnosis is to give the excessive pain complaint a name.

Given the laboratory test motif so common in medicine, the pain psychologist will inevitably encounter the plaintive request: "Can't you just give us a good screening tool for determining who is malingering or has other psychological problems?" The desire for an efficient "blood test" equivalent can mask the HCP's desire to shunt patients effortlessly to the correct specialists, rather than to participate in a serious collaborative effort to manage pain. Many HCPs need to improve their skills at working with patients with psychosocial issues more than they need "screens" to deflect such patients, since it has been estimated between 50% and 80% of all patients encountered in the amubulatory care setting have some degree of psychological dysfunction (e.g., Rogers, 1977). On the positive side, paradigm shifts in psychology over the past two decades have made communication somewhat easier for the psychologist. The currently popular behavioral and cognitive-behavioral paradigms appear to the average physician to be more scientific, and to lead to more obvious clinical strategies, than the paradigms that were in favor during the earlier psychoanalytic era of psychosomatic medicine.

The "What" of Feedback Communication

The feedback should consist of information that can facilitate improvement in the working relationship between the patient and the health care system. For example, a consultant may convey why a patient is so concerned about cancer, or state why he or she believes narcotics do or do not appear to facilitate this patient's functioning. The consultant should clarify the patient's goals and indicate whether the goals are realistic and can serve as a positive source of motivation. The consultee should be informed regarding what aspects of pain treatment this patient understands, and what aspects still require further clarification.

Every consultation should be perceived as an opportunity to educate the referral source in cognitive and emotional management of pain. This is especially important for a patient population in which the failure to benefit from treatment so readily leads to anger, frustration, and blaming on both sides. The HCPs with whom a psychologist consults—be they physicians, nurses, physical and occupational therapists, or other specialized therapists—must become knowledgeable about the basic facts of chronic pain, such as the difference between pain sensation and pain behavior. They must be aware of pain behavior as a form of interpersonal communication. They must give up oversimplified notions of malingering and realize that even blatant pain behavior is rarely a matter of conscious intent. Likewise, they must see motivation as more than a matter of conscious choice. Written reports by the consultant should be educative as well, not just for the present consultees but for future readers of the patient's records.

If the consultant can establish rapport with the patient, that rapport can become a springboard for more positive patient rapport with other staff members. There is overwhelming empirical evidence that good doctor–patient rapport improves treatment outcomes. Studies with chronic disease patients (e.g., Kaplan, Greenfield, & Ware, 1989) and patients recovering from surgery and heart attacks (e.g., Mumford, Schelsinger, & Glass, 1982) illustrate this point.

Case Examples of Outpatient Consultation

In these and all other case examples in this chapter, names and other identifying details have been disguised.

Understanding Anger: Mike

Mike was a 26-year-old married man who worked (when he was able) as a self-employed gardener and tree trimmer. Four years earlier he had undergone a a complex operation for an aortic aneurysm after appearing in the hospital emergency room with sudden-onset severe chest pain. While recovering in the hospital, he was informed that his cardiovascular emergency was a result of a chronic condition in which his liver failed to produce a necessary protein, and that he would probably require a liver transplant in the near future. Ever since the surgery, he had experienced exertional pain in the general area of his incision, and recently the pain had worsened. No treatment had a significant impact. Two months ago he had quit working entirely because his physically demanding job appeared to trigger the pain episodes. He was referred to our pain center by his cardiovascular surgeon with the diagnosis of probable incisional neuropathic pain.

Our pain center physicians found Mike's symptoms incompatible with neuropathic pain, and concluded that the exertional pain was either of muscular origin or related to his underlying cardiovascular pathology. A psychological consultation was requested after the examining physician found communication with him difficult because of a distant, vague, and hostile interaction style. During the early stages of a psychological interview, he likewise seemed irritable and spontaneously offered little information. However, expected issues of narcotic use or disability compensation did not appear to underlie his anger. Paradoxically, despite his irritability, he was quite open about psychosocial matters, readily acknowledging that his pain gave him a bad temper.

In a rather adolescent-like fashion, Mike angrily complained that it was a waste of time to keep going to doctors, because "they don't do anything for me, and just give me pills that don't help and I can't afford." When sympathetically he was asked, "What do you think you should do?" he responded in an ironic, forlorn manner: "Sue every damn doctor." At that point his affect was strikingly inconsistent with the content of the statement. It seemed that he just had no other way to express his fear and confusion. His father had died relatively young a few years earlier, after years of chest pain, of a heart attack. Mike, at only age 22, had already experienced a life-threatening event, which left him with severe exertional pain similar to his father's pain. He had remarkably little information regarding how to understand and deal with this pain as well as with his general high-risk health situation. His communication skills were very limited. He seemed to know neither how to ask questions nor how to process medical information. He worried constantly about his heart and liver, but had no idea how to go about calming his fears. He was never able to communicate his real agenda, yet he interpreted doctors' giving him "useless" pills as their not caring.

Mike could have been diagnosed as having a passive–aggressive personality, probably with borderline intelligence. But beyond reinforcing the status quo, what benefit could possibly come from such a diagnosis? Instead, the consultant urged his physician to view the patient as an adolescent who was acting out his anxiety rather than internalizing it, because he had no words to communicate his distress. Mike needed more straightforward communications from his doctors about whether his pain was benign or dangerous. He also needed activity guidelines to help him reduce his constant fear of sudden death. Following this single consultation and the resultant change in the physicians' communication pattern, Mike appeared on the way to becoming a more cooperative patient.

Perceived Noncompliance: Ruth

Ruth was a woman in her late 50s who had been a very physically active gardener before suffering a severely ruptured disk 2 years ago. Unfortunately, there were complications with her surgery, which left her with partial motor and sensory loss and severe neuropathic pain in her right leg. She could now walk only with a leg brace and cane. She struck her treating physician as angry, depressed, and coping poorly; he also felt that she was noncompliant with recommended drug therapies.

Ruth told the consultant psychologist that after 2 years she just did not want to take any more drugs. She had an objection to every class of pain medications: Nonsteroidals caused her stomach pain; narcotics caused nausea, dizziness, and constipation; and antidepressants and anticonvulsants made her feel weak and "out of my mind." She did not want her doctors to think she was uncooperative, but felt angry if they tried to make her feel guilty.

The psychologist's impression was that by all standard criteria Ruth was a woman who was coping very well with a serious physical disability. He urged her physicians to be supportive and available, but to cease insisting that she should take medication. After a couple of brief follow-up counseling visits, she seemed much happier and much more secure in her ability to count on her doctors to support her, even if she would not take their medications.

INPATIENT MEDICAL
AND SURGICAL PAIN CONSULTATION

Our experience in the acute care inpatient setting has been with an acute pain service (APS) based in an anesthesiology department. The psychology component of this service appears to be unique, and its development and functioning are described elsewhere (Dane, Rowlingson, & Eksterowicz, 1994). Referrals are received both from the APS medical staff and from other medical and nursing staffs throughout a 550-bed university teaching hospital. As in the outpatient setting, the expectation is both for consultation and provision of psychological intervention.

In the inpatient medical setting, it is useful to distinguish between referrals involving *de novo* (or "naive") acute pain patients (i.e., ones who are facing severe pain for the first time) and those involving patients dealing with painful exacerbations or recurrences of ongoing, chronic medical conditions. This acute versus chronic distinction is well recognized by most pain psychologists, but it is surprising to find how novel and useful it can be in an acute medical setting.

The most common inpatient referrals to the pain psychologists in our setting involve cases of problematic pain accompanying hospitalizations that are unexpectedly prolonged, often because of medical or situational complications. Such cases typically involve our most extensive, most time-consuming, and most valued input. This is not to say that effective provision of self-regulation and coping skills training for patients with *de novo* acute pain have not been gratifying or fully appreciated by referral sources. However, many caregivers, particularly nursing staff members, are already skilled in these types of interventions. The uniqueness of the pain psychologists' input has been in addressing complex cases by interweaving a particular perspective on chronicity with brief psychotherapy, coping skills training, and the highly proactive use of therapeutically refined interpersonal skills. For this reason, we focus in this section on consultation with the more complex and challenging types of acute pain referrals. The following case example is provided to help illustrate various concepts to be presented in this section.

Case Example: Sharon

Sharon was a 31-year-old woman hospitalized for severe abdominal distention and pain. She had carried a diagnosis of idiopathic intestinal pseudo-obstruction for the past 12 years. This is a relatively rare and poorly understood type of congenital neuropathy of the myenteric plexus (enteric nervous system) involving sudden interruption of bowel motility and consequent accumulation of gas, resulting in significant abdominal bloating and severe colicky pain. Corrective efforts had included exhaustive bowel motility studies and recourse to manipulations of the hormonal system. Routine clinical management, however, was limited to pain medication and aggressive programs of bowel lavage while waiting for each recurrent episode to resolve spontaneously. The patient had experienced a gradual increase in the frequency and duration of her hospitalizations, with constantly escalating doses of Demerol. The referring service was very concerned that narcotic-induced ileus (bowel immotility) was prolonging the duration of her episodes, since she was currently using more narcotic than most of the house staff had ever seen used, even for terminally ill cancer patients. The patient was blatantly hostile toward any reduction in her use of Demerol. She had a history of sensitivity to other medications, and in her experience, Demerol was the only medication that gave her reasonable relief.

Consistent with her long history of having to "fight" for whatever pain relief she could obtain, Sharon's interaction style with caregivers was irritable, accusatory, and argumentative. She was inconsistently cooperative with an aggressive bowel regimen for constipation, and engaged in a constant battle with her caregivers as to what constituted appropriate treatment. The situation was exacerbated by her frequent trips to the hospital's smoking deck area two floors away, and her pattern of socializing there with other patients who had similar reputations in the hospital for unreasonable pain medication usage. Although the extent of her abdominal distention was impressive, and she looked exhausted and in marked discomfort, Sharon was quickly labeled by most of her caregivers as a "narcotic seeker." They clearly responded to her as if there were something intentional in her condition: "If she can spend all her time up on the smoking deck, she must not be hurting that badly." Frustration levels were extremely high on all sides; no real progress was being made medically; and caregivers were in disarray as to how to deal with Sharon. Her case is described further below.

Distinctions between Outpatient and Inpatient Pain Consultation

A major difference between inpatient and outpatient pain consultation is the interpersonal intensity generated by the "captive" nature of the former setting. In the outpatient setting, time and geographic distance normally help soothe ruffled feelings and mollify the effects of negative interactions between patients and physicians. By contrast, in the inpatient setting, physicians, other staff members, and patients must contend with one another on a daily basis, with considerable pressure for immediate results. In addition, the "hothouse" environment of the inpatient setting can often lead to miscommunication and interpersonal distortions. When these problems are fueled by pre-existing psychological vulnerabilities in both patients and staff members, the circumstances can become very problematic.

It is therefore not surprising that the inpatient consultant frequently encounters misunderstanding and interpersonal strife, which lead to overly personalized reactions and stereotypic thinking in both patients and staff. As difficulties centering around pain management escalate, severe disagreement and open conflict can be generated. Even more difficult is when the severity of conflict is camouflaged by "absenteeism" from, or frank avoidance of, pertinent discussions on the part of crucial staff members. The level of conflict can become quite dysfunctional.

This was essentially the situation when a consultant was approached in Sharon's case. She was showing no improvement in her condition. Her attending physician and house staff were adamant about the need for reduction in her use of narcotics. Sharon perceived herself as unjustly labeled as a "bad patient" and experienced her caregivers as unjustifiably withholding badly needed relief. Her defense was to become increasingly demanding and intransigent, vehemently arguing that the prescribed regimens of intestinal lavage had repeatedly been ineffective in the past, and that what was needed was more effort to "fix the problem rather than just treat the symptoms." In short, the atmosphere was one of mutual blame and criticism, held in place by the medical realities of severe abdominal distention and risk of bowel perforation, but responded to with the tacit invitation to "just go somewhere else if you don't like how we do it here."

Inpatient pain management can become especially conflictual in a teaching hospital, where the cast of essential players is constantly changing. Development of treatment plans and coordination among the many different services is particularly difficult when many of the staff members may rotate on a daily or weekly basis. Even the attending physician can change several times over a course of a long hospitalization, and particularly over repeated hospitalizations. Simply achieving some form of continuity in management of a patient's pain becomes a challenge. However, since pain is an issue that pervades the patient's entire treatment, the consulting psychologist can become pivotal in both establishing and maintaining such continuity. The consultant's impact is particularly enhanced if he or she can add self-regulation training, which may improve the patient's capacity to cope, and if effective recommendations for management of medication regimens are consistently available from the APS with which the consultant is attached. Furthermore, in cases where interpersonal strife is rampant and the opportunity for an individual medical staff member to avoid a patient is built into the system through staff rotation and scheduling conflicts, the pain psychologist is often the individual best suited to maintain rapport with the patient and over time to help pilot a consistent course of pain management.

However, we should emphasize that in order to establish and maintain such a role, we have found it necessary to take a more proactive stance than is usually the case in the outpatient setting, and possibly a more proactive stance than some psychologists may find comfortable. In this sense, our earlier definition of pain consultation can be further elaborated for application to the inpatient setting: Effective pain consultation involves communication of information about the psychosocial variables that influence pain management in a way that facilitates therapeutic interaction between a consultee and a patient, and that clarifies and precipitates effective action—either by the consultant, the patient, the consultee, or some combination of these.

Yet another factor that may distinguish inpatient from outpatient pain consultation is the degree of relevance of the patient's medical condition to treatment and consultation decisions. It is crucial for the pain psychologist to maintain close alliance with competent physicians whose specialty is the medical management of pain. Only with such backing is it possible to gain the "clout" that is often necessary to help coordinate and implement recommendations for crucial medication adjustments, which may not be popular or easily understood by the treating staff. It is not uncommon that new residents, or even more experienced members of the house staff, will flatly refuse to implement APS recommendations for medication because of their misinformed but real fears of potentially lethal side effects, such as respiratory arrest or seizures.

The house staff's reaction was initially a major stumbling block in implementing treatment recommendations for Sharon. A common initial strategy for dealing with intractable pain, and the one employed with Sharon, is to assess the baseline need for pain medication by allowing patients to medicate themselves to a level of comfort through use of a patient-controlled analgesia (PCA) pump. In Sharon's case, as is not uncommon, problems with implementing this strategy were most likely to occur at night, when coverage was provided by less experienced house staff members who had no personal knowledge of the patient's circumstances, and they were backed by nurses who were isolated from reliable information that might help counter the patient's negative reputation. Left to their own judgment, the night nursing staff chose to withhold "as-needed" medications that had been duly authorized by the daytime staff. Sharon insisted on talking with "the doctor," and the on-call resident found himself in the middle of the night confronted by an angry patient demanding more pain medication than the staff had ever seen administered to any other patient. When confidently reassured by the nursing staff that this patient was "just an angry druggie," the resident had no difficulty in refusing Sharon's demands. These circumstances in turn generated valid accusations by the patient that she was being "tortured" by the night staff, who "won't give me my pain medication even though the doctor has ordered it."

In such instances, the pain psychologist may need to convince the immediate care-givers of the wisdom of obtaining additional specialized medical and nursing input, as well as to provide specific psychological treatment for the patient. In our setting, assistance from the nurse coordinator of the APS has been especially important in this regard. She has a recognition of psychological issues in patients' care, as well as relevant medical knowledge and experience. She can more readily attract the attention of the medical staff when she emphasizes certain issues as medical rather than "just" psychological. Her role has been crucial in gradually developing a pain management milieu in which patient psychology is viewed on a par with patient physiology.

For example, when Sharon's abdominal distention had finally subsided and she was ready for discharge, she remained in need of weaning from high levels of narcotics. It had not been possible to transfer her from PCA to comparable oral doses because of poor intestinal absorption. Clinical wisdom dictated sending her home on PCA rather than needlessly prolonging her hospitalization. However, her primary physician was initially adamant that "I've never sent anyone home on PCA, and I'm certainly not going to start for a case like this!" He only relented following considerable reassurance from the APS physicians that this plan was appropriate and that the APS nurse coordinator would assist in setting up the requisite home care services to help monitor medication usage. Home detoxification was in fact successful, although it was necessary to monitor the process at every stage in order to manage the inevitable obstacles that presented themselves.

A final distinction between outpatient and inpatient pain consultation is the inordinate amount of time that can be required for effective consultation, especially with complex cases. This can have significant financial implications in a fee-for-service setting, since the proportion of nonbillable to billable time can be troublesome. In addition, medical colleagues in the inpatient setting are especially intolerant of "wasted time." They often would like more to be done faster with more patients. The only antidotes we have found to this environmental demand have been establishing a record of generally effective treatment, and gradually educating staff members about the contingencies of psychological treatment.

Representative Problems in Complex Inpatient Pain Consultations

Table 15.1 summarizes representative types of problems often seen in more complex referrals. Problems are organized according to patient-specific, interpersonal, and hospital systems levels.

Several items in this table deserve comment. The first is "smoking." Like Sharon, some patients continue to go to the hospital's smoking area and socialize with other patients, despite clear indications that smoking may be contributing to their pain (as with vascular disorders) or interfering with their healing. A typical reaction from staff members is that such patients "must not be in that much pain" if they are able to engage spontaneously in this behavior. Our experience is that smoking as a way of socializing is more often an integral part of the patient's pain coping behavior, not an index of malingering or hysteria. Patients themselves may be able to verbalize their awareness of and even agreement with their physicians' concerns. But they typically claim they are unable to muster the energy and self-discipline necessary to overcome a nicotine addiction in the face of deal-

TABLE 15.1. Representative Problems in Complex Inpatient Pain Consultations

I. Patient level
   A. Extreme/inconsistent pain behaviors.
      1. Smoking
      2. Socializing with other patients
   B. Drug seeking
   C. Drug abuse
   D. Medical noncompliance
      1. Disregard for activity restrictions
      2. Poor wound self-care
      3. Poor or no participation in needed medical procedures
II. Interpersonal level
   A. "Manipulative" behavior
   B. Generalized frustration/anger
   C. Difficult/abusive interactions between patients and caregivers
   D. Animosity between patient and caregivers
   E. Animosity between services
III. Systems level
   A. Discontinuous approaches to pain management
      1. Discontinuity internal to treating institution
      2. Discontinuity between treating institution and local physician
   B. Confusion about/lack of discharge planning
   C. Desperate crescendo of increasingly invasive medical procedures

ing with their pain. Wisely or not, we generally avoid making smoking an issue; we attempt to frame it as a regrettable but effective pain coping behavior with concerned staff members; and we reserve our energy for other battles that will need to be fought and have a higher likelihood of success.

A second item deserving comment is "drug seeking." It is important to distinguish between behavior that appears to be a function of physical or psychological addiction and behavior that is a response to inadequately treated pain. It is discouraging to recognize how frequently pain is either minimized or disregarded in the hospital setting, even with obvious sources of pain such as surgery. Fortunately, such instances are increasingly rare, and the need for staff education and patient advocacy is clear when they do occur.

More difficult is determining whether, and to what extent, one should take an advocacy position for patients who are embroiled in conflicts exacerbated by the patients' own self-defeating or "manipulative" behavior. Perhaps the most that can be said is that making this determination is a matter of clinical judgment, and that errors will occur in both directions. Our own experience, however, is that with sufficient knowledge of patients' history and psychological functioning, and an adequate appreciation of the interpersonal dynamics and contingencies of each patient's situation (which itself assumes adequate rapport and alliance with the treating caretakers), it is usually possible to discriminate among patients who warrant proactive advocacy in support of better pain control; patients who warrant a more behavioral approach to containing their behavior through contracting, limit setting, and contingency management; and patients who warrant some combination of these.

Sharon's case is a good example of this experience. Interviews revealed an articulate woman in considerable distress. Her initial interaction with the consultant was belligerent and uncooperative, seemingly based on a set of beliefs and attitudes about her condition that predestined her to conflict upon entering the hospital. She reported that her local physicians had already explained to her that "pain clinics can't help me, because I have acute pain, not chronic pain." She insisted that pain management techniques outside of medication usage had never been discussed with her. Further discussion revealed that she had achieved a position of considerable responsibility in her work until approximately 2 years previously, when frequent absences because of her condition had led to conflicts with her employer. She was now on medical leave of absence and considering applying for disability.

Sharon recounted a long and escalating history of emergency room visits with severe abdominal bloating and pain, and feeling "just dismissed as a druggie." She was furious with doctors who "get me addicted to this stuff and then tell me I can't have it, even if I need it." With regard to her past treatment, she expressed considerable frustration: "All they did was keep giving me pain medication. They weren't doing anything to fix the problem." She stated that she had come to our hospital despite the absence of approval from her insurance company, because she was convinced that the gastroenterology specialist in our institution would be in a better position to do more for her.

Sharon denied any previous psychiatric history, and adamantly denied any history of excessive drug use outside of episodes of severe abdominal pain. This information was later corroborated by collateral sources. Further discussion clarified that she was not opposed to the idea of self-regulation training to assist in managing her pain "if it could work." However, her chief interest was in "getting the problem fixed rather than just putting all these Band-Aids on it." It became abundantly clear that she had never accepted the inevitable chronicity of her condition, and was still approaching the situation from an "acute pain" perspective. Within our nested-matrix model, she could be described as lodged in the anger, denial, and bargaining stages of an arrested grief response, and would need to be treated accordingly (for details of this formulation, see Dane & Kessler, 1994, pp. 58–59 and 70–71).

In attempting to distinguish which patients warrant an advocacy position, it is important to determine exactly what is meant in any given instance by the ubiquitous accusation of "manipulative behavior." By focusing with staff members on specific patient behaviors and attitudes that have contributed to the sense of being manipulated, the pain psychologist can often identify sources of difficulty and targets for intervention. In Sharon's case, the staff members were complaining about the frequency with which she would go two floors away to the smoking deck. Staff interpretations of this behavior included statements that it was an effort to "get sympathy by looking so pathetic as she mopes around dragging her IV pole with her," and that it was evidence that "she must not really be hurting all that much." "This isn't the Holiday Inn, you know!" was a frequently heard comment from both physicians and other members of the staff.

Direct discussion of these behaviors with Sharon yielded a very different perspective. She explained that although it was difficult, walking was one of the few things that could help reduce her severe colic pain. Walking seemed to help because it helped move the air lodged in her abdomen. She acknowledged that cigarette smoking was not healthy, but stated that she was under enough stress without adding nicotine withdrawal to her problems. Sharon also lived in a distant city, missed her family's support a great deal, and found solace in commiserating with other patients with similar difficulties. She also openly acknowledged her desire to "avoid being around those doctors and nurses" as much as possible, since "they just treat me like a druggie anyway." It was clear that considerable work would be needed to establish rapport and mutual understanding before any effective negotiations could take place about a mutually acceptable balance between self-care and the need to be available for medical treatment.

A Treatment Model Based on Interpersonal Influence

By "interpersonal influence" we are referring to interpersonal skills and competencies in rapidly establishing and maintaining therapeutic rapport and alliance, even in the face of conflict. In particular, these include the abilities to assess the interpersonal dynamics of a situation, to avoid personalizing the extreme reactions one can encounter, to maintain a sense of calm in the face of extreme conflict, and to generate in others the willingness to examine their own behavior and attitudes. As already discussed in regard to the outpatient situation, the role of the consulting pain psychologist is to assist in rehumanizing the interactions among all parties involved, through recognition and clarification of the patient's agenda based on his or her unique systems of beliefs and perceptions. This can allow parties in conflict to experience one another as caring human beings who can make mistakes but who are essentially of good will. Once this "rehumanization" occurs, cooperation and problem solving tend to emerge.

The Pain Psychologist as "Leverage Point"

Despite having a central role in establishing and maintaining continuity in approach, the pain psychologist cannot have primary responsibility for the patient's pain management. This is clearly the responsibility of the attending physicians and treatment team. However, when considerable interpersonal strife is associated with a task, teams often become disorganized and dysfunctional, and lose flexibility and continuity of approach. For the majority of harried physicians and nurses, dealing with problematic behavioral issues has little reinforcement value by comparison with "real" medical concerns. Thus, they often simply desire to have the psychologist "straighten out" the problem. However, since most complex pain problems have become complex precisely because of psychosocial and personality issues, avoidance can become an acceptable norm for dealing with pain problems. It becomes the consulting psychologist's task to translate interpersonal concerns from stumbling blocks into incentives for effective action and coordination of care.

In addition to direct communication with specific individuals, one of the most effective strategies in this translation process can be the psychologist's willingness to precipitate "useful crises." As we describe in more detail below, this means creating a therapeutic context in which difficult issues both can and must be addressed, decisions made, and treatment plans implemented. In this sense, the pain consultant becomes both a fulcrum and a leverage point for effective action.

Understanding Leverage: When, Where, How Much, and What Kind

The psychologist should first take whatever time is needed to evaluate the situation before taking any action. Resisting the push for immediate action can be difficult, especially with patients whose pain behavior is creating havoc with staff members and interfering with appropriate medical care. In complex situations, it can require several days to develop the rapport necessary to understand what is going on from the patient's perspective. The delays may be mechanical, such as the patient's being off the floor for medical procedures when the psychologist is available. Or a particular staff member who has crucial information based on his or her personal experience of the patient may be off work that day. The patient's own internal dynamics may also interfere with the easy development of rapport, or the patient may simply be too physically and emotionally exhausted to interact at a given time.

The psychologist's flexibility and tenacity in gaining access to the patient become important messages to the patient and caregivers. They indicate how serious the psychologist is (or isn't) about helping with a difficult situation that may have already "chased off" a number of potential helpers. The willingness simply to keep showing up at the patient's room can ultimately produce rapport, particularly when the patient is initially diffident or offended about the idea of talking with a psychologist. Demonstration of respect for timing and for the patient's sense of control over boundary issues can go a long way toward overcoming such initial reluctance. In addition, the psychologist's demonstration of tenacity may be the patient's (and staff's) first experience of hope about achieving some understanding of his or her situation.

Some Basic Principles of Intervention

Within the process of consultation and treatment, we identify five basic principles that help define and organize our activities. The first posits that with regard to communication, human beings tend to repeat themselves until they feel "heard." This phenomenon has as much to do with acknowledging the speaker's affective status as with acknowledging the intellectual or factual content of what is communicated. Since pain behavior is a form of communication, patients are likely to "repeat themselves" (perseverate in pain behavior) until they are heard. Once they feel genuinely heard and believed, there can be less emphasis on communication (pain behavior) and more on problem solving (e.g., development of self-regulation strategies). This principle is especially relevant in decisions about to what degree one should serve as the patient's advocate in contentious settings. For example, Sharon's ability to accept additional goals beyond mere reliance on medication (i.e., training in self-hypnosis) helped discriminate her as a patient who warranted advocacy. However, given her level of emotional distress, she would have been unable even to consider the relevance of alternative goals without first feeling heard.

A second organizing principle is that the pragmatics and contingencies of medical urgency dictate automated and stereotypic thinking when possible. Since interpersonal dynamics necessarily have low priority in the face of medical urgency, stereotypic and automated thinking is the norm with regard to the psychosocial aspects of acute pain management. The pain consultant's role is therefore to help consultees (i.e., both patients and caregivers) identify and counteract this tendency in themselves, and to establish circumstances and provide information that help counteract effects of this tendency. This often means helping staff members to understand their patients as specific human beings with specific wants, needs, and personal circumstances that have become lost in the pull for stereotyping.

An important part of communicating this information to caregivers is via progress notes in each patient's medical chart. Here, use of formal diagnoses is generally less helpful than communicating specific information about prior functioning and specific psychosocial circumstances or stressors. Such information communicates a sense of the person who exists outside the immediate circumstances of pain complaints and interpersonal strife. The absence of such information is especially damaging to patients who are only known to staff members when they repeatedly show up at the hospital, disheveled and in pain, "seeking medications." Knowledge that an individual also has two children in college, is devoted to his or her family, and is an active member of a church can go a long way toward mitigating erroneous impressions based on limited experience of the patient's total life situation.

When one is writing in the patient's chart, it is also useful to communicate some sense of the patient's intra- and interpersonal dynamics and coping style. However, this information must be communicated in a way that gives a practical basis for understanding and interacting with the patient with regard to the presenting problem. Formal psychological terms such as "regression" and "transference" can be translated into less formal language such as "emotional age" and "personality template."

Rehumanizing caregivers' perceptions of their patients is not limited to written or verbal descriptions, however, as Sharon's case illustrates. A particularly effective strategy in this regard involved Sharon's returning for a social visit to the unit after she had successfully discontinued all narcotics, contrary to most of her caretakers' expectations. There was a stark and unmistakable contrast between the svelte, stylishly dressed, and pleasant young woman of obvious competence who returned to visit the unit and the bedraggled creature who had been sent off with such strong misgivings and dire predictions. She was a remarkable example of the blatant interpersonal misconceptions that can be generated by misperceived pain and suffering.

Counteracting the pull for stereotyping may also mean helping patients such as Sharon to understand and recognize the concepts of transferential reactions and self-defeating behaviors (the psychodynamic correlates of "automated thinking"), and to facilitate more adaptive responses in light of this understanding. In Sharon's case, the consultant focused on her own behaviors and attitudes that were contributing to her problems in obtaining appropriate care. Specifically, the consultant identified with her a pattern of generating interpersonal "storms" and emotional upset as a way to deflect and avoid confronting difficult realities that she did not want to accept (e.g., that her condition was indeed chronic and no ready "fix" was available). This preparation was quite useful in countering a tendency toward similar behavior during subsequent hospitalizations.

A third organizing principle for consultation and intervention has to do with the phenomenon of "personalizing" others' reactions. Both caregivers and patients need to become inoculated to the debilitating impact of inappropriate overpersonalization by identifying it as a phenomenon, pointing it out when it occurs, and suitably reinforcing improved handling of the phenomenon. This strategy can have an impact when one is faced with what can appear to be impossibly tangled webs of reactions between patients and caregivers. It seems to provide both a refreshing reminder of appropriate professional behavior and a face-saving mechanism to justify rapid reversal of previously intransigent positions and attitudes. Implementation of this principle involves the psychodynamic notion of providing a "container" for the considerable affect that can be generated in both patients and staff during conflicts centering around pain management. This simply means allowing open expression of affect in others (i.e., emotional ventilation) without adding one's own affect to the situation. This neutral acceptance and tolerance of emotion without retribution both models appropriate professional behavior for distraught caregivers, and reassures regressed patients that their own affect can be tolerated and therefore "contained" by a trusted adult figure.

The fourth and final principle is the need to take a gradual or shaping approach to altering human behavior. This means that targeted goals, such as improved trust and rapport and reduced medication consumption, may require from several days to several hospitalizations to achieve. Maintaining this perspective is not easy in the inpatient setting, but it is a crucial antidote to unrealistic expectations.

Sharon's case again illustrates our point. At this writing, she has gone through two additional hospitalizations. Her referring physician is impressed with the extended length of time between hospital admissions, and with Sharon's use of self-regulation strategies to tolerate minor flare-ups in her condition, which previously would have triggered yet another bout of escalating narcotic usage. It is now possible to meet and discuss options with Sharon in a calm setting on an outpatient basis. As an outpatient she is able to consider and discuss her options rationally, free from the distractions, distortions, and potential avoidance of uncomfortable reality issues afforded by dealing with severe acute pain. This has only become possible through a gradual shaping effort by the consulting psychologist, who has maintained rapport with both the patient and the ever-changing cast of caretakers involved across successive hospitalizations.

Therapeutic Sleuthing as a Consulting Strategy

When dealing with complex pain problems, a consultant may encounter reports from reasonable and reliable staff members about the attitudes and actions of seemingly villainous others, who are described as either over- or undermedicating the patient out of ignorance or ill will. It is important, however, that the consultant *not* accept such reports at face value, and do a thorough investigation of his or her own. The situation frankly does sometimes resemble that of a detective attempting to solve a mystery. However, the goal is not to determine who is "guilty," but to identify potential targets for intervention. Often, what is needed may be readily apparent, since the problem is simply that no one has had the time or energy to obtain the information needed to coordinate an effective solution. At other times, frank intransigence and avoidance may have resulted in deadlock.

The process of therapeutic sleuthing is one of becoming adequately immersed in the perspectives of the various personnel involved (who are often "too busy" to communicate with one another), and then attempting to foster a spirit and context of mutual education and negotiation among those perspectives. Therapeutic sleuthing can be greatly facilitated or hindered by the quality of rapport with the nursing staff. In a teaching hospital, nurses can become the *de facto* purveyors of continuity in care, since they are often the only unchanging elements across multiple readmissions of a given patient. Their support and cooperation are crucial to the implementation of any long-term treatment plan. We have therefore found it useful to make a habit of daily contact with the nurses assigned to a patient for a given day. This practice is typically very well received by nurses, who can often feel ignored and undervalued in patients' care, especially when they are dealing with complex and hostile patients who are frankly being avoided by their physicians.

Daily contact between nurses and the pain psychologist serves a number of additional functions. Since the nursing staff holds the key to perpetuating or altering a patient's reputation within the hospital, this alliance can provide important leverage in dealing with new attending physicians or house staff members who are unfamiliar with a given patient. Daily contact with the nursing staff also helps the psychologist to monitor and potentially influence the interpersonal "tone" surrounding a patient's care. This tone is most often communicated to patients through their daily contacts with nurses. In addition, daily conversations with the nursing staff permit the psychologist to monitor a broader range of the patient's functioning than would otherwise be possible. This provides a sort of early warning detection system for potential areas of need for troubleshooting.

Precipitating Useful Crises

At times, the extent of interpersonal toxicity and the consequent damage to a patient's reputation with the staff can lead to a degree of deadlock in the patient's care that requires a "miniexplosion" to dislodge. In such situations, it can be helpful to generate a "useful crisis." By this we mean highlighting or amplifying situations or circumstances that are not being addressed, but that can no longer be tolerated (e.g., inconsistencies among nursing shifts in willingness to administer prescribed levels of pain medications).

In precipitating useful crises, the trick is to generate a situation that is perceived by physicians and the hospital staff as appropriately unavoidable, in the same way that medical crises are unavoidable. We believe that this model of managing the pain consultation process via successive levels of "managed crises" can be effective because it is already familiar to medical personnel. When a patient is dying, something has to be done immediately. By judicious orchestration of challenging personal interactions, the pain psychologist can elevate the status of a patient's pain complaints from a nuisance to be avoided to a medical necessity that logically must be addressed. Unpleasant and uncomfortable as they may be, medical crises must be dealt with. Even beleaguered staff members can feel good about confronting difficult challenges, despite ultimately negative outcomes. Appropriate support to staff members may consist simply in maintaining a sense of humor and detachment as they discuss the most recent vitriolic attack by the patient on the staff members' professional competence for failure to deliver pain medication exactly on time. Like most medical crises, however, most pain crises can be dealt with successfully. All that is generally needed is facilitation of communication and understanding between patients and caregivers, through identifying and countering stereotypic thinking and overpersonalized reactions.

In more complex cases, a primary vehicle for dealing with crisis can be the multidisciplinary patient care conference. It is here that the pain psychologist's interpersonal skills may be the most severely taxed. Arranging such conferences requires that those requested to attend feel both that they must attend and that the patient's care will benefit from their attendance. There may be strongly conflicting opinions about what should be done about the problem to be addressed, not to mention considerable interpersonal friction between those asked to attend. Schedules crowded with valid demands provide built-in excuses for not attending. And in an extreme case, the patient's behavior may have so thoroughly alienated most caregivers that there is little sympathy for "sacrificing" even more time and energy in what can feel like a worthless cause. It is in this scenario that the role of consulting psychologist as proactive stage manager and role juggler becomes most prominent.

In preparation for a patient care conference, it is essential that the patient be adequately prepared, and that the pain psychologist have some sense of the patient's response to issues that are likely to be raised in the conference. This includes assessment of the patient's capacity to tolerate and respond appropriately to the inevitable stress of such a meeting. Precipitation of a "test" minicrisis can be useful in this process.

For example, the consultant working with Sharon identified a pattern of blaming and focusing on emotional upset with others, rather than on acceptance of her condition and on problem solving (as noted earlier). This pattern was normalized and therefore depersonalized by framing it as a common expression of the "bargaining" phase of an arrested grief response. It was unclear, however, whether Sharon was capable of self-monitoring or altering this pattern. If not, it would be counterproductive to include her in a patient care conference, since her behavior would only be likely to confirm impressions of her as "impossible to deal with." Just prior to initiating a request for a conference, the consultant therefore chose to risk confronting her about this behavior in a way that would clearly stretch the therapeutic alliance (i.e., interpreting the possible role of this behavior in the history of three previous marriages). As predicted, Sharon became quite upset and even threatened to leave the hospital. Agreeing that leaving was one of her choices, the consultant requested that she examine her response as a possible example of the very behavior they had been discussing (i.e., avoidance), and that she indicate within the next hour or so whether she would be leaving or staying. She ultimately chose to stay, and the outcome of the subsequent patient care conference was remarkably positive. Sharon was able to avoid defensive posturing and to present herself and her history in a convincing manner that elicited compassion and understanding from her caregivers. This became a major turning point in forging a more global therapeutic alliance that had begun several weeks previously as a hostile interaction with "some damn shrink who thinks it's all in my head!"

In general, it has been gratifying to see how readily caregivers and sufficiently adaptive patients have been able to make use of experiences and conceptual frameworks that help to rehumanize the patients and establish a useful understanding of relevant interpersonal dynamics, which permits a move to more solution-oriented behaviors. As Sharon's case readily illustrates, consultation with medical and surgical inpatients can be a challenge to all the skills of a pain psychologist. However, the inpatient setting remains a highly underdeveloped arena for psychological consultation.

INTEGRATION OF INDIVIDUAL AND SYSTEMS CONSULTATION: SPECIAL PROBLEMS OF WORKPLACE INJURIES

Case Example: From Acute Back Pain to Chronic Disability

The case of Bill, a 45-year-old married man with four children and limited formal education, illustrates several commonplace problems associated with blue-collar workplace injuries. For 18 years Bill had operated a stamping press requiring hundreds of repetitive insertions and removals of small pieces of metal per hour, periodically punctuated by moving 40-pound trays of unstamped pieces and shaped parts. Lifting these trays from knee level gradually became more difficult, as over the years Bill gained weight and lost some of his former strength and flexibility. Some days his back ached so much he could barely make his minimum quota, and a couple of times he asked the plant nurse for some aspirin to help him complete the day. One morning a metal piece became jammed in the mechanism of the press. As he had done many times before, Bill reached in and pulled as hard as he could, but this time he felt a sharp stabbing pain in his lower back. Bent over with pain, Bill went to the first aid station, where a nurse gave him some analgesic medication and permission to take off the remainder of the day. The next morning he could hardly move, and his wife called in sick for him. He continued with several more days of rest and analgesics, but finally went to his family doctor, who diagnosed a sprain/strain back injury and recommended more rest and medication. But after 3 weeks without improvement, the family doctor made a referral to an orthopedic surgeon.

Now, nearly a month after the injury, the surgeon saw a physically unfit, anxious, and depressed-appearing middle-aged man with what appeared to be a sprain/strain soft-tissue injury superimposed on a benign postural back condition. In light of Bill's fear of losing his job, the surgeon reluctantly admitted him to a hospital for a complete workup. The tests were tedious and painful, and the myelogram left him with a terrible headache. Bill was greatly disappointed when he was informed that he did not have a surgically correctable problem. He left the hospital thoroughly confused and angry, especially about the implication that there was nothing seriously wrong with his aching back. Out of desperation he saw another doctor, who reached the same conclusion, but did recommend that he begin a course of intensive physical therapy. But because Bill's problems were now compounded by nearly 2 months of inactivity, the physical therapy seemed excessively difficult, and he feared it might be dangerous and make his pain even worse. Most of all, he wondered whether the doctors did not care what happens to him or had made some terrible mistake in their diagnosis.

Meanwhile, Bill's employer and compensation carrier were demanding to know what was "really wrong" with him. In turn, he was beginning to feel frantic. He had a family to support, and who else would hire him at his age? His doctors resented being caught in the middle of his dilemma, but one of them finally cleared him for "light duty." Reluctantly the employer agreed, but after weeks of inactivity, Bill was slow-moving and requested numerous rest breaks. This irritated his coworkers, who implied that he was a "goldbricker." Feeling increasingly alienated and depressed, he complained to his foreman that the work was too hard, which elicited this response: "If you don't like it, you can quit." After a few more days he decided that he could tolerate the pain no longer and he did quit, immediately canceling all of his benefits. On the basis of nursing records that he had earlier sought aspirin for back pain, he was told that he was ineligible for workers' compensation because of a "prior condition." He was furious that he had given "the best years of my life" to an employer who was now "treating me like dirt." Driven by anxiety and desperation, he went to a lawyer for help. He felt that his life was now controlled by powerful others, none of whom could be trusted. Further visits to doctors were at the request of "the system" and were therapeutically futile. He no longer expected to improve; he only wanted to prove the legitimacy of his pain and see that justice was served.

Consultation with the Individual Worker

In Western society, almost nothing is more threatening to a person's identity than the loss of earning potential. Such circumstances inevitably give rise to self-protective cognitions and behaviors by which the individual attempts to maintain a sense of internal direction. Bill's scenario is not at all uncommon; in fact, sometimes the picture is even worse. Included may be numerous unsuccessful surgical procedures; drug addiction; severe family disruption and divorce; or, more rarely, serious depression accompanied by threats of suicide and/or homicide.

More so than any other type of case, the pain patient reporting problems with medical or disability insurance payments raises the apprehension of an HCP. Experience tells the clinician that this patient will generate a lot of paperwork, but may still be distraught and may well fail to respond to treatment efforts. Furthermore, the HCP may end up obligated to determine the patient's work fitness (or disability), whether or not he or she feels qualified to do so.

It is crucial that the consultant be alerted to the fact that a case involves workers' compensation, and therefore that he or she thoroughly explore the patient's view of the work environment and perceptions of future options. Patients such as Bill, who all too often appear desperately pleading or demanding that they be certified as having "legitimate" pain, must be handled sympathetically but firmly. We try to reassure such patients that although we recognize their concerns, we are not all-powerful parents who can instantly relieve all their anxiety about the future. Generally, we inform these patients that we will be willing to deal with their "determinations" at the appropriate time, after we have sufficient information and a meaningful relationship has been established.

It is not unusual for individuals injured at work to report that their employer was initially sympathetic, but began to demonstrate a perceptible shift in attitude after the passage of several weeks. Employers and their insurance carriers understand actuarial tables. Ninety percent of laborers with back injuries return to work in 6 weeks or less (Spitzer et al., 1987); however, those who fail to return within this relatively brief time window are at very high risk for long-term disability. This is a turning point at which the employer and insurance carrier may latch onto any possible excuse to challenge the legitimacy of the claim. With many soft-tissue injury pain cases, physical findings are vague, some prior history of pain is common, and motivation to return to work can always be questioned. The employer/insurer challenge, as in the case of Bill, can initiate a rapid polarization of opinion about fault, responsibility, and entitlement, prompting a mutual adversarial stance. The patient suddenly feels abandoned and persecuted by those he or she feels should be helping.

Once the worker and employer/insurer began their adversarial standoff, it is a very difficult time for an HCP to step in and successfully treat the pain. Instead of a single patient to please, the HCP now encounters a cast of characters with mutually exclusive goals. Nevertheless, the consultant must encourage all parties to avoid the uniformity myth that all patients presenting with employment/insurance conflicts have the single goal of becoming certified as disabled in order to procure financial entitlements. Even though many workplace-injured pain patients may superficially appear alike, consistently presenting as frustrated, angry, and depressed, one must still listen to the details of the individual story. A key element to monitor is the degree to which the patient has already become identified with the disability role. At least three quite different patient subgroups can be recognized:

1. *Patients with a firmly established disability identity.* Unfortunately, such an individual does correspond to the negative stereotype. His or her identity is that of a disabled person with little residual energy remaining for investment in alternative roles. This patient seeks credentials that will legitimize his or her disability status—not just for the present, but for the future as well, since there is no expectation of returning to work. There is also minimal or no expectation of ever receiving help with pain; consistent with the identity, a primary reason for accepting a referral, besides fear of being seen as noncompliant, is to prove the ineffectiveness of all treatments. The disability identity may be entirely justified by physical condition or circumstances, or, at the other extreme, may appear absurd. The consultant should warn HCPs against the low return on risky medical interventions directed at a behavioral pattern that is unlikely to change. Such patients must, of course, receive essential medical care, and insurance companies are best advised to reach a settlement appropriate to the actual facts in the case as quickly as possible.

2. *Patients with a temporary disability identity.* A second set of patients may appear similarly emotionally upset. Such a patient may have recently been denied medical and wage benefits, or his or her employment may have been abruptly terminated. Again, the physical findings and circumstantial facts may or may not fit the patient's view. However, this individual simply wants justice relative to the perceived injury. The person does not expect the pain to last forever, nor is his or her self-esteem tied to remaining permanently

disabled. This patient can still benefit from treatment and will often return to work as soon as the case is resolved. Clues regarding disability identity can often be elicited by a question like this: "What do you expect to do in the future?" Patients in this second sub-type will have plans and will be eager to seek information about options.

3. *Patients with an ambivalent disability identity.* An uncertain identity, unfortunately, is often the plight of an older worker such as Bill. The person's self-esteem may still be tied to the job, but he or she fears that there may no longer be any viable employment opportunities remaining. Bill clearly feared returning to the job; he doubted his ability to do a full day's work, and therefore feared being fired. Disability compensation was not his preferred route, but it rapidly become his only perceived option. Some ambivalent patients will respond well to work reconditioning programs. (e.g., see Feuerstein, 1991). Also, allowance for a trial of part-time work and/or light duty can be extremely helpful in preventing a premature formation of a rigid disability identity.

Cast of Characters in the Disability Scenario

The consultant's task with the workplace-injured patient can be complicated by the vested interests of least three different groups: (1) the patient and his or her family; (2) the health care system; and (3) the employer, the insurance company, and the legal system. It is especially difficult to coordinate these diverse interests when the patient arrives after adversarial positions have already been staked out. A consultant may wish to view himself or herself as the patient's advocate, but must also recognize that access to his or her services may be entirely controlled by the third-party payer. Under such circumstances, the consultant's greatest value may be the ability to bring a systems perspective to the problem. In the midst of the adversarial posturing, the consultant must try to emphasize the need to maintain a "reality" focus, rather than a "magical wish" or "blaming focus."

Maintaining a Focus on Reality

The patient must be educated as to how the workplace insurance system works, and counseled to try not to take challenges to his or her credibility so personally. The "reality" the patient must face is not only medical, but psychosocial as well. For example, we will alert a 30-year-old patient with a benign back injury that a failure to return to work within a month will predictably lead to a questioning of motivation. With that in mind, we may tell the patient something to this effect:

> "You must be prepared to do what seems to be in your best interests. That is usually to get back to work as soon as possible, but if you feel that you cannot or should not, you must get yourself retrained or repositioned toward another type of work. Otherwise, you must be prepared to fight a battle with the insurance carrier—a battle you are probably going to lose. In the meantime, we will urge your insurer to give you some time to sort this out, but we are going to have to suggest a time limit by which a decision (returning to work, moving toward some other type of work, or being ready to reach a reasonable settlement) can be reached."

The patient may not like this message, but being informed encourages the formation of an adaptive perspective that may have been previously absent. In contrast to the younger worker, a middle-aged patient with similar symptoms may be counseled to seek lighter work, early retirement, or even medical disability. Sometimes social system prob-

lems masquerade as medical problems. When after only 10 seasons a professional foot-
ball player loses a step, it is time for him to retire—we don't expect doctors to fix him. But
the medical system may be expected to "fix" and return to the starting lineup a 60-year-
old coal miner who is no longer able to work on his knees in cold, damp conditions. We
advocate that all concerned must face the reality of such a situation and stop pretending
that blaming the patient, or the doctors, is going to solve any problems.

Insurance and Legal Consultation

The effective pain consultant must learn to work with insurance representatives, most
often those identified as "rehabilitation case managers" or "rehabilitation specialists."
Access to psychological services may be entirely controlled by such individuals. Case
managers vary a great deal in their background, training, knowledge, and style of handling cases. They can be burdened by large caseloads, which leave them with little ability
to respond to the nuances of individual cases. Some are helpful and sympathetic to
patients' needs, others can be unwaveringly bureaucratic and view the patients as "en-
emies." Most work under a mandate to try to resolve cases as rapidly and cheaply as possible. Naturally, their greatest fear is open-ended treatment during which a patient receives full medical coverage and lost wages.

A consultant must try to understand the contingencies under which case managers
work, while simultaneously attempting to educate them to the reality of each patient's
situation. Ignoring the case manager will only make things worse for the patient. The
manager should be reassured that the consultant's goal is to help with reaching decisions
within certain time limits, no matter what the improvement level of the patient may be.
The consultant should provide as much as possible of the requested documentation, even
when endless rounds of redundant forms are required; insurance company employees
function in an environment where supervisors will question any judgments unsupported
by written documentation.

The consultant may, by agreement or subpoena, become involved in legal proceedings. The courtroom culture can be disconcerting to the uninitiated psychologist. Legal
proceedings are by their very nature adversarial, with one side winning and the other
side losing. This environment fosters little appreciation for the subtleties of psychosocial
contributions to chronic pain. Complex issues are reduced to binary assertions that a
patient is either telling the truth or faking for reasons of secondary gain. Although a
psychologist can try to educate, even in court, attention must be given to communicating
in a clear and concise manner. Becoming too esoteric about cognitive-behavioral nuances
can produce increased confusion.

The nature of the questioning faced by the pain psychologist in court is usually quite
predictable. The attorney representing the insurance company will attempt to use psychological testimony to support the argument that the patient has a pre-existing history
of poor social, vocational, and emotional functioning, or has current personal or family
reasons beyond the actual injury for having insufficient motivation to get better and
return to work. The patient's lawyer, in turn, will wish to establish that whatever mood,
behavioral, or other documentable psychosocial problems may be evident are the results
of pain in a person who would otherwise be functioning well. A careful social and vocational history, as well as knowledge of the patient's current beliefs and attitudes about
the injury, can be useful in addressing these issues.

Obviously, to maintain personal integrity and credibility, the consultant must present
as sworn testimony only what he or she considers to be the truth. Because we presume

that many patients are unaware that information gathered by a consultant may be used against them in a court proceeding, we are reluctant to testify in a manner that will harm a patient's case. If we are requested to testify regarding a patient for whom we believe our information will not be helpful, we let the patient's attorney know about our belief. Quite naturally, doing so nearly always results in a withdrawal of the request for our participation. When consultants are subpoenaed in such cases by the opposition, the best strategy seems to be to stick as close to the facts as possible, offering minimal comment or interpretation. Cases with little merit will seldom go far in the legal system. When our information will be supportive of the client's claims, we will similarly report facts; however, we liberally add comments about the danger of stereotyping pain patients, point out potential abuses where they seem to occur, and emphasize where accusations made about the patient's motives and character seem improbable in light of his or her past social and work history.

A Systems Approach to Pain and Disability Management

Many years of observing how disability is amplified by pain transformed into an adversarial legal event, as well as our own research on injury management systems (see, e.g., Carron, DeGood, & Tait, 1985), have led us to the conclusion that if employers and their insurance carriers can develop an adequate humanitarian plan for dealing with patients' needs and concerns following injuries, they will find that such a plan can end up saving them money. Concerns similar to those seen in the individual case require attention, but these concerns must be analyzed from the perspective of the systems in which the patient functions. It is no longer only the individual patient's beliefs that require appraisal, but rather the beliefs and attitudes that characterize an entire system of management and labor.

Prevention of Pain Disability

The case of Bill is a good starting point for dealing with systems. Bill had a good premorbid social and work history; yet only a few weeks after a relatively minor injury, he was involved in an adversarial struggle with his employer and insurer, which almost guaranteed his prematurely slipping into the disability trap. He rapidly acquired a disability identity not merely to preserve self-esteem, but to protect himself against the fear of unemployability.

The groundwork for understanding and reducing long-term pain-related disability in the workplace comes from studies (e.g., Bigos & Battie, 1987; Bigos et al., 1992; Frymoyer, 1992) suggesting that psychosocial factors are more instrumental than physical factors in failure to return to work after a back injury. These psychosocial factors include perception of fault, perception of compensability for an injury, lawyer involvement, low job satisfaction, expectation of continued disability, and few transferable vocational skills. But these same studies also suggest that preventive measures can be taken to reduce the occurrence of disability resulting from chronic pain. We have consulted for some time with a private psychological practice and a group of orthopedic physicians working with local employers on implementing such an effort.

There is no special magic that will eliminate all workplace disability. Some individuals are going to sustain serious injuries and become disabled. Likewise, there will always be disgruntled employees with limited coping skills and a strong sense of entitlement, who will strive to establish their disability credentials even with little physical evidence. But what can be dramatically reduced is system-generated disability—that is, disability that results from poor handling of injury cases, leading to premature polarization of opinion and adversarial posturing. Too often, the shortsighted approach with employees like Bill has been to "get tough" by cutting off compensation after a few weeks, thus challenging the employees to "prove" in court that they are truly deserving. There is an ample supply of lawyers who specialize in "helping" people like Bill seek redress for their perceived injustice. The immediate effect is for these injured workers to divert effort that might be put into rehabilitation into proving that they deserve disability benefits.

Several strategies that employers can adopt to reduce premature polarization of beliefs and attitudes include the following:

1. Employers should demonstrate a positive interest in injured or sick employees, by having the health/safety staff and supervisors show positive concern.

2. Whenever feasible, injuries and lost wages should be covered immediately with sickness and accident insurance. A patient who is out of work for only a brief time should not be forced to resort to adversarial tactics to cover his or her losses.

3. Meaningful light duty should be made available. This may be the single most important factor in keeping a patient out of the sickness/disability role. The work must not be so aversive or meaningless that it is perceived as punishment.

4. Employers should not reflexively challenge all workers' compensation claims, but should develop a sufficient information network that allows sound discrimination between deserving and truly questionable claims. When nearly all employees' claims are challenged as a matter of policy, employees will assume that they have no choice but to seek an attorney promptly or be vulnerable to capricious treatment.

5. Employers should establish an injury management protocol that begins immediately after an acute injury, and make sure it is someone's responsibility to make sure that the protocol is being followed.

An Injury Management Protocol

1. *Immediately following injury.* If the patient does not return to work on the day of the injury or the next day, the patient is examined by a doctor. Conservative care is initiated, but bed rest is avoided unless absolutely necessary. An educational videotape about the conservative management of back pain (or other conditions) is viewed by the patient, and a brief questionnaire designed to assess the patient's perception of the injury and expectations about his or her recovery is completed. Return to light-duty work is arranged as soon as the patient feels ready. For the small fraction of patients for whom the physical exam indicates a need for a presurgical diagnostic workup, this workup is begun within a few days. Medical bills and lost wages are covered without question, and the immediate supervisor is urged to call the patient at home to express his or her concern.

2. *From 2 to 4 weeks after injury.* If no significant improvement occurs within 2 to 4 weeks, a second medical opinion is sought, with responsibility for coordinating care remaining with the first doctor. A decision is made whether to hospitalize the patient for more comprehensive and expensive diagnostic testing. If the test results are negative, conservative therapy is continued (especially physical therapy), with a target date set for return to light duty. A brief psychological consultation is obtained to assess the patient's perception of the situation, and to collect some information about relevant past history and stressors in the current work and family situation that might hamper progress. Counseling is provided if indicated.

3. *From 6 to 10 weeks after injury.* If there is still no progress, the employer and the medical and psychological team try to reach a decision about what treatments should be continued, when the patient should be ready to attempt a return to work, whether the patient should change jobs, whether retraining for a different line of work should be encouraged, or whether reaching an insurance settlement should be considered. After nearly 3 months of no improvement, if physical evidence is not supportive of the level of pain behavior and/or unresolvable psychosocial factors appear prominent, the patient is clearly told the nature of the team's concern. The case may become adversarial at this time, but this need not be the case. If the patient chooses to seek legal redress, both parties have the advantage of access to an orderly body of information.

The key to the success of the plan is for the entire process to be handled in an orderly and fair manner, with all parties having full access to all information and opinions. There are no lengthy time gaps or mysterious, hidden decision-making processes in the protocol that will cause the patient to begin feeling abandoned or confused. Polarization of opinion, which can lead to adversarial positioning, is reduced. It has been a personally rewarding experience for us to see that the principles learned in years of consultation with individual chronic pain patients can be applied and can make a difference at a systems level.

CONCLUSION

The routine of the psychological pain consultant can be quite different from expected stereotypes about pain and psychology. Patients often fear that the purpose of referral to a psychologist is for a "sanity check" because someone believes the pain is "all in my head." In turn, the referral source may harbor an equally distorted notion that psychologists can use some mysterious and potent magic to turn a fearful, angry, and demanding behavioral problem into a happy and compliant patient. In contrast to such expectations, the effort that may actually make the most difference is for the consultant to act as a patient advocate, referee, negotiator, or stage manager who attempts to help the patient navigate the treacherous shoals of chronic pain and deal with the cast of characters that may be encountered along the way. As detailed in this chapter, this effort can occur in a variety of settings and can include both individual and systems interventions.

REFERENCES

Beutler, L. E., Engle, D., Oro'-Beutler, E., Daldrup, R., & Meredith, K. (1986). Inability to express intense affect: A common link between depression and pain. *Journal of Consulting and Clinical Psychology, 54*, 752–759.

Bieliauskas, L. A. (1991). Critical issues in consultation and liaison: Adults. In J. J. Sweet, R. H. Rozensky, & S. M. Tovian (Eds.), *Handbook of clinical psychology in medical settings* (pp. 187–200). New York: Plenum Press.

Bigos, S. J., & Battie, M. C. (1987). Acute care to prevent back disability. *Clinical Orthopaedics and Related Research, 221*, 121–130.

Bigos, S. J., Battie, M. C., Spengler, D. M., Fisher, L. D., Fordyce, W. E., Hansson, T., Nachemson, A. L., & Zeh, J. (1992). A longitudinal, prospective study of industrial back injury reporting. *Clinical Orthopaedics and Related Research, 279*, 21–34.

Carron, H., DeGood, D. E., & Tait, R. (1985). A comparison of low back pain patients in the United States and New Zealand: Psychosocial and economic factors affecting severity of disability. *Pain, 21,* 77–89.

Dane, J. R., & Kessler, R. S. (1994). A matrix model for the psychological assessment and treatment of acute pain. In R. J. Hamill & J. C. Rowlingson (Eds.), *Handbook of critical care pain management* (pp. 53–81). New York: McGraw-Hill.

Dane, J. R., Rowlingson, J. C., & Eksterowicz, N. R. (1994). *Development and utilization of a psychology service in an anesthesia-based acute pain service.* Poster presented at the 13th Annual Scientific Meeting of the American Pain Society, Miami, FL.

DeGood, D. E. (1983). Reducing medical patients' reluctance to participate in psychological therapies: The initial session. *Professional Psychology, 14,* 570–579.

DeGood, D. E. (1988). A rationale and format for psychosocial evaluation of pain patients. In N. T. Lynch & S.V. Vasudevan (Eds.), *Persistent pain: Psychosocial assessment and intervention* (pp. 1–22). Boston: Kluwer.

DeGood, D. E., & Kiernan, B. (in press). Perception of fault in patients with chronic pain. *Pain.*

DeGood, D. E., & Shutty, M. S. (1992). Assessment of pain beliefs, coping, and self-efficacy. In D. C. Turk & R. Melzack (Eds.), *Handbook of pain assessment* (pp. 214–234). New York: Guilford Press.

Feuerstein, M. (1991). A multidisciplinary approach to the prevention, evaluation and management of work disability. *Journal for Occupational Rehabilitation, 1,* 5–12.

Forsterling, F. (1988). *Attribution theory in clinical psychology.* New York: Wiley.

Frymoyer, J. W. (1992). Predicting disability from low back pain. *Clinical Orthopaedics and Related Research, 279,* 101–109.

Gentry, W. D. (1984). Behavioral medicine: A new research paradigm. In W. D. Gentry (Ed.), *Handbook of behavioral medicine* (pp. 1–12). New York: Guilford Press.

Hickling, E. J., Sison, G. F. P., & Holtz, J. L. (1985). Role of psychologists in multidisciplinary pain clinics: A national survey. *Professional Psychology: Research and Practice, 16,* 868–880.

Huszti, H. D., & Walker, C. E. (1991). Critical issues in consultation and liaison: Pediatrics. In J. J. Sweet, R. H. Rozensky, & S. M. Tovian (Eds.), *Handbook of clinical psychology in medical settings* (pp. 165–186). New York: Plenum Press.

Ingram, R. E. (1986). *Information processing approaches to clinical psychology.* New York: Academic Press.

Jensen, M. P., Turner, J. A., & Romano, J. M. (1994). Beliefs about pain predict treatment response. *Clinician's Research Digest, 12,* 4.

Kaplan, S. H., Greenfield, S., & Ware J. E. (1989). Impact of the doctor–patient relationship on the outcome of chronic disease. In M. Stewart & D. Roter (Eds.), *Communicating with medical patients* (pp. 228–245). London: Sage.

Kerns, R. D., Rosenberg, R., & Jacob, M. C. (1994). Anger expression and chronic pain. *Journal of Behavioral Medicine, 17,* 57–68.

Kingsbury, S. J. (1987). Cognitive differences between clinical psychologists and psychiatrists. *American Psychologist, 42,* 152–156.

Malamed, B. C., & Siegel, L. J. (1980). *Behavioral medicine: Practical applications in health care.* New York: Springer.

Maloney, M. P., & Ward, M. P. (1976). *Psychological assessment: A conceptual approach.* New York: Oxford University Press.

Mumford, E., Schelsinger, H. J., & Glass, G. V. (1982). The effects of psychological intervention on recovery from surgery and heart attacks: An analysis of the literature. *American Journal of Public Health, 72,* 141–151.

Pilowsky, I., & Spence, N. D. (1976). Illness behavior syndromes associated with intractable pain. *Pain, 2,* 61–71.

Rowlingson, J. C., Kessler, R. S., Dane, J. R., & Hamill, R. J. (1994). Adjunctive therapy for acute pain. In R. J. Hamill & J. R. Rowlingson (Eds.), *Handbook of critical care pain management* (pp. 229–250). New York: McGraw-Hill.

Rogers, D. E. (1977). The challenge of primary care. In J. Knowles (Ed.), *Doing better, feeling worse* (pp. 81–104). New York: Norton.

Seligman, M. E. P. (1975). *Helplessness: On depression, development, and death.* San Francisco: W. H. Freeman.

Selvini-Palazzoli, M., Cecchin, G., Prata, G., & Boscolo, L. (1978). *Paradox and counterparadox.* New York: Jason Aronson.

Shutty, M. S., DeGood, D. E., & Tuttle, D. H. (1990). Chronic pain patients' beliefs about their pain and treatment outcomes. *Archives of Physical Medicine and Rehabilitation, 71*, 128–132.

Spitzer, W. O., LeBlanc, F. E., Dupuis, M., et al. (1987). Scientific approach to the assessment and management of activity-related spinal disorders: A monograph for clinicians. Report of the Quebec Task Force on Spinal Disorders [Special issue]. *Spine, 12*(1).

Turk, D. C., & Melzack, R. (Eds.). (1992). *Handbook of pain assessment.* New York: Guilford Press.

Strategies for the Prevention of Chronic Pain

Steven J. Linton
Laurence A. Bradley

This chapter describes recently developed strategies for the prevention of chronic musculoskeletal pain (MSP). Although not fatal, chronic MSP inflicts immeasurable suffering and is extremely costly; consequently, in spite of pain treatment advances, this problem has demanded preventive action. Yet, until recently, surprisingly few resources have been directed toward prevention, and relatively little effort has been devoted to evaluating preventive interventions. Over the past few years, however, various attempts at prevention have been made and a considerable amount of knowledge has been generated.

After briefly reviewing the need for prevention of MSP and a model of its development, we describe and evaluate a number of possible strategies for the secondary prevention of chronic MSP. We consider secondary prevention because it is most relevant to health care providers and has some documented success. "Secondary prevention" is defined here as initiatives taken from the point of the first reported injury until a full chronic problem has developed (pain that continues after 6 months of health care or sick leave).

THE NEED FOR PREVENTION

A large number of people in the industrialized world will suffer from MSP at some time during their lives. Various cross-sectional studies show, for example, that roughly 50–75% of adults report having had low back pain at some point (Frymoyer, 1992; Pope, Andersson, Frymoyer, & Chaffin, 1991; Skovron, 1992), and that 25% have suffered back pain within the past year (Skovron, 1992). Add to this the other sorts of MSP (e.g., neck and shoulder pain), and the problem takes on gigantic proportions.

Although many people suffer from MSP, a relatively small number develop chronic pain and thereby consume most of the resources devoted to the problem. It is estimated that between 3% and 7% of those with current acute back pain will develop chronic pain in the forthcoming year (Frymoyer, 1992; Nachemson, 1992). And fewer than 10% of back pain patients account for more than 75% of the costs (Nachemson, 1992). Thus, these sufferers may be the primary targets for secondary prevention.

However, there is mounting evidence that MSP problems are typically *recurrent*. Rather than experiencing a single incident that either remits quickly or results in a chronic syndrome, most patients seem to have recurrent problems and eventually may develop chronic problems even if they are not off work (VonKorff, 1994). VonKorff points out that many patients in primary care have chronic/recurrent pain. For example, Philips and Grant (1991) found that among acute-onset back pain patients, 40% still reported pain at a 6-month follow-up. VonKorff (1994) has also found that 34% of primary care back pain patients who were followed for 1 year reported "chronic pain," defined as pain present on at least half the days in the prior 6 months.

Given the size of the MSP problem, it is not surprising that it is also costly. The direct costs for treating MSP (i.e., inpatient and outpatient services) in 1990 were estimated to be $50 billion in the United States alone (Frymoyer, 1992). The demand for medical care for back pain is so great that it accounts for the second highest number of physician visits in the United States (Skovron, 1992). However, a large number of such health care consultations are "repeat" consultations with chronic sufferers that do not seem to result in significant improvements (Davies, Crombie, Macrae, & Rogers, 1992). It should be emphasized, though, that indirect costs—mainly in the form of sick leave, compensation, and early retirements—probably account for a majority of the expenses associated with MSP. In Sweden, for example, about 85% of the total costs for MSP are related to various compensation benefits (National Board of Social Welfare, 1987). The combination of direct (health care utilization) costs and indirect (compensation) costs results in staggering amounts of money. For our purposes, the exact cost is not important; it is sufficient to point out that expensive health care utilization and loss of work are two major results of MSP, especially chronic MSP. These are great problems not only for individual chronic MSP sufferers but for the other members of society, who together must devote their economic resources to pay for the high costs of health care and compensation. Thus, there is a very real need for effective interventions to prevent the development of chronic MSP.

A MODEL OF THE DEVELOPMENT OF CHRONIC MUSCULOSKELETAL PAIN

Although MSP is often ascribed to multidimensional processes, psychological variables are now believed to be crucial in the development of chronic pain (Linton, 1994b). Recently, psychosocial factors have been causally implicated in the etiology of even acute MSP. Regardless of the origins of acute pain, however, psychological factors are believed to play a vital role in the development of chronic problems.

The events that occur between the onset of acute injury and a full chronic state are important in understanding the development of the problem, as well as in identifying possible secondary prevention techniques. A progressive disease or disorder is the rare exception rather than the rule for MSP (Frymoyer, 1992; Nachemson, 1992). Fordyce (1976) instead has maintained that as the tissue injury heals over time, learning processes may act to support pain behaviors so that the problem persists or actually increases. Cognitive processes are also involved in a reciprocal process, in which attributions, pain beliefs, coping, and the like are linked to the development of chronic pain. An essential ingredient for this to take place is time. The longer a person has the problem, the more time psychological factors (e.g., learning) have to operate and thereby to establish and maintain "sick role" behaviors. Consequently, although considerable healing may actually take place, psychosocial factors may come to maintain and even exacerbate the perception of pain, pain behaviors, and suffering. More detailed descriptions of this developmental process are available elsewhere (Fordyce, 1976; Linton, 1994a; Turk, Meichenbaum, & Genest, 1983).

Again, our purpose in this chapter is to examine several strategies for the secondary prevention of chronic MSP, based on the model we have sketched briefly here. Since this area is truly in its infancy, detailed, tried-and-proven programs cannot be presented. Rather, we present methods currently being employed that are believed to be of help in preventing chronic pain problems. We hope that our review of current strategies will promote understanding of the area, as well as the development of successful, standard-ized preventive methods for clinical use in the future.

RISK ASSESSMENT SCREENING

Screening offers the advantage of being able to allocate restricted resources to those who may benefit the most from them. In fact, prevention ordinarily presumes some form of risk assessment. However, identifying potent risk factors so that systematic screening procedures can be developed has been a tedious task. Part of this problem has stemmed from difficulty in defining what it is we are actually trying to prevent. Unlike diseases with identifiable pathophysiology (e.g., cancer), MSP is a syndrome consisting of a col-lection of symptoms. Thus, it is not possible to prevent MSP by targeting particular bio-logical tissue states. Pragmatic objectives have been put forward, such as preventing reinjury or the sick role. Nevertheless, these range from preventing the experience of pain itself to reducing relapse, or minimizing work loss.

Another problem is that the development of chronic MSP is a dynamic process. Therefore, the type of variable that may serve as a "risk factor" presumably varies over time for the same person. Moreover, risk factors may be related to predisposition, trig-ger, buffer, maintenance, or hindrance variables.

Given the devastating effects of chronic MSP as discussed earlier, we argue that pre-vention should be oriented toward preventing dysfunction, including time off work, reinjury, and side effects of improper self-care, in addition to reducing the subjective experience of pain. From an economic point of view, a reduction in the number of MSP sufferers who would ordinarily develop chronic problems should be a top priority. Although other preventive orientations may certainly be worthwhile, "usual" bouts of acute MSP are probably natural parts of life and do not require extra resources; these cases remit with, and often even without, medical treatment of the symptoms.

Risk Factors

Because standardized screening procedures are not yet available, we need to inspect known risk factors to understand more fully how we may conduct clinical risk assessments. Although much work remains to be done, a few factors are definite candidates for screen-ing procedures.

Medical Factors, Demographic Factors, and Duration of Pain

First, it is clear that the results of physical examinations for MSP have been disappoint-ing as risk factors, but they are still important in ruling out progressive diseases/disor-ders. Medical diagnosis, for example, has little relationship with long-term back pain outcome, and only about 1% of patients have clearly diagnosable problems such as fractures, tumors, or infections (Frymoyer, 1992). On the other hand, some clinical factors—for instance, limited range of motion, impairments in straight-leg raising, sciatica, and pain provoked during range of motion—have been found to be connected with long-term pain problems (Frymoyer, 1992; Hellsing, Linton, & Kälvemark, 1994).

Medical history, the so-called "time factor," and demographic factors have also been associated with the development of chronic problems. Age and employability (education, work experience, etc.) are established risk factors (Frymoyer, 1992; Linton, 1994a). Perhaps the best-known risks, however, are related to pain history: The longer the duration of pain and the greater the number of treatments, the worse the prognosis seems to be (Frymoyer, 1992; Nachemson, 1992). The time factor is an important risk factor, since it provides an opportunity for psychosocial processes to operate. Consequently, the time factor is central in screening procedures. Figure 16.1 graphically depicts the relationship between time off work and the probability of returning to work.

All of these factors have some disadvantages, however. These factors may not be causal factors (i.e., they may not contribute to the course of chronic pain), and their importance may vary tremendously among individual patients. Furthermore, many of these factors are difficult or impossible to alter; thus, although these factors may predict chronicity to some degree, they provide no avenue for prevention. Finally, it is important to keep in mind in regard to the time factor that, by definition, chronic problems are related to longer periods of pain and disability; thus, the time factor per se may not be very informative.

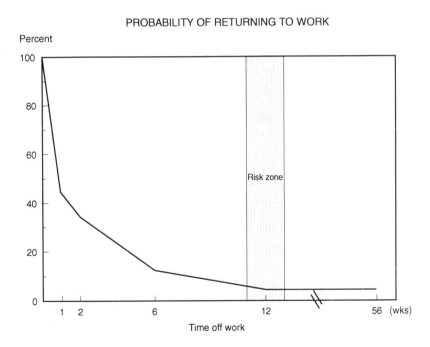

FIGURE 16.1. Relationship between time off work after the development of pain and the probability of returning to work.

Psychological Factors

A number of psychological risk factors that appear to be crucial in assessment and screening procedures have been isolated during the past decade. These may be divided into factors concerning the work situation, the family, and the individual himself or herself.

Work Situation. Several recent studies have shown that psychosocial factors at work are related to MSP (Bongers, Winter, Komper, & Hildebrandt, 1993; Linton, 1994b). These factors are often believed to maintain or enhance the pain problem, as well as hindering return to work. Those with low job satisfaction suffer from MSP problems more frequently than those who are satisfied with their work. For example, among 145 industrial workers, low job satisfaction increased the risk for having had back pain during the previous year by sevenfold (Linton & Warg, 1993). Two prospective studies have causally linked job satisfaction to future pain reports (Bigos et al., 1991; Niemcryk, Jenkins, Rose, & Hurst, 1987).

Social factors at work seem to be instrumental determinants of return to work. How well one gets along with coworkers and supervisors has been related to the maintenance of pain problems and sick leave (Bigos et al., 1991; Bigos & Battié, 1992; Skovron, Szpalski, Nordin, Melot, & Cukier, 1994). As an illustration, both Feuerstein and Thebarge (1991) and we ourselves (Linton & Bradley, 1992) have discovered that supervisor support is a key variable associated with return to work.

Various forms of stress at work have also been linked to MSP. Perceived workload, job demands, and stress symptoms have all been found to be associated with MSP (Bongers et al., 1993, Frymoyer, 1992; Linton, 1994b). Time pressure also may be related to back pain, although research results are mixed (Bongers et al., 1993). Finally, boring, repetitive work has been shown to be related to back pain (Bongers et al., 1993; Linton, 1990; Svensson & Andersson, 1983).

Psychosocial factors at work thus appear to be important in the etiology and development of pain problems and may constitute a major stumbling block for a return to work after injury. Still, there are limitations in the research. There have been few prospective studies, for example, and many of the variables examined may actually be interconnected. Moreover, some of the factors have been rather broadly defined (e.g. "stress," "job satisfaction") and thus have been difficult to operationalize for study.

Family. The patient's family situation represents a remarkable, but often neglected, set of potential risk factors. Evidence indicates that family members may serve as models for coping with pain problems (Bradley, Haile, & Jaworski, 1992a). Thus, the risk of developing chronic pain increases for patients who have a family member with a chronic health problem (Crook, Rideout, & Browne, 1984; Turkat & Noskins, 1983).

Family members also may be an important source of reinforcement for pain behaviors. Patients' reports of pain and dysfunction increase, for instance, when they experience their spouses' response as supportive or solicitous (Bradley et al., 1992a; Romano et al., 1991). Since patients spend considerable time with their families, especially if they are on sick leave, the interaction may be a central determinant of chronicity.

A final issue is sexual and physical abuse by family members. Those patients who have been or are currently being abused are more likely to suffer pain without a specific precipitating injury (Bradley et al., 1992a). In addition, abused patients report higher levels of disability and more frequently use health care resources than patients without histories of abuse (Scarinci, Haile, Bradley, & Richter, 1994).

Individual. Psychopathology, pain behaviors, and cognitive processes are all related to the development of chronicity. Various forms of psychopathology, such as depression, anxiety, and excessive somatic awareness, have been shown to be correlated to the development of long-term back pain problems. Moreover, pain behaviors (e.g., low activity levels, limping, guarding, etc.) are also risk factors. Pain behaviors appear to be central in avoidance generated by fear, and the level of pain behaviors has been found to increase with the number of failed treatments (Lacroix et al., 1990; Waddell, Bircher, Finlaysson, & Main, 1984).

A patient's beliefs, attributions, and perceptions of pain offer new avenues for risk assessment. Specifically, a patient's beliefs about the relationship between pain and activity have proven critical in MSP problems (Jensen & Karoly, 1992; Jensen, Turner, Romano, & Lawler, 1994; Riley, Ahern, & Follick, 1988; Vlaeyen, Kole-Snijders, Boeren, & van Eek, 1995). Waddell, Newton, Henderson, Somerville, & Main, (1993) have found that a patient's level of fear–avoidance, as seen in perceptions of the relationship between physical activity and pain, is strongly related to sick absenteeism. In short, the literature indicates that beliefs that activity will provoke pain increase the risk for further development of a pain problem.

Maladaptive thoughts and coping strategies also may exacerbate the problem. Williams and Thorn (1989) showed that negative cognitions, including self-blame and views of the pain as unending and mysterious, predicted treatment outcome. Perceptions of being "disabled" or permanently "injured" are additional examples of negative cognitions related to MSP problems. Finally, the type of coping strategy employed by a patient has been firmly related to long-term outcome. Those patients who use passive techniques (e.g., hoping, praying, and catastrophizing) tend to do poorly, whereas those using active strategies (e.g., ignoring or reinterpreting the pain) tend to do relatively well (Jensen, Turner, Romano, & Karoly, 1991).

Screening Procedures

Translating risk factors into active and effective screening procedures is unfortunately not a straightforward process, and no standardized evaluation system is currently available. Nevertheless, we provide some suggestions for clinical use after examining some difficulties in directly generalizing findings from the literature reviewed above.

Problems in Generalizing Research Findings

Problems in generalizing research findings directly to the clinical screening situation are important, since they set limits that must be considered. First, the population studied may not completely correspond to the patients being screened; thus, the reported research results may not be directly applicable. Second, because of the large variance reported in the research investigations, and because these studies are on the group level, it may be very difficult to generalize findings to individual patients. Thus, although the results may be valid, individual variation may still render the variables insensitive. Third, some of the factors isolated are most likely intercorrelated. This means that adding the variables together does not necessarily mean that predictive power will be improved. Fourth, some of the variables described in the literature have not been defined sufficiently (as noted earlier in regard to the research on the work situation); this increases the likelihood of error in assessment. Fifth, cutoff points are almost never reported, and thus a clinician may have difficulty evaluating whether a given score is low, normal, or high. As a result of these problems, some unsuccessful attempts at screening have been reported (Lehmann, Spratt, & Lehmann, 1993).

Still, there is every reason to employ screening procedures. For example, some studies have reported very accurate predictions of various outcomes, such as working versus not working (Feuerstein & Thebarge, 1991; Iezzi, Adams, Stokes, Pilon, & Ault, 1992). Above all, even simple screening procedures should prove better than the usual current state of affairs—unsystematic assessment or no assessment at all. Consequently, although it may appear difficult to screen patients, improvements in current routines can be expected when screening procedures are implemented.

Clinical Procedures

We suggest a two-step approach to screening. The first step is designed to provide a rough idea of the level of risk. Screening methods in this step should be simple and time-efficient. The main goal is to isolate patients at high risk for developing chronic problems and thereby to reduce the number of patients targeted for preventive interventions. We believe that these procedures should be especially useful and cost-effective at an early stage of acute pain, since they tend to be relatively brief and inexpensive (e.g., self-administered questionnaires, simple examinations, and interviews). The second step should provide a more in-depth assessment, and those found to be at clear risk will need to be directed immediately to an intervention program.

The First Step: General Screening. An outline of important factors that ought to be evaluated in the first step of the assessment is provided in Table 16.1. It is essential to record previous history accurately, as chronic problems tend to develop over rather long

TABLE 16.1. Important Factors to Assess in the First Stage of Screening for Risk of Developing Chronic Pain

Essential variables	Points to be covered
Previous history	Is pain recurrent?
	Number of previous visits
	Number of absences from work
Time factor	Duration of current problem
	Total duration
Pain beliefs	Fear–avoidance
	Belief that activity increases pain
	Belief that work causes pain
Pain behavior	Does the patient exhibit excessive amounts?
Work situation	High stress levels?
	Heavy physical work?
	Does patient have *poor* relations with supervisors or workmates?
Coping ability/self-efficacy	Does patient cope well with pain?
	Active vs. passive coping strategies
	Does patient believe in own potential to deal with pain, return to work, etc.?
Anxiety/depression	Are these present to a significant extent?
Hindrances	What hindrances does patient perceive to a return to work and normal life?
Information deficits	Does patient understand problem (e.g., cause, prognosis, self-care, activity)?
Current pain/dysfunction	High levels of pain or dysfunction

time periods, in which recurrent bouts become more frequent with longer periods of pain (VonKorff, 1994; Rossignol, Suissa, & Abenhaim, 1992). The current duration of the problem is also of interest, as is the current duration of time off work. These variables can usually be readily ascertained from the patient's journal or in an interview.

Pain beliefs, especially fear–avoidance, may also be assessed as early as the first visit. These beliefs may well be related to actual pain behaviors. Whether these are reinforced will depend on the patient's family and work situation. Thus, establishing how the family reacts to the patients' pain behavior may be very revealing. Changes in everyday routines may also reflect the probability of developing chronic problems. The patient's ability to cope with pain may also be screened, as well as the presence of anxiety or depression. The patient's own belief in his or her potential to return to work, a form of self-efficacy, seems to be a particularly potent predictor of actual development. Information deficits regarding the problem, its cause, and its prognosis should also be evaluated. Finally, the patient may be asked to describe any hindrances to a return to work.

Taken together, the data from the first step should provide considerable information about the patient's risk for developing chronic problems. The point in time at which the assessment is conducted, however, is vital in interpreting the results. For example, information deficits appear to be easier to deal with early, and psychopathology is generally deemed a more potent risk factor in acute as opposed to subacute pain. Moreover, in the early acute state, missing a person at risk for chronic problems is not as critical as it may be later, since such a patient will almost certainly present again with the problem. Statistically, few acute back pain patients actually develop chronic problems. Thus, to reduce costs, one may want to concentrate resources only on those patients with a very high likelihood of developing chronic problems (good sensitivity). A somewhat different strategy is to identify those *not* at risk of developing chronic problems, so that extra resources will not be expended unnecessarily on them (good specificity). However, when patients have reached the subacute stage or have had several recurrences, it becomes much more important that no patient at risk be actually "missed."

The Second Step: Risk Assessment. The second step in assessment involves bringing the patient into the clinic for more thorough testing and assessment procedures, including an interview. The techniques employed may be similar to those employed with other pain patients; detailed descriptions of these assessment procedures are available elsewhere (Turk & Melzack, 1992). We recommend an assessment procedure that includes a semistructured interview and a small number of self-report questionnaires.

The semistructured interview has five objectives. The first of these is to obtain a more complete history of the patient's pain. This should include eliciting the patient's beliefs regarding events that may have precipitated the onset of pain, as well as determining the course of the patient's pain over time with regard to intensity, frequency, sensory and affective qualities, and location (Bradley et al., 1992a). The identification of physical (e.g., work or home injuries) and emotional (e.g., marital discord, abuse, loss of loved ones) traumatic events that preceded the onset of pain is important, given that these events tend to be associated with high levels of disability and work loss (Greenfield, Fitzcharles, & Esdaile, 1992). Patients with emotional trauma may be particularly good candidates for early preventive intervention programs; relative to those with physical trauma, these patients report higher levels of fatigue, more daily stressors, and greater usage of maladaptive pain coping strategies (Aaron et al., 1994).

Reports of high pain levels and poor health, or frequent displays of pain behavior, should also receive special attention. It has been found that among blue-collar workers with subacute low back pain, observed pain behaviors and ratings of general and back strength are strong predictors of return to work and work absenteeism over a 2-year period (Öhlund et al., 1994).

The second objective of the interview is to identify events that reliably precede exacerbations in the patient's pain perceptions or pain behaviors, as well as the events that reliably follow these exacerbations. As noted in the discussion of family risk factors, it is particularly important to focus on solicitous responses (e.g., offers of assistance or concern regarding pain) emitted by a spouse or significant other in the patient's environment. Romano et al. (1992) have shown that spouses' solicitous behaviors often precede and follow patients' displays of verbal and nonverbal pain behaviors. We recommend adminstration of Part II of the West Haven–Yale Multidimensional Pain Inventory (WHYMPI; Kerns, Turk, & Rudy, 1985) to both patients and spouses or significant others as a relatively brief screen for frequent solicitous behaviors. The WHYMPI also permits assessment of distracting spouse responses, such as attempts to divert attention from pain, that may reinforce pain behavior in some patients (Bradley, Richter, Scarinci, Haile, & Schan, 1992b). It is important to evaluate the perceptions of both patients and spouses, given that patients' perceptions may not always be as accurate as those of their spouses (Lousberg, Schmidt, & Groenman, 1992).

The third objective of the interview is to assess functioning and determine (1) how the patient usually spends his or her time, (2) what activities have been performed more or less often since the onset of pain, and (3) whether any activities have been modified or eliminated since pain onset. This information may allow one to generate hypotheses regarding reinforcement contingencies related to the patient's pain behavior, in addition to solicitous or distracting responses by the spouse or others (Bradley et al., 1992a). For example, if the performance of physically demanding pleasurable activities has not decreased greatly, but the performance of aversive tasks with similar physical demands has been substantially reduced, one might infer that the patient's behavior has been influenced by negative reinforcement (Romano, Turner, & Moore, 1989).

Interview items concerning changes in daily activities may be supplemented by open-ended questions or self-report measures regarding job satisfaction. Patients' reports of work dissatisfaction, in conjunction with decreases in aversive physical activities, may be important in identifying persons who are especially good candidates for early preventive interventions.

The fourth objective of the interview is to determine whether the patient has any relatives or friends who suffer from pain problems similar to the patient's or who have become disabled because of pain. We have noted earlier that previous experiences with pain and disability may foster a patient's formation of maladaptive beliefs or behaviors, such as inappropriate usage of medication or health care services. These beliefs or behaviors, in turn, may eventually contribute to the development of chronic pain (Chun, Turner, & Romano, 1993; Gamsa & Vikis-Freibergs, 1991).

The final objective of the interview is to evaluate the degree to which the patient is experiencing affective disturbance or engaging in maladaptive cognitive or behavioral coping strategies. Several recent prospective studies have shown that depression and other dimensions of psychological distress are reliable predictors of MSP, headache, and chest pain (Leino & Magni, 1993; Magni, Moreschi, Rigatti-Luchini, & Merskey, 1994; Pietri-Taleb, Rjihimäki, Viikari-Juntura, & Lindström, 1994; VonKorff, LeResche, & Dworkin, 1993b). It should be stressed, however, that these studies also suggest that the relationship between psychological distress and pain onset or chronicity is not consistent across all patient groups or pain syndromes.

With regard to maladaptive cognitions and behaviors, many reliable and valid questionnaires for assessing these variables exist. We believe that all patient evaluations should include at a minimum one measure of psychological distress, one measure of coping strategies, and one measure of pain beliefs or other cognitions. For example, we regularly use the Center for Epidemiologic Studies Depression Scale (Radloff, 1977), the Pain Beliefs and Perceptions Inventory (Williams & Thorn, 1989), and the Coping Strategies Questionnaire (Rosenstiel & Keefe, 1983) for patients with MSP who are referred to our clinics. However, before selecting a battery of questionnaires from the large number of available instruments, the reader should consult the reviews by Bradley et al. (1992a) and DeGood and Shutty (1992) for discussions of the strengths and weaknesses of the major measures of psychological status.

PREVENTIVE INTERVENTIONS

Providing medically and psychologically sound treatment the very first time a patient seeks help for MSP may be an excellent form of secondary prevention. It would appear superior to initiating intervention only after patients actually begin to develop problems (e.g., subacute, relapse, or prechronic). Furnishing thorough information concerning the cause of the pain, its probable prognosis, and ways in which the problem may be best tackled should reduce anxiety and fear levels. Providing sound management for the experience of acute pain is also important. Furthermore, issues concerning activity limitations may be addressed before learning or secondary gains have had an opportunity to operate.

In short, early intervention efforts should be directed toward prevention of the development of the sick role. Moreover, self-help activities can be taught that may provide the patient with more control over the pain problem and encourage the patient to be an active participant in the treatment. Finally, barriers to full recovery, including a return to work, can be identified and addressed at their source. These advantages are discussed in more detail by VonKorff (1994).

Even though there are many potential benefits associated with delivering preventive strategies to patients with acute MSP, developing a program may not be easy. Organizational problems may arise, since effective prevention programs usually require an entire staff to work together to provide a very consistent line of information and treatment. These programs also may involve extensive cooperation with families, workplaces, insurance carriers, and government authorities; this requires time and patience. Cost containment issues arise as well, since prevention programs to date have been provided for all acute sufferers—a considerable number of patients. Lastly, those incurring the costs of a program may not be the ones receiving the financial benefits it produces.

Secondary Prevention Programs for Acute Pain

Several studies of the outcomes produced by secondary prevention programs for acute MSP have been described in the literature. Deyo, Diehl, and Rosenthal (1986) reported one of the first studies of secondary prevention of acute back pain. These investigators randomly assigned 203 patients with mechanical back pain in a primary care setting to one of two medical recommendation groups: bed rest for 2 days (Group I) or bed rest for 7 days (Group II). Their rationale was that for patients without disk herniation or neurological deficits, activity might be more beneficial than rest in healing soft tissues and joints. Patients' self-reports revealed that the Group I patients maintained bed rest for a mean period of 2.3 days; Group II patients maintained bed rest for a mean period of 3.9 days. Despite this modest difference in bed rest, a 3-week follow-up period demonstrated that the Group I patients were characterized by significantly lower work absenteeism than patients in Group II (3.1 vs. 5.6 days). Indeed, the U.S. Public Health Service now recommends that bed rest for acute back pain should be limited to 4 days (Bigos et al., 1994).

Fordyce, Brockway, Bergman, and Spengler (1986) designed a special behavioral program for patients with acute back pain, to prevent reinforcement of dysfunction and medication overuse. A total of 107 patients with pain onset during the preceding 10 days were randomly assigned to a usual-treatment control group or a preventive intervention. The controls received analgesics and recommendations for rest and for activity restriction on an as-needed (i.e., pain-contingent) basis. By contrast, subjects in the prevention group were administered behavioral time contingencies, so that pain behaviors would not be reinforced. For example, analgesics, if used, were taken on a fixed time schedule, and the prescriptions were strictly limited. Similarly, activity restrictions, if any, were based on specified time intervals rather than on the occurrence of pain, and exercises were performed on a fixed time schedule. Follow-up results showed that whereas the usual-treatment group displayed increased levels of impairment compared to baseline, the prevention group had returned to preonset levels of function. Thus, the method of delivering care was shown to be effective in preventing dysfunction.

Philips, Grant, and Berkowitz (1991) reported a comparison of time-contingent versus "Let pain be your guide" recommendations for resuming normal activities among 117 patients with recent onset (<15 days) of back or neck pain. They also subdivided the groups receiving the two types of recommendations so that half of each group received minimal (45 minutes) behavioral counseling and half received nondirective psychotherapy. Surprisingly, they found no significant difference between the time-contingent and "Let pain be your guide" groups with regard to reactivation, but there was a trend for the behavioral counseling to produce more patients with no pain at a 6-month follow-up than the nondirective psychotherapy. Still, referral to a minimal behavioral counseling did not seem to have sufficient therapeutic effect. One explanation of the lack of effect could be that the intervention was too little. Another possible explanation is that the intentions of the time-contingent program did not coincide with information being provided by the patients' referring doctors, and thus patients did not comply with the program.

A somewhat different approach at the workplace has been reported by Haig, Linton, McIntosh, Moneta, and Mead (1990). Hospital employees who were off work 2 days or more for MSP were included in a preventive program. The intervention concentrated on establishing good communication with each patient, identifying factors delaying a return to work, and maintaining communication with the workplace to facilitate a modified or early return to work. Although this was not a controlled study, Haig et al. were able to show a 33% improvement in return to work, compared to a period before the preventive program was initiated. This suggests that communication and return-to-work issues may be important in prevention.

Linton, Hellsing, and Andersson (1993) have investigated the effects of an early, active behavioral program for first-time sufferers of acute MSP. A total of 198 patients seeking health care for acute MSP were randomly allocated to treatment as usual or to a prevention group. The prevention program reinforced functional and other well behaviors, and underscored the importance of maintaining everyday activities and a return to work. Usual treatment consisted, after a short waiting period, of a prescription for analgesics and advice to rest as needed. Sick leave records indicated that about half the participants had actually had a history of previous MSP problems during the past 2 years (Study I), whereas the other half were true first-time sufferers (Study II). For those with a previous history in Study I, both treatment conditions produced great improvements at the 1-year follow-up compared to pretest, but there were virtually no differences between the treatment conditions. However, for the first-timers in Study II, there were dramatic differences between treatments. Patients in both treatment conditions made great improvements, but the prevention group had significantly less dysfunction and less sick leave than did the control group. The risk of developing chronic pain was, in fact, reduced by more than eight times.

The studies described above thus show that the method of delivering care at the acute stage may have a profound effect on the development of chronic problems.

Secondary Prevention Programs for Subacute Pain

Three groups of investigators have evaluated the effects of secondary prevention programs for workers with subacute MSP. We and our colleagues carried out the first controlled study of such a secondary prevention program; our subjects were nurses who had been sick-listed for back pain during the previous 2-year period (Linton, Bradley, Jensen, Spangfort, & Sundell, 1989). Given the relatively long time period since the onset of pain, the secondary prevention program was more complex than those used for the prevention of acute pain. The program included exercise, training in ergonomics (e.g., improved ways of lifting and transferring patients), and a cognitive-behavioral intervention designed to reduce pain and to help reduce the risk of reinjury following program termination. The program also included four "booster sessions" during the 6-month follow-up period, in which the nurses met in small groups to reinforce the problem-solving skills that were learned during the cognitive-behavioral training.

We found at the 6-month follow-up that the program, relative to a waiting-list control condition, produced significant improvements on a large number of outcome variables: ratings of pain intensity, fatigue, anxiety, helplessness, and satisfaction with daily activities. The program also produced a significant decrease in the nurses' observable displays of pain behavior, which was maintained at follow-up. An 18-month follow-up of the nurses who had received this intervention showed that they had maintained their improvements in ratings of pain intensity, fatigue, satisfaction with daily activities, and helplessness. Reductions in anxiety were not maintained, and pain behavior was not assessed (Linton & Bradley, 1992).

Donchin, Woolf, Kaplan, and Floman (1990) examined the efficacy of a 3-month program of flexion and pelvic tilt exercises in reducing back pain among 142 hospital employees who had experienced at least three back pain episodes during the previous year. Consistent with the unidimensional nature of the prevention program, the only pain-related outcome measure evaluated was the number of months during a 1-year period in which back pain was experienced. Nevertheless, relative to an educational program and a no-treatment control condition, the prevention program produced a significant reduction in "painful months."

Finally, Lindström et al. (1992) studied the effects of a graded exercise and operant conditioning program on 103 automobile workers who had been sick-listed for 8 weeks because of subacute back pain. This program required a physical therapist to establish a set of individualized exercise quotas for each patient and to positively reinforce these quotas and increasing functional capacity. It was reported that patients who participated in the prevention program, relative to those who received standard medical care, required signficantly less time to return to work. However, an analysis by gender showed that this effect was found primarily among the men rather than the women patients. Similarly, the prevention program, relative to standard care, was associated with significantly fewer sick leave weeks only among the men during a 2-year follow-up.

The studies reviewed above suggest that it is possible to reduce pain, psychological distress, and work absenteeism among patients with subacute back pain. However, patients with subacute pain tend to require more complex interventions than those needed at the acute stage. In addition, the effects of these complex interventions may not be consistent across all outcome variables or patient groups. As noted earlier, a key dimension in the long-term success of preventive interventions at the subacute stage of pain may be the use of booster sessions to reduce relapse (Keefe & Van Horn, 1993; Linton et al., 1989, Linton & Bradley, 1992).

Specific Strategies for Prevention

Recommendations concerning specific, concrete clinical methods for secondary prevention must necessarily be tentative. There are simply insufficient data and experience concerning what works best and why. And, unfortunately, not all early efforts are effective. For example, Mitchell and Carmen (1994) found that an early functional restoration program for patients with MSP of 90 days' duration did *not* produce significantly better results than a control condition consisting of "usual" treatment managed by patients' primary care providers. Similarly, Faas, Chavannes, van Eijk, and Gubbels (1993) could not substantiate any significant differences between acute back pain patients receiving an exercise program or ultrasound treatment. Nevertheless, clinicians need clear advice when developing a prevention program. Rather than advocate dubious routines, we attempt to delineate some strategies that we believe characterize successful secondary MSP prevention programs.

Probably the most frequently employed strategy involves three aspects: Interventions should be early, active, and oriented toward health behaviors. In regard to the first critical feature, earliness, time since onset (often measured in days off work) is used to initiate the preventive intervention. The critical period is believed to lie between 4 and 12 weeks, although recent work by VonKorff, Deyo, Cherkin, and Barlow (1993a) and Philips and Grant (1991) suggests that a wider time period, beginning sooner after onset, may be relevant, and that pain-related factors rather than time per se may be the actual predictors of outcome. As a result, there is no obvious reason to wait before employing preventive strategies.

To offset the negative effects of bed rest, rest in general, and being off work, the interventions focus on being active and health-oriented. This means prescribing what the patients should be doing during recovery, not what they should avoid doing. Some programs may simply stress physical activity. However, the crucial element in success, according to cognitive-behavioral theory, should be preventing the reinforcement of specific "sick" behaviors and thoughts (e.g., dysfunction, medication overuse, and the view that activity will increase pain). Similarly, fear–avoidance mechanisms and beliefs about the pain—in particular, the relationship between the pain and activity—would seem to be quite important. In fact, we suggest that some programs may not be successful because they inadvertently reinforce the sick behaviors they aspire to prevent. This unintended reinforcement of illness behavior may occur when attempts are made blindly to "activate" the patient, but do not consider specific contingencies. Thus, intervening early with programs that actively reinforce "well" behaviors and cognitions is a clear strategy for preventing the development of pain behaviors, such as inactivity/dysfunction and over-reliance on analgesics.

A second strategy that appears to be important is that the patient is incorporated into the intervention as an active partner. Since there is seldom a medical cure for MSP, a prerequisite for successful prevention seems to be the patient's participation. Motivation is consequently an essential element and represents one method of increasing compliance. It is hoped that patients will not only follow the recommended program, but also believe in its utility and perceive that it enhances their ability to control the pain problem. Therefore, successful secondary prevention programs seem to make special efforts to employ the patient as an active participant. For example, rather than being treated as a traditional patient, the pain sufferer may be given the role of a "student." Moreover, the student is given considerable control in developing the prevention strategy. Commitment is thereby increased, as the student is also involved in the decision-making process.

A third strategy is the promotion of good communication. The interaction among the patient, his or her family, the workplace, the insurance carrier, and the health care unit appears to be vital to ensure recovery and especially a return to work. For example, patients who believe that the workplace or insurance carrier is not sincerely interested in their case may be more likely to pursue litigation. Philips and Grant (1991) found that 48% of patients with acute back or neck pain had contacted a lawyer within 7 days of pain onset. Moreover, we (Linton & Bradley, 1992) found that patients returning to work often did not feel that their supervisors provided active support for a return to work, and that this seemed to be associated with poor outcome.

Daltroy et al. (1993) also documented this phenomenon. They found that an educational program designed to reinforce injury prevention changes among urban postal workers did not change worker behavior or back complaints at a 2½-year follow-up assessment. This negative effect was associated with workers' perceptions that their coworkers and supervisors failed to engage in appropriate helping behaviors or in reinforcement of safe lifting behaviors. Similarly, Feuerstein and Thebarge (1991) found that relations with the supervisor was one of four variables discriminating between pain patients who were working and those who were off work.

Moreover, a major hindrance in delivering proper treatment and rehabilitation services may be a lack of coordination of services. Waiting periods caused by administrative bureaucracy seem to be detrimental, whether they are related to aspects of care (e.g., referrals) or to decisions about compensation or special help in returning to work. Consequently, good communication may "oil the wheels" of intervention to provide maximum preventive impact. The study by Haig et al. (1990), described above, seems mainly to have resulted in improved communication and better-coordinated services, as was also the case in the Linton et al. (1993) study.

A fourth strategy consists of follow-up and maintenance of good adherence. Although follow-up and adherence have been highlighted for successful treatment of chronic pain (Turk & Rudy, 1991; Nicholas, 1992), these issues may be overlooked in secondary prevention. Nevertheless, there is reason to believe that compliance and follow-up are important for long-term outcome. Several of the programs described above explicitly provided follow-up or booster sessions, and most of the programs have been adapted to include recommendations for enhancing adherence.

Since outcome may be related to pain and disability (VonKorff, 1994; Philips & Grant, 1991) strategies to deal with flare-ups of pain may be particularly relevant (Nicholas, 1992). Keefe and Van Horn (1993) have provided a model for helping individuals maintain good adherence and prevent relapse following termination of behavioral interventions for pain. The model consists of two stages. First, individuals are taught to identify high-risk situations that tend to be associated with flare-ups of pain and that may compromise their coping abilities (e.g., interpersonal distress, increases in depression or anxiety). Next, individuals are taught to rehearse different coping efforts for various high-risk situations and to apply their coping skills soon after recognizing that they are in such a situation.

Some of the strategies described here may be incorporated into a unified program for maximum effectiveness. The content, administration, and timing of the intervention will undoubtedly be important determinants of success, as we have seen that seemingly similar programs have produced surprisingly different results.

Cost-Effectiveness of Preventive Interventions

Although cost reduction is a frequently used argument for providing chronic pain prevention programs, few adequate analyses have been reported. Nevertheless, a small number of well-designed studies have shown that preventive interventions may reduce work absenteeism, health care utilization, and other sources of high costs. For example, although "back schools" have generally produced modest results (Bigos et al., 1994), two studies have demonstrated that this approach can produce cost-effective changes among large groups of workers. Brown, Sirles, Hilyer, and Thomas (1992) studied the effects of a back school, consisting of 6 weeks of exercise training and education, on 144 city employees with previous occupationally related back injuries. It was found that the back school, relative to a no-intervention control condition, produced a significant reduction in number of injuries (16 vs. 33) and medical costs ($24,000 vs. $34,000) during a 6-month follow-up period. Similarly, Versloot, Rozeman, van Son, and van Akkerweeken (1992) studied the effects of a back school program on 500 city bus drivers. This back school program consisted of three sessions in which instruction was provided regarding responsibility for personal health, stress and coping strategies, body mechanics, and exercise. It was shown that over a 2-year follow-up period, the back school program, relative to a no-intervention control condition, reduced absenteeism by at least 5 days per year per employee. This translated into an annual saving of $900 per employee, or $103,400 for the entire sample, even after the costs of the program were controlled for.

Two groups of investigators have examined the effects of interventions that offer more intensive treatments than back schools do. Mitchell and Carmen (1990) reported the results of a multicenter trial that involved over 3,000 patients with acute soft-tissue and back injuries. The intervention consisted of education and an intensive exercise and work conditioning program. Patients who received the intervention were compared to matched control patients who received standard treatments at other facilities. It was found that during a 5-month follow-up period, the savings produced by the intervention in wage loss and health care costs ranged each month from approximately $1 million to $1.5 million. A continuation of this research with 542 patients (Mitchell & Carmen, 1994) showed that the early preventive intervention produced lower costs than the control condition; although the difference was not statistically significant, the projected amount saved was about $5,000 per patient, or an astounding $1.3 million over a period of 30 months.

We examined the effects of our secondary prevention program on sick-listing and associated costs among nurses with subacute back pain (Linton et al., 1989). We found at a 6-month follow-up that the program, relative to the waiting-list control condition, was associated with significantly fewer days off work than would have been expected on the basis of pretreatment trends. An 18-month follow-up of the nurses who had received this intervention showed that, relative to pretreatment trends, the mean reduction in sick days for pain was 76.5 days per person. It was estimated that this reduction in sick days had saved the nurses' employer nearly $10,000 per person, or approximately twice the cost of the intervention (Linton & Bradley, 1992).

In summary, the studies reviewed above suggest that secondary prevention programs, if properly implemented and evaluated, can produce substantial savings to employers and insurance providers. It should be noted, however, that these programs vary greatly in their structure and in the magnitude of their effects. In addition, the financial benefits for such programs have been found over relatively short time periods, ranging from 5 to 18 months. The long-term program benefits have not been documented. Finally, given that journals tend to reject manuscripts with negative results, we do not know the number of preventive interventions that have failed to produce favorable outcomes (e.g., Daltroy et al., 1993). We believe, therefore, that effort must be devoted to two areas. First, it is necessary to determine what components of these preventive interventions are necessary and sufficient to produce cost-effective benefits for specific worker groups. In addition, it is necessary to determine whether the financial benefits of secondary prevention are maintained over long time periods without retraining. If effects are not maintained, further effort should be directed toward developing relapse prevention components (Keefe & Van Horn, 1993) that may be administered as part of the prevention programs or in booster sessions following treatment.

SUMMARY

The humanitarian, medical, and economic need for the prevention of chronic MSP is distinct. Although experience is limited and the research is often equivocal, effective secondary prevention of chronic MSP appears to be possible if the proper intervention is provided at the right time point and administered in an appropriate way. Despite the difficulty, successful programs have been able to reduce the risk of developing chronic problems by as much as eightfold.

Three approaches to secondary prevention have been attempted. First, screening routines hold the promise of isolating patients who are likely to develop chronic problems, so that resources may be allocated efficiently. Even though no standardized method is currently available for clinical use, risk factors have been delineated. These offer the advantage of helping to identify patients at risk very early. For example, some studies suggest that it may be possible to predict which patients are likely to have problems returning to work. Many of the variables suggested to be crucial are in the psychosocial realm. A good deal of research is needed before psychometrically sound methods will become available. Yet there is apparently sufficient knowledge to allow the clinician to improve routines.

A second approach involves preventive measures provided for patients with subacute MSP. This is the best-documented approach, with results generally indicating significant improvements relative to no intervention or to traditional interventions. Cognitive-behavioral methods applied in treating chronic pain sufferers have usually been employed at an earlier time point in these programs than in traditional rehabilitation efforts.

A third approach consists of preventive measures provided for patients with acute MSP. Medically and psychologically sound treatment provided at the very first treatment for acute MSP would seem to be an effective way of preventing the development of chronic

MSP behaviors. Programs vary considerably, but frequently emphasize reactivation, prevention of the conditioning of fear–avoidance for movement, and prevention of the reinforcement of pain behaviors.

Since the prevention of chronic MSP is in its infancy, no complete, tried-and-proven program may be recommended. However, certain strategies that appear at this time to be important have been delineated above. Successful programs appear to provide early, active interventions that focus on the patient's health behaviors. Furthermore, these programs stress the incorporation of the patient as an active partner in preventing chronic problems. Therefore, good communication with the patient as well as with other actors on the rehabilitation stage (e.g., the family, workplace, insurance carrier, and government agencies) is deemed important. Finally, successful programs seem to provide follow-up and measures to ensure adherence.

Taken together, the information available today suggests that it is quite possible to prevent the development of chronic MSP. However, if this goal is to be met, we need to continue to make bold attempts—both clinically and scientifically—to provide effective secondary prevention measures. Research to date has provided a very good beginning, but the details have yet to be worked out. If the promise of prevention is to be fully realized, these details are urgently needed.

REFERENCES

Aaron, L. A., Bradley, L. A., Triana, M., Alexander, R. W., Martin, M., Alberts, K., Alarcón, G. S., Stewart, K. E., & McCurley, H. (1994). Correlates of physical and emotional trauma in fibromyalgia. *Arthritis and Rheumatism, 37*(Suppl.), S297. (Abstract)

Bigos, S. J., & Battié, M. C. (1992) Risk factors for industrial problems. *Seminars in Spine Surgery, 4,* 2–11.

Bigos, S. J., Battié, M. C., Spengler, D. M., Fisher, L. D., Fordyce, W. E., Hansson, T. H., Nachemson, A. L., & Wortley, M. D. (1991). A prospective study of work perceptions and psychosocial factors affecting the report of back injury. *Spine, 16,* 1–6.

Bigos, S., et al. (1994). *Acute low back problems in adults* (Clinical Practice Guideline No. 14, AHCPR Publication No. 95-0642). Rockville, MD: U.S. Department of Health and Human Services.

Bongers, P. M., de Winter, C. R., Komper, M. A. J., & Hildebrandt, V. H. (1993). Psychosocial factors at work and musculoskeletal disease. *Scandinavian Journal of Work and Environmental Health, 19,* 297–312.

Bradley, L. A., Haile, J. M., & Jaworski, T. M. (1992a). Assessment of psychological status using interviews and self-report instruments. In D. C. Turk & R. Melzack (Eds.), *Handbook of pain assessment* (pp. 193–213). New York: Guilford Press.

Bradley, L. A., Richter, J. E., Scarinci, I. C., Haile, J. M., & Schan, C. A. (1992b). Psychosocial and psychophysical assessments of patients with unexplained chest pain. *American Journal of Medicine, 96*(Suppl.), 65S–73S.

Brown, K. C., Sirles, A. T., Hilyer, J. C., & Thomas, M. J. (1992). Cost-effectivness of a back school intervention for municipal employees. *Spine, 17,* 1224–1228.

Chun, D. Y., Turner, J. A., & Romano, J. M. (1993). Children of chronic pain patients: Risk factors for maladjustment. *Pain, 52,* 311–317.

Crook, J., Rideout, E., & Browne, G. (1984). The prevalence of pain complaints in a general population. *Pain, 18,* 299–314.

Daltroy, L. H., Iverson, M. D., Larson, M. G., Ryan, J., Zwerling, C., Fossel, A. H., & Liang, M. H. (1993). Teaching and social supports: Effects on knowledge, attitudes, and behaviors to prevent low back injuries in industry. *Health Education Quarterly, 20,* 43–62.

Davies, H. T. O., Crombie, I. K., Macrae, W. A., & Rogers, K. M. (1992). Pain clinic patients in northern Britain. *The Pain Clinic, 5,* 129–135.

DeGood, D. E., & Shutty, M. S. (1992). Assessment of pain beliefs, coping, and self-efficacy. In D. C. Turk & R. Melzack (Eds.), *Handbook of pain assessment* (pp. 214–234). New York: Guilford Press.

Deyo, R. A., Diehl, A. K., & Rosenthal, M. (1986). How many days of bed rest for acute low back pain? A randomized clinical trial. *New England Journal of Medicine, 315,* 1064–1070.

Donchin, M., Woolf, O., Kaplan, L., & Forman, T. (1990). Secondary prevention of low-back pain: A clinical trial. *Spine, 15,* 1317–1320.

Faas, A., Chavannes, A. W., van Eijk, J. T. M., & Gubbels, J. W. (1993). A randomized, placebo-controlled trial of exercise therapy in patients with acute low back pain. *Spine, 18,* 1388–1395.

Feuerstein, M., & Thebarge, R. W. (1991). Perceptions of disability and occupational stress as discriminators of work disability in patients with chronic pain. *Journal of Occupational Rehabilitation, 1,* 185–195.

Fordyce, W. E. (1976). *Behavioral methods for chronic pain and illness.* St. Louis, MO: C. V. Mosby.

Fordyce, W. E., Brockway, J. A., Bergman, J. A., & Spengler, D. (1986). Acute back pain: A control-group comparison of behavioral vs traditional management methods. *Journal of Behavioral Medicine, 9,* 127–140.

Frymoyer, J. W. (1992). Predicting disability from low back pain. *Clinical Orthopaedics and Related Research, 279,* 101–109.

Gamsa, A., & Vikis-Freibergs, V. (1991). Psychological events are both risk factors in, and consequences of chronic pain. *Pain, 44,* 271–277.

Greenfield, S., Fitzcharles, M. A., & Esdaile, J. M. (1992). Reactive fibromyalgia syndrome. *Arthritis and Rheumatism, 35,* 678–681.

Haig, A. J., Linton, P., McIntosh, M., Moneta, L., & Mead, P. B. (1990). Aggressive early medical management by a specialist in physical medicine and rehabilitation. *Journal of Occupational Medicine, 32,* 241–244.

Hellsing, A. L., Linton, S. J., & Kälvemark, M. (1994). A prospective study of patients with acute back and neck pain in Sweden. *Physical Therapy, 74,* 116–124.

Iezzi, A., Adams, H. E., Stokes, G. S., Pilon, R. N., & Ault, L. C. (1992). An identification of low back pain groups using biobehavioral variables. *Journal of Occupational Rehabilitation, 2,* 19–33.

Jensen, M. P., & Karoly, P. (1992). Pain-specific beliefs, perceived symptom severity and adjustment to chronic pain. *Clinical Journal of Pain, 8,* 123–130.

Jensen, M. P., Turner, J. A., Romano, J. M., & Karoly, P. (1991). Coping with chronic pain: A critical review of the literature. *Pain, 47,* 249–283.

Jensen, M. P., Turner, J. A., Romano, J. M., & Lawler, B. K. (1994). Relationship of pain-specific beliefs to chronic pain adjustment. *Pain, 57,* 301–309.

Keefe, F. J., & Van Horn, Y. (1993). Cognitive-behavioral treatment of rheumatoid arthritis pain: Maintaining treatment gains. *Arthritis Care and Research, 6,* 213–222.

Kerns, R. D., Turk, D. C., & Rudy, T. E. (1985). The West Haven–Yale Multidimensional Pain Inventory. *Pain, 23,* 345–356.

Lacroix, J. M., Powell, J., Lloyd, G. J., Doxey, M. C. S., Mitson, G. L., & Aldam, C. F. (1990). Low-back pain: Factors of value in predicting outcome. *Spine, 15,* 495–499.

Lehmann, T. R., Spratt, K. F., & Lehmann, K. K. (1993). Predicting long-term disability in low back injured workers presenting to a spine consultant. *Spine, 18,* 1103–1112.

Leino, P., & Magni, G. (1993). Depressive and distress symptoms as predictors of low back pain, neck–shoulder pain, and other musculoskeletal morbidity: A 10 year follow-up of metal industry employees. *Pain, 53,* 89–94.

Lindström, I., Öhlund, C., Eek, C., Wallin, L., Peterson, L. W., Fordyce, W. E., & Nachemson, A. L. (1992). The effect of graded activity on patients with subacute low back pain: A randomized prospective clinical study with an operant-conditioning behavioral approach. *Physical Therapy, 72,* 279–290.

Linton, S. J. (1990). Risk factors for neck and back pain in a working population in Sweden. *Work and Stress, 4,* 41–49.

Linton, S. J. (1994a). The challenge of preventing chronic musculoskeletal pain. In G. F. Gebhart, D. L. Hammond, & T. S. Jensen (Eds.), *Progress in pain research and management: Vol. 2. Proceedings of the 7th World Congress on Pain* (pp. 149–166). Seattle, WA: International Association for the Study of Pain Press.

Linton, S. J. (1994b). The role of psychological factors in back pain and its remediation. *Pain Reviews, 1*, 231–243.

Linton, S. J., & Bradley, L. A. (1992). An 18-month follow-up of a secondary prevention program for back pain: Help and hindrance factors related to outcome maintenance. *Clinical Journal of Pain, 8*, 227–236.

Linton, S. J., Bradley, L. A., Jensen, I., Spangfort, E., & Sundell, L. (1989). The secondary prevention of low back pain: A controlled study with follow-up. *Pain, 36*, 197–207.

Linton, S. J., Hellsing, A. L., & Andersson, D. (1993). A controlled study of the effects of an early intervention on acute musculoskeletal pain problems. *Pain, 54*, 353–359.

Linton, S. J., & Warg, L. W. (1993). The effects of attributions (beliefs) and job satisfaction on back pain. *Perceptual and Motor Skills, 76*, 51–62.

Lousberg, R., Schmidt, A. J. M., & Groeman, N. H. (1992). The relationship between spouse solicitousness and pain behavior: Searching for more experimental evidence. *Pain, 51*, 75–79.

Magni, G., Moreschi, C., Rigatti-Luchini, S., & Merskey, H. (1994). Prospective study on the relationship between depressive symptoms and chronic musculoskeletal pain. *Pain, 56*, 289–297.

Mitchell, R. I., & Carmen, G. M. (1990). Results of a multicenter trial using an intensive active exercise program for the treatment of acute soft tissue and back injuries. *Spine, 15*, 514–521.

Mitchell, R. I., & Carmen, G. M. (1994). The functional restoration approach to the treatment of chronic pain in patients with soft tissue and back injuries. *Spine, 19*, 633–642.

Nachemson, A. L. (1992). Newest knowledge of low back pain. *Clinical Orthopaedics and Related Research, 279*, 8–20.

National Board of Social Welfare. (1987). *Att förebygga sjukdomar is rörelseorganen [Preventing musculoskeletal illnesses]*. Stockholm: Author.

Niemcryk, S. J., Jenkins, C. D., Rose, R. M., & Hurst, M. W. (1987). The prospective impact of psychosocial variables on rates of illness and injury in professional employees. *Journal of Occupational Medicine, 29*, 645–652.

Nicholas, M. K. (1992). Chronic pain. In P. H. Wilson (Ed.), *Principles and practice of relapse prevention* (pp. 255–289). New York: Guilford Press.

Öhlund, C., Lindström, I., Areskourg, B., Eek, C., Peterson, L. E., & Nachemson, A. (1994). Pain behavior in industrial subacute low back pain: Part I. Reliability: Concurrent and predictive validity of pain behavior assessments. *Pain, 58*, 201–209.

Philips, H. C., & Grant, L. (1991). The evolution of chronic back pain problems: A longitudinal study. *Behaviour Research and Therapy, 29*, 435–441.

Philips, H. C., Grant, L., & Berkowitz, J. (1991). The prevention of chronic pain and disability: A preliminary investigation. *Behaviour Research and Therapy, 29*, 443–450.

Pietri-Taleb, F., Riihimäki, H., Viikari-Juntura, E., & Lindström, K. (1994). Longitudinal study on the role of personality characteristics and psycholgical distress in neck trouble among working men. *Pain, 58*, 261–267.

Pope, M. H., Anderson, G. B., Frymoyer, J., & Chaffin, D. B. (1991). *Occupational low back pain: Assessment, treatment, and prevention*. St. Louis: Mosby–Year Book.

Radloff, L. (1977). The CES-D Scale: A self-report depression scale for research in the general population. *Applied Psychological Measurement, 1*, 385–401.

Riley, J. F., Ahern, D. K., & Follick, M. J. (1988). Chronic pain and functional impairment: Assessing beliefs about their relationship. *Archives of Physical Medicine and Rehabilitation, 59*, 579–582.

Romano, J. M., Turner, J. A., Friedman, L. S., Bulcroft, R. A., Jensen, M. P., & Hops, H. (1991). Observable assessment of chronic pain patient–spouse behavioral interactions. *Behavior Therapy, 22*, 549–567.

Romano, J. M., Turner, J. A., Friedman, L. S., Bulcroft, R. A., Jensen, M. P., Hops, H., & Wright, S. F. (1992). Sequential analysis of chronic pain behaviors and spouse responses. *Journal of Consulting and Clinical Psychology, 60*, 777–782.

Romano, J. M., Turner, J. A., & Moore, J. E. (1989). Psychological evaluation. In C. D. Tollison (Ed.), *Handbook of chronic pain management* (pp. 38–51). Baltimore: Williams & Wilkins.

Rosenstiel, A. K., & Keefe, F. J. (1983). The use of coping strategies in low-back pain patients: Relationship to patient characteristics and current adjustment. *Pain, 17,* 33–40.

Rossignol, M., Suissa, S., & Abenhaim, L. (1992). The evolution of compensated occupational spinal injuries. *Spine, 17,* 1043–1047.

Scarinci, I. C., Haile, J. M., Bradley, L. A., & Richter, J. E. (1994). Altered pain perception and psychosocial features among women with gastrointestinal disorders and history of abuse: A preliminary model. *American Journal of Medicine, 97,* 107–118.

Skovron, M. L. (1992). Epidemiology of low back pain. *Bailliére's Clinical Rheumatology, 6,* 559–573.

Skovron, M. L., Szpalski, M., Nordin, M., Melot, C., & Cukier, D. (1994). Sociocultural factors in back pain: A population based study in Belgian adults. *Spine, 19,* 129–137.

Svensson, H. O., & Andersson, G. B. J. (1983). Low back pain in 40 to 47 year old men: Work history and work environment factors. *Spine, 8,* 272–276.

Turk, D. C., Meichenbaum, D., & Genest, M. (1983). *Pain and behavioral medicine: A cognitive-behavioral perspective.* New York: Guilford Press.

Turk, D. C., & Melzack, R. (Eds.). (1992). *Handbook of pain assessment.* New York: Guilford Press.

Turk, D. C., & Rudy, T. E. (1991). Neglected topics in the treatment of chronic pain patients: Relapse, noncompliance, and adherence enhancement. *Pain, 44,* 5–28.

Turkat, I. D., & Noskins, D. E. (1983). Vicarious and operant experiences in the etiology of illness behavior: A replication with healthy individuals. *Behaviour Research and Therapy, 21,* 169–172.

Versloot, J. M., Rozeman, A., van Son, A. M., & van Akkerweeken, P. F. (1992). The cost-effectiveness of a back school program in industry: A longitudinal controlled field study. *Spine, 17,* 22–27.

Vlaeyen, J. W. S., Kole-Snijders, A. M. J., Boeren, R. G. B., & van Eek, H. (1995). Fear of movement/(re)injury in chronic low back pain and its relation to behavioral performance. *Pain, 62,* 363–372.

VonKorff, M. (1994). Perspectives on management of back pain in primary care. In, G. F. Gebhart, D. L. Hammond, & T. S. Jensen (Eds.), *Progress in pain research and management: Vol. 2. Proceedings of the 7th World Congress on Pain* (pp. 97–110). Seattle, WA: International Association for the Study of Pain Press.

VonKorff, M., Deyo, R. A., Cherkin, D., & Barlow, W. (1993a). Back pain in primary care. *Spine, 18,* 855–862.

VonKorff, M., LeResche, L., & Dworkin, S. F. (1993b). First onset of common pain symptoms: A prospective study of depression as a risk factor. *Pain, 55,* 251–158.

Waddell, G., Bircher, M., Finlaysson, D., & Main, C. J. (1984). Symptoms and signs: Physical disease or illness behaviour? *British Medical Journal, 289,* 739–741.

Waddell, G., Newton, M., Henderson, I., Somerville, D., & Main, C. J. (1993). A Fear–Avoidance Beliefs Questionnaire and the role of fear–avoidance beliefs in chronic low back pain and disability. *Pain, 52,* 157–168.

Williams, D. A., & Thorn, B. E. (1989). An empirical assessment of pain beliefs. *Pain, 36,* 351–358.

CHAPTER 17

Occupational Rehabilitation

Multidisciplinary Management of Work-Related Musculoskeletal Pain and Disability

Michael Feuerstein
Thomas R. Zastowny

The prevalence, incidence, and associated economic and personal impact of work-related musculoskeletal disorders of the spine and upper extremities and associated work disability have reached crisis proportions for businesses and governments around the world. This situation has stimulated much research and spawned a wide range of approaches to prevention, evaluation, and rehabilitation. Health care providers, risk managers, health/safety and human resource personnel, insurance carriers, unions, state organizations, and national and international policy makers have all been actively working toward curbing the impact of this escalating problem. One promising approach has evolved from an integration of principles and techniques in pain treatment, sports medicine, ergonomics, rehabilitation and occupational medicine, orthopedics, vocational rehabilitation, and behavorial medicine. This approach has focused on evaluation and rehabilitation of chronic work disability secondary to occupational musculoskeletal disorders (OMDs), and typically involves a multidisciplinary team of providers. It has been referred to as "occupational rehabilitation" because of its emphasis on return to work (RTW) in patients with occupationally related disorders. Table 17.1 presents the components typically included in multidisciplinary rehabilitation of OMDs and work disability.

The occupational rehabilitation approach described here is broader in scope than work hardening or work conditioning, in that the treatment is tailored to a diverse set of presenting problems and includes (when appropriate) medical management, physical conditioning, work conditioning, pain and stress management, workplace psychosocial and ergonomic consultation, and vocational counseling and placement. Although occupational rehabilitation possesses many of the characteristics of functional restoration as developed by Mayer, Gatchel, and colleagues (Kinney, Gatchel, Polatin, & Mayer, 1991; Mayer & Gatchel, 1988; Mayer et al., 1987), it places a greater emphasis on the workplace and on specific interventions directed at workplace factors (ergonomic, psychosocial) assumed to inhibit RTW (e.g., Feuerstein & Hickey, 1992; Feuerstein et al., 1993).

The opinions or assertions contained herein are the private ones of the author(s) and are not to be construed as official or reflecting the views of the Department of Defense or the Uniformed Services University of the Health Sciences.

TABLE 17.1. Components of Multidisciplinary Rehabilitation for Work Disability Secondary to OMDs

Medical	Physical	Psychoeducational/ psychosocial	Ergonomic	Vocational
Further diagnostic evaluation	Therapeutic exercise/ physical conditioning	Cognitive-behavioral therapy	Worksite ergonomic job analysis	Counseling
Medication management	Work conditioning/ simulation	Stress management	Redesign of work station/ work method to reduce risk	Placement
Physician education of injured worker	Physical therapy modalities	Pain managment	Assistance with reasonable job modifications	Retraining
Case management/ follow-up		Back school		
		Operant conditioning		

With an increasing awareness of the role of psychosocial factors in the etiology, exacerbation, and maintenance of OMDs and concomitant work disability among a broad range of providers and payers, as well as the contribution of various psychological approaches in the rehabilitation and RTW process (both in the clinic and at the workplace), psychologists can play an ever-increasing role in the management and prevention of OMDs and work disability. However, a major shift in the conceptualization of these disorders and their treatment appears necessary for successful integration of psychological services within the workers' compensation health care system and occupational health care more generally.

This chapter first provides a brief overview of the magnitude of OMDs and associated disability. Following this, a summary of the conceptual basis for a multidisciplinary approach and a treatment model for rehabilitation of work disability associated with the OMDs is presented. Particular emphasis is placed on the role of psychological factors in OMDs and work disability. A brief review of the outpatient multidisciplinary rehabilitation outcome literature for treatment programs (for back pain only) using variations of the approach is also provided. Areas where the occupational rehabilitation approach requires a different focus or set of different considerations are identified, and important elements that may enhance outcomes are identified. A summary of knowledge areas that we have found helpful in making a transition from classic approaches to pain evaluation and treatment to working with OMDs and work disability is also presented.

The occupational rehabilitation approach is only briefly outlined in this chapter. For a more detailed consideration of this approach, the reader should refer to Feuerstein and Zastowny (in press). It is also important to note that this approach has been applied to *prevention* of OMDs with some preliminary success (Feuerstein, Carosella, & Lackner, 1994). Moreover, occupational rehabilitation is an area in which psychologists working directly at the workplace with a multispecialty team of managers, health/safety personnel, physical therapists, ergonomists, and physicians can contribute to effective management of OMDs and work disability. Although the present chapter focuses on the clinic-based treatment setting, much can be accomplished directly at the workplace if programs are designed, coordinated, and implemented in a cost-effective manner. Finally, although the comprehensive and intensive approach described in this chapter was developed primarily for the complex chronic patient who has received multiple attempts at physical therapy and pain management but remains work-disabled, variations of the approach can be applied to those individuals with less chronic levels of disability.

WORK-RELATED MUSCULOSKELETAL DISORDERS

Problems associated with OMDs and related work disability are increasingly common (Bureau of Labor Statistics, 1991) and can often evolve into more chronic conditions (Chaffin & Fine, 1992). Musculoskeletal disorders have been classified as a major occupational health problem by the National Institute of Occupational Safety and Health (NIOSH) since 1983, based upon the following characteristics of these disorders: (1) They represent a leading cause of disability during a person's working years; (2) they are ranked highly among health problems affecting the overall quality of life; (3) they exert a significant cost impact in terms of lost earnings and workers' compensation payments; and (4) they are projected to increase, based on the sociodemography of the workforce (Chaffin & Fine, 1992). Despite the recognition of OMDs as a major source of disability in the U.S. workforce over a decade ago, Dr. Donald Millard, former director of NIOSH, in his opening remarks to a conference held in 1991 on the state of the art in research on OMDs, stated: "Occupational musculoskeletal injuries represent a pandemic problem in the United States with gigantic effects on the quality of millions of people's lives every year" (Chaffin & Fine, 1992, p. 1).

Data from the U.S. Department of Labor indicate that in 1992 disorders of the musculoskeletal system that involved damage to the tendons, tendon sheaths, and related bones, muscles, and nerves of the hands, wrists, elbows, arms, back, or legs, and were associated with some type of repetitive motion, represented over 60% of all occupational illnesses (Bureau of Labor Statistics, 1991). In addition, pain complaints related to the musculoskeletal system in general are the most frequent causes of clinic visits in primary care settings (Deyo & Tsui-Wu, 1987).

These disorders, which are wide-ranging and heterogeneous in both etiology and course, typically include activity-related spinal disorders of the upper, middle, and lower spine (Spitzer, LeBlanc, & Dupuis, 1987), as well as the upper-extremity cumulative trauma disorders (UECTDs), including a range of nerve entrapment and tendinitis-related disorders (Putz-Anderson, 1988). In many cases, symptoms are self-limiting. However, if acute medical management is not successful and pain persists, these disorders can result in persistent pain and disability. Some individuals will never return to work and remain totally occupationally disabled.

The epidemiology of occupational low back pain has been reviewed in detail elsewhere (Andersson, Pope, Frymoyer, & Snook, 1991). Back problems accounted for 19% of all workers' compensation claims in the United States, resulting in 400,000 claims in 1978 (Klein, Jensen, & Sanderson, 1984). More recent data from New York State indicate that low back pain accounted for 34% of all compensated closed cases in 1987 (Feuerstein, 1991). The Liberty Mutual Insurance Company reports annual rates of work-related low back pain ranging from 1% to 15% (Snook, 1982). The total compensable cost for all occupational low back pain in the United States has recently been estimated at $11.1 billion (Webster & Snook, 1990a). The natural history of RTW following an activity-related spinal disorder, based upon an analysis of 45, 858 claims (Spitzer et al., 1987), is as follows: 74% of cases return to work within 1 month, 83% return at 7 weeks, 87% return at 3 months, and 92% re-enter the workforce between 3 and 6 months after injury. The remaining 7–8% remain work-disabled beyond 6 months. It is interesting to note that this latter group accounted for 76% of the total compensation costs for spinal disorders and 21% of total compensation costs for all injuries within the Quebec Workers' Compensation System in 1981 (Spitzer et al., 1987). It is also important to note that only 14% of these costs were related to medical care, while 86% were allocated to salary replacement, indicating the importance of efforts to facilitate timely RTW.

Equally important, but far less studied than low back pain, are the UECTDs. Unlike low back problems, which have been prevalent for a number of years, UECTDs have appeared to increase significantly in recent years (from 23,000 in 1981 to 223,600 in 1991). UECTDs accounted for only 18% of all occupational illness in 1981, but represented 61% as of 1991. The costs for the UECTDs have become significant as well. Webster and Snook (1990b) studied insurance company claims files ($n = 6,067$) and found the mean cost per UECTD case was $8,070 in 1989. From this analysis, they estimate the total compensable costs for UECTDs in the United States at approximately $563 million. Similar data for low back pain in another article by Webster and Snook (1990a) estimated average cost per case as $6,087 in 1986, with total compensable costs across the United States at $11.1 billion, as noted above. The total costs for UECTDs have not reached the level of those for back disorders, the average cost per case is quite similar in 1989 dollars. Tables 17.2 and 17.3 list common variants of low back disorders and UECTDs, respectively, that can be work-related and can contribute to recurrent or chronic work disability.

PSYCHOLOGICAL FACTORS RELATED TO WORK DISABILITY: IMPLICATIONS FOR TREATMENT

Converging Forces

The clinical evaluation and rehabilitation of patients with persistent work disability associated with OMDs represent a major challenge to the health care system. A prominent

TABLE 17.2. Common ICD-9-CM Diagnostic Categories for Patients with Work-Related Low Back Pain

Diagnostic category	ICD-9-CM codes	Definition
Herniated lumbar disk	722.10	Displacement disk, no myelopathy
	722.73	Disk disorder with myelopathy
Probable degenerative changes	721.3	Spondylosis without myelopathy
	722.52	Degeneration of disk
	722.93	Other and unspecified disk disorder
Spinal stenosis	721.42	Spondylogenic compression of cord
	724.02	Lumbar stenosis
Possible instability	724.6	Disorders of sacrum, including lumbosacral joint instability
	738.4	Acquired spondylolisthesis
	756.11	Spondylolysis
	756.12	Spondylolisthesis
Nonspecific backache	724.2	Lumbago
	846.0–9, 847.2, 847.3	Sprains and strains
Miscellaneous	722.83	Post laminectomy syndrome
	724.3	Sciatica
	739.3–4	Nonallopathic lesions

TABLE 17.3. Common IC9-9-CM Diagnostic Categories for Patients with Work-Related UECTDs

Nerve-related
353 Nerve root and plexus disorders
    353.0   Brachial plexus lesions
              Cervical rib syndrome
              Costoclavicular syndrome
              Scalenus anticus syndrome
              Thoracic outlet syndrome
    353.9   Unspecified nerve root and plexus disorder

354 Mononeuritis of upper limb and mononeuritis multiplex
    354.0   Carpal tunnel syndrome (median nerve entrapment)
    354.2   Lesions of the ulnar nerve
              Cubital tunnel syndrome
              Tardy ulnar nerve palsy
    354.3   Lesions of the radial nerve
    354.9   Mononeuritis of upper limbs, unspecified

Tendon/muscle-related
723 Other disorders of cervical region
    723.1   Cervicalgia
              Pain in neck
    723.3   Cervicobrachial syndrome (diffuse)
    723.9   Unspecified musuloskeletal disorders and symptoms referable to neck
              (cervical disorder, NOS)

726 Peripheral enthesopathies and allied syndromes
    (Enthesopathies are disorders of peripheral ligamentous or muscular attachments)
    726.1   Rotator cuff syndrome or shoulder and allied disorders
              726.10   Disorders of bursae and tendons in shoulder region:
                        Rotator cuff syndrome
                        Supraspinatus syndrome
              726.12   Bicipital tenosynovitis
    726.3   Enthesopathy of elbow region
              726.31   Medial epicondylitis
              726.32   Lateral epicondylitis (tennis elbow)
    726.9   Unspecified enthesopathy

727 Other disorders of synovium, tendon, and bursa
    727.0   Synovitis and tenosynovitis
              727.03   Trigger finger (acquired)
              727.04   Radial styloid tenosynovitis (de Quervain's)
              727.05   Other tenosynovitis of hand and wrist
    727.2   Specific bursitides, often of occupational origin
    727.9   Unspecified disorder of synovium, tendon, and bursa

728 Disorders of muscle, ligament, and fascia
    728.8   Other disorders of muscle, ligament, and fascia
              728.85   Spasm of muscle
    728.9   Unspecified disorder of muscle, ligament, and fascia

729 Other disorders of soft tissues
    729.1   Myalgia and myositis, unspecified (fibromyositis)
    729.8   Other musculoskeletal symptoms referable to limbs
              729.81   Swelling of limb
              729.82   Cramp
    729.9   Other and unspecified disorders of soft tissue

component of both the evaluation and rehabilitation of these patients involves access to psychological services.

A number of historical and contemporary forces have combined to heighten the importance of psychological factors in the assessment and rehabilitation of OMDs and associated work disability. The first is the recognition of the limitations of traditional medical management of OMDs, and related shortfalls of classic models of disease in explaining the common discrepancies between perceived disability and documented pathology (Waddell & Main, 1984; Waddell, McColloch, Kummel, & Venner, 1980; Waddell, Somerville, Henderson, & Newton, 1992). A second factor has been the emergence of multidimensional and multifaceted assessment and treatment models, which involve the use of multidisciplinary teams in treatment of these disorders and the theoretical bases for such approaches (Engle, 1977). Furthermore, there is increasing recognition that OMDs and work disability (particularly in more chronic situations) are likely to be the consequences of a complex interaction of multiple factors, including medical status, physical capabilities in relation to work demands (biomechanical, metabolic, and psychological) and psychological and behavioral resources. Finally, research on the psychosocial dimensions of these disorders suggests that effective management often involves engagement of the patient's motivation, sense of self-efficacy, and ability to manage pain and distress.

An Integrated Model of Work Disability

Before we examine specific psychological procedures for the assessment and management of OMDs and associated work disability, a review of the integrated model on which these procedures are based is worthwhile. Early in its history, the Center for Occupational Rehabilitation at the University of Rochester Medical Center developed an approach to evaluation and rehabilitation of OMD-related work disability, using an integrated model of work disability (Feuerstein, 1991). The "Rochester model," as it has become known, highlights the potential interaction of a patient's medical condition and ability to meet physical and psychological demands at work. It also emphasizes the importance of psychological factors (such as fear of reinjury, expectations of RTW, perception of disability, illness behavior, and pain and stress coping skills) in rehabilitation efforts directed at RTW.

Equally important, the model serves as a framework to (1) guide clinical evaluation, (2) identify barriers to work re-entry, (3) develop targeted interventions to reduce the impact of these barriers, and (4) provide rehabilitation services. Figure 17.1 presents the model and highlights the multiple factors potentially affecting RTW following occupational musculoskeletal illness and injury. The model assumes that RTW is often a complex function of multiple factors (medical status, physical capabilities, and psychological and behavioral resources). Detailed psychological assessment using this approach also includes preinjury work traits, personal workstyle, psychological readiness for RTW, ability to manage pain and distress, and identification of psychiatric symptoms (if present). The role of problem-solving skills regarding symptom management, and ability to manage musculoskeletal health and safety at work, are also considered. Successful RTW is seen as a cumulative outcome achieved through multidisciplinary treatment. Other outcomes of interest are increased physical capacity in relation to work demands, improved symptom management, and ability to self-manage personal workplace health and safety more efficiently.

The Rochester model provides a particularly effective paradigm for tracing contributory biobehavioral factors (psychological, environmental, and physiological processes that

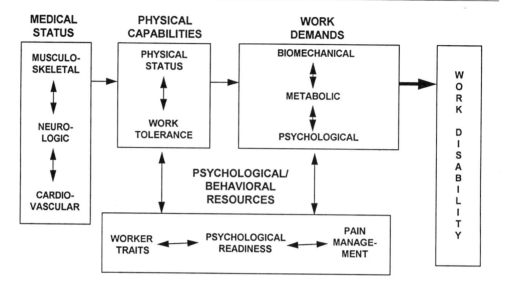

FIGURE 17.1. Rochester model of work disability. From Feuerstein (1991). Copyright 1991 by Plenum Press. Reprinted by permission.

can attenuate or exacerbate the discrepancy among pathology, impairment, pain, and functional limitation) often seen in the clinical presentation of OMDs and resulting disability. The model was developed in part as a response to a need for a broader understanding of the complexities of these disorders, which could lead to the integration of existing diverse treatment approaches and the development of innovative interventions.

PSYCHOLOGICAL APPROACHES
IN OCCUPATIONAL REHABILITATION

Using the Rochester model of work disability as a conceptual platform, we can further highlight the role and importance of key psychological factors, and return to the discussion of psychological factors in OMD assessment and management from a broader perspective.

Evaluation

Psychological factors that have had a demonstrated influence on the presentation, assessment, and treatment of OMDs are wide-ranging and involve numerous domains. Broadly, these factors can be divided into three categories: (1) cognitive/perceptual, (2) behavioral/environmental, and (3) psychophysiological. Overall, the evaluation of the work-disabled patient is most concerned with cognitive, perceptual, and behavioral factors that influence an individual's ability to adapt effectively to personal challenge (e.g., persistent and recurrent pain, loss of physical function) and return to a higher level of function and to work. More specific constructs that have been identified that are of potential significance include disease conviction (Pilowsky, 1978), perceived control over pain (Jensen, Turner, & Romano, 1991), perceived disability (Waddell & Main 1984; Waddell et al., 1980, 1992), fear of pain (Lethem, Slade, Troup, & Bentley, 1983; McCracken, Zayfert, & Gross, 1992), perception of the workplace and family (Bigos et al., 1991; Feuerstein, Sult, & Houle, 1985; Feuerstein & Thebarge, 1991), perceived self-efficacy (Bandura, 1977; Jensen et al., 1991), pain behaviors (Keefe & Williams, 1992; Fordyce, 1976), autonomic and musculoskeletal reactivity (Feuerstein, Papciak, & Hoon, 1987; Feuerstein, Labbe, & Kuczmierczyk, 1986), and personal workstyle (Feuerstein, in press).

As with any comprehensive pain evaluation, many of these factors are routinely included in the psychological assessment. However, the focus in occupational rehabilitation is not primarily on factors affecting pain, but rather on those affecting functional improvement and work re-entry. Table 17.4 presents common areas of psychological assessment that our group has found useful in the evaluation of OMDs. These areas encompass five broad categories (symptoms/pain, function, workplace, family, and secondary psychiatric features) that are assumed to influence work disability. These areas of inquiry are integrated into a multidisciplinary functional capacity evaluation (FCE) that assesses each of the dimensions of the Rochester model of work disability, including medical status; physical capabilities in relation to work demands (biomechanical, metabolic, psychological); and the individual patient's psychological and behavioral resources, including worker traits, psychological readiness for work (e.g., supervisor support, family support, personal expectation), and ability to manage pain and other symptoms.

Predictors of RTW following multidisciplinary rehabilitation for chronic back pain should also be assessed during the initial evaluation. In a recent review of the outcome literature related to multidisciplinary rehabilitation directed at facilitating return to work in work-disabled chronic back pain patients, we (Feuerstein, Menz, Zastowny, & Barron, 1994) categorized the variables predicting RTW 1 year after treatment into five groups: medical history, demographics, physical findings, pain, and psychological indices. Results from these studies indicated that the following psychological factors were predictive of RTW: lower pain severity (Barnes, Smith, Gatchel, & Mayer, 1989; Polatin & Mayer, 1992), and pain drawing scores (Barnes et al., 1989), higher levels of satisfaction with treatment (Hazard, Haugh, Green, & Jones, 1994), higher cooperativeness during treatment (Barnes et al., 1989), lower levels of hypochondriasis (Barnes et al., 1989), distrust/stubbornness (Barnes et al., 1989), depression (Barnes et al., 1989), and "premorbid pessimism" (Barnes et al., 1989). Although the relative predictive strength of each of these variables cannot be determined at present, given the limited number and the diversity of studies to date, these findings indicate the importance of a range of biobehavioral factors as prospective correlates of outcome. In addition, Carosella, Lackner, and Feuerstein (1994) recently reported that those patients who were more likely to drop out of an occupational rehabilitation treatment program were younger; had a longer duration of work disability; reported lower RTW expectations; and had higher levels of perceived disability, pain severity, and preoccupation with bodily sensations (higher scores on the Somatization subscale of the Million Clinical Multiaxial Inventory-II). These findings as a whole indicate that assessment of the correlates of RTW outcome and early discharge should also be made during the initial evaluation of these patients, and that efforts to enhance outcome through strategic interventions directed at high-risk patients should be initiated.

TABLE 17.4. Psychological Aspects of Assessment in Occupational Rehabilitation

Symptoms/pain
  Disease conviction
  Fear of reinjury
  Subjective pain
  Distress
  Pain coping
  Fear of pain and reinjury
  Impact of pain symptoms on quality of life
Function
  Perceived disability
  Perceived coping with residual loss of function
  Activities of daily living
  Perceived self-efficacy regarding function
  Adaptation to disability
  Areas of function (maximum, minimum)
  Factors limiting function
Workplace
  Expectation of RTW
  Work demands
  Worksite ergonomic job analysis (ergonomic risk factors with emphasis
    on work organization)
  Job stress
  Assertiveness/negotiation skills
  Safe work behavior/body mechanics
  Workstyle
  Work characteristics
  "Worker–environment fit"
  Prospective job targets
Family
  Beliefs of current disability status and ability to return to work
  Degree of family support for work re-entry
  Current family structure
  Current family needs/demands
  Quality of family life
  Relation of disability to current family function
Secondary psychiatric features
  Anxiety
  Depression
  Substance abuse
  Personality disorder
  Psychiatric crisis
  Somatoform features
  Personality profile

Treatment

Following the comprehensive FCE, a detailed treatment plan is formulated. The psychological treatment component is best characterized as a stepped intervention that includes both psychoeducational group sessions and brief individual sessions provided on an as-needed basis. Each patient receives basic information in group sessions that meet for approximately 1 hour daily. On the basis of information obtained in the evaluation and via staff observation during the program (e.g., during the physical conditioning phase), problem areas that emerge (e.g., increased fear of reinjury) are targeted for additional treatment. This treatment is provided during the as-needed time and involves the use of a problem-focused protocol. This stepped intervention strategy represents a time-efficient approach to the delivery of psychological services. Such an approach provides patients with a general set of skills to assist them with work re-entry and with maintaining a safe work environment and optimal musculoskeletal health, in addition to providing targeted interventions for individual problem areas (e.g., fear of reinjury, depression, anxiety, or supervisor or coworker difficulties). The problem-focused protocols require that (1) the psychologist work with the client and/or his or her family and supervisor on an individual basis; and (2) the psychologist work with staff members in program areas (i.e., physical conditioning, work conditioning) to facilitate goal achievement for each of the identified problem areas.

Table 17.5 provides a summary of the target areas typically addressed in the psychological intervention component and specifically covered in the psychoeducational group sessions over a typical 4-week duration. The coverage of each area typically goes beyond a single session. Also, it is important to re-emphasize that selected patients receive concurrent brief (15- to 20-minute) interventions by the psychologist to augment the acquisition of skills and strategies presented in the group or to discuss areas that are particularly significant for a given patient. Table 17.6 presents a summary of the psychoeducational group sessions for a typical 4-week period. As the table indicates, several topics covered in these sessions are related to classic pain management approaches. Detailed considerations of these approaches are included in select chapters in this book and are not discussed in this chapter. (See especially Sanders, Chapter 5; Bradley, Chapter 6; Blanchard & Arena, Chapter 8; Keefe, Beaupré, & Gil, Chapter 10; and Kerns & Payne, Chapter 11.) Although certain generic pain management approaches are included in the group meetings, the emphasis is on the application of these skills to the workplace and the RTW process. We believe this emphasis is necessary to facilitate the acquisition of skills and attitudes that will help the patient move beyond disability and attempt an RTW.

TABLE 17.5. Major Problem Areas
Targeted for Psychological Intervention
in Occupational Rehabilitation

I. *Managing pain*
   Pain and symptom focus
   Behavioral dysregulation
   Fear of pain
   Fear of failure
II. *Managing stress*
   Marital stress
   Family stress
   Job stress
   Communication problems
III. *Managing emotions*
   Generalized anxiety
   Depression
   Anger/hostility
IV. *Work re-entry*
   Direct communication
   Workstyle modification
   Facilitating support
   Using coping strategies
V. *Relapse prevention*

TABLE 17.6. Psychoeducational Group Sessions Provided in an Occupational Rehabilitation Program

Session 1	Session 2	Session 3	Session 4	Session 5
		Week 1		
Pain Models and Disability Describe models of pain Describe pain components Define difference between pain and disability Debunk myths about pain Present model and rationale for behavioral treatment Introduce idea of goal setting and its purpose	*Goal Setting* Define short- and long-range goals and their importance Discuss the attainment of intermediate goals Explain the idea of "perspective" in rehabilitation Provide examples of unrealistic goal setting (e.g., "back to normal" now) Discuss behavior change and reinforcement Discuss shaping and success motivation	*Behavioral Dysregulation* Define avoidance and excessive activity Explain pain's influence on behavior Explore alternative ways of behaving	*Stress and Pain* Define stress Explore how stress is manifested physically and emotionally; differentiate between adaptive and maladaptive methods Discuss simple ways of coping with stress (exercise, relaxation, distraction, nutrition)	*Fear of Pain and Reinjury, Part I; Understanding Generalization* Discuss the components of fear (bodily reactions, thoughts/memories) Discuss how fear influences behavior (e.g., avoidance) Describe how pain is a signal for fear Describe how fears gain and maintain their strength Define generalization; describe how to use it, how to put it to work Discuss why generalization is important—practice makes it easier
		Week 2		
Fear of Pain and Reinjury, Part II Discuss major fears: reinjury, increased pain Describe ways of combating fear	*Thinking and Pain/Fear* Discuss how thinking influences the way we feel and in turn our pain Discuss how we make judgments about situations and how our beliefs influence how we behave Provide a model relating thoughts and feelings to pain	*Feeling Good Again: Controlling the Way You Think* Discuss how we think influences the way we view the world and ourselves Discuss how negative thoughts can get us feeling down, frustrated, angry Describe how we can control how we think: thought refocusing, thought stopping, reframing	*Assertiveness* Define assertiveness Explore examples of assertive behavior—view videotapes Conduct personal assessment of assertive behavior Discuss the importance of accurate communication Discuss methods to communicate directly and accurately	*Assertiveness: Generalization of What You Have Learned* Discuss how assertiveness can be used at home, at work, and socially Ask: What can assertiveness do for you in your own life? Role-play situations with video feedback Reinforce attempts at practicing cognitive strategies and assertive behavior

468

Week 3

Putting It All Together	Family and the Influences of Pain	Family and the Influences of Pain	Coping with Job Stress	Problem Solving: Generalization of What You Have Learned
Discuss different components of pain management and how they fit together to assist in managing pain and stress (pain sensation strategies—relaxation, sensory alteration, pain inoculation, imagery; pacing; stress management)	Discuss the positive and negative ways family members deal with pain Discuss the role of reinforcement and pain maintenance Discuss pain as a means of communication Stress importance of doing something together—learning to have fun together again	Discuss disability and role changes Discuss the role of pain-related moods in family Discuss the expectations of family members for a person in pain Examine family problem solving	Discuss sources of job stress Discuss controllable vs. uncontrollable job stress Discuss interaction of employee and supervisor Discuss the perception of the job itself Review methods for managing job stress more effectively	Define problem solving Define problem-solving model Discuss ways of adaptive and maladaptive problem solving Discuss enlisting the help of others Reinforce patients' attempts at practicing pain management skills, reducing pain behavior, and increasing family communication Introduce relapse prevention

Week 4

Pacing Behavior	Family and the Influence of Pain	Putting It All Together	Planning for the Future	Planning for the Future; Goal Setting; Generalizing; Graduation
Reinforce use of pacing behavior Discuss how pacing can be used in the work and home situations Use examples of what patients have found helpful to stimulate group discussion Use videotapes of work samples from work conditioning areas to illustrate good and bad pacing	Ask: How can you begin to make changes in how you relate to your family? Ask: How can you reintegrate into the family and get your needs met? Ask: How can you positively ask for help?	Discuss how patients have used the strategies thus far Discuss picking and choosing what works best for them Discuss the need to integrate these strategies into a way of life Discuss how they can be used in the family and at work	Discuss future in blocks of time Discuss realistic vs. unrealistic goals Discuss dealing with social pressure "now that you are better" Discuss setting realistic goals Emphasize the use of information for different settings Discuss relapse prevention: what happens when the pain increases again	Setting goals for work and family Reinforce patients' using the strategies and making them part of their lifestyle Provide a reminder sheet Pass out graduation certificates

Note. It is important to emphasize that not all topics are covered in detail; the therapist tailors the approach to the specific needs of the patient group. The group is both psychoeducation- and process-oriented.

OUTCOME RESEARCH ON MULTIDISCIPLINARY OCCUPATIONAL REHABILITATION FOR CHRONIC BACK PAIN AND CONCOMITANT WORK DISABILITY[1]

In search of obtaining benchmarks for specific RTW percentages following work reha-bilitation, we recently conducted a review of multidisciplinary occupational rehabilita-tion outcome studies. We were also interested in highlighting common components of multidisciplinary rehabilitation programs. In accord with these aims, a Medline search was conducted to identify occupational-rehabilitation-related outcome studies for chronic back pain published between 1984 and 1994. Key terms used in the search included "back pain," "musculoskeletal disorders," "occupational diseases," "return to work," and "rehabilitation." The criteria for including an outcome study in this review were as fol-lows: (1) The subjects had diagnoses of back pain, low back pain, or spinal disorder (spe-cific and nonspecific diagnoses); (2) back pain was chronic, either lasting longer than 3 months since injury of involving an absence from work longer than 3 months; (3) treatment included a multidisciplinary rehabilitation approach (also referred to as multi-disciplinary occupational or work rehabilitation) that utilized some combination of medical management, physical conditioning, pain and stress management, ergonomic consulta-tion, vocational counseling/placement, and education regarding back safety and health (refer to Table 17.1 for a summary of the components often included in multidisciplinary occupational rehabilitation); (4) treatment was provided on an outpatient basis; and (5) work re-entry was the *primary* focus of outcome. There were an additional five studies in the literature that assessed the effects of multidisciplinary inpatient rehabilitation pro-grams on RTW (Mellin et al., 1993; Altmaier et al., 1992; Estlander, Mellin, Vanharanta, & Hupli, 1991; Cassisi, Sypert, Salamon, & Kapel, 1989; McArthur, Cohen, Gottleib, Naliboff, & Schandler, 1987). These were not included in the review. The rationale for exclusion of these studies was based upon the growing trend away from inpatient treat-ment of pain and disability (particularly for occupational back pain), given the higher cost of such interventions and absence of superior outcomes in relation to outpatient treatment.[2]

For the purposes of this review, RTW was defined as (1) return to preinjury position on a full-time basis; (2) return to any job (preinjury, modified, or new) on a part-time or full-time basis; or (3) state-supported participation in vocational rehabilitation (coun-seling, training, placement). Although there are many other outcomes resulting from multidisciplinary rehabilitation, including improvement in functioning, pain, and distress, the justification for selecting RTW as the exclusive outcome measure of interest in this review was based upon the following assumptions: (1) RTW represents an outcome mea-sure with a relatively clear dichotomous endpoint (i.e., return—yes or no); (2) RTW is frequently the ultimate goal of rehabilitation of individuals with occupational back pain; (3) RTW can theoretically have an impact on workers' compensation indemnity and medical costs; and (4) RTW can be associated with improved quality of life. It is impor-tant to note that some studies have included participation in state-supported vocational rehabilitation services (counseling, placement, and training) in their RTW rate figures. "Ready for vocational rehabilitation" was another measure of vocational outcome reported

---

[1] Parts of this section are adapted from Feuerstein, Menz, Zastowny, and Barron (1994). Copyright 1994 by Plenum Press. Adapted by permission.

[2] In the past, inpatient treatment has been reserved for the highly disabled patient with excessive levels of pain behavior, depression, and narcotic analgesic abuse.

in one study. Also, when vocational rehabilitation was included in the calculation of RTW outcome, it is specified below in Figure 17.2. Although the original intent of this review was to identify outcome studies that included individuals with occupational low back pain receiving workers' compensation benefits, this was not feasible because all investigations did not include this group of patients exclusively.

Of the outcome studies published through March 1994, 42 articles related to back pain rehabilitation were identified. Of these 42, 9 articles met the criteria stated above and were included in this review. Two of the nine articles (Mayer et al., 1987; Hazard et al., 1994) reported long-term follow-up of the original studies in separate papers (Hazard, Haugh, Green, & Jones, 1989; Mayer 1985), but in each case the original and follow-up studies were classified in this review as a single study. Five studies evaluated outpatient rehabilitation programs exclusively (Hazard et al., 1989, 1994; Mitchell & Carmen, 1994; Mayer et al., 1985, 1987; Tollison, 1991; Sachs, David, Olimpio, Scala, & Lacroix, 1990). Two additional studies evaluated both outpatient and inpatient programs (Fredrickson, Trief, VanBeveren, Yuan, & Baum, 1988; Cairns, Mooney, & Crane, 1984). Although the Fredrickson et al. (1988) study did not specify the exact number of cases in each type of program, it was decided to include the outcome from this study in the review because both the outpatient and impatient options provided the multidisciplinary rehabilitation approach described above. The Cairns et al. (1984) study compared an outpatient to an inpatient intervention, and the data related to the outpatient intervention were used in the review.

Methodological Observations

All seven studies utilized a prospective design. In contrast, only one out of the seven studies randomly assigned subjects to treatment or control groups (Mitchell & Carmen, 1994). Even the Mitchell and Carmen (1994) study did not employ completely random assignment, in that subjects with more severe illness behavior were referred to the treatment group. Across most studies, there was a general tendency to assign individuals who either were denied access to treatment by their insurance carrier or had dropped out of programs to usual-care groups. In general, these comparison or control groups were exposed to unspecified interventions, with possible access to physical therapy, medication, work hardening, back school, acupuncture, active exercise, manipulation, or psychological intervention directed at enhancing pain and stress management skills.

Studies included a variety of diagnostic categories ranging from nonspecific low back pain to specific diskogenic disorders. The Mitchell and Carmen (1994) study also included "nonback" cases: 77% of the treatment group and 78% of controls had "back" disorders, whereas 23% of the treatment group and 22% of the control group had "nonback" disorders. The authors defined "back" disorders as low back injuries involving the lumbar and lumbosacral regions, and "nonback" disorders as soft-tissue injuries to "other anatomical locations." The results of the literature as a whole did not distinguish diagnostic groups in terms of RTW outcomes. Prior history of surgical treatment, psychological disorders, litigation status, workers' compensation status, and presence and duration of work disability varied across studies when specified. Type of work in terms of physical demands, job availability, availability of necessary job modifications or other accommodations, and insurance status (workers' compensation, Social Security Disability Insurance, Medicaid) were not consistently reported across studies.

The treatment rationale for the various multidisciplinary rehabilitation programs directed at RTW was reported in all studies. Treatment goals were also reported and generally included (1) restoration of general physical function by increasing flexibility, strength, and endurance; (2) improvement in work specific physical function; (3) enhanced pain management; (4) enhanced psychological coping skills; and (5) improved knowledge related to body mechanics and back pain risk reduction techniques.

In terms of subject size per group, the smallest study included 45 treatment cases and 33 in a comparison group (Sachs et al., 1990); the largest study included 271 cases receiving treatment and 271 controls (Mitchell & Carmen, 1994). Across all studies, the average number of subjects in the multidisciplinary treatment group was 104, whereas the average number of subjects in the comparison group was 74. Two of the seven studies reported patients who dropped out of the rehabilitation program (Mayer et al., 1987; Hazard et al., 1994), who accounted for 2% of the total number of patients entering treatment. Four studies (Tollison, 1991; Mayer et al., 1987; Hazard et al., 1994; Sachs et al., 1990) reported an inability to locate a subset of patients for follow-up. Based on available data, the mean age of subjects in both treatment and control groups was 40 years, ranging from 20 to 69 years. The average duration of work disability was approximately 16 months, ranging from (this was calculated by combining the mean duration of work disability or age reported across the treatment, comparison, and dropout groups for each study, followed by calculating the combined mean from each individual study). The average values could not be weighted for subject size, since individual case information was not provided in every study.

Definitions of RTW outcome were also variable across studies. In only one of the seven studies was return to full-time employment used as the exclusive operational definition of vocational outcome (Mitchell & Carmen, 1994). Only four of the seven studies reported subjects participating in vocational training separately from those subjects who were employed full-time or part-time (Fredrickson et al., 1988; Sachs et al., 1990; Cairns et al., 1984).

Return-to-Work Outcome

Outpatient multidisciplinary rehabilitation for chronic back pain demonstrated a mean RTW rate of 71%, ranging from 59% to 85%. This rate was calculated by averaging the 12-month follow-up data for six of the seven studies and posttreatment data for the remaining study, using the broader definition of RTW (including vocational training). In contrast, in corresponding comparison groups for which treatment was generally unknown, 44% were working at the 12-month follow-up. The range for the comparison groups, 20% to 78% ($\Delta 57\%$), was more than twice that of the treatment groups ($\Delta 26\%$). When the average RTW rate was calculated according to a more conservative definition (i.e., excluding vocational training outcome), the mean rate in the multidisciplinary rehabilitation groups was 67% at the 12-month follow-up (vs. 44% for the control groups). The outcome results are displayed in Figure 17.2.

When the RTW rate at the 12-month follow-up was based on totaling the individual cases for each study rather than averaging the percentages reported in each study, the rate increased to 74% for the treatment groups and 64% for the control groups when the Mitchell and Carmen (1994) "control" group was included. When eliminating the control group from the Mitchell and Carmen (1994) study, because of the questionable status of the group as a control (i.e., it is very likely that this group received a set of interventions similar to those for the treatment group), the overall RTW rate for the control or comparison groups was 39%. It is interesting to note that the difference between the RTW rates obtained according to the two methods for calculating RTW outcome is minimal.

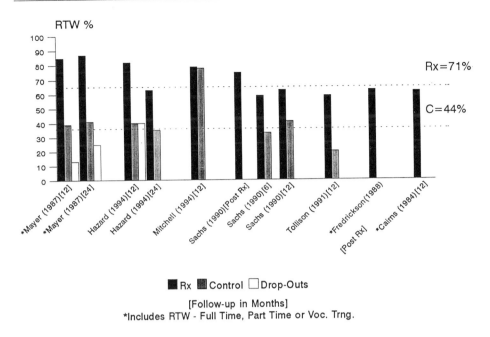

RTW %

■ Rx ▦ Control □ Drop-Outs

[Follow-up in Months]
*Includes RTW - Full Time, Part Time or Voc. Trng.

FIGURE 17.2. RTW outcomes for chronic low back pain in studies of outpatient multidisciplinary rehabilitation. From Feuerstein, Menz, Zastowny, and Barron (1994). Copyright 1994 by Plenum Press. Reprinted by permission.

Although RTW was the primary focus of this review, the research reviewed measured other outcomes, including trunk strength, trunk range of motion, aerobic capacity, pain levels, mood levels, and lifting capacity. In general, the research indicated significant improvements in many of these measures in the treatment groups in contrast to controls (Cairns et al., 1984; Frederickson et al., 1988; Hazard et al., 1989, 1994; Mayer et al., 1985, 1987; Mitchell & Carmen, 1994; Sachs et al., 1990; Tollison, 1991). It is beyond the scope of this chapter to detail these outcomes. An outcome study directed at occupational UECTDs also suggests that the approach is helpful in facilitating RTW in patients with these disorders (Feuerstein et al., 1993). However, this research is limited in terms of number of patients, its exclusive focus on RTW, and absence of randomized assignment.

BEYOND PAIN MANAGEMENT: THE NEED FOR A DIFFERENT APPROACH

When we consider the findings from these outcome studies and the experience from our center and that of similar rehabilitation facilities, it appears that to be maximally effective in the management of these cases, it is essential to move beyond traditional approaches to pain management. Health care providers, including psychologists with expertise and experience in pain assessment and treatment, need to approach the problem of OMDs from a different perspective. The problem of OMD-related work disability requires a treatment paradigm shift, including identified targets for intervention, evaluation approach, approach to treatment, and practice management. Another factor in this change involves the presence of managed care. Although managed care has relatively recently moved into mental health practice more generally, the evaluation and treatment of OMD-related pain and disability have been conducted under variations of managed care for many years. Although in need of major improvements, this area of practice is far ahead of health care systems not based on workers' compensation in terms of the significant involvement of third- and fourth-party reviewers in the management of treatment. This situation requires that the psychologist understand the "mind-set" of the approach and goals of those who manage workers' compensation cases, and be knowledgeable concerning fees and health care delivery system requirements in order to operate successfully within this area of practice. The following discussion highlights key aspects of the paradigm shift and some of the major issues in this area, in an effort to sensitize those interested in working in this area of practice.

Outcome Targets

Although similar issues regarding pain management exist with both generic pain disorders and the OMDs, there are many non-pain-related concerns that need to be addressed in the effective management of these cases. The first area to be discussed relates to selection of outcome targets for intervention. In contrast to traditional approaches to pain management, it should be clear at this point that the focus of treatment efforts with OMDs is most commonly on functional restoration and ultimate RTW. The goal of RTW is frequently the primary reason why a patient is referred for occupational rehabilitation. Although it appears on the surface that RTW may represent a fairly straightforward goal, in practice it is often difficult to achieve, particularly in cases with prolonged or recurrent episodes of work disability. Indeed, the longer an individual is out of work because of an OMD, the less likely RTW ultimately becomes (Spitzer et al., 1987).

A second outcome target change involves pain management. Whereas enhanced pain management also represents a goal of a comprehensive approach to occupational rehabilitation, it is not the primary goal of such interventions, as indicated earlier. Indeed, often patients achieve RTW but have residual pain. In such cases, secondary goals of the intervention include assisting the patients in reducing the likelihood that certain dimensions of work (physical, ergonomic, and psychosocial) will increase this residual pain, as well as improving the patients' use of pain management skills at the workplace.

Additionally and parenthetically, the better the consensus regarding target outcomes, the better the chance of success. From a practical perspective, when the RTW goal is explicit and is mutually agreed upon by patient, employer, attending and referring physician(s), case manager, and rehabilitation team providers, the outcome can be more easily achieved. However, when multiple parties are unclear regarding the RTW treatment goal, when the goal has not been agreed upon by all parties, or when such a goal has not been made explicit, it becomes much more difficult to achieve such an outcome.

It has been our experience that the RTW treatment goal appears to represent a more challenging outcome than improvement in pain coping skills or reductions in distress and pain alone. First, achievement of the outcome is quite clear on one level: Either the patient is or is not back to work at a given point in time. An "easily defined" outcome, it is also one that is relatively easily measured and therefore open to scrutiny by a number of interested parties. Often this exposure places much pressure on the rehabilitation team to produce such an outcome. Moreover, certain insurance carriers and case managers base positive outcome exclusively on RTW and will not refer or approve rehabilitation to those providers who do not achieve relatively high rates of RTW.

However, in practice, RTW is often both difficult to measure and hard to achieve. A sometimes unstated complication associated with a primary focus on RTW, of which providers should be aware, is that there appear to be qualitatively different outcomes associated with a "positive" RTW. For example, patients can go back to work at their former job, a new job, or a modified job at either their former workplace or a new one. Depending upon the job, the salary may differ drastically (e.g., a shift from a construction position to a service job); this affects not only the injured worker, but the carrier and employer as well, in terms of payment of lost wages (the difference between the former and the new salary). Often the optimal outcome is a return to the former job with the former employer; however, there are circumstances where that is not feasible from medical, physical demand, psychological, or economic perspectives. There are also certain cases in which individuals simply cannot continue to expose themselves to physical demands of a certain job, with or without modifications. This necessitates the very difficult decision to seek alternative work. Often these decisions are delayed until multiple RTW failures are experienced or a reinjury occurs. Thus, as noted above, RTW as a clinical outcome is deceptively complex (see also Fishbain et al., 1993, especially the comments on RTW classification). It is beyond the scope of this chapter to discuss all the nuances of this clinical goal. Suffice it to say that a shift from a primary goal of improved pain and stress management to a goal of RTW requires an awareness of multiple factors within the workplace, the patient, and the health care and workers' compensation systems that can affect such an outcome.

In summary, the psychologist can no longer simply attempt to improve a patient's psychological coping skills, but needs to help facilitate attitude and related behavior change regarding work re-entry. Often this must be accomplished through the collaboration of multiple care providers, including physical therapists, ergonomists, health/safety personnel, exercise psychologists, and physicians (in orthopedics, physical medicine, and rehabilitation/occupational medicine). Such an approach goes well beyond an exclusive focus on pain, distress, and concurrent psychopathology. To manage such cases effectively, a keen awareness of workplace ergonomic and psychosocial factors, a knowledge of each patient's physical capabilities in contrast to work demands, and an understanding of what can reasonably be achieved in the areas of enhancing physical capabilities and work tolerances is most helpful.

Evaluation Approach

In relation to the need for a more comprehensive understanding of the multiple factors contributing to work disability and inhibiting RTW, the psychologist must shift the focus of the evaluation. Rather than diagnosing concurrent psychopathology and the impact pain has had on functioning (psychological and physical), an important role for the psychologist is the identification of psychological and environmental factors that appear to be inhibiting the RTW process. RTW expectations, fear of reinjury, and specific workplace and family stressors, in addition to the existence of depression, anxiety, substance abuse, and/or personality disorders, are areas of interest for assessment.

The goal of all evaluations of patients with OMDs is *not* to provide a formal psychiatric diagnosis. Indeed, such a diagnosis will often serve to alienate a patient and carrier from the psychologist, because of the potential for misinterpretation that the diagnosis is the explanation or cause of the pain and disability; this can have the effect of negating and minimizing the pathophysiological basis. Moreover, such diagnoses are greatly feared by carriers, because they may invoke a secondary "mental health claim" that can further escalate claim costs and prolong recovery. Such a situation can also fuel the friction between the patient and carrier, increasing the patient's distress and pain, and potentially prolonging disability. It is highly recommended that the psychologist probe for factors that may be exacerbating or prolonging disability, identify these, and make specific recommendations for interventions directed at reducing the impact of these factors to assist the patient in a safe RTW.

The FCE, referred to earlier, is a commonly used evaluation method for patients with OMD and work disability. The evaluation is generally an assessment of physical function (flexibility, strength, endurance) and work-related function (lifting, pushing–pulling, carrying, climbing, etc.). These evaluations are typically conducted by a physical or occupational therapist or exercise physiologist. Frequently, they also include some global index of distress, reliability, and motivation to participate in rehabilitation. At present, the role of the clinical psychologist in conducting these evaluations varies from facility to facility and state to state. Some states (e.g., New York) have indicated that a psychological evaluation is not included in the FCE, but must be requested separately. Although the specific utility of the FCE in general and of FCEs that include a psychological component in particular needs to be empirically determined, it has been our clinical experience that the psychologist can be effectively used to identify abnormal illness behavior, barriers to RTW, and existing psychopathology. This clinical description (in the FCE writeup or companion documents) must be presented in a nontechnical manner to avoid some of the problems discussed earlier. Whether this psychological assessment is included in the FCE or is conducted separately, it must differ from the traditional psychological evaluation for either pain or more general mental health problems.

Treatment Approach

As in evaluation, there is also a need for the psychologist to function in a different manner in treatment. In many occupational rehabilitation settings, the psychologist is operating within a milieu environment. Patients are involved in half-day or full-day rehabilitation programs (i.e., treatment blocks) that involve physical conditioning, work conditioning, safety training, and health education. Often the psychological interventions are administered "on the floor," while a patient is exercising on a treadmill or simulating a work task. Here the psychologist can utilize in vivo procedures to facilitate learning and promote rapid generalization of a range of pain and stress management skills. This environment also promotes more rapid desensitization of fear of pain/reinjury, and can enhance interventions directed at facilitating self-efficacy regarding the ability to perform certain functions with pain. This latter area represents a unique and highly promising area for psychological research and treatment (Lackner, Carosella, & Feuerstein, 1994).

As previously indicated, many of the psychological interventions are conducted in a group format. Here the psychologist can instruct patients in specific cognitive-behavioral skills, as well as provide opportunities to deal more effectively with workplace stress and fear of reinjury. The frustrations and anger frequently associated with the workers' compensation and health care systems are also common topics. In addition, the psychologist may visit the workplace and meet with the supervisor and patient to work out any communication problems that are inhibiting effective RTW. This model of practice is quite different from the individual treatment model of 15 to 20 one-hour sessions per week that is commonly used in pain management and other areas of clinical psychology. Classic pain treatment and other cognitive-behavioral approaches are reserved for more chronic cases or cases where pain or significant levels of distress appear to be predominant barriers to work re-entry. The psychological intervention typically taken within occupational rehabilitation can be best described as a rapid, brief, and efficient use of a range of psychological approaches in the clinic *and* workplace, directed at improving problem-solving skills and the use of a variety of pain and stress management strategies.

Multidisciplinary Team

An important role of the psychologist in occupational rehabilitation involves participation as a member of the multidisciplinary treatment team, providing consultation to the other team members. In the multidisciplinary case staffing, each professional involved in the assessment presents his or her findings and recommendations, typically in a round-table discussion format. As the professionals report their findings, the conceptualization of the case continues to evolve; the extent to which a patient meets program admission criteria is considered, and specific target areas are identified for intervention. By the completion of the round-table review, a tentative decision is reached and presented to the group for consensus review. The psychologist often plays an instrumental role in the case conceptualization and identification of treatment targets/goals.

Although the multidisciplinary approach has a scientific basis in both epidemiological and clinical outcome research, much remains to be learned about the mechanisms and managment of work disability. Many practical challenges also accompany the implementation of such an approach; these make its effective management at times frustrating and complex. Working with multiple disciplines, each with its own biases, can be difficult. Although task clarity is helpful, it is also important for cross-training to occur and for team members to participate in multiple levels of decision making and clinical service delivery, provided they have demonstrated the relevant competencies.

The strategy of flexible roles is also not without its difficulties. For such an approach to work, it is essential that the various team members recognize the limitations of their knowledge and skills, and not simply apply what appears to be a "common-sense" approach to problems. This requires a highly skilled group that works with the best available empirical knowledge and clearly defined treatment goals. For example, a physical therapist or an occupational therapist who does not fully understand specific techniques to facilitate attitude and behavior change, but uses "pop psychology" to deal with these problems, can be ineffective and even counterproductive. Similarly, a psychologist or other mental health provider who happens to have a cursory understanding of exercise prescriptions should not be prescribing or supervising therapeutic exercise (e.g., exercise recommendations for a back client with significant nerve root irritation). A basic understanding of the principles and techniques of each discipline, as well as respect for the contribution of each team member, is critical. Managers and others involved in the development and management of teams required to operate in complex environments may find the "team effectiveness model" of Tannenbaum, Beard, and Salas (1992) useful in providing a framework for understanding factors affecting teams and strategies for facilitating team development. This model has evolved from human factors research on effective teams operating under conditions that at times can characterize the occupational rehabilitation work environment.

With this model as a guide, some processes that characterize effective teams include (1) continual monitoring of performance against well-defined objectives, (2) self-correction of errors, (3) adaptation to unpredictable events, (4) use of "closed-loop communications," (5) ability to predict team members' behavior, and (6) functioning under a shared model of the task and team. Working as a multidisciplinary team is an important component of a successful program and must be an ongoing process, with all team members continually striving to develop and improve these skills.

REQUISITE NEW KNOWLEDGE

Given the emphasis on safe RTW, clinical practice in occupational rehabilitation of work disability associated with OMDs requires a specialized knowledge base different from classic clinical psychology training, as well as a willingness to enter new practice areas (e.g., the worksite). Clearly, the traditional skills in assessment and treatment of pain, psychiatric/psychological disorders, and problems generally seen by clinical psychologists involved in clinical health psychology/behavioral medicine constitute an ideal foundation to build on when one is expanding one's clinical services to OMDs and work disability. In addition to this knowledge and skill base, additional information in the areas of occupational safety and health, work physiology, ergonomics, exercise physiology and conditioning, industrial/organizational psychology, and workers' compensation law can be very useful in the evaluation and management of work disability associated with OMDs. In addition, a basic understanding of orthopedics, physical therapy, physical medicine, and rehabilitation/occupational medicine as they pertain to examination and treatment of the range of occupational spinal disorders and UECTDs is helpful. Such knowledge is particularly useful when communicating and collaborating with the clinical services typically involved in the treatment process. An understanding of the role of the occupational health nurse, rehabilitation nurse, and vocational counselor is also critical, given the privotal role of these care providers in the RTW process.

Perhaps one of the most useful areas in which there is a substantial knowledge base in terms of assessment and intervention techniques is the area of ergonomics (Marras, Karwowski, Smith, & Pacholski, 1994). The application of principles and techniques in ergonomics to occupational rehabilitation represents an area with much potential (Feuerstein & Hickey, 1993). From the perspective of a clinical psychologist attempting to assist in the RTW process, techniques from ergonomics can provide a useful set of tools to facilitate re-entry into a work environment designed to be less stressful physically and psychologically (Feuerstein & Hickey, 1993). Although ergonomic intervention is typically accomplished by an occupational health and/or safety staff member at a patient's company, a physical therapist, an occupational therapist, or an exercise physiologist, an awareness by the psychologist of the concepts and approaches taken to reduce ergonomic stressors can be quite helpful in work with these patients.

At our Center for Occupational Rehabilitation, the psychologists on our rehabilitation teams frequently collaborate in the ergonomic assessments and interventions for given cases. The contribution of the psychologists has been fundamental in case conceptualization, ensuring that these assessments lead to suggested interventions and that the outcomes of the interventions are measured to determine the effects on symptoms, fatigue, and productivity. These functions can facilitate completion of an ergonomic consultation, assist in addressing problems that may arise throughout the process, and ensure that the ergonomic factors considered go beyond physical stressors to workplace organizational job stress and workstyle factors as well (Feuerstein & Hickey, 1993). Research and clinical experience suggest that these latter factors play an important role in conjunction with the classic ergonomic risk factors of excessive force, repetition, awkward posture, vibration, and extreme temperatures. Indeed, this complex interaction among medical, physical, psychosocial, and behavioral factors is what may contribute to prolonged disability in complex cases, thus justifying the involvement of the occupationally oriented clinical (health) psychologist.

Knowledge in ergonomics can be obtained through excellent professional continuing education courses provided by the University of Michigan Center for Ergonomics or the Harvard University School of Public Health. These courses are taught by leaders in the field of occupational ergonomics who are also excellent teachers. Although there are many courses available, we highly recommend these two. There are also excellent textbooks in the area (Ayoub & Mital, 1989; Burke, 1992; Chaffin & Andersson, 1991; Fraser & Pityn, 1994; Marras et al., 1994; Salvendy, 1987).

A second area that is quite helpful for working with occupational problems is the area of work and exercise physiology. There are several textbooks in this area that can provide useful information (Eastman Kodak Company, 1986; McArdle, Katch, & Katch, 1986; Astrand & Rodahl, 1986). The American College of Sports Medicine offers workshops at its annual meetings, as do the various industrial engineering and ergonomics groups. Of particular importance is an understanding of the physiological demands of various types of work, as well as a knowledge of concepts of capacity and recovery. An understanding of factors that affect physical conditioning and of techniques to maximize outcome of exercise interventions is also important (Blair, Painter, Pate, Smith, & Taylor, 1988).

Another area that many psychologists are not aware of is the area of workers' compensation laws and the relationship of these laws to health care practice. Each state has its own set of workers' compensation laws; there are also various federal workers' compensation laws. An excellent review of workers' compensation laws for each state can be found in DeCarlo and Minkowitz (1989). Also, each state publishes an annual update of workers' compensation laws (e.g., *Gould Workers' Compensation Law Handbook of New York*, 1993). It is helpful to meet with workers' compensation counselors and attorneys as well, in order to obtain firsthand information regarding new trends and policies that emerge. With the crisis in workers' compensation in the United States, rapid changes are occurring at both the state and national levels. These changes can affect the definitions of work-relatedness of an injury, reimbursement of certain procedures by certain providers, limits on number of sessions, prior authorization for treatment procedures, documentation requirements, and a range of practical operational issues. Other related laws, such as the Americans with Disabilities Act and proposed guidelines (e.g., U.S. Department of Labor, 1991, 1992), can also affect practice approaches; knowledge of these policies is very useful in working with injured employees and their employers.

An understanding of the practice approaches of other health care providers, including underlying principles of practice, goals, treatment approaches, and expected outcomes, is most helpful. This information can be obtained from textbooks in each of the clinical fields involved in occupational rehabilitation and from reviews in various professional journals (e.g., *Journal of Hand Therapy*, *Spine*, *Archives of Physical Medicine and Rehabilitation*, *Physical Therapy*, *Occupational Therapy*, *Journal of Hand Surgery*, *Journal of Occupational Rehabilitation*).

FUTURE TRENDS

Although it is difficult to predict the future of rehabilitation of OMDs and related work disability, a number of emerging trends suggest that if multidisciplinary approaches to work disability can evolve to such an extent that cost-effective, comprehensive intervention can be provided for each level of work diability (acute, subacute, chronic), the future will be positive. The continued recognition of the multiply determined nature of OMDs and work disability, recently translated into legislative reform (Minnesota Department of Labor and Industry, 1993), suggests that a scope of practice going beyond the classic medical model for these disorders is likely to emerge. This will particularly be the case if epidemiological and clinical research continues to provide empirical support for the role of psychological factors in the etiology of OMDs, and if research on work disability and clinical outcome also indicates that the "psychological intervention components" of the multicomponent treatment are effective.

The exact nature of occupational rehabilitation interventions in the future is less clear. Comprehensive yet inexpensive variations of the multidisciplinary approach reviewed in this chapter are likely to continue to evolve. There has also been a major shift away from clinic-based treatment toward workplace-based rehabilitation. Although there are few outcome studies available to determine the efficacy of such an approach, early anecdotal reports suggest that workplace-based treatment is significantly less costly and assists in retaining a worker's ability to remain at work during the recovery process. At present, workplace-based rehabilitation approaches primarily involve physical therapy; however, it is not inconceivable that brief clinical health psychology/behavioral medicine interventions for selected workers to enhance pain and stress coping skills will be offered in conjunction with physical therapy. It may also be possible to identify injured workers at risk for prolonged work disability who may benefit from more intensive behavioral medicine interventions. However, it will be essential first to demonstrate the utility of these psychological approaches, and subsequently to advocate for them and to educate payers and employers. Finally, there is also a trend toward earlier intervention to prevent the negative sequelae that can occur with an OMD. Such early intervention is also typically provided by a physical therapist or occupational physician. In the future, brief psychological interventions (e.g., interventions limited in the length and number of sessions) may prove useful in this clinical situation as well. Given the current environment of cost containment, interventions will need to be cost-competitive and cost-effective.

From a policy perspective, it is clear that the emphasis on multidisciplinary approaches to prevention of OMDs and work disability continues to increase (Feuerstein, 1993). Large-scale reform efforts that clearly emphasize the need to reduce risk factors associated with OMDs have been launched by many countries (e.g., Ministry of Social Affairs and Employment, The Netherlands, 1994). These reform efforts also emphasize the importance of RTW as the primary goal of rehabilitation efforts. It is expected that the U.S. Department of Labor's Occupational Safety and Health Administration will publish an ergonomics standard to help reduce the prevalence of OMDs and disability in the workplace (see U.S. Department of Labor, 1992). This standard will emphasize the need to address the multiple factors that are currently assumed to play a role in the etiology of OMDs and work disability, and to provide guidelines for developing safer work environments from the perspective of musculoskeletal safety and health.

Lastly, various states have developed standards of care for certain OMDs (e.g., Minnesota Department of Labor and Industry, 1993; Wegner, 1993). The standards, which are detailed in state law, identify appropriate outcomes to target (primarily function-based outcomes), as well as time intervals that should trigger various levels of care, depending upon functional status. These guidelines address a variety of "treatment parameters" related to the management of workers' compensation cases: (1) definitions of assessment and treatment; (2) specification of outcome goals; (3) delineation of general and specific treatment approaches, including psychological services; (4) more detailed guidelines for diagnosis of low back disorders and UECTDs; (5) guidelines for surgical treatment; and (6) specification of responsibilities of providers. The standards also state mandatory requirements for providers to participate in outcome studies on efficacy. Although the utility of such standards remains to be empirically determined, they are being developed by a number of states. In many instances, such guidelines cap psychological evaluation and treatment services (e.g., they specify intensity and frequency). Despite this, such standards may actually facilitate access to appropriate care when required, reducing the need for restrictive case management practices, which at times limit access to psychological treatment for individuals who could potentially benefit from such intervention. Although research should assist in answering questions regarding the clinical effectiveness of access to psychological services and the optimal intensity, frequency, and type of such services, reform appears to be moving the complex management of OMDs and work disability from a fragmented, market-driven enterprise to a more integrated and coordinated approach.

It should be emphasized that although the role of the psychologist in prevention, evaluation, and rehabilitation of OMDs and work disability appears to be expanding, future involvement will be determined by (1) the evoulation of sound empirical support for the role of psychological factors in the etiology, exacerbation, and maintenance of OMDs and work disability; (2) findings from outcome research supporting the specific role of various psychological interventions; (3) the ability of psychologists to develop effective collaborative advocacy efforts at a national level, with diverse provider, funding, and legislative groups involved in the various aspects of disability prevention and management; (4) the ability to develop and provide brief, cost-effective interventions in a manner acceptable to a diverse group of end users (injured workers, supervisors, insurance carriers, physicians, etc.); (5) the ability to ensure that psychological services are included in workers' compensation legislation on a state-by-state basis; and (6) the creation and maintenance of effective and strategic collaborative liaisons with the network of local medical and rehabilitation providers typically involved in the care of specific patients with OMDs.

CONCLUSIONS

Over the past decade, a number of innovative treatment approaches have evolved directed at facilitating RTW in patients with OMDs and work disability. This shift from symptom relief to symptom management to functional restoration and RTW continues to gain momentum, and the emphasis on RTW has been recently adopted by various health care professional groups, legislative bodies, and third-party carriers. Simultaneously, there is an increasing recognition of the role psychological factors can play in recovery of function following an OMD and in facilitating RTW, particularly in complicated cases with a history of recurrent or chronic work disability. This scientific, legislative, and clinical recognition bodes well for the potential role of psychologists in occupational rehabilitation.

However, the approach psychologists need to take will differ from their traditional roles in pain clinics. Although pain and stress management will continue to be important aspects for the overall management of these cases, much more is required. The requisite skills and knowledge base for effective work in this area have been briefly summarized here. Many of the basic skills are no doubt present in the current repertoire of the clinical psychologist; however, there is a need for a greater understanding of the workplace, the worker, and the overall workers' compensation system that goes beyond the traditional patient–psychologist relationship. With such understanding, and with an appreciation for the roles of others in and outside the workplace involved in the RTW process of those with work disability, clinical psychologists can expand their scope of activities and facilitate more effective work re-entry in these complex cases. When this goal is achieved, the patients and all others involved benefit.

ACKNOWLEDGMENTS

The writing of this chapter was supported in part by a Research and Demonstration Grant from the National Institute on Disability and Rehabilitation Research awarded to Michael Feuerstein (Grant No. H133A00040), and in part by National Institute of Occupational Safety and Health Grant No. U60/CCU106156 to the New England Center for Occupational Musculoskeletal Disorders. We wish to thank Jennifer Boehles for assistance with manuscript preparation.

REFERENCES

Altmaier, E. M., Lehmann, T. R., Russell, D. W., Weinstein, J. N., & Kao, C. F. (1992). The effectiveness of psychological interventions for the rehabilitation of low back pain: A randomized controlled trial evaluation. *Pain, 49*, 329–335.

Andersson, G. B. J., Pope, M. H., Frymoyer, J. W., & Snook, S. (1991). Epidemiology and cost. In M. H. Pope, G. B. J. Andersson, J. W. Frymoyer, & D. B. Chaffin (Eds.), *Occupational low back pain: Assessment, treatment and prevention* (pp. 95–113). St. Louis, MO: Mosby–Year Book.

Astrand, P. O., & Rodahl, K. (1986). *Textbook of work physiology: Psychological bases of exercise.* New York: McGraw-Hill.

Ayoub, M. M., & Mital, A. (1989). *Manual materials handling.* Bristol, PA: Taylor & Francis.

Bandura, A. (1977). Self-efficacy: Toward a unifying theory of behavioral change. *Psychological Bulletin, 80*, 286–303.

Barnes, D., Smith, D., Gatchel, R. J., & Mayer, T. G. (1989). Psychosocioeconomic predictors of treatment success/failure in chronic low-back pain patients. *Spine, 14*, 427–430.

Blair, S. N., Painter, P., Pate, R. R., Smith, L. K., & Taylor, C. B. (1988). *Resource manual for guidelines for exercise testing and prescription: American College of Sports Medicine.* Philadelphia: Lea & Febiger.

Bigos, S. J., Battie, M. C., Spengler, D. M., Fisher, L. D., Fordyce, W. E., Hansson, T. H., Nachemson, A. L., & Wortley, M. D. (1991). A prospective study of work perceptions and psychosocial factors affecting the report of back injury. *Spine, 16*, 1–6.

Bureau of Labor Statistics. (1991). *Occupational injuries and illnesses in the United States by industry, 1989* (U.S. Department of Labor, Bulletin No. 2379). Washington, DC: U.S. Government Printing Office.

Bureau of Labor Statistics. (1994, April 26). *Work injuries and illnesses by selected characteristics, 1992* (U.S. Department of Labor, Technical Release No. USDL-94-213). Washington, DC: U.S. Government Printing Office.

Burke, M. (1992). *Applied ergonomics handbook.* Ann Arbor, MI: Lewis.

Cairns, D., Mooney, V., & Crane, P. (1984). Spinal pain rehabilitation: Inpatient and outpatient treatment results and development of predictors for outcome. *Spine, 9*, 91–95.

Carosella, A. M., Lackner, J. M., & Feuerstein, M. (1994). Factors associated with early discharge from a multidisciplinary work rehabilitation program for chronic low back pain. *Pain, 57,* 69–76.

Cassisi, J., Sypert, G., Salamon, A., & Kapel, L. (1989). Independent evaluation of a multidisciplinary rehabilitation program for chronic low back pain. *Neurosurgery, 25,* 877–883.

Chaffin, D. B., & Andersson, G. B. (1991). *Occupational biomechanics* (2nd ed.). New York: Wiley.

Chaffin, D. B., & Fine, L. J. (1992, November). *A national strategy for occupational musculoskeletal injuries: Implementation issues and research needs* (DHHS Publication No. NIOSH 93-101). Washington, DC: U.S. Government Printing Office.

DeCarlo, D. T., & Minkowitz, M. (1989). *Workers compensation insurance and law practice: The next generation.* Fort Washington, PA: LRP.

Deyo, R. A., & Tsui-Wu, Y.-J. (1987). Descriptive epidemiology of low back pain and its related medical care in the United States. *Spine, 12,* 264–268.

Eastman Kodak Company, Ergonomics Group. (1986). *Ergonomic design for people at work* (2 vols.). New York: Van Nostrand Reinhold.

Engle, G. L. (1977). The need for a new medical model: A challenge for biomedicine. *Science, 196,* 129–136.

Estlander, A. M., Mellin, G., Vanharanta, H., & Hupli, M. (1991). Effects and follow-up of a multimodal treatment program including intensive physical training for low back pain patients. *Scandinavian Journal of Rehabilitation Medicine, 23,* 97–102.

Feuerstein, M. (1991). A multidisciplinary approach to the prevention, evaluation, and management of work disability. *Journal of Occupational Rehabilitation, 1,* 5–12.

Feuerstein, M. (1993). Workers' compensation reform in New York State: A proposal to address medical, ergonomic, and psychological factors associated with work disability. *Journal of Occupational Rehabilitation, 3,* 125–134.

Feuerstein, M. (in press). Workstyle: Definition, empirical support and implications for prevention, evaluation and rehabilitation of occupational upper extremity disorders. In S. Moon & S. Sauter (Eds.), *Beyond biomechanics: Psychosocial influences on cumulative trauma disorders in office workers.* London: Taylor & Francis.

Feuerstein, M., Callen-Harris, S., Hickey, P., Dyer, D., Armbruster, W., & Carosella, A. M. (1993). Multidisciplinary rehabilitation of chronic work-related upper extremity disorders: Long term effects. *Journal of Occupational Medicine, 35,* 396–403.

Feuerstein, M., Carosella, A. M., & Lackner, J. (1994, April). *Factors associated with work disability in an occupational group at risk for upper extremity disorders.* Paper presented at the 15th annual meeting of the Society for Behavioral Medicine, Boston.

Feuerstein, M., & Hickey, P. F. (1992). Ergonomic approaches in the clinical assessment of occupational musculoskeletal disorders. In D. C. Turk & R. Melzack (Eds.), *Handbook of pain assessment* (pp. 71–99). New York: Guilford Press.

Feuerstein, M., & Hickey, P. F. (1993). Clinical ergonomic job analysis and consultation: Facilitating work reentry in a case with upper extremity cumulative trauma-related disability. *Journal of Occupational Rehabilitation, 3,* 159–166.

Feuerstein, M., Labbe, E. E., & Kuczmierczyk, A. R. (1986). *Health psychology: A Psychobiological perspective.* New York: Plenum Press.

Feuerstein, M., Menz, L., Zastowny, T. R., & Barron, B. A. (1994). Chronic back pain and work disability: Vocational outcomes following multidisciplinary rehabilitation. *Journal of Occupational Rehabilitation, 4,* 229–251.

Feuerstein, M., Papciak, A., & Hoon, P. (1987). Biobehavioral mechanisms of chronic low back pain. *Clinical Psychology Review, 7,* 243–263.

Feuerstein, M., Sult, S., & Houle, M. (1985). Environmental stressors and chronic low back pain: Life events, family and work environment. *Pain, 22,* 295–307.

Feuerstein, M., & Thebarge, R. W. (1991). Perceptions of disability and occupational stress as discriminators of work disability in patients with chronic pain. *Journal of Occupational Rehabilitation, 1,* 185–195.

Feuerstein, M., & Zastowny, T. R. (in press). *Occupational musculoskeletal disorders and work disability: A multidisciplinary approach.* New York: Plenum Press.

Fishbain, D. A., Rosomoff, H. L., Goldberg, M., Cutler, R., Abdel-Moty, E., Khalil, T. M., & Rosomoff, R. S. (1993). The prediction of return to the workplace after multidisciplinary pain center treatment. *Clinical Journal of Pain, 9,* 3–15.

Fordyce, W. E. (1976). *Behavioral methods for chronic pain and illness.* St. Louis, MO: C. V. Mosby.

Fraser, T. M., & Pityn, P. J. (1994). *Work, productivity, and human performance.* Springfield, IL: Charles C Thomas.

Fredrickson, B. E., Trief, P. M., VanBeveren, P., Yuan, H. A., & Baum, G. (1988). Rehabilitation of the patient with chronic back pain: A search for outcome predictors. *Spine, 13,* 351–353.

Gould Workers' Compensation Law Handbook of New York. (1993). Binghamton, NY: Gould.

Hazard, R. G., Fenwick, J. W., Kalisch, S. M., Redmond, J., Reeves, V., Reid, S., & Frymoyer, J. W. (1989). Functional restoration with behavioral support: A one year prospective study of patients with chronic low-back pain. *Spine, 14,* 157–161.

Hazard, R. G., Haugh, L., Green, P., & Jones, P. (1994). Chronic low back pain: The relationship between patient satisfaction and pain, impairment and disability outcomes. *Spine, 19,* 881–887.

Jensen, M. P., Turner, J. A., & Romano, J. M. (1991). Self-efficacy and outcome expectancies: Relationship to chronic pain coping strategies and adjustment. *Pain, 44,* 263–269.

Keefe, F. J., & Williams, D. A. (1992). Assessment of pain behaviors. In D. C. Turk & R. Melzack (Eds.), *Handbook of pain assessment* (pp. 275–294). New York: Guilford Press.

Kinney, R. K., Gatchel, R. J., Polatin, P. B., & Mayer, T. G. (1991). The functional restoration approach for chronic spinal disability. *Journal of Occupational Rehabilitation, 1,* 235–244.

Klein, P. B., Jensen, R. C., & Sanderson, L. M. (1984). Assessment of workers' compensation claims for back strains/sprains. *Journal of Occupational Medicine, 26,* 443–448.

Lackner, J., Carosella, A. M., & Feuerstein, M. (1994, April). *Functional self efficacy, fear of pain, and fear of injury as cognitive mediators of work related function among chronic low back patients.* Paper presented at the 15th annual meeting of the Society for Behavioral Medicine, Boston.

Lethem, J., Slade, P. D., Troup, J. D. G., & Bentley, G. (1983). Outline of a fear-avoidance model of exaggerated pain perception: I. *Behaviour Research and Therapy, 21,* 401–408.

Marras, W. S., Karwowski, W., Smith, J. L., & Pacholski, L. (Eds.). (1994). *The ergonomics of manual work.* Washington, DC: Taylor & Francis.

Mayer, T. G., & Gatchel, R. J. (1988). *Functional restoration for spinal disorders: The sports medicine approach.* Philadelphia: Lea & Febiger.

Mayer, T. G., Gatchel, R. J., Kishino, N. D., Keeley, J., Capra, P., Mayer, H., Barnett, J., & Mooney, V. (1985). Objective assessment of spine function following industrial injury: A prospective study with comparison group and one-year follow-up. *Spine, 10,* 482–493.

Mayer, T. G., Gatchel, R. J., Mayer, H., Kishino, N. D., Keeley, J., & Mooney, V. (1987). A prospective two-year study of functional restoration in industrial low back injury. *Journal of the American Medical Association, 258,* 1763–1767.

McArdle, W. D., Katch, F. I., & Katch, V. L. (1986). *Exercise physiology: Energy, nutrition, and human performance* (2nd ed.). Philadelphia: Lea & Febiger.

McArthur, D., Cohen, M., Gottlieb, H., Naliboff, B. D., & Schandler, S. L. (1987). Treating chronic low back pain: I. Admission to initial follow-up. II. Long term follow-up. *Pain, 29,* 1–38.

McCracken, L. M., Zayfert, C., & Gross, R. T. (1992). The Pain Anxiety Symptoms Scale: Development and validation of a scale to measure fear of pain. *Pain, 50,* 67–73.

Mellin, F., Harkapaa, K., Vanharanta, H., Hupli, M., Heinonen, R., & Järvikoski, A. (1993). Outcome of a multi-modal treatment including intensive physical training of patients with chronic low back pain. *Spine, 18,* 825–829.

Ministry of Social Affairs and Employment, The Netherlands. (1994). *Measures to reduce sick leave and improve labour conditions.* The Hague: Author.

Minnesota Department of Labor and Industry. (1993). *State of Minnesota emergency rules relating to workers' compensation: Treatment parameters* (Code No. 3-72s1). St. Paul: Author.

Mitchell, R. I., & Carmen, G. M. (1994). The functional restoration approach to the treatment of chronic pain in patients with soft tissue and back injuries. *Spine, 19,* 633–642.

Pilowsky, I. (1978). A general classification of abnormal illness behaviors. *British Journal of Medical Psychiatry, 51,* 131–137.

Polatin, P. B., & Mayer, T. G. (1992). Quantification of function in chronic low back pain. In D. C. Turk & R. Melzack (Eds.), *Handbook of pain assessment* (pp. 37–48). New York: Guilford Press.

Putz-Anderson, V. (Ed.). (1988). *Cumulative trauma disorder: A manual for musculoskeletal diseases of the upper extremity.* Philadelphia: Taylor & Francis.

Robertshaw, C. (1991). *Rehabilitating Alberta's injured workers: A framework for the 90's.* Edmonton: Workers Compensation Board.

Sachs, B., David, J., Olimpo, D., & Scalia, A. D. (1990). Spinal rehabilitation by work tolerance based on objective physical capacity assessment of dysfunction: A prospective study with control subjects and twelve-month review. *Spine, 15,* 1325–1332.

Salvendy, G. (Ed.). (1987). *Handbook of human factors.* New York: Wiley-Interscience.

Snook, S. H. (1982). Low back pain in industry. In A. A. White & S. L. Gordon (Eds.), *Symposium on idiopathic low back pain* (pp. 23–28). St. Louis, MO: Mosby–Year Book.

Spitzer, W. O., LeBlanc, F. E., & Dupuis, M. (1987). A scientific approach to the assessment and management of activity-related spinal disorders: A monograph for clinicians. Report of the Quebec Task Force on Spinal Disorders. *Spine, 12*(Suppl. 75), S3–S59.

Tannenbaum, S. I., Beard, R. L., & Salas, E. (1992). Team building and its influence on team effectiveness: An examination of conceptual and empirical developments. In K. Kelley (Ed.), *Issues, theory and research in industrial/organizational psychology* (pp. 117–153). Amsterdam: Elsevier.

Tollison, C. (1991). Comprehensive treatment approach for lower back workers' compensation injuries. *Journal of Occupational Rehabilitation, 1,* 281–287.

U.S. Department of Labor. (1991, July). Americans with Disabilities Act: Equal Employment Opportunity Commission. Occupational Safety and Health Administration. *Federal Register, 56,* 35725–35756.

U.S. Department of Labor. (1992, August). Ergonomic Safety and health Managment. Occupational Safety and Health Administration. *Federal Register, 57,* 34192–34200.

Waddell, G., & Main, C. J. (1984). Assessment of severity in low back pain disorders. *Spine, 9,* 204–208.

Waddell, G., McColloch, J. A., Kummel, E. G., & Venner, R. M. (1980). Nonorganic physical signs in low back pain. *Spine, 5,* 117–125.

Waddell, G., Somerville, D., Henderson, I., & Newton, M. (1992). Objective clinical evaluation of physical impairment in chronic low back pain. *Spine, 17,* 617–628.

Webster, B. S., & Snook, S. H. (1990a). The cost of compensable low back pain. *Journal of Occupational Medicine, 32,* 13–15.

Webster, B. S., & Snook, S. H. (1990b). The cost of compensable upper extremity cumulative trauma disorders. *Journal of Occupational Medicine, 36,* 713–717.

Wegner, J. A. (1993). Treatment standards for work-related injuries. *Journal of Occupational Rehabilitation, 3,* 135–144.

CHAPTER 18

Program Evaluation Methods for Documenting Pain Management Effectiveness

Thomas E. Rudy
John A. Kubinski

The treatment of pain, particularly when it becomes prolonged, is a major health care problem in the United States and many other countries. Patients suffering from chronic pain conditions consume billions of health care dollars annually, and the amount of human suffering and lost productivity is immeasurable. Although numerous studies that report on the efficacy of a wide range of treatment programs for chronic pain patients have appeared in the literature over the past decade, these studies are not without substantial methodological problems and limitations (Hoffman, Turner, Cherkin, Deyo, & Herron, 1994; Turk & Rudy, 1990, 1991). Thus, additional controlled, systematic evaluations of the efficacy of pain treatment programs are crucial if the field is to advance or perhaps even survive (Rosomoff, 1993).

Determining treatment outcome remains a formidable challenge to both clinicians and researchers, in part because outcome, like the pain experience itself, is a complex, multidimensional phenomenon. Despite many hotly debated and controversial aspects of health care reform, including managed competition, cost containment, and selective reimbursement, one issue appears certain: The distinction between the clinician and the researcher is becoming increasingly blurred and artificial. A new era of accountability is emerging in pain management practice that will require the close collaboration of clinicians and investigators. Reimbursement will increasingly be contingent on demonstrated outcomes, including not only "success rates" but cost effectiveness. To address program outcomes in a way that is satisfactory to third-party payers, managed care consortiums, governmental agencies, and patients themselves, it is essential to merge clinical practice standards with scientific principles.

The days of poorly controlled clinical studies and haphazard or incomplete evaluations of program outcomes are past. The outlook for the field of chronic pain treatment appears similar to current trends in other areas of clinical practice: Powerful external forces will be scrutinizing tradition or professional consensus unsubstantiated by scientific evidence, wide variations and discrepancies in current treatment practices for patients, the lack of standards for defining successful treatment outcomes, the maintenance of treatment effects, and probably the field in general. For example, the formation of the Agency for Health Care Policy and Research (AHCPR) in 1989 is already having a substantial impact. Government standards and clinical practice guidelines have been implemented or soon will be in pain practice areas as diverse as the management of acute pain, cancer pain, acute low back pain, and headache. It is simply a matter of time before AHCPR and/or other U.S. government agencies turn their attention to chronic pain treatment.

In this chapter, we focus on a number of practical strategies and issues related to conducting program evaluation in chronic pain treatment programs. Although program evaluation can serve many purposes, some of which are reviewed briefly in this chapter, much of our focus is on evaluating treatment effectiveness—that is, patient-oriented outcomes. Several proposed guidelines for program evaluation of chronic pain treatment programs are reviewed, as well as the domains of measurement considered important in these evaluations. We have resisted conducting an extensive review of pain measurement instruments, however, since comprehensive reviews of pain assessment measures are readily available (e.g., Turk & Melzack, 1992). Rather, it is our experience that pain investigators and clinicians tend to debate which specific measures are best, and to neglect important conceptual, methodological, and logistical issues related to program evaluation. Because neglecting these factors can seriously affect the success of a program evaluation, in terms of both its implementation and the utility of the information collected, we have chosen to focus on what we consider four necessary phases in developing a sound and productive evaluation program. Finally, we present a case example of a small program evaluation strategy that we developed to meet a specific need.

DEFINING PROGRAM EVALUATION

A simple yet perhaps adequate definition of program evaluation is as follows: A "program" is anything tried because it is thought to lead to positive effects, and "evaluation" is a systematic collection of information to show how the program operates, to determine the effects it may be having, or to answer other questions of interest that can be operationalized and measured (e.g., referral satisfaction). More formally, "program evaluation," as defined by the Commission on Accreditation of Rehabilitation Facilities (CARF), is the systematic process of determining how effectively and efficiently improvements in a client's functional status are achieved (CARF, 1991). "Effectiveness" is defined as the extent to which a program's performance is congruent with its expectations. "Efficiency" is concerned with the association between a program's "outputs" (e.g., quality of treatment outcomes) and the program's "inputs" (e.g., cost of providing the treatment services). Thus, efficiency involves considering a program's effectiveness with respect to the resources consumed.

Traditionally, program evaluation has been considered from the standpoint of providing information to make decisions regarding a program's performance. These decisions involve judgments about the quality and standards of a program, particularly from a client-centered, outcomes-based perspective. Thus, the primary objectives of a program evaluation are to identify aspects of care, to establish thresholds of care, to collect and organize data, to evaluate and compare data against thresholds, and to use these results to assess the effectiveness of actions taken in relation to client care.

As described below, the traditional view of program evaluation, though important, is rather limited and restrictive. Program evaluation should be conceptualized more broadly, since program evaluations can serve many different purposes and audiences. In the sections that follow, some of these purposes are described. More important, we propose that individuals who want to establish an effective evaluation system give careful consideration to what we believe are four essential phases of developing such a system: setting evaluation boundaries, selecting appropriate evaluation methods, collecting the data, and reporting findings (Herman, Morris, & Fitz-Gibbon, 1987).

PHASE 1: SETTING EVALUATION BOUNDARIES

A common pitfall in many program evaluation systems is that the need for a data base is seen as paramount, and therefore the data collection phase drives or defines the evaluation system. In other words, the collection of data is seen as the essential component of program evaluation, rather than as a result of an explicit prospective plan. Considerable work and planning should occur before the actual implementation of the data collection phase.

Defining the Purposes of the Evaluation

Before a program evaluation system is designed and implemented, it is important to recognize that an evaluation system can serve many purposes. Without an explicit statement of these purposes, it is difficult or impossible to define the measurement instruments, data collection procedures, and implementation strategies needed to achieve the intended evaluation objectives.

The designers of the evaluation system need to ask two basic questions: (1) Who or what is the focus of the evaluation, and (2) who is the intended audience of the information that will be obtained? For example, it is important to decide whether the evaluation will be primarily patient-oriented, staff-oriented, program-oriented, or some combination of these. In addition, is the purpose to (1) increase the benefits to patients (i.e., clinical effectiveness and outcome); (2) increase program productivity and cost-effectiveness; (3) conduct a needs assessment to identify goals, problems, or conditions that should be addressed in future program planning; (4) identify current levels of patient, referral, and/ or staff satisfaction; or (5) help administrators, third-party payers, community groups, or government agencies determine the extent to which the program is successful, and perhaps the program's ultimate fate? Finally, it is essential to identify beforehand who will have access to the information obtained and what the intended audiences will accept as credible information. Failure to address these types of preliminary questions often results in an evaluation system that is burdensome to the staff members responsible for its implementation and produces information that is of little value to anyone.

Identifying Organizational Resources and Barriers

Another essential first step is to conduct a preliminary assessment of the level of organizational interest in and support of an evaluation system. Simply getting administrative agreement that an evaluation system is a good idea is not enough. A careful, detailed determination of the level of support is required, because even a simple evaluation system can have substantial organizational costs and consequences. Some of the many issues to resolve at this stage are as follows: (1) deciding which staff members will assume primary responsibility for designing, implementing, monitoring, and reporting the results of the evaluation system; (2) reaching a general consensus regarding the goals or purposes of the evaluation system and their related priorities (e.g., is measuring client outcomes more important than determining the level of staff satisfaction?); (3) establishing a working timetable for each phase of the program evaluation; (4) making time available to professional staff members to participate in the evaluation (e.g., for collecting and completing additional forms as part of their clinical evaluations and/or treatment sessions, for conducting follow-up phone interviews); (5) making secretarial support available (e.g., for sending mailings, for entering data); and (6) committing the necessary financial resources to purchase outside services (e.g., a programmer to develop and maintain a computerized data base, microcomputer work stations, a statistician to assist with data analyses).

The answers to these and the many other issues that will emerge in this phase of planning are likely to determine the feasibility and success of the evaluation system. For example, if there is administrative interest in an evaluation system, perhaps to assist with program management and the marketing of services, but staff members' time is not allocated because "we are already understaffed and they are overloaded," the evaluation system is doomed to failure. In other words, without the organizational commitment to make staff adjustments (e.g., reducing a nurse's direct clinic time by 20% so that he or she can conduct telephone interviews, or reducing a secretary's typing load by 4 hours per week so that he or she can enter data), we believe that it will be futile to continue with subsequent phases of program evaluation.

Anticipating Negative Side Effects

Apart from patients' telling us things about our programs that we would rather not hear, or discovering that our programs are not as effective as we would like to believe, program evaluations can have many unanticipated negative consequences. For example, overly elaborate or comprehensive evaluation strategies can be too disruptive to the normal operations of a clinic. Also, it is important to recognize that "information is power." If administrators who control program resources are to have access to the data collected, and those data are not very complimentary of the program's effectiveness and/or efficiency, obviously the evaluators' primary intent of collecting information to improve the program may be overlooked and the data may be used instead to reduce resources or eliminate the program entirely. Thus, although the latter may be an extreme example of the negative side effects of evaluation systems, the planners of the evaluation system need to consider the possibilities of adverse organizational and programmatic consequences.

PHASE 2: SELECTING APPROPRIATE EVALUATION METHODS

In Phase 1, the staff and administration reach a common understanding regarding the primary purposes of the program evaluation, as well as the general availability of resources for the evaluation. In Phase 2, this understanding needs to be developed into a clearly specified, program-sensitive set of data collection procedures and measurement instruments. Aside from lack of adequate administrative support, this phase is perhaps the most crucial in that the decisions made in this phase can adversely affect subsequent phases; in the worst possible cases, the resulting evaluation plan is costly but produces uninterpretable data.

The detailed specification of evaluation procedures involves a complex interplay among a number of interlocking decisions: (1) determining the specific aspects of the program, processes, and outcomes that will be the focus of the evaluation; (2) evaluating the most feasible methods to measure or observe those program aspects; (3) deciding on the design and sampling plan for administering or implementing the selected measurement methods; and (4) determining the logistical plan that will permit the evaluation tasks to be completed within a specified schedule.

Table 18.1 presents what we believe are 10 essential steps that should be followed in this phase of developing a program evaluation system. Some of the more difficult or problematic steps outlined in Table 18.1 are discussed in more detail below.

Choosing Outcome Domains and Criteria

Deciding what to measure and how best to measure it presents unique challenges to evaluators of pain rehabilitation programs. Since pain by definition is a complex, multidimensional phenomenon comprised of biomedical, psychosocial, and behavioral/functional factors (Turk, Rudy, & Stieg, 1988), the evaluation of program outcomes requires a comprehensive, multidimensional perspective. A persistent problem in the pain literature, however, is that investigators simply do not agree about how outcomes or clinical improvement should be determined (Turk, Rudy, & Sorkin, 1993). To complicate matters further, what is considered a "successful" outcome is largely in the "eyes of the beholder" and varies widely among those parties interested in treatment outcomes. For example, patients may define "success" as a substantial reduction in their pain severity; clinicians may define "success" in terms of an increase in functional capacities; and third-party payers may be unimpressed with either of these outcomes and choose instead to focus on whether patients return to gainful employment. Furthermore, program administrators may deemphasize patient outcomes per se, and choose rather to adopt a cost–benefit or cost–effectiveness perspective in their evaluation of program efficacy.

Some of the earliest guidelines addressing measurement domains for program evaluation in chronic pain management were established by CARF (1987). Ten program objectives and measurement areas were identified, each of which is described briefly below. These areas were selected primarily to provide a conceptual framework to help ensure that an evaluation system is comprehensive and well balanced. An additional strength of these guidelines is that they not only are patient-oriented, but focus on program delivery aspects as well.

• *Area 1: Productivity status.* Measures designed to assess productivity following treatment are considered essential by CARF, because they reflect the practical impact of the

---

TABLE 18.1. Ten Essential Steps to Consider in Phase 2

1. Choose the outcome domains and criteria.
2. Choose data collection approaches and measures.
3. Consolidate the measures into a few instruments.
4. Plan the construction and/or acquisition of instruments.
5. Choose evaluation designs.
6. Choose a sampling strategy for conducting data collection.
7. Plan the data analyses to be performed with the results from each instrument, within the context of the evaluation design selected.
8. Design a plan for monitoring program implementation.
9. Estimate the cost of the evaluation.
10. Come to a final arrangement about staff and patient responsibilities.

program on the patients served—not only by providing evidence that patients are better able to cope with chronic pain, but also that the program results in economic benefits for them, their families, and the community. Although this area may appear unidimensional (i.e., a patient does or does not return to employment), a broader definition can include other productive roles (e.g., engaging in community volunteer work, returning to school, or successfully managing a household).

• *Area 2: Use of health care resources.* This area is concerned with patients' continued use of various types of health care services following participation in a treatment program. If a pain rehabilitation program is successful in helping individuals cope better with their chronic pain conditions, then visits to health care providers for their pain conditions should be less frequent.

• *Area 3: Physical activity.* A common feature of individuals with persistent pain is the reduction in their amount of physical activity and/or increases in the amount of time that they spend lying down, resting, and sleeping. Thus, program effectiveness should lead to an increase in desirable activities and a reduction in "downtime."

• *Area 4: Use of medications.* When appropriate, a common goal of many pain treatment programs is to reduce patients' dependence on or misuse of pain medications. These medications may be narrowly defined (e.g., only prescription, "habit-forming" drugs), or may be more generally defined as all substances used in excess to cope with pain (e.g., alcohol, aspirin).

• *Area 5: Program costs.* Although many of the CARF guidelines for program evaluation of chronic pain management programs focus on the benefits to the individuals served, these guidelines also recommend that treatment costs be evaluated, because cost is an important issue for patients, program administrators, and third-party payers.

• *Area 6: Program productivity.* This area of evaluation essentially measures program *outputs* (e.g., the number and extent of services received by individuals) in relationship to program *inputs* (e.g., the number of services available, the amount of money spent to provide these services).

• *Area 7: Patients' assessment of pain.* This area, which is familiar to all pain practitioners, is concerned with the measurement of how patients perceive their pain, particularly its intensity. Despite the difficulties of measuring a perception as private and subjective as pain, the CARF guidelines consider its measurement an essential evaluation component.

• *Area 8: Psychological adjustment.* This area is concerned with patients' overall adjustment to their chronic pain condition, and may include standardized psychological measures that evaluate levels of depression, perceived coping or self-efficacy, anxiety, and so forth.

• *Area 9: Medical findings.* Although biomedical findings constitute an essential component in the initial evaluation of patients, this area focuses on those findings that can be expected to change as a result of treatment (e.g., range of motion, gait, and posture). The CARF program evaluation guidelines, however, place little emphasis on medical findings, and suggest that the primary treatment objectives of most pain treatment programs is not to achieve reductions in pathology. Thus, no specific measures are recommended for this area of evaluation.

• *Area 10: Improved independence in activities of daily living (ADLs), Increased social activity.* As in the case of medical findings, the CARF guidelines provide little discussion of or emphasis on measuring changes in ADLs. The primary rationale provided is that not all pain treatment programs provide services (e.g., occupational therapy) that address these areas of a patient's life. However, we disagree with this position and believe that this is an important area of assessment, because increases in patients' ability to perform common ADLs, as well as increases in their social and recreational activities, are closely associated with individuals' perceptions of the quality of their lives.

Developing an Outcomes Table

Table 18.2 presents an example of a five-column outcomes table that can be used to consolidate program evaluation plans related to the specific outcomes that will be measured; the general measurement domain (e.g., biomedical, psychosocial, behavioral/functional); the methods that will be used to collect the information; who will be the source of that information; and whether instruments exist to measure the specific outcome desired or whether an instrument needs to be developed to measure a unique program component or specific area of interest. Considerable time should be devoted to the development of such a table, since it has important implications for data collection methods and their related costs.

Recently, there has been what seems like an avalanche of new measurement instruments appearing in the pain-related literature. However, these instruments vary widely in quality. The mere fact that an instrument is published does not make it a psychometrically sound measure or necessarily well suited for program evaluation purposes. Instruments that perform well in terms of the initial evaluation and diagnosis of chronic pain patients may not be appropriate for outcome assessment. Some instruments are too long and difficult to complete to include within a program evaluation plan. Similarly, some measures work well with one particular type of administration format (e.g., paper-and-pencil self-reports), but are impossible to administer by other means (e.g., telephone follow-up interviews). Table 18.3 outlines some of the many issues that need to be considered when evaluators are selecting existing instruments to measure program outcomes.

Writing New Questions for Evaluations

Although test construction and psychometric issues are rapidly improving in the area of pain assessment, unfortunately we believe that many existing measures are inadequate for the purposes of program evaluation. Thus, program evaluators are likely to write their own questions for specialized components of the program evaluation because a published

TABLE 18.2. Developing an Outcomes Table

Specific outcome	Measurement domain	Data collection method	Source of data	Existing instrument, or does one need to be developed?
1. Reduction in depression	Psychosocial	Paper and pencil	Patient	Existing—Beck Depression Inventory (Beck et al., 1961)
2. Increased mobility	Behavioral/ functional	Observational	Patient, physical therapist	Existing— Hall-walking time
3. Medication reduction	Biomedical	Interview	Patient, nurse	Existing—Medication Quantification Scale (Steedman et al., 1992)
Etc.				

TABLE 18.3. Issues to Consider in Selecting Outcome Measures

Psychometric issues
- Does the instrument have published reliability indices (e.g., internal consistency, test–retest stability, interrater reliability)?
- Does the instrument have published validity coefficients (e.g., construct validity–correlational analyses with other validated instruments; predictive validity–analyses related to the instruments' ability to predict outcome or other future events)?
- Has the instrument been demonstrated to have good sensitivity in its ability to detect treatment effects?
- Are norms available for the type of sample that will be used in the program evaluation?
- Has the necessary psychometric work been done if the instrument developers claim that multiple administration formats can be used?

Administration issues
- Does the instrument have face and content validity? That is, will the items appear directly relevant to respondents?
- From a respondent's perspective, is the content (including the instructions, questions, and response categories), easy to understand?
- Can the instrument be administered in multiple ways (e.g., self-administered, interview format)?
- Is special training and/or equipment (e.g., a computer) needed to administer the instrument?

Cost issues
- How easy is the instrument to score (e.g., is a computer needed, does it need to be sent to an outside scoring service)?
- Are shorter, less time-consuming instruments available that measure the same construct or domain of interest?
- Are professional staff members needed to administer or score the instrument, or can the support/secretarial staff be used?
- What purchase fees and copyright issues are involved in using the instrument?

instrument cannot be found to meet their needs, or because existing instruments would be too costly to use. In addition, the guidelines reviewed below may be useful for evaluators as they critique existing instruments being considered as part of the program evaluation data collection plan.

From a scientific perspective, the "goodness" of questions, questionnaires, and interviews may be evaluated in terms of their reliability, their validity, and (when applicable) their clinical utility. From this perspective, having an accepted set of guidelines that defines the characteristics necessary for pain questionnaires and interviews to produce reliable, valid, and useful information would be highly desirable. Unfortunately, such guidelines do not exist. However, the literature on survey methodology has addressed this issue in the form of qualitative, descriptive propositions regarding what constitutes a "good" question, questionnaire, or interview. These principles lead to better-designed pain-related measures (Danchik & Drury, 1988) and are outlined below.

- *Type of introductions.* The nature and content of the introductory statements of each section of a measurement instrument should be evaluated closely, because the type, content, and readability of these statements and instructions can influence behavioral reports, increase bias and random responding, and reduce response consistency.
- *Uniformity of wording.* Item wording and the way questions are asked should be examined for uniformity and standardization. Instructions and items should be evaluated to eliminate (1) jargon or technical terms; (2) excessive use of polysyllabic words; (3) biased words that may prompt specific responses; and (4) words with idiosyncratic meaning for different cultural, gender, or age groups.

• *Readability*. The reading level of all instructions and questions should be considered. Many software programs are now available that compute several quantitative indices, including readability level and percentage of polysyllabic words. We recommend that instructions and question content be kept to an eighth-grade reading level or below.

• *Frame of reference*. Questions should be phrased in such a way as to take into account the frame of reference that respondents bring to the subject under discussion. Specifically, items should be linked directly to the impact of pain on a respondent's physical, psychological, social, and behavioral functioning. Frames of reference should be explicit and precise. For example, the question "How much does your pain interfere with your life?" does not contain an explicit reference to a specific area of the respondent's life and is likely to lead to vague, unanchored responses or numerous questions on the part of respondents (e.g., "You mean work or socially or sleep or my walking ability?").

• *Reference period*. The optimal time frame for each question should be evaluated to reduce sampling errors. These errors increase with decreases in the length of the reference period. However, a tradeoff in increasing the reference period is that the accuracy of the information obtained decreases with an increase in the length of the reference period. In determining the length of the reference period, evaluators should consider both recall loss and telescoping errors (i.e., the tendency for respondents to transport events that occurred before the reference period forward or backward in time; Sudman & Bradburn, 1982). The time frame of the question should be congruent with the substantive objectives of the question and should be anchored appropriately.

• *Singleness of purpose*. Each question should be examined to decide whether it has a single and unambiguous referent, and whether, with respect to the respondent, a single proposition or point of view is clearly present. In addition, the specific topic or focus of each question should be such that the intent of the item is clear, unambiguous, and unidimensional.

• *Completeness*. Each question should be scrutinized to establish whether the wording of a question "prepares" the respondent to answer it. That is, the question should be self-contained to reduce time-consuming "questions about the questions."

• *Length*. Ideally, questions should be brief, but if they are too short, respondent recall and understanding are compromised. Longer questions may increase the quality of the data if they do not add to the complexity of the question. Each item should be examined for complexity and ambiguity versus clarity and length.

• *Subjective context*. Attention must be given to the subjective context of the respondent, to control for confounding variables such as anxiety or potential embarrassment. Offensiveness or appearance of "bias" should also be considered; that is, questions that may lead to biased responding as a result of gender, ethnic, or cultural group membership should be reworded to have a neutral context.

• *Response set*. The wording of items should be viewed to make sure that there is variability in form, to avoid response set bias.

Designing Answer Categories

In devising answer categories for the questions they write, evaluators should consider these criteria:

• *Clarity*. Response categories should be meaningful and unambiguous.
• *Dimensionality*. The response alternatives offered should be unidimensional. Compound alternatives should be rewritten as separate response categories.

- *Completeness.* All meaningful answer categories that can possibly be anticipated from respondents must be represented for accurate data collection.
- *Exclusivity.* Response alternatives offered must be mutually exclusive—that is, non-overlapping.
- *Number of responses.* The number of response categories available to the respondent can significantly affect the reliability of a question. For example, Cicchetti, Showalter, and Tyrer (1985) found that reliability increased steadily from 2 to 7 points on a scale, beyond which no substantial increase occurred. Moreover, they found that the largest increase in reliability occurred between 2- and 3-point scales. Thus, dichotomization of a response scale should be avoided whenever possible, because of the substantial loss of information and accuracy (Cohen, 1983). However, there is a tradeoff between the number of response categories and interrater reliability (Rudy, Turk, & Brena, 1988).
- *Order.* Response alternatives offered should be presented in logical sequence, because the order of alternatives can significantly affect response frequencies. For example, "often, rarely, or sometimes" is a confusing response sequence.
- *Standard response categories.* Response categories should avoid vague terms that require excessive subjectivity and thus idiosyncratic interpretation (e.g., "often," "frequently"). Rather, the categories selected should have clearly understood or specified definitions (particularly when used within an interview format), or large individual differences in interpretation will result that are unrelated to the content of the question. Standard response categories (e.g., "none, mild, moderate, severe") have wide applicability, are easy for most respondents to understand, and are adaptable to lists of items.
- *Ease of completion.* Responses to questions must allow a rating response. The degree of subjective interpretation must be reduced to increase reliability. Thus, the match between question and response alternatives needs to be examined, to ensure that responses are appropriate for the questions asked and that a minimal interpretive burden is imposed.

Overall Instrument Design

The general design of the instrument, particularly if it is to be used within an interview format, should be evaluated by the following criteria:

- *"Flow" and naturalness.* The instrument needs to be evaluated for its natural flow, clarity, and "sensible" or coherent arrangement.
- *Order of questions.* The order of questions can have significant influence on respondents' accuracy and truthfulness. The instrument (particularly if it is used in a structured interview format) should be evaluated for question order, to ensure that less sensitive "warm-up" questions precede those of a more sensitive nature. A sequence of questions that looks good on paper or eases data entry may not work as well when it is applied within an interview format.
- *Use of prompts and probes.* Questions asked in an interview format need to be examined to determine whether specific prompts and probes (including avoidance of inappropriate interviewer responses) should be developed, either for inclusion within the form itself or for use in training materials. To maximize completeness of data and uniformity of administration, standardized procedures for addressing respondent questions and confusion should be developed (Means, Nigam, Zarrow, Loftus, & Donaldson, 1989).

Choosing Evaluation Designs and Sampling Strategies

Table 18.4 presents several of the many possible designs that can be used to conduct a program evaluation. At one end of the continuum is the "gold standard" for clinical research—that is, the controlled clinical trial in which patients are randomly assigned to treatment conditions. This prospective design has numerous scientific advantages (e.g., determining the relative efficacy of different treatment approaches), but may be too expensive or impractical to conduct within the confines of a program evaluation system. Alternative "quasi-experimental" designs are available, with their associated strengths and weaknesses (Cook & Campbell, 1979). A program evaluator, for example, may only be interested in evaluating the magnitude of changes over time for a specific treatment program, and may thus select a single-group time series design. Although this type of design does not permit the evaluator to make causative statements about the treatment program, nonetheless outcome effect sizes can be determined and compared with other published treatment studies or meta-analyses (e.g., Flor, Fydrich, & Turk, 1992).

Selecting a sampling strategy involves deciding whom to measure and how frequently. A common problem in many chronic pain treatment outcome studies is that the sample included in the study is not truly representative of the population of interest, and therefore significantly reduces the generalizability of the study (Turk & Rudy, 1990). If the volume of the program to be evaluated is small, sampling difficulties can be avoided by evaluating *all* participants. In larger programs, however, the costs of this strategy may be prohibitive. Thus, an evaluator needs to develop a scientifically sound random sampling plan. We do not believe that using a convenient sample or a retrospective chart review, for example, is adequate for the purposes of program evaluation.

The frequency of data collection has major implications for the cost of the evaluation program. Our own particular bias is that evaluators should reduce the amount of information collected to the bare essentials, while still operationalizing the outcome domains that are considered most important, and should collect that information more frequently. At a minimum, three waves of data collection should be conducted: at pretreatment, immediately following treatment completion, and at a predetermined follow-up time. Although the length of the follow-up time is frequently debated, we believe that for patients with long-standing pain problems, a minimum of 1 year after treatment is required. If the necessary resources are available, two follow-up phases should be used—for example, one at 6 months after treatment and another at 1 or 2 years after treatment.

Estimating Costs

A well-designed evaluation system can have a substantial impact on a program's budget. Obvious potential costs include postage, photocopying/printing, long-distance phone calls, the purchase and scoring of measurement instruments, consultants, and data processing. These costs are relatively minor, however, compared to the personnel costs that can be associated with the evaluation system. For example, if members of the clinical staff are involved with some of the data collection components of the evaluation, this involvement is likely to result in a reduction in the percentage of their time that is billable. Similarly, if secretarial services are needed for data entry and mailing purposes, their normal duties related to important business aspects of the program (e.g., timely letters and reports to referral sources) can be adversely affected. Once an evaluator has completed the outcomes table (see Table 18.2), selected an evaluation design, and determined the dura-

TABLE 18.4. Some Possible Evaluation Designs

1. True control or comparison group (e.g., patients are randomly assigned to two existing treatment programs).
2. Nonequivalent control or comparison group (e.g., a cohort comparison group of patients who receive a treatment program other than the one under evaluation, but who are not randomly assigned to that program, is employed).
3. Time series with nonequivalent control group (i.e., two groups of patients receiving two different treatment program to which they were not randomly assigned receive multiple assessments over time).
4. Single-group time series (i.e., multiple assessments are conducted over time).

tion of the evaluation project, the personnel time commitment and related costs to process a single participant through the evaluation system should be calculated. At this point the evaluator will need to meet again with the program administration and provide concrete cost estimates. Depending on available resources, the magnitude of the program evaluation strategy and the number of participants may need to be revised.

PHASE 3: COLLECTING THE DATA

During Phase 3, the data collection plans developed in Phase 2 are put into effect. At this stage of the program evaluation, what remains is to see that everything proceeds as planned—that is, that deadlines are met; that design and sampling plans are implemented correctly; that instruments are administered at the proper times; that interviews and observations are conducted and coded in standardized ways; and that the data are entered accurately into a computerized data base.

Training and Pilot Testing

Despite the best plans developed in Phase 2, our experience is that Murphy's law is always a reality. Before the formal collection of evaluation data begins, it is important to train staff members in specific data collection procedures, and also to inform them of the overall evaluation plan. Particularly for interview and observational or examination methods of data collection, written procedural manuals should be developed to ensure that data collection methods are consistent within and across the staff members participating in the evaluation system.

Pilot testing on several program participants should be conducted, to evaluate whether the proposed data collection methods are feasible within the actual operations of the clinic. We have also found that pilot testing uncovers oversights in the intended procedures and scoring methods. Moreover, the pilot testing may lead to significant revisions in the estimated time to conduct certain aspects of the data collection.

Data Base Design

The computerized data base should also be developed during the pilot-testing phase. Several issues that should be considered in the development of a computerized data base include the following:

1. If possible, raw scores rather than scale scores should always be entered; this will permit psychometric analyses if needed, as well as increase the accuracy and reduce staff time if software routines are used to score the instruments.
2. Flexibility should be designed into the data base, and significant software changes should be expected as the evaluation program proceeds.
3. Methods for regularly monitoring the integrity and accuracy of the data base should be developed (see Freedland & Carney, 1992).
4. If an outside consultant is employed to develop the data base software, an evaluator should make sure that the language or development package used is a common one that can be modified or "debugged" by someone other than the developer.
5. Frequent, regularly scheduled backups of the data base should be made, and these should be stored off site.

Periodic Program Monitoring

After pilot testing and the necessary revisions have been completed and the final evaluation plan has been started, an evaluator should conduct periodic monitoring of all program aspects. This includes ensuring that the randomization or participant selection plan is being conducted as designed, that forms are administered and completed at the predesignated periods, and that the staff members involved in data collection are adhering to the written protocols established. The last of these is particularly important, since as the evaluation progresses and staff members become more familiar and/or bored with the procedures, considerable drifting from protocols often occurs.

PHASE 4: REPORTING FINDINGS

The level of statistical analyses and reporting mode for program evaluations varies considerably, depending on the program setting and the primary purpose for the evaluation system. At a minimum, an evaluator should develop a written summary report of evaluation findings that carefully documents the activities and findings of the evaluation, including aspects of the evaluation system that worked well and those that will need to be revised or eliminated in future program evaluations. Typically, multiple summary reports will need to be written that are tailored to the intended audiences.

A program evaluator should also provide oral reports to the staff and administrative personnel who participated in the development and/or implementation of the evaluation system. These face-to-face meetings provide an important forum for active involvement in program planning and evaluation; for discussion, clarification, and detailed elaboration of the evaluation's findings; and for making suggestions about additional evaluation activities that may be needed. This is an important time to solve logistical problems, data collection difficulties, and cost containment issues if subsequent evaluations are planned.

Depending on the complexity of the design and the data collected, statistical consultation may be needed during this phase to analyze the data collected and interpret the findings. As we have emphasized in our discussion of Phase 2, statistical consultation should have been obtained *before the data are collected*. If diverse methods of data collection are used (e.g., self-report, observational ratings, relapse rates) across multiple time periods, an evaluator will invariably need the assistance of an expert in multivariate analysis, since specialized statistical procedures will be needed (e.g., "conditional" logistic regression, survival analysis).

CASE STUDY

The case study presented in this section concerns a recent small patient-oriented program evaluation that we conducted as part of a larger project. We present this example not with great pride (i.e., not as an illustration of "how to do program evaluation properly"), since, as will become apparent, this section could be subtitled "How to Make a Silk Purse out of a Sow's Ear." Rather, it is intended to illustrate many of the practical and often less than ideal decisions that must be made in the development of an evaluation system. In addition, this example highlights the necessity of customizing evaluation procedures to the specific program and intended purposes of the evaluation system.

A randomized, controlled clinical trial that compared several conservative treatment approaches for temporomandibular disorders (TMDs) was conducted with funding from the National Institutes of Health. This study included the necessary funding for posttreatment follow-ups of patients for 6 months following treatment completion. It was apparent from the outset that extending the outcome study beyond the funded 6-month period would improve the practical significance of the study considerably. However, since additional funds were not available to conduct the same intensive follow-up assessments used at the time of the 6-month follow-up (i.e., a comprehensive dental examination, a battery of self-report instruments, and a clinical interview by a psychologist, which were similar to the assessments used at pre- and posttreatment), an alternative, cost-effective strategy was needed.

Obviously, we realize in retrospect that for scientific reasons, the budget should have allowed for the same level of evaluation at 1 year after treatment. Nonetheless, we decided to conduct a 1-year follow-up with the primary objective of maintaining the high completion rate established for the 6-month follow-up, which was 88% and most likely the result of budgeting funds to pay patients to return to the clinic for these evaluations.

Many practical problems had to be addressed. For example, there was the problem of losing patients to follow-up because they had moved out of the geographic region, or might simply be unwilling to extend the period during which they would make themselves available for evaluation. That is, following the initial evaluation, all study participants committed themselves to completing the six treatment sessions and returning to the clinic for follow-up at 6 months. Now, however, we were changing the game plan and seeking an additional time commitment from them.

The specifics of the patient population also had to be considered when we are developing the extended follow-up evaluation plan. It is important to note that most of the patients in this study had full-time jobs and were busy raising families (88% were females, with a mean age of 33.1 years). The clinic was located in a congested area of the city, and many patients had to travel up to an hour each way to reach the clinic; thus, any return visits to the clinic would entail substantial inconvenience to the patients. In addition, we did not have the necessary funds to reimburse patients for the costs associated with a return visit to the clinic.

Costs could be reduced substantially, and patients would probably be more available, through either phone or mail contact. Patients had completed printed questionnaires at pretreatment, at midtreatment, at treatment completion, and again at the 6-month follow-up evaluation. Thus, it made some sense to send patients the same materials to complete at the 1-year follow-up. However, the self-report assessment inventories used when patients attended the clinic were lengthy, and we questioned the rate of return from a general mailing. More specifically, our previous experience with this patient sample and also with other pain populations suggested that the return rate was likely to be substantially below the 88% rate we had achieved for the 6-month follow-up. We also considered the option of conducting an evaluation by mail, followed by phone contacts of those patients who failed to return the questionnaires. The additional cost was a concern, as was the problem of how to aggregate data collected in the two different ways.

Perhaps of most importance in determining the follow-up evaluation strategy that we finally selected was a realistic appraisal of what information we were seeking. The primary study objective was to evaluate a multidimensional treatment approach for TMD patients. Therefore, a multidimensional assessment strategy was used throughout the study; it addressed the behavioral, cognitive, and affective dimensions of TMD symptoms. Although few patients reported being completely symptom-free by the end of the 6-week treatment period, nearly all patients noted marked pain reduction and improvement in mood and quality of life, and few patients indicated a need for any additional treatment for their TMD condition. Such positive results at treatment completion were encouraging, but we knew that evaluating whether treatment gains continued over an extended period of time was essential.

Like patients with other prolonged pain conditions, TMD patients frequently obtain symptom relief in the short term following treatment, but often fail to maintain these gains over time. Although multidimensional evaluations were considered essential at the initial assessment through the 6-month follow-up, we decided that a more global outcome evaluation would be adequate for the 1-year follow-up. This decision was driven by the practical concerns noted above; it is a concrete example of the need to balance more rigorous scientific approaches with more pragmatic concerns of clinical services when program evaluations are being conducted.

Our final decision was to use a brief, structured telephone interview, which went through several iterations before a final format was reached. The initial phone interview schedule included questions asked of patients throughout the earlier evaluations; our hope was that we would be able to compare responses across time. One clear problem was that responses to questions in a paper-and-pencil instrument could not be assumed to be directly comparable to responses to the same questions asked in a phone interview. An even more important problem was that the phone interview quickly became longer than was practical. To contain costs, the interviews were to be conducted as much as possible during the usual working hours of the clinic, and this meant contacting many patients at their work phones. We felt that we were more likely to obtain patients' cooperation with a brief interview. Thus, our final working objective was to be able to develop an interview instrument that would permit us to inform patients that the interview would only take 5 minutes of their time to complete.

It was a difficult task to select which items to include in an interview of this brief duration. Which items would be the best indices of success? Unfortunately, there were no easy and uniform answers to this question. After careful deliberations related to the specific pain population under consideration and the outcomes we believed TMD patients would consider most important, intensity, duration, and frequency of pain were selected as primary content areas that should be covered in the interview. As often happens when evaluators are designing pain-related questions, a compromise was reached between our desire for concrete patient responses and the reality that an individual's pain symptoms vary across time.

The final structured telephone interview form that emerged is presented in Appendix 18.1. It is important to note that the patients enrolled in this study were those who had been experiencing pain symptoms for a minimum of 3 months and at least twice per week. As can be seen in the appendix, at the 1-year follow-up, patients who had not experienced pain in the previous month were not asked to provide any further information about their pain experience. Although this strategy could have missed information about a patient who might have had an unusual pain-free month, we were willing to allow for this possibility in order to keep the interview brief. We found that it was too difficult to obtain more concrete information about the nature of patients' pain if it had not occurred within a relatively recent period of time.

Following information about patients' pain experience since treatment completion, we were interested in determining what strategies the patients used to help reduce their pain. Information gained from patients during our 6-month follow-ups helped shape our questions related to the strategies that patients used to reduce their pain. The 6-month assessment included the Coping Strategies Questionnaire (Rosenstiel & Keefe, 1983), which requires patients to rate the frequency with which they use a variety of cognitive and behavioral coping strategies when they are in pain. A helpful patient indicated to us, however, that he had not used any of the strategies because he had not experienced any pain for several months. This provided a remarkably different picture of the patient than we would have formed from the scores he provided on this self-report instrument, had he not volunteered information beyond what the instrument asked of him.

Accordingly, we only asked patients about the use of pain management strategies if they reported having had pain within the previous 6 months. Patients were asked an open-ended question to elicit any strategies they used to help reduce their pain once it occurred, and their responses then were coded according to pre-established categories (see Appendix 18.1). When patients offered a response that could not be categorized unambiguously, they were asked to describe the strategy further. We chose not to prompt patients with types of strategies, to reduce the likelihood that patients would simply respond to the demand characteristics inherent in the question. A similar question was asked of patients regarding their use of strategies for preventing TMD symptoms from occurring. Again, patients were asked to give more details to allow categorization of their responses, without leading them to provide particular responses.

Patients then were asked to provide a global assessment of their current level of symptoms, compared to how they felt before treatment (see Appendix 18.1). Although this type of question involves the obvious problem of a difficult reference point (i.e., memories that were now at least a year old), it did have face validity for patients and was likely to be a good indicator of overall patient satisfaction with treatment. It did, however, probably contain considerable demand characteristics.

Finally, patients were asked whether they had received any other treatment, and if not, why not (see Appendix18.1). We felt that it was important to distinguish patients who did not seek additional treatment because they felt no need for such treatment from those patients who did not pursue other treatments either because they could not afford it or had simply given up and felt further treatment would be useless.

The final interview schedule was a result of many adaptations, based on a pilot trial of the interview. The most obvious change was the continual shortening of the instrument to fit our goal of minimal demand on patients' time. Another change was to have the clinician who provided the treatment to a particular patient conduct the phone interview of that patient. This decision was not without its problems. The cost of clinician time was one factor mitigating against the decision, but the question of the potential demand characteristics was more critical, as it had implications for the validity of the data collected. The very factor that we believed would help increase the response rate—namely, contact by the treating therapist—might increase the tendency of patients to respond in ways they deemed more socially desirable. Nevertheless, we decided that having the clinicians conduct the interviews would be the best way of gaining patients' cooperation. Furthermore, the clinicians would need the least amount of training to establish consistent use of the question categories, as they had been involved in the initial development of the treatment protocols and were familiar with various ways of referring to specific pain management strategies.

In summary, it is important to recognize that the simple, brief phone interview displayed in Appendix 18.1 went through several iterations and pilot testing during a period of more than 2 months. The commitment to conducting the 1-year follow-up was maintained, despite the obvious drawbacks of completing the project on "a shoestring." To date, of the 210 TMD patients who completed the 6-month follow-up, we have successfully completed the 1-year phone interview on 90% of these patients. Although these data have some substantial limitations, we believe that they are far superior to no longer-term data at all. Many decisions were the result of choosing one potential problem over an alternative, perhaps more crucial one. It is helpful to bear in mind that data flawed by choosing what is practical or possible over what is the ideal strategy can provide some progress in the evaluation of clinical services, whereas waiting for "untainted" data may mean never obtaining outcome data.

CONCLUSIONS

In this chapter, we have highlighted the many challenges involved in developing and implementing a program evaluation system for measuring chronic pain treatment outcomes. We have recommended that evaluators follow four primary phases, not only to simplify this difficult task, but more importantly to illustrate that program evaluation involves much more than simply collecting data. Careful planning—particularly in terms of administrative and staff support; the selection of evaluation methods, instruments, and study design; and the monitoring of the integrity of program implementation—is needed if the evaluation system is to produce valid and useful information.

We have also emphasized that program evaluations can be designed for multiple purposes. Our primary emphasis has been on evaluating patient outcomes, but the reader should recognize that program productivity and cost-effectiveness, and patient, staff, or referral satisfaction, are also important areas to consider in the evaluation of chronic pain treatment programs.

Finally, we have concluded with a case example illustrating some of the hard decisions that must be made in the selection of an evaluation strategy. Achieving scientific perfection when one is designing evaluation systems is simply not possible. Costs, available resources, and program objectives will always dictate the final evaluation design. It is our hope that the many hurdles encountered in planning an evaluation program described in this chapter will not deter the reader. Our patients, our staff, and those who have a financial stake in our programs deserve the substantial improvements that can be realized from our willingness to evaluate ourselves.

APPENDIX 18.1. FOLLOW-UP PHONE INTERVIEW:
TEMPOROMANDIBULAR DISORDERS (TMD) PROJECT

Name:_____ ID #:_____

Home phone: _____ Work phone: _____

Post-Tx. date: _____ Follow-up date: _____

1. Do you have any TMJ pain right now? (No = 0. If yes: Which word on the following scale best describes your pain now?

No pain	Mild	Discomforting	Distressing	Horrible	Excruciating
0	1	2	3	4	5

2. During the past month, have you experienced any TMJ pain symptoms?
   ☐ 1 Yes   ☐ 2   No (skip to #6)

3. Constant pain/ache: ☐ 1 Yes   ☐ 2 No

4. If yes (to #2), how often? (frequency of flares)
   ☐ 1 >5/week   ☐ 2 2–4/week   ☐ 3 1/week
   ☐ 4 <1/week   ☐ 5 <1/month   ☐ 6 No flares

5. How long does pain continue, once it begins?
   ☐ 1 <1 hr.   ☐ 2 1–2 hr.   ☐ 3 2–4 hr.   ☐ 4 4–8 hrs.
   ☐ 5 8–12 hrs.   ☐ 6 12 hr.–constant   ☐ 7 No flares

If you have had any TMJ pain in the past 6 months, what did you do to reduce it?
(If no pain in last 6 months, skip to #22)

6. ☐ 0 NA   ☐ 1 Yes   ☐ 2 No: Relaxation (protocol-based)
7. ☐ 0 NA   ☐ 1 Yes   ☐ 2 No: Rest or sleep
8. ☐ 0 NA   ☐ 1 Yes   ☐ 2 No: Medication
9. ☐ 0 NA   ☐ 1 Yes   ☐ 2 No: Splint use
10. ☐ 0 NA   ☐ 1 Yes   ☐ 2 No: Cognitive technique (protocol-based)
11. ☐ 0 NA   ☐ 1 Yes   ☐ 2 No: other (adaptive—e.g., yoga) _____
12. ☐ 0 NA   ☐ 1 Yes   ☐ 2 No: Distracting behavior
13. ☐ 0 NA   ☐ 1 Yes   ☐ 2 No: Nothing or maladaptive (e.g., alcohol use)
14. Do you use any medications for TMJ pain? (If yes:) What do you take and how often do you take them in the course of a week?

    <u>Pain medication</u>   <u>How often</u>

_____

_____

What do you do to prevent TMJ pain from occurring?

15. ☐ 0 NA   ☐ 1 Yes   ☐ 2 No: Progressive muscle relaxation exercise
16. ☐ 0 NA   ☐ 1 Yes   ☐ 2 No: Jaw relaxation
17. ☐ 0 NA   ☐ 1 Yes   ☐ 2 No: Oral habits
18. ☐ 0 NA   ☐ 1 Yes   ☐ 2 No: Splint use
19. ☐ 0 NA   ☐ 1 Yes   ☐ 2 No: Stress management technique
20. ☐ 0 NA   ☐ 1 Yes   ☐ 2 No: Diet restrictions
21. ☐ 0 NA   ☐ 1 Yes   ☐ 2 No: Nothing or maladaptive
22. Think about the symptoms you had before you started treatment at the Pain Institute. Is the TMJ problem now worse, the same, or improved? If improved, do you feel you have gained a small, moderate, or major improvement?
    ☐ 1 Problem is worse than before treatment
    ☐ 2 No change (same as before treatment)
    ☐ 3 Small improvement
    ☐ 4 Moderate improvement
    ☐ 5 Major improvement

23. Have you received any treatment for TMJ symptoms since completing treatment at the Pain Institute?
    ☐ 1 Yes ☐ 2 No
    If yes, what kind?
    _____

24. If no, is that because you have not needed any treatment or is there some other reason?
    ☐ 0 NA (had other tx.)   ☐ 1 No need   ☐ 2 Couldn't afford it
    ☐ 3 Other _____

25. Do you have any comments about the treatment you received here?

ACKNOWLEDGMENTS

Preparation of this chapter was supported in part by Research Grants No. R01 AR38698 from the National Institute of Arthritis and Musculoskeletal and Skin Diseases, and No. R01 DE07514 from the National Institute of Dental Research, National Institutes of Health.

REFERENCES

Beck, A. T., Ward, C. H., Mendelson, M., Mock, J., & Erbaugh, J. (1961). An inventory for measuring depression. *Archives of General Psychiatry, 4,* 461–471.

Cicchetti, D. V., Showalter, D., & Tyrer, P. J. (1985). The effect of number of rating scale categories on levels of interrater reliability: A Monte Carlo investigation. *Applied Psychological Measurement, 9,* 31–36.

Cohen, J. (1983). The cost of dichotomization. *Applied Psychological Measurement, 7,* 249–253.

Commission on Accreditation of Rehabilitation Facilities (CARF). (1987). *Program evaluation in chronic pain management programs.* Tucson, AZ: Author.

Commission on Accreditation of Rehabilitation Facilities (CARF). (1991). *Standards manual for organizations serving people with disabilities.* Tucson, AZ: Author.

Cook, T. D., & Campbell, D. T. (1979). *Quasi-experimentation: Design and analysis issues for field settings.* Chicago: Rand McNally.

Danchik, K. M., & Drury, T. F. (1988). *Asking about chronic pain in general population surveys.* Paper presented at the Canadian and American Pain Societies Joint Meeting, Toronto, Canada.

Flor, H., Fydrich, T., & Turk, D. C. (1992). Efficacy of multidisciplinary pain treatment centers: A meta-analytic review. *Pain, 49,* 221–230.

Freedland, K. E., & Carney, R. M. (1992). Data management and accountability in behavioral and biomedical research. *American Psychologist, 47,* 640–645.

Herman, J. L., Morris, L. L., & Fitz-Gibbon, C. T. (1987). *Evaluator's handbook.* Newbury Park, CA: Sage.

Hoffman, R. M., Turner, J. A., Cherkin, D. C., Deyo, R. A., & Herron, L. D. (1994). Therapeutic trials for low back pain. *Spine, 19,* 2068S–2075S.

Means, B., Nigam, A., Zarrow, M., Loftus, E. F., & Donaldson, M. S. (1989). Autobiographical memory for health-related events. *Vital Health Statistics, 6*(2),

Rosenstiel, A., & Keefe, F. J. (1983). The use of coping strategies in chronic low back pain patients: Relationship to patient characteristics and adjustments. *Pain, 17,* 33–44.

Rosomoff, H. L. (1993). President's message. *American Pain Society, 3*(4), 3–4.

Rudy, T. E., Turk, D. C., & Brena, S. F. (1988). Differential utility of medical procedures in the assessment of chronic pain patients. *Pain, 34,* 53–60.

Steedman, S. M., Middaugh, S. J., Kee, W. G., Carson, D. S., Harden, R. N., & Miller, M. C. (1992). Chronic-pain medications: Equivalence levels and method of quantifying usage. *Clinical Journal of Pain, 8,* 204–214.

Sudman, S., & Bradburn, N. M. (1982). *Asking questions*. San Francisco: Jossey-Bass.

Turk, D. C., & Melzack, R. (Eds.). (1992). *Handbook of pain assessment*. New York: Guilford Press.

Turk, D. C., & Rudy, T. E. (1990). Neglected factors in chronic pain treatment outcome studies: Referral patterns, failure to enter treatment, and attrition. *Pain, 43,* 7–25.

Turk, D. C., & Rudy, T. E. (1991). Neglected topics in the treatment of chronic pain patients: Relapse, noncompliance, and adherence enhancement. *Pain, 44,* 5–28.

Turk, D. C., Rudy, T. E., & Sorkin, B. A. (1993). Neglected topics in chronic pain treatment outcome studies: Determination of success. *Pain, 53,* 3–16.

Turk, D. C., Rudy, T. E., & Stieg, R. L. (1988). Disability determination dilemma: Towards a multiaxial taxometric solution. *Pain, 34,* 217–229.

Index